Law and Practice

Essays on Reform

Law and Practice

Essays on Reform

Edited by

Eoin O'Dell

&

Geoffrey Shannon

CLARUS PRESS

Law Society of Ireland

Published by
Clarus Press Ltd,
Griffith Campus,
South Circular Road,
Dublin 8.

Typeset by
Compuscript Ltd,
Bay 11A, Shannon Industrial Estate,
Shannon, Co. Clare

Printed by
MPG Books Ltd
Victoria Square, Bodmin, Cornwall.

ISBN
978-1-905536-12-2

Preface

The impetus behind the concept of the Annual Student Law Reform Essay Prize is to foster an interest in law reform in the future practitioners and teachers of law in Ireland. From its inception, the quality of the entries received has never failed to disappoint. Disparate issues have been discussed, analysed and reformed by the entrants. The essays chosen for this collection demonstrate the level of originality of thought, complexity, practicality, research and presentation skills that has gone into the development of these remarkable law reform proposals. Some of the essays will be of tremendous interest to academics; others may stimulate more curiosity in the practitioner, but all have the potential to "make a very significant impact on the lives of the community at large".[1]

The necessity to tackle the concept of law reform in a serious manner has long been evident to the legal profession and the State. Bodies such as the Law Reform Committee of the Law Society and the Law Reform Commission play an essential role in analysing complex areas of law and suggesting fundamental reforms. The courts in the administration of justice often signpost important law reform initiatives and implement necessary reforms. Universities and other academic institutions encourage discussion of law reform through academic discourse and scrutiny.

However, such investigations cannot be conducted without the initial identification of the area in need of reform. This may often transpire where a law is applied in a manner which is unreasonable in all the circumstances or where a situation arises which cannot be dealt with under the existing legal regime. The Annual Student Law Reform Essay Prize has the distinct advantage of operating outside this realm and provides significant insight into issues which are causing injustice and which require suitable reform. The reader should be mindful that many of the essays were written in advance of reforms and may therefore misrepresent the current state of Irish Law. However, the contributors to this competition have inspired reports by the Law Reform Committee and indeed many of the essays contained in this collection have anticipated legislative change.

---

[1] North "Problems of Law Reform" (2002) *New Zealand Law Review* 338 at p 401.

The sheer extent of the essays that have been included in this publication reflects the great variety of topics that are in need of substantial reform. Many of the contributions have been influenced by the changes that have occurred in Irish society in recent years. The theme of commercial law features strongly in this publication with issues such as non-life insurance regulation, limited liability partnerships, cyber uncertainty, privity of contract and third party rights, the concept of subject to contract in Irish law, the duty of care and skill of company directors and on-line education and copyright law all receiving individual attention. The contributions also discuss technological issues such as stem cell research.

Several of the essays in this publication refer exclusively to criminal law and the law of evidence, reflecting the recent focus in Ireland on the criminal justice system. The issues raised in such contributions begin with the pre-trial procedure, with particular focus on the concepts of the right of access to a lawyer and the interrogation of suspects in the pre-trial process. The trial process is also considered with the constitutionality of procedures in the Special Criminal Court, the rule on double jeopardy, the defence of provocation, the rule against hearsay and infanticide, all receiving particular attention. Other issues, including diversion programmes for young offenders were also addressed.

The laws in relation to employment, the family, the environment and consumer protection were among the other issues identified by the contributors as deserving of consideration. Trade union representation, forestry, unmarried fathers, the law on nullity, gender and marriage, the guardian *ad litem* procedure, arbitration and the rights of transsexuals were all investigated and submissions for reform were proposed. The law in relation to the sale of goods also figured strongly, with many essays examining the legislation on sale by description, the passing of property, the *nemo dat* rule, the presumption of advancement and the law on fundraising.

The area of practice and procedure in the court process in Ireland also faced scrutiny from the contributors and interesting reform proposals were advanced. The public interest was a key factor in an examination of the constitutional role of the Attorney General as well as in other areas of practise, including: the concept of the undertaking as to damages, the more appropriate modes of address for judges in Irish courts, the role of expert witnesses, the development of a catastrophe law in Ireland and pre-emptive cost orders. Despite being inherently practical in focus, the contributors managed to engage in academic discussions as to the most effective proposals for reform of the current court procedures.

However, law reform is not just about originality of thought. Good law reformers will be conscious that the need for, and practicality of, the proposals advanced are also pertinent to the determination of the impact of reform on the legal system. With this in mind, it is essential that those engaging in law reform do not ignore the complex in favour of the more simple features of the legal system The essays produced here could not be described as lacking in importance, practicality or complexity. Importantly, this embracing of complex legal problems has not prevented the contributors from developing "practical and workable solutions"[2] to the legal problems they have identified.

The level of research involved in any law reform initiative will always be immense, incorporating as it does a detailed analysis of the current law, a critical appraisal of its virtues and problems and the detailing of a viable solution. The essays in this collection are vastly researched, a fact that can be evidenced by the quality and value of the final contributions. While, it is often effortless to condemn law reform proposals as incomplete or lacking extraneous analysis, this would not do justice to the breadth of knowledge and insight that has gone into the final proposals.

While originality, necessity, importance, complexity and research are essential to a law reform proposal, it must be remembered that unless the suggestion is capable of being interpreted and comprehended, then it may well be as deficient as the law it is endeavouring to reform. Without the exceptional flourish, flair and writing skills of the authors in this contribution, the solutions advanced in this publication could not be viewed as valuable law reform initiatives.

Over the years, numerous judges have volunteered their time and valuable experience to read, examine and most difficult of all, choose winners. It is a testament to the quality of the entrants that the judges, academics and practitioners who judged the prize were happy to contribute their time. Perhaps this is because throughout the legal profession there is an understanding that law reform is, in itself, an essential part of the legal system and is in need of cultivation and development. Often those involved intimately in the legal process are unable to see the simple solution to the many problems they encounter on a daily basis or are too afraid to cause controversy among their peers. This publication is a tribute to all those students who took the time to read, research and write and who were not afraid to tackle the complex, the difficult or the unreasonable features of our legal system.

---

[2] North "Problems of Law Reform" (2002) *New Zealand Law Review* 338 at p 401.

Acknowledgements

The Law Reform Committee of the Law Society of Ireland would like to thank the many people who helped, both directly and indirectly, in writing this book. The Committee owe a great deal of gratitude to the contributors, the editors, the publishers and the Committee members who all encouraged and supported this publication. While it is impossible to name all those who assisted in making this publication a reality, there are a few who are deserving of special mention.

It has been a privilege to work with the many contributors who made this publication possible. Without their enthusiasm, patience and acute legal minds, this vision could never have been made a reality. Special thanks must be paid to the editors of this publication, Geoffrey Shannon and Dr. Eoin O' Dell, who generously gave their time and expertise to read, proof and edit the essays for this publication. The Committee extends their heartfelt thanks to them both. Similarly, the Committee would like to extend their gratitude to the publisher, Clarus Press, and in particular to David McCartney for his constant patience and helpfulness. Finally, the Committee would like to extend their special thanks to Alma Clissmann and Elaine Dewhurst, who worked behind the scenes to bring this publication to fruition.

The Committee would also like to extend their warm gratitude to all the law students who have taken the trouble and effort over the years to challenge the Irish legal system and to make suggestions for reform. Thanks must also be extended to all the law teachers all over Ireland who have encouraged their students to partake in the Annual Law Reform Essay Prize and who have stimulated in their students a questioning interest in the law. Sincere thanks must also be paid to the various judges of the Law Reform Essay Prize for their time and patience in reading scripts and bringing their experience and expertise to the judging of this competition.

The Committee hopes that this publication will inspire others to take the initiative to take up the mantle of law reform and continue the important and inspiring work of the contributors to this collection. To everyone involved, thank you.

Contents

Privity of Contract and Third Party Rights: An Unnecessary and Complex Anomaly in Need of Reform

by

Ronan MacSweeney*

Introduction

Under the Irish law of contract a third party may not enforce a benefit afforded to him by a contract to which he is not privy. This rule of law, commonly referred to as the doctrine of privity, is one which has been described as just and sensible.[1] While some argue that there is a sound theoretical basis for the exclusion of third party rights it can, on occasion, cause considerable inconvenience, apparent injustice and unnecessary complexity in legal transactions. Ireland is one of the few remaining jurisdictions that refuses to allow third parties to enforce contractual rights granted to them by a contract.[2] As the privity rule is honoured now more in theory than in practice, reform of this anomaly is warranted.

In this essay it is proposed to outline in brief the current state of our law in relation to third party rights in contract law, highlighting the exceptions that have been developed so as to circumvent the problems to which the privity doctrine gives rise. I will consider the theoretical basis for, and note the inconsistencies that exist in, the law in this area, and examine how reform might be achieved. This analysis will be illuminated by drawing comparisons with other jurisdictions where appropriate.

---

* Ronan MacSweeney BA, LLB (NUI), LLM (Edin), Senior Associate, Minter Ellison Lawyers, Sydney, Australia. This essay was awarded first prize in the Law Society of Ireland, *Student Law Reform Essay Competition 1999.*

[1] Treitel, *The Law of Contract* (11th ed, Sweet & Maxwell Limited, London 2003), p 580.

[2] In Ireland there are a number of statutory exceptions already in place, such as the *Married Women's Status Act* 1957 and s 76(1) of *Road Traffic Act* 1961.

Theoretical Justification for the Doctrine of Privity

The reason why the doctrine of privity excludes third parties from the right to rely on the provisions of a contract is linked to the doctrine of consideration. However, Flannagan goes further and argues that privity and consideration are but different ways of saying the same thing.[3] As he puts it, the privity rule is merely the result demanded by the doctrine of consideration.[4] The creation of a separate privity rule, he believes, may have come about through the usage of loose language as the earliest case law on this matter seems to concentrate on whether or not the party was a stranger to the consideration provided.[5] *Zweigert & Kotz* describe the relationship between consideration and privity as the *vinculum juris* of contract law, where only the parties to the contract can generate rights for and against each other.[6] Despite criticism of this approach by various quarters neither the courts nor the legislature in Ireland have been moved to change.[7]

It is generally accepted that no one should find themselves under a legal obligation without being a party to a contract by consent. Thus, the decision in the Irish case *Barry v Barry*[8] was based on the reasoning that the doctrine is designed to prevent persons who are simply the objects of a gratuitous promise from suing others in contract. However, that this should then exclude a third party from acquiring rights under a contract does not necessarily follow. The doctrine of privity supposedly creates a notional cocoon around the contracting parties, within which they may do as they please. If this is so, then surely the doctrine is undermined when the wishes of the contracting parties, to allow a third party to acquire rights under the contract, cannot thereby be realised. Indeed it was in this regard that Steyn LJ remarked in *Darlington Borough Council v Wiltshire Northern Ltd.*[9] that the reason for recognising third party rights was:

> "...simple and straightforward. The autonomy of the will of the parties should be respected. The law of contract should give effect to the reasonable expectations of contracting parties. There is no doctrinal, logical or policy reason why the law should deny effectiveness to a contract for the benefit of

---

3 Flannagan, "Privity —The End of an Era (Error)" (1987) 103 LQR 568.
4 *ibid.*
5 See *Price v Easton* (1833) 4 B & Ad 433.
6 Zweigert & Kotz, *Introduction to Comparative Law (Oxford, 1998),* p 457.
7 For example Flannagan, above, n 3, at 568.
8 (1891) 28 L R (Jr) 45.
9 [1995] l WLR 68.

> a third party, where that is the expressed intention of the parties. Moreover, often the parties organise their affairs on the faith of the contract. They rely on the contract. It is therefore unjust to deny effectiveness to such a contract."[10]

Certainly the common law has not always set itself against the idea of affording third parties rights under the terms of a contract to which they are not a party. As Denning LJ once said third party rights were settled law for 200 years before 1861.[11] Indeed it was only following the case of *Tweddle v Atkinson*[12] that the courts set themselves firmly against the idea of affording third parties rights within contracts, by adopting an earlier precedent from the case of *Price v Easton.*[13] However, that case was based not only on privity but also on the fact that the plaintiff had failed to provide any consideration to the agreement.[14] In his decision in the case, Wightman J. said in regard to third party rights that it is now established that no stranger to consideration can take advantage of the contract, although made for his benefit.[15] In making such a resolute statement, one could reasonably expect that the learned judge would have put forward strong arguments and reasons in favour of the privity rule. However, it is quite astonishing that the learned judge's decision contained no such reasoning or explanation. Nonetheless, this decision was readily adopted in subsequent Irish cases such as *Murphy v Bower.*[16]

It is argued therefore, that *Tweddle* does not stand as authority for an independent privity doctrine. Flannagan argues that the case could be viewed as having been decided solely on the basis of the absence of consideration moving from the third party and so by basing his decision on the rule that consideration of the contract

---

10 *ibid* at 72.

11 *Drive Yourself Hire Co (London) v Strutt* [1954] 1 QB 250 at 272.

12 (1861) I B & S 393 [hereinafter referred to as *Tweddle*].

13 See above, n 5.

14 The facts of *Tweddle* were that the plaintiff sought to enforce an agreement between his father and his father in-law which involved the payment of money to the plaintiff in consideration of a marriage. It was held as the plaintiff was not a party to the contract he could not enforce the contract. It would seem bizarre, however, that the plaintiff could be regarded as a stranger to the contract in any sense, for without him the basis of the contract, the marriage itself, would be negated.

15 *ibid* at 457.

16 (1868) IR 2 CL 506 at 512, where Monahan CJ said it has been decided that where the foundation of the right of action is rested upon contract, no one can maintain an action who is not a party to the contract.

must move from the promisee, the learned judge over emphasised the identification of contract as a bargain.[17] As such, the rule was merely an insular reflection of a general assumption that a contract is an intimate and exclusive product of the parties that made it.[18] Even if this was not the case, it is still submitted that the refusal to allow third parties to enforce rights granted to them in a contract should not necessarily be a consequence of the principle of privity of contract.

Under the French *Code Civil,* for example, we meet once again the concept of the *vinculum juris* described by Zweigert and Kotz.[19] The governing principle in French contract law is laid down as follows:

> "On ne peut, en general, ni s'engager, ni stipuler en son propre nom, que pour soi-meme (Article 1119),[20] and
>
> Les conventions n'ont d'effet qu'entre les parties contractantes (Article 1165),"[21]

However, this guiding principle is subsequently modified by the provision of Article 1121 which reads:

> "On peut stipuler au profit d'un tiers, lorsque telle est la condition d'une stipulation que l'on fait pour soi-meme ou d' une donation que l'on fait a un autre."[22]

In this way, Dickson explains that the French courts have been able to admit exceptions without engaging in the "serpentine reasoning" to which the courts of common law jurisdictions have had to resort so as to accommodate exceptions to the privity rule.[23] There are now numerous exceptions in law that have been applied in the most circuitous fashion so as to mitigate against what would otherwise be clear injustice. These exceptions operate to make the law more complicated and intricate than should be the case.

---

[17] Flannagan, above, n 3, at 565.

[18] See Cheshire, Fifoot & Furmston, *Law of Contract* (14th ed, Butterworths London 2001), p 500.

[19] Zweigert & Kotz, above, n 6, at 462.

[20] Dickson, *Introduction to French Law* (London, 1994), p 141. The article states that, in general, one can only bind oneself or make promises on one's own behalf.

[21] *ibid.* The article states that agreements can effect only the parties to them.

[22] Above, n 20, at 142. The article states that one can promise something to a third party if this is the condition upon which something was promised to oneself or upon which one has made a gift to another.

[23] *ibid.*

Multiple Exceptions Negating the Doctrine of Privity

Many of these privity exceptions were developed in response to the complex commercial relationships that are necessary for the functioning of modern business and commerce. The courts of equity have adopted a characteristically flexible position in this area. Towards the end of the last century they began to employ the device of the trust to allow circuitously a degree of third party rights into contractual arrangements. So it was that the constructive trust was used whenever a contract purported to confer rights on third parties. The third party could claim that a trust in its favour had been created, thereby enforcing its rights by way of trust when unable to do so through normal contractual rules.

However, the courts have clung with remarkable tenacity to the doctrine of privity and have indicated a reluctance to go down this path.[24] Many within the judiciary have recognised the artificial nature of the trust system in this context. Lord Wright described the trust system in terms of a mechanism to overcome the doctrine of privity as a "cumbrous fiction".[25] Moreover, a trust may not always be an adequate remedy, as was seen in the *Schebsman* case.[26] In his decision in that case Du Parcq LJ held, *inter alia,* that "unless an intention to create a trust is clearly to be collected from the language used and the circumstances of the case, I think that the court ought not to be astute to discover indications of such an intention".[27] A similar attitude was discernible in *Green v Russell.*[28] Indeed, it is now necessary to satisfy certain definite criteria before a trust in favour of a third party will be construed.[29]

---

[24] Zweigert & Kotz, above, n 6, at 468.

[25] Wright (1939) 55 LQR 189 at 208.

[26] *Re Schebsman, Official Receiver v Cargo Superintendents (London) Lt. and Schebsman* [1944] Ch 83. The facts of the case were as follows: A was employed by two companies. By a contract made between him and these two companies, one of the companies agreed in certain eventualities that they would pay the sum of £5,500 to A's widow and daughter. It was held that the contract did not create a trust in favour of the widow and daughter.

[27] *ibid* at 104.

[28] [1959] 2 QB 226. Romer LJ said that an intention to provide benefits for someone else and to pay for them does not in itself give rise to a trusteeship.

[29] *Landepitte v Preferred Accident Insurance Corporation* [1933] AC 70 it was held that the intention to create a trust must be irrevocable and that there must also be more than a mere intention to benefit the third party. Furthermore, in *Re Englebach's Estate* [1924] 2 Ch 348 it was held that the courts will refuse to find a trust where a promise, with a clear intention to benefit a third party, cannot be distinguished from a mere intention to create a gift.

The courts will not simply apply the trust concept to get around every problem that involves third parties. In many cases the courts have rejected arguments founded on equity that third parties are entitled to enforce contracts made for their benefit.[30] Clearly it is not an absolute substitute for recognition of third party rights in contract.[31]

However, it is important to note that the willingness of the courts to apply the trust concept in very many situations does seem to negate the very *raison d'être* of the privity rule.

In the area of property law, attempts have been made to bridge the gap between it and contract. Leases are remarkable examples of the trade-off between the two. When two parties execute a lease they enter into certain contractual obligations. However, these obligations are intended to apply to the parties as landlord and tenant respectively. So if the tenant assigns his lease, the new tenant can be sued for breach of his obligations, for example, for failure to pay rent. Likewise, if the landlord sells his freehold, the new landlord may sue or be sued for failure to abide by the terms of the tenancy agreement. Again, it should be noted that the courts, by admitting this exception, are bending the principle that lies behind the privity doctrine.

Modern contract law also allows a contracting party to transfer or assign his rights to a third party. In practice, assignment is almost as good as legal title except that it is an equitable right and the assignor may have to be joined as a party to an action by the assignee against the debtor. There are two rules limiting the extent of the right. First, the debtor must have notice of the assignment or he is not affected. Secondly, assignments are subject to equities. So the debtor may employ any defence which he had against the assignor against the assignee also. While it is common to assign debts and other commercial rights, it is not quite so easy to assign certain contractual rights. Nevertheless, assignment represents yet another attempt to avoid the difficulties of a strict application of the privity rule. It also shows up another significant anomaly in the law, namely, the willingness to allow a contracting party to assign its rights to a third party but its steadfastness in refusing third parties the right to benefit directly from a contract itself.[32]

---

30 Treitel, above, n 1, at 651.

31 It is also notable that the trust concept has traditionally been confined only to the promise to pay money or to transfer property.

32 Atiyah, *An Introduction to the Law of Contract* (Oxford University Press, Oxford 1984) at p 364.

Again with the law of agency, deviation occurs. Of course, it could be said here that ordinarily the agent is merely acting for the principal, and that so long as he states that this is what he is doing then there is no conflict with the doctrine of privity. However, the agent can normally extend his role beyond this under what is known as the doctrine of the undisclosed principal.[33] This doctrine is of course limited by certain rules to protect the interests of third parties.[34] So while it is clear that the law on agency does not create a *carte blanche* to conclude contracts without disclosing the true role that one is playing, it is submitted nonetheless that the rule of agency amounts to a controversial instance of where the law must admit exceptions to the doctrine of privity so as to reflect commercial and business reality.[35]

Certain exceptions do not fall neatly into legal theory.[36] These exceptions have either been created simply on the basis that the courts have said that an exception should exist or because of the numerous statutory exceptions that have resulted over the years. In commercial law several exceptions have been admitted to the privity rule, most notably in the area of negotiable instruments. When transferring bills of lading, the normal privity rules are ignored. The consignor will normally have made a contract with the carrier which is then evidenced in a bill of lading. The subsequent transfer of the bill of lading to the consignee is treated as a transfer of the whole contract of carriage. In banking law, bankers' commercial credits do not fall within the doctrine of privity, while in insurance law the concept of subrogation has had to be invented.

With respect to exclusion clauses the courts have, however, tended to show more leniency than might be expected. Indeed, in *Elder, Dempster and Co v Paterson, Zochonis & Co*[37] the court seemed to suggest that the benefit of an exclusion clause could be used by a non-party to the contract, while this was rejected in *Scruttons v Midland Silicines Ltd.*[38] The net effect of these decisions appears to be that the application of exclusion clauses has become riddled with so many exceptions that it amounts to yet another diversion from the traditional privity doctrine.

---

[33] This rule compels a third party to meet the contractual obligations of a contract with a principal, of whose existence he had no knowledge; the reason for this compulsion being based solely on the subjective intention of the agent.

[34] These are that: the third party can always enforce the agreement against the agent; the principal must be able to prove that the principal did have the requisite authority at the time the decision was made; and finally the contract cannot be of a personal nature.

[35] Clark, *Contract Law in Ireland,* (4th ed, Sweet & Maxwell, Dublin, 1998), p 402.

[36] Friel, "The Failed Experiment with Privity" (1996) 14 *Irish Law Times* (NS) 86.

[37] [1924] AC 522.

[38] [1962] AC 446.

Furthermore, several statutory exceptions to the privity rule exist in Ireland.[39] For example, under the Married Women's Status Act 1957, a life insurance policy taken out expressly for the benefit of a spouse or child can be enforced by the beneficiary, although the latter may have no claim at common law. Yet there are a whole variety of insurance contracts that cannot avail of the same third party privileges as the above example.[40]

The last major exception whose evolution has been shaped by the existence of the privity doctrine is to be found in the law of tort. In the landmark case *Donoghue v Stevenson,*[41] despite the lack of a contract between the parties, the court saw no reason to deny the plaintiff a remedy in tort. This principle has been greatly extended.[42] It is worth pointing out, however, that the House of Lords has signalled on several occasions that many of these problems would be better resolved by applying certain contractual concepts.[43] Indeed, the decision in *Junior Books*[44] has been described as an illegitimate use of tort law to evade the privity principle.[45]

---

[39] For example, a life insurance policy taken out expressly for the benefit of a spouse or child can be enforced by the beneficiary, under the Married Women's Status Act 1957, although the latter may have no claim at common law. There are of course a whole variety of insurance contracts that cannot avail of the same third party privileges as the above example.

[40] Another good example of a statutory exception is s 76(1) of the Road Traffic Act 1961, which affords a person claiming against an insured motorist certain remedies against the insured. Section 13(2) of the *Sale of Goods and Supply of Services Act* 1980 created an implied condition in sales by a dealer of a motor vehicle to the effect that the vehicle is, at the time of delivery, free from any defect which would render it a danger to the public, including persons travelling in the vehicle with the consent of the buyer. Such third parties who are injured through a breach of the implied condition of s 13 may bring an action against the vendor as if he were the buyer.

[41] [1932] AC 562. A consumer was permitted to sue the manufacturer for injuries suffered as a result of its faulty production of its product.

[42] It includes a duty of an occupier towards a visitor and the duly of a professional towards his or her clients.

[43] *Junior Books Ltd v Veitchi Co. Ltd* [1983] 1 AC 52 [hereinafter referred to as *Junior Books*] was a particularly controversial extension of tort liability. Later authorities have sought to emphasise the exceptional nature of this case namely *Henderson v Merritt Syndicates* [1994] 3 WLR 761 and White *v* Jones [1995] 2 WLR 187. In short, the facts of *Junior Books* were that A undertook to build a factory for B. A contracted with C for the laying of a floor. B and C had no contract. However, when the floor subsequently cracked, it was held that C was liable to B as the floor had to be laid again.

[44] *ibid.*

[45] Atiyah, above, n 32, at 382.

It may be argued then, that while the above exceptions represent a serious weakening of the doctrine of privity, they can only partially compensate for the absence of third party rights. Further, if third parties were to have rights under contract law these exceptions would be circumvented and the law in this area could be applied in a much simpler and clearer fashion.

Steps Toward Reform—Other Jurisdictions

The majority opinion in the English Law Commission's detailed report on this issue set out strong arguments in favour of reform.[46] These were, first, that the privity rule frustrates the intentions of the party to a contract, which as has already been argued seems to undermine the general justification of contract theory itself. Secondly, the Commission focused on the injustice to the third party, who may have engendered reasonable expectations as to the outcome of a particular contract. Thirdly, it pointed to the clear injustice in the law as it stands, where a person who has suffered no loss can sue on a contract if that person is a party to it while, perversely, a third party who has suffered loss cannot. Fourthly, the Commission said that while the promisee may be able to obtain a remedy for the aggrieved third party, he may not wish to do so.

A minority view in the Commission made a number of arguments against reform. First, it said that reform was unnecessary because the doctrine caused little or no difficulty in practice. Second, the minority argued that a change in the *status quo* would create uncertainty as to how the law stands. It is submitted that reform in this area, if it served to create greater clarity and a more just system, without the numerous exceptions that are currently employed, would, on the contrary, lend itself to greater certitude.

Statutory Reform—England and Wales

The majority proposals of the English Law Commission helped to mould the Contracts (Rights of Third Parties) Act 1999 (hereinafter referred to as the English Act) which received Royal Assent on 11 November 1999. The English Act radically alters the long-standing position with regard to privity of contract within England and Wales[47] and further serves to highlight the anomaly of the current position in Irish law.

---

[46] English Law Commission, *Privity of Contracts: Contracts for the Benefit of Third Parties*, Consultation Paper 242 (London: HMSO, 1996).

[47] Bates and Cowper, "Third parties' contractual rights—Radical changes to the basic principles" [1999] PLC 21.

The English Act defines a third party as a person who is not a party to the contract and gives that person the right to enforce a term of a contract if either of the following two conditions apply:

(i) if the contract expressly provides that the third party may enforce a term of the contract; or

(ii) if the terms of the contract purport to confer a benefit on the third party, unless on a proper construction of the contract it appears that the parties did not intend the term to be enforceable by the third party.

This second provision was always liable to create some uncertainty as to whether a promise to confer a benefit had actually been made in any given case. It would seem, though, that as soon as it can be shown that a contractual term purports to confer a benefit on the third party, there will be, in effect, a rebuttable presumption that it is enforceable by the third party.[48] So it was that in the first English case to consider the English Act, *Nisshin Shipping Co Ltd v Cleaves & Co Ltd and others*[49] the English High Court adopted a broad interpretation of the provisions of the English Act and in particular as to when a benefit is deemed to be conferred on a third party.[50] In his decision in the case, Colman J warmly welcomed the introduction of the new Act and signalled a judicial willingness to interpret the provisions of the English Act widely.[51]

---

[48] *ibid* at p 22.

[49] [2004] 1 All ER (Comm) 481.

[50] The facts of the case were as follows: A number of similar charter-parties containing an arbitration clause were entered into between owners and charterers, which provided that the owners would pay commission to a third party broker. The owners challenged the broker's entitlement to payment on the basis that certain conduct on the broker's part had amounted to a repudiatory breach of the agency relationship. The broker referred the issue of entitlement to arbitration in accordance with the charter-parties' arbitration clause and the arbitrator ruled that the effect of ss 1 and 8 of the English Act was that the arbitrator had jurisdiction. The owners challenged this finding under s 67 of the Arbitration Act 1996. In the English High Court it was held that notwithstanding that none of the charter-parties expressly provided that the brokers could enforce payment against the owners through arbitration, and that although the charter-parties were silent as to whether there was an intention to confer a benefit on the broker, the effect of the Act was to make the broker the statutory assignee of the charterers right of action against the owners.

[51] Colman J referred to the Contracts (Rights of Third Parties) Act 1999 as "a long overdue body blow to the doctrine of privity of contract".

Statutory Reform—Australia

In contrast, while Australian state and territory legislatures were among the first to recognise the inconsistency in the law in this area and take steps toward reform, the courts have adopted a more cautious approach.[52]

In the Northern Territory, Western Australia and Queensland legislative reform has, for the most part, led to the abolition of the privity rule.[53] Although by no means indistinguishable from each other, the relevant legislative provisions in these Australian jurisdictions entitle a third party beneficiary to enforce the contract, allow the contracting parties to vary or discharge the contract prior to its being "adopted" (in Western Australia) or "accepted" (in Queensland and the Northern Territory) by the third party beneficiary but not thereafter and can subject the third party beneficiary to obligations which the contract purports to impose on it prior to it being able to enforce a benefit.[54]

There has been limited case law on the effect of the relevant provisions in Western Australia and none indeed in the Northern Territory.[55] However, there has been a reasonable amount of judicial consideration of the relevant Queensland provisions where the issue as to what degree a contract can be deemed to confer a benefit on a third party and to what extent that third party must be identified in the relevant contract has been the focus of a reasonable amount of deliberation.

The kernel of the Property Law Act 1974 (Qld), s 55 (hereinafter referred to as the Queensland Act) provides that:

> "A promisor who, for a valuable consideration moving from the promisee, promises to do or refrain from doing an act for the benefit of a beneficiary shall, upon acceptance of the beneficiary, be subject to a duty enforceable by the beneficiary to perform that promise."[56]

---

[52] In addition, in *Trident General Insurance Co Ltd v McNeice Bros Ltd* (1988) 165 CLR 107, the Australian High Court abolished the common law doctrine of privity as it relates to insurance contract, although the court did not explicitly reject or abandon the rule itself.

[53] See: Law of Property Act 2000 (NT), s 56, Property Law Act 1974 (Qld), s 55 and Property Law Act 1969 (WA), s 11.

[54] Carter and Harland, *Contract Law in Australia* (Butterworths, Chatswood 2002) at p 352.

[55] To date there have been only 14 cases in Western Australia, where the relevant Western Australia legislation has been reviewed.

[56] Butler, "Enforcement of Third Party Rights in Queensland pursuant to Property Law Act 1974 (Qld), s 55" (1998) 14 QUTLJ 73.

The Queensland Supreme Court has held that a beneficiary must be named as such and cannot be an incidental beneficiary in order to enforce a benefit.[57] In *Northern Sandblasting Pty Limited v Harris,*[58] the High Court of Australia held that a beneficiary must be ascertainable from the terms of the promise made. The court cautioned that the application of a more expansive interpretation as to who a beneficiary was would make it impossible to predict how wide the category of beneficiaries might be. The court also rejected the idea that a promise could be inferred in the absence of an intention to make a promise. It held that the relevant section of the Queensland Act could only apply if there was a clear intention in the relevant agreement to benefit the third party. In other words, in contrast to the equivalent English provision, a benefit to a third party cannot be implied into a contract by statute. It is submitted that the narrow interpretation adopted by the Australian courts has meant that third parties may not as readily enforce what might otherwise be thought to be a benefit flowing to a third party under a contract as is likely to be the case in England and Wales when the jurisprudence in this area has developed further.

Proposed Reform

While it has been said that reform could best be achieved through common law decisions in the courts,[59] it is submitted that statutory reform is preferable. It would establish a clean break with past case law. It would also lessen any teething problems, that would be necessitated by the inevitable court litigation that would be required to tease out the exact nature of the third party right, if established through common law decisions. Nor, of course, is there any indication that the courts would take steps to reform the common law. Indeed everything to date points to an unwillingness to do just that without legislative guidance.

---

57 See: *Robt Jones (363 Adelaide Street) Pty Ltd v First Abbott Corporation Pty Ltd*, unreported, Qld SC, White J, 28 October 1997. In this case it was held that the owners of a defective property could not claim the benefit of obligations under the building contract where the builder was required to obtain certain warranties from subcontractors although they clearly stood to benefit incidentally from such warranties.

58 (1997) 188 CLR 313. The facts of the case were that a landlord of a residential premises undertook to have a defective electrical appliance repaired before his tenants entered into possession. The plaintiff, the daughter of the tenant subsequently suffered severe injuries from an electrical shock. The High Court of Australia found for the plaintiff on a number of different grounds. However, it flatly rejected the argument that the tenant was a beneficiary of a promise in accordance with s 55 of the Queensland Act.

59 *op. cit* at 54.

An important issue is whether contracting parties, who have created rights in favour of third parties, are at liberty to rescind or vary such rights at a later date. All English and Australian Acts provide that, where a third party has a right to enforce a term of a contract under the Act, the parties may not, by agreement, rescind or vary the contract in a way that would adversely affect the third parties rights where such rights have crystallised.[60] This crystallization will occur when, first, the third party has communicated his assent to the term to the promisor; secondly, where the promisor is aware that the third party has relied on the term; or thirdly, the promisor can reasonably be expected to have foreseen that the third party would rely on the term and the third party has in fact relied on it.

Of course, it is probably fair to say that rights granted to a third party in accordance with such legislation are less satisfactory than rights directly granted to contracting parties. First, it may be difficult for a third party to be certain that the contract on which that party is being asked to rely was validly created. Nor indeed will a third party always be certain that its rights have actually crystallised under a contract. Thirdly, if the contract is breached on grounds of misrepresentation, for example, the third party will have no rights.

Despite this, it is submitted that such legislation in Ireland would make the application of the law fairer and, theoretically, more sound. Although, as we have seen, its success will depend on the clarity of draftsmanship within the legislation as to what constitutes a promise and as to who the beneficiary of that promise may be.

Conclusion

In conclusion, we have seen that the doctrine of privity is built on an unsteady foundation of case law. It has been referred to as one of the "most reviled legal doctrines ever to have gained such widespread acceptance".[61] The numerous exceptions that have been developed to counteract its harshness seem to negate the *de facto* operation of the doctrine, while also creating a degree of complexity that could otherwise be avoided. Reform in England, Australia and elsewhere has highlighted the anomaly within our own jurisdiction. There is no valid reason why the law must resort to such numerous exceptions and other imaginative but intricate reasoning to achieve simple objectives. As Cheshire, Fifoot & Furmston put it, "these inconsistent exceptions

[60] s 2(1), Contract (Rights of Third Parties) Act 1999.

[61] Friel, above, n 36 at 89.

render the operation of the law uncertain [and] so the rule may often disappoint the reasonable expectations of the third parties".[62]

Reform of this area of contract law is needed. It is true, as Zweigert and Katz assert, that one advantage of the common law is that it has been "able to adapt itself quickly to changes in economic and social circumstances by modifying legal principles and standards".[63] However, the courts have consistently failed to abolish the privity rule despite its inadequacies and while it is conceded that success of such legislation would depend on how the Irish courts applied the new law, it is argued that statutory reform is now long overdue and is surely the most appropriate way of protecting the expectations of third parties under Irish contract law.

---

62 Cheshire, Fifoot & Furmston, *Law of Contract,* (13th ed, Butterworths, London 1995), at p 454.
63 Zweigert & Katz, above, n 6, at 466.

The Law of Fundraising: Rumblings in the Coffers?

by
Geoff Moore*

Introduction

Charitable and philanthropic purposes have traditionally enjoyed widespread public support in this jurisdiction, with numerous types of fundraising techniques being employed at any one time. Collections and flag days, lotteries, sale of goods and services, fundraising social events and appeals through the mass media are all commonplace. Despite the dedicated work of thousands of volunteers, the potential for abuse is huge. In 1994, total charitable donations in this jurisdiction were estimated to range up to £251 million.[1] The figure is undoubtedly significantly higher now. Ultimately the actions of a handful of fundraisers whose *bona fides* may be questionable can bring the voluntary sector as a whole into disrepute.

While the statute books contain several Acts relating to charity law in general,[2] it has become increasingly obvious in recent years that the area of fundraising suffers from a marked lack of modern legislative control. On addressing the opening meeting of the Committee on Fundraising Activities for Charitable Purposes (the "Costello Committee") in early 1989, the then Minister for Justice, Mr Gerard Collins TD, stated:

> "Over the last year or so a great deal of public disquiet and unease has been expressed about possible abuses in fundraising for charitable purposes,

---

* Geoff Moore, BCL (NUI (UCC)), M. Litt. (Dublin). Mr Moore is a Senior Associate in the Corporate Department of Arthur Cox, Dublin, and is admitted to practice in Ireland, England and Wales and New York. An earlier version of this article was awarded joint second place by the Law Society of Ireland *Student Law Reform Essay Competition 1999.*

[1] See the Gaming and Lotteries (Amendment) Bill 1996, Explanatory Memorandum.

[2] See, for example, the Charities Acts of 1961 and 1973.

about alleged inadequacies in existing legislation in relation to fundraising and the way in which proceeds are accounted for and distributed."[3]

Regrettably, the comprehensive report of the Costello committee was not acted upon for many years, and accordingly the deficiencies in the existing structure need to be highlighted once again.

The Inadequacies of the Existing Regime

The Street and House to House Collections Act 1962

At present the major statutory controls relating to fundraising in this jurisdiction are contained in the Street and House to House Collections Act 1962.[4] The Act, as the name implies, contains controls of fundraising by means of street collections and house-to-house collections which are undertaken both for charitable and non-charitable purposes. These controls are supplemented by regulations made under s 28 of the Act, namely the Street and House to House Collections (Prescribed Forms) Regulations 1962.[5] It is the scheme of the Act to prohibit "collections" (as defined),[6] which are held without a permit issued under the provisions of the Act.

Under s 3 it is an offence for any person to carry out an unauthorised collection. The authority designated by the Act to grant a collection permit is the chief superintendent of the locality where it is proposed to hold the collection.[7] This locality is in practice the respective Garda division.[8] The reference to "locality" has the effect of ensuring that a permit issued by a Superintendent is only valid for a collection within the division of which he has charge. It also results in the cumbersome situation whereby, if it is proposed to hold a collection in various parts of the country (as is often the case in modern fundraising campaigns) separate

3 Report of the Committee on Fundraising for Charitable and Other Purposes, Pl. 7028 [1990], Appendix 1. (Hereafter the "Costello Report", named after the committee's chairman, Mr Justice Declan Costello).

4 No. 13 of 1962.

5 SI No. 134 of 1962. The then Garda Commissioner, Mr Daniel Costigan, introduced these regulations in August 1962, which relate to the form to be used by an applicant for a collection permit. This form is known as "Form SC1" and requires that would-be collectors furnish a minimum amount of information relating to the collection.

6 SI No. 134 of 1962.

7 s 5.

8 For a discussion of Garda divisions, see the Costello Report, para 4.4.

applications have to be made for each Garda division in which the collection is proposed to take place.

Several points of criticism arise from an examination of the Act. It contains no provision relating to the accountability of the collector or the permit holder. The Bill as originally drafted did contain a provision for the post-collection accounts to be submitted to the chief superintendent. However, Mr Michael O'Higgins TD was of the opinion that the obligation to account would prove to be excessively onerous. He felt that if the licensing authority (namely the chief superintendent) was satisfied with the objects of the collection and the character and *bona fides* of the people carrying it out, then such a provision was unnecessary.[9] Accordingly, the section was deleted.[10] Nowadays, however, a need for accountability clearly exists when public collections of this sort are made, and indeed the Costello Report expressly recognised this in its recommendation that a provision for the submission of accounts to the chief superintendent within one month of the completion of the collection be incorporated into any new legislation.[11] It was also felt that these accounts should be available for public inspection in a place designated in the application for the permit.[12]

Penalties for breach of the Act are completely inadequate. While the Act creates a number of offences, the only penalty outlined is that contained in s 25, whereby a person guilty of an offence under the Act is liable to a fine not exceeding £50 or to imprisonment for a term not exceeding six months or to both fine and imprisonment. These penalties need to be increased in line with inflation and current penalties, for at their present levels they do little more than serve to make a mockery of the potential financial gravity of a modern-day offence under the Act.

The Act deals obliquely with the thorny issue of payment of commission to collectors and fundraisers. This practice has escalated in recent times whereby payment of commission is made to collectors taking up collections under the Act. The Costello committee, while acknowledging that the extent of the practice was not easy to ascertain, were nevertheless satisfied that it existed on a significant scale.[13]

---

9 See 193 Dáil Debates Col 510.

10 Note the comments of the then Minister for Justice, Mr Charles Haughey TD, who felt that a prudent person would keep these accounts irrespective of any statutory duty to do so.

11 Costello Report, para 5.24.

12 *ibid.*

13 *ibid* para 5.26.

Reference is made in the Act to the fact that collectors may obtain "reasonable commission for their services",[14] but unfortunately the legislature did not see fit to expand on this or to specify what percentage of commission would constitute a "reasonable" proportion. The Costello Report presented two possible solutions to the problem:[15] either the payment of collectors could be made expressly illegal by statute, or alternatively, collectors could be required to make known to the public that they are in receipt of payment. The latter option was correctly rejected as it was felt that it would do nothing to preserve the public perception of unselfish volunteers giving their time and energy in the interests of others which undoubtedly plays a part in the public's response to charitable appeals. In relation to the former option it can be argued that the introduction of such a measure is not necessary as the claiming of commission by collectors is contrary to trust law in any event. In this regard the judgment of Brightman J in the *Sanctuary*[16] case is particularly interesting:

> "Another point which has troubled me in this case is the legality of commissions charged by persons who take round, charity collecting boxes. A collecting box which names a charity as the recipient of a donation represents that the money placed in the box goes for the charity. If a collector retains 35% commission, all the money does not go to the named charity. The collector is collecting as 65% of the charity and 35% for himself. This is contrary to the representation on the collecting box and contrary to the belief of most people who place money in the box. Therefore, on that ground, I have grave doubt as to the legality of such a commission. Furthermore, a person who solicits money for a charity is a trustee of the money for the purpose of handing it to the charity. A member of the public who puts money in the box is a donor of his own contribution, not distinguishable in principle from any other donor or settlor of trust funds. Unless the collector makes known to the donor his intention to retain a percentage of the contribution for himself, it seems to me that he has no possible title to that percentage. If the collector makes clear to all concerned that a specified percentage of the contribution will be retained by him, there can be no objection to the retention of that percentage however high it may be. If, however, the collector fails to disclose that he

14 s 9(f) of the 1962 Act.

15 See Costello Report, para 5.26.

16 *Jones v Attorney-General*, *The Times*, 10 November 1976.

> is keeping something for himself, there is every objection to the retention of that percentage. This appears to me to be elementary trust law. I fail to discern any reason why it should not apply just as much to collection boxes as to other fiduciary activities."

What the learned judge has stated would appear to apply with equal force to other fundraising methods also.

The Gaming and Lotteries Act 1956

The second set of statutory controls on fundraising in this jurisdiction are those pertaining to lotteries that are found in the Gaming and Lotteries Act 1956.[17] Part IV of the Act is important in relation to the law of fundraising in that it relates to lotteries. Interestingly, the term "lottery" is not defined in the Act. The Act makes all lotteries lawful other than those which the Act declares not to be unlawful. Part IV states that certain types of lottery are not unlawful; namely certain private lotteries,[18] lotteries promoted at dances and concerts,[19] those promoted at carnivals and other like events,[20] those held under a permit granted by a superintendent of the Gárda Siochána[21] or those held under a licence granted by the District Court.[22]

The statute came under greater scrutiny following the enactment of the National Lottery Act 1986.[23] It had been claimed that the voluntary charitable agencies would be placed in a very unfair position as a result of this legislation since under s 22 of the 1956 Act they were prevented from advertising and publicising their lotteries, and also they were limited to offering prizes of a certain value.[24] As part of the Government's response to the concern expressed by the charitable agencies that their fundraising abilities would be lessened as a result of competition from the National Lottery, power was given to the Minister for Justice by s 33(2) of the 1986 Act to alter the amount specified for the value of prizes under ss 27 and 28. Under

17 No 2 of 1956.

18 s 23.

19 s 24.

20 s 25.

21 s 27.

22 s 28.

23 No 28 of 1986.

24 See *Irish Current Law Studies Annotated* [1986], p 28–20.

the Lottery Prizes Regulations 1987,[25] the then Minister for Justice, Mr Alan Dukes, TD, increased the maximum prize money under s 27 from IR£300 to IR£3000, and in the case of s 28, from IR£500 to IR£10,000. Regrettably, while maximum prize values are imposed, there is no limit to the proportion of the proceeds that may be taken as commission or used as promotional expenses.[26] The 1986 Act did not, however, empower the Minister to alter the IR£25 limit on prizes contained in s 24 relating to lotteries promoted. The preservation of the status quo by the Minister at the time was questionable at best. It appears illogical that the prize values were amended in relation to ss 27 and 28 and not s 24, since this section could also be relevant to charitable objects.

Rumblings of Reform

In an attempt to level the playing pitch for the major Irish charities by removing the restrictions which had been placed on lotteries for charitable purposes, a Private Members Bill was placed before Dáil Eireann by Mr Michael Woods, TD, in May 1996.[27] The Bill was rejected on the basis of an undertaking given by the then Minister for State at the Department of Justice, Ms Joan Burton, TD, that a Charities Bill was soon to be published that would herald a comprehensive reform of the legislative framework within which fundraising organisations operate.[28] This was to prove an overly optimistic statement, and for several years more no such Bill was published.

In 2002, the Law Reform Committee of the Law Society of Ireland published a comprehensive report entitled "Charity Law: The Case for Reform", which set out a host of recommendations relating to Irish charity law, including fundraising.

In particular, the Law Reform Committee recommended that an independent statutory office should be created and known as the Registrar of Charities. Subject to consultation with that body, the Commissioners for Charitable Donations and Requests should be reconstituted as an advisory board under the title of the Charities Board. The Charities Registrar should be a member of the board *ex offico*. Both the Registrar and the Board should be supported by a Charities Office. Specifically, in

---

[25] SI No 72 of 1987.

[26] Costello Report, para 4.12.

[27] Gaming and Lotteries (Amendment) Bill 1996 (No 24 of 1996).

[28] See 467 Dáil Debates Col 313.

relation to fundraising, the report recommended that the Charities Office, in consultation with the Charities sector and the Irish Institute of Fundraisers, should develop best practice guidelines for fundraising and a system for certification or self-certification. The purpose of this would be for participating organisations to certify their fundraising procedures in the manner of quality assurance. The report also recommended that the Charities Office should take responsibility for the granting of permits and licences for fundraising with appeals against decision of the Board to the District Court. The report also recommended that the current exclusion from regulation of fundraising by means of charitable street trading should be reviewed and that such fundraising should be made subject to controls as to dates and locations in the interest of the fair sharing of dates and locations between all charities. Such fundraising should also be brought under the same controls of regulation and accountability of street collections in the public interest. Finally, the sale of items for charity or promotions in conjunction with charities should clearly state the amount or percentage which is payable to the charity.

Shortly after the publication of the Law Society report, the pressure for reform mounted with the publication by the Department of Community Rural and Gaeltacht Affairs in 2003 of a Consultation Paper entitled "Establishing a Modern Statutory Framework for Charities".[29] The consultation paper highlighted that there was a need for an integrated approach to the regulation of charities because there is:

- no body that has the specific aim of regulatory charities;
- no complete register of charities;
- no legal requirement for charities that are not Companies to provide regular accounts to any supervisory body;
- no legal requirement for the registration of professional fundraisers employed by charities.

It is clear than any new legislation needs to encompass a variety of issues. The existing statutory framework is clearly outdated. At one end of the spectrum it fails to demand an acceptable level of accountability in relation to funds which are raised, yet at the other end it places those running charitable lotteries in a position where effective fundraising is almost impossible given the ultra-stiff competition from the Irish and British National Lotteries and the Euro Millions Lottery. Examining the existing legislation with a view to forming the core of any reform is to plough much too narrow a furrow, however. Many other issues also need to be addressed that have

[29] December 2003.

hitherto not been incorporated in legislation in any guise or form. In this regard, the position of professional fundraisers is one that needs to be urgently considered.

The regulation of professional fundraisers was thoroughly considered in the Costello Report,[30] and it was recommended that legislation be introduced to ensure that their activities do not harm the reputation of the charitable sector in any way. The report recommended a system of registration similar to that already in place for auctioneers under the Auctioneers and House Agents Act 1947.[31] The requirement for written contracts between professional fundraisers and consultants, on the one hand, and charitable organisations, on the other, was also recommended, with the contract written on a form to be prescribed by ministerial regulation.[32] In this regard, the enactment of the Charities Act 1992[33] in England and Wales provides very useful comparative legislation.

The UK Charities Act grew out of a National Council for Voluntary Organisations report entitled "Malpractice in Fundraising for Charity" and a subsequent report carried out by Sir Philip Woodfield entitled "Efficiency Scrutiny for the Supervision of Charities", both of which recognised that fundraising practices have developed and become more sophisticated in response to the rising tide of demand for funds. It was acknowledged that while many potential fundraisers are highly reputable, there are others who, because of the methods they use or the fees or commission that they charge, bring the profession (and also the voluntary sector) into disrepute. The legislation introduced, contained in Pt 11 of the 1992 UK Act, is a comprehensive statutory regime aimed at controlling agreements between the two parties by ensuring that all agreements are in writing and that the terms of any agreement are clearly specified.

It is noteworthy that the profession itself recognises that regulation is necessary. The Irish Institute of Fundraisers was set up in 1996 with the purpose of improving the ethical standards and ability of fundraising managers and providing training facilities. While self-regulation is to be commended, fundraising also has to be accountable to the public. Reliance on personal integrity alone is insufficient. As Ms Burton noted as far back as 1996, there needs to be a system of controls in place that are thorough yet are not unduly cumbersome.

---

30 Chap 6.

31 Costello Report, para 6.8.

32 *ibid*, para 6.9.

33 1992 c 41.

In voting against the Private Members Gaming and Lotteries Bill in 1996, the then Government correctly recognised that piecemeal reform of charitable fundraising laws is insufficient and that widespread legislative change is instead needed. Ten years later, the proposed legislative amendments have only recently seen the light of day.

The Charities Regulation Bill 2006[34] was published in March 2006 and presents a scheme for the wholesale reform of Irish charity law. While the majority of the proposed reforms are outside the scope of this paper, Pt VI of the Bill addresses charitable fundraising.

The introduction to Pt VI of the Bill notes that the approach now proposed with respect to the regulation of charitable fundraising is to develop a three-pronged mixed regulatory model by:

- modernising and streamlining the 1962 provisions by providing a statutory framework to safeguard the public interest and the more uniform application of permits for charitable fundraising;
- giving the requisite powers to a newly created body with responsibility for charitable regulation to require charities to provide information concerning their fundraising activities; and
- implementing agreed codes of good practice in relation to the actual fundraising operations, while retaining reserve powers for the Minister for Community, Rural and Gaeltacht affairs to bring in statutory regulation if this approach proves ineffective.

The Bill is only in draft form, although the proposed approach in relation to the regulation of fundraising is to be welcomed. The Bill has not yet been introduced to the Dáil or the Seanad—it appears unlikely that this will occur prior to 2007—meaning that there is no guarantee that it will become law in its current form. It is however hoped that it will serve as a suitable platform to remedy the various deficiencies in the existing legislation relating to charitable fundraising. The disquiet and unease that Mr Collins spoke of fully 17 years ago has neither silenced nor soothed—the time is nigh.

34 General scheme for the Charities Regulation Bill 2006 (*for the information of the public*).

The Law of Nullity — Current Defects and Suggested Reforms

by
Muireann McEnery*

Introduction

Justice Kenny remarked in *S v S* that the act of 1870[1] "did not have the effect of fossilizing the law in its state in that year"[2] and that advances made in psychological medicine should be acknowledged. This acknowledgement took place, at first cautiously and without injustice, but several decisions, particularly those made in the late 1990s, are cause for concern. The development of two new grounds, the "inability ground" and the "inadequate or defective knowledge ground" are particularly troublesome. The trouble arises not so much from the creation of the grounds themselves but rather the manner in which these grounds have been developed.

The "inability to enter into and sustain a normal marital relationship" as a ground for obtaining a decree of nullity is divisible into three principle grounds: mental illness, immaturity and homosexuality. Two of these grounds, mental illness and immaturity, have developed without any semblance of coherency.

Mental Illness

The world of psychological and psychiatric medicine is constantly evolving, and it is, perhaps this evolution, which in a time when divorce was unavailable in this jurisdiction, provided the judiciary with a means of creatively providing petitioners with an escape from doomed marriages. The judiciary, while adamant not to

* This essay was awarded joint second place in the Law Society of Ireland, *Student Law Reform Competition 1999.*

[1] Matrimonial Causes and Marriage Law (Ireland) (Amendment) Act 1870.

[2] Unreported, Supreme Court, July 1976.

"abdicate its function"[3] to experts in deciding such cases, should perhaps be careful not to rush in where even experts may fear to tread. In many of the cases I am about to discuss, however, this creativity in interpreting "mental illness" and "immaturity" as grounds for the granting of a decree of nullity created inconsistency, uncertainty and an "unprecedented relaxation in the conditions upon which a marriage would be deemed null and void".[4]

When dealing with these grounds of nullity, in the words of Keane J "[w]e move from the cold objectivity of ascertainable clinical findings to the elusive and impalpable area of emotions".[5] The cases being referred to by Justice Keane are *RSJ v JSJ*[6] and *D v C*.[7]

These cases, both concerning mental illnesses, were the first to give credence to the inability ground. Justice Barrington stated in *RSJ v JSJ*:

> "If it could be shown that at the date of the marriage, the petitioner, through illness lacked the capacity to form a caring relationship with his wife, I would be prepared to entertain this as a ground upon which a decree of nullity *might* be granted."[8]

A number of observations can be made about this statement. First, on the facts of the case, no decree was granted even though it was acknowledged that the petitioner had assaulted, hurt and frightened his wife. It was also acknowledged that the petitioner suffered from "some form of personality defect or illness similar to schizophrenia" and that this would cause problems for any marriage. Notwithstanding these concessions, because he wasn't satisfied that the petitioner had proved the necessary incapacity on the date of his wedding, as already stated, Barrington J refused a decree. Also to be noted is the use of the words "Illness at the date of the marriage" and "caring relationship", neither of which are defined or elaborated upon. Exactly what type of illness is being referred to? Is the non existence of the illness at the date of the marriage fatal to a decree on its basis in all situations

---

3 *KWT v DAT* [1992] 2 IR 11.

4 Ryan, *"Family Law – Reversal of Fortune – Nullity in the Age of Divorce"* (2000) DULJ at p 224.

5 *UF v JC* [1991] 2 IR 330.

6 [1982] ILRM 263.

7 [1984] 4 ILRM 175.

8 [1982] ILRM at 265.

or is this case to be confined to its facts? And what exactly is a caring relationship? Is it the same as a "considerate relationship", a "normal interpersonal relationship" or "some form of society"?[9] Looking at the facts of the present case, only the most insensitive of human beings could infer that a relationship where one spouse had occasion to assault and frighten the other is any of the above, and indeed nowhere does the court try to suggest as such. It seems therefore that the decisive factor was the petitioner's failure to prove that on the date of his wedding he was so incapacitated as to make the marriage void or voidable. The use of the word illness, without elaboration or definition, is also dangerous in that it could be extended to almost any physical ailment regardless of its true effect on a marital relationship. Does lack of knowledge of the illness at the date of the marriage by one or both of the parties have to be shown? Or is one spouse to be discarded if several years after his or her wedding ceremony some genetic imperfection manifests itself? What if a marriage fails due to the personality of one of the spouses? Eccentricity, insensitivity and other flaws can undoubtedly result in an uncaring relationship but the question is, should they result in the granting of an annulment?[10] The origins of this new inability ground stem from impotence; however, in relation to impotence, curability, if proven, could have the effect of removing the grounds for a decree, yet curability in relation to psychological inability is not mentioned here. Does it matter that the illness in question is treatable? It has been stated that physicians are too cautious to testify in absolute terms that *any* condition is incurable.[11] Does this mean that any illness, whether or not it is psychological or existed at the time of the marriage, and may be curable can still result in a decree of nullity?

Two years after this landmark decision another somewhat similar case,[12] in which *RSJ v JSJ* was cited as an authority, appeared before the courts. The petitioner's claims were based on the existence of a mental illness affecting both the respondent's ability to understand the marriage contract and also to sustain a normal marital relationship. The court rejected the argument that the respondent was unable to fully understand the nature, purpose and consequences of the marriage but a decree was granted on the ground that the respondent was unable "to enter into and sustain a normal marital relationship with the petitioner". Again the court failed to define

---

9 *W v P*, unreported, High Court, 7 June 1984.

10 This appears to have occurred to some extent in a 2003 decision *MO'C v MO'C*, unreported, High Court, 10 July 2003, discussed below.

11 Professor Homer Clark.

12 *D v C* [1984] 4 ILRM 175.

exactly what is meant by a normal marital relationship, and while *RSJ v JSJ* was cited as an authority, there was one fundamental difference in the wording used. Justice Costello, unlike Justice Barrington, restricted the type of illness to "psychiatric illness". Another difference between the two cases is one relating to the criteria that the illness should exist at the date of the marriage. This was one of the decisive factors in the *RSJ* case, yet Justice Costello, some 10 years after the date of the marriage in *D v C*, on the evidence of the petitioner and a psychiatrist employed by the petitioner, was satisfied that the respondent was at the time of the marriage suffering from a psychiatric illness and also that this illness precluded him from sustaining a normal marriage relationship. Viewed in this light, it seems that the tentative extension by Justice Barrington has been distorted even further. The subjective opinion of judge and petitioner, 10 years after a marriage, are being substituted for objectivity and ascertainable facts. Justice Costello's recognition that "the law should have regard to the emotional and psychological relationship" is laudable, but he refrains from instilling any clarity into this new ground.

The subsequent case law gave immediate support to this ground, many of the cases involving instances of schizophrenia.[13] Schizophrenia is undoubtedly an "illness" and relatively easy to prove, coming within what Justice Keane termed "ascertainable clinical findings"[14] and therefore free of the anomalies that are encountered where the incapacity stems from something less well defined. One of the many examples of this is *S v K*.[15] The parties in this case were a young couple who married, probably as a result of an unplanned pregnancy; the subsequent marriage was a turbulent one, nothing short of a disaster and a decree was granted on the inability ground. The incapacity arose from many things, including a schizoaffective disorder and immaturity on both sides. The fact that both parties were, at the time of the hearing, in stable relationships with other people was regarded as irrelevant to the relationship in question. But for the sake of argument, perhaps it could be used in combination with several other factors to argue against a decree of nullity. In concluding his opinion in *S v K*, the judge applied the analogy of impotence in stating that the incapacity could be in relation to a particular person (as found in *S v S*[16]). A

13 *R v R*, unreported, High Court, 21 December 1984; *DC v DW* [1987] ILRM 58; *WK v MC* 31 July 1992.

14 *UF v JC* [1991] 2 IR 330.

15 [1993] 1 Fam LJ 31.

16 Unreported, Supreme Court, July 1976.

difference between the two cases is the extent to which post-marital circumstances were a catalyst for the incapacities. If we look again at the facts of *S v K*, we see two young immature people, consigned by an accidental pregnancy and no doubt the views of society at that time to marriage. Inexperienced in the ways of the world, unable to provide, both emotionally and financially, for each other or their child and both with unhappy childhoods.

The fact that subsequent to their marriage, they were able to form stable relationships highlights the extent to which this particular marriage was a bad if not a disastrous decision. Their age, the pregnancy, the emotional baggage they both had to deal with and the timing of the entire ordeal could have led to nothing other than a breakdown. But it was the circumstances of the marriage which "triggered" the incapacity, and not the reverse, which was the scenario in *S v S*. To put it another way, a marriage cannot be impugned "merely because it could be considered to have been an unwise decision". A case in 1996 seems to add another layer of confusion.[17] Here the judge stated, "I do not think the law has been extended so far as to say that a decree of nullity may be granted where a person suffered from a latent illness which did not affect the ability to enter into a marriage, but which might subsequently affect the ability to sustain that marriage".

This seems to be at odds with the outcome of *S v K*, especially when the illness was just one of the many deleterious circumstances affecting the marriage. However, it was found on the facts in that case that at the time of the marriage, while the respondent suffered from a latent illness, that illness did not render her incapable of forming and sustaining a normal life-long marital relationship. This statement was made even though on the wedding day, the respondent started to laugh and cry during the taking of the vows. Also, the fact that the illness in question could have been kept under control by the earlier use of lithium seemed to play a part in the denial of the decree. This possibly relates to the curability element. But one could also apply this reasoning to the *S v K* decision; the subsequent formation of stable relationships by both parties involved seems to demonstrate curability.

Looking back at the pioneer case *RSJ v JSJ*, it appears that the essential requirement that the illness existed at the time of the marriage has been phased out over time and to the point where the requirement of a "mental illness" may no longer be an

---

[17] *SC v PD*(C), unreported, High Court, 14 March 1996.

essential prerequisite.[18] In *W v P*,[19] "emotional disability or incapacity" was accepted as warranting the granting of an annulment.

Immaturity

The nature of some of the cases brought before the courts on the basis of immaturity show the whimsical character of this ground. Cases which perhaps would not have stood a chance of success under any other heading of the inability ground were framed in terms of immaturity. One such case is *AB v EB*.[20] The petitioner based his claim on what he considered the respondent's failure to perform sexually at the level of his desires and expectations. Thankfully, the Supreme Court rejected this notion of sexual inadequacy. *PC v CM*[21] proffered the respondent's promiscuity as the basis for nullity, which was again rejected. Another tragic and curious case is *DMcC v EC*,[22] where a combination of factors brought about the marriage breakdown. These stemmed from the abusive childhood of the respondent leading later in life to alcoholism and other emotional dysfunctions. The inability of the respondent to sustain a functional marriage was easily believed, but again, is nullity warranted? The following statement by Justice O'Hanlon statement in *PC v VC*[23] was cited as supporting the outcome of this case:

> "as both parties entered into the marriage contract innocently, being unaware of factors connected with personality and psychology".

However, it must be noted that the petitioner and the respondent met in AA meetings and so knowledge of at least some of these factors seems to be an unavoidable inference. In addition, the problems suffered by the respondent, while serious, fall short of the label "mental illness". They are a result of the tragic circumstances of his upbringing and possibly treatable to a large extent by counselling. Strangely enough, inalterability or curability is not referred to in the context of immaturity, as already noted in relation to *S v K*.

---

[18] This observation was made by Keane J in *UF v JC*, unreported, High Court, 25 May 1989.

[19] Unreported, High Court, 7 June 1984.

[20] [1994] 2 Fam LJ 36; Unreported, Supreme Court, 31 July 1995.

[21] [1996] 3 Fam LJ 78.

[22] Unreported, High Court, 6 July 1998.

[23] [1990] 2 IR 91.

The original legal requirements—that the grounds for nullity had to exist at the date of the marriage, and that this has to be established to a high degree of probability—are being overlooked. The existence of a defect without more seems enough to obtain nullity in the cases discussed above.

More recent case law does little to curb the arbitrary extension of this particular ground of nullity. In *MO'C v MO'C,*[24] Ms Justice Finlay Geoghegan granted a decree of nullity on the grounds that the respondent suffered a personality disorder, which was characterised by a "self-obsession" and " lack of insight" and a "failure to take responsibility and accept blame". The facts are remotely similar to *S v K,* discussed earlier, in that the pregnancy of the petitioner in both instances seemed to have moved the parties towards getting married; and in *MO'C v MO'C,* the parties proceeded with the marriage despite the marked deterioration in the relationship before the actual wedding. If the granting of a decree was questionable in *S v K,* given that the parties were both in stable relationships at the time of the granting of the decree, then it is more so on the facts of *MO'C v MO'C* where the personality disorder is explicitly stated as not being psychiatric or a mental illness. In *S v K,* the incapacity was at least based on a schizoaffective disorder. *MO'C v MO'C* would seem to be another instance of a bad decision on behalf of the parties to the marriage, but is a decree of nullity warranted?

Another recent case, *LB v TmacC,*[25] thankfully seems to indicate a more cautious approach and an attempt to draw a distinction between bad marriages where the more appropriate remedy is divorce and instances where a party to the marriage genuinely lacks the capacity to sustain a normal marital relationship as a result of a diagnosable mental illness.

The petitioner in this instance sought a decree of nullity on the grounds that the respondent had misrepresented fundamental facts of his personal circumstances and also on the ground that he was psychologically immature, incapable of maintaining a normal marital relationship and pathologically given to deception and concealment in relation to his circumstances, intentions and emotions. Higgins J refused to grant a decree of nullity, stating that " he was not satisfied that the totality of the evidence disclosed that the personality traits of the respondent were so outside the norm as

[24] Unreported, High Court, 10 July 2003.

[25] Unreported, High Court, 20 December 2004.

would preclude him from contracting to a valid marriage". He went on the say that although the respondent was selfish, egotistical, deceitful and dishonest, this did not warrant the granting of a decree of nullity. This description could arguably be applied to the respondent in *MO'C v MO'C,* where, conversely, a decree was granted.

Defective Knowledge

The case of *N v K*[26] decided in 1986 introduced the concept of "informed consent" into the law of nullity, also expressed as "full and free consent" and "adequate knowledge". This concept, as used in that case, itself is fully comprehensible. While not defined extensively, it is self explanatory within the context of the facts. Unfortunately, this concept as enunciated in *N v K* was subsequently taken out of context and misconstrued in cases where the granting of a nullity decree was somewhat dubious.

First, let's examine the meaning of "informed consent", or rather lack of, in its original context. The elements of *N v K,* which are the basis for this concept, are found in other similar cases. Perhaps the proper identification of these elements will show the intended meaning of "informed consent". The cases of *N v K, B v O'R*[27] and *MK v FMcC*[28] all possess these elements.

In *N v K,* the petitioner was found to be "a quiet, unassertive girl…always obedient to her parents…little more than a schoolgirl….acquiescent in her parents wishes". It was also found that she got no advice on what alternatives she had and couldn't think clearly. The following is a passage from *MK v FMcC* :

> "The petitioner gave the impression of being a shy, reserved, and very sensitive type of girl, closely-attached to both her parents and very dependent on them...the respondent…felt himself condemned by his parents and by anyone he turned to for advice; any decision was effectively taken out of his hands by the joint meeting of the parents, who obviously considered they were in a position to impose their will on both the petitioner and the respondent, and this occurred in fact".

---

26 [1986] ILRM 75.

27 [1991] 1 IR 289.

28 [1982] ILRM 277.

B v O'R is an even more acute version of the above situations. It involved an arranged marriage of an orphan. The orphan in question was 15 years old and had lived all her life in an orphanage and received no independent advice on the alternatives available to her. One possible meaning, therefore, that can be ascribed to lack of informed consent is a situation involving young people; not necessarily immature but perhaps lacking in the wisdom life itself bestows. In all of these cases circumstance has cast them in a situation where they are forced to make important decisions and are subject to pressure from those they trust. Their judgment is further clouded by the seriousness of the situation they find themselves in.

There has always been an abhorrence to applying the same standard to marriage contracts as that which exists in commercial contracts. These cases, while they do not expressly use the term "undue influence", seem to be nonetheless describing this principle. Perhaps there is no need to give the collective circumstances in these cases a name, but the following cases show how the concept of "informed consent", taken in isolation, can have disastrous results.

M'OM v BO'C[29] and *BJM v CJM*,[30] both 1996 cases, granted decrees of nullity on questionable if not ridiculous grounds, yet the former, as a Supreme Court decision, represented the law until 2001. The following extract from Justice Blayney's decision highlights the irrationality of this decision.

> "The test is subjective. Because of this, great weight must be attached to the wife's evidence that had she known that the husband had attended Dr O'S, for approximately six years she would not have married him. It is possible that another person would not have reacted in the same way, but this was the wife's evidence of how she would have reacted if she had known."

The petitioner succeeded in obtaining a decree simply on the basis that she was unaware that her husband had attended a psychiatrist even though "there was no evidence that the husband suffered from" a psychiatric illness. *BJM v CJM* is perhaps even more difficult to accept. Here again, the petitioner succeeded because he was ignorant of his wife's significant disfigurement due to extensive burns she received as a child. While *N v K* is not specifically referred to in this judgment it is apparent from the language used that the "inadequate knowledge" criteria is being extended

---

29 [1996] 1 IR 208.

30 [1996] 2 IR 574.

to cover the situation in this case. The flaws in this reasoning are many. First, the acceptance of the subjective opinion of the petitioners in both cases is opening the oft-cited floodgates and allowing the most frivolous grounds as potential bases for annulment. The attempt to base these decisions on the inadequate knowledge ground is stretching the limits of this principle. If the explanation of inadequate knowledge as already set out is accepted then it is inapplicable to these facts. The case of *AB v EB*[31] provides an interesting comparison. That case involved what could be termed as "psychological disfigurement" as opposed to the "physical disfigurement" involved in *BJM,* yet a decree was refused in *AB v EB.* In addition, the parties to the proceeding in *BJM* remained married for 17 years after the revelation of the disfigurement and had children during this relationship, yet on the request of the petitioner his wife's physical form was held grounds for annulment. Why is approbation not mentioned? Surely a 17-year physical and emotional relationship constitutes acceptance of his wife's deformities. If *AB v EB* had been decided after these cases, it seems probable that the outcome would be different. Is it justifiable that a decree could be granted where a spouse bases his or her claim on an inadequate sex life? Sadly, this is what these recent cases seem to be saying. Since time immemorial the "reasonable man" standard has been employed, albeit in the commercial setting, to provide some guideline as to what is acceptable for attempting to end contracts. Yet, in the most volatile contract of them all, the subjective opinion of the person involved was accepted as sufficient grounds for voidability.

The dissenting judgment of Henchy J in *N v K* was an honest look at the law of nullity as it then stood, and it provided possible solutions to the astounding incoherency in this area. "In my view, the furthest the wife's case can be put is to say that she entered into the marriage because she was unduly influenced by the wishes of her parents. But undue influence, as the law stands, is not a ground for nullifying a marriage." He later goes on to say, "[r]egardless of today's result, this case may be said to emphasize the need for a modern statute providing for the grant of decrees of nullity of marriage on fair, reasonable and clearly stated grounds".

Justice Henchy is applying the law honestly without attempting to use linguistic acrobatics to extend it. The outcome of *N v K* is just, but a new ground was carelessly created to facilitate it. Justice Henchy acknowledged the shortcomings of the law as it stood, seeing perhaps the chaos which might ensue from the decision in *N v K.* His call for statutory reform remains sadly neglected but the wisdom of his words are

[31] [1994] 2 Fam LJ 36; Unreported, Supreme Court, 31 July 1995.

evident. Perhaps the inadequate knowledge ground as used in *N v K* and *B v O'R* is better expressed in terms of undue influence, "the unconscious use of power or authority by one person over another".[32] In *M'Mackin v Hibernian Bank* the following statement was made:

> "The law recognizes that a young person living with or under the influence of a parent, is likely to remain for some time under parental dominion and is at an impressionable age when gratitude affection and respect for a parent are fresh and strong, while knowledge and experience of the stress and struggle and varied obligations of human life have yet to be acquired."[33]

There is no comparison between the facts of *N v K* and *BJM* and *MOM.* It was somewhat bizarre to have extended a principle created in one to explain the outcome of the others.

Thankfully, a 2001 Supreme Court decision addresses the flaws in the above decisions and attempts to distinguish *MO'M* on its facts by stating that it was not the mere fact of the respondent's attendance at a psychiatrist but rather the implication that he was mentally unstable which allowed for the granting of a decree of nullity in that instance. This seems to be a somewhat superficial distinction and one which wasn't explicitly made in that decision itself. However, any attempt to limit the granting of decrees of nullity in circumstances where they are clearly not warranted and restore a degree of certainty is welcome. In *PF V GO'M,*[34] the petitioner sought a decree of nullity on the ground of misrepresentation on the basis that the respondent had been having an affair during the engagement and for several years after the parties were married. The petitioner claimed that had he been aware of this affair, he would not have married the respondent. One can see the similarity to *MO'M v BO'C.* Thankfully, however, McGuinness J in the Supreme Court was able to draw a distinction between the cases as outlined above and refused to grant a decree of nullity, stating that the principles of that case could not "be extended to cover concealed misconduct and other forms of misrepresentation".

32 *Per* Keeton and Sheridan *Equity.*

33 [1905] 1 IR 296.

34 Unreported, Supreme Court, 28 November 2000.

Conclusion

The above discussion highlights the lack of coherent development in this area of the law, much of which can be explained by the difficult cases presented to the courts, particularly those which arose when divorce was not available as an escape from failed marriages in a conservative society still dominated by the tenets of Catholicism. The courts can hardly be faulted for providing petitioners an escape in such circumstances, albeit sacrificing certainty and foreseeability along the way. As recent decisions highlight, there has been a welcome acknowledgement of this lack of certainty and a repeated call to "provide a clear statutory code setting out both the grounds for nullity and its ancillary consequences, both for parties and for any possible children".[35] This sentiment echoes the Law Reform Commission report of 1984 and Justice Henchy's warning in 1986.[36] There seems to be no further excuse in restricting the granting of decrees of nullity given the availability of divorce and the more liberal views towards divorce and separation. More disturbingly, however, is the fact that nullity applications have actually increased since 1997,[37] potentially supporting the observation that nullity is being used as a tactical device to deprive dependent spouses of ancillary relief otherwise available in separation and divorce.[38] While the original and still present need to provide certainty and clarity in this area of the law still exists it has surprisingly become more urgent for different reasons something which is unexpected in the wake of the introduction of divorce. One hopes that codification is imminent and that in the interim case law will continue to redefine the lines between cases where a decree of nullity is genuinely warranted and those in which divorce is the more appropriate remedy.

---

35 *ibid* at 33-34.

36 *N v K* [1986] ILRM 75.

37 Horgan, "Divorce – The Irish Experience" in *The Divorce Act in Practice* (1999).

38 Shatter, *Family Law in the Republic of Ireland* (Wolfhound Press, 1997).

Cyber Certainty: Definite Legal Rights in the Digital Domain

by

Mark Browne*

The potential offered by electronic commerce on open interactive systems such as the Internet is now clear. The particular benefits offered to peripheral nations with modern communication networks and an educated workforce are especially apparent, and in order to facilitate development in this jurisdiction the Irish Government has sought to address some of the preliminary legal uncertainties surrounding electronic commerce via the draft Electronic Communications Bill.[1] However, although this legislation addresses prominent contract related issues, such as the legal enforceability of digital signatures, it is apparent from an examination of emerging overseas case law and current litigation that the areas addressed are merely the tip of the iceberg in terms of the legal issues raised by this new business paradigm.

In fact, the Internet is affecting such change that it will require a re-examination of current interpretations of existing terms and the modification of broad areas of legislation to ensure the applicability of appropriate provisions.[2] Providing legal certainty in the area will promote the development of the online industry in this jurisdiction and attract related investment. However, in addition to requiring a re-

* This essay was awarded joint second by the Law Society of Ireland, *Student Law Reform Essay Competition 2000.*

[1] This piece was originally written and submitted as a topic for law reform in early 2000. The draft legislation mentioned was enacted as the Electronic Commerce Act 2000 shortly thereafter.

[2] In the original work it was noted that the meaning and use of terms such as "premises" or "location" will probably have to be re-examined in the light of the internet and that changes to the tax system would probably be necessitated to limit the scope for both avoidance and evasion. Indeed such were the concerns regarding the potential impact of e-commerce at the time of writing that the OECD established the "Electronic Commerce Tax Study Group" to re-examine core definitions in taxation, such as "permanent establishment", in order to explore the extent to which the underlying concepts of OECD tax codes needed to be redefined. A number of recommendations were issued by this body.

examination of existing legislative provisions, the internet is also generating completely new issues.[3] This work seeks to address a topic which is generating increasing litigation worldwide and is a central feature in the practical operation of the World Wide Web, but which is surrounded in legal uncertainty: the legality of hypertext links to third party sites.

The Issue

A hypertext link is a reference to another document or part thereof which, when activated by means of a mouse click, causes the document which is the subject of the link to be displayed. Hypertext links are a ubiquitous element of websites and a core element of the internet. The link itself merely comprises a reference to the web address or Uniform Resource Locator (URL) (e.g. http://www.bloggs.ie) of the linked site in the Hyper Text Mark-Up Language (HTML) source code for the linking page and this link can be graphically represented in any manner.

Not only are such links found on a substantial number of websites, but they are also the basis of the services offered by some of the most popular sites operated on the internet, such as those of "Yahoo" or "Alta Vista", However, although many sites welcome links, or even pay substantial sums to others to provide links to their sites, others view them as a means of unfairly taking advantage of their work. Especially controversial, is the practice of "deep linking" whereby a link is provided, not to the home page of the third party site but rather to a specific item within it.[4] Direct access to such a page may allow the visitor to bypass advertising, as well as legal notices and warnings on the site and generally reduce the marketing impact of carefully designed sites.

Even more controversial is the use of "frames". These make it possible to display two or more different web pages simultaneously on a single page by means of HTML coding which divides the screen into sections called frames. Such technology allows the user to access numerous sites at the same time and to change or browse the sites in one or more of these "frames" without changing the others. The term "frame" is

---

[3] Examples of other issues generated by use of the internet include the extent to which entities are liable for illegal content, such a pirated materials etc, available on third party sites they link to.

[4] The URL of a home page is usually composed of only the hostname and protocol information, i.e. the domain name including the high level domain details e.g. http://www.bloggs.ie or http://www,bloggs.com. "Deeplinking" involves the inclusion of the file-path information as well, e.g. http://www.blogg.ie/wigdets.html.

something of a misnomer as unlike a picture frame, for example, a frame on a website does not have to surround an internal picture (although a series of frames could in fact be designed to achieve such an effect) but rather it allows a single website to incorporate a number of others in a variety of different formats. Creation of such a feature on a web site merely requires the use of the "framed" site's URLs in the source code of the "framing" site. Again, some site owners view the use of frames as unfairly taking advantage of their work as, for example, they allow framing sites to display advertisements from one site and content from another.

The use of links and frames therefore prompts the question: is it legally possible to stop third parties making your site the target of links or frames contained on their site?[5]

Legal Analysis of Current Position

Where a site operator wishes to prevent third parties linking to his site there are a number of legal bases which he may attempt to use. These include both contractual remedies and rights arising from intellectual property laws regarding patents, copyright or trademarks.[6]

Contract

Where a website's terms of use include a restriction on creating links without express authorisation then this may be effective in requiring such authorisation to be granted

---

[5] There has been a variety of case law from around the world on this point since this work was first written. Examples include: *Ticketmaster Corp. v Tickets.com,* 2000 US Dist LEXIS 4553 (CD Cal 2000) or *Hard Rock Café Int'l v Morton,* 999 US Dist LEXIS 13760 (SDNY 1999). Technical means may be developed from time to time to either prevent linking or to attempt to overcome technical measures used as blocks. However, the fact that there have been cases on this issue as recently as October 2005 (e.g. *Agence France-Presse v Google, Inc,* No. 1:05-cv-00546 (DDC filed March 17 2005, motion filed by Google 12 October 2005), illustrates that it has not yet been clearly resolved. The advantage of ensuring legal certainty on this point is that regardless of the technology involved or how it evolves, entities will have clear legal rights and where technical means are used to attempt to circumvent these, a legal remedy will exist.

[6] Plaintiffs have also attempted to prevent linking in recent years on the grounds of unfair competition, e.g. *SNC Havas Numerique v SA Kelijob,* (France, 2001), or infringement of rights in a database, e.g. Hyperlink-Datenbank, 28 O 216/98, LG Köln, (Germany, 1998)—with varying degrees of success. Such causes of action may be of use in specific circumstances, but a more generic solution would clearly be preferable to the issue.

and give the "linkee" a right of action for breach of contract where the clause itself is effective against the "linker". For example a warning in the terms on a homepage (e.g. http://www.bloggs.ie) may impose various conditions on browsers who wish to use the site and deem that these are accepted if they browse further (e.g. to http://www.bloggs.ie/widgetnaufacture,htmI). Therefore, where the browser goes on to view such a page he will do so subject to such conditions, which may include a restriction on creating links to the site.

However, in order to mount a successful action it will be necessary to prove that the linker was in fact subject to the terms of such clause and that he had visited the site and got the address there, rather than from another source, such as a third party. Furthermore, as such terms are unusual they would have to be specifically drawn to the visitors' attention to be enforceable.

Therefore, in practice, contract will not be a suitable method of preventing third parties from establishing links to a site as it will often be impossible to prove that the third parties were subject to the conditions limiting the creation of a link, rather than being made aware of the site's address indirectly by some anonymous third party (who was subject to the terms), or indeed through a process of random searching.

In fact, in order to allow site operators to stop third parties providing links to their sites what is needed is for the site owner to demonstrate intellectual property rights in the web address itself (i.e. for example http://www.bloggs.ie/widgetmaufacture.html). Such a right would allow the linkee to legally prevent third parties creating links to the site regardless of how they discovered the site or the lack of any contractual relationship between the two parties, Such intellectual property rights could theoretically arise from patent, copyright or trademark law.[7]

Patent

It will not normally be possible to obtain protection under patent law for a web address as it will not satisfy the necessary criteria for patentability contained in the Patents Act 1992 and the European Patent Convention. For example, the Irish Act specifically excludes the presentation of information or aesthetic creations from

[7] Passing off is not considered as this would apply where confusion is created by the appearance of one party's site (or its address) as against another's rather than where the actual site of the other party is being used, as in this case.

being the subject of patents and requires an inventive step or innovation to qualify for a patent. Case law also supports the notion that words or new combinations of letters are generally not patentable.[8] In any event, apart from the difficulty in meeting the required criteria, the expense, trouble and time limits inherent in patent applications and patent protection mean that this is a fundamentally unsuitable basis upon which to build legal protection for web addresses.

Copyright

Copyright law may offer some protection,[9] but it is important to remember that as only the web address is being copied by the link, it is this which must be the subject of copyright protection, rather than the work on the relevant webpage, in order for there to be a right of action using this legal basis.

In fact, although there are no direct precedents in relation to the internet in this jurisdiction, existing case law illustrates that it will not normally be possible to obtain copyright protection for web addresses. This arises because titles are not usually capable of being copyrighted,[10] and neither are invented words or new combinations of letters,[11] which would appear to include web addresses.

In any event, it is submitted that copyright is an unsuitable legal means of protecting web addresses as it confers a statutory right to individuals to control the use of a form of expression which they have created and therefore, if extended to include web addresses, this would allow third parties to obtain copyright in phrases, even where they did not own the domain names or trademarks which formed part of such phrases. As such, it would effectively lead to the imposition of restrictions on site owners and hinder the development of electronic commerce in this jurisdiction.

For example, where Bloggs Limited established a site then, were it possible to obtain copyright protection for web addresses, third parties could seek to get copyright in the phrases which Bloggs might logically want to use as file-paths such as

[8] *Exxon v Exxon Insurance Co.* [1982) 3 AER 241.

[9] See *Shetland Times v Shetland News*, JITL, 30/11/96 where alleged copyright infringement was used to obtain a preliminary injunction to prevent linkage. This initial ruling was widely criticised and the rational behind it appears flawed.

[10] *Francis, Day and Hunter v Twentieth Century Fox* [1963] 2 AER 16 CA.

[11] *Exxon v Exxon Insurance Co.* (1982) 3 AER 241. See also *Hollinbrake v Trustwell* [1894) 3 CLI 420.

http://www.bloggs.ie/products.html or http://www.bloggs.ie/sales.html by being the first to "create" these copyrightable works and then seek to sell these to Bloggs, or its competitors, and thus hinder attempts to develop the site. Similarly, where a new higher level domain was being proposed, such as "shop", individuals could obtain copyright in the proposed domains prior to possible registration and then take legal action against persons who registered in the new domain.

Therefore, it is submitted that copyright should not be extended to incorporate this area as it would only lead to the hijacking of potential addresses and a repeat of the problems caused by the "cyber-squatting" issue, which is currently being addressed by ICANN.[12]

Finally, copyright, like patenting, grants rights subject to a strictly limited time period, which appears an inappropriate concept in this area. Legal rights to protect a site should exist for as long as the site itself is maintained.

Trademark

Where a domain name incorporates a trademark, it may be possible to prevent third parties linking to the site in the course of trade by arguing that the use of the trademark in the link constitutes infringement. For example, where "Bloggs" is a registered trademark, then the creation of any link to the home site :/Jwn,blog4_e, or any page forming part of this website (i.e. "deep" pages including file-paths in the URL, e.g. http://w.bloggs.ie/widgets.html) will require the linker to reproduce the trademark either on his webpage or in the code thereof.[13]

There is a specific defence in the Irish trade mark legislation where a third party's trade mark is used for the purposes of identifying goods or services as those of the proprietor or licensee of the registered trade mark, but this only applies where the use is in accordance with honest practices in industrial or commercial matters and does not, without due cause, take unfair advantage of, or is detrimental to, the distinctive

[12] As mentioned at n 1, above, this article was originally written in early 2000. The Uniform Domain Name Dispute Resolution Procedure had only recently been finalised at that stage.

[13] The actual representation of the trademark, in the coding of the linking site may differ from the standard format used by the trademark owner (unless the trademark has been registered in the format used in the code), but nevertheless, such a representation of the trademark would appear to come within the auspices of the protection afforded by ss 14(2) and (3) of the Trademarks Act 1996 as it will, at the very least, be a similar mark used for an identical purpose.

character or reputation of the trade mark,[14] Therefore, where the terms of use of a website require that permission is received prior to establishing a link and the linker was aware of this term, then failure to get such authorisation may fall foul of the obligation to comply with honest practices. Similarly, if a court took the view that the link took unfair advantage of, or is detrimental to, the distinctive character or reputation of the trade mark then this could give rise to infringement and constitute grounds for having the link removed. However, it is debatable whether a link would, in fact have such negative effects and therefore under the current law this issue is likely to be a source of expensive litigation as it would be necessary to make such a finding on the specific facts applicable in each individual case.

Moreover, if such a finding was made on a general basis, this would significantly impede the development of electronic commerce as it would mean that a site owner could always prevent the creation of links to any part of his site and therefore established businesses could use this power to effectively curtail the development of, for example, online brokerage sites, which are widely viewed as posing a key benefit for consumers from b-commerce due to their facilitation of more efficient markets.

The Need for Reform

There is a need for reform in this area as the law is unclear and inevitably this is leading to injustice and market inefficiency. For example, smaller businesses with sites offering brokerage or referral services are being subjected to threats of litigation and effectively being obliged to shut down or curtail their services, even though they view such services as legitimate, because they cannot afford the risk of loosing a legal battle on this issue. On the other hand, many smaller businesses offering content on their sites feel aggrieved at what they view as unfair exploitation of their work by third parties through the use of links or frames, but they lack the necessary funds to take legal action and respond instead by reducing the amount of content on their sites or by protecting such content by password pages, etc, which merely slow up online research. Apart from directly limiting growth in the area by small and medium enterprises, the uncertainty and threat of litigation must in the long-term raise the cost of capital to firms planning operations in this area and thus lead to further indirect restrictions on electronic commerce.

Particularly unsettling is the fact that the current highly uncertain position is giving rise to injustices whereby financially secure undertakings can use links or frames to

[14] s 14 (6) Trade Marks Act 1996.

third party sites immune from protestations from small online undertakings which lack the financial resources to embark on highly risky legal action against them while at the same time they can exploit the legal uncertainty in the area by threatening legal action against other sites creating links to their site in a manner they wish to prevent. A solution is therefore needed which would create clear legal rights and allow a degree of protection from perceived exploitation while at the same time ensuring that the development of electronic commerce was not hindered and that the considerable benefits which it can bring through creating more efficient market conditions were not lost through regulatory impediments.

The Proposed Solution

In order to create legal certainty while simultaneously protecting the legitimate interests of site operators and ensure that the possible efficiencies which the internet offers are protected, it is proposed that the Trade Marks Act 1996 be amended to include the following:

Definitions: Homepage:	A homepage shall be deemed only to be a web page whose Uniform Resource Locator ((URL), or web address, is limited to its host name, i.e. a domain name ending in a high level domain, such as but not limited to ".ie" or ".co".' Where the URL includes a filepath this shall not be deemed to be a homepage.·[15]
s 14 (7)	For the absence of doubt, the use of a trade mark in a website, regardless of the representation such mark is given in the graphical interface of the website, shall constitute "use" of the trademark for the purposes of this Act.[16]

[15] The file-path is essentially used to indicate specific pages beyond the site entrance page. Deeplinking or deepframing therefore requires the use of a file-path. Due to length limitations, it is not possible to define all the technical terms used in this work,

[16] It is proposed to include this provision as a similarly worded provision was included in the Electronic Communication Bill in relation to digital signatures to afford certainty and prevent litigation on this matter despite the fact that in that case, just as in this, pre-existing statutory provisions could have been interpreted as meaning there was no need for legislation on the area (in that case s 36 of the Interpretation Act 1937).

s 15 (5)(a)	Any use of a registered trademark in or on a website shall not be deemed infringement under the terms of this Act in so far as the trademark is being used to indicate the homepage of any party with a right to use such trademark by means of a hypertext link.[17]
(b)	Where a trade mark is being used to indicate any page on a website other than the homepage of a party with a right to use such trademark then this shall automatically be deemed to constitute dishonest use of the trademark under the terms of the s 14 (6) of this Act in the absence of any express representation from the trademark owner or its licensee, either on that website or elsewhere, to the contrary.

These amendments to the Trade Marks Act 1996 would have the following specific benefits:

- Unauthorised "deeplinking", i.e. linking to specific pages within a website, would be preventable and therefore site owners would be able to protect themselves from perceived exploitation;
- The changes would ensure some linking (i.e. to home pages) was legally protected and therefore the potential for more efficient markets offered by electronic commerce would not be lost through regulatory impediments;
- It would provide legal certainty and a level pitch for all online businesses, thereby ensuring that site owners and operators were not exposed to unknown liability or the threat of being obliged to discontinue their services.

The proposed amendments seem broad enough to catch not only both linking and framing but other potential technical means of accessing third party sites which may be developed on the internet. At the same time they include the option of waiving such rights for the many sites which wish to encourage linking by third parties and also ensure trademarks continue to be protected by allowing litigation where the use of the trademark was for purposes other than merely indicating the site (e.g. fraud,

[17] The term "hypertext link" is currently already used in legislation, for example—the Prospectus (Directive 2003/71/EC) Regulations 2005, SI No 324 of 2005.

defamatory comments etc.) or where the link was to a site which had no rights to the trademark and had been established for such fraudulent or defamatory purposes (e.g. links to http://www.bloggsiscrap.com).[18]

In addition to protecting interests in websites such an amendment in the law would bolster the Irish electronic commerce industry generally by indicating further willingness by the Government to address the legal issues being raised in this area and to provide clear legal solutions in a manner designed to accommodate the interests of all those involved. As such, it would encourage parties to rely on Irish law in the terms of use applicable to their websites, to host their websites in this jurisdiction and to consider basing their online operations in Ireland.

---

[18] Use of trademarks in such a scenario could still be acceptable using a "fair use" defence. It is not suggested that any additional statutory protection be extended in such situations to that already afforded by the current law on the basis that it is not clear that any such extension would provide any benefit to development of electronic commerce (as opposed to facilitating free speech).

The Undertaking as to Damages in Interlocutory Remedies: An Argument for Access to Justice

by
Marsha Coghlan*

Interlocutory remedies[1] are arguably the most powerful tools available to the modern day litigant;[2] they are, as one jurist has noted, the most striking remedy issued by contemporary courts.[3] They have the capacity to ensure the effective dissolution of a business.[4] It is precisely because of the lethal effects which these orders can produce that the courts may require a cross-undertaking as to damages as a prerequisite to the exercise of its equitable jurisdiction. This undertaking lends legitimacy to an intervention by the court which, but for the undertaking, may be contrary to the principle of equality before the law.[5] This requirement is the main obstacle that the impecunious litigant must overcome when seeking an interlocutory order. She must

---

* Apprentice Solicitor. This essay was awarded a prize by the Law Society of Ireland for the *Student Law Reform Essay Competition 2000.*

1 The criteria to be applied when making the decision to grant an interlocutory injunction were established in the landmark decision of the House of Lords in *American Cyanamid v. Ethicon* [1975] AC 396. See: Prescott (1975) 91 LQR 68 for comment on the case. This test was given express approval by the Irish Supreme Court in *Campus Oil Ltd v Minister for Industry and Energy (No 2)* [1983] IR 88. For a general overview of this area see: Courtney, *Mareva Injunctions and Related Interlocutory Orders* (Butterworths, Dublin, 1998) and Delany, *Equity and the Law of Trusts in Ireland*, (2nd ed, (Roundhall Sweet & Maxwell, Dublin, 1999).

2 Injunctions are on a statutory footing in England since the Common Law Procedure Act 1854 (17 & 18 Vict. C. 125) (UK) which gave to common law courts a power to grant injunctions in certain cases.

3 Leubsdorf, "The Standard for Preliminary Injunctions" (1978) 91 Harvard LR 525.

4 This is a fact that has been recognised by the courts. For example, see *Columbia Pictures Inc. & Ors. v Robinson* [1986] WLR 542 at 566–567.

5 Article 40.3, Bunreacht na hÉireann, 1937.

convince the court to accept a possibly worthless undertaking as to damages in order to obtain a remedy.[6]

In light of this problem, it is argued that the undertaking as to damages needs to be reassessed and adjusted to take into account a broader range of rights and considerations. The primary aim of this reform would be focused on improving access to the courts for the impecunious litigant, litigants acting in the public interest and litigants seeking to uphold a statutory provision.

The Rationale Underlying the Undertaking as to Damages

The undertaking as to damages is clearly necessary in any system of justice which purports to accord equal protection before the law to the parties that interact with it.[7]

It serves to protect the substantive rights of the defendant, *viz,* the right of the defendant to receive damages if the imposition of the injunction interfered with his legitimate rights and he suffers direct loss, for example, his business goes into liquidation. However, the undertaking also serves to safeguard the procedural rights of the defendant, *viz,* the infringement of his rights as a result of the adjudication of his case on an *ex-parte* basis.[8] As one writer points out, although litigants are not entitled to insist that the State provide them with the best and most accurate procedure regardless of expense, they are entitled to a procedure that is even-handed and that treats opponents as equals before the law.[9] It is precisely for this reason that the issue of impecuniosity raises problems as the cross-undertaking represents the

---

[6] The only Irish decision which was considered the issue of the impecuniosity of a plaintiff is *Moloney v Laurib Investments Ltd,* unreported, High Court, Lynch J, 20 July 1993. Here the court refused to grant a *mareva* order because the balance of convenience did not favour granting the order sought. Therefore, the plaintiff was not deprived the order for reasons relating solely to her impecuniosity. For comment on this case see Courtney, "Mareva Injunctions in Personal Injuries Actions" (1995) *The Western Law Gazette* 107. Undoubtedly there has been more than one adjudication of this point. However, interlocutory applications are rarely reported which provides at least a possible explanation for the apparent sparsity of precedent on the point.

[7] See Courtney, above, n 1, at pp 322–334, for an excellent overview of the treatment of the requirement of the undertaking as to damages in the Irish context.

[8] See further: Zuckerman, "The Undertaking in Damages—Substantive and Procedural Dimensions" (1994) 53 *Cambridge Law Journal* 546.

[9] Zuckerman, "Interlocutory Remedies in Quest of Procedural Fairness" (1993) 56 *Modern Law Review* 325.

commitment by the court to according equal protection to the rights of both parties. It is not possible to achieve this protection in the way the current law is structured for the reasons discussed, below.

When the problem of the impecuniosity of a litigant arises, the court finds itself in the awkward position of attempting to strike a fair balance between the defendant's right to have his rights protected in the form of security provided by the cross-undertaking, and the competing right of the plaintiff to have an alleged breach of his rights adjudicated upon, and further his right not to be discriminated against by virtue of his financial position. This balance is neither easy nor, it could be argued, possible to achieve to the satisfaction of either party because of the conflict of rights that ensues. If the court decides to dispense with the requirement of the requirement of the undertaking on the grounds of the plaintiff's impecuniosity, the defendant's rights to equal protection are eroded on at least two related grounds.

First, it accords inadequate protection to the defendant's potential rights at final trial. If the defendant is ultimately successful at final trial; and he proves that his rights were unjustifiably interfered with, he cannot obtain compensation from the plaintiff in respect of the damage arising from the imposition of the injunction itself. Secondly, the defendant is placed in an inferior position pertaining to settlement as the defendant is in a subordinate bargaining position *vis-á-vis* the plaintiff. This arises because if the defendant is aware that he will receive no compensation for any harm rendered by the imposition of an injunction, even if it is proved subsequently that it was granted, he has no reason to go to final trial. This may render a premature result regardless of whether or not the plaintiff's claim is legitimate.

Equally, however, the decision by the court to insist on the undertaking in all circumstances regardless of either the consequences or the relative strength of the parties involved is problematic. Not only could this approach have the result of effectively denying the plaintiff's right of access to the courts on purely financial grounds, but this injustice is further aggravated if the plaintiff's rights are in fact infringed. This is manifestly unfair because it has the result of effectively placing limits on the procedural rights of the plaintiff to have his claim adjudicated upon.

The preceding discussion serves to illustrate the particular problems which both the plaintiff and the defendant may encounter in respect of the undertaking as to damages. The following restructured hierarchy is suggested as a framework for achieving a compromise which strikes a balance between the rights of both parties, and in addition, allows the court to take other factors into consideration when determining the nature of the undertaking.

Nominal Undertaking where the litigant is challenging an action on the grounds of the "public interest" or where the plaintiff is impecunious but it is highly probable that he will succeed at trial

A nominal undertaking as to damages could be accepted where the litigant in question is indigent and there is a point of considerable public importance[10] which merits consideration by the courts. Variations of this type of an exception are already in evidence in English[11], American[12], and Canadian[13] systems. For example, one possible area where a nominal undertaking could serve as a means of protecting the public interest is in the area of environmental law. The importance of protecting the public interest has already been recognised in this area of injunctions by virtue of s 27 of the Local Government (Planning and Development) Act 1976, which deals with *locus standi.* This allows the High Court "on the application of a planning authority or any other person, *whether or not the person has an interest in the land,* by order prohibit the continuance of the development or unauthorised use".[14] This prohibition may take the form of either an interim or an interlocutory order.[15]

This is the antithesis of the normal requirements relating to *locus standi* in that it does not require the party in question to have any interest at all in the proceedings to make an application. There is no reason why the Irish courts could not also allow a similar exception in respect of the undertaking where the public interest is at issue. Arguably, it may ensure that the provisions of s 27 operate effectively as it might ensure that a plaintiff having established *locus standi* will not fall at the damages hurdle as a result of his inability to offer a worthwhile undertaking.

---

[10] A discussion of public interest litigation is outside the scope of this article. However, for a recent discussion of this litigation in England see *R.v Lord Chancellor ex p Child Poverty Action Group* (1998) 148 *New Law Journal* 205 (QBD).

[11] See *Hoffman-Law Roche & Co. v Secretary of State for Trade and Industry* [1974] 2 All ER 1128, which held that the undertaking should be dispensed with when the Crown seeks an injunction to enforce the law. This was extended to local authorities in *Kirkless Metropolitan Borough Council v Wickes Building Supplies* [1991] 4 All ER 240.

[12] A nominal bond under 65(c), Federal Rules of Civil Procedure, by the courts in some states where the public interest is at issue. See further Dobbs, "Should Security be Required as a Pre-Condition to Provisional Injunctive Relief?"(1974) 52 *North Carolina LR* 1091 for detailed discussion of this jurisprudence.

[13] For example, see: *Hunt v Halcan Log Services* [1987] 34 DLR (4th) 504; *University of Alberta* [1995] 52 DLR (4th) 46; and *Pasco v Canadian National Railway Co* [1986] 1 CNLR 35.

[14] s 27(1) (emphasis added).

[15] s 27(3).

Equally, a nominal undertaking could be accepted where the plaintiff is impecunious, but on an overall assessment of the merits of the action it is highly probable that the plaintiff will succeed at final trial. A nominal undertaking would be accepted here in order to ensure that a poor litigant is not denied access to the courts because he cannot offer a worthwhile undertaking. In this scenario there will be a more onerous burden would be placed on the plaintiff to demonstrate to the court the merits of his case, and in this way justify the nominal nature of the undertaking.

Limited undertaking where the litigant is exercising duties of a statutory nature and the injunction is sought to restrain a breach of Statute

The most compelling and obvious situation arises in the context of insolvency proceedings, where a liquidator or examiner seeks an interlocutory order. He has no personal interest in the outcome of the proceedings and is only acting in the performance of his statutory duties. Therefore, he has nothing to gain by giving an unlimited undertaking which the insolvent company could not ultimately finance if the defendant is subsequently adjudicated to have been wrongfully enjoined. Indeed, it could be argued that there is a danger of being found to be in breach of the fiduciary obligations imposed by such an appointment if he intentionally commits the company to the possibility of payment such monies and the company is in danger of going into insolvency.

This was the exact scenario which the Irish Supreme Court had to grapple with in the decision of *O'Mahony v. Horgan.*[16] The applicant liquidator was appointed on a petition by the Revenue Commissioners. Due to alleged irregularities in the conduct of the company's affairs, the liquidator sought an order making the respondents personally liable for some of the company's debts. On foot of this order the applicant sought a *mareva* order against the second respondent restraining him from disposing of money imminently due to him under an insurance policy. In the High Court, Murphy J granted the injunction and limited the applicants undertaking to £25,000.

On appeal to the Supreme Court, this limitation on the undertaking was overturned. In the words of O'Flaherty J:

> "I know of no case where a limit has been out on the amount that may be required to be paid, if it is held that the injunction was improperly

[16] [1995] 2 IR 411; for comment on this case see Courtney, "Providing an Intention to Frustrate Judgement" (1996) 3 *Commercial Law Practitioner*.

> obtained, nor do I think it right in principle that such a limit should be placed in view of the far-reaching implications involved in any restraint that is imposed on a party by reason of such an injunction prior to judgment"[17]

Hamilton CJ, whilst expressly inclining towards the views of O'Flaherty J, was not as trenchant in his opposition to a limitation being placed upon an undertaking. In the instant case he felt that the prerequisite "intention to dissipate" monies had not been established. Therefore, he felt it unnecessary to consider the issue of the limited undertaking.[18] However, he further opined that "I will reserve for future consideration the powers of the court in this regard should it arise in the future."[19]

Although, the Chief Justice did hint at the possibility of considering this issue again in the future, the net effect of the decision is such as to veto a limitation ever being placed on an undertaking, regardless of the facts or merits of a particular case. This is open to criticism as there may be circumstances which merit a departure from the normal requirement of an unlimited undertaking.

One such potential situation arose before the English courts in the case of *In Re DPR Futures Ltd.*[20] The facts concerned an application by the joint liquidators of a company to continue *Mareva* orders against three former directors. Section 330 prohibits the making of loans to directors. Here, neither of the joint liquidators felt that they had the authority to commit the firm to the theoretically open-ended liability of the undertaking as there was no large creditors who might be expected to indemnify them and their own insurance did not cover such a situation.

Millet J held that the liquidators should not be required to give an unlimited cross-undertaking, and thus the undertaking was limited to an amount commensurate with the size of the company's assets. He justified his decision on the grounds that:

> "the joint liquidators [had] no personal interest in the outcome of the proceedings. They [were] acting in the performance of their statutory duties. They [sought] to recover for the benefit of a large number of small creditors from whom it [was] impractical to obtain an indemnity ..."[21]

---

[17] *ibid* at 422.

[18] *ibid* at 421.

[19] See above, n 19.

[20] [1989] 1 WLR 778.

[21] *ibid* at 785.

In Ireland, irrespective of the merits of the company's claim an unlimited undertaking would appear to be required. It is suggested that the approach adopted in this latter decision is to be preferred as it would allow protection of the potential assets of a company. It should also allow the liquidator to properly exercise and vindicate his statutory duties without the threat of being in breach if his fiduciary duties. It strikes the appropriate balance between protection of the defendant's right to damages and proper enforcement of the law relating to the winding-up of companies.

Unlimited undertaking where the court orders it on an overall assessment of the merits of an action

In every other situation there is no justification for ordering anything except an unlimited undertaking as to damages. The preceding exceptions are tailored to accommodate the exceptional applications for interlocutory remedies. In every other scenario there is no justification for requiring anything less than a full, unlimited undertaking.

Conclusion

This commentary demonstrates that although the rationale underlying the undertaking the requirement of an undertaking as to damages is a laudable one, it can also act as a double edged sword, depriving some litigants of the opportunity to obtain these remedies. Lord Justice Woolf, commenting on his proposals in the United Kingdom, made the following comment in an address to an Irish Conference on civil reform:

> "I wanted to make the system more equal. By more equal I mean achieving a situation in which it is not possible for a party to use greater resources to deprive the party who has less resources of the opportunity of obtaining justice."[22]

This is an aspiration which should not be overlooked when considering the future role of the impecunious litigant in the interlocutory context. Interlocutory remedies undoubtedly have a role to play in the 21st century. The challenge lies in striking the appropriate balance between protection of rights and ensuring that these remedies remain accessible to all, regardless of their means.

---

[22] Woolf LJ, "Judicial Case Management:Crucial to the Changes Necessary in the Civil Justice System in England and Wales" in *Working Group on a Courts Commission:Conference on Case Management* (Government Publications Office, Dublin, 1997), at p 19.

A Director's Duty of Care, Skill and Diligence: Reforming the Standard

by

David Naughton*

Introduction

Under present Irish common law, whether or not the duty of care, skill and diligence[1] owed by a director to his or her company in the performance of his or her functions has been discharged is judged by a low standard of care.[2] As a result, it is very difficult to sue a director for the negligent performance of his functions where the company is trading as a going concern.[3] The Republic of Ireland is one of those jurisdictions that have not modified the common law in this area by imposing a

* BBLS (NUI), LLM (Dub), Solicitor, A&L Goodbody, Dublin. This essay was awarded first place in the Law Society of Ireland *Student Law Reform Essay Competition 2000.*

1 As Courtney notes, "Directors owe duties of care, skill and diligence to their company. In essence, a director must not act negligently or conduct the business of his company in an inept manner. These duties arise not only from the directors' fiduciary duties as agents ...but also because directors owe duties of care in tort to persons who foreseeably rely on their actions". Courtney, *The Law of Private Companies* (Butterworths, 1994), at para 8.042. Thus where the liability of company directors is being determined, the general principles of the law of negligence apply. See generally, McMahon & Binchy, *Irish Law of Torts* (2nd ed, Butterworths, 1990), Cha. 14.

2 So much so that one commentator has remarked "the common law operates to give directors a remarkable freedom to manage companies incompetently". See Finch, "Company Directors: Who Cares about Skill and Care?" (1992) 55 *Modern Law Review* 179.

3 This is so as, provided a director's behaviour falls short of the grossest negligence, he is unlikely to be held to account due to this low standard of care and, as company controllers are slow to sue themselves, action will often only be taken against inept directors where a company is being wound up. In such a situation, the liquidator may bring misfeasance proceedings under s 298 of the 1963 Companies Act against the inept directors if their negligence was compounded by impropriety on their part. *See Re Contract Packaging Limited,* High Court, 16 January 1992, reported in *The Irish Times,* 17 January 1992.

statutory duty to act as a reasonable competent director.[4] Considering that statutory standards of care in other respects have been raised considerably[5] and the strong public perception that requiring only a low standard of care of directors is unacceptable in the existing commercial climate, reform of the law in this area is warranted. This will produce clearer law without unnecessary burdens being placed on business.

This paper will briefly outline the current common law position in relation to the standard of care owed by directors. It will then examine the justifications for, and inadequacies of, this low standard and outline proposals for amendment of the law.

Current position in Respect of the Standard of Care

Traditionally, the common law has imposed a low standard of care upon directors.[6] In *Overend, Gurney & Co v Gibb and Gibb*[7], Lord Hatherley LC put forward a test of "ordinary prudence" which set out a basic level of competence to be demanded of directors. Directors will only be held liable if they are guilty of gross negligence; that is where:

> "they were cognisant of facts of such a character, so plain, so manifest, and so simple of appreciation, that no men with any ordinary degree of prudence, acting on their own behalf, would have entered into such a transaction as they entered into."

In *Re Brazilian Rubber Plantations and Estates Ltd*,[8] Neville J held that a director was:

---

4 See, for example, the legislative reform of this area in Germany (Art 93(1) of the Stock Corporation Act), New Zealand (s 137 of the Companies Act 1993), Australia (s 232(4) of the Corporations Act, 1989) and Canada (s 122(1) of the Business Corporations Act, 1985). The Law Commission of England and Wales and the Scottish Law Commission have recommended legislative reform in this area. See "*Company Directors: Regulating Conflicts of Interest and Formulating a Statement of Duties*" (1999) Report No 261 at 5.20 and below.

5 See, for example, the fraudulent trading provisions in s 297A of the Companies Act 1990 and *Re Hunting Lodges Ltd* [1985] ILRM 75; s 204 of the 1990 Act and *Re Mantruck Services Ltd; Mehigan v Duigan* [1997] 1 IR 340 and n 3, above.

6 See generally, Dwight, "Liability of Corporate Directors" (1907) 17 *Yale Law Journal* 33; Trebilcock, "The Liability of Company Directors for Negligence" (1969) 32 *Modern Law Review* 499; McKenzie, "A Company Director's Obligations of Care and Skill" [1982] *Journal of Business Law* 460.

7 (1872) LR 5 HL 40, 486–7.

8 [1911] 1 Ch 425.

> "not bound to bring any special qualifications to his office and may undertake the management of a rubber company in complete ignorance of everything connected with rubber without incurring responsibility for the mistakes which may result from such ignorance."

However, it was also held in *Re Brazilian Rubber* that if a director brought special expertise to his office, he was bound to give the company the advantage of it and would be judged accordingly.[9]

This stream of largely 19th century cases culminated in *Re City and Equitable Fire Insurance Company*,[10] wherein Romer J, whilst noting that the authorities were not entirely clear,[11] reviewed and summarised them. He held, *inter alia*, that:

> "A director need not exhibit in the performance of his duties a greater degree of skill than may reasonably be expected from a person with *his* knowledge and experience ... it is perhaps only another way of stating the same proposition to say that directors are not liable for mere errors of judgment."[12]

An Irish case on this issue is that of *Re Mont Clare Hotel Ltd: Jackson v Mortell*,[13] wherein Costello J held that "it seems to be that something more than mere carelessness is required...[what is required is] some act that perhaps may amount to gross negligence in failing to carry out a duty owed by a director to his company".

---

9 "If he is acquainted with the rubber business he must give the company the advantage of his knowledge when transacting the company's business"—*ibid* at 437. In *Pavlides v Jensen* [1956] Ch 565 the Court held that the directors were free to be an amiable set of lunatics; any remedy for dissatisfaction with the directors lay with the shareholders. They could vote for a new set of directors. However this ignores the principle that in a plc the board will often control the voting at shareholder meetings through proxies.

10 [1925] Ch 407.

11 *ibid*, at 427.

12 *ibid*, at 428–429 (emphasis added). This test contains an objective element because the director could be held liable for failing on a particular occasion to live up to the standard of which he is in fact capable of reaching, but the stronger element in the proposition is the subjective one, meaning that the director can never be required to achieve a standard higher than that which he is personally capable of reaching.

13 High Court, Unreported, 2 December 1986.

In summary, the position in this jurisdiction is that directors' discharge their duty of care, skill and diligence if they exercise such a standard of care as is reasonably to be expected of them, *having regard to their knowledge and experience.* They are not required to act, for example, as persons in a leading and responsible position who are managers of other persons' property in a specific enterprise.[14] Therefore, there is no fixed minimum standard of care for all directors; the standard that a director must satisfy is what one can reasonably expect of that person with his own background and experience.[15] As a consequence, what may be regarded as negligent for an accountant-director may not render a "country gentleman" liable.[16]

Justifications for a Low Standard of Care

In September 1998 the Law Commission of England and Wales and the Scottish Law Commission issued a joint consultation paper entitled "Company Directors: Regulating Conflicts of Interests and Formulating a Statement of Duties",[17] which dealt, in part, with this area of the law.

The consultation paper outlined the justifications for a low standard of care. First, management is not a profession and directors do not need particular skills. Secondly, to raise the standard of care may encourage litigation whereas management should be supervised by shareholders, not the courts. Thirdly, the courts are not well placed to second-guess matters of business judgement[18] and, fourthly, many directors are appointed for their in-depth knowledge in a particular area outside of the business realm; thus, the law should take account of their lack of knowledge and skill in this regard.[19] Otherwise directors would be reluctant to become directors.

---

[14] This being the standard of care imposed upon German directors under Art 93(1) of the German Stock Corporation Act. This is an objective test and individual abilities are not taken account of.

[15] As Trebilcock, above, n 6, at 501 states, "The director is obliged only to do as much as could be expected from someone as incompetent and foolish as he happens to be".

[16] See *Re Denham & Co Ltd* [1884] 25 Ch D 752.

[17] (1998) Consultation Paper No 153; Discussion Paper No 105.

[18] See *Shareholder Remedies*, Law Commission Consultation Paper No 142, paras 9.44–9.48, for a discussion of the English court's reluctance to hold that anything less than serious mismanagement could amount to unfair prejudice.

[19] Above, n 17, at 289.

Inadequacies of a Low Standard of Care

However, as against these justifications, the consultation paper posited the following arguments.[20] First, many areas of business now require specialised skills and knowledge beyond those possessed by the layman, which warrants a higher standard of care.[21] Secondly, it is doubtful how often the power of shareholders to remove directors at any time by ordinary resolution of the company in general meeting[22] is actually utilised. Since the turn of the last century, shareholders have had virtually no general supervisory power over the board; therefore a higher standard of care of directors whilst a company is a going concern would alleviate this situation.[23]

Thirdly, a low standard of care of directors is out of line with the standard generally imposed on persons who agree to provide services. In relation to employees, the common law has long recognised that if an employee holds himself out as having a particular skill, the employee will be held to an objective standard of reasonableness in its exercise.[24]

Fourthly, the present law fails to provide an adequate sanction for mismanagement. This gap in the law has to some extent been filled by Chap 2 of Pt VII of the 1963 Companies Act in this jurisdiction which provides, *inter alia,* that the court may disqualify a director whose conduct makes him unfit to be a director.[25] However, a serious case of negligence would have to be made out if the only allegation against a director was one of mismanagement. Moreover, disqualification serves the purpose of protecting the public for the future. It does not provide compensation for the company, which has lost money through the mismanagement. Finally, there are many other jurisdictions where directors are bound to act as reasonable competent directors.[26]

---

[20] Above, n 17, at 289.

[21] This has been recognised by the Institute of Directors of England and Wales which, in June 1999, introduced a new examined qualification for company directors, that of Chartered Director.

[22] Provided for in this jurisdiction by s 182 of the Companies Act 1963.

[23] Article 80 of Table A of the Companies Act 1963, which confers on directors the power to manage the company's business, is subject only to the provisions of the Act and to regulations prescribed by the company in general meeting but this has been held not to entitle shareholders to control the directors by ordinary resolution. See *Quinn & Axtens v Salmon* [1909] AC 442 and *Clark v Workman* [1920] 1 IR 107.

[24] See *Lister v Romford Ice and Cold Storage Co. Ltd* [1957] AC 555.

[25] See s 160 of the 1963 Act applied in *La Moselle Clothing Ltd v Soualhi* [1998] ILRM 345.

[26] Above, n 4, for examples of such jurisdictions.

Reform of the Standard of Care

It is submitted that statutory reform of the standard of care required of directors is warranted. This would state the law clearly, make it more accessible to directors and, by stating the essential proposition of law in modern language, should make it a more effective controlling device of potentially rogue directors. In addition, statutory reform would reduce any initial difficulties otherwise encountered by the axiomatic litigation following the establishment of a modern standard of care through the common law.

In its report on the issue, the Law Commissions' recommended reform of the common law standard of care through the introduction in statute of a twofold subjective/objective test[27] based on that contained in s 214(4) of the Insolvency Act 1986 (UK).[28] Under this test a director owes a duty to his company to exercise the care, skill and diligence that would be expected of a reasonable person in the same circumstances having both (a) the knowledge and experience that may reasonably be expected of a person in the same position as the director, and (b) the director's knowledge and experience. Thus, this requires the conduct of directors to be judged both objectively and subjectively by reference to their own personal characteristics.[29]

This recommended reform has been followed by the publication of a company law reform bill in the UK during November 2005 which provides, in part, that directors, in carrying out their duties, will be required to exercise the:

> care, skill and diligence that would be exercised by a reasonably diligent person with –
>
> (i) the knowledge, skill and experience that may reasonably be expected of a person carrying out the functions carried out by the director in relation to the company, and

---

27 Above, n 4, at 5.20.

28 The English courts have recently used this section as the basis for a more modern standard of care, which a director must show under the common law. See *Norman v Theodore Goddard* [1992] BCC 14 and *Re D'Jan of London Ltd* [1993] BCC 646 which were followed by Nelson J in *Bairstow v Queen's Moat Houses plc* [2002] 2 BCLC 531. The reasoning behind the adoption of s 214(4) as the basis of the standard of care is that, firstly, directors will have to discharge the same standard of care while the company operates as a going concern as when it approaches insolvent liquidation. Secondly, the English courts have over 13 years' experience interpreting this section. It is envisaged that a new s 309A of the Companies Act 1985 will shortly be enacted by statutory instrument to put *Re D'Jan of London* on a statutory footing.

29 Above, n 17, at 291.

(ii) the general knowledge, skill and experience, which he has.

The important difference between this formulation of the standard of care and that of Romer J[30] is that in the latter the director's subjective level of skill set the standard required of the director,[31] whereas under the former the director's subjective level does so only if it improves upon the objective standard of the reasonable director. Limb (a) of the recommended reform sets a standard which all directors must meet and it is not one dependent on the particular director's capabilities; limb (b) then adds a subjective standard which can operate only to increase the standard of care required of the director.[32]

In summary, a director will no longer be able to rely on his own particular lack of knowledge or experience to avoid being subject to the general minimum standard of care to be required of all directors.

During 2002, the company law review group, an advisory body charged with advising the Minister for Enterprise, Trade and Employment on the review and development of Irish company law, issued a draft Companies Bill with the stated aim of simplifying company law. The draft Bill, in part, provides a statement of the fiduciary duty of care, skill and diligence owed by a director to his company which reads as follows:

> "A director owes the company a duty to exercise the care, skill and diligence which would be exercised in the same circumstances by a reasonable person having both –
>
> (i) the knowledge and experience that may reasonably be expected of a person in the same position as the director, and
> (ii) the knowledge and experience which the director has."

---

30 And the adoption of which would make it an important reform of Irish law.

31 See n 12, above.

32 This reform of the common law standard of care attributes to the director the knowledge, skill and experience of *both* the reasonable man and the particular director in question, so the latter is important only when it *adds* to the attributes of the reasonable person. As was stated in the Law Commissions' Report, above, n 4, at 5.9, "We thought that it was only fair that a director with some special expertise should be bound to exercise it. Accordingly, it was our view that the subjective limb could operate only as a requirement in addition to the objective standard and could not be used by the director to avoid being subject to the minimum standard of care required by every director". *It is important to note that a purely objective test would be too low for skilled directors who would not be obliged to use them.*

Conclusion

In conclusion, the common law standard of care owed by directors in the performance of their functions in this jurisdiction is low, as the relevant test contains a strong subjective element.[33] Indeed Courtney notes, "subjectivity in this context has been interpreted as meaning that an idiot, provided he is honest, can avoid liability".[34]

There is no justifiable reason why the common law should continue to impose this low standard, which, in practice, has been a toothless tiger.[35] As Dent comments: "The duty of care has been a problem child of corporate law. Its command that directors and officers perform their duties with reasonable prudence appears on its face to provide a significant constraint on directors and officers, especially in an age when control has become divorced from ownership in public corporations. In practice, however, the duty of care has proved almost totally ineffectual".[36] Notwithstanding the current position, the recent proposed reform by the Company Law Review Group is a step in the right direction.

It is submitted that statutory reform[37] similar to that proposed by the Company Law Review Group should be adopted. In this jurisdiction, that would entail statutory reform, based upon s 297A of the Companies Act, 1963 (which is the equivalent fraudulent trading provision to that in England[38]) which would provide that the standard of care which a director must now show under the general law requires the director to act as a reasonably diligent person having not only the same general knowledge and experience as the director but has also the general knowledge and skill to be expected of a person having the same functions.[39] The task of investigating and enforcing suspected breaches of this reformed standard could possibly be assigned to the statutory officer, the Director of Corporate Enforcement, following complaint by interested stakeholders.[40]

---

33 See n 12, above.

34 Above, n 1, at 8.044.

35 See *Inadequacies of a low standard of care* see "paragraph above".

36 Dent, "The Revolution in Corporate Governance, The Monitoring Board and the Director's Duty of Care" (1981) 61 *Boston University Law Review* 623, 624.

37 In the form of a Statutory Instrument.

38 s 214(4) of the Insolvency Act 1986.

39 See *Gower's Principles of Modern Company Law* (6th ed, 1997), at pp 641–664.

40 This new office has been recommended to be established by the Working Group on Company Law Compliance and Enforcement—See the Report of the Working Group, 30 November, 1998 (Govt Pubs).

A Glitch on the Path Towards *Nova Hibernia*: The Case for Partial Reform of Ireland's Non-life Insurance Legislation

by

Max Barrett*

Aficionados of Joyce will be familiar with the scene from *Ulysses* in which Leopold Bloom speaks with his friend Daedalus of transforming Dublin into "the golden city which is to be the new Bloomusalem in the *Nova Hibernia* of the future".[1] A major step towards bringing about a new Ireland was taken in 1987, with the establishment of an International Financial Services Centre (the "IFSC") in Dublin. The success of the IFSC, and the boost it has given to the financial services sector generally, have been significant factors in Ireland's recent economic success.[2] This centrality of the financial services sector to Ireland's present economic well-being is evidenced by the number of legislative measures enacted in recent years, aimed wholly or partly at encouraging and facilitating the performance of financial services in Ireland.[3] Still, problems remain. One problem concerns Ireland's non-life insurance legislation. It is a problem that has the potential to affect many transactions that involve the giving of guarantees. It is also a problem that has the potential to adversely impact on Ireland's burgeoning popularity as an international financial services centre. However, it is not an irremediable problem. Indeed, this essay advocates a legislative solution to the problem. To understand this solution, it is first necessary to consider the problem in some detail.

---

* This essay was awarded a prize by the Law Society of Ireland for the *Student Law Reform Essay Competition 2001.*

[1] See Joyce, *Ulysses,* (Penguin Books, London 1992) p 606.

[2] For an account of the success of the IFSC, see the IFSC's own website at www.ifsc.ie. For an account of the success of the financial services sector in Ireland generally, see Hughes, *"Financial Services Reaps the Benefits of Booming Economy"* in the *Sunday Business Post Online* at www.sbpost.ie.

[3] See, for example, the Investment Limited Partnerships Act 1994, the Investment Intermediaries Act 1995, the Netting of Financial Contracts Act 1995, the Securitisation (Proceeds of Certain Mortgages) Act 1995, the Investor Compensation Act 1998, the Companies Amendment (No 2) Act 1999, and the Electronic Commerce Act 2000.

The Problem—One Aspect

Underpinning many credit transactions is a contract of guarantee whereby a third-party guarantor promises that in the event of a repayment default by the party obtaining credit, the guarantor will indemnify the disappointed creditor. Without such a guarantee, the risk of default would be too great a risk for many creditors to bear.

In a colloquial sense, contracts of guarantee can be described as forms of insurance. They are, after all, agreements whereby one party agrees to pay money to another upon a certain event occurring (much as an insurer will agree to pay money upon a particular event transpiring). However, in a legal sense it is important to distinguish contracts of guarantee from contracts of insurance. Two good reasons for this are provided by s 9 of the Insurance Act 1936,[4] and Art 6 of the EC (Non-Life Insurance) Framework Regulations 1994[5] (s 9 of the 1936 Act and Art 6 of the 1994 Regulations are hereafter jointly referred to as "the Problem Provisions").

Section 9 of the 1936 Act makes it a criminal offence "to effect or endeavour to effect any contract of assurance with an assurance company or any other person which or who is not the holder of an assurance licence entitling such company or person to effect contracts of insurance of the kind so effected."

Article 6 of the 1994 Regulations provides that "an insurance undertaking shall not carry on the business of non-life insurance unless it is the holder of an authorisation".[6] Breach of Art 6 is a criminal offence.[7]

The combined effect of the Problem Provisions has been to create apprehension that if contracts concluded as contracts of guarantee are later deemed by the courts to be contracts of insurance unlawfully effected in contravention of s 9 of the 1936 Act and unlawfully issued by an unauthorised insurer in contravention of Art 6 of the 1994 Regulations, those contracts will be so tainted by illegality as to be void.

---

4 No 45 of 1936 (hereafter "the 1936 Act").

5 SI No 359 of 1994 (hereafter "the 1994 Regulations").

6 This authorisation requirement is mandated by Art 4 of the Third Non-Life Insurance Framework Directive (Council Directive 92/49/EEC of 18 June 1992 on the coordination of laws, regulations and administrative provisions relating to direct insurance other than life insurance (OJ L228, 11.8.1992, p l)) (hereafter "the Third Non-Life Directive").

7 Per Art 59 of the 1994 Regulations.

Undoubtedly the courts, when asked to determine the true nature of a purported guarantee, i.e. whether it is a contract of guarantee or a contract of insurance, would have regard to the intention of the parties to that contract at the time it was entered into. However, it is possible for parties not to be in agreement as to the nature of a contract into which they enter. Moreover, it is possible that an unscrupulous guarantor asked to honour a guarantee might seek to avoid liability there-under by claiming that the relevant contract of guarantee is actually a contract of insurance, that a duty of good faith existed at the time of its formulation, that this duty was breached and that consequently the guarantor/insurer is not liable under the contract. Unfortunately, with Ireland's non-life insurance law as it presently stands, there is scope for such mischief.[8]

An Aside on Some Relevant Case Law

Even when parties are acting honestly, disputes can arise as to whether a particular contract constitutes a contract of guarantee or one of insurance. Case law shows this to be so. Take, for example, the case of *International Commerce Bank plc v Insurance Corporation of Ireland.*[9]

Mr Kazantzis was the co-owner of Amaxa SA (hereafter "Amaxa"), which wanted to borrow money for a particular purpose but was unable to offer adequate security. It

[8] The "duty of good faith" mentioned above is also known as the "duty of uberrima fides". Both phrases can note a basic principle on which insurance law has been based for the last two centuries or so, namely that a party seeking insurance has a duty to reveal to an insurer all material facts which would influence a prudent insurer when fixing a premium or deciding whether to accept a risk (for a classic exposition of this duty, see the judgment of Mansfield LCJ in *Carter v Boehem* [1766] 3 Burr 1905). The duty of good faith flows from a contract being a contract of insurance. It is not an *a priori* criterion by which one can determine whether a particular contract is a contract of insurance. As Lord Justice Romer (as he then was) stated in the seminal English insurance law case of *Seaton v Heath* [1899] QB 782 at 792, "Whether...[a] contract be one requiring uberrima fides or not must depend upon its substantial character and how it came to be effected". In short, one must first determine whether a contract is a contract of insurance before one can state that a duty of good faith arises in respect of it. In his judgment Romer LJ moves on to consider some of the factors relevant to such a determination.

[9] [1991] ILRM 726. The case is hereafter referred to as "the *ICB* case", International Commerce Bank as "ICB", and Insurance Corporation of Ireland as "ICI". Another case of interest is *Kreglinger and Fernau Limited v Irish National Insurance Company Limited* [1956] IR 116, in which Davitt P decided that a particular performance bond constituted a contract of insurance and not a contract of guarantee.

was suggested to Mr Kazantzis that a loan might be forthcoming if Amaxa was to enter into a "credit guarantee insurance" contract, the counterparty to which would promise to recompense any disappointed creditors in the event of a repayment default by Amaxa on the loan sought. ICI agreed to enter into such a contract. ICB was then approached to make a loan to Amaxa. In light of the proposed credit guarantee insurance contract, ICB agreed to make the loan. The loan was made. ICI and ICB entered into the credit guarantee insurance contract. Amaxa subsequently defaulted on repayment of the loan. ICB then sought recompense from ICI. However, ICI repudiated liability under the credit guarantee insurance agreement on the basis that it was a contract of insurance and that there had been a breach of the duty of good faith that arises when parties enter into an insurance contract (the alleged breach being that ICI had not been informed that the intended use of the loan money was unlawful). ICB did not accept this repudiation of liability under what it considered to be a contract of guarantee.

In the High Court, Blayney J concluded that the disputed contract was a contract of guarantee. In doing so Blayney J concluded to the fact that ICI and ICB had roughly equivalent knowledge of the risk involved. The purported insurer (ICI) was not dependent on the purportedly insured party (ICB) for its knowledge of the risk involved (as would be the case in a typical insurance situation). Blayney J pointed to the fact that the contract of credit guarantee insurance had been procured by the principal debtor (Amaxa), not by the "insured" party, a typical feature of guarantees. Blayney J also adverted to the fact that in form the contract resembled the standard guarantee precedent in *Butterworth's Encyclopaedia of Forms and Precedents.* One aspect of the transaction gave Blayney J some difficulty, namely that ICI had entered into the contract of credit guarantee insurance in return for a premium-style payment. However, the learned judge concluded that this was not fatal to his finding that the disputed contract was a contract of guarantee as the general weight of the evidence before him pointed to it being so.[10]

Although the Problem Provisions were not in issue in the *ICB* case, the uncertainty that can exist when it comes to determining whether a particular contract is a contract of insurance or a contract of guarantee, an uncertainty amply evidenced by the facts in that case, shows that it is right to be concerned about the potential

[10] In the course of a related appeal to the Supreme Court, Blayney J's decision was affirmed in a brief judgment for that Court delivered by McCarthy J. See *Hong Kong and Shanghai Banking Corporation v Icarom plc (Meadows Indemnity Limited, Third Party),* Unreported, Supreme Court, 31 July 1992.

implications of the Problem Provisions. Of course the substantial character of any purported contract of guarantee and how it came to be effected will generally be determinative of its true nature. Still, potential for uncertainty remains. This uncertainty is not what the Problem Provisions were intended to achieve. They belong to a body of legislation that seeks to ensure the stability of the insurance industry by regulating the manner in which insurers do business. That legislation cannot be said to be serving society entirely well when it contains provisions that preclude lawyers from being able to advise with confidence on the validity of certain contracts of guarantee, and so exposes commercial players to the possibly devastating risk that voidance of a guarantee could entail. This uncertainty does not just affect ordinary individuals. It has the potential to affect financial institutions, including those international financial institutions which have so recently located in Ireland, and from whose presence and activities so much of Ireland's current prosperity derives. These institutions could readily scale down their presence in Ireland if they were to decide that the Irish legal system is not conducive to the safe performance of certain legitimate financial transactions. As it happens, financial service providers have particular reason to be concerned about Ireland's non-life insurance laws.

The Problem—Another Aspect

In the last quarter-century derivative instruments have formed an increasing component of global financial market activity.[11] One of the more recent innovations is the credit derivative. This instrument enables a party to protect itself from the loss it might suffer in the event of a credit default by some third party who is a stranger to the derivative transaction. The party seeking protection will pay money to another party, typically a bank or some other financial services provider. That other party will agree that if a specified event occurs it will pay a sum of money to the protection-seeker. The protection-seeker thus hedges itself against the possibility of future loss while the protection-provider seeks to make a quick penny now, in the considered belief that a default event will never occur and it will never have to payout. Just in case the protection-provider does have to payout, it may enter into a synthesised credit transaction. As part of that transaction it will issue commercial notes to professional investors who are effectively asked to speculate on whether the protection-provider issuing the notes will ever have to honour the liability it assumed

[11] For an account of the comparatively recent explosion in derivatives activity on world markets, see Foy, *The Capital Markets* (Round Hall Sweet and Maxwell, Dublin, 1998) at paras 1–150 to 1–154. The IFSC is home to two derivatives exchanges, FINEX Europe and the New York Cotton Exchange.

under the original credit derivative. If it does, the protection-provider will use the principal paid by the investors for the notes to meet that liability. If it does not, the protection-provider will instead pay an attractive rate of interest to the note-holders.

The difficulty with the above-described derivative transactions (and many variants thereof which exist in practice) is they could be argued to constitute non-life insurance contracts. Thus, it could be suggested that in the original derivative transaction the protection-provider is offering a type of insurance to the protection-seeker and that the money paid by the latter in return for being granted protection is essentially a premium. Similarly, it could be argued, perhaps less convincingly, that in the synthesised credit transaction the investors are offering a form of insurance to the protection-provider against any liability to payout that may arise under the original derivative transaction, the interest payments on the notes being a sophisticated form of premium payment. The substantial character of a given derivative transaction, and how it came to be effected, will determine how persuasively these arguments can be made and whether they can be rebutted by reference to the intention of the parties, the absence of a duty of good faith and, in certain derivative transactions, the possible absence of an insurable interest and of a promise to indemnify.[12] In this context it is worth noting the possible comfort offered by a fairly recent decision of the English High Court which suggests that, for the purposes of English law, the relationship between the parties to certain derivative transactions is not of a kind that would necessarily place those transactions within the realm of insurance law.[13] Notwithstanding this, the combined effect of the Problem Provisions and the absence of any Irish case law along the lines of the English case just mentioned means that there cannot be any real certainty under Ireland's non-life insurance legislation as it presently stands that particular credit derivatives do not constitute void non-life insurance agreements. With Ireland putting itself forward as a global financial services centre, it is lamentable that this should be so.

Proposed Reform

What reform would remedy the legal uncertainty described above? A single section in any statute touching upon financial affairs should suffice. The section would be composed of five subsections:

---

[12] See further Breslin, *"Credit Derivatives:* The Need For Legislative Clarification" (1998) 5 *Commerical Law Practitioner* 219.

[13] *Bankers Trust International plc v PT Dharmala Sakti Sejahtera and Others* [1995] 4 *Bank Law Reform* 382.

- The first subsection would repeal s 9 of the 1936 Act.

  Repeal of s 9 would clear the way for better regulation of this area of the law and is also prompted by the notion that while it is important for customers and the reputation of the insurance industry, and while it is a requirement of the Third Non-Life Directive, that only authorised insurers be allowed enter into non-life insurance contracts, it does not follow (and it is not a requirement of the Third Non-Life Directive) that the honest beneficiary of a guarantee which turns out to be an insurance contract should be exposed to criminal liability (as provided in s 9).
- The second subsection would revoke Art 6 of the 1994 Regulations.
  Revocation of Art 6 would clear the way for better regulation of this area of the law.
- The third subsection would leave it a criminal offence for an unauthorised undertaking to transact non-life insurance business with a consumer or a small or medium sized enterprise (hereafter a "SME").[14]

  This subsection recognises that consumers and SMEs, either because of a weak bargaining position or because of unfamiliarity with the financial services world, merit special protection under the law. Keeping it a criminal offence to engage in unauthorised non-life insurance with consumers or SMEs should help to deter those who might otherwise prey on these vulnerable categories of financial service users.[15]
- The fourth subsection would impose a statutory duty on any institution authorised to act as a bank or as an investment services provider or as a life insurer in Ireland, not to act as insurer in a non-life insurance transaction with another such institution without first obtaining a non-life insurance authorisation. Breach of this statutory duty, the fourth subsection would provide, would be a civil transgression actionable by the State and by affected private individuals but would not give rise to criminal liability.

---

[14] "Consumer" could be defined by reference to the definition of that term in s 2(1) of the Consumer Credit Act 1995, i.e. as "a natural person acting outside his trade, business or profession". What constitutes a SME could be defined by reference to a factor such as mutual turnover or profit.

[15] The notion that SMEs should be afforded protection similar to that enjoyed by consumers is inspired by the *Report of the Implementation Advisory Group on the establishment of a Single Regulatory Authority jar the Financial Services Sector* (Dublin: Stationery Office, 1999), the "McDowell Report", which states (at para 4.9) that in the financial services context the term "consumer" should include both private individuals and business interests.

This proposed subsection recognises that financial service providers when dealing with each other do not require the same level of statutory protection as consumers and SMEs.[16] Thus, it maintains in place the authorisation requirement mandated by Art 4 of the Third Non-Life Directive without recourse to a criminal sanction. Instead, contravention of the authorisation requirement would give rise to civil liability for breach of statutory duty, i.e. to strict liability sounding in both general and special damages.[17] These damages could on occasion exceed the amount insured under a disputed contract. Such exposure to additional cash liability should deter unauthorised financial institutions from transacting non-life insurance business, much as civil liability to pay compensation has been used to deter insider dealing.[18]

- The fifth subsection would provide that no contract or part of any contract would be considered void solely because it had been concluded in contravention of either the new section proposed in this essay or the problem provisions which that section would replace.

This sub-section copper-fastens the broad thrust of the preceding reforms. It ensures that no honest beneficiary of an insurance contract concluded with a non-life insurer would run the risk of substantial financial loss that could follow the voidance of such a contract pursuant to the non-life insurance legislation.

Together, the proposed fourth and fifth subsections, in ending criminal liability for unauthorised wholesale non-life insurers and creating new certainty regarding the payment liabilities of such insurers, go as far as is possible within the constraints of the authorisation requirement mandated by the Third Non-Life Directive, to ensure that financial institutions do not seek to avoid doing certain wholesale business in Ireland altogether.

---

[16] The idea that wholesale financing should be regulated differently from retail financing already finds expression in the Consumer Credit Act 1995, which applies to retail leases but not wholesale leases, and in the Netting of Financial Contracts Act 1995, which allows the parties to "financial contracts", effectively wholesale financial transactions, to set off the liabilities owing under various financial contracts between them and so to arrive at a net amount due.

[17] On liability for breach of statutory duty, see Hogan and Morgan, *Administrative Law in Ireland,* (3rd ed, (Round Hall Sweet and Maxwell, Dublin) 1998), at p 816 *et seq.*

[18] See s 109 of the Companies (Amendment Act) 1990.

Conclusion

Arrian[19] recounts the tale of "Alexander the Great" and the "Gordian Knot". Many men had expended their energies puzzling over the intricacies of the Knot. Alexander cut clean through the Knot with his sword. The Problem Provisions present a troublesome legal knot which only the Oireachtas can cut through by using the sharp sword of legislation and implementing the reform outlined above.

19 See Arrian, *History of Alexander,* trans, P A Brunt (Heinemann, London 1976), at 1.29.6.

The Origins and Evolution of the Special Criminal Court

by

Julie Anne Sweeney*

> "Rightly or not, trial by jury has for centuries been regarded popularly as a most important safeguard for the individual, a protection alike against the zeal of an enthusiastic executive or the rigidity of ultra-conservative judiciary. Especially was this so in the history of Ireland."[1]

One of the most fundamental concepts in Irish law is the right of the individual to trial by jury. However, this right is increasingly being curtailed through the use of the special criminal court for "ordinary crime".

Article 38(3) of the Irish Constitution provides for the establishment of special criminal courts for the trial of offences in cases "where it may be determined in accordance with such laws that the ordinary courts are inadequate to secure the effective administration of justice and preservation of public peace and order". Part V of the Offences against the State Act 1939 reiterates this constitutional provision word for word and so provides the legislative basis for the special criminal court (herein after "the Court").

In order for Pt V of the Act to come into effect, the Government must issue a proclamation stating that the ordinary courts are inadequate to secure the effective administration of justice and preservation of public peace and order. Such a proclamation was issued in 1939, and the Court remained in operation until 1946. The present Court was established by such a proclamation in 1972 and has been in

---

* This essay was awarded joint second place in the Law Society of Ireland, *Student Law Reform Essay Competition* 2001.

[1] Per Kingsmill Moore J in *Melling v O'Mathghamhna* [1962] IR 97.

operation to date. The problem of Northern Ireland and the ensuing paramilitary activities has been the primary reason given by the Government, on numerous occasions, for the establishment of the current Court. Recently however the reasons for its retention have included jury and witnesses intimidation not only by paramilitaries but also by members of organised criminal gangs.[2]

Background to the Introduction of the Offences against the State Act 1939

The Oireachtas debates of 1939 illustrate not only the circumstances and events surrounding the introduction of the Offences against the State Act 1939 but also provide an insight into the initial intention of the Oireachtas in passing the Act.

The Offences against the State Bill 1939 was introduced when the Irish State was in its infancy, the country had recently emerged from a bitter civil war and dissident political views regarding partition were rife. In trying to combat threats made by the IRA, the Government decided to introduce an Act conferring on itself special powers.

Introducing the Bill the then Minister for Justice, Mr Rutteledge, outlined its sole objective as being "to prevent the display, the use or the advocacy of force as a method to achieve political or social aims."[3] By including the phrase "social aims", the parameters of the Bill were rendered sufficiently broad so as to encompass crimes not related to subversive activity.

However, the Dáil debates indicate that the initial intention was to use these measures to combat politically motivated violence. The Bill, and in particular Pt V, relating to the Courts, was defined as an "emergency provision". The emergency to which the Minister referred was a proclamation made by the IRA purporting to be the true government of the State with the right to declare war. Thus, the primary grounds given for the Bill was that the security of the State was under threat.

The speeches made by Dáil Deputies during the debates may indicate the intentions of the legislature regarding the Bill. For example, Professor O'Sullivan (Deputy for North Kerry) said: "It is a bill which is clear from its content is designed to deal with what I might call dangerous political disorder". But even in the initial stages of the

---

[2] B Lenihan, Seanad Debates on the Criminal Justice (Terrorist Offences) Bill 2002. Dated, Tuesday, 10 February 2005.

[3] 74 Dáil Debates Col 1283.

Bill's passage some Deputies' voiced their fears about its potential for abuse. Professor O'Sullivan highlighted the dangers of certain sections of the Bill "to the ordinary citizen who may be guilty of anything that could be interpreted as upsetting the State or leading to the upsetting of the State".[4]

As will be outlined below, this danger has already been realised through the use of the Court for the trial of non-subversive crimes, such as manslaughter and drug trafficking.

Certification by the Director of Public Prosecutions

Section s 46 and 47 of the Act authorise the Director of Public of Prosecutions (DPP) to issue certificates deeming the ordinary courts "inadequate to secure the effective administration of justice and preservation of public peace and order" in relation to *any* case/offence. Upon certification by the DPP, these cases must be sent for trial in the Court. There is no limit on the type of offence that may be certified by the DPP and no reason need be given as to why the ordinary courts would be inadequate in that particular case. The decision of the DPP is not subject to judicial review unless there is evidence of *mala fides* (see *Kavanagh v the Government of Ireland, the DPP and the Special Criminal Court* [1996] IR 321).

The question of whether the certificate of the DPP could be subject to judicial review was examined in *Savage v DPP* [1982] ILRM 385. Relying on In *Re McCurtain* [1941] IR 83, Finlay J held that the only function of the judiciary in this area was to ascertain whether the certificate was valid in that it was (a) issued by the DPP and (b) that he had reached an opinion as expressed in that certificate. Nevertheless the basis on which the opinion was formed is not subject to review: "the opinion of the AG is not reviewable by the courts".[5]

Relying on *Savage v DPP* in her High Court decision of *Kavanagh v Ireland*,[6] Laffoy J outlined one of the reasons why the certificate of the DPP should not be subject to judicial review. She stated that "the revealing of such information in open court ... would be a security impossibility".[7] However, as commentators have argued, this

[4] 74 Dáil Debates Col 1307.

[5] *Savage v The Director of Public Prosecutions* [1982] ILRM 388.

[6] *Kavanagh v Ireland* [1996] IR 321.

[7] *ibid.*

concern could be met by following the ruling in *Murphy v Dublin Corporation*,[8] under which court proceedings, which include sensitive material from a security point of view, may be held *in camera*. Yet, in the case of *O'Reilly & Judge v the DPP*,[9] it was held that "based on the terms of Article 38(3) (1) of the Constitution and the authorities to date the opinion of the DPP is not reviewable by the courts whether in open court or as private investigation".

Moreover, the certificate is not reviewable even in cases which contain no subversive elements or security hazards. In *Byrne v Dempsey*[10] the plaintiffs argued that the DPP's decision should be subject to review by the ordinary courts as "the upholders and protectors of the constitutional rights of the citizens". As in the previous decisions, it was held that the power of the DPP to transfer cases derived from the legislature, which vested this power solely in the executive. As such, in the absence of *mala fides* the DPP could not be called upon to explain his decision, give reasons for it or reveal the sources of information on which it was based. Thus, there has been little development in this area and little leeway is afforded to the judiciary to examine the decision of the DPP. The accused cannot contend his right to jury trial as he cannot avail of any opportunity to dispute the allegation that the ordinary courts are inadequate to secure justice in his particular case.

The Special Criminal Court and Ordinary Crime

There is now a commonly held and not unsubstantiated fear among human rights organisations that the jury trial is slowly being abolished "by the backdoor".[11]

This fear has developed due to the increasing use of the Court to try offences with no subversive connections. For example, between 1999 and 2001 the Irish Council for Civil Liberties recorded that approximately one third of the cases dealt with by the Court related to offences with no paramilitary connections.[12]

The ICCL has also documented the wide range of ordinary crime that has been charged before the Court via the certificate of the DPP. Charges such as arson, the unlawful taking of a motorcar, receiving a stolen caravan and its contents and the

---

8 *Murphy v Dublin Corporation* [1972] IR 215.

9 [1984] ILRM 229.

10 Unreported, Supreme Court, March 1999.

11 Robinson, *The Special Criminal Court* (1974), at p 7.

12 Farrell, *The Special Criminal Court – The Facts* (Irish Council for Civil Liberties, 1997).

theft of cigarettes and £150.00 from a small shop have all been heard before the Court.

The contention that the Act could be extended into ordinary crime was dealt with extensively in *People v Quilligan and O'Reilly.*[13] This case concerned an appeal made by the DPP against the ruling of the trial judge pertaining to the arrest of Mr Quilligan under the Offences against the State Act. Quilligan was charged with murder. Barr J, in the Central Criminal Court, divided offences into two broad categories for the purposes of determining the intention of the Act: those which were "ordinary crimes" and those defined as "subversive crimes". He held that as the offence with which the accused had been charged contained no subversive element, an arrest under the Offences against the State Act was unlawful and so any statements made whilst in police custody were inadmissible.

In coming to this conclusion, Barr J held that "[the Act's] general purpose is to deal with political or quasi political crimes against the states, its organs or personnel". Furthermore, he held that "the adequacy or otherwise of the ordinary courts to conduct and dispose of criminal business arises only in connection with subversive crime". On appeal the Supreme Court held that Barr J had erred in his interpretation of the Act by limiting its application to subversive offences.

In the Supreme Court, Walsh J outlined the jurisdiction of the Court as being:

> " restricted to the offences in relation to which the government is satisfied that the ordinary courts are inadequate to secure the effective administration of justice and preservation of public peace and order which have been "scheduled" by the government in the proscribed manner and to any offences in respect of which there is a certificate by the Attorney General or now also the DPP that the ordinary courts are in his opinion inadequate to secure the administration of justice and the preservation of public peace and order in respect of the trial of the offence in question".[14]

Considering that the certificate of the DPP is in reality unreviewable by the courts and neither the DPP's nor the Government's reasoning as to the adequacy of the

[13] [1986] IR 495.

[14] *People (at the suits of the DPP) v Christopher Quilligan and Patrick O'Reilly* [1986] IR 429 at 506.

courts are fully disclosed, this effectively means that there is little or no limit to the jurisdiction of the Court.

In holding that the Act could be extended to ordinary crime, Walsh J referred to actions which contained no paramilitary element yet could be economically injurious to the State and used the black market cases which were heard by the Court to illustrate this. However, these cases were heard during the late war years when Ireland was in a state of emergency. As the Dáil debates of 1939 demonstrate, the Act was set up to deal with issues affecting the functioning of the State whilst experiencing emergency conditions.

Walsh J then continued his analysis for allowing the Act to encapsulate ordinary crime by citing the reasoning of the legislature in 1939 for the Court, which envisaged the possibility of jury intimidation. He argued that "ordinary gangsterism or well organised drug dealing" could just as equally pose as great a threat to juries as subversives. This argument carries weight but ignores the fact that the intention of the Act, as demonstrated in the Dáil debates of 1939, was to deal with crime affecting the security of the State in a time of emergency. Unfortunately, large scale drug trafficking is quite common in many countries and would not constitute an "extraordinary circumstance" in modern society.

It has also been argued that if a jury is at risk of tampering then there are more effective ways of dealing with this issue than dispensing with them completely.[15] Other jurisdictions, such as the United States, deal quite effectively with high profile drug and gang related cases where juries may be at risk of intimidation without doing away with juries all together.

The courts have conceded that the maintenance of the Special Criminal Court is primarily a political question. As was stated in the 1996 case *Joseph Kavanagh (Applicant) v The Government of Ireland, the DPP, the Attorney General and the Special Criminal Court*: "It is natural that such a political decision should be primarily subject to political control".[16] However, in this case Keane J also acknowledged that the Government's decision on the adequacy of the ordinary courts "cannot be regarded as forever beyond judicial control".

---

[15] The submission from the Law Society's Criminal Law committee to the Hederman Committee to review the Offences against the State Acts 1939 to 1998 and related matters, p 11.

[16] [1996] IR 321 at 355.

Keane J also recognised that, as per *Crotty v An Taoiseach* [1987] IR 713, judicial review of the decision by the Government is dependent on the actual infringement of the rights of individual citizens. Such an infringement may be indicated by "a clear disregard by the governments of the powers and duties conferred upon them by the constitution".

In *Byrne v Ireland,*[17] the appellants were transferred to the Court on foot of a certificate of the DPP while nine of their co-accused were sent for trial in the ordinary courts. On appeal, the appellants contended the validity of the certificate and relied on unfair discrimination in violation of Art 40.1 of the Constitution.

In particular, they relied upon this statement made by Henchy J in the *Stardust Victims Tribunal*: "I would accept that Article 40.1 of the constitution requires that people who appear before the courts in essentially the same circumstances should be dealt with in essentially the same manner". The appellants and their nine co-accused were charged with the same offences arising out of the same set of circumstances. Hamilton CJ justified the situation in which the appellants found themselves by stating that "what distinguishes the appellants from their co-accused is that, in respect of them only, the DPP has certified that the ordinary courts are inadequate to secure the effective administration of justice and preservation of public peace and order". He stated that the DPP is directly authorised by statue "to issue a certificate and thereby make this distinction between citizens".

By contrast, Keane J in *Kavanagh v Ireland* stated that "save in exceptional circumstances of war and national emergency envisaged by Article 28(3) the courts at all times retain their jurisdiction to interfere so as to ensure that the exercise of these drastic powers to abridge citizens' rights is not abused by the arm of the government to which they have been entrusted".[18]

It could be argued that the distinction by the DPP in *Byrne* between 11 people charged with identical crimes arising out of identical circumstances was an infringement of an individual's right to equality, which based on *Crotty v An Taoiseach* the courts claim authority to protect.

---

[17] Unreported, Supreme Court, 11 March 1999.

[18] [1996] IR 321 at 366.

The Recommendations of the Hederman Committee

The Hederman Committee was established to review the Offences against the State Act and related matters. The Committee heard submissions from all interested parties, including human rights organisations. The report of the Committee documents that reviews as to the necessity for the keeping in operation of the Court took place in 1997, 1998, 1999 and 2000 and involved consultations with the Department of Justice, Equality and Law Reform, the Attorney General, the DPP and the Gardai. The reasons advanced by these groups for the Courts, continuance was the continued threat of subversives to the security of the State, the ruthlessness of organised criminal gangs and the threat which these groups pose to juries.

A majority of the committee was of the opinion that the security risk to the State alone was a sufficient reason for the retention of the Court. The majority also accepted that the risk to jury intimidation was a very real risk should jury trial be restored in these cases.[19] The Committee recommended that the necessity of the Court be kept under regular review. To this end the Committee was of the opinion that the Government should amend the legislation to provide that the resolution establishing the Court should automatically lapse unless it is positively affirmed by resolutions passed by both Houses of the Oireachtas at three yearly intervals. These resolutions should state the basis on which the Court is being established or continuing in force. The legislation should also provide for a three-yearly report on the need for the Court.

Moreover, the Hederman Committee recommended four alternative suggestions which would ensure that the certificate of the DPP could be reviewed. These were outlined at para 9.67 of the report as follows:

(i) A review by the High Court following *inter partes* hearing;
(ii) An *ex-partes* application to the High Court *in camera*;
(iii) An administrative review of the certificate by a retired judge;
(iv) Review of the certificate by a judge in the Supreme Court.

The dissenting members of the Hedermann Committee[20] were of the view that the justification of jury intimidation was not a sufficient reason for the retention of the Court. The minority made the point that no other common law

[19] The Report of the Hederman Committee on the Offences against the State Act 1939 and related matters at Chap 9, para 9.29.

[20] The Hon. Justice Anthony J Hederman, Professor William Binchy and Professor Dermot Walsh.

jurisdiction has come to the conclusion that the risk of jury intimidation warrants non-jury trial. They were of the view that if juries were both anonymous and kept at a secret and secure location then the risk of effective jury intimidation would not be very great. Regarding the certificate of the DPP, the minority opined that the DPP

> "represents one side of an adversarial process. As an active participant in that adversarial process, it is not just that he should be given powers relating to the trial of the accused which can detrimentally affect the interest of the accused. Even if these powers were to be exercised in good faith in all cases they do not have the appearance of the impartial and objective protection of the right of the accused persons to a fair trial".[21]

Despite the recommendations of the Committee, the Government arrived at a decision on 14 December 2004 to introduce a second Special Criminal Court. A factor behind the Government's decision to establish a second Court was stated as a need to avoid any difficulty or challenge on the basis that persons are held on remand for undue periods pending trial.[22]

The evolution of the Court has witnessed somewhat of a snowball effect: it began as a means to combat political crime. It is now increasingly being applied to try any sort of offence, regardless of classification, where the DPP is of the opinion that the ordinary courts cannot secure justice. The adequacy or otherwise of the ordinary courts is determined by two subjective sources: the Government, which has an interest in ensuring that crimes are prosecuted, and the DPP, who will be prosecuting the case.

This fact, coupled with the evasion of the judiciary in adopting a supervisory role in relation to the certificate, highlights the need for well-defined conditions under which the Court should be used. A starting point should be the implementation of all the recommendations of the Hederman report regarding the Court.

The most obvious and persistent criticism of the Offences against the State Act 1939 and the Court is that it was not intended that ordinary criminal cases should fall within its ambit. These cases are being tried under an emergency procedure which could be said to contravene the initial intention of the Oireachtas. To use Pt V of the

---

[21] The Report of the Hederman Committee on the Offences against the State Act 1939 and related matters at Chap 9, para 9.44.

[22] Minister McDowell, Dáil Eireann Debates dated Wednesday 16 February 2005.

Act in ordinary crime without adequate justification is not only incorrect but also disconcerting.

If emergency measures are used and normalised within this jurisdiction, we may witness the degeneration of the criminal justice system into one of double standards where, for unexplained reasons, certain individuals are granted their right to jury trial while others are denied it.

A Right to Be Represented by a Trade Union in the Irish Constitutional Context?

by

Eoin Carolan*

Introduction

Although the organised labour movement in Ireland has never experienced the sort of institutionalised state opposition to its existence that was evident in the United Kingdom during the 1980s, legal protection of trade union activities in this jurisdiction has, in certain senses, proved something of a disappointment. The commonly celebrated system of social partnership, which has become the norm in the Irish industrial relations sphere, may have given trade unions increased access to the creation and development of social policy in this country, but there remain many areas of particularly private enterprise from which the labour movement finds itself entirely excluded. The experience amongst European unions has been of a dramatic drop in trade union membership,[1] due, according to some writers,[2] to the increased instances of de-recognition occurring across the continent.[3] Although Irish membership levels have, to an extent, bucked this continent-wide trend, a closer examination of the statistics reveal that all may not be well in the domestic system

* Junior Sophister Law, Trinity College, Dublin. This essay was awarded a prize by the Law Society of Ireland for the *Student Law Reform Essay Competition 2001.*

[1] See, for example, Kerr and Waddington, "Membership Retention in the Public Sector" (1999) 30 IRJ 151; Hendy, *Every Worker Shall Have the Right to be Represented at Work by a Trade Union* (Institute of Employment Rights, 1998).

[2] *ibid.*

[3] See Gall and McKay, "Trade Union Derecognition in Britain 1988–94" (1994) 32 BJIR 433, where the authors discovered that "union recognition and organisation in many small workplaces has collapsed". Given that such de-recognition deprives trade union of much of their attraction for members, it is not difficult to discern a link between unions' inability to represent their members and the progressive decline in membership levels across Europe.

either.[4] Examples remain of individual firms which steadfastly refuse to entertain even the simplest representations of trade unions acting on behalf of the company's employees, unwilling to extend even the most basic of representation rights to employee associations, engendering an atmosphere of antagonism and mistrust hardly conducive to industrial peace.

Arguably, the institution of a legal or constitutional obligation on employers to allow a union act in a representative capacity would encourage the development of a more efficient industrial relations system. Certainly, there would appear to be obvious benefits to a structure under the auspices of which the employer is kept informed of the complaints and opinions of his employees. More importantly, however, such a right would give full effect to the Irish constitutional guarantee of freedom of association, arid to the apparent theory underlying our law's attitude to industrial relations. After all, if labour law is truly to proceed on the basis of eradicating the inherent inequality of bargaining power present in the employment relationship,[5] it appears somewhat of an inconsistency for it to allow workers to be deprived of their only obvious means of equalisation.

In its contravention of established common law principles, however, proponents of a right of representation could find themselves faced with immense difficulties in securing judicial recognition of the asserted right. The common law, both historically and institutionally, has had an uneasy relationship with the organised labour movement. Although its initial antagonism was in part motivated by the social origins of those judges who applied it, there existed also a philosophical foundation for the judiciary's deep-seated distrust of collective action. Benthamite liberalism, atomic[6] and individualist in character, and Malthusian economics, abstentionist in

---

[4] This downward drift was initially also replicated in Ireland as union membership fell from 499,744 in 1980 to 482,990 in 1990. The number of Irish trade unionists has, however, increased again to 561,793 in 1999. (<www.lrc.ie/labour_relations_in_ireland/trade_unions.htm#TRADEUNION MEMBERSHIP 1980-1999>). Nonetheless, there has been a noticeable decline in the percentage of the Irish workforce who are also members of a trade union, dropping from 57 per cent in 1980 to 50 per cent in 1990 and 38 per cent in 1995. See Hendy, *op. cit,* p 6. CSO figures, available at <www.cso.ie/principa1stats/pristaZjab.ht~J>, for the total number of people in employment in Ireland for 1999 (1,591,000) indicate a continued fall in this figure to 35 per cent. If the total available labour force is taken as the determining criteria, the figure is a mere 33 per cent.

[5] For an analysis of competing theories of the proper role of labour law, see Von, Prondynski, *Freedom of Association and Industrial Relations, A Comparative Study* (Mansell, 1987).

[6] Laski, *Liberty in the Modern State* (Allen & Unwin, 1930), p 180.

approach, combined to cast the efforts of trade unionists in an unfavourable light, portraying them as the oppressive, coercive actions of organisations intent on interfering in the vital freedom of the marketplace. Unions, by their very existence, sought to subvert economic precepts sanctified as fundamental laws of nature.[7] The judicial doctrines of conspiracy and restraint of trade were applied so as to stifle the labour movement, undermining as it did that panacea of the 19th century court—freedom of contract.[8] Although overtaken by a more benevolent statutory approach, the underlying common law principles remained almost unremittingly hostile.

The enactment of Art 9 of the Irish Free State Constitution, followed subsequently in 1937 by Art 40.6.l(iii) of Bunreacht na hÉireann, ought to have marked the emergence of a new legal regime under which, rather than receiving grudging exemption from the full rigours of the law, unions would be positively protected in the pursuit of their essential objectives. In practice, however, this has not proved to be the case. Instead, the Irish courts have invariably interpreted Art 40.6.1(iii) as a safeguard for individuals against the possible abuse of organisational power,[9] an interpretation undoubtedly influenced by the underlying legal hostility to the trade union movement.[10] Yet, the constitutional text, as outlined below, would appear to envisage at least some measure of protection for trade union activities. Thus, if the courts are not to deprive this Article of real meaning and effect, protection of the basic trade union activity of representation appears unavoidable. After all, if the freedom of association guarantee fails to incorporate this most foundational union

---

[7] Dicey, *Law and Public Opinion in England* (Macmillan, 1914), p 199, cited in Von Prondynski, *Freedom of Association and Industrial Relations A Comparative Study* (Manswell, 1987), p 4.

[8] What Lord Wedderburn has described (Wedderburn, *The Worker and the Law* (3rd ed, Sweet & Maxwell, 1986), p 318) as "the pervasive individualism of the common law, its unshakeable belief in the reality of apparent market relationships and the accompanying ideology" was reflected in the many 19th-century examples of judges attempting to undermine statutory reforms. See, for example, how the courts declared certain trade unions to be lawful, with the effect that they could not claim the protection of s 4 of the Trade Disputes Act 1906 in *Swaine v Wilson* [1889] 24 KB 252; *Gozney v Bristol Trade & Provident Society* [1909] 1 KB 901; or where severability of objects was permitted so as to render an association lawful at common law in *Russell v* ASCJ [1912] AC 421.

[9] See *Educational Company v Fitzpatrick* (No 2) [1961] IR 345; *Meskell v CIE* [1973] IR 121; *Rodgers v ITGWU* [1978] ILRM 51; *Doyle v Croke* [1988] 7 JISSL 150.

[10] An individualist emphasis, characteristic of the common law, has been a notable feature of Irish freedom of association jurisprudence. See *R(IUDWC) v Rathmines UDC* [1928] JR 260; *NUR v Sullivan* [1947] JR 77; *Educational Company v Fitzpatrick (No 2)* [1961] JR 345; *Meskell v CIE* [1973] JR 121.

function, it would appear an inescapable conclusion that Irish law continues to regard the organised labour movement with residual antipathy, as little more than the undeserving recipient of legislative reform.

The International Perspective

The right to be represented by a trade union is widely regarded as the most basic right inherent in trade union membership. Although most common law countries[11] appear to favour the restrictive view of freedom of association expressed in *Collymore v AG*,[12] the majority of international and European conventions regard the right rather as "the visible and external manifestation of trade union membership".[13] Even the case law of the ECHR, criticised as "skewed towards an individualistic interpretation",[14] protects representation as one of the basic activities of trade unions.[15]

---

11 *Banton v Alcoa Minerals of Jamaica Ltd* [1971] 17 WJR 275; *All India Bank Employees Association v National Industrial Tribunal* AIR (1962) 29 AIR 171.

12 [1970] AC 538; [1970] 2 WLR 233. This restrictive view of the concept has been described as "the grim reduction of freedom of association to the right to associate together for some purpose or other, however restricted". Wedderburn, "Freedom of Association or Right to Organise: The Common Law and International Sources", in *Employment Rights in Britain and Europe* (Institute of Employment Rights, 1991), p 146.

13 *Discount Tobacco & Confectionery v Armitage* [1990] IRLR 15 at 16.

14 Wedderburn, "Freedom of Association or Right to Organise: The Common Law and International Sources", in *Employment Rights in Britain and Europe* (Institute of Employment Rights, 1991), p 143.

15 The Art 11 case law of the European Court of Human Rights recognises an obligation to protect "the occupational interests of trade union members by trade union action, the conduct and development of which the Contracting States must both permit and make possible"—*Swedish Engine Drivers Union* (1975) 1 EHRR 578 at para 40. Although the Court's approach has been criticised for its holding that Art 11 does not secure any particular treatment of trade unions, it is clear from the case law that freedom of association in an ECHR context requires, at a minimum, that trade unions be able "to strive for the protection of members' interests". That even this low-level protection incorporates the suggested right to be represented is obvious. As one Irish writer has remarked, "It is clear that freedom of association under the Convention includes the right to have one's union make representations on one's behalf, though not the right to compel employers to negotiate with that union. Thus any provision in Irish law which would entitle a citizen to join a union but then deny that union the right to represent him would appear to be in violation of the European Convention", Whyte, "Right of Workers to Choose their Collective Bargaining Agents" (1981) 75 *GILSI* 53 at p 55 although to this must be added the *caveat* that, in Whyte's view, such protection extends only to representation in relation to individual grievances.

When it is considered that this ECHR protection lags far behind that of either the ILO[16] or European Social Charter,[17] the fundamental nature of the asserted right is very much in evidence.

"Right of Representation" in Irish Law

The lush position on the suggested constitutional right to be represented by a trade union is uncertain.[18] Nonetheless, despite the absence of detailed examination of the asserted right by the Irish courts, the case law remains useful, in the sense that it illustrates the underlying factors discouraging the courts from the recognition of such a right. Courts have three primary concerns with regard to recognising a constitutional right to representation—its nature as a collective right, its imposition of a duty to entertain representations upon the employer and the trespass into the legislative domain which its recognition appears to entail.

---

16 Art 5 of the European Social Charter guarantees to "all workers ... freedom of association ... for the protection of their economic and social interests" while Art 6 protects the right to bargain collectively. These articles clearly envisage a measure of protection for trade union activities and have been interpreted as giving rise to a right to be represented by a trade union. See Walton and Hendy, "An Individual Right to Union Representation in International Law" (1997) 26 III International Labour 205 at p 217.

17 ILO Conventions do not expressly provide for the right to be represented by a trade union. Article 4 of ILO Convention No 98 on the Right to Organise and Bargain Collectively (1949) does, however, commit states to the adoption of measures "to encourage and promote the full development and utilisation of machinery for voluntary negotiation between employers and ... workers' organisations", albeit in the context of collective bargaining over terms and conditions of employment. See Wedderburn, *op. cit,* n 7. Given its expansive view of freedom of association, the ILO Convention No 98 would undoubtedly endorse the position that "the right to union membership is not restricted to the right to hold a membership card", Walton and Hendy, *op. cit,* p 221.

18 Although references to a right of representation abound in the constitutional case law—see *Abbott and Whelan v ITGWU and SHB* (1982)1 JISSL 56; *Dublin Colleges ASA v City of Dublin VEC* (1982) 1 JISSL 73; *Association of General Medical Practitioners v Minister for Health* [1995] 2 11RM 481—the right, as it appears in this essay, has arguably never received significant judicial attention. See Hendy, who feels that Irish courts have "negated the right of representation (save in disciplinary matters—*Devlin v Player Wills (Ire) Ltd* UD 90/1978)", Hendy, *op. cit,* p 35. On the whole, Irish courts have found themselves faced rather with the assertion by a trade union of a right to negotiate, or with an attempt to obtain exclusive recognition rights for the purposes of collective bargaining. The distinction between this right to negotiate with a trade union and the right of that union to represent its members was recognised by Walsh J in *El v Kennedy Co.* [1968] JR 69, although the point was not decisive of the case at issue. The English courts, too, have noted the "clear linguistic distinction" between representation and negotiation. See Wedderburn, *The Worker and The Law* (3rd ed, Sweet & Maxwell, 1986), p 285, relying on *R. v CAC, ex parte BTP Tioxide* [1981] ICR 843.

Common Law Opposition

It is well known that common law courts, both in principle and in procedure, find it difficult to balance collective rights with those of the individual.[19] Adversarial in approach, these courts are unused to subjugating the legal rights of the individual to the interests of the overall good.[20] Traditionally, there existed also a judicial fear that attaching rights to the collective entity would enable it to act to the detriment of its own individual members.[21] These concerns are answered by the fact that the right, as it is envisaged here, would be individual in nature, vesting not in the collective entity that is the trade union but, rather, in the individual member who finds himself deprived of the representation to which he is arguably due.

The issue of the imposition of a duty upon an employer is rather more troublesome. Irish judges have been clear[22] that this would be anathema to both the emphasis placed by the common law on individual rights and also to the tradition of voluntariness[23] in Irish industrial relations.[24] Representation, however, entails the

---

19 See Cousins, "The Protection of Collective Rights Before the Irish Courts" (1996) 14 ILT 110 at p 134.

20 Obviously this difficulty is less in Ireland in light of the courts' experience of judicial review, with its associated task of reconciling competing constitutional rights.

21 The comments of Murnaghan J in *R (IUDWC) v Rathmines* UDC [1928] JR 260 at 306 exemplify this emphasis on the primacy of individual rights over those of the collective entity, when he asked rhetorically: "Is the will of those members to prevail, or are they to be taken to have surrendered their liberty of action to the Union?"

22 Speaking generally in the context of an asserted right to compel an employer to negotiate with a particular trade union. See *Abbott and Whelan v ITGWU and SHB* (1982) 1 JISSL 56; *El Co. v Kennedy* [1968] IR 69; *Association of General Medical Practitioners v Minister for Health* [1995] 2 1LRM 481.

23 Emphasised in the *Report of the Constitution Review Group* (Stationary Office, 1996) and in the recent Seanad debates on the Industrial Relations Bill 2000. See the comments of Mr Tom Kitt, Minister of State at the Department of Enterprise, Trade and Employment at <www.irlgovie/debates-00/s l4june/sectl .htm#ind.> that the "imposition of a legal award ... [is] a last resort in Irish industrial relations".

24 Irish case law is replete with judicial *dicta* emphasising the abhorrent nature of any suggested imposition of a duty to bargain on an unwilling employer. McWilliam J insisted that "There is no duty placed on any employer to negotiate with any particular citizen or body of citizens"—*Abbott and Whelan v ITGWU and SHB* (1982) 1 JISSL 56 at 59, while Walsh J in *El Co. v Kennedy* [1968] JR 69 was of the view that "[i]n law an employer is not obliged to meet anybody as the representative of his worker, nor indeed is he obliged to meet the worker himself for the purpose of discussing any demand which the worker may make", at 89. O'Hanlon J expressed his agreement with this point of view in the recent High Court case of *Associated General Medical Practitioners v Minister for Health* [1995] 2 1LRM 481:

mere articulation of a demand, requiring neither negotiation nor bargaining. Thus, the extent of the duty imposed upon the employer is minimal. The suggested right of representation does not even require an employer to provide reasons for any conclusions to which he may come. Rather, he must simply give due consideration to any representative request.[25] Such a diluted duty would not doubt be less likely to "stick in judicial gorges"[26] than past efforts to impose an enforceable duty to bargain.

One final issue, however, falls to be addressed—how the Irish courts would regard the creation of a new constitutional right in light of the modern judiciary's instinctive restraint in the industrial relations sphere.[27] Such judicial restraint has been the decisive consideration in whole, proved willing to examine the actions of the executive and the Oireachtas wherever there might exist a possible infringement of

---

"I do not consider that there is any obligation imposed ... by the Constitution on an employer to consult with or negotiate with any organisation representing his employees ... when the conditions of employment are to be ... reviewed. The employer is left with a freedom of choice as to whether he will negotiate with any organisation ... and is also free to give a right of audience to one representative body and refuse it to another, if he chooses to do so."

[25] Similar to the *droit d'expression* enacted in French law in 1982. See Wedderburn, above, n 3, at p 281.

[26] *Express Newspapers Ltd v McShane* [1980] AC 672 at 687.

[27] Arguably, it was this sense of judicial restraint which divided the court in the key *Re Public Services Employee Relations Act* (1987) 38 DLR (4th) 161 case. A telling indication of this divergence of attitudes was the respective judges differing views on the significance of *R. v Big M Drug Mart* (1985) 18 DLR (4th) 321. Where Dickson CJC, dissenting, saw the case as authorising the adoption of "a generous rather than a legalistic [interpretation], aimed at fulfilling the purpose of the guarantee", at 195, McIntyre J, for the majority, construed it as requiring caution lest the court "overshoot the actual purpose of the right or freedom in question" with the effect that the courts come to regard the Charter "as an empty vessel to be filled with whatever meaning we might wish from time to time", at 217. The majority felt ill-equipped to adjudicate on the "delicate balancing" required by the immense political and social sensitivity of this area, regarding it as almost entirely within the legislative domain. Such a view was again evident in the recent *Delisle v Canada (Deputy AG)* (1999) 176 DLR (4th) 513 decision where the court again split on a view of the required judicial restraint. The majority felt that to recognise a right of participation for RCMP employee organisations in the particular statutory scheme would be to "enter the complex and political field of socio-economic rights, and unjustifiably encroach-upon the prerogative of Parliament ... [T]his kind of recognition would unduly limit the ability of Parliament ... to regulate labour relations", *per* Bastarche J at 531, 536.

constitutional rights,[28] the immense social and political sensitivity of industrial relations could dissuade them from endorsing the existence of a constitutional right of representation, thereby intimately involving the judiciary in affairs with which it generally feels ill-equipped to deal. Just as in Canada, this sense of judicial restraint could prove decisive. Any analysis of the right's possible existence in the Irish Constitution must thus be undertaken with such considerations in mind.

Art 40.6.1(iii): An Expansive Interpretation?

It is at least arguable that the Irish Constitution supplies a degree of textual justification for recognition of the right. Unless the Irish courts were to adopt the Privy Council's view of freedom of association,[29] some measure of trade union activities must be protected[30]—and as the most basic right of a trade union member is to have the union act on his behalf,[31] such an activity would appear to be the minimum encompassed by constitutional protection.[32]

---

[28] See, for example, *Crowley v Ireland* [1980] JR 102; *Crotty v An Taoiseach* [1987] JR 713; [1987] ILRM 400; *DB v Minister for Education* [1999] 1 IR 29, [1999] 1 ILRM 93.

[29] *Collymore v AG* [19701 AC 538; [1970] 2 WLR 233.

[30] Most countries see freedom of association as extending protection to some degree of trade union activities. For example, Italian law is of the opinion that a "right to associate in trade unions can be meaningful only as a right to organise for at least some normal union purpose". The German Constitutional Court has meanwhile interpreted their constitutional guarantee "as making sense only if the associations themselves are given the opportunity to engage in activities typically undertaken by such associations", while s 7 of the Swedish Joint Regulation of Working Life Act 1976 provides for a right to "make use of membership" of a trade union. Wedderburn, above, n 7, pp 149–150.

[31] Knox J in *Discount Tobacco & Confectionery v Armitage* [1990] IRLR 15 saw representation as "the outward and visible manifestation of union membership", at 16, declaring that he saw "no genuine distinction between membership of the union on the one hand, and making use of the essential services of a union on the other". This was regarded as "unquestionably correct" by the Court of Appeal in *Associated Newspapers v Wilson* [1994] ICR 92 at 110, but was overruled on appeal by the House of Lords [1995] 2 AC 454. Lord Lloyd, at 484, felt unable to accede to the "broad proposition ... that membership of the union, and making use of the union services, are in some way to be equated."

[32] It is pertinent to note that, although heavily criticised for adopting an overly-restrictive view of the freedom of association concept, (Christian and Ewing, "Labouring under the Canadian Constitution" (1988) 17 JU 73) the Canadian courts are clear that it encompasses a right to be represented by a trade union. Cory and Lacobucci JJ, dissenting, in *Delisle v Canada (Deputy AG)* (1999) 176 DLR (4th) 513 relied on Le Dam J's insistence in *Re Public Services Employee Relations Act* (1987) 38 DLR (4th) 161 at 239 on the importance of protecting the "freedom to belong to an association, to maintain it, and to participate in its lawful activity ..." to support their view that the RCMP ought to be able to be represented by their employee associations under the Public Service Staff Relations Act

The express reference to "unions" in Art 40.6.1(iii) clearly envisages its application in an industrial relations context and would appear to imply an intention on the part of the framers for the courts to pursue a purposive approach to freedom of association.[33] Arguably this in itself is sufficient to justify the Irish courts intervening to ensure that this 'fundamental purpose of trade union membership',[34] the *raison d'etre* that is representation, is not denied. Constitutional case law provides judicial *dicta* in support of either interpretation,[35] with *Doyle v Croke*[36] and

regime. For the majority, Bastarche J was content to uphold the restriction, noting that it satisfied the constitutional guarantee by allowing RCMP members to "freely set up an independent employee association ... which may carry on any lawful activity that is members may carry on individually, including representing their interests". This was followed subsequently in *Ontario Teachers Federation v Ontario (AG)* (2000) 188 DLR (4th) 333 at 348, when a prohibition on the membership of trade unions by school principals and vice-principals was upheld as constitutional because "it does not preclude Principals and Vice-Principals from establishing their own association to seek to persuade school boards to voluntarily bargain terms and conditions outside of the statutory framework of collective bargaining", thus preserving the right to form an association able to make representations as to its members interests.

[33] Art 19(1)(c) of the Indian Constitution contains the same "associations and unions" phrasing but has been held not to authorise such an approach. In *All India Bank Employees Association v National Industrial Tribunal* (1962) 29 AIR 171 at 180, Ayangar J said that "to read each guaranteed right as involving or including concomitant rights necessary to achieve the object ... [underlying] the grant of each of these rights-...- would by a series of ever-expanding concentric circles in the shape of rights concomitant to concomitant rights ... lead to an almost grotesque result". Casey, however, has argued that this judgment was "so heavily influenced by special features of the Indian Constitution that it could hardly be regarded as suggestive of the way in which the Irish courts might approach this issue." See Casey, "Reform of Collective Bargaining Law: Some Constitutional Implications" (1972) 7 *Ir. Jur.* 1 at pp 5–6.

[34] Hendy, *op. cit.*, p 8.

[35] In the manner in which the mere fact of association appeared to exhaust the Art 40.6.1(iii) guarantee in *Aughey v Ireland* [1989] JR 87 and *PMPS v AG* [1983] JR 339, certain Irish cases do seem to favour the constitutive construction of *Collymore* over the more purposive interpretation argued for here. On the other hand, there exist the comments of Costello J in *Doyle v Croke* (1988) 7 JISSL 150, where he derived the right to participate in the decision-making process of the organisation in part from Art 40.6.1(iii), observing (at 159) that "to be effective", the constitutional guarantee had to imply this protection of the individual's rights. This case could, of course, be characterised as yet another example of the courts defending the rights of the individual against potential abuse of organisational power, but it nonetheless remains an example of a High Court judge looking behind the text of the freedom of association guarantee to give effect to the intention arguably underlying it, as the Supreme Court itself also purported to do in *Educational Co. v Fitzpatrick (No 2)* [1961] JR 345. If Irish courts are to be consistent in having regard to such an intention, the express reference to unions in the Art 40.6.1(iii) text would appear to extend a degree of positive protection to the trade union movement. In such a scenario, "the basic human right" (Walton and Hendy, *op. cit,* p 211) to be represented would surely qualify for constitutional protection.

[36] (1988) 7 JISSL 150.

Fitzpatrick[37] arguably acting as authority for the adoption of a teleological interpretation of the Article at issue. Another argument in favour of this more expansive approach is that the level of protection entailed by the concept in *Collymore*[38] would appear to be already supplied by the freedom of assembly provision. Constitutional protection of the mere fact of association would not require the courts to protect any particular group activity, regardless of the extent to which that activity encapsulated the essence of the organisation. Once the law allowed its members to meet, assemble and associate—even if the purpose for which they wish to do so was proscribed—the *Collymore*[39] concept of freedom of association would be satisfied. Little, if anything, appears to separate this from freedom of assembly. The framers ought not to be taken to have intended differing constitutional provisions to have nothing more than identical effect. Freedom of association[40] must, at base, protect the lawful activities essential to an association, if it is not to seem simply to re-enact the freedom of assembly guarantee.[41]

Interfering in the Oireachtas Domain?

Of course, any judicial acceptance of a constitutional right to be represented by a trade union would have repercussions for the "delicate balancing" required in the industrial relations area. Courts have been traditionally cautious of involvement in this area,[42] aware of their own limitations in considering a question involving so

37 *Educational Co. v Fitzpatrick (no 2)* [1961] JR 345.

38 [1970] AC 538; [1970] 2 WLR 233.

39 [1970] AC 538; [1970] 2 WLR 233.

40 Which, it ought to be remembered, safeguards also the formation of political parties or religious groups.

41 Dickson CJC's example of a law allowing marriage but prohibiting procreation, cohabitation or the raising of children is entirely apposite. If mere association is to act as the parameter of constitutional protection, there would be nothing to prevent the Oireachtas enacting such a law (ignoring of course the content of Arts 41 and 42 of the Constitution). See *Re Public Services Employee Relations Act* (1987) 38 DLR (4th) 161 at 195.

42 This lay at the heart of the Canadian Supreme Court's rejection of a suggested right to strike in *Re Public Services Employees Act* (1987) 38 DLR (4th) 161. As McIntyre J put it (at 233–234):

> "The balance between the two forces [of capital, and organised labour] is delicate ... There is no clearly correct balance which may be struck giving permanent satisfaction to the two groups, as well-as securing the public interest. The whole process is inherently dynamic and unstable ... To intervene in that dynamic process ... by implying constitutional protection for a right to strike would ... give to one of the contending forces an economic weapon removed from, and made immune from, legislative control which could go far towards freezing the development of labour relations and curtailing the process of evolution necessary to meet the changing circumstances of a modem society on a modem world."

many social, political and economic elements. However, judicial recognition of the inherent limits to their own competence, welcome though it may be, should not be allowed to act as a pretext for abstention from the labour law area entirely. Constitutional rights and duties remain at issue, rights which Irish judges are under an obligation to uphold. Judges also ought not to underestimate the law's capability to evolve to take account of changing social circumstances. Primary power in this area may be ceded to the Oireachtas,[43] but judges must still be conscious at all times of their obligation, and indeed ability,[44] to ensure that the freedom of association guarantee, "a *sine qua non* of any democratic society",[45] be given its intended effect.

Thus, it is at least arguable that the Art 40.6.1.(iii) guarantee is capable of including an individual right to be represented by a trade union. The constitutional nature of the right could, however, present obstacles to its acceptance by the Irish courts, with the judiciary probably unwilling to excessively fetter the exercise by the legislature of its statutory powers. Thus, the focus must turn to the impact any recognition of the asserted right may have upon Ireland's statutory framework for industrial relations.

Effect on Statutory Policy

Government policy since the foundation of the Free State has focused on removing trade union multiplicity, with all its associated problems. Given that the right outlined above is one which vests in the individual worker, trade union fragmentation appears to be an obvious potential danger. An absolute constitutional right could conceivably lead to the emergence of a host of new trade

---

[43] The fact that industrial relations difficulties were more appropriate to legislative solutions played a significant role in ensuring the Constitution Review Group was "not persuaded" that Art 40.6.1(iii) ought to be extended to encompass a right to negotiate. Constitution Review Group, *Report of the Constitution Review Group* (Stationary Office, 1996), at p 316.

[44] Impossible as McIntyre J in *Re Public Services Employee Relations Act* (1987) 38 DLR (4th) 161 at 248 may have found it to state with certainty that collective bargaining will still continue to form a central strand of the fabric of industrial relations half a century from now, it is equally impossible to envisage a trade union movement which does not purport to represent its members in their engagements with employers. Should the day ever dawn when unions no longer act in a representative capacity, they would surely be unable to assert the same constitutional protection which they arguably now enjoy. Unions which do not represent their members were not within the intended ambit of Art 40.6.1 (iii). Thus court action in this area is hardly likely to lapse easily into anachronism. *Cf* Gall, "Freedom of Association and Trade Unions: A Double-Edged Constitutional Sword" in *Litigating the Values of a Nation: The Canadian Charter of Rights and Freedoms* (Carswell, 1986).

[45] *Per* Dickson CJC in *Re Public Services Employee Relations Act* (1987) 38 DLR (4th) 161 at 173.

unions, able, under the aegis of this new right, to circumvent the current statutory restrictions on their existence. It has been argued that the union movement could itself contain and limit the potential for inter-union rivalry,[46] but statistics suggest that this, of itself, may not be sufficient.[47] Recognition of the asserted right would, *prima facie,* also pose problems with regard to its interaction with the criminal offence created by s 6 of the Trade Union Act 1941.[48] These difficulties are, however, based on the concept of an absolute Art 40.6.1(iii) right. The qualifications of "regulation and control" contained in the constitutional text clearly would not support such an interpretation. Rather, they would allow the Oireachtas to continue the operation of some form of regulatory policy aimed at minimising trade union multiplicity.

The obvious solution of sole recognition rights could be constitutionally suspect,[49] as well as presenting practical problems of administration[50] in relation to the

46 Hendy relies on Kahn-Freund's view that multi-unionism is "innocuous so long as it does not become 'rival unionism'" (Kahn-Freund, *Labour and The Law* (2nd ed, 1977), p 7) and argues that the Bridlington principles guard against this. Hendy, *op. cit,* p 65.

47 A survey of the experience of the operation of the Bridlington principles in the 1970s and 1980s has led some to conclude that while there is "still a role for [an arbitration-like mechanism of] inter-union disputes ... the experience of 1974–1991 shows that there are limits beyond which it is unlikely to be an effective one." Elgar and Simpson, "A Final Appraisal of Bridlington? An Evaluation of the TUC Disputes Committee's Decisions 1974–1991" (1994) 32 BJIR 47.

48 Although any constitutional obligation imposed on an employer to entertain the representations of a trade union without a negotiation licence would fall short of s 6 criminal "negotiation", any further engagement between the two sides could arguably lead them into illegality. The artificiality of the fine line which would separate the exercise of a constitutional right from the commission of a criminal offence would be unsatisfactory in the extreme, depending as it would upon the most Jesuitical of distinctions (although the constitutional right would obviously be superior, I am assuming that any potential for conflict would discourage judicial recognition of the right). Such a system would also breed damaging uncertainty in the conduct of industrial relations.

49 *NUR. v Sullivan* [1947] JR 77.

50 Fennelly J admitted as such in the recent decision of *larnród Éireann v Holbrooke,* unreported, Supreme Court, 25 January 2001. The judge was clear that the difficulties involved in a "genuine dispute as to the representativeness of trade unions ... are potentially extremely complex and delicate." A reluctance to force either the Oireachtas or the courts to embark on an examination of such complex problems could conceivably prove decisive in convincing our courts not to recognise the asserted right in the Irish constitutional context. The text of the judgment is available at <www.ireland.comlnewspaper/specialI200l/irishraillindex.htm>.

imposition of arbitrary thresholds of trade union representativeness.[51] The most satisfactory solution would thus be one which does not necessitate a radical overhaul of the Irish statutory system. The needs of industrial order obviously require that an employer not be compelled to negotiate with any trade union of which an employee of his happens to be a member. Equally however employees ought not be deprived of their right to be represented by a trade union. Such a constitutional right would seem to be satisfied by the existence of a limited choice of associations empowered to act on the workers' behalf, amounting to a legitimate interference within the constitutional qualifications of 'regulation' and 'control'.[52]

The paradigm case requiring a right of representation occurs however in the situation where an individual employee finds himself without any form of authorised representation. S.6 should be read so as allow for the possibility of exceptions in such instances.[53] What this would amount to would be the individual entitlement of each worker to request that a trade union act on his behalf, even if he is not a member.[54]

---

[51] The "Byzantine complexity" (Antill, "Collective and Individual Representation at Work" (1999) 149 NLJ 1334) of the procedures established under the most recent English attempt to tackle this thorny issue—the Employment Relations Act 1999—ought to act as a warning to Ireland of the difficulties involved in seeking to strike an appropriate balance between the rights of individuals to be represented by a trade union of their choice and, on the other hand, regulation of the exercise of that right so as to avoid the problems of excessive trade union multiplicity. Such a statutory system would inevitably lead to the imposition of arbitrary thresholds of trade union representativeness, such as the English Act's minimum 21-employee requirement, and would also force the courts into making difficult assessments as to whether a union adequately represented a given workforce. This has, however, been done by English courts in the past. See *NCB v NUM* [1986] ICR 736; *Grifin v SW Water Plc* [1994] IRLR 121.

[52] Such a reform of the system could also move Ireland closer to fulfilling its international obligations under the European Social Charter. Ireland's negotiation licence system has been consistently found to be in breach of Arts 5 and 6 of the ESC. In the most recent report of the Joint Committee of Independent Experts, published in June 2000, the committee again found "the conditions imposed for obtaining a negotiation licence" to be "incompatible with the Charter" on various grounds. The Committee also requested that Ireland's next report contain information "on the right of union representatives to access the workplace", a situation which would arguably be addressed by the recognition of the suggested right. See<www.humanrights.coe.intlcseweblFRlPDF/html%20concs/ Conslusions%20xvi%20ireland.htm>.

[53] This should not be taken to imply that non-members be given a right to join a trade union, or even that members be entitled to demand representation on any issue.

[54] Obviously with some sort of provision to come to an arrangement to cover costs.

In the event of their refusing to do so, the worker would then be allowed to require the employer to entertain the representations of an association of his choice, be they authorised or unauthorised. Thus, the authorised union's primacy is maintained while the employee's right to have a union official act on his behalf remains unaffected, regardless of the decision of the primary trade union. The Supreme Court could therefore require that s 6 be read so as to render negotiations by an unauthorised body illegal[55]—except where an employee finds the existing unions in his place of employment unwilling to act on his behalf.

Is the Right Necessary?

Another important consideration is whether the right would in fact be necessary in light of the range of statutory protections currently available to authorised trade unions.[56] The Irish situation on this issue is certainly not as serious as that in the United Kingdom, from whence the loudest demands for reform of this area have come.[57] Arguably, however, the nature of our statutory approach, dependent as it is upon a system of legal immunities, risks leaving some employees outside the embrace of Acts focused only on specific situations.

Industrial Action?

Given that recognition disputes have been held to come within the ambit of the statutory definition of a trade dispute, industrial action in pursuit of representation rights is one option available to a trade union. Such an approach—presupposing as it does a certain level of strength in the trade union involved—is appropriate, however, only in certain situations and available only to certain unions.[58] In practice,

---

[55] Much as it held in *Educational Co. v Fitzpatrick (No 2)* [1961] IR 345 that the Constitution could be used to require that the Trade Disputes Act 1906 be read "as if there were attached thereto the words 'Provided that a dispute ... having as its object the frustration of the right of any person to choose with whom he will or will not be associated ... shall not be deemed to be a trade dispute for the purposes of this Act.'", *per* Kingsmill Moore J at 398.

[56] Especially considering the risks of trade union fragmentation outlined above.

[57] See Mortimer, *In Defence of Trade Unionism* (Institute of Employment Rights, 1998); Hendy and Walton, "An Individual Right to Union Representation in International Law" (1997) 26 ILI 205.

[58] Industrial action can have a debilitating effect upon union resources and morale, meaning that a union executive is likely to look on this option with considerable caution. Such action is only likely to occur when the trade union is in a sufficiently strong position to feel confident that there exists a definite possibility of success. Unless a union is able to call upon the support of a significant number of workers from a specific enterprise, the chances of their success remain slim. However, there is

the amount of unions availing of this option suggest its benefit is of negligible value only.[59]

Industrial Relations (Amendment) Bill 2000

A more considered response to the issue of union representation is the Industrial Relations (Amendment) Bill 2000. Although the Bill is a welcome attempt at legislative regulation of situations "where negotiating procedures are not in place", arguably it would serve only to supplement the suggested constitutional right rather than render its acceptance by the Irish courts unnecessary. The lengthy delay[60] between the initiation of proceedings by the applicant trade union and the final determination of the Labour Court eventually becoming legally binding presents certain problems. This delay would allow an intransigent employer to ignore the Labour Court recommendations with impunity for a significant period of time. Given the evidence that a trade union without representation rights finds it immensely difficulty to attract new recruits,[61] and that the Labour Court's ultimate recommendations will no doubt be influenced by existing union membership levels within the particular business, the potential exists for trade unions to find themselves trapped in a vicious circle whereby they are unable to attract members because of the

considerable evidence that unions find it difficult to recruit new members until workers are convinced that membership would be of benefit to them; for example a Unison survey in the UK found that "most members stay in their union because of the collective security deriving from their membership and not for peripheral reasons such as financial ... services", Antill, *op. cit,* p 1337. If a union finds itself unable even to obtain an audience with an employer, it is less likely to be able to attract new recruits and is therefore less likely to be able to draw upon the collective strength necessary to mount a successful campaign of industrial action in pursuit of representation rights.

59 The Irish Government admitted in its most recent report to the Committee of Independent Experts of the European Social Charter that less than 1 per cent of trade disputes in Ireland are related to issues of recognition rights. See <www.humanrights.coe.intlcseweb/GBIPDFe/R181Re.pdf>.

60 After an initial investigation and recommendation, and subsequent determination where the dispute remains unresolved, s 9 provides that the Labour Court cannot intervene again until one year has elapsed and either of the parties applies for a review. After this takes place, a further six weeks is allowed before the determination becomes cognisable by the Circuit Court.

61 See Waddington and Whitstone, "Why do people join unions in a period of membership decline?" (1997) 35 BJIR 515; Hendy, *op. cit,* at pp 5–9 ; Rain and Price, *Industrial Relations in Britain* (Blackwell, 1983); Waddington and Kerr, "Membership Retention in the Public Sector" (1999) 30 IRJ 151. It was also noticeable in *Delisle v Canada (Deputy AG)* (1999) 176 DLR (4th) 513 that the RCMP employee associations, without either a strong tradition or representation rights, were described by the Supreme Court judges as weak and ineffective, without large numbers of members.

attitude of their employer and yet are unable to compel that employer to entertain their representations because of their low levels of membership.

Such concerns are exacerbated by the fact that an application under the Bill leaves the trade union involved effectively emasculated[62]—without representation rights and unable to embark upon industrial action[63]—for a lengthy period of time. Such an association is hardly likely to command the support of workers in any large numbers. The Bill thus arguably fails to address adequately the very situation on which its provisions could exercise the most positive effect—that of an employer actively hostile to the establishment of a trade union in his own enterprise.[64]

Were there to be a constitutional right to be represented, membership levels could provide a more accurate indicator of the level of support for a particular union in an individual company and therefore allow the Labour Court to form a more accurate view of the issues arising within the particular enterprise.[65]

Obviously, therefore, the Bill does not render recognition of a constitutional right otiose. Rather, it provides a statutory scheme which could usefully act as the Oireachtas' attempt at regulation and control of the suggested constitutional right.

---

62 Galligan J was of the opinion that a trade union which is "not free to take such lawful steps that they see as reasonable to advance [their common interests] ... as a practical matter ... is a barren and useless thing". *Re Service Employees International Union Loc. 204 and Broadway A'fonnr Nursing Home* [1984] 4 DLR (4th) 231 at 248.

63 s 8 provides that the Labour Court shall "cease its investigation or review ...., and withdraw any recommendation where ... the Court has satisfied itself that industrial action in relation to the dispute of an investigation has taken place". This commits the parties to the statutory mechanism while the investigation is taking place. Subsection 2 makes clear, however, that this restriction applies only to the investigation and recommendation stages and also only to action in relation to the dispute at issue—unions are still able to embark upon industrial action in the one-year "cooling-off" period.

64 It should be noted, however, that the Government has committed itself to re-examining the fixed statutory 12-month period before presenting the Bill to the Dáil, as a response to a suggested Seanad amendment which would have allowed the Labour Court to specify the suitable delay between determination and enforcement on the basis of the circumstances of the case before it. Mr Tom Kitt, TD, commented that this proposal "raised a number of interesting points". See <www.irlgov.ie/debates-00/sjunel4/sectl .htm#ind>.

65 A more fundamental objection to the statutory scheme as set out in the Bill (but one in substance considered above in the context of s 6 of the Trade Union Act 1941) is the fact that its application is limited to authorised trade unions and "excepted bodies". The Bill thus leaves open the possibility of an individual worker being denied representation by a trade union if the relevant organisations who have obtained statutory representation rights refuse to exercise them on his behalf. Thus, it too would have to be read in light of the constitutional representation right, as set out above for s 6.

"Floor of Rights"

The concept of a "floor of rights" has received some recognition in Irish law, with certain statutes[66] setting minimum standards from which all employers ought to proceed.[67] In their operation, these Acts satisfy many of the same concerns which give rise to arguments in favour of a constitutional right to be represented by a trade union. They may even, in certain situations, go further than the asserted constitutional right.[68] Nonetheless, the fact that these statutory provisions provide greater protection in specific areas than would arise solely from a constitutional right to representation should not conceal the potential problems inherent in the Oireachtas' necessarily piecemeal approach.

The registration facility provided for in Pt III of the Industrial Relations Act 1946 offers perhaps the most significant protection for employees bereft of trade union representation, allowing them to obtain the benefits of trade union efforts even where their own employer operates an anti-union policy.[69] Obviously, this removes much of the need for the right outlined above. That it is not to say, however, that the issues which arise are entirely addressed by the statutory scheme. Part III can obviously only apply once a collective agreement has been registered with the Labour Court. Until such a time as this occurs, workers will still—if their employer refuses to entertain its representations—find themselves unable to make effective use of their trade union membership.

Similar considerations apply if the agreements, once registered, fail to address issues of particular importance to workers in an individual firm. Collective agreements

---

66 See for example the Anti-Discrimination (Pay) Act 1974 and the Unfair Dismissals Act 1977.

67 These Acts invariably render void the relevant provisions of any employment agreement which seeks to contract out of the statutory protection, providing vital protection for those individual workers who find themselves unable to rely on the collective strength of a trade union, whether through non-membership of a union, derecognition, or the adoption of various other anti-union measures by their employer.

68 A duty is imposed on employers to consult with trade unions over certain issues, for example, impending redundancies under the Protection of Employment Act 1977 or a transfer of undertakings under the European Communities (Safeguarding of Employee's Rights on Transfer of Ownership) Regulations 1980 (SI No 306 of 1980).

69 In a similar vein, the Oireachtas has addressed the problems posed by sectors where collective bargaining in practice does not operate effectively, owing to low levels of trade union membership or the absence of a tradition of organised labour, having established the auxiliary mechanism of the Joint Labour Committee in ss 34–45 of the Industrial Relations Act 1946 as a fall-back institution, empowered to set a standard minimum wage in such sectors.

negotiated at national or sectoral level, no mater how all-embracing, can never hope to cover the concerns of individual workers in every firm.[70] This is where the need for trade union representations at a local level becomes significant, so as to ensure complete protection of workers rights and occupational interests, even those specific to an individual employee.

It is this sort of concern which explains the continued need for an individual right to be represented by a trade union, regardless of the quality of statutory protection available. Given the negative nature of the Irish statutory scheme, there will always be certain firms, specific individual concerns, given situations which are outside statutory control.[71] A floor of rights aims to establish certain minimum standards, below which no worker ought to be forced into employment.[72] However, as long as Irish protection of trade unions depends upon a system of negative statutory immunities, some workers will inevitably slip through the cracks.[73] Recognition of a positive constitutional right to representation would effect a fundamental change in Ireland's legislative policy in this area, allowing the Oireachtas to exempt specific areas from the operation of this right, assured in the knowledge it is unlikely to unwittingly produce an adverse impact upon employees in other areas.[74]

Conclusion

Such a system, even to the extent of its limited recognition of a right to representation, could be of much use. Hendy has remarked that judicial acceptance of this right "would make a dramatic inroad into the wasteland of derecognition", a

---

[70] Such comments apply even more so to the Joint Labour Committees, adjudicating as they do usually only on the issue of pay, although they may submit Employment Regulation Orders to the Labour Court on conditions of employment as well.

[71] For example, the Unfair Dismissals Act 1977 applies only to certain situations, the Transnational Information and Consultation of Employees Act 1996 applies only to EU-wide enterprises, while the Trade Union Act 1946, as we have seen above, cannot completely protect workers whose employers refuse to allow their union make their case.

[72] In this, it operate similarly to the European "inderogabilite" principle. See Wedderburn, "Collective Bargaining at European Level: The Inderogability Problem" in *Labour Law and Freedom* (Lawrence & Wishart, 1995).

[73] At present, the Oireachtas finds itself forced to enact statutes to deal with the situation in specific industries and economic sectors, with the enduring risk therefore of unintentionally overlooking the claims of workers in an individual area.

[74] Given the extensive nature of Oireachtas reform on this issue, it is clear that the political consensus is generally in favour of facilitating the regular interaction of employers and unions.

statement which holds true even for the restricted form of the right outlined above.[75] Arguments regarding the asserted constitutional right as an unnecessary complication to Ireland's statutory industrial relations system also neglect the fundamentally unsound legal foundations upon which Irish unions depend.[76] A positive right to representation would give real meaning to freedom of association in the Irish constitutional context, extending protection to the most essential of associational activities and above that of the *Collymore*[77] mere fact of association. This is especially true in light of the express reference to unions contained in Art 40.6.1(iii). Recognition of the right would serve also to reorient the focus of statutory intervention so as to provide a truly even floor of rights. In its individualist character, and the minimal burden it imposes on employers, the right has few of the abrasive characteristics likely to offend the foundational philosophies of the common law. Furthermore, once the risks of fragmentation are avoided, the right in its operation chimes closely with the Oireachtas' consistent statutory policy of encouraging interaction—even to the minimum extent—between workers and employers.[78] Were the right to receive constitutional protection, the petty disputes over the preliminary issue of whether a request will be entertained or not, the like of which has led to many a damaging trade dispute, could become a thing of the past. That is not to say the right will have a radically positive effect on an already strained relationship between hostile unions and employers—rather, it will simply ensure that each side will, at least, be less likely to act in misinformed ignorance of the other side's opinions. In this, if in nothing else, it might do some good.

---

75 Studies in Europe have demonstrated a continued trend towards derecognition, especially in relation to small to medium-sized industries without a strong trade union tradition. Given that the economic consensus is that the majority of new jobs will be created in small to medium-sized enterprises (Antill, *op. cit*) the danger to the organised labour movement is clear. The impending introduction of the Industrial Relations (Amendment) Bill goes some way towards answering these concerns but, as we have seen, falls short of establishing a completely satisfactory system.

76 The English experience ought to act as a warning against an overly-complacent reliance on statutory immunities which may, all too easily, be seen as "privileges", of which the trade union movement is essentially undeserving. For an analysis of how something similar occurred under the Conservative governments in the United Kingdom in the 1980s, see Wedderburn, "Freedom of Association and Philosophies of Labour Law"(1989) 18 IU 1.

77 *Collymore v AG* [1970] AC 538; [1970] 2 WLR 233.

78 With derecognition an increasing trend in the United Kingdom, the experience has been of a decrease, both qualitatively and quantitatively, in collective bargaining. See Kerr and Waddington. "Membership Retention in the Public Sector" (1999) 30 IRJ 151.

Catastrophe Law and the Irish Legal System: All Crass and No Class?

by

Genevieve Coonan*

Ni neart go cur le cheile – With unity comes strength

Old Irish Proverb

Introduction

Man's achievements in the fields of medicine and science have brought about huge improvements in standards of health. That is beyond doubt. However, there is inevitably an upshot to significant technological advancement. Unknown and potentially hazardous consequences can accompany the implementation of new inventions. Each discovery of a new "wonder" drug carries with it the danger of ill side-effects. In some cases, that danger materializes and manifests itself in catastrophic form because it is likely that defects in widely used products, such as medicines, will affect a wide range of people. Where this occurs, the resulting onslaught of litigation can often prove difficult for the courts to handle.[1]

The example of the wonder-drug-found-out-to-be-defective does not, however, exhaust the situations where the law falters when applied to catastrophes. Indeed, the same can be said for any mass-victim incident irrespective of whether its genesis is directly attributable to some technological advancement or to any mass-victim incident in general (e.g. the army deafness fiasco). The point is a simple one — court

---

* This essay was awarded a prize by the Law Society of Ireland for the *Student Law Reform Essay Competition 2005*.

[1] This was an argument put forward by the National Consumer Council in its submission to Lord Woolf, as noted in his *Access to Justice Final Report By The Right Honourable the Lord Woolf, Master of the Rolls* (July 1996, HMSO). The Council said:

> "As we become an increasingly mass producing and mass consuming society, one product or service with a flaw has the potential to injure or cause other loss to more and more people. Yet our civil justice system has not adapted to mass legal actions. We still largely treat them as a collection of individual cases, with the findings in one case having only limited relevance in law to all the others."

practice does not fare well when it attempts to accommodate catastrophe victim's access to justice. This article seeks to build on these points. It discusses the efficiency and suitability of the mechanisms already in place to deal with mass tort litigation and furthermore, endeavours to address the manner in which the law of practice and procedure should accommodate it.

Catastrophes and Irish Law

For the purposes of this article, a catastrophe may be defined as an event attributable to a tortious act which results in loss of such an extraordinary magnitude that the ordinary law of practice and procedure is incapable of providing redress to victims in an efficient manner. There are two categories of catastrophe, distinguishable by whether they are of a "sudden" or "creeping" nature. The primary difference between the two is the presence of an identical act of causation. For example, where a "sudden" disaster occurs, the causative link between the tortious act and the damage suffered by all the victims is usually identical[2] and readily identifiable. Such catastrophes will often incur widespread and immediate damage to a large yet specific number of people. In Ireland, classic illustrations of this type of disaster include the devastating fire in the Stardust Ballroom[3] and the explosion which occurred on the oil tanker *Betelgeuse* while docked in the Whiddy Oil Terminal.[4]

With "creeping" disasters, on the other hand, although the tortious act may be easily ascertainable, the manner in which the resulting damage is incurred can vary from victim to victim.[5] "Creeping" disasters often arise where the same defective product has injured a large number of claimants. Usual problems in this area revolve around proof of causation. For example, the symptoms of an illness may not surface for some time after use of the product in question. Furthermore, where the product is a drug,

---

[2] As the Scottish Law Commission noted in its *Report on Multi-Party Actions*, "all the people share the causal relationship between the event and the resulting loss, injury or damage" — see *Report on Multi-Party Actions: Report on a reference under s 3(1)(e) of the Law Commissions Act 1965*, Scot Law Com. No 154, at 6.

[3] See *Report of the Tribunal of Inquiry: Fire at the Stardust Artane, Dublin* (PI 853) and the *Report of the Stardust Victims Compensation Tribunal* (PI 7831 1987).

[4] See *Report of the Tribunal of Inquiry: Disaster at Whiddy Island Bantry Co Cork* (PI 8911).

[5] The Scottish Law Commission in its *Report on Multi-Party Actions* has argued that the term relates to those situations where a number of persons have similar claims "attributable to a single cause but occurring at different times and in different circumstances" — see *Report on Multi-Party Actions: Report on a reference under section 3(1)(e) of the Law Commissions Act 1965*, Scot Law Com. No 154, at 6.

for example, it is often difficult to ascertain whether the injuries sustained are attributable to the drug's usage or the illness being treated. During the 1980s, much public debate surrounding these issues when it was discovered that some 1,500 young mothers had contracted Hepatitus C through the blood product anti-D supplied to them by the Blood Transfusion Board.[6]

In spite of their differences, the obvious factor that all catastrophes will have in common is that of numerosity. In many cases, the huge number of litigants produced can render the pursuit of claims on an individual basis uneconomical and inefficient. It is proposed that some procedure for combining claims and presenting them to the courts in a consolidated format should be adopted. The term "catastrophe law" may be used to describe the procedural mechanism best suited to this task. Its primary aim should be to present claims to the courts in a manner that benefits both plaintiffs and defendants alike. Such a mechanism could even be of some public benefit, as it could potentially reduce the length of court lists and, in turn, the waiting time for other litigants. It will be argued later in this article that the class action procedure is one such mechanism and should be adopted into Irish law,[7] especially when one considers the great financial strain that litigation surrounding catastrophes has placed on State resources in recent years.

Indeed, an examination of the procedures presently available to victims of mass torts highlights the great need for the introduction of an Irish catastrophe law. At present, where a tortious disaster occurs, it may be said that there are, in general, just two options available to persons who have suffered loss. They may choose to take their complaints straight to the courts (bearing in mind, obviously, the new role of PIAB)[8] and litigate them individually, or they may campaign within the political sector for the

---

[6] See *Report of the Tribunal of Inquiry into the Blood Transfusion Service Board* (Pn 3695) and *The Scheme to Compensate certain persons who have contracted Hepatitus C from the use of the human immunoglobulin-Ant-D, whole blood or other blood products* which was laid before the Oireachtas in December, 1995.

[7] Although it must be noted that s 11 of the Human Rights Commission Act, 2000 allows the Commission to institute proceedings "for the purpose of obtaining relief of a declaratory or other nature in respect of any matter concerning the human rights of any person or class of persons", this mechanism can only be called in aid where a breach of an individual's constitutional rights or human rights (governed by any treaties to which Ireland is a signatory) occurs. Furthermore, it is arguable that s 11 will not allow the pursuit of concrete modes of redress (such as damages). Although it states that "relief of a declaratory or other nature" may be granted, it is unlikely that this will include damages as traditionally the only redress available for breach of one's constitutional rights was that of declaratory relief.

[8] For the sake of completeness it should be noted that there is nothing in the Personal Injuries Assessment Board Act 2003 which contains special procedures for PIAB to deal with multi-victim claims.

establishment of a public inquiry, followed by a compensation tribunal. Unfortunately, in terms of affording redress to mass tort victims in an efficient manner, it must be said that both of these mechanisms fall far short of what is necessary.

Where a mass tort occurs, the primary drawback of litigating each claim individually is that the patent similarities between them are disregarded and the possibility of consolidating all claims abandoned. As Donaldson MR noted in *Davies v Eli Lilly & Co.*:[9]

> "Trying 1,500 cases together is much cheaper than trying 1,500 cases separately, so the plaintiffs as a group can spend more before they reach the economic limit."[10]

Failing to avail of the cost-saving potential, which a class action procedure could provide, can seem even more neglectful where many victims are unable to pursue their claims on an individual basis due to economic disadvantage. Another difficulty is that many of the issues common to each claim will not be adequately dealt with by the courts until a significant number of claims have filtered through the system.[11] The result can be that plaintiffs whose claims had been stronger than earlier ones are unsuccessful or vice versa. In addition, defendants can become burdened with awards made against them which, under the law as amended, would not have been granted. All of these shortcomings can be seen through an examination of the course of the hearing loss litigation.

For example, in the test case of *Greene v Minister for Defence*[12] the High Court awarded the claimant £3,000 in damages for a two percent hearing disability incurred during his 35-year service. However, two years before that decision was handed down, the High Court had awarded £30,000 to an unnamed soldier with six years service for a three per cent hearing disability.[13] These disproportionate verdicts highlight the problems outlined above. To put it simply, the difference in these two

---

[9] [1987] 3 All ER 94.

[10] *ibid* at 10.

[11] This assertion is supported by the fact that in relation to the hearing loss litigation the Minister for Defence has acknowledged that although the evidence presented in the *Greene* case was comprehensive, a "single test case could not answer every possible question arising in the complex technical area of disability assessment"—see the comments of Deputy Minister Molloy in the *Estimates for Public Services, 1998: Report of Select Committee,* Dáil Debates, 18 June 1998.

[12] Unreported, High Court, Lavan J 3 June 1998.

[13] Estimates for Public Services, *1998: Report of Select Committee,* Dáil Debates, 18 June 1998.

awards reflect the fact that the law in this area changed once *Greene* was decided. It was not until *Greene* that the issue of tinnitus[14] was adequately dealt with and from that point onward a higher standard had to be satisfied if a claim in damages for tinnitus was to succeed.[15] It is arguable that had this issue been dealt with at the beginning of the hearing loss litigation (which it arguably would have had if it had been brought within a class action) this would have had a radical impact on the finances of the Defence Department.

In addition, it must be noted that expenses are not limited to the Defence Department alone. As all 12,000 hearing loss claims filter through the courts, they have slowly siphoned off the income of the Department of Justice Equality and Law Reform. Representation for each litigant must be paid for, legal aid accounted for in respect of those who need it and with each sitting so increases the costs for both sides as well as the State. To reduce these costs, even minimally, would be of some public benefit. In addition to the inflation of costs, the absence of a class action procedure can also cause court lists to become clogged up, thus preventing claims from being dealt with expeditiously. Although class actions can also require the investment of a Herculean amount of time and resources, this will often be much less than that required for the litigation of 12,000 individual, albeit quite similar cases.[16] In an area where medical expenses can increase significantly in very short periods of time, one is constantly reminded of the maxim "justice delayed is justice denied".

Unlike litigation, the establishment of a public inquiry, followed by that of a compensation tribunal, can, in theory, provide some sort of wholesale redress to catastrophe victims.[17] However, the great disadvantage of this mechanism is that

---

[14] Tinnitus is a subjective aspect of hearing disability and, as a result, it can be difficult to ascertain liability and the extent of damage incurred.

[15] The High Court held that in order for tinnitus to be viewed as a compensable injury, the plaintiff must establish a track record of complaints about it to a medical practitioner before they institute legal proceedings.

[16] See Lord Donaldson's comment above, n 9.

[17] Examples of circumstances in which such relief has been provided include the Stardust Tragedy (see *Report of the Tribunal of Inquiry: Fire at the Stardust Artane, Dublin* (PI 853) and the *Report of the Stardust Victims Compensation Tribunal* (PI 7831 1987)), the Hepatitus C scandal (see *Report of the Tribunal of Inquiry into the Blood Transfusion Service Board* (Pn 3695) and the *Scheme to Compensate certain persons who have contracted Hepatitus C from the use of the human immunoglobulin-Ant-D, whole blood or other blood products* which was laid before the Oireachtas in December, 1995) and more recently the child abuse which has occurred in State-run institutions (see the *Commission to Inquire into Child Abuse Act 2000* and the Residential Institutional Redress Board, which was set up to decide issues of quantum in relation to claims of victims already heard before the Commission).

control over the entire process falls squarely in the hands of the Oireachtas. The legislation in this area[18] provides that it is solely upon the initiation of the Government that tribunals may be set up and in reality this only occurs in the face of public indignation and disgust, with victims being forced to campaign publicly for the vindication of their rights. In *Redmond v Flood*,[19] the Supreme Court implicitly accepted this, stating that, "it is of the essence of such inquiries that they be held in public for the purpose of allaying the public disquiet that led to their appointment".[20]

Of course, the requirement of governmental accession is clearly rational when one considers the differences between tribunals and courts. As Michael Collins SC has pointed out:

> "tribunals of inquiry tend to resemble courts, have many of the features, at least superficially, of adversarial litigation such as examination and cross examination of witnesses, orders for discovery and so forth. But fairly quickly dawns the disconcerting realisation that all is not what it seems. For those accustomed to plying their trade in courts, tribunals of inquiry are the forensic equivalent of a Star Trek transport to a parallel dimension, a world superficially similar to one's own but which on investigation transpires to be both different and potentially dangerous."[21]

Although in recent times the courts have held that natural and constitutional justice requires that certain procedures followed in the courtroom must also be observed by tribunals,[22] the fundamental differences between these two worlds remains, in essence, the same.[23] Unlike litigation, the purpose of a public inquiry is not to "settle

[18] See Tribunals of Inquiry (Evidence) Act 1921 as amended by the Tribunals of Inquiry (Evidence) (Amendment) Act, 1979 as amended by the Tribunals of Inquiry (Evidence) (Amendment) Act 1997.

[19] (1999) 1 ILRM 241.

[20] (1999) 1 ILRM 241 at 250.

[21] Michael Collins, "Continuing Legal Education: Tribunals of Inquiry (Booklet Two)" (*Law Society of Ireland).*

[22] See *O'Callaghan v Judge Mahon* (Unreported, Supreme Court, 9 March 2005).

[23] In *Haughey & Others v Mr Justice Michael Moriarty & Others* [1999] 3 IR 1 the Supreme Court held that the function of a court is to hear evidence and adjudicate and the function of a tribunal is to inquire and gather information. In its final stages, a tribunal will prepare a report and make recommendations based on its findings. A court will give concrete and immediate results upon deciding a case while the recommendations of a tribunal will fluctuate from extremely convincing arguments for reform to weak contemplations on the state of the area in question.

disputes between private parties about private rights"[24] but rather to ascertain, in the interests of the public good, whether a wrong against society has been committed. At a fundamental level, tribunals are inquisitorial in nature while litigation is an adversarial process. These differences will have a knock-on effect on the procedures governing both mechanisms. Tribunals often operate in the absence of many of the evidential requirements and procedural restrictions imposed upon the courts.

With that point in mind, it is arguable that some more fundamental restriction on the power wielded by tribunals is necessary. Perhaps it may be said in this respect that the requirement of accession fills a necessary gap. If a tribunal could be set up at the initiation of any disgruntled section of the public, no matter how well justified their complaints, it is arguable that, in the absence of the procedures which govern litigation before the courts, such an inquiry would quickly degenerate into a "witch-hunt". Unfortunately, such a justification offers little solace to victims of mass torts, especially where litigation on an individual basis may not always be a feasible option. In such circumstances, victims may, quite simply, have no concrete options of redress open to them. Although they are certainly entitled to campaign within the public arena for the establishment of a public inquiry or compensation tribunal, the requirement of governmental accession ensures that they remain in essence powerless. In the absence of a class action procedure, there is little to be said for the argument that in such circumstances the autonomy of victims is respected.

The Need for an Irish Catastrophe Law

Despite its problems, tribunal procedure has undoubtedly had some success in providing redress to catastrophe victims on a more widespread basis. Litigation also has its benefits. As the Irish legal system venerates the autonomy of the individual, there are, in general, no procedural limitations imposed on the right of access to the courts. Thus, if a mass tort victim has the means to do so, there is nothing to prevent them from pursing their claim before the courts. Unfortunately, there is no mechanism in Irish law which merges these two qualities. This can cause problems in certain cases. For example, where there is no possibility of a tribunal being established to provide redress and where the tortious act in question results in the creation of a large number of small claims which it would not be economically viable to pursue on an individual basis, victims are in effect rendered powerless and abandoned in a legal no man's land. This lacuna in Irish law is highlighted further by

[24] Chayes, "The Role of the Judge in Public Law Litigation" (1976) 89 *Harv. L. Rev.* 1281 at p 1282.

the fact that the courts have refused to extend the application of the representative action procedure provided for by Ord 15, r 9 of the Rules of the Superior Courts, 1986,[25] to actions founded in tort.[26]

In fact, even if the representative action procedure applied to tortious claims, it would be of little use to victims of large-scale disasters. This is due to the fact that it is subject to a number of limitations. In the first instance, the proposed representative must obtain authorisation to act on behalf of all members of the injured class.[27] This will be difficult where the class of injured persons is quite large or where creeping disasters occur. This assertion is supported by the fact that the procedure has so far only ever been used in cases where the class is relatively small.[28] Furthermore, members of the class must have "the same interest" in the cause of action or matter and this requirement has been adhered to strictly by the courts.[29] Again, particularly in cases where a creeping disaster arises, it is obvious that this requirement would be difficult to satisfy.

Thus, it seems that at present we have no suitable catastrophe law in Ireland. The introduction of a class action procedure could change all that. The Australian Law Reform Commission has described the class action as a procedure:

> "which enables the claims of a number of persons against the same defendant to be determined in the one action. In a class action one or more persons ('the plaintiff) may sue on his own behalf and on behalf of a large

---

25 Which states in full: "Where there are numerous persons having the same interest in one cause or matter, one or more of such persons may sue or be sued, or may be authorized by the Court to defend, in such cause or matter, on behalf, or for the benefit of all persons so interested."

26 In *Moore v Attorney General (No 2)* [1930] IR 471 Kennedy CJ held, at 490, that Ord 15, r 9 did not apply to tort actions, relying in this regard on "an apparent consensus of judicial opinion in England". In fact, this approach is supported by the wording of Ord 6, r 10 of the Circuit Court Rules, 2001, which expressly excludes representative actions founded on tort. That rule states:
"Save in actions founded on tort, when there are numerous persons having the same interest in one action or matter, one or more of such persons may sue or be sued, or may be authorised by the Judge to defend, in such action or matter, on behalf of or for the benefit of all persons so interested."

27 See the decision of O'Hanlon J in *Madigan v Attorney General* [1986] ILRM 136.

28 See *Brennan v Attorney General* [1984] ILRM 355; *Greene Minister for Agriculture* [1990] 2 IR 17; *McMenamin v Ireland* [1996] 3 IR 100; *Rafferty v Bus Eireann* [1997] 2 IR 424.

29 *Markt & Co Ltd v Knight Steamship Co* [1910] 2 KB 1021; *Barker v Allanson* [1937] 1 KB 463 and *Roche v Sherrington* [1982] 1 WLR 599.

> number of other persons ('the class') who have the same interest in the subject matter of the action as the plaintiff. The class members are not usually named as individual parties but are merely described. Although they usually do not take any active part in the litigation, they may nevertheless be bound by the result. It is, thus, a device for multi-party litigation where the interests of a number of parties can be combined in the suit."[30]

The aims of the class action procedure are clear—it seeks to bring efficiency and economy into the courtroom while preserving procedural fairness. It strives to provide access to justice for victims whose claims all derive from the same tortious act and whose loss, even if minimal, will be shared by many others. It also endeavours to provide:

> "expeditious, effective and proportionate methods of resolving cases, where individual damages are large enough to justify individual action but where the number of claimants and the nature of the issues involved mean that the cases cannot be managed satisfactorily in accordance with normal procedure."[31]

Other jurisdictions experiencing problems with catastrophes have also seen the advantages of the class action. As Arnup J noted in *Naku v General Motors of Canada Ltd*[32]:

> "In these days of mass merchandising of consumer goods, accompanied as it often is by widespread or national advertising, large numbers of persons are almost inevitably going to find themselves in approximately the same situation if the article in question has a defect that turns when the article is put to use. In many instances the pecuniary damages suffered by one purchaser may be small, even if the article is useless. It is not practical for any one purchaser to sue a huge manufacturer for his individual damages, but the sum of the damages suffered by each individual purchaser may be very large indeed. In such cases it would clearly be both convenient and in the public interest if some mechanism or procedure existed whereby the

---

30 Australian Law Reform Commission, "Access to the Courts—Class Actions", Discussion Paper No.11, (1979).

31 *ibid*, p 2.

32 92 DLR (3d) 100.

> purchasers could sue as a class, with appropriate safeguards for defendants, who ought not to be subjected to expensive law suits by class action plaintiffs who cannot pay costs if they lose."[33]

In the US, in order for a class action to come into being, certification must first be obtained. Rule 23 of the US Federal Rules of Civil Procedure lists the "pre-requisites" to certifying a class action (more commonly known as numerosity, commonality, typicality and adequacy) as:

> "1) the class is so numerous that joinder of all members is impracticable;
> 2) there are questions of law or fact common to all;
> 3) claims or defences of representative parties are typical of claims/defences of class; and
> 4) representative parties will fairly and adequately protect the interests of the class."

Prior to certification, the US courts will also consider whether a class action would be "superior" to normal litigation. Determining this issue requires consideration of whether common questions of law or fact predominate over questions affecting individual claims, whether the size of the class will make management difficult and whether prosecutions of separate claims would create varying adjudications or incompatible standards of conduct or impair the ability of individuals to protect their own interests.

In spite of the obvious advantages of the class action procedure, it is open to abuse when unaccompanied by adequate controls. In the absence of regulation such abuse can become rampant, resulting in various different problems ranging from disagreement among the class itself as to the generic issues of the case as a whole to the promotion of a tense atmosphere between the parties. Discovery exercises can also spiral out of control as both sides struggle to establish the factual limits of the dispute, while costs and delay can expand as large numbers of claimants are likely to become organisation orientated, thus neglecting to discuss whether the "ends" justify the "means". Class actions run much more efficiently upon a foundation of rules. As a result, legislation purporting to introduce the procedure should set out precisely what those rules are and how they are to be implemented. It must be noted that this in turn will have the effect of placing more power in the hands of the judiciary who

[33] 92 DLR (3d) 100 at 104.

inevitably will have to exercise considerably more control in the courtroom. They will be required to certify the class action, supervise the establishment of generic issues and the sub-classification of generic issues, appoint lead lawyers, approve settlements and balance the wishes of the plaintiff against those of the defendant. In fact, it is submitted that this is not dissimilar to how the new Commercial Court deals with actions contained in its list.

However, it is submitted that before carrying out any of these tasks, the presiding judge must first decide whether an "opt-in" or "opt-out" approach is to be adopted. This is necessary as the approach which is adopted will identify the limits of the "class" in question. One of the most fundamental differences between these two approaches is the extent to which they impinge upon the autonomy of the individual's decision to sue. For example, the opt-in approach involves the registration of all claimants as members of the class prior to certification. Any persons not so registered remain free to pursue litigation on an individual basis. Unfortunately, the opt-in approach can lead to the swamping of valid claims with weaker ones and additional claimants may surface years after the class action has been resolved, leaving the defendants in a position of financial uncertainty.[34] The opt-out approach, on the other hand, allows the determination of the rights of all victims of a catastrophe unless they 'opt-out' of the class by making their wish to be excluded known prior to the expiration of a specified time period. The disadvantage of this is that a victim may be joined in a class action without his knowledge, let alone his consent. In this way the opt-out approach tends to negate the principle of individual autonomy which is at the root of the Irish legal system.

Although many jurisdictions favour the opt-out approach,[35] it is submitted that the responsibility of determining which approach should be adopted should lie with the court. This is primarily because one should adopt the approach best suited to deal with the needs of the particular catastrophe in question. As the nature of every catastrophe will vary with the facts of each case, this is a matter that should be left up to the presiding judge. For example, creeping disasters may be more suited to an

---

[34] Many defendants try to avoid this. Lennox points out that in a recent $368.5 billion US cigarette company settlement, one of the terms of the settlement was that the cigarette companies would be immune from all future class action suits as they posed the most financial risk to the cigarette companies—see Lennox, "Toxic Torts now a reality in Ireland" (1997) 15 ILT 236.

[35] Including the US (see *Federal Rule of Civil Procedure* 23(c)), Australia (see s 33J of the Federal Court of Australia Act, 1976) and Canada (see s 16(1) of the Class Proceedings Act 1995 (British Columbia) and s 9 of the Class Proceedings Act 1992, (Ontario)).

opt-in approach, as symptoms of an illness may not come to light until years after the tortious act causing them. In turn, sudden disasters may be better suited to an opt-out approach as victims may be readily identifiable. Thus, legislation allowing for the certification of class actions should distinguish between the opt-in and opt-out approach and should also vest in the presiding judge a discretion to decide which should be adopted in accordance with the facts of each case.

Conclusion

Over the course of the past century a plethora of catastrophes have wreaked havoc on our society. It is only natural that victims will seek redress for the injuries caused. However, in the absence of a suitable multi-party procedure, the courts have difficulties processing each and every claim in an efficient and cost effective manner. As a result, America, Australia and Canada have all enacted legislation providing for a class action procedure, and its introduction has also been debated in Scotland and England. The time is now ripe for a similar discussion in Ireland. Our ever increasing rate of litigation has resulted in longer court lists and waiting times.[36] Where catastrophes occur, the courts become bombarded with claims which, in turn, exacerbate these problems. It is submitted that in order to avoid such difficulties, a class action procedure must be introduced. By consolidating victims' claims within a defined "class", time, energy and money will be saved, in turn benefiting both plaintiffs and defendants as well as serving a valuable public purpose.

Post-Script: This is a modified version of an essay submitted to the Law Society Law Reform Competition in 2001. Since that time, the Law Reform Commission, in 2003, has published a Consultation Paper on Multi-Party Litigation (Class Actions), which discusses the possibility for adoption of a class-action procedure in Ireland. However, any worthwhile discussion of the Consultation Paper would bring this essay far beyond its original scope, form and size.

---

36 See *Annual Report of the Courts Service 2004.*

The Guardian *Ad Litem* in Irish Law: Where Do We Go From Here?

by

Lillian O'Sullivan*

> "The importance of legislation as a symbol cannot be under-estimated; but the true recognition of children's rights requires implementation in practice. Indeed, unimplemented, partially implemented or badly implemented law may actually do children more harm than good."[1]

Ten years after the birth of the guardian *ad litem* in Irish law, judges, practitioners and children alike are still confused by this new "animal in the jungle" of Irish legal procedure. Besides heralding its introduction, the legislation fails to contribute to the definition of the role of the guardian *ad litem*. Practitioners are given no guidance regarding their functions, duties, qualifications or extent of use in public and private law. Furthermore, no facilities for the administration and research of the system are in place. Voluntary organisations[2] and independent practitioners have taken up the challenge of providing a guardian *ad litem* service in the absence of an organised system. However, the chaos which characterises the developing model leaves Ireland in breach of its international obligations[3] and muffles the voice of the child in whose interests the legislation was introduced. Regulations are urgently needed to impose order on this chaotic system. The following attempts to contribute to the debate about the manner in which the guardian *ad litem* system should be developed in Ireland.

---

* BCL L.L.M. (NUI). This essay was awarded joint second place in the Law Society of Ireland *Student Law Reform Essay Competition 2001.*

1 Freeman, "Taking Children's Rights More Seriously" in *Children, Rights and the Law* (Alston, P, Parker, S, Seymour, J, eds, Clarendon Press, 1992), p 52 at p 60.

2 ISPCC has a panel of eight to ten guardians *ad litem;* Barnardos has a five-member panel: approximately three independent practitioners with various qualifications also provide the service in Dublin.

3 Under the United Nations Convention on the Rights of the Child (UNCRC) and the European Convention on the Exercise of Children's Rights (ECECR).

Outline of the Law

Section 24 of the Child Care Act 1991 directly recognises the child's right to have its voice heard in proceedings affecting its welfare. This provision is complemented by s 26, which introduces an intermediary through whom the wishes of the child can be presented to the court. Section 26(1) states:

> "If, in any proceedings under Parts IV or VI, the child to whom the proceedings relate is not a party, the court may, if it is satisfied that it is necessary in the interests of the child and in the interests of justice to do so, appoint a guardian *ad litem* for the child".

This advancement in public law procedure is reflected in private law. The guardian *ad litem* was formally made available to the court in certain private law proceedings in s 28 of the Guardianship of Infants Act 1964 as amended by s 11 of the Children Act, 1997 (henceforth, s 28).[4] This section states:

> "If, in proceedings under Section 6A, 11 or 11A, the child to whom the proceedings relate is not a the court may, if it is satisfied that, having regard to the special circumstances of the case it is necessary in the best interests of the child to do so, appoint a guardian *ad litem* for the child."

Section 28 will not become operative until enacted by the Ministerial Order.[5]

Role of the Guardian *ad litem*

Neither the 1991 Act nor the 1997 Act offer a definition of the role of the guardian *ad litem.* The strict definition of the term is "guardian for the purposes of litigation".[6] In practice, the guardian *ad litem* is an officer of the court appointed by

---

4 Strong recommendations were made for the extension of the service into private law proceedings in the Law Reform Commission's (LRC) Report (1996) and Consultation Paper (1994) on Family Courts.

5 Apparently, the Ministerial Order has been postponed until problems with Pt IV of the Act can be dealt with.

6 Presenting s 26 of the 1991 Act to the Dáil, the Minister for Justice, Equality and Law Reform outlined the role of the guardian *ad litem* as being "to represent the child, take care of the child, observe the child and ensure that the child's interests are protected beyond any doubt in the care proceedings...", 419 Dáil Debates Col 439. Similarly, during the Second Stage of the Children Bill in the Dáil, the Minister stated: "This role of the guardian *ad litem* will be to interview the child," 480 Dáil Debates Col 1321. See also Senator David Norris's submission in Seanad Debates Cols 2088–2089.

the judge to act independently of parents and health boards on behalf of the child whose interests are in question during legal proceedings. In the absence of any legislative guidelines for how the role of the guardian *ad litem* is to develop, the courts and practitioners are defining the role on a case basis, having regard to the English model for guidance.[7]

This approach entails the guardian *ad litem* objectively making recommendations on the child's welfare while drawing attention to the child's wishes when presenting their report to the court (even if these wishes are contrary to what he believes to be in best interests of the child).[8] Despite the argument of some critics that the court will always take the side of the professional without giving adequate regard to the views of the child,[9] it is submitted that this role should be maintained. Regulations should, however, reinforce the child's position with *express* obligations on:

- the guardian *ad litem* to draw attention to the child's wishes and any conflict between those wishes and his recommendations and
- the court to have due regard to the wishes of the child.[10]

In addition, under the current regime, the *manner* in which the guardian *ad litem* performs his role varies according to the qualifications of the representative. This practice has evoked deep confusion over the distinction between the role of the guardian *ad litem* and the legal representative, confusion which has been exacerbated by the courts' frequent appointment of solicitors as guardians *ad litem* for practical convenience and in an effort to conserve resources. Order 7 of the District Court Rules further complicates matters by bestowing on the guardian *ad litem* a duty to "defend" the child in proceedings, thereby suggesting an advocate-style role.

Although in some jurisdictions (i.e. the US under the CASA system) the role adopted by the child's separate representative is that of *amicus curia*, in others, the role resembles that of an advocate (i.e. Australia and some Canadian states). However, it is submitted that the role of the guardian *ad litem* should not include

[7] See empirical research in unpublished thesis: "The Guardian *Ad Litem* In Irish Law: Where Do We Go From Here?"

[8] This approach is in line with Art 10 of the ECECR and its Explanatory Report.

[9] See Bennett, "Giving a Voice to Children", presentation to the Family Law Committee of the Law Society of Ireland, 10 October 1998.

[10] As under s 24 of the Child Care Act 1991 and s 25 of the Children Act 1997.

aspects of advocacy, not least because the individuals who are best qualified to represent the child in this capacity are not solicitors and, usually, are not trained in advocacy.

Who should be the Guardian *Ad Litem?*

The absence of regulations has given Irish courts a *carte blanche* to appoint anyone, regardless of their qualifications, training or experience, to the post of guardian *ad litem.* The result has been that some of those selected have been clearly unsuited to the role.

The ECECR offers no guidance concerning the experience and qualifications required by the guardian *ad litem.* Ideally, he should possess qualifications and experience rendering him suitable for interacting with children, thereby maximising his possibility of ascertaining and informing the court as to the wishes of the child. Further, he should be qualified to make an objective and informed decision regarding the child's welfare.

Opinions diverge as to what qualifications a guardian *ad litem* should have. Some argue for "some background in a therapeutic child-centred setting".[11] Others suggest that he should be "a social worker or another child-care specialist".[12]

It is submitted that once a candidate has professional expertise in caring for and dealing with children there should be no difficulty in drawing guardians *ad litem* from different disciplines. A candidate should not be barred due to the nature of his qualifications. Rather, he should be included on the basis of the expertise which renders him suitable to represent and interact with children.

Functions and Powers

Currently the ISPCC and Barnardos are instructing their guardians *ad litem* to carry out functions identical to those carried out by their English equivalent.[13] The primary functions are investigation, representation, explanation and development of

---

[11] Kelly, "The Guardian *ad Litem* Service in Ireland – A Service or Disservice?", Trinity College, Dublin (1998) – unpublished.

[12] Shannon, "The Guardian *ad Litem* Reviewed", unpublished article (1999).

[13] Timm's *Manual of Practice Guidance for Guardians ad litem.*

recommendations concerning the child's welfare. This list allows the guardian *ad litem* to fulfil his role as safeguarder and promoter of the interest of the child. An equivalent list should be clearly outlined in Irish regulations.

In England the guardian *ad litem* also has case management duties, enabling him to track the implementation of orders and minimise opportunities for delay. As Irish guardians *ad litem* have experienced difficulties in asserting such a role in practice, these functions should be included in regulations in order to avoid further confusion.[14]

Furthermore, the guardian *ad litem* must be officially conferred with a number of powers, as the foundation upon which his interaction with other agencies and the legal process can develop. Rights of access to all files concerning the child, access to the child and access to all persons related to or connected with the child in order to conduct interviews must be assured. The power to request examination of the child by a medical, psychiatric or other expert should also be guaranteed along with the power to appeal any decision with which the child is not comfortable or which does not appear to be in the child's best interests.[15]

When to Appoint a Guardian *Ad Litem*

Under both sections, appointment of the guardian *ad litem* is at the discretion of the court. However, each section requires the court to take different issues into account when ruminating on the necessity of making an order for appointment. The 1991 Act requires the court to "decide to appoint a guardian *ad litem* if it is necessary in the interest of justice." However, the elusive "interests of justice" is not defined. The section also requires the court to have regard to the "interests of the child". Meanwhile in private law proceedings, s 28(2) advances a list of criteria to which the court should pay particular attention when making its decision.[16] As an aid and

---

[14] Above, n 7.

[15] Guardians *ad litem* in the English system have these powers.

[16] "(a) the age and understanding of the child.
(b) any report or any question affecting the welfare of the child that is furnished to the court under Section 47 of the Act of 1995.
(c) the welfare of the child.
(d) whether and to what extent the child should be given the opportunity to express his wishes in the proceedings, taking into account any statement in relation to those matters in any report under Section 47 of the Act of 1995.
(e) any submission made in relation to the appointment as a guardian *ad litem* that is made to the court by or an behalf of a party to the proceedings or any other person to whom it relates."

direction to the court, while contributing to the accountability of the court in its decision-making, the absence of such a list in s 26 of the 1991 Act is a significant void.

Section 28 also requires the court to have regard to the "special circumstances of the case"[17] and whether the appointment of a guardian *ad litem* is necessary in the best interests of the child. This requirement coupled with the absence of a reference to the "interests of justice" renders the test more child-centred. Indeed, it is difficult to see a case where it would not be in the child's best interests to have his wishes presented independently to the court. However, the legislation does not allow for a mandatory service across the board, providing instead that the court decide on "the special circumstances" case by case.

In England the court appoints the guardian *ad litem* unless it is satisfied that it is not necessary in order to safeguard the child's interests. It is an unusual case where the court decides that the services of a guardian *ad litem* are not required. It is proposed that this positive duty to appoint a guardian *ad litem* should be extended to Ireland for both public and private law proceedings. Application for the appointment of a guardian *ad litem* by the parties to the proceedings should not be necessary. Rather, the guardian *ad litem* should be appointed by the court at the beginning of the proceedings and he should see the case through to its conclusion. Such a development would not provide a luxury service to children but would merely acknowledge every child's basic human rights to participate and to be represented in proceedings which affect his or her welfare.

Should the Guardian *Ad Litem* have Legal Representation?

A significant difference between the 1997 Act and the 1991 Act is that s 28(4) of the 1997 Act expressly provides for legal representation to be appointed for the guardian *ad litem*. Effectively, this section potentially safeguards the position of the guardian *ad litem* in court and facilitates him with a medium through whom he can understand his part in the legal process and maximise his (and thereby the child's) participation therein.

---

[17] Paul Ward, in the annotated version of the Child Care Act 1991, notes that a case where the "special circumstances" were taken into account was the C Case: *In Re A and B v The Eastern Health Board and the Attorney General* [1998] ILRM 460.

No express provision is made in the 1991 Act for legal representation of the guardian *ad litem.* A loophole has, however, been located to enable practitioners to evade this inconvenience. Section 26(3) obliges the health board to pay "any costs incurred by a person acting as a guardian *ad litem* under [s 26]". It could be argued that "any cost" includes cost of legal advice and representation.[18] In practice, guardians *ad litem* acting on the ISPCC panel immediately apply for (and are granted) legal representation when they are appointed under the 1991 Act.

It appears, therefore, that through legislation and in judicial practice, there has been a clear acknowledgement of the guardian *ad litem's* need for legal representation. This need should not vary from public to private law proceedings.

The consequence of providing suitably qualified guardians *ad litem* is that such persons usually will not have legal qualifications. Therefore, the guardian *ad litem* may need access to a lawyer at many stages during the case.[19] By not providing legal representation for the guardian *ad litem* in public law cases and only in limited circumstances in private law cases, the legislation is indirectly weakening the child's position before the court and undermining the principle that the court should regard the welfare of the child as its first and paramount consideration. It is crucial that in all proceedings (whether public or private) where a guardian *ad litem* is appointed that he always have access to legal advice and the benefit of the skills and expertise of his own legal representative. It is proposed that regulations should be formulated to ensure that this is so.

Legal Representation for the Child

A detailed examination of the complex question of legal representation for children is outside the scope of this article, but because the relevant sections of the 1991 and 1997 Acts deal with the issue, some brief comments must be made.

Section 26 of the 1991 Act requires that representation of the child by a guardian *ad litem* and a legal representative are mutually exclusive. Meanwhile, under the 1997 Act, the child is not permitted to have legal representation or to be joined as a party to the proceedings in family law disputes under any circumstances.

---

[18] See Kelly, "Practical Difficulties Regarding Guardian *ad Litem* in Cases Involving the Welfare of Children" (1978) unpublished paper.

[19] From the investigation stages to presenting evidence and being subject to vigorous cross-examination.

While it is accepted that a number of economic[20] and child-centred reasons militate against the introduction of mandatory dual representation of the child in Ireland, it is submitted that the judge should retain discretion to appoint a lawyer:

- in particularly contentious cases;
- where there is a deep conflict between the wishes of the child who has sufficient age and understanding and the recommendations of the guardian *ad litem*; and
- where the guardian *ad litem* wishes to exercise a right of appeal.

Independence of the Guardian *Ad Litem*

A central characteristic of the guardian *ad litem* is that he acts as an independent representative of the child. He must be independent of the health board, the parents and, in some ways, independent of the child.[21] No provisions exist to guarantee the independence of the guardian *ad litem* in Irish law.[22] Timms[23] recognises four main aspects of the guardian *ad litem's* independence:

(i) Independence of professional opinion;
(ii) Personal independence;
(iii) Perceived independence;
(iv) Administrative independence.

It is submitted that equivalent Irish terms of reference would be useful to practitioners.

---

[20] The strain which dual representation placed on the English model for many years was at the heart of recent cutbacks and reform of that system.

[21] This is so particularly if the guardian *ad litem* disagrees with the child's wishes.

[22] In England and Wales Regulation 2.4 of the "Children Act, 1989, Guidance and Regulations" Volume 7 states:

> "It is essential that GALRO's in researching their judgment about the welfare of each child should continue to be independent of the local authority or other organisation providing that service. Arrangements of the management of the panel and the day-to-day work of the GALRO must take full account of this requirement."

[23] In *Manual of Practice Guidance for Guardians ad litem and Reporting Officers*, (London, HMSO, 1992), p 3.

Administration of an Irish Guardian *Ad Litem* System

The legislation fails to allocate responsibility for administration of a guardian *ad litem* service to any body. Voluntary bodies (i.e. the ISPCC and Barnardos) have set the administrative ball rolling by providing and training panels of guardians *ad litem.* However, in view of their limited resources, these organisations do not have the capacity to provide a comprehensive national service. Regulations are required to create an independent body to perform the tasks of establishing, co-ordinating, administering and financing an Irish guardian *ad litem* service.

Health boards, which are responsible for paying any costs incurred by the guardian *ad litem* appointed under s 26 of the 1991 Act, should not be given this responsibility. Ireland should learn from the mistakes of our neighbours in England and Wales. Although local authorities administered the system there since its inception, grave concerns surrounding the guardian *ad litem's* independence have prompted extensive recent reform.[24]

As the body required should be independent, apolitical and specifically orientated towards children, it is submitted that the Office of Children's Ombudsman (OCO), soon to be established, may represent an ideal mechanism through which the Irish guardian *ad litem* system should be administered. This central administrative office should have responsibility for:

- Establishing a national panel system, co-ordinated by panel managers;
- Training guardians *ad litem* on the panel;
- Educating judges, lawyers, other court officials and health boards on the role of the guardian *ad litem* so as to promote inter-agency co-operation and awareness;
- Education of the general public on the role of the guardian *ad litem*;[25]
- Establishing a complaints procedure;
- Establishing aftercare facilities — giving the child an opportunity to detach from and "say goodbye" to the guardian *ad litem;*
- Developing a multi-disciplinary forum for discussion to carry out research and hear feedback from the children to whom the service is provided. Perhaps this body could consider the legislation's application to complicated, yet common, situations where the mother of a child represented by a guardian *ad litem* is

[24] See also Corrigan and Forde's idealistic yet complex suggestion in "Separate Representatives for Children", Coolock Community Law Centre, 1995.

[25] As per our obligations under the ECECR.

herself a child. Clearly, she will require independent representation even though she is not the subject of the proceedings;

- Funding the system: the OCO would be funded directly by the Exchequer and this office should fund the service in both public and private law proceedings.[26] Furthermore, regulations should clarify that the costs of the guardian *ad litem* will extend to costs of experts whose assistance he or she may employ, including counsel, should the case go to the higher courts.

Finally, it appears that the Children's Act 1997 contains no authority for regulations to be issued on foot of its provisions. This may require amendment to include express permission to draw up regulations.

The Guardian *Ad Litem* outside Legal Proceedings

While detailed analysis of this issue is also outside the scope of this paper, it is submitted that one exception to a general rule that the guardian *ad litem* should not represent children outside legal proceedings should apply.

It has been argued that proceedings before An Bord Uchtala could be categorised as "administrative proceedings" for the purposes of Art 12 of the UNCRC.[27] Section 3(2) of the Adoption Act 1988 requires the court to give due consideration to the wishes of the child concerned, having regard to his or her age and understanding. In view of the finality of the consequences of adoption proceedings and the danger that, from time to time, the proceedings may focus on the intentions of the parties rather than on the interests and wishes of the child, the extension of the guardian *ad litem* service into adoption proceedings would be a significant improvement in Irish law.

English Model

As some core aspects of the developing Irish guardian *ad litem* system are borrowed from the English model, it could be tempting to decide to transpose the system in its entirety into Ireland. However, this should be avoided. Certainly, our neighbour's

---

[26] This would be a vast improvement to the 1997 Act's impractical obligation on the parties to the proceedings to pay the costs.

[27] LRC Consultation Paper on Family Courts, pp 86–87. See also The Children's Rights Alliance "Small Voices: Vital Rights" (1997) and Review Committee on Adoption Services Report, (1984). In the UK in 1995, 36.9 per cent of applications for guardians *ad litem* were made for adoption proceedings.

model has some attributes which would benefit an Irish equivalent. The welfare checklist to which the court must have regard when considering whether to make and order appointing a guardian *ad litem* is very useful.[28] It would serve us well to have regard to the duties and powers of our English counterparts when developing regulations. In addition, detailed recruitment and training practices should act as a blueprint for the developing Irish model. However, as regards administration of the guardian *ad litem* system in England and Wales, it is submitted that we should learn from the mistakes of our neighbours. The local authority administration of the system failed for its inability to guarantee professional and financial independence. Similar difficulties would surely arise in Ireland if health boards were given equivalent administrative responsibilities.

It may, however, be instructive to have regard to the extensive research carried out before the recent establishment of the Children and Family Court Advisory Service, which replaces the old administrative system and is financed by the Lord Chancellor's Office. Although still only finding its feet, observation of this system may have some valuable lessons to offer the seedling Irish system. An eye should also be cast to practice in other jurisdictions[29] in order to draw on their strengths and avoid their weaknesses.[30]

Conclusion

By facilitating the appointment of the guardian *ad litem* in both public and private law proceedings, Ireland can be praised for being at the forefront of international legal procedure in this respect. However, the Irish guardian *ad litem* system, as it is developing today, is disjointed and inadequate. Regulations are needed to provide guidelines and directions to ensure the smooth operation of the system for all involved—the court and court officers, the guardian *ad litem* himself and the participants in the guardian *ad litem's* investigations, especially the child. It is crucial that Ireland fulfil her international obligations by guaranteeing to every child the right to participate and be represented in legal proceedings affecting his welfare—sooner rather than later.

[28] s 1(3), Children Act 1989.

[29] For example, in Australia a scandalous practice has developed whereby the child's representative "may discount, editionalise or reject the child's wishes and argue the case in accordance with his or her own views of the child's best interests." See the *Australian Law Reform Commission Report,* 1998.

[30] See also Canada, America, Scotland and Northern Ireland.

Limiting the Liability of Partnerships

by

Brendan Kirwan*

Partnership is defined in the seminal Partnership Act 1890 ("the 1890 Act") as "the relation which subsists between persons carrying on a business in common with a view of profit".[1] Introduced to regulate the burgeoning number of partnerships, the 1890 Act provided the statutory basis for what has proven to be a popular vehicle for the carrying on of business. Indeed, some professions are constrained legislatively from operating other than as partnerships.[2] A number of beneficial features flow from operating as a partnership[3]: partnerships are not obliged to file annual reports or accounts, and so have significant freedom in how they structure and operate their business. Partnerships attract more favourable tax regimes than those imposed on a limited company. Management structures within partnerships also tend to be much more flexible than their equivalent in other business structures.[4] However, the price to be paid for such benefits is the unlimited liability of every partner for the debts and obligations of the partnership which they make up and the joint and several liability of each and every partner for the debts and obligations of other partners.[5] In

* This essay was awarded joint second place in the Law Society of Ireland, *Student Law Reform Essay Competition 2002.*

[1] See generally Twomey, *Partnership Law* (2000, Butterworths, Dublin) chap 1; for a succinct overview of the legislative history in relation to partnerships, see the British House of Commons Select Committee on Trade and Industry Fourth Report, 16 February 1999, paras 7–10.

[2] In the case of solicitors, by s 64 of the Solicitors Act 1954. Vets are similarly constrained by virtue of s 47(2) of the Veterinary Surgeons Act 1931, as are dentists, under s 52(1) of the Dentists Act 1985.

[3] See generally Twomey, "The Legal Requirements for the Establishment of a Partnership Under Irish Law" (1996) CLP 178.

[4] For other examples, see Twomey, above, n 1 at paras 1.09–1.13.

[5] Under s 9 of the Partnership Act 1890, which states that 'Every partner in a firm is liable jointly with the other partners...for all debts and obligations of the firm incurred while he is a partner'. Section 10 states that every partner is jointly liable for wrongful acts or omissions.

a climate of increased litigation for professional negligence and the related size of such claims, partnership as a business model has thus come under greater scrutiny. Consideration has been given in a number of jurisdictions to finding a model which would preserve the benefits of partnership whilst limiting the apparent downsides. A model which has found favour is the Limited Liability Partnership (LLP), a vehicle which would be of considerable benefit to businesses in Ireland were it to be introduced here.

Background to the Need for Reform

The Partnership Act 1890 remained virtually untouched until the late 1990s in both Britain and Ireland and to date has not been significantly amended in this jurisdiction. However, the British House of Commons Committee on Trade and Industry, reporting in 1999, identified the traditional partnership as being "under strain" due to a number of factors, including in particular the growth of "mega-partnerships" on a global basis.[6] The suggestion was that the partners who make up such behemoths barely know each other, if at all. Yet in the context of litigation, due to the twin principles of unlimited liability and joint and several liability, the assets of partners can be put at risk by the actions of partners over whom they have no control and of whom they potentially have little or no knowledge. A dramatic example of such litigation is the English case of *ADT Limited v BDO Binder Hamlyn*,[7] in which an assurance from one of the defendant's audit partners as to the accuracy of the audited accounts of a takeover target company was found to have been misleading. By giving such an assurance, the court found that the defendant firm, and not just the audit partner who gave the assurance, assumed responsibility to the plaintiffs.[8]

In looking at responses to increased litigation, there is also an argument that partnerships need some form of extra protection because they are perceived, fairly or otherwise, to be the preserve of well-insured and well-heeled professionals and, as such, represent the "easiest and potentially most rewarding 'targets'".[9] Whilst this

[6] Select Committee on Trade and Industry Fourth Report, above, n 1, para 13. See also the Explanatory Notes to the British Limited Liability Partnerships Act 2000, at para 9.

[7] *ADT Limited v BDO Binder Hamlyn* (1996) BCC 808. Indeed, auditors may find themselves at the wrong end of a litigation suit in circumstances where a company's directors may be more at fault due to the perceived depth of the pool of assets available to partners.

[8] The case was ultimately settled for a sum of in the order of GBP50 million.

[9] This argument was identified by the Select Committee on Trade and Industry, above, n 1, at para. 19. See also Freedman and Finch, "Limited Liability Partnerships: Have Accountants Sewn Up the 'Deep Pockets' Debate" (1997) JBL 387.

concern should not lead to attempts to circumnavigate the rigours of professional responsibility, the reality is that if there is a perception that partnerships are an easy mark, there is certainly a case to be made for some form of additional protection for them.

Other factors which contribute to the strain on partnerships in the context of litigation include an increase in specialisations among partners coupled with an increase in multi-disciplinary partnerships. This can lead to a lack of knowledge by partners of each other's activities and corresponding lessening of control. Of course, such factors would appear to apply primarily to larger partnerships, but that is not to say that smaller partnerships should not also have concerns; indeed the latter, particularly in high risk areas such as in the construction and related sectors, "may also face claims which go far beyond their insured cover, discouraging them from undertaking high-risk work or driving them to seek other means of restricting their liabilities".[10]

Ireland is not immune from such concerns; partnerships—both indigenous and "local" partnerships which form part of a much bigger global organisation—are also a popular commercial vehicle in this country. A further factor to be considered is the need to maintain a competitive legal framework within which businesses operate. This was one of the key considerations in Britain in its Government's review of the area, perhaps best summarised by the view that:

> "[t]oo long a delay in the introduction of a vehicle for doing business for which there are good arguments at the time can lead to commercial law structures missing the boat, with real if incalculable effects on competitiveness".[11]

That the Irish legislature is clearly alive to the need to modernise and improve the laws relating to business in broad terms is evident from its creation of the Company Law Review Group (CLRG) in this jurisdiction, charged with, *inter alia*, monitoring, reviewing and advising on matters concerning companies legislation.[12]

---

[10] British House of Commons Select Committee on Trade and Industry Fourth Report, above, n 1, para 14.

[11] This argument was identified by the Select Committee on Trade and Industry, above, n 1, at para 19.

[12] *et seq.* of the Company Law Enforcement Act 2001 s 67 sets out the statutory role and advisory responsibilities of the CLRG.

It would seem to be somewhat remiss if, in the context of such review, the CLRG did not at a minimum have regard to the arguments which informed the introduction of the LLP in Britain.[13]

Options for Reform

To promote the LLP as a suitable commercial vehicle for this jurisdiction without considering other options in detail is somewhat akin to the Queen in *Alice in Wonderland* seeking a sentence before a verdict. Yet, even a cursory consideration of the alternatives throws a favourable light upon the LLP structure. To reconstitute partnerships as companies with limited liability, which is one obvious option, would be to cause businesses to sacrifice many of the benefits which make partnership such an attractive option in the first place, for example in terms of tax and management structures. That partnership has proven a popular option as a means of conducting business, notwithstanding the availability of other corporate vehicles, would also suggest that the wholesale dismantling of the partnership structure would not be particularly helpful.[14] Other piecemeal alternatives which have been suggested include reforming unlimited liability, introducing proportionate liability, abolishing joint and several liability, excluding liability, capping damages[15] and the conferring of corporate personality without limited liability on partnerships.[16] It is submitted that the better approach is to introduce an LLP structure, which preserves the partnership structure, provides a degree of protection to partners from the risk of unlimited and joint and several liability yet does not diminish the ability of third parties to sue.

Before examining the structure of an LLP in more detail, it is important to distinguish the structure from that of a limited partnership (LP): the latter, provided

[13] It was identified as a flaw in the process in Britain that the proposal to introduce LLPs had not emerged from, or been referred to, the groups reviewing company law and partnership law. See Select Committee on Trade and Industry, above, n 1, at para 10(f). In relation to the proposed changes to partnership law, see Law Com No.283 "Partnership Law", November 2003. When asked in the Dáil whether she had any plans to reform partnership law, including the introduction of limited liability partnerships, the then Minister for Enterprise, Trade and Employment replied that she would consider whether to refer such matters to the CLRG: Dáil Debates Vol 524 12 October 2000.

[14] Although it has been recognised in other jurisdictions that there is some need for reform of existing partnership law; see the paper produced by the English Law Commission: Law Com No 283 "Partnership Law", November 2003.

[15] See Glanville, *Partnerships: A Limited Future?* (1998) LSG 12, 13.

[16] Select Committee on Trade and Industry Fourth Report, above, n 1, para 9.

for under the Limited Partnership Act 1907,[17] whilst allowing for limited liability for partnerships, does so at the expense of the ability to undertake management functions.[18] What this means in practice is that a limited partnership firm will be made up of one or more partners who will be liable for all the debts and obligations of the firm, who will manage the firm, and one or more partners whose debts and obligations are limited but who cannot undertake any management role.[19]

The Development of Limited Liability Partnerships

The first law allowing for the creation of a limited liability partnership was enacted in the United States in 1991, in Texas, as a direct response to the large suits brought against law and accountancy partnerships as a result of the collapse of many US savings and loan associations in the late 1980s.[20] The LLP was viewed as a device to protect lawyers or accountants in partnerships from exposure to claims on a massive scale. It was developed as a corporate vehicle which would allow its members to organise themselves along traditional partnership lines yet which relieved those same members of all or part of their personal liability for partnership liabilities, debts and obligations.[21] Refinement of the initial laws was felt necessary, and this refinement encompassed protection for partners from personal liability for any partnership obligations or liabilities arising from the malpractice of a co-partner or other person not under the partner's supervision and control.[22]

Other questions which subsequently fell to be addressed by state legislatures included that of whether there would be a recontribution obligation on partners in the event

[17] According to the Companies Report 2003 issued by the Department of Enterprise, Trade and Employment, there were only 456 limited partnerships registered in Ireland at the end of 2003, out of a total of 148,303 companies on the Register of Companies at that date.

[18] In Joint Consultation Paper No 161, the English Law Commission notes that the limited partnership is a useful vehicle for those investors who do not wish to take an active role in the management of their funds. The Investment Limited Partnerships Act 1994 is on the Irish statute books, but such investment limited partnerships are highly specialised.

[19] For a further discussion of limited partnerships, see Henning, *Limited Liability Partnerships, Limited Partnerships and Limited Liability Limited Partnerships* (2000) *Company Lawyer* 165. The article also discusses limited liability limited partnerships (LLLP), a hybrid form of LP and LLP. See also l'Anson, *Lindley & Banks on Partnership* (18th ed, Sweet & Maxwell, London, 2002) pp 844–845.

[20] For an overview of LLPs in the United States, see Callison, *Limited Liability Partnerships & Limited Liability Limited Partnerships* at www.lectlaw.com. The limited liability company ("LLC") has now been introduced in the United States, based on the model more familiar in civil law jurisdictions.

[21] It should of course be noted that LLP status will do little to protect a firm against intra–partner disputes.

[22] See ABA Model Rule 5.1(c)(1).

of negligence being found. The application of similar conditions to dissimilar practice areas also gave rise to debate, on the basis that some areas of partnership work, particularly in large, multi-discipline firms, are more susceptible to claims of malpractice and are perceived to be higher risk. These and other arguments also fell for consideration in more recent years in Britain and, as such, bear a degree of scrutiny in order to highlight how an LLP works in practice and also to demonstrate some of the key issues which would have to be addressed before an LLP-type vehicle could be introduced in this jurisdiction.[23]

Arising out of a review by the Department of Trade and Industry initiated in 1996,[24] the Limited Liability Partnerships Act 2000 came into force on 6 April 2001.[25] Maintaining competitiveness was one obvious factor informing the introduction of the Act, particularly in circumstances where offshore LLPs could be established in Jersey.[26] In the context of proposed reform and how it could be effected, it also appears that there was considerable demand for

> "the highly flexible management structure appropriate to an organisation where there is a commonality of interest between capital and management, and a shared motivation…with some at least of the external features of a company, including in particular limited liability".[27]

The Limited Liability Partnerships Act 2000

Under the provisions of the 2000 Act, an LLP involves two or more people "associated for carrying on a lawful business with a view to profit".[28] These people are known as members rather than partners.[29] The LLP operates as a body corporate which exists separate from its members, and to which the 1890 Act does not apply.[30]

23 LLP status is also available in, *inter alia*, Australia and Canada.

24 See Consultation paper: "Limited Liability Partnerships: A New Form of Business Association for Professions" URN 97/597.

25 See l'Anson, *Lindley & Banks on Partnership* (18th ed, Sweet & Maxwell, London, 2002) pp 23–25.

26 Under the Limited Liability (Jersey) Law 1996. See Payne, *The Limited Liability Partnership Bill* (2000) *Company Lawyer* 133.

27 Select Committee on Trade and Industry, above, n 1, at para 23.

28 s 2(1)(a) of the 2000 Act.

29 See s 4 of the 2000 Act.

30 ss 1(2) and 1(5) of the 2000 Act. However, various of the provisions of the 1890 Act are effectively incorporated into the 2000 Act.

Members are agents of the LLP[31] and are thus not personally responsible for each other's acts, although the firm will be responsible for the actions of its members acting in the ordinary course of business.[32] In contrast to partnerships, where each partner is liable personally for the debts of the firm, under the LLP structure a party contracts with a legal entity separate from the partners. The debts of the firm are thus the responsibility of the firm and the individual members of the firm may not, in broad terms, be sued for them on a personal basis. Individual members' liability is limited to the extent of their stake in the firm and personal assets are, in the normal course of events, protected from creditors.

Although these provisions create the impression of a body that is more akin to a limited company than a partnership, LLPs are treated as partnerships for the purposes of income tax, capital gains tax and insurance.[33] Related to this, members of an LLP can distribute profits as they see fit, subject to a provision concerning the insolvency-related claw back of drawings by members.[34]

The benefits identified come at a price, however. By virtue of s 15 of the Act, provision is made for the application of company law and insolvency law, with any necessary modifications, to LLPs. The Limited Liability Partnerships Regulations 2001 subsequently applied parts of the British Companies Act 1985 (as amended) to LLPs. The result of this is to provide for the public disclosure of information about LLPs, including in particular their finances, as well as the disclosure of information about what happens when an LLP becomes insolvent.[35] Such disclosure may seem a small price to pay for the protections afforded by the LLP structure. Indeed, the impact is softened by the fact that the agreement between members of an LLP—which in effect is determined by the members themselves, thus affording great flexibility[36]—remains

---

[31] s 6(1) of the 2000 Act.

[32] s 6(4) of the 2000 Act.

[33] ss 10–13 of the 2000 Act; for example, members will be taxed as partners rather than as employees.

[34] s 214A of the Insolvency Act 1986, inserted by Sched 3 of the Limited Liability Partnerships Regulations 2001.

[35] See in particular Pts II and IV of the 2001 Regulations.

[36] Referred to in the 2001 Regulations as a "limited liability partnership agreement". This has been criticised on the basis that in the absence of a model agreement, members of LLPs would fall back on limited default provisions. Boundy, "LLP: The Final Straw or the Post-Enron Panacea?" *Accountancy Age* 3 April 2002. The risk inherent in such an approach is that the boundary lines between the application of company law and partnership law to LLPs is somewhat blurred and is best dealt with by drafting all-encompassing agreements: See Comment, "Limited Liability Partnerships: Available at Last" (2001) 22(3) *Company Lawyer* at 65.

private; no equivalent of the articles of association need be filed. Yet, firms used to non-disclosure may find it very difficult to open up for inspection information they view as highly sensitive. This is particularly so in the professional services industries, where personal contacts and relationships are critical. Furthermore, many firms may have partner pension liabilities that would have to be disclosed under LLP rules, although this is an issue which might be more of concern to partners than parties dealing with them in a professional capacity.[37] At a more prosaic level, limited liability partnership would increase the rigours of corporate governance on a partnership. However, although this may not be welcomed wholeheartedly by every partnership, in the climate of corporate enforcement which now prevails in this jurisdiction, as evidenced by, *inter alia*, the regime established under the Corporate Law Enforcement Act 2001, this is hardly a tenable stance to maintain.

On balance, the benefits of the introduction of an LLP corporate vehicle would appear to greatly outweigh the downsides, certainly from the perspective of those who wish to take advantage of such a new corporate structure. However, a frequent criticism is that the creation of an LLP structure in Britain essentially provided for the freedom of the professions to enjoy all the benefits of partnership without the usually associated liabilities.[38] Of course such an argument, certainly at a superficial level, ignores the fact that the LLP does not deprive a third party of the right to sue an LLP as a corporate entity; indeed, whilst undoubtedly focused on protecting individual partners, the legislation does not deprive third parties of any rights. In order to assuage any doubts in this regard, the Jersey LLP legislation requires a £5 million bond in order to ensure the availability of funds on liquidation.[39] This was not introduced in the British legislation, but professionals will still be required to take out professional indemnity insurance, and it is unlikely that insurance companies are not alive to the link between taking out this insurance and its relevance in the context of the LLP structure; indeed, it was suggested that such insurance could be raised for professionals operating within an LLP structure.[40]

---

37 Partnerships would not be unique in this regard. See the comments of Alan Broxson of Irish Pensions Trust, Tuesday, 21 October 2003, at the Trustee Forum of the Irish Association of Pension Funds (IAPF): www.iapf.ie in relation to concerns that Irish pension funds have been through a "pensions hurricane", leading to shortfalls in funds.

38 Select Committee on Trade and Industry, above, n 1, at para 6. However, eligibility to operate as an LLP is not restricted to the regulated professions.

39 See Art 6 of the Limited Partnerships (Jersey) Law 1996.

40 Select Committee on Trade and Industry, above, n 1, at para 35.

A Limited Liability Partnerships Law for Ireland

The pressures and considerations identified above, many of which brought the Limited Liability Partnerships Act 2000 into being in Britain, are equally applicable in Ireland and require some form of response.[41] It is submitted that the introduction of the LLP as a corporate vehicle in this jurisdiction would be a positive step, not just for larger partnerships, but also for small incorporated business and quasi-partnerships, which could benefit from limited liability without having to cloak themselves in the effective fiction that they are a limited liability company. Of course, the introduction of LLP status could also prove attractive to existing limited liability companies, as distinct from partnerships. Such considerations clearly highlight the importance of ensuring that any debate in relation to LLPs should ideally be ventilated in the context of review of company law by the CLRG. This dovetails neatly with consideration of the uses of limited liability, a debate which has effectively been rehearsed already in the context of the House of Lords decision in *Salomon v Salomon*.[42] In framing a law providing for LLPs, concerns that the structure could be taken advantage of to promote fraud and the evasion of legal obligations would clearly have to be taken into account. An LLP should not be the vehicle by which the more unscrupulous could abuse the advantages of limited liability.

In the context of considering the introduction of LLPs in this jurisdiction, it would also appear to make sense to carry out a general housekeeping exercise in relation to existing partnership law. Were LLPs to be introduced, it is important that they would not simply be a stopgap attempt to remedy some of the deficiencies and anachronisms evident in partnership law. Examples of such anachronisms which survive and which should be tackled from a legislative perspective include the provision first set out in the Joint Stock Companies Act 1844,[43] that partnerships of more than 20 members are unlawful (this figure was reduced to 10 in the case of banking).[44] Another quirk

---

[41] The President of the Institute of Chartered Accountants has called for limited liability partnership structures on the basis of "making this country a worthwhile place to do business and a recognition that professional services will soon become an international traded commodity like never before": *Irish Independent,* 18 April 2005. The total number of registrations of LLPs in Britain to 31 March 2004 was 7,396 DTI "Companies in 2003–2004".

[42] *Salomon v Salomon* [1897] AC 22. See Puig, "A Two Edged Sword: Salomon and the Separate Legal Entity Doctrine" 7(3) *Murdoch University Electronic Journal of Law* (September 2000).

[43] As subsequently replaced by s 4 of the Joint Stock Companies Act of 1856.

[44] The rationale for this rule, namely the requirement to join each and every partner in any action against a given firm, has been done away with as it is now possible to sue partnerships in their firm name. That this rule provided little benefit is evident from the number of devices used to get around it; see generally Twomey, above, n 1, para 4.26 *et seq.*

of partnership law is that if a partner dies, his or her estate can force the sale of the practice, regardless of profitability, damage to goodwill or to the wishes of the surviving partners subject, of course, to any partnership agreements in place.[45] The terms implied into partnership law, furthermore, effectively do not entitle partners to expel another partner.

A balance would also need to be struck between responding to pressures from the business world but at the same time ensuring that any legislation introduced adequately dealt with the variety of issues arising. LLPs, as introduced in Britain, are body corporates, whereas under the Partnership Act 1890, partnerships are treated as an aggregate of individuals. This is a significant and fundamental change and gives rise to a number of issues. Taxation neutrality in terms of choosing between a partnership or limited liability partnership[46] is a key consideration. The related effect on employees must be borne in mind. The distinction between existing companies or partnerships applying to change their status to that of LLP and those which are constituting as a new business would also have to be considered. This is particularly relevant in light of the need to consider to what degree the original capital investment of a person entering a partnership should be protected and whether a rescaling or redistribution of such capital would be required. Furthermore, to justify the creation of a legal LLP structure, professions which are compelled to operate as partnerships under legislation would need to be freed from such obligations and given the option to constitute or reconstitute as LLPs.

Given such issues, although seductively simple, it is clear that if a British style LLP was to be introduced, the amendment of existing partnership laws in order to give birth to limited liability partnerships would seem inappropriate. Nor would building on the legal construct of limited partnerships be appropriate, as they still expose any given number of partners to full liability and, as such, are much closer in form and spirit to partnerships than LLPs. A standalone Limited Liability Partnerships statute would thus represent, it is submitted, the cleanest and simplest way of introducing a modern and useful structure into the world of business. Of course, whilst there is much merit in the creation of a limited liability partnership corporate vehicle, the development of legislation allowing for this should not be treated lightly. In reviewing the manner in which the legislature created LLPs in Britain, one somewhat sceptical commentator had recourse to the adage that "a camel is a horse created by

[45] s 33(1) and s 39 of the 1890 Act.

[46] Achieved by taxing the profits of LLPs as a partnership rather than a body corporate.

a committee".[47] There is little point in responding to the pressures that inform reform of the law if such a response only creates further pressures at a time when many bodies require clear, sensible and practical legislation.

---

[47] Boundy, "LLP: The Final Straw or the Post-Enron Panacea?" *Accountancy Age*, 3 April 2002.

The Presumption of Advancement and Unlawful Fraudulent Conduct

by

Laura McGowan*

The Irish Law: Coherent at First Sight

One of the best-known cases to establish the principle that unlawful fraudulent conduct cannot be relied upon to rebut the presumption of advancement is *Gascoigne v Gascoigne.*[1] A husband had conveyed property into his wife's name to protect it from his creditors. The court held he could not rely on this fraudulent purpose to rebut the presumption of advancement, which arose in his wife's favour, despite the fact the wife also knew of the purpose behind the conveyance. This was followed in the Irish case of *Parkes v Parkes.*[2] The defendant husband wanted to buy land, and to avoid the statutory requirements which would arise because he was not an Irish citizen, he conveyed it into his wife's name. The parties later divorced. The husband registered an inhibition on the land and the wife instituted proceedings claiming it was wrongly registered. The defendant counterclaimed for a declaration that he was entitled to the beneficial ownership.

Justice Costello reviewed the case law. He accepted that *Gascoigne* established the basic principle that a party cannot rebut a presumption, which the law raises, by setting up his own illegality and fraud, and obtain relief in equity. This principle was applied in *Re Emery's Investment Trusts.*[3] The husband registered American securities

* This essay was awarded first prize by the Law Society of Ireland, *Student Law Reform Essay Competition 2002.*

1 [1918] KB 223.

2 [1980] ILRM 137.

3 [1959] 1 Ch 410. In this case the plaintiff was a British subject and husband of the defendant. He purchased American savings bonds and registered them in the name of his wife with the husband expressly named as beneficiary with her. The bonds were then changed for common stock in American securities in the wife's name.

in the name of his wife with the intention that the beneficial interest in the securities should be held equally between them. To avoid payment of American withholding tax, to which he was liable as a non-US citizen, no mention was made of his beneficial interest. After the wife had sold the securities, the husband applied to the English courts for a declaration that at the date of the removal and sale of the securities the wife held them as to one half for him. The husband's claim failed.[4] Wynn-Parry J found that there was a clear breach of US federal law in the way the transactions were carried out by the husband's non-disclosure of his beneficial interest in the securities, and he concluded that the plaintiff could not seek the aid of equity in such circumstances.

Costello J then considered the Court of Appeal case of *Tinker v Tinker*[5] which was different on the facts from other cases but in which the basic principle of *Gascoigne* was restated. Salomon LJ held:

> "It is trite law that anyone coming to equity to be relieved against his own act must come with clean hands. If in a case such as the present, he were to put forward, as a reason for being relieved against his own act, a dishonest plot on his part, for example to defraud his own creditors the court would refuse him relief and must say: let the estate lie where it falls."[6]

Finally, Costello J considered the Northern Irish case of *McEvoy v Belfast Banking Ltd.*[7] This concerned a deposit of £1,000 made by a father in the joint names of himself and his son, although there was no intention on the father's part to benefit the son. The object of the deposit was to avoid death duties. The court held it could not have regard to the evidence, which established this fact, "because of its illegal intent".

Following these cases, Costello J held that the court should not grant relief to a person who had placed property in his wife's name for the purposes of evading the

[4] Wynn-Parry J pointed out that had the tax involved been UK tax the case would have been covered be Gascoigne and concluded against the plaintiff.

[5] [1970] P 136. The husband intended to buy a house in his own name but was advised by his solicitors that if the new business venture he was then entering failed, the house could be taken by his creditors as part of his business assets and his solicitors recommended that it should be put in his wife's name. This was done and the house was conveyed to her. The marriage broke down and the wife claimed the house as her own. It was held on the evidence that the husband had an honest intention at the time of the conveyance that the house would belong to his wife and therefore the wife's claim to the property succeeded.

[6] At 143.

[7] [1934] NI 67; [1935] AC 24.

law relating to transfer of land.[8] Echoing Salomon LJ in *Tinker v Tinker*,[9] he held "The estate must lie where it falls".[10]

This principle of non-recovery applies in cases involving the presumption of advancement. However, as will be outlined in the following cases, the courts find themselves in great difficulty when the presumption of advancement does not arise. Costello J stated that "the whole transaction is tainted with illegality", yet he allowed the initial phase of the transaction, being the presumption of advancement, to stand despite the fraudulent intent which existed in order for this presumption to operate. It was only the second phase, in which the plaintiff relied on the illegality to rebut the presumption, which the courts prevent from operating. It is this writer's contention that once an illegal intention is found, the entire transaction is tainted with illegality and therefore is void *ab intio.* The result would be that the party who has received property must give it back to the other. This argument is developed further below.

The 1990s: the Danger of Non-recovery and Arbitrary Distinctions

In the 1990s the English courts were faced with a number of cases concerning fraudulent conduct. To avoid applying the non-recovery rule, as applied in the Irish courts, the courts had recourse to a number of illogical distinctions. The House of Lords, in the 1993 case of *Tinsley v Milligan,*[11] allowed recovery for a defendant despite being aware of an illegal intention. The plaintiff and the defendant were two single women and formed a joint business venture to run lodging houses. Using funds generated by the business, they purchased a house in which they lived together. The house was vested in the sole name of the plaintiff on the understanding that they were joint beneficial owners of the property. The purpose of the arrangement was to defraud the Department of Health and Social Services. Over a number of years, the defendant, with the knowledge of the plaintiff, made false claims on the DHSS. The

---

[8] In relation to Mr Parkes, Costello Justice held (at 144): "It suffices in this case that he knowingly authorised the commission of that which was prohibited by the section for the purpose of evading the statute. As a result the whole transaction is tainted with illegality. Mr Parkes is in the same inescapable dilemma in which the plaintiff in *Tinker's* case found himself. If he acted honestly and the certificate was a true one the property belongs to his wife, if he acted dishonestly and the certificate was a false one the court will not allow him take advantage of his own dishonesty."

[9] *ibid.*

[10] At 145.

[11] [1993] 3 WLR 126.

plaintiff did the same. The parties had a disagreement and the plaintiff moved out, leaving the defendant in possession. The plaintiff then gave the defendant notice to quit and brought proceedings against the defendant claiming possession and asserting sole ownership of the property. The defendant counterclaimed for an order for sale and for a declaration that the property was held by the plaintiff on trust for the parties in equal shares. The judge dismissed the plaintiff's claim and allowed the counterclaim. On appeal by the plaintiff, the Court of Appeal dismissed the appeal. The case came before the House of Lords, which, by a majority of 3:2 found for the defendant and dismissed the appeal.

The judgment reviewed the status of illegal contracts as a whole. Lowry, Jauncey and Browne-Wilkinson LJ were in the majority and rejected the main principle relied on by the minority, Goff and Keith LJ. The rejected principle was that of Lord Eldon LC set out in *Muckleston v Brown,*[12] stating that:

> "the plaintiff, had he been guilty of a fraud upon the law to evade, to disappoint, the provision of the legislature, to which he is bound to submit, and coming to equity to be relieved against his own act, and the defence being dishonest, between the two species of dishonesty the court would not act; but would say, let the estate lie where it falls."[13]

Thus it would seem that on this principle, once the court was aware of the illegal intention, even if it was not being relied on as a defence, the court would not intervene but would "let the estate lie where it falls".[14] Browne Wilkinson LJ laid out the clearest judgment for the majority. He reviewed the overall position at law of illegal contracts and held that three principles emerged:

> "(1) Property in chattels and land can pass under a contract which is illegal and therefore would have been unenforceable as a contract;(2) a plaintiff

[12] 6 Ves 52 at p 69.

[13] Lord Eldon reiterated this principle in *Curtis v Perry* 6 Ves 739, where he stated: "the moment the purpose to defeat the policy of the law by fraudulently concealing, that this was his property, is admitted, it is very clear, he ought not to be heard in this court to say, that this is his property."

[14] The court also rejected the "public conscience test" favoured by the Court of Appeal which involved "The court looking at the quality of the illegality relied on by the defendant and all the surrounding circumstances, without fine distinction and seeking to answer two question; first, whether there had been illegality of which the court should take notice and second, whether in all the circumstances it would be an affront to the public conscience if by affording him relief sought the court was seen to be indirectly assisting or encouraging the plaintiff in his criminal act."

> can at law enforce property rights so acquired provided that he does not need to rely on the illegal contract for any purpose other than providing the basis of his claim to a property right;(3) it is irrelevant that the illegality of the underlying agreement was either pleaded or emerged in evidence: if the plaintiff has acquired legal title under the illegal contract that is enough."[15]

He then examined the cases where a presumption of advancement arose. He held that although recovery was not allowed in such circumstances, this was because the party seeking recovery had to rely directly on his own illegality. He went on:

> "Although reference was made to Lord Eldon's principle none of those cases were decided on the simple ground (if it were good law) that equity would not in any circumstances enforce a resulting trust in such circumstances. On the contrary in each case the rule was stated to be that the plaintiff could not recover because he had to rely on the illegality to rebut the presumption of advancement".[16]

Thus it was the reliance on the illegality and not the court's awareness of it that Browne-Wilkinson LJ felt was fatal to the claim.[17] Therefore the court found for Miss Milligan, the defendant.[18] At no time did she have to rely on her fraudulent intention. The court merely became aware of it during examination of the witnesses. The decision was criticised by the Australian High Court in *Nelson v Nelson*[19] because the outcome of the case was dependent on presumptions. One commentator

[15] At 147. His Lordship also rejected drawing a distinction between property rights enforceable at law and those which require the intervention of equity as "more than 100 years has elapsed since law and equity became fused".

[16] At 151.

[17] His Lordship gave an explanation for the departure from Lord Eldon's absolute rule of non-intervention that being the fusion of law and equity has led the courts to adopt a single rule (application both at law and in equity) as to the circumstances in which the court will enforce property interests acquired in pursuance of an illegal transaction *viz*, the *Howmakers rule* [1945] KB 65. A party to an illegality can recover by virtue of a legal or equitable property interest if but only if, he can establish his title without relying on his own illegality at 151.

[18] Milligan established a resulting trust by showing that she had contributed to the purchase price of the property and that there was a common understanding that the house would be shared equally. Having proved theses facts the defendant raised a presumption of resulting trust and there was no evidence to rebut. Lord Browne-Wilkinson relied on the reasoning adopted by the Ontario court of Appeal in *Gorog v Kiss* (1977) 78 DLR (3d) 690.

[19] (1995) 132 ALR 133.

disliked that approach of the majority because "it appears to regard the accomplishment of the fraud as immaterial and I do not think that is right."[20]

This result does produce a number of arbitrary distinctions. Under this law a different outcome will be produced depending on the parties' gender and relationship.[21] It is particularly harsh on husbands and fathers who wish to recover property from a divorced wife or estranged child as a presumption of advancement arises in both cases and the father or husband will have to rely directly on the illegal intention to rebut the presumption. However, the law is kinder to wives or mothers as a presumption does not arise when property is transferred by a wife to a husband or by a mother to a child. This situation could be changed somewhat if the recommendations by the Law Reform Commission were implemented.[22] Further, if the legislature were to legislate for civil unions between same sex couples, cases with facts similar to those in *Tinsley v Milligan* could have a different outcome. It does seem somewhat unfair that the law will aid the recovery of land despite an illegal intention existing in relation to strangers, or same sex couples, or wives and mothers, and yet directly penalise a father or husband. All categories are coming to equity with unclean hands yet the courts are relying directly on now scorned discriminations to aid recovery in the aforementioned categories.

A further distinction between an illegal intention existing and being brought into effect was then introduced by the case of *Tribe v Tribe.*[23] A father (the plaintiff) had transferred shares in his company to his son, to avoid repair notices claimed by his landlords. Before the illegality was brought into effect the father reached a compromise with the landlord and then sought a transfer of the shares back to him, but his son refused. The son claimed a presumption of advancement arose which could not be rebutted by the father because it would mean him relying on his own illegality. The Court of Appeal however found for the father. The court found as a general rule that the presumption could not be rebutted by the plaintiff relying on his own illegality, but that where the illegal purpose had not been carried into effect, the plaintiff could rely on it to rebut the presumption of advancement.[24] Nourse LJ

---

20 JD Davies in *Presumptions and Illegality* SLC PC 14499 James Joyce Library UCD at 5.

21 This was highlighted by Hanbury and Martin in *The Modern Law of Equity* at chap 10.

22 The 6th Report of the Law Reform Commission (LRC 56). It recommended that the doctrine of advancement should be extended to a gift from wife to husband and mother to child.

23 [1996] Ch 107.

24 Millet LJ stressed that the transferor must have withdrawn from the transaction while his dishonesty lay in intention only: "The law draws the line once intention has been wholly or partly carried into effect."

held that he was bound by *Tinsley v Milligan* in relation to when a presumption of advancement arises and when it does not but was in agreement with Judge Weeks QC in the lower court who said:

> "Finally it is not for me to criticise their Lordships' reasoning but with the greatest respect I find it difficult to see why the outcome in cases such as the present one should depend to such a large extent on arbitrary factors, such as whether the claim is brought by a father against a son, or a mother against a son or a grandfather against a grandson."[25]

Nourse LJ went on: "I see much force in those observations. If the defendant had been his brother, grandson, nephew or son-in-law the plaintiff would have succeeded without further inquiry."[26] Nourse LJ felt that drawing a distinction between when an illegal intention exists and where one is brought into effect was consistent with the view as set out in *Tinsley v Milligan.*[27] However is should be noted that this distinction has been departed from in Australia in *Nelson v Nelson.*[28]

Reform: Restoring the Dignity of the Courts

From the case law it is clear that the law regarding recovery in the circumstances of illegality is in a state in flux.[29] At present it is not even clear whether there are two or

---

[25] At 1003.

[26] Nourse LJ again upheld the distinction in *Tinsley v Milligan* in *Lawson v Coombes* [1999] CH 373.

[27] Nourse LI said "Be that as it may, we are bound by *Tinsley v Milligan* [1994] 1 AC 340 for what it decided. It decided that where the presumption of advancement arises the general rule applies. It did not decide that there is no exception where the illegal purpose has not been carried into effect. If anything, it may be said to support the existence of the exception in such a case. See Lord Goff's reference at p 356H to *Perpetual Executors and Trustees Association of Australia Ltd v Wright* (1917) 23 CTLR 185. However, Browne-Wilkinson LJ, in the same judgment, commented that "the principle of *locus poenitentiae* is in my judgment irreconcilable with any rule that where property is transferred for an illegal purpose no equitable proprietary right exists. The existence of the equitable interest cannot depend upon events occurring after that date." At 150.

[28] (1995) 132 ALR 133. A mother transferred her house into the names of her son and daughter in order to obtain a subsidy for the purchase of a subsequent house. After the sale of the original house the daughter claimed a half share as the mother could not adduce evidence of the illegal purpose to rebut the presumption of advancement which arose in her favour. The New South Wales Court of Appeal decided against the mother holding that she could not rely on her illegal intention to rebut the presumption of advancement which occurred. However the Australian HC overturned this and accepted the evidence to rebut the presumption even though it showed an illegal intention which had been carried into effect.

[29] See Enonchong, "Illegality in French and English Law" *International and Comparative Law Quarterly* (1955) at p 200.

three rules in existence. The first can be identified as the traditional rule on non-recovery as laid out in *Holman v Johnson.*[30] The basic principle is that he who comes to equity must come with clean hands or *neom auditur propriam turpitudinem allegans.* Therefore those who must rely on their own turpitude (as will be the case where one wishes to rebut a presumption) will fail to recover. This is less strict than Lord Eldon's rule of absolute non-recovery, that once the court becomes aware of the fraudulent intention recovery is not permitted, irrespective of whether it was actually relied upon. Finally there is the *Bowmaker rule* which has since been split into two. The plaintiff will be permitted to recover even though he is *in pari delicto,* as long as he does not have to rely on his own turpitude. This was applied in *Tinsley v Milligan.* However this has been altered by *Tribe v Tribe* where a plaintiff can rely directly on a fraudulent intention, so long as it has not been brought into effect. The Irish courts have adopted the non-recovery, non-intervention rule by refusing to allow recovery where the applicant has to rely directly on his own turpitude.[31] However there are a number of criticisms of this policy.

The first is that it is discriminatory in nature as outlined previously. Secondly it raises the presumption of advancement to a decisive new level, when it has already been viewed as inadequate. Nourse LJ, in *Tribe v Tribe,* highlighted this when he stated "Moreover in times when the presumption of advancement has for other purposes fallen into disfavour (see for example, the observations of Lord Reid, Lord Hodson and Lord Diplock in *Petti v Petti* [1970] AC 777, 793, 811, 824) there seems to be some perversity in its elevation to a decisive status in the context of illegality".[32] Further, it leads to unjust enrichment of one party over another, "when usually both are equally guilty of the fraud".[33] Finally the combination of these factors has the effect that it

---

30 (1775) 1 Comp 341.

31 This was also the case in Roman law. Pothier drew a distinction between agreements where one party was guilty and agreements where both parties were guilty. Recovery was allowed in the first but not in the second. The rule was expressed *as in pari causa turpitudinis cessat repetitio.* This seems the most perverse of all the rules. Surely where both parties are guilty, the recovery should be mutual; allowing recovery to only one party, *i.e.* the guilty party where only one party was guilty strikes the author as being nonsense.

32 At 118. In *McGrath v Wallis* [1995] 2 FLR 114 Nourse LJ commented that presumptions should only be used as a last resort. Also, JD Davies commented that "Presumptions are not as innocuous as they seem. They create awkwardness in the law distorting issues and affecting adversely the manner in which cases are decided." *Presumption and Illegality, ibid* at 1

33 This was one of the main reasons why the HC in Australia allowed recovery to the mother in *Nelson v Nelson.* Millet J, in *Tribe v Tribe,* commented that the doctrine of *locus peonitentiae* was an exception which operates to mitigate the harshness of the primary rule.

reduces the authority and credibility of the courts because they are rewarding fraudulent conduct (where there is unjust enrichment) or scurrying around for technical distinctions in order to aid recovery to a party who has little regard for the law anyway.[34]

It is submitted that the most effective way of reforming the law would be to deprive such illegal agreements of any effect. If the courts adopted a policy of recovery it would bring much needed clarity to the area and restore respect to the courts. Therefore the party who has received a windfall must give back what he received from the other. It is a policy of intervention.

This policy is the one adopted in the French Civil code under Art 1131. One of the earliest cases to rely on this was in *Chedeville v Delarnotte*,[35] where it was decided that since illegal agreements can have no effect, money paid or property transferred under such an agreement must be recoverable. This principle of mutual recovery has a number of advantages. First, it brings a single, definite clear rule to a much confused area. Illegal agreements can have no effect, therefore the *status quo ante* must be restored. Second, the courts do not have to rely on a presumption of advancement or indeed a presumption of resulting trust; thus the discriminatory and indeed paternalistic nature behind these presumptions is nullified. Third, as there is mutual recovery, there is no unjust windfall to one of the parties. In cases where one party transfers property to another, the other party is usually aware of the fraudulent purpose behind it. The receiving parties are equally guilty of the turpitude and should not be excused by the court just because they were not the pro-active parties. They are guilty by their acquiescence. Indeed they could be the initiating parties, but because of their gender are favoured by the courts.[36] Fourth, it prevents the courts having to rely upon senseless distinctions, such as allowing recovery where the party does not have to rely directly upon the illegality,[37] or the even more dubious distinction that an applicant can rely on his or her own illegal intention so long as it is not brought into effect.[38] In both of these instances the plaintiffs are guilty of fraud

---

34 *Tribe v Tribe* [1996] Ch 107.

35 S.1844 I. 582.

36 For example, where a husband transfers property to his wife, his wife may have been the motivating factor but under the law at present she would benefit as the husband would have to rely on the (mutual) illegal intention to rebut the presumption of advancement.

37 The *Bowmaker* rule as applied in *Tinsley v Milligan*. However, on this principle the court can never refuse recovery even where the turpitude of the plaintiff is excessively offensive. This has already been greeted with judicial contempt, see Goff LJ in *Tinsley* at 79.

38 *Tribe v Tribe* [1996] Ch 107.

against the law. They should not be saved by distinctions invented by the courts when they have tried to evade the requirements made by the very law which the guilty parties had so little respect. Fifth, the principle of mutual recovery, because it is based on the rule that illegal contracts can have no effect, is a principle of policy and justice. This is in contrast to the Irish approach of non-recovery, which is a principle of policy only.[39] Finally, the combination of the above points acts to restore dignity and status to the courts. The courts by advocating a policy that illegal contracts have no effect, therefore restoring the parties to their pre-contract position, are seen as being pro-active and applying a coherent logical rule that fraudulent conduct will not be rewarded.

One criticism of the proposed reform could be that it would be a weak deterrent to those wishing to avoid the law.[40] However, in answering this criticism the author suggests that the present law is also an inadequate deterrent. In certain circumstances it can even be employed directly as a means of acting fraudulently. For instance, a plaintiff could act with fraudulent intent but withdraw from the transaction before it is complete. The law, however, allows the plaintiff to rely directly on his or her fraudulent intention to rebut any presumption of advancement which may arise. It should be noted that in *Tribe v Tribe* the creditors did not know of the father's intention to deceive them. However, because he transferred his assets, a false impression was given to the creditors. The fact that the plan to deceive them had been carried to the stage of transferring the assets did not prevent recovery.[41] Also because the law is in such a confused state it is unlikely that it will act as a deterrent to anyone other than lawyers and unfortunate law students. Finally, the best deterrent against acting fraudulently should be provided by the legislation in each specific area and not case law in equity.[42]

---

[39] It was admitted in *Tinsley v Milligan* that as it was a principle of policy and not justice unjust outcomes will result, at 72, 83.

[40] If the parties are restored to their original position they could commit fraud against the law and not lose anything directly under this policy as all property is returned.

[41] Thus, a plaintiff father could transfer property to his son to protect it from his creditors. He could then inform his creditors that they will be unable to recover any property from him because it is out of their and indeed his reach (he does not have to disclose why). Therefore, they are pressured into negotiating with the father to reduce the debt owed. The father can then seek the return of the property. On the authority of *Tribe v Tribe*, the plaintiff father will recover.

[42] Such as transferring shares out of the reach of creditors' hands (*Tribe v Tribe*), avoiding legal requirements when buying land (*Gascoigne v Gascoigne*), defrauding the DHSS (*Tinsley v Milligan*).

In conclusion, Goff LJ in *Tinsley v Milligan*[43] entreated Parliament to reform the law. It is submitted that before the Irish courts embark on the slippery slope of technical discriminations, the Irish parliament should at least direct the Law Reform Commission to examine the law and possible solutions.[44] However, it is more likely that the courts will find themselves in the legal quagmire that is presumptions and illegality before parliament takes such an initiative. If such a case should arise it should be treated with caution and with particular wariness when looking across the water.

---

43 [1993] 3 AER 65.

44 The New Zealand legislature stepped in over 20 years ago, introducing the New Zealand Illegal Contracts Act 1970.

Arbitration as an Alternative Means of Resolution of Family Law Disputes

by
Mary-Jo Butler*

Introduction

Lawyers, judges and clients, as well as other professionals involved in family law disputes in Ireland have long questioned whether society is best served by using litigation to decide such matters. This is particularly true in cases involving children, such as custody and access.

This paper attempts to analyse the benefits of arbitration as an option for settling such disputes by looking at the advantages of such a system and critically evaluating the alleged detriments.

Other Jurisdictions

In other jurisdictions, arbitration as an alternative form of dispute resolution is at varying stages of acceptance in family law matters.

In Australia, arbitration for disputes about property is possible under the regulations of the Family Law Amendment Act 2000 that came into effect on March 1 2000. Arbitration of disputes is voluntary (unlike some US states, such as Oregon, where the court may order family law matters to be arbitrated)[1]. Coupled with the Howard Government's family law reforms, including the introduction of binding financial

---

* This essay was awarded joint second place by the Law Society of Ireland for the *Student Law Reform Essay 2002*. The law is as stated in 2002. The author wrote this essay while employed as a Child Protection Social Work Team Leader with the Health Service Executive. She is now a practicing barrister.

[1] The court orders a case into arbitration in relation to domestic relations or family law cases where the parties are arguing about matters other than custody or support. In addition, parties can agree to arbitrate disagreements about support. See http://www.osbar.org/legal1inks/oregonlaw/TelLaw/1216.htm.

agreements, these regulations give couples unprecedented choice as to how to manage their financial affairs without recourse to the courts.[2]

This would appear to be the first step in that jurisdiction towards the resolution of domestic disputes by arbitration.

In the United States, the majority of states have a general arbitration statute, and it is common for property and alimony disputes to be arbitrated upon.[3] However, the arbitration of disputes involving children has been received with mixed reactions in different states, as will be discussed below.

The Basic Elements of Arbitration

The basis of any arbitration process is the parties' agreement to arbitration, which will outline the parameters of the process, including who the arbitrator is, their powers under the agreement and the subject matter of the arbitration.

These basic elements not only outline the benefits of arbitration as a form of conflict resolution in family law matters but also act as a counter-argument for the alleged disadvantages.

The Advantages of Arbitration

(1) Speed

A factor frequently cited in favour of arbitration is the speed of the process. Instead of waiting for a hearing date, waiting lists now being quite considerable, the parties can also get a full hearing, uninterrupted by other court matters, practically on a mutually agreeable date.

In litigation, if there is any complexity to the case, the case may be heard for a few days at a time over a number of months. At each hearing, the parties waste time

---

2 "Arbitration Now A Reality For Family Law Matters", news release of the Attorney General, The Hon. Daryl Williams, AM QC MP, 8 March 2000—http://www.law.gov.au/rninisters/attorney-~eneral/mediamn.htrnl.

3 http://consumer.pub.findlaw.com/newcontent/flaw/chp15_c.htmlmime

reminding the judge of significant details. Meanwhile, the parties cannot separate themselves from the case since it involves matters that are extremely personal to them in their everyday lives.

Delay can also place non-custodial parents at a disadvantage, and not only due to their separation from their child; practice can show that delay can decrease the chance of the non-custodial parent being awarded custody of the child.[4]

Delay can also be highly prejudicial for a party seeking access for similar reasons.

The fact that the arbitration process would be more expeditious would reduce the length of time that the parties, including children, are exposed to the stress and anxiety involved due to the lack of certainty as to the outcome.

The Cost of Litigation

Due to the fact that a matter submitted to arbitration usually results in a quick hearing and decision, the costs involved can be greatly reduced.[5] This is particularly important as the costs of both parties are likely to be coming from the same pool of family resources, which can often reduce the parties' future standard of living, or even result in situations of financial hardship.

It has also been argued that the high costs of the litigation process have also led to a two-tier system developing whereby the poorer, often unrepresented, litigants seek summary judgment in the District Court whilst their wealthier neighbours apply for the most sophisticated Circuit Court remedies.[6] According to Fahey and Lyons,[7] less well off couples in the lower tier are restricted to resolving limited, discrete aspects of their difficulties, whereas the better off, in the upper tier, can seek fully fledged resolutions.

---

[4] Jay Romano, "Divorce Logjam Leads to Alternatives", *New York Times*, 26 July 1992 (quoting nationally recognised expert on child custody, Dr. Richard A. Gardner: "The longer a custody battle goes on...the more likely it is that the court will award custody to the parent with whom the child is living...Even if that parent is the less desirable one, the child will become more bonded and won't want to change...As a result...the court will be less willing to order a change.")

[5] Block, "Divorce Arbitration An Alternative to Mediation" 4 *Fairshare* 784 at p 786.

[6] Law Reform Commission on Family Courts [LRC Report No 52, Dublin, 1996], p iii.

[7] *Marital Breakdown and Family Law in Ireland—a Sociological Study*, 1995, p 122.

With the lower costs of arbitration, resolution can be sought in all matters at a price more affordable and, therefore, accessible to parties, and make better use of resources. The promotion of a more cost efficient method of resolution in family matters was also recommended by the Report of the Joint Oireachtas Committee on Marriage Breakdown.[8] However, nothing has developed in relation to having any State-funded professionals, such as child psychologists and other relevant services, to assist the courts in its current structure, which results in parties having to pay for same from their own resources. In addition the issue of legal representation at an arbitration would have to be addressed, as it would be unfair if one side only had such representation.

Informalities of the Process

The arbitration process can be far less formal than that of litigation, depending upon the agreement of the parties. A more relaxed and less formal approach involves less stress than the formal courtroom setting, resulting in less animosity amongst the parties involved. The parties can decide on the location of the arbitration, which would avoid the situation where, "at the moment, many cases are heard in inadequate and unsuitable accommodation..."[9]

The sense of inhibition engendered by the formalities of the court process is obviously an issue mooted by the legislature, which has made specific provisions in ss 33 and 45 of the Judicial Separation and Family Law Reform Act 1989. These require that family law proceedings before the District Court, Circuit and High Courts "shall be as informal as is practicable and consistent with the administration of justice".

Psychological research has shown that intimidation and stress can decrease a person's willingness and ability to retrieve information from memory.[10] Thus, a more informal setting, coupled with a chosen arbitrator in whom the couples have confidence and whom they respect, would result in more accurate information being given during the process, inevitably leading to a more equitable outcome. This clearly has benefits for cases involving children. Given that children are generally

---

8 *Report of the Joint Oireachtas Committee on Marriage Breakdown* (Dublin Stationery Office, 1985).

9 *ibid.*

10 Goodman and Helgeson, "Child sexual assault : children's memory and the law" (1985) *University of Miami Law Review* 40 at pp 181–208.

more impressionable than adults, it is especially important to limit as much as possible the ill effects of such fears. This has also been recommended as a way of reducing suggestibility.[11] The majority of children have no clear idea of what court involves. Their views are mainly composed of distorted images committed to memory from over-dramatised television dramas or movies. Research has shown that most children believe that court is a "bad" place and that only "bad" people go to court.[12] Children tend to view the courtroom as a threatening place, a place in which "if the witness gives the wrong answer, he will go to jail".[13] If children are required by the judge to attend court, which is increasingly becoming the norm for older children in other jurisdictions, this can, as a result, be an extremely stressful experience for them. (At present in this jurisdiction the views of children tend to be elucidated through a child professional, though this may change in the future.)

The importance of minimising animosity between parties in family law matters cannot be over-emphasised, particularly where children are involved. It is important, regardless of the outcome of the decision-making process, that the parties can remain civil towards each other to reduce the effect of the difficulties on the children. In family matters, particularly where children are involved, unlike other areas of the law, parties need to maintain a continuing relationship, and it is important that this remains as positive as possible.

The current system is an adversarial one, where the process can lead to each party making accusation and counter-accusation against each other in an attempt to prove the other less fit to care for the child or children, which can further exacerbate the damaging effects of the divorce or separation on the child or children.

Arbitration conducted in a less formal atmosphere, often in a shorter time span than litigation, and with an arbitrator of the parties' own choosing, will undoubtedly be less antagonistic and hostile than a courtroom setting. The fact that the parties ultimately have more control over the process themselves, including the choosing of

---

11 Perry and Wrightsman, *The Child Witness* (Ca, 1991), p 120.

12 Flin, Davies and Stevenson, Y, (1987), "Children as witnesses psychological aspects of the English and Scottish system" *Medicine and Law* (1987) 6 at pp 275–291; Warren-Leubecker, Tate, Hinton and Ozbeck, "What do children know about the legal system and when do they know it?: First steps down a less travelled path in child witness research" in *Perspectives on Children's Testimony (*Ceci, Ross Toglia, eds, Springer Verlag, New York or Berlin, 1989), pp 158–183.

13 Saywitz, "Children's conceptions of the legal system: Court is a place to play basketball", in *Perspectives on Children's Testimony (*Ceci, Ross Toglia, eds, Springer Verlag, New York or Berlin, 1989), p 150.

the arbitrator, is likely to reduce their anxiety and animosity towards each other and should result in a decision that will be respected and more likely to be adhered to.

In its 1996 report, the Law Reform Commission proposed a strategy that would involve a combination of measures designed to promote agreement and avoid litigation in order to avoid, as far as possible, the use of procedures which may further damage family relationships, or may cause harm or unnecessary distress to family members, especially children, or may even hinder or deter reconciliation.[14] In addition, the parties may request that the arbitrator address future issues regarding the children, a matter with which the courts are reluctant to become involved.

Indeed, as suggested by Forde,[15] in certain cases the adjudicator may even seek to mediate the dispute.

Choice of Adjudicator

This is probably the most significant advantage of the arbitration process in family matters.

Litigation affords the parties no say in who adjudicates the issues in hand. The appointment of the judge involved is merely dictated by chance. It is a common complaint from clients, professionals in child care matters and, indeed, judges themselves, that childcare matters are extremely complex and conclusions difficult to reach.[16] The judge often has to absorb information amidst an overloaded listing and often amongst other unrelated types of cases. Additionally, the legislature has failed to provide any specific training for members of the judiciary presiding over child-related or family law matters.

The Law Reform Commission has been critical of the lack of such training.[17] Legislation has provided some assistance to the courts when making child-related decisions.[18] Despite this, it is the contention of the Law Reform Commission that

---

[14] LRC report, *op. cit*, para 3.02.

[15] Forde, *Arbitration—Law and Procedure* (Dublin, 1994), p 2.

[16] *O'Shea v Breannan* 387 NYS 2d.

[17] LRC report, *op. cit*, p. ii, suggests that special training is required to deal with such matters as judges dealing with family disputes do not always have the necessary experience or aptitude.

[18] Child Care Act 1991, s 20; Family Law Act 1995, s 47.

the courts lack adequate support services, in particular the independent diagnostic services so important in resolving child-related issues.[19]

Arbitration could, as a matter of course, provide this. The parties involved could choose someone with the relevant experience, skill and expertise to deal with such complex and sensitive matters. In Australia, following recent amendments to their Family Law Regulations, parties can choose to have financial disputes in family matters decided by a private arbitrator instead of a judge or magistrate. A list of approved arbitrators, who must be accredited family law specialists who have completed arbitration training, is provided. A similar system could be employed here, ensuring skilled and highly qualified arbitrators of family issues.

As outlined above, trust and confidence in the arbitrator can result in greater respect for the decision made by the arbitrator.

The Disadvantages of the Arbitration of Domestic Disputes

Parties are not protected by rules of discovery

As outlined above, part of the arbitration agreement will involve deciding on the powers of the arbitrator. Negotiating the terms of the arbitration agreement and ensuring that the agreement provides for discovery would cover this aspect. In other jurisdictions, this is managed by arranging for the arbitrator to supervise discovery or for the parties to complete court-enforced discovery.[20] However, in more complex cases, this might not be achievable.

Arbitrators are not bound by rules of evidence

Similar to above, any arbitration is pursuant to contract and the provisions of the arbitration agreement can provide for the extent to which the arbitrator will follow the rules of evidence thus providing for a relaxation of the strict rules of evidence.

Family law proceedings in Ireland have traditionally been conducted by application of adversarial procedures. However, developments in case law and statutes have led to the judiciary exercising an inquisitorial role when determining some issues of

[19] LRC report, *op. cit.*

[20] Tupman, "Discovery and Evidence in U.S. Arbitration: The Prevailing Views" 44 ARB J 27.

family conflict. Inquisitorial procedures have been particularly applied to proceedings in which the welfare of either party or children is an issue.[21]

Can there be a final and binding determination made by an arbitrator?

This has often been cited as the main disadvantage of using arbitration in family law disputes involving children, given that the intention of such decisions to be binding is an essential characteristic of arbitration. However, this is equally a difficulty for judicial decisions in that custody and access matters are always subject to review.

In the United States, however, case law would indicate reluctance on the part of the family courts to allow such matters to be submitted for arbitration. In most states, husbands and wives are permitted to arbitrate issues of property and alimony, but the courts in those states are not likely to approve binding arbitration of custody and child support. The reasoning for same is that courts usually view themselves as ultimately responsible for protecting a child's welfare *(parens patriae),* a responsibility which they are reluctant to transfer to an outside arbitrator.[22]

A New York appellate court in 1964, in *Sheets v Sheets,* held that parties do have the right to choose arbitration for resolving child custody disputes but reserved the right to conduct a *de novo* review if the decision of the arbitrator might be contrary to the best interests of the child.[23]

The court stated that although the parents could be bound by an arbitrator's decision, the child's interest could never be completely bound by an arbitrator because of the court's continued interest in protecting the child. In addition, the court found that a dissatisfied parent could not challenge the award merely because it "affected the child". It must be shown that that the award "adversely affects the welfare and best interests of the child."[24]

The Supreme Court of North Carolina, in *Crutchley v Crutchley,* stated that while the parties could settle issues of custody and child support by arbitration, such decisions would always be reviewable by the court, given its inherent and statutory authority to protect the interests of *their* children.[25]

---

[21] Shatter, *Family Law* (4th ed, Dublin, 1997), p 116.

[22] Mustill and Boyd, *Commercial Arbitration,* (2nd ed, 1989).

[23] *Sheets v Sheets* 22 A.D.2d 176 (N.Y. App. Div. 1964).

[24] *ibid* at 179.

[25] 293 S.E 2d at 797.

Similar findings have been made by the courts in various other cases, such as *Spencer v Spencer* [26] and *Keim v Keim.*[27]

Despite the seeming trend for the court to retain some kind of supervisory role, intervening when decisions are made contrary to the best interests of the child, it is unclear as to exactly what those circumstances may be and when they may arise.

In *Dick v Dick,*[28] the Michigan Court of Appeals held that arbitration of child custody matters was proper and binding within the meaning of the Uniform Arbitration Act and that the court may only intervene upon allegations of fraud, duress or other undue means. The Court, in this case, treated child custody matters as they would any other matter for arbitration, thus limiting the parties' right of appeal and moving towards the idea of final and binding decisions in arbitration of child custody issues.

The Use of Arbitration by Lawyers

Given the lack of certainty regarding the binding nature of the decisions, it is interesting to note that parties in dispute in the United States continue to use arbitration as a means of resolving domestic disputes, and their lawyers continue to promote the process.

The reasons for this are likely to include the advantages of the process, as outlined above. In addition, the courts have a tendency to rush cases, given the heavy demands on their time and couples can feel that their issues have not been heard, thus heightening their sense of anxiety, making it impossible for the parties to get on amicably, or to reach a compromise. The quick resolution of the dispute by a skilled expert who will "listen to their side of the story" is, in these circumstances, in everyone's interests.

Is there a Future for Arbitration of Child Related Matters?

Uncertainty as to the binding nature of decisions in the arbitration of family disputes may not be the longer-term position of the courts. As seen in *Dick v Dick,*[29] arbitration decisions are rarely overturned, and only in circumstances where the

[26] 494 A.2d 1279 (D.C. Cir 1985).

[27] 623 N.E. 2d 39 (Ohio 1993).

[28] *Dick v Dick* 534 N.W. 2d 185 (Mich Ct App 1995).

[29] *ibid.*

decisions are erroneous and in direct conflict with the best interests of the child. The judge in *Faherty v Faherty*[30] outlined the fact that family courts are, at present, reluctant to relinquish their protection over the child, but as they gain experience in the arbitration of child support and custody disputes, it may become evident that a child's best interests are as well protected by an arbitrator as by a judge. The ultimate finding in *Dick v Dick*[31] showed a definite move towards affording decisions of arbitration in family matters the binding nature afforded to other, non-family matters.

Whether or not arbitration will continue to be used as an alternative method of dispute resolution will largely depend on the viewpoint of the lawyers involved. In reality, if they do not endorse the process, it is hardly likely that clients will utilise it.

The American Academy of Matrimonial Lawyers undertook a survey of 1,500 of its members in the autumn of 1996.[32] The survey was posted to the members and consisted of both multiple choice questions and open-ended questions. Of these, 123 were returned. Some 67 of these attorneys responded that arbitration was used in their jurisdiction.

The survey indicated that arbitration is most frequently used to resolve economic issues, such as property division issues (100 respondents), and less so for spousal support (54) and child support (48). The use of arbitration to resolve child custody or visitation matters was not as popular an option (35). This is not surprising, given the uncertainty surrounding the binding nature of the arbitrator's decision in such cases.

More than half of the respondents (57) found that the parties could agree to make the decision binding in their jurisdiction, with a small number (20) finding that the decision was not always binding.

In general, it was found that arbitration in relation to family disputes, where it was available, was well received.

---

30 477 A. 2d 1257 (N.J. 1984) at 1263.

31 *op. cit*, n 28.

32 Available in its entirety from University of Missouri-Kansas City, School of Law 5100, Rockfield Road, Kansas City, MO.

Conclusion

In order for a viable family law arbitration process to be put in place in Ireland, it is imperative that the arbitrator be an expert in the field of family law and childcare matters, and thus ensure that decisions are made in the child's best interests. These experts could be drawn from the ranks of a number of professions with skills, training and experience in family law and child care matters.[33]

Although decisions of arbitrators in family disputes do not necessarily require the supervision or review of the courts, it is probable that the courts would retain some supervisory role, as discussed above. Perhaps the appointment of a skilled and qualified *guardian ad litem* (as in current complex child care cases) to represent the interests and wishes of the child in the arbitration process would go some way to bolstering confidence in the arbitration process. Current legislation, which provides for a limited right of access to the High Court to set aside a decision or to refer a matter by way of case stated to the High Court, could be utilised in child care matters also or perhaps the legislation could be amended to allow for a referral to the Circuit Family Court in order to minimise costs. This could provide parties with some right of appeal in circumstances where the decision of the arbitrator is irrational or perverse, where the arbitrator was found to have misconducted the arbitration or where the there is gross injustice on the face of the decision itself.[34] In the absence of such a finding, the courts would, as is the case in other matters subject to the arbitration process, be very reluctant to intervene. Where cases are already before the court, a stay could be applied for,[35] as in non-family matters, allowing that court to then confirm the arbitrator's decision, leaving it subject to enforcement like any other judgment of the court.

Given the qualifications that arbitrators would ideally possess, they would be well placed to decide not only on the less contentious, less emotional issues involved in family disputes, such as property division and financial matters, but also on the more delicate issues, such as custody and access, which require a degree of inter-personal skills and sensitivity.

However, there would be little point in this reform unless the concerns raised in this essay were addressed, namely, that arbitrators had the specialist knowledge in family law, there was a discovery process, and that there was some state founded service

---

33 This adherence to the law would naturally incorporate the best interests of the child.

34 *Doyle v Kildare County Council* [1995] 2 IR 424.

35 Under s 5 of the 1980 Act.

providing for child professionals such as psychologists or other specialists to assist in custody and access disputes.

Parties should have a right to choose their own method of dispute resolution. This, coupled with the advantages of arbitration as an alternative method of dispute resolution, as outlined above, both in relation to the parties involved, the children of those parties and, indeed, the state, the arbitration of family disputes is an option that is worthy of consideration.

Commercial Law

by
Audrey Huggard*

Sections 16 to 18 of the Sale of Goods Act 1893 (the "1893 Act") contain a number of legal rules which govern the time and circumstances in which property passes from a seller to a buyer of goods. To those who have not come across the concept of passing of property, I ought to explain that the location of property plays a crucial role in determining the legal rights of the parties to a contract for the sale of goods.[1] Furthermore our law, as it stands, recognises that property may pass from a seller to a buyer of goods long before the goods are delivered.[2] Sections 16 to 18 of the 1893 Act specify exactly when this may happen. Before delving any further, this is perhaps an apt time to explore how and why the legal rules governing the passing of property have come to have such an important role in our legal system.

The impetus behind the creation of the concept of passing of property stems from the fact that when disputes arise between buyers and sellers it is the courts who were called upon to resolve these disputes with answers to questions about legal rights such as:

- Which party bears the risk of loss or damage to the goods?
- Has a seller a right to demand the price of the damaged or lost goods from the buyer?

---

* This essay was awarded first place in the Law Society of Ireland, *Student Law Reform Essay Competition 2003.*

1 For instance, should the seller become insolvent before delivery of the goods, a buyer will be entitled to claim the goods if property has passed. If property has not passed the buyer will have to share the goods with the insolvent sellers other creditors.

2 See reference to Atiyah, who contrasts what he sees as our general rule that property passes when contractual terms are agreed upon with the general rule under Roman law that property passes on delivery.

- Has a buyer a right to claim the goods from an insolvent seller?

Early common law judges provided answers by reference to the location of property. But how did this common law concept become a statutory one? For a long time it has been widely acknowledged that legal certainty is an imperative if our commercial world is to operate effectively and efficiently as it allows definite procedures to be followed and costly litigation to be avoided. Towards the end of the nineteenth century most agreed the legal rules governing the sale of goods as embodied in the common law, that is various judicial decisions recorded from the time of King Edward III, were too fragmentary to meet the requirement of legal certainty.[3] In an attempt to introduce greater legal certainty, Sir Mackenzie Chalmers[4] sought to clarify the sale of goods aspect of commercial law by converting it from a common law based subject to a statutory one. While the fruit of his efforts, the 1893 Act, did not dramatically alter the pre-existing legal rules governing the sale of goods, it did convert the subject from a common law to a statutory, or codified, one. Codification rendered the legal rules governing the sale of goods more accessible and simplified the process of legal reasoning.[5] The third advantage of the 1893 Act was ensuring that a standard set of legal rules existed throughout the United Kingdom, as the Scottish common law, which the 1893 Act also superseded, was based on principles of Roman law, unlike its English and Irish counterparts.

Thus, the pre-existing common law concept of the passing of property came to play a "pivotal"[6] role in the Sale of Goods Act 1893. Most accept that the 1893 Act benefited the commercial community of the late nineteenth century by making, amongst other things, the legal rules governing the time and circumstances in which property passes less fragmentary. A little over a century later, this paper sets out the following:

(i) first, the existing legal rules governing the passing of property;
(ii) secondly, why the traditional legal concept of the passing of an explanation as to property and the existing legal rules are not suitable to govern commercial transactions in Ireland today; and

[3] There was voluminous case law on certain topics which was at times irreconcilable. Other topics, on the other hand, lacked judicial decisions as for years they did not arise for authoritative decision.
[4] 1847–1919. During his lifetime Chalmers codified three areas of English commercial law, namely: sales law; banking; and marine insurance.
[5] Judges no longer had to trawl through masses of case law to find the answers to legal problems before them as the judicial approach to interpreting codifying statutes did not favour recourse to pre-existing case law. See *Bank of England v Vagliano Brothers* (1891) AC 107.
[6] Goode, *Proprietary Rights & Insolvency in Sales Contracts* (1985) p 12.

(iii) thirdly, an examination of the reform options open to our Parliament (the "Oireachtas").

Sections 16 to 18 of the 1893 Act—The Existing Legal Rules

Section 17 of the 1893 Act lays down the general principle that property passes in accordance with the parties' intentions provided the goods are ascertained.[7] Goods can be said to be ascertained when they have been identified as the goods to be used in the performance of the contract.[8] The qualification to the s 17 general principle is reinforced by s 16 of the 1893 Act, which provides that property cannot pass before unascertained goods are ascertained. Section 16 has been interpreted as a fundamental rule of law which cannot be contracted out of.

Should a court be unable to discern the intentions of the parties in circumstances where the intention of the parties as to when property passes is paramount (i.e. where the goods have been ascertained) a number of presumptive rules can be found in s 18 of the 1893 Act to aid a court. For instance, s 18, r 1 of the 1893 Act is useful where there has been an unconditional sale[9] of specific goods. In those circumstances

---

[7]Although the term ascertained goods is referred to in the 1893 Act, it is not defined. On the other hand, specific goods are defined in s 61(1) of the 1893 Act to mean "goods identified and agreed upon at the time of the contract of sale". By a process of elimination it can thus be inferred that ascertained goods are goods identified as the goods to be used in the performance of the contract subsequent to contractual agreement.

[8] This can be done in one of three ways, namely (i) by the parties themselves (see *re Stapleton Fletcher* (1994) WLR 1181 where the contract goods, cases of wine, were found to have been appropriated by the parties when physically separated from the sellers trading assets) (ii) by the operation of the legal presumption in s 18, rule 5 of the 1893 Act if the intention of the parties is unclear and (iii) by the operation of a doctrine, known as exhaustion, developed by the English High Court in *Wait & James v Midland Bank* (1926) 31 Com Cas 172 and endorsed by the House of Lords in *The Elafi* (1982) ER 208 (note in *Wait & James v Midland Bank* (1926) ascertainment was found to have taken place when a bulk of 1250 quarters of wheat was reduced to 850 quarters (the quantity due to the buyer under the contract) after all the other purchasers had taken their respective quantities from the bulk.

[9] Chanel J's broad interpretation of a conditional sale in *Varley v Whip* (1900) QB 573 has been widely critiqued. Atiyah suggests the court adopted this "forced interpretation" in order to avoid the conclusion that property had passed because under the pre-existing law the right to reject the goods was lost once the property had passed. He argues that if the same facts arose today, the court ought to conclude property had passed. Conditional contract should be confined to those subject to a condition precedent.

if the intention of the parties is not obvious the court may presume property in the goods passed at the time the contract was made or agreed regardless of time of payment and delivery.

Section 18, rr 2 to 4 of the 1893 Act deal with conditional sales of specific goods. There, if the intention of the parties is not obvious, the presumed intent differs depending on the type of conditional sale. Thus, if the contract goods have been identified at the time of contractual agreement, the intention of the parties is unclear as to when property passes and:

(i) the goods are not in a deliverable state, r 2 allows the court to presume property does not pass until the buyer has notice that the goods are in a deliverable state;[10]

(ii) the goods are in a deliverable state but the seller is bound to weigh or do some other act to the goods to fix the price, r 3 indicates it ought to be presumed property does not pass until the buyer has notice the action in question has been performed;

(iii) the goods are supplied on a sale or return basis, sale on approval basis or on similar terms, r 4 indicates the court should presume property has passed if the contract of bailment coupled with the option to buy becomes a contract of sale. This will happen if the buyer signifies his approval or acceptance by word[11] or action. Sub-rule 4 (2) deems a contract of sale to have been created if the buyer fails to signify his approval or acceptance within a reasonable time.[12]

Finally, s 18, r 5 of the 1893 Act deals with situations where previously ascertained goods have been ascertained. In the absence of any evidence of the parties' intention as to when the property in the goods is to pass, s 18, r 5 permits a court to presume property was intended to pass at the moment the unascertained goods are unconditionally[13] appropriated by one party for the performance of the contract

[10] This terms definition in s 62 of the 1893 Act is not comprehensive: *Underwood Ltd v Burgh Castle Brick* (1922) KB 343.

[11] In *Atari Corporation Ltd* (1998) LWLR 66 the English courts considered the form and standard notices of rejection should take and at what stage must the goods be made available for collection.

[12] Sub-rule 4(2) does not apply where the goods are detained by someone for whose acts the buyer is not responsible (for example, the buyers creditors): See *re Ferrier* (1944) Ch 295.

[13] Contrast conditional appropriation where the party performing the act of appropriation reserves the right to substitute the goods. Section 19 of the 1893 Act deals with some important types of conditional appropriation.

with the assent[14] of the other party. Sub-rule 5(2) of the 1893 Act provides an illustration of where the goods may be considered unconditionally appropriated to a contract, namely where goods are delivered to a carrier for shipment to the buyer.[15]

Why Irish Law, as Embodied in Sections 16 to 18 of the 1893 Act, Does not Serve the Needs of Modern Commerce in Ireland

Section 16 and Quasi-Specific Goods[16]

As we have discovered s 16 of the 1893 Act prevents property passing until the goods are ascertained no matter what the parties might otherwise intend. This fundamental rule has given rise to much debate regarding the statutory protection, or lack of it, offered to a pre-paid purchaser of a quantity of unascertained goods forming part of a bulk identified in the contract, such as a cargo or warehouse for instance. The classic illustration of how the rule can defy commercial expectations is illustrated by *Re Wait.*[17] In *Re Wait* the buyer paid the seller, Wait, for 500 tons of wheat in advance of delivery. It was agreed his order was to come from a 1000 tonne cargo being shipped aboard the Challenger. Wait went bankrupt four days before the Challenger docked. Although the buyer had not received a bill of lading or any other document of title representing the goods, the buyer assumed property had passed giving the buyer a better claim than Wait's other creditors to the 500 tons of wheat. But the buyer was mistaken as the operation of s 16 of the 1893 Act prevented property passing as his 500 tons had not been ascertained from the 1000 ton bulk.[18] This

[14] As Goode points out, appropriation is a contractual act therefore is only effective if carried out in conformity with the contract. If the seller purports to appropriate goods different to those specified in the contract, the appropriation is ineffective unless the buyer has given or subsequently assents (for example, by dispatching an invoice) to the change of identity. *Commercial Law* (1995), p 221.

[15] Sub-rule 5(2) must be read subject to s 16 of the 1893 Act. *Healy v Howlett* (1917) B 337 is used by Atiyah to illustrate this point—seller delivers the goods to the carrier but no property passed the fact (even though delivery to a carrier had earlier been held to amount to unconditional appropriation) as the goods were unascertained: Sale of Goods (1998), p 329.

[16] This is the term used by Goode to describe unascertained goods forming part of an identified bulk, such as a cargo or warehouse, as opposed to wholly unascertained goods whose source is not be identified in the contract. Commercial Law (1995), chap 6.

[17] (1937) CH 606. See also the Scottish case of *Hayman v McLintock* (1907) SC 936.

[18] The buyer was a mere unsecured creditor battling other creditors to obtain the money he paid over.

meant Wait's creditors enjoyed a windfall as s 16 of the 1893 Act permitted them to retain the 500 tons of wheat as well as the buyer's purchase moneys.

Agreement to buy specific quantities of goods from bulk has become increasingly popular in recent years as advances in technology have led to ships and therefore cargoes becoming larger, and cash flow problems in recent years have led buyers to prefer to make frequent purchases of small quantities rather than carry large reserves.[19] While the average commercial trader probably presumes these agreements pose no particular problems, a number of decisions of the English courts endorsing the result in *Re Wait, Re Gosforth*[20] and *Re London Wine Shippers Ltd*,[21] for instance, have shattered any such presumptions for English traders. Although the decisions of the English courts are not binding on the Irish courts they will be regarded as persuasive authorities should the matter come before the Irish courts. Given that there are no Irish authorities on the matter, *Re Gosforth* and *Re London Wine Shippers Ltd* highlight that prepaid buyers of quantities of goods from cargoes and warehouses are more than likely to be left victims to fortune due to the operation of s 16 of the 1893 Act. A leading commentator, Goode, describes the latter case as a

> "graphic illustration of the risks run by a buyer who purchases or a bank which lends on the security of an unidentified part of bulk and leaves it in storage with the seller or third party without ensuring its segregation and appropriation to purchasers or security interest".[22]

The offering of this s 16 type statutory protection to pre-paid buyers of quantity from bulk cannot be in the interests of Irish commerce as it can only repel international traders from concluding contracts in Ireland in favour of the commercial convenience of concluding agreements in other jurisdictions which now offer greater protection.[23]

---

[19] These concerns were identified by the English Law Commission their report on a "*Right to Goods in Bulk*" WP No 112(89), para 1.2.

[20] (1985) Sen S 91. Where the buyer received a bill of lading in respect of pellets aboard the Gosforth without payment. The prepaid sub-buyers were given a delivery note in respect of their quantities. When the buyer failed to pay the price the sub-buyers were unable to claim their goods from the seller as no property had passed due to the operation of s 16 of the 1893 Act.

[21] (1986) PCC 121, where Oliver J rejected the prepaid buyers argument that lack of precise identification was no barrier to their claim based on s 16 of the 1893 Act.

[22] Proprietary Rights & Insolvency in Sales Transaction (1989), p 25.

[23] In England, Germany, Canada and the US.

In the domestic context, traders will either have to avoid buying from bulk as a method of trading or obtain costly legal advice on how to draft suitably worded contracts, as developed in England, to avoid the harsh effects of s 16 of the 1893 Act which either stipulate:

(a) any advance payments will be held on trust for the buyer in a separate bank account. This means that in the event of the seller becoming insolvent it would give the buyer a proprietary interest in the trust fund as a beneficiary under the trust;[24]

(b) the sellers' bank will provide a bond guaranteeing repayment in the event of insolvency; or

(c) the presumption in s 20(1) of the 1893 Act, which in the absence of evidence of a contrary intention allows a court to presume the parties intended that the risk passes with property, does not apply to their contract which would give the buyer the insurable interest required to obtain insurance.

While these precautions go some way towards ameliorating the harsh effect of s 16 of the 1893 Act on pre-paid buyer of quasi-specific goods,[25] they nevertheless cost pre-paid buyers time, money and convenience. Trading on the basis of such "legally sophisticated terms"[26] should not be burdened upon our domestic traders. Guidance should be taken from other jurisdictions that now offer more efficient procedures to conclude bargains.

A wider commercial concern that has been mooted is that s 16 of the 1893 Act threatens the common commercial practice whereby a buyer offers documents of title such as a bill of lading[27] to a bank as a security for a loan.[28] The question arising is whether these documents of title relate to unidentified goods in an identified bulk if the parties intended title should pass with this document. If the goods form an

---

[24] *Re Kayford Ltd (in liquidation)* (1975) ER 604.

[25] Burns, "Better Late Than Never" (1996) MLR 260 at p 272.

[26] Scottish & English law Commissions Report 1993, para 3.7.

[27] In general this is perceived to be a document of title in the commercial sector. Note in *Sewell v Burdick* (1884) AC 74 the House of Lords held that bills of lading in the legal arena represent possession and not ownership but that possession raises the presumption of ownership.

[28] See Burns, "Better Late Than Never" (1996) MLR 260 at p 261. An example of a case giving cause for concern is *Re London Wine Shippers Ltd* (1986) PCC 121, where the buyers believed the delivery notes they were given represented the title documents of the goods.

unidentified part of an identified bulk s 16 of the 1893 Act means this question must be answered in the negative and thus frustrates the parties' intentions.

Section 18

Commentators[29] criticise r 1 as it is not necessarily appropriate for the law to presume property has passed to an unwitting consumer[30] at the moment of contract. Their household insurance is unlikely to protect them against the risk of loss or damage to the goods before delivery. However, the risk could be covered with little extra cost to the seller. Therefore, unsurprisingly "in modern times very little is needed to give rise to the intention that the property in specific goods is to pass only on delivery or payment".[31] Rule 2 does give the buyer time to arrange insurance but perhaps it would be better in the interests of certainty if "deliverable state" defined more comprehensively. Rule 3 seems somewhat pointless as it is difficult to imagine circumstances in which the presumption will not be displaced by evidence of contrary intention. Like all such provisions it should perhaps be abolished as it only causes uncertainty. Rule 4 meets the needs of commerce as it provides both parties with protection against various commercial risks,[32] but the diverging interpretation of "unconditional appropriation" contained in rule 5 causes uncertainty as to what action suffices to constitute unconditional[33] appropriation.[34]

---

29 Bradgate, *Commercial Law* (2002).

30 On the other hand, it could be argued traders ought to be aware of the Acts, "policy" that property passes on contract. Risk will be presumed to pass with property under s 20(1) of the 1893 Act. This will enable them to insure against the risk of loss or damage to the goods before delivery as they will have an insurable interest.

31 Per Lord Diplock in *RV Ward v Bignall* (1967).

32 Sealey maintains this is re enforced by the English Court of Appeals interpretation of what constitutes an effective notice of rejection in *Atari Corporation* (1998). See his case note at (1998) CLJ 451.

33 English and Irish authorities appear to be out of sync in relation as to what constitutes unconditional appropriation. In *Hendy v Lennox* (1984) 2 ER 152 the English Courts found the generators were unconditionally appropriated to the contract in question when their serial numbers were communicated to the buyers by phone. However, Walsh J appears to be implicitly rejecting such a conclusion in *Flynn v Macken*, where it was found the question had not been unconditionally appropriated to the contract despite the fact its registration number was communicated by phone to the buyer. Such divergence in interpretation is apt to cause confusion in a sector which thrives on certainty.

34 Courts have also had difficulty attempting to define what action suffices to constitute appropriation. In *Carlos Federspiel* (1957) LR 240, Pearson J suggested "usually but not necessarily, the appropriating act is the last act to be performed by the seller."

Reform Options Open to the Oireachtas—Modernisation of the Existing Rules or More Radical Reform

Sections 16 to 18 of the 1893 Act have not been amended or reformed since their enactment, which means the rules governing the passing of property in Irish law have remained unchanged for a staggering 111 years. Commercial practice, on the other hand, has undergone rapid advancement over the last 100 years due to technological and communications developments. I have attempted to prove that these stagnant rules are incompatible with the needs of the modern commercial world as they fail to meet the needs of modern commerce and, indeed, hinder commercial transactions in certain circumstances. The legislator in England and other countries whose sales law was modelled on the Sale of Goods Act 1893 have acknowledged that these traditional rules governing the passing of property are inadequate in facilitating commercial transactions. Those jurisdictions have taken different steps towards reform. Perhaps it is time the Oireachtas took a look at their experiences for inspiration and guidance. If it does so, it will discover there are two options open to it. The first is to modify the concept of the passing of property. The second is to abandon the concept altogether. Both "options" will now be briefly outlined.

Option One—Modify the Rules Regarding the Passing of Property

A leading commentator, Atiyah, has observed that "[t]he Sale of Goods adopted the policy of allowing property to be transferred by contract alone, and then contained many elaborate provisions designed to reverse the practical effects of that policy".[35] In light of his view that the exceptions to this policy "sometimes seem to eat up the rule", earlier editions of Atiyah's text book suggested this unsatisfactory state of affairs could be remedied by altering the current policy that property passes on contractual agreement. The alternative policy he pointed to is to be found in a maxim developed by Roman law: *maxim traditionibus et usucapionibus non nudis pactis, transfunctur verum domincia,* whereby the general rule would be that property passes on delivery of the contract goods as opposed to when the contract was merely agreed upon. It should be noted that actual delivery was not always necessary under Roman law as there was recognition of constructive delivery of the contract goods on delivery of the documents of title. As mentioned earlier, the 1893 Act was extended to replace the Scottish common law on sale of goods, which was based on this principle of Roman

[35] Atiyah, *Sale of Goods* (1998), p 314.

law.[36] It is interesting to note that many Scottish jurists have criticised that extension.[37] They argued that many of the inadequacies of the statutory rules governing the passing of property, such as the lack of protection offered to pre-paid buyers of quasi-specific goods, would not have arisen under the Scottish common law. Contributors to later editions of Atiyah's textbook seem to have abandoned Atiyah's suggested substitution of the Roman general rule to the concept of passing of property as many of the problems generated by the current rules on the passing of property and will not be eliminated by such a change. Nevertheless, it is argued that the Oireachtas ought to consider this option of reform as it appears that the Roman rules will at least reduce the exceptions and commercial inadequacies of the current policy and rules respectively.[38]

Turning our attention to s 16 of the 1893 Act, one wonders should we abolish this provision given the injustices and the commercial harm it is capable of giving rise to if sophisticated drafting is not utilised to avoid its effects? If we struck s 16 of the 1893 Act from the statute books we would allow property to pass in unascertained goods when the parties so intend. This would be an unwise course of action given it is widely accepted that the rationale behind s 16—namely one cannot say to what one's proprietary interest attaches until one can identify those goods—is sensible for wholly unascertained goods. This is reflected in Lord Mustill's observation "common sense dictates that the buyer cannot acquire title until it is known to what goods the title relates".[39] Nevertheless, concern has been raised about the plight of the prepaid buyers of wholly unascertained goods whose seller goes bankrupt before the goods are ascertained. The risks facing those buyers are illustrated by the facts of *re Goldcorp*,[40] where over 100 New Zealanders were persuaded by colourful sales literature to buy gold from Goldcorp Ltd. Upon payment no gold was handed over but each customer was given a certificate which described him as the owner of the gold bought. It also promised that the company would keep sufficient stocks of gold to meet its obligations but that it would be held on a non-allocated basis. When the seller became insolvent the pre-paid buyers were deemed to be mere unsecured creditors due to the operation of s 16 of the 1893 Act, given that no gold had ever been appropriated to any of the contracts. As the bank had a floating charge over the

---

36 See above.

37 See Burns, "Better Late Than Never" (1996) MLR at p 261.

38 Note under the US Universal Commercial Code risk generally follows the passing of possession. See $2–509.

39 In *Re Goldcorp* (1995) AC 74.

40 (1995) AC 74.

company assets, it was given priority as a secured creditor to the company's stocks of gold. The prepaid buyers were left deprived of both their gold and their purchase price. This unjust result has led one commentator to suggest that in the absence of provisions permitting property to pass in such circumstances the legislator should enable the courts to infer a floating trust[41] in favour of the buyer.

The rationale behind s 16 of the 1893 Act does not have as much force when it comes to quasi-specific goods as one can identify the bulk, albeit contained in cargo or a warehouse, to which one's proprietary interest should attach.[42] Given that the courts are reluctant to upset the statutory rules of insolvency distribution,[43] the Oireachtas could make a policy choice to give the pre-paid buyers of identified bulk priority over other creditors. One method of doing this is to follow the English modification of the rules regarding the passing concept of property in 1995. This option of reform would amend s 16 rather than abolish it entirely.

The enactment of the English and Scottish Law Reform Commission's recommendations has been described as "a balancing act; by limiting the reform to pre-paying buyers from an identified bulk, this would not affect the insolvency rules too severely but would satisfy the main concerns of international traders."[44] The

41 Described as "been reminiscent of a banks floating charge over the company's assets but, in contrast would not be disclosed" by Ulph in her article, "Sale of Goods Act 1995" (1996) LMCLQ 93 at p 96.

42 Note dicta in *re Wait* suggests an equitable interest in favour of the bulk will arise where the contract is for the purchase of a share (as opposed to a specific quantity) of the bulk. In that case counsel for the buyer tried to avoid the harsh effects of s 16 of the 1893 Act by arguing that the buyer had an equitable interest over the 500 tons of wheat by relying on comments of Lord Watson in *Taliboy v Official Receiver* suggesting although the common law (existing prior to 1893) required goods to be ascertained before property could pass, equity was less stringent. Aitken LJ rejected the buyer's argument by stating the equitable doctrine of *Taliboy* did not apply to a contract to purchase a specific quantity of goods contained in an identified bulk but did concede that an equitable interest could arise if the contract specifically referred to the fact it was an agreement to buy a share of the bulk. If the Irish courts follow this English authority, it appears a co-ownership could arise in the interim period before the goods are ascertained with the aid of a suitably drafted contract, for example, if the contract indicated I am to purchase half the cargo I would have an entitlement to the bulk as tenant in common. On the other hand, if it stated I was to purchase 1/2kg from the cargo, no proprietary interest would arise.

43 At present the prepaid buyer of a quantity of quasi-specific good is a mere unsecured creditor if the seller becomes insolvent. His creditors enjoy a "windfall". Due to the operation of s 16 of the 1893 Act, they are entitled to maintain the goods as well as the buyers purchase moneys. See Goode, *Proprietary Rights & Insolvency in Sale Transaction* (1989), p 26.

44 Ulph, "Sale of Goods Act 1995" (1996) LMCLQ 93.

English Sale of Goods (Amendment) Act 1995 (the "1995 Act") permits an interim statutory proprietary interest[45] in an identified bulk[46] to arise in favour of the prepaid buyer of quantity, pending the passing of property. Section 20A of the 1893 Act, as amended, provides that should the bulk be smaller than anticipated, the buyer's interest in the bulk will be reduced proportionately. Section 20B of the 1893 Act, as amended, highlights the difference between this statutory interim interest and an equitable interim interest capable of arising prior to 1995.[47] The statutory interim interest does not require the consent of his interim co-owners to deal with his interest. Thus, buyers who take delivery are not liable to his interim co-owners should there be a shortfall in their subsequent delivery.[48] The Act does not alter s 17 of the 1893 Act, which means the parties can still agree property will not pass until payment. Section 18, r 4 provides that goods can be ascertained once the bulk is reduced by a process of exhaustion to the quantity the buyer had agreed to buy or to the aggregate of the quantities due to the buyer under separate contracts giving statutory recognition to the third method of ascertainment developed by the courts in cases such as *Wait & James* and the *Elafi*.[49]

It must be pointed out that the "English solution" to the inadequacies of ss 16 to 18 of the 1893 Act is directed specifically at solving the prepaid buyers of goods in bulk problem rather than reforming the law in a wider context.[50] One should not be under any allusions that the these type of prepaid buyers are now offered absolute statutory protection having regard to the fact:

(i) Under s 18, r 3, prepaid buyers of a quantity of goods forming part of a bulk will not be protected from the "rogue" seller who subsequently sells their undivided share to a bona fida purchaser without notice as under s 24 of the 1893 Act the second buyer will obtain good title. The first prepaid buyer will be unable liable to claim the goods from the second buyer. His only remedy is to sue the "rogue" seller (if he can still be found!) for non-delivery.[51]

---

[45] The buyer is entitled to an undivided share of the bulk as a tenant in common.

[46] A sellers stock does *not* come within the definition of bulk under the 1995 Act.

[47] See above.

[48] This section was considered necessary for "commercial convenience as a carrier cannot be expected to check the whole bulk before releasing it…[it also]means liquidators or other officers will not be sued in conversion by co-owners"—per Gullifer, "Constructive Possession " (1999) LMCLQ 93.

[49] See above.

[50] So prepaid buyers, such as those in *re Goldcorp*, would not be offered protection under the 1995 Act.

[51] See further, Ulph, "Sale of Goods Act 1995..." (1996) LMCLQ 93.

(ii) There is no special statutory adjustment scheme for shortfalls which might be triggered on insolvency. Although the Scottish and English Law Reform Commission did consider three possible schemes,[52] they were all rejected in its recommendations. It foresaw these complex schemes proving to be highly difficult for the courts and insolvency practitioners to operate and burdensome in terms of time and money. But as Burns[53] points out, this leaves these types of prepaid buyers who suffer a shortfall in their expected delivery vulnerable to the prospect of great loss. Delays in delivery and subsequent court action against the seller will be costly in terms of time and money. The rule governing this interim statutory co-ownership can be displaced if the parties stipulate their contractual obligations as co-owners. But drafting such legally sophisticated contracts, although perhaps not as cumbersome as their 1995 counterparts, still cost in terms of convenience, time and money.

Option Two—Abandon the Concept of the Passing of Property

The location of property has a long history in the common law as being the "chief determinant"[54] for the allocation of legal rights arising from a contract for the sale of goods. As mentioned earlier, this conceptual approach survived the enactment of the Sale of Goods Act 1893 and remains the governing concept in Irish sales law today. This conceptual approach has the advantage of flexibility in resolving disputes where novel questions are referred to the courts. The *Span Terza*[55] provides an example of the concepts ability to meet new legal problems. There, the House of Lords answered the question as to who owned the fuel oil on board chartered vessels (namely the charterer or the mortgagee) by reference to the fact that property had not passed on sale to the ship owners. Therefore, the charterer still owned the oil and had a better claim than the mortgagees.

However, the concept also has its disadvantages. Atiyah[56] points to the fact the exceptions at times appear to eat up the general rule resulting in somewhat complex

---

52 The three schemes were as follows: (A) a statutory *pro rata* apportionment scheme to be administered by insolvency office holders; (B) a statutory monetary adjustment scheme between co-owning buyers; and (C) legislation giving the courts the powers to make equitable adjustments amongst co-owning buyers.

53 "Better Late Than Never" (1996) MLR 260.

54 *ibid.*

55 (1984) LR 119.

56 *Sale of Goods Act* (1998), p 314.

legal rules. Many feel the concept is outdated as it fails to meet the needs of modern commercial traders. This criticism carries strong force in particular circumstances; the risk faced by pre-paid buyers of unidentified goods forming part of an identified bulk is a stark example. Karl Llewylln[57] regarded reference to the concept as being a "silly issue"[58] and inappropriate in determining the legal consequences of commercial transactions. He favoured the legal abandonment of what he saw as the over-reliance on a concept in governing the economic well-being of society. His proposed alternative was a functionalist approach. The functionalist approach answered questions about the legal rights of the parties to a contract for the sale of goods by reference to the specific policy considerations involved, totally divorced from the concept of property. Perhaps the classic example of legislatures abandoning this conceptual approach in favour of the functionalist approach is the adoption of the Universal Commercial Code ("the UCC") across the United States in the 1950s. I will briefly outline why this option of reform was chosen and how the Code operates in practice.

The original model sales law of the United States was contained in the Sales Act 1906 and incorporated much of the Sale of Goods Act 1893; thus the concept of passing of property was the model method of determining the legal consequences arising from the contract for the sale of goods.[59] Shortly after World War II the American commercial sector became increasingly unhappy with the rules governing the passing of property. These rules tended to produce legal answers contrary to commercial expectations and were not being interpreted in a uniform manner from State to State. It was agreed reform of these rules would be required to make them more sensitive to meet changing commercial patterns. The National Conference on Uniform State Laws[60] was charged with the task of reforming the law. Initial plans to merely modernise the rules were abandoned in favour of undertaking a more radical reform when it decided to place Llewellyn in charge of constructing his proposed Commercial Code, which was seen as the best method of modernising and

---

[57] 1893–1962. He was amongst the concept's, bitterest critics as a member of the American realist school of jurisprudence.

[58] "Through Title to Contract and Beyond a Bit" (1937–1962) NYULR 159.

[59] While generally following the English 1893 Act, the 1906 Act did take a different stance on the protection offered to prepaid buyer of a quantity of unidentified goods from an identified bulk. Section 6 of the Model Sales Act 1906 provided the buyer became an owner in common of the bulk. This reflected the policy choice that it was unjustified to allow the seller's creditors enjoy a windfall. Section 6(2) gave statutory recognition to exhaustion, the third process of ascertainment (See above).

[60] Established in the late nineteenth century on the prompting of the American Bar Association, which felt it desirable to have particular points regulated identically in all States. Each State is required to send three representatives.

simplifying the law. Under this Code the intentions of the parties are paramount. Only if the parties fail to answer the questions arising from the dispute in their contract is recourse to the answers provided by the Code necessary. It took almost ten years for the code to be drawn up. In 1952 the first draft was submitted to thousands of merchants, commercial agents, bailment carriers and warehousemen for comment and criticism. In 1956 the final version appeared and was adopted in its entirety by all the States except Louisiana.

I will furnish two examples of how the UCC tackles two commercial concerns alluded to in this essay in its step by step manner, providing answers based on sound policy considerations:

(i) the first relates to the position of a prepaid buyer of a quantity of goods within an identified bulk. Most would agree it would be unjustified to allow the seller's creditors to enjoy a windfall at the expense of such a buyer by allowing them to keep the goods as well as the purchase price. After due consideration it was decided the policy choice reflected in s 6 of the 1906 Act ought to be retained;[61] and

(ii) the second relates to whether documents of title may relate to portions of an identified bulk. Most would agree it ought to in order to facilitate the speed of commercial transactions in which time can cost money due to fluctuating prices, depending on the supply and demand of the goods. In addition, it would facilitate the commercial practice whereby buyers give documents of title as security for a loan advanced. After due consideration it was decided documents of title over part of the bulk should be as effective as documents of title over ascertained goods.[62]

Conclusion

This paper started by explaining how the rules on the passing of property came and continue to play such a crucial role in the main body of sales law in Ireland, the Sale

---

61 Therefore $2–105(4) provides "an individual share in a an identified bulk of fungible goods is sufficiently identified to be sold although the quantity of the bulk is not determined, any agreed portion of such bulk of any quantity…may to the extent of the sellers interest be sold to the buyer who then becomes the tenant in common".

62 See $1–201(15).

of Goods Act 1893. While no doubt their incorporation was welcomed by the commercial world in 1893, their stagnancy places a legal hurdle in the path of Irish commercial development in 2005. So these rules are in need of reform.

We must look at what reform has brought to commercial and legal practice of other countries in the common law world, particularly England, the United States and Canada. We can also seek guidance on how to answer our problems from those countries who have faced similar decisions in the past. The American "answer" has the potential to deal with these problems in a more coherent and comprehensive manner. The construction of a similar Irish Code will require a commitment of more time, resources and effort than the English "answer."Should we choose to allow the concept of the passing of property to continue to govern the Irish commercial scene, a more comprehensive modification of this concept than undertaken by English in 1995 deserves consideration. Perhaps we ought to look at the principles of Roman law in this regard. Openness to new ideas and new perspectives will ultimately benefit Irish commerce and thus the economic well-being of society as a whole. For that, reform would be worthwhile.

Losing Nemo?
Reform of the *Nemo Dat* Rule in Ireland

by
Cliona Kelly*

Introduction

If S, in possession of goods with the consent of their owner O, wrongfully sells them to an innocent third party, B, and then absconds or becomes insolvent, there is left the dilemma of who, between the two innocent parties, owns the goods.[1] The conflict that arises is essentially one between the protection of the rights of the original owner and the promotion of certainty and finality in commercial transactions. These two interests have "striven for mastery" in the development of the law.[2]

The common law has traditionally preferred the preservation of the property rights of the original owner and relied on the maxim *Nemo dat quod non habet*: you cannot pass on that which you do not have.[3] This principle is embodied in s 21 of the Sale of Goods Act 1893, which states:

> "Subject to the provisions of this Act, where goods are sold by a person who is not the owner thereof, and who does not sell them under the authority or

* B.C.L. (NUI); PhD Student at UCD; IRCHSS Government of Ireland Scholar. This essay was awarded joint second place in the Law Society of Ireland, *Student Law Reform Essay Competition 2003*.

[1] It is important to differentiate this situation from one where an action can be taken directly against S. If S enters an agreement for the sale of goods to B, but in fact the goods belong to O, no title can pass to B because of the principle *Nemo dat quod non habet*. However, B may have an action against S under Section 12 of the Sale of Goods Act 1893 for breach of the implied condition that the seller has title to sell the goods. For a recent example of such a situation, see *Mallett & Son Ltd v Rogers* Unreported, High Court, Quirke J, 12 May 2005.

[2] *Bishopsgate Motor Finance Corporation Ltd v Transport Brakes Ltd* [1949] 1 KB 322 at 336 per Lord Denning.

[3] Hereinafter referred to as the *Nemo Dat* rule.

> with the consent of the owner, the buyer acquires no better title to the goods than the seller had, unless the owner is by his conduct precluded from denying the seller's authority to sell."

Although this part of s 21 clearly anticipates an exception to the general rule—namely that the owner of the goods may be by his conduct precluded from denying the seller's authority to sell—in practice, the courts have taken a narrow view of this exception and favoured the rights of the original owner. The wording of s 21 ("under the authority or with the consent of the owner") also indicates that the ordinary rules of agency will apply to bind an owner of goods if the seller has actual or apparent authority from the owner to make the sale. Section 21(2) contains more specific exceptions, providing that nothing in the Act affects the provisions of the Factors Acts[4] or the validity of certain common law and statutory powers of sale, or sales under a court order. Further exceptions to the general rule can be found in ss 22 to 25 of the 1893 Act.[5] However, the scope of these exceptions, and the rationale behind some of them, is unclear and it has been commented that there is "little or no discernible policy" linking them.[6]

As a result of a general dissatisfaction with the state of the law, Law Reform Commissions and similar institutions in various jurisdictions have examined and recommended reforms of various aspects of the *Nemo Dat* rule.[7] In England alone, there have been four such reports since the 1960s.[8] Although no such report has been

---

4 See in particular the Factors Act 1889.

5 There are also exceptions to the *Nemo dat* principle at common law and in legislation such as The Factors Act 1888. However, the scope of this article is limited to the exceptions found in ss 22 to 25 of the Sale of Goods Act 1893.

6 Bradgate, *Commercial Law* (3rd ed, 2000), p 411.

7 See for example: Ontario Law Reform Commission, *Report on Sale of Goods* (1979), Volume II, Chap 12, "The 'Nemo Dat' Doctrine and Sales Transactions", which forms the basis for the Canadian Uniform Sale of Goods Act; New South Wales Law Reform Commission *Sale of Goods Issues Paper* (1988); Law Reform Commission of Western Australia *Project No 89: Report on the Sale of Goods Act 1895* (1998); Law Reform Commission of Hong Kong *Contracts for the Supply of Goods* (2002).

8 These are: (1) The English Law Reform Committee *Twelfth Report on the Transfer of Title to Chattels* Cmnd. 2958 (1966) (Report noted by Diamond "Law Reform Committee: Twelfth Report on the Transfer of Title to Chattels" (1966) 29 MLR 413; Atiyah, "Law Reform Committee: Twelfth Report" (1966) 29 MLR 541; Thornely "Transfer of Title to Chattels by Non-Owners" [1966] CLJ 24.) (2) *Report of the Crowther Committee on Consumer Credit* Cmnd. 4596 (1974) (3) A Department of Trade and Industry Report carried out by Professor Diamond, entitled *A Review of Security Interests in Property* (1989) (4) A rather short consultation paper of the Department of Trade and Industry, entitled, *Transfer of Title: Sections 21 to 26 of the Sale of Goods Act 1979: A Consultation Document* (1994).

carried out in Ireland, the Irish Law Reform Commission is due to investigate the *Nemo Dat* rule as part of its Second Programme of Reform, showing that there is an awareness that the law in this area needs some clarification and change.[9]

This article outlines the scope of the rule in Ireland, focusing on the "conduct" exception in s 21, and the exceptions relating to a sale by a seller or buyer in possession (s 25), a sale under voidable title (s 23), and a sale in market overt (s 22). In particular it aims to show how the unclear policy of the 1893 Act has resulted in overly technical results and confusion, and to highlight areas where reform is necessary.[10]

An Overview of the Competing Claims

The original owner's claim is based on the protection of property rights and a reluctance on the part of the legal system to be seen to be condoning theft and the sale of stolen property. The law does not expect an owner of goods to actively take precautions against burglary or theft, or act as constant vigilantes of goods:

> "[I]t is not consistent with the general spirit of the law to hold innocent persons responsible for not taking measures to prevent the commission of a crime which they may have no reason to anticipate."[11]

On a practical level, it is argued that the onus on the buyer to check that goods are not stolen is much less onerous than the onus on the owner goods to constantly check that they are not stolen from him:

> "A buyer can protect himself by inquiring as to the source of the goods, going to more reputable shops, etc. It could be argued that an owner can also protect himself by taking precautions against burglary and robbery, but sometimes burglary and robbery cannot be prevented no matter how

---

[9] See: http://www.lawreform.ie/lawunderreview/secondproglawreform.htm (Accessed 30 August 2005).

[10] For detailed analysis of some of the more technical aspects of the *Nemo dat* rule and the exceptions thereto see: Atiyah, Adams & McQueen, *The Sale of Goods,* (10th ed, 2001), p 368 *et seq*; Goode, *Commercial Law* (3rd ed, 2004), p 415 *et seq*; Bradgate, *Commercial Law* (3rd ed, 2000), p 408 *et seq*; Ulph, "Conflicts of Title and the Obligations of the Seller" in McKendrick (ed), *Sale of Goods* (2000), p 165 *et seq*; For an academic analysis of some of the issues involved see Davies, "Transferability and Sale of Goods" (1987) 7 *Legal Studies 1.*

[11] per Lord Watson *Scholfield v The Earl of Londesborough* [1896] AC 514 at 537.

> cautious an owner is. An owner is in a more passive position than a buyer, who can take a more active role to protect himself."[12]

It is thus generally accepted that goods which are stolen outright from their owner will always be reclaimable as against an innocent purchaser in good faith.[13] Any other stance is merely seen as creating a paradise for thieves and an easy defence for those who purchase stolen property.

This argument has been extended to protect an owner even where the owner is arguably careless with his goods:

> "If a person leaves a watch or a ring on a seat in the park or on a table at a café and it ultimately gets into the hands of a bona fide purchaser it is no answer to the true owner to say that it was his carelessness and nothing else that enabled the finder to pass it off as his own."[14]

In favour of such an extension of protection of ownership rights is the argument that in either case a crime or fraud has been committed and the law should not appear to encourage that fraud by facilitating transactions which are based on it. Why should the civil law uphold a distinction that does not exist in criminal law? Are crimes such as fraudulent misappropriation and embezzlement not just as wrong as outright theft?[15] Thus, the argument goes, it should make no difference to the owner of the goods how exactly his goods were taken: what is important is that a crime was committed, and crime should not destroy one's property rights.

However, those that favour the rights of the purchaser argue that although the law is ostensibly choosing between two innocent parties, it is possible that the owner is more to blame than the purchaser and it would be wrong for the law to turn a blind eye to the behaviour of the owner as regards his own goods. Thus, the conduct of the owner should be taken into account. This argument thus upholds in a very general manner the distinction between outright theft and other forms of fraud:

> "Theft, and to some extent loss, have the unpredictability of lightning, and there is relatively little the owner can do to protect himself against them. It

---

[12] Law Reform Commission of Hong Kong, *Contracts for the Supply of Goods* (2002), p 235.

[13] See however the market overt rule, discussed below.

[14] per Lord McNaghten in *Farquharson Bros & Co v C King & Co* [1902] AC 325 at 336.

[15] On the distinction in the criminal law between various forms of theft, deception and fraud, see The Criminal Justice (Theft and Fraud Offences) Act 2001.

is of his own free will, on the other hand, that the owner parts with possession of goods of his own to another by way of loan, lease, deposit, pledge, etc., and he has every opportunity of investigating the integrity of that person before doing so. It is only fair and equitable, therefore, that the risk should fall on him rather than on the innocent purchaser. The fact that he has, in the first instance, voluntarily parted with possession swings the delicate balance of equity in [the purchaser's] favour."[16]

Similarly, Goode has stated:

> "In principle, the protection of the innocent buyer is a more sensible and more realistic approach. If the owner of goods voluntarily parts with possession of them, he takes upon himself certain risks. He can make his own judgment as to the creditworthiness of the party to whom he gives possession, and if his trust turns out to be ill-founded, he ought not to put the consequences of his own mistaken judgment on to the shoulders of a blameless third party.[17]

Futhermore, an approach favouring the innocent purchaser is seen as one which protects commercial transactions and encourages trade. It has been argued that if goods are to move freely down the distributive chain, it is important that buyers should be able to "rely on possession as evidence of a right to dispose"[18] and purchase with confidence in the strength of the seller's title.[19] However, it is generally a *sine qua non* of these cases that the purchaser did in fact rely on possession, either of goods or title deeds, when he bought the goods. Taken to its logical end, therefore, an argument based purely on possession and the sanctity of commercial transactions could obviously result in an overruling of the *nemo dat* principle, even in cases of pure theft. It is thus proposed that any attempt to resolve this problem and reform this area of law should focus on the conduct of the owner.[20]

---

16 Hahlo, *Sale of another person's property* (Quebec Civil Code Revision Commission), cited in Bradgate, *op. cit,* p 421.

17 Goode, *op. cit,* p 416–417.

18 Goode, "The Dispositive Effect of a Seller's Repossession" (1972) 35 MLR 186 at p 189.

19 Goode, *op. cit,* p 417.

20 Assuming, of course, that the purchaser buys in good faith, without notice of the owner's title to the goods, and that the claim is in good faith. For an example of a case where the purchaser's claim was not made in good faith as the purchaser had not in fact paid for the vehicle see: *Shaw v Commissioner of Metropolitan Police* [1987] 1 WLR 1332. See: Gill, "Transfer of Title to Goods by Non Owner" (1987) ILT 276.

Exceptions to the *Nemo Dat* Rule

Estoppel

Section 21 of the Sale of Goods Act 1893 codifies the *Nemo Dat* principle but also makes room for an exception whereby the owner of the goods may be "by his conduct precluded from denying the seller's authority to sell". This would seem at first glance to adopt an approach whereby the more careless of the two innocents should bear the loss: if the owner is careless with his goods, or entrusts them to a rogue, he should be estopped from asserting his title because of his conduct. Such an interpretation would reflect the following rather wide assertion of Ashurst J in *Lickbarrow v Mason*:

> "Wherever one of two innocent persons must suffer by the acts of a third, he who enabled the person to occasion the loss must sustain it."[21]

The courts have however been very reluctant to apply this exception to the *Nemo Dat* rule, confining it to cases where there can be said to be a "representation" by the owner, i.e. a positive assertion or action, as opposed to mere carelessness or inactivity.[22] There would thus appear to be no room in this context for "estoppel by negligence," a rather overused phrase[23] which in the context denotes the imposition of a duty of care on the owner of goods not to cause loss to a third party purchaser of the goods.[24] Even in the

---

[21] *Lickbarrow v Mason* (1787) 2 TR 63. This statement has been criticised as too wide: see for example the comments of Lord Lindley in *Farquharson Bros v King* [1902] AC 325 at 343. An obvious difficulty with this statement is that "enable" is a broad phrase. In *Farquharson Bros v King* [1902] AC 325 the Earl of Halsbury LC focused on the difference between "enabling" somebody to do something which causes harm to a third party, and being guilty of an "indiscretion" which results in harm to a third party. Entrusting an employee with certain duties may "enable" him to take your goods and pass them off as his own, just as selling guns may "enable" somebody to commit murder. However, there is no question of there being any indiscretion on the part of the employer/seller in these cases. See also: *Central Newbury Car Auctions Ltd v Unity Finance Ltd* [1957] 1 QB 371 at 389–390, per Hodson LJ.

[22] For examples of representation made by the owners which have successfully estopped the owners from claiming the goods in dispute see: *Henderson & Co v Wiliams* [1895] 1 QB 521; *Abigail v Lapin* [1934] AC 491; *Rimmer v Webster* [1902] 2 Ch 163; *Fuller v Glyn, Mills, Currie & Co* [1914] 2 KB 168; *Eastern Distributors v Goldring* [1957] 2 QB 600.

[23] *See* Atiyah, Adams and MacQueen, *op. cit,* p 372, where it is stated that "strictly speaking" there is no such thing as "estoppel by negligence".

[24] Exceptionally, in *Mercantile Credit Co Ltd v Hamblin* [1964] 3 WLR 798 such a duty of care was held to exist but on the facts there was no breach of that duty. On this case see: Sealy, "Sale of Goods and Transfer of Title by Estoppel" [1965] CLJ 21; Atiyah, Adams and MacQueen, *op. cit,* p 378–379.

case of "estoppel by representation" the courts will not easily allow a defence. The representation must be made voluntarily[25] by the owner[26] and be unequivocal—the person who relies on the representation cannot simply rely on an interpretation which is reasonable in the given circumstances.[27] There is a distinction between a representation that the seller has authority to sell the goods as an agent and a representation that the seller is the owner of the goods. In the former case, the purchaser can only rely on estoppel if the apparent agent sells the goods in the ordinary course of business. There is no such restriction if the seller is represented as the owner of the goods.[28]

It would be relatively easy to form an argument based on estoppel by representation if an owner expressly stated "[t]his car belongs to X and it is his to sell" or "X is my agent and has full authority to sell this car". However, in many instances the purchaser is duped not because the owner has spoken directly to him but because the owner has given the seller possession of the chattel in question or some form of documentation which implies ownership of the chattel. In this situation it must be determined whether or not possession alone constitutes a representation by the owner which will estop him from claiming title.

This was an issue in *Mercantile Bank of India Ltd v Central Bank of India*,[29] where it was held that although railway receipts were documents of title to certain goods, the mere fact that they were in the possession of X with the consent of the owner did not mean that the true owner of the goods was estopped from claiming title. Possession of the railway receipts "no more conveyed a representation that [X] were entitled to dispose of the property than the actual possession of the goods

---

[25] See: *Debs v Sibec Developments Ltd* [1990] 3 RTR 91, where a representation by the owner that the goods belonged to a third party was not binding when the representation was induced by threats of violence. For a commentary on this case see: "Economic Loss and the Duty to Speak" (1989) JBL 284.

[26] Whether or not the party making the alleged representation to the purchaser was an agent of the owner was an issue in *Moorgate Mercantile Co Ltd v Twitching* [1977] AC 890.

[27] See per Lord Wilberforce in *Moorgate Mercantile Co Ltd v Twitching* [1977] AC 890 at 902; There are judicial dicta in favour of giving such a representation its "reasonable" interpretation: see for example the dicta of Bowen LJ in *Low v Bouverie* (1891) 3 Ch 82 at 106 and of Lord Wright in *Canada and Dominion Sugar Ltd v Canadian National (West Indies) Steamships Ltd* [1947] AC 46 at 55.

[28] See Atiyah, Adams and McQueen, *op. cit*, p 376–377; Goode, *op. cit*, p 423; Bradgate, *op. cit*, p 418.

[29] [1938] AC 287.

themselves would have done".[30] The failure to make a distinction between possession of the goods themselves and possession of documents of title to the goods has been criticised:

> "The possession of documents of title is a great deal less ambiguous in character than the possession of goods. Goods may be delivered and held for use, for repair, for letting out on hire or for safe custody. Documents of title, on the other hand, are not taken for any of these purposes except safe custody; and the range of persons whose business it is to hold documents for safe keeping is very much narrower than in the case of goods."[31]

The relevance of possession of both the chattel and documents of title was at issue in the Court of Appeal decision of *Central Newbury Car Auctions v Unity Finance Ltd*,[32] although the decision of both the majority and the minority leaves much room for debate. In this case the plaintiff car dealer had entered into a contract with X whereby the car dealer would sell a car to a finance company, which would then enter into a hire purchase agreement with X, under which X would have possession of the car. However, the plaintiff handed over possession of the car and the registration book to X before the finance company had formally accepted any hire purchase agreement thereon. The finance company subsequently refused to accept the agreement, but not before X had sold the car on to another car dealer. The original car dealer, on discovering what had happened, brought an action for damages for conversion against the second car dealer. A majority of the Court of Appeal held that there was no representation by the plaintiff that the car was X's to sell, and hence the plaintiff's action succeeded. The majority was swayed by the argument that a registration book is not a document of title and in fact on each page of the book there was a warning that the person in whose name a vehicle is registered may not be the legal owner of the vehicle. Hodson LJ stated:

> "The mere handing over of a chattel to another does not create an estoppel and there will be no estoppel unless the doctrine of ostensible ownership

---

30 [1938] AC 287 at 303, per Lord Wright.

31 Goode, *op. cit*, p 421. See however the comments of Ulph, *op. cit*, p 181: "[D]ocuments are transferred to others, such as solicitors or banks, for security reasons; property may also be transferred to another as trustee. This is so common place that the owner's conduct could not and should not be viewed as inconsistent with his own property rights. Furthermore, if the owner has, in depositing documents of title, acted in the ordinary manner in which business in his field is conducted, then it would be out of line with commercial expectations to divest the owner of the property by way of estoppel.".

32 [1957] 1 QB 371.

applies, as for example, when the owner gives the recipient a document of title or, has often been said, invests him with the indicia of ownership. . . The book itself is not a document of title; its terms negative ownership and it contains no representation by the plaintiffs or anyone else that the thief was entitled to deal with the car as his own."[33]

The majority was thus prepared to admit that the seller's possession, with the owner's consent, of the indicia of title would possibly prevent the owner from claiming the goods, but on the facts refused to hold that a registration book constituted evidence of ownership. Lord Denning, on the other hand, was of the opinion that the registration book was "good evidence of title"[34] but was not content to base a defence of estoppel on possession alone:

"[T]he mere fact that the true owner consents to someone else being in possession of his goods or of the indicia of title to the goods is not sufficient to prevent him afterwards asserting his title to them."[35]

Lord Denning took it as a given that the seller relied on the possession of the car and registration book, and instead looked to the conduct of the owner in deciding which claim should succeed. In particular, Lord Denning focused on the intention of the owner when he parted with the car:

"It is one thing to part with possession of your goods. It is quite another to part with the property in them ... if a man intends to part not only with the possession of goods but also with the property in them or the power of disposing them—or behaves as if he had that intention by arming the recipient with all the documents necessary to that end—he is not entitled to recover them from an innocent purchaser."[36]

What the owners in fact lost here was not the car itself but rather the money they expected to receive from the car—a bad debt which was entirely their own fault because they parted with the car before they were supposed to. When they handed their car to the rogue they intended to part with all their property in it. In contrast,

---

33 [1957] 1 QB 371 at 388. See the similar comments in *Shaw v Comr. of Police of the Metropolis* [1987]. 3 All ER 405.

34 [1957] 1 QB 384.

35 [1957] 1 QB 371 at 381.

36 [1957] 1 QB 371 at 382.

if the owners had simply been careless with the car and registration book—for example, by entrusting them to a fraudulent employee, or leaving the book in the car and the car unlocked—then the owners would not have intended to part with the property in the car and would have retained title as against a *bona fide* purchaser for value.[37]

It can be seen from Lord Denning's dissent in *Central Newbury Car Auctions* that even when the courts attempt to serve "the needs of a commercial country"[38] and preserve the sanctity of commercial transactions over the rights of owners, they will not condemn an owner for merely being careless with his goods. Indeed, Lord MacNaghten once stated:

> "The right of the true owner is not prejudiced or affected by his carelessness in losing the chattel, however gross it may have been."[39]

It is highly questionable whether the absolute nature of ownership should be accepted even in the presence of 'gross' carelessness, especially when the purchaser would have no way of establishing that the seller had no title. Bradgate has argued that such a principle goes too far in its protection of the original owner:

> "By allowing the owner of goods to be recklessly careless with them and yet recover them from a bona fide purchaser, the law allows the owner to act with flagrant disregard for the effect of his conduct on others."[40]

The dilemma in these cases is supposed to be the question of who, as between two equally innocent parties, should bear the loss. If one of those parties was grossly careless the scales should weigh in favour of he who is perhaps the only truly

---

[37] Unless the purchaser bought the goods in market overt.

[38] [1957] 1 QB 371 at 381 per Lord Denning.

[39] *Farquharson Bros v King* [1902] AC 325 at 335. This was approved by Lord Fraser in *Moorgate Mercantile Co Ltd v Twitchings* [1977] AC 890 at 925: "The owner of property is entitled to be careless with it if he likes, and even extreme carelessness with his own property will not preclude him from recovering it from a person who has bought it from someone who dishonestly purported to sell it." The same principle has been applied with regards to instruments such as corporate seals, cheque books and bills of exchange, so there is no duty to protect these instruments from fraudsters: see: *Bank of Ireland v Evan's Trustees* (1855) 5 HLC 389 and *Scholfield v Lord Londesborough* [1896] AC 514.

[40] Bradgate, *op. cit,* p 421.

innocent party in the whole affair—the purchaser. If this approach was taken, a solution "approaching justice" could possibly be achieved.[41]

The harshness of a strict adherence to the *Nemo Dat* principle in such circumstances can be seen in *Moorgate Mercantile Co Ltd v Twitchings*.[42] The facts of this case centered around a voluntary hire purchase registration system run by Hire Purchase Information Ltd. (HPI). Members of HPI would register any hire purchase agreements they entered into, and in turn would have access to the records of the H.P.I. when purchasing cars, in order to check that the cars were not the subject of any other hire purchase agreement. In effect this system was an attempt at a practical, market-based solution to a problem which the law had failed to effectively address, for example, by a State system of compulsory registration of hire purchase agreements.[43] This dispute arose, however, when the plaintiff failed to register an agreement to sell a car on hire purchase to M. M subsequently offered the car to a dealer who, on checking the hire purchase register, had no reason to believe the car was the subject of any other agreements, and bought the car. The plaintiffs later sued the dealer for conversion and the defendants argued that the plaintiffs were estopped from asserting their title.

This defence was rejected in the House of Lords. The House of Lords first rejected the argument that the plaintiff was estopped by the representation that HPI had made to the defendants. The representation made by HPI did not unequivocally

41 Sealy, "Sale of Goods and Transfer of Title by Estoppel" [1965] CLJ 21. The author points out (p 22) that the "most just" solution would be one where neither party would suffer loss for the wrongdoing of a stranger.

42 [1977] AC 890; For commentary on this case see Kanjian, "The *Nemo Dat* Rule and Estoppel by Representation and Estoppel by Negligence" (1977–1979) 8 *Sydney Law Review* 698; Atiyah, Adams and MacQueen, *op. cit,* p 379–380; Ulph, *op. cit,* p 184.

43 See the comments of Lord Wilberforce: [1977] AC 890 at 901: "[T]his case arises out of a hire purchase agreement of a motor car, a type of transaction which has provoked much litigation in which hardship to individuals is frequently revealed. This is due to the perennial failure of English law to develop a proper method of charging movable property. The hire purchase agreement is an ingenious invention which has proved itself as a very convenient and economically stimulating method of financing sales of chattels. But by divorcing ownership (vested in a finance company) from possession (held by a dealer or private hirer), by permitting the latter to retain documents of title without any endorsement of the interest of others, and by not requiring registration, in an accessible register, of the agreement, it lends itself, almost ideally, to fraudulent dispositions. In order to reduce these risks the finance companies in about 1938 devised a registration machinery of their own, through a company called Hire Purchase Information Ltd. (HPI) with which the great majority of hire purchase agreements are registered."

state that there was no hire purchase agreement whatsoever in relation to the car, only that there was no such registered agreement. As only 98 per cent of hire purchase companies were members of HPI, it was possible the car was registered under a hire purchase agreement with a company not a member of HPI. The dealer's check with HPI could not therefore be regarded as conclusive evidence that M had title to sell. Furthermore, there was considerable doubt as to whether HPI could be said to be an agent of the plaintiff, so that a representation by it would be binding on the plaintiff. A majority of the House of Lords further rejected the idea that the plaintiff was under a duty to the defendants to register the agreement, such that breach of that duty would estop the plaintiffs from claiming title:

> "It is, of course, desirable that finance companies who are members of HPI should promptly and accurately notify HPI of any new agreement entered into, and this both in their own interest and in that of dealer-members of that organisation . . . In most situations it is better to be careful than careless, but it is quite another thing to elevate all carelessness into a tort. Liability has to be based on a legal duty not to be careless, and I can find none in this case."[44]

It was stressed that no such duty was imposed in the contract between the plaintiff and HPI and it would be odd if a finance company which, "without obligation, takes the precaution of joining HPI, is thereby placed under a higher duty than those who refrain from joining".[45]

However, this view ignores the commercial reality of the situation. Even if 2 per cent of hire purchase companies are not members of HPI, it is certainly reasonably foreseeable by anybody who is a member of the organisation that information which they put forward will be relied upon by other members in commercial transactions, and that an absence of information will equally be relied upon:

> "The appellants as members of HPI would necessarily be aware that their omission to register their hire purchase agreements with HPI would be likely to cause financial loss to any member dealers to whom the vehicle the subject matter of such agreement might be offered. All the members of HPI are in such close business propinquity with each other that they are in my

[44] per Lord Edmund-Davies [1977] AC 890 at 919.

[45] per Lord Edmund Davies [1977] AC 890 at 919.

> view clearly "neighbours" within the meaning of that word as used by Lord Atkin."[46]

Furthermore, members of HPI are not at any disadvantage to non-members as they also reap the benefits of membership:

> "Those which join HPI gain considerable benefits, in the form of mutual protection, and saving of administrative costs. They substantially reduce their risk of loss, and if, in the course of doing so, they come under other risks, which must certainly be exceptional, these must be outweighed by the benefit of the scheme."[47]

It has been argued that this case is explicable as part of a general trend restricting the growth of liability in negligence,[48] but although this may be an explanation of this case, it is by no means a justification. It is important to remember here that this is not simply a tortious action in negligence but rather a situation where the courts must choose between two supposedly innocent parties. As is argued above, it would seem logical to let the loss fall where the blame lies. Even if the courts or legislature are reluctant to develop a general duty not to be careless with one's goods,[49] Lord

---

[46] per Lord Salmon [1977] AC 890 at 908. The reference to Lord Atkin is of course a reference to the famous principle in *Donaghue v Stevenson* [1932] AC 562 at 580: "The rule that you are to love your neighbour becomes in law, you must not injure your neighbour; and the lawyer's question, Who is my neighbour? receives a restricted reply. You must take reasonable care to avoid acts or omissions which you can reasonably foresee would be likely to injure your neighbour. Who, then, in law is my neighbour? The answer seems to be—persons who are so closely and directly affected by my act that I ought reasonably to have them in contemplation as being so affected when I am directing my mind to the acts or omissions which are called in question."

[47] per Lord Wilberforce [1977] AC 890 at 906. See also the comment of Lord Salmon [1977] AC 890 at 909.

[48] Atiyah, Adams and MacQueen, *op. cit,* p 380.

[49] In this regard, note should be made of the Irish decision in *Breslin v Corcoran and the Motor Insurers Bureau of Ireland* [2003] 2 ILRM 189. In this case, the owner of a car left his car unattended, with the keys in the ignition, and the car was stolen by a joyrider who crashed into a plaintiff, causing injury to him. The plaintiff sued the owner of the car for negligence in leaving his car unattended. It was held in the Supreme Court that the owner was not negligent, on the basis that, although it was reasonably foreseeable that the car would be stolen if the keys were left in the ignition, there was nothing to suggest that the defendant should have anticipated as a reasonable probability that the car, if stolen, would be driven so carelessly as to cause injury to another user of the road. For a similar English decision see: *Topp v London Country Bus (South West) Limited* [1993] 3 All ER 448. See however, the contrasting previous Irish decisions of *Dockery v O'Brien* [1975] ILTR 127 and *Cahill v Kenneally (1955–1956)* Ir Jur Rep 127.

Denning's dissent in *Central Newbury Car Auctions* could provide an intermediate solution: namely that where there is a voluntary disposition of goods and the original owner intends to part with the property in the chattel the owner should be estopped from claiming title to the chattel. Certainly, on the facts of *Moorgate Mercantile* the original owner intended to part with the property in the car. It could be said that the owner lost not the car itself but rather the money that was supposed to be paid in instalments. Once they put the car in the possession of a third party they should have taken what measures they could—for example registration with HPI—to protect both their ownership rights and innocent third parties.

In England in 1994, a consultation document from the Department of Trade and Industry recommended legislative intervention to reverse the result in the Moorgate decision, although no moves in this direction have yet been made.[50] In England, legislation exists—and was in existence at the time of the Moorgate decision—to protect a private purchaser in good faith of a motor vehicle which in fact was subject to a hire purchase agreement.[51] It has been argued that this protection should be extended by legislation to protect a trade dealer in motor vehicles[52] and, indeed, to protect goods other than motor vehicles. This has effectively been done in Ireland by virtue of s 70 of the Consumer Credit Act 1995, which states:

> "Where goods of any class or description are let under a hire-purchase agreement to a dealer who deals in goods of that class or description and the dealer sells the goods when ostensibly acting in the ordinary course of his business, the sale shall be valid as if the dealer were expressly authorised by the owner to make the sale:

[50] Department of Trade and Industry, *Transfer of Title: Sections 21 to 26 of the Sale of Goods Act 1979: A Consultation Document* (1994).

[51] s 27 of the Hire Purchase Act 1964 protects the purchasers of motor vehicles. It applies where a motor vehicle "has been bailed or (in Scotland) hired under a hire-purchase agreement, or has been agreed to be sold under a conditional sale agreement, and, before the property in the vehicle has become vested in the debtor, he disposes of the vehicle to another person" and provides that where the purchaser is a "private purchaser" of the motor vehicle "in good faith without notice of the hire-purchase or conditional sale agreement" that disposition shall have effect "as if the creditor's title to the vehicle has been vested in the debtor immediately before that disposition." For commentary on these provisions see Davies, "Wrongful Dispositions of Motorvehicles—A Legal Quagmire" [1995] JBL 36; Atiyah, Adams and MacQueen, *op. cit,* p 408–411; Goode, *op. cit,* p 438–443; Bradgate, *op. cit,* p 432–433.

[52] This was suggested by Lord Edmund Davies in the *Moorgate* decision: [1977] AC 890 at 922.

> Provided that the buyer acts in good faith and has not at the time of the sale notice that the dealer has no authority to make the sale."[53]

Although the protection of consumers is laudable, it is argued that this goes too far in its protection of trade purchasers: what incentive would there be to check, before purchasing, whether particular goods belonged to somebody else if you would acquire good title to those goods regardless? Arguably, a better alternative would be to introduce a suitable system of compulsory registration of hire purchase agreements.[54] This would have the advantage of having a preventative effect, reducing the number of incidents where a rogue can pass off somebody else's goods as his own and hence the number of disputes arising out of such a situation. Furthermore, it would mean that the owner of goods (i.e. the finance company) would not lose title to the goods automatically, but only if it failed to register the hire purchase agreement. The purchaser of goods would be expected to check the register before purchasing goods, but would be able to rely conclusively on that register as evidence of the seller's good title—at least as against an owner who should have registered the agreement on the register.[55]

In situations which fall outside these reforms, i.e. where the facts do not concern registered hire purchase agreements, it is proposed that the courts should adopt a broader interpretation of s 21 of the 1893 Act as regards the owner's conduct. In other words, where there is evidence that an owner was careless with his goods and gave possession to another who wrongfully sold them on, the courts should be prepared to find that title to the goods rests with the purchaser of the goods and not the owner. The requirement that the owner voluntarily hand over possession to the seller means the owner would be protected in the case of outright theft, even if he

---

53 s 28 of the now repealed Hire Purchase (Amendment) Act 1960 was of the same effect.

54 This was suggested by the Court of Appeal in *United Dominions Trust (Commercial) Ltd. v Cartwright* [1961] CLY 3925 and by Lord Edmund Davies (for the majority) in *Moorgate* [1977] AC 890 at 922. It was also suggested in the *Crowther Report on Consumer Credit* (Cmnd 4596, 1971).The possibility of an ownership register is reviewed in Davies, "Wrongful Dispositions of Motorvehicles—A Legal Quagmire" [1995] JBL 36 at pp 52–55. See also the suggestion of Scott LJ in *Norman v Pitt* [1948] WN 270; (1948) 92 S.J. 514, that reference in a car registration book to any hire-purchase agreement to which the car is subject should be required by statute.

55 It has been pointed out (Atiyah, Adam and MacQueen, *op. cit,* p 110) that such a register would have made no difference in a situation such as that in *Central Newbury Car Auctions,* as here the owner of the car was not the finance company (which, it will be remembered, refused to enter into a hire purchase agreement) but rather a motor dealer. However, this situation could be dealt with under an expanded concept of estoppel by negligence, discussed below.

was arguably careless with his goods. For example, if he leaves his keys in a car and the car is stolen, the owner will still retain title to the car as against a purchaser in good faith. Furthermore, this proposition is not as wide as Ashurt J's statement in *Lickbarrow v Mason*: it is not enough that the owner "enabled" the fraud by handing over possession of the goods; there must also be evidence of carelessness or recklessness on his part. Inevitably there will occur situations where the purchaser of goods was also careless—for example, where the purchaser is a trade dealer in that type of good and should have realised that the goods were stolen. It should of course be open to the courts to find against the purchaser in such a situation, most obviously on the basis that the purchaser had actual or constructive notice of the owner's title and is not really a purchaser in good faith.

If it is felt that this proposed solution goes too far in favour of the purchaser, there is always the possibility of the intermediate solution suggested by Lord Denning in *Central Newbury Car Auctions*: namely, that when the owner of goods voluntarily parts with possession of those goods, and *intends to part with the property in them*, the owner should be estopped from claiming title to the goods as against an innocent purchaser in good faith. The main argument in favour of this approach is that the owner of goods has simply entered a bad commercial transaction and suffered a bad debt, and this should not stop title from passing onto a third party. Thus, for example, where an owner enters an agreement for the sale of goods and hands over possession of those goods before being paid, and the buyer sells on the goods and absconds, the facts of the situation merely concern bad debts and not any question of title.

Seller in Possession

Section 25(1) of the 1893 Act deals with a situation where S sells goods to B1 but retains possession of the goods and proceeds to sell them a second time to B2. This section attempts to resolve whether B1 or B2 is the true owner of the goods. It states:

> "Where a person having sold goods continues or is in possession of the goods ... the delivery or transfer by that person ... of the goods ... under any sale, pledge or other disposition thereof, to any person receiving the same in good faith and without notice of the previous sale, shall have the same effect as if the person making the delivery or transfer were expressly authorised by the owner of the goods to make the same."[56]

[56] See the similar (but slightly wider) wording of s 8 of the Factors Act 1889. In England, s 25(1) of the 1893 Act was reproduced as s 24 of the Sale of Goods Act 1979.

Section 25(1) was applied by Kinlen J in the Irish High Court in *Michael Hanley v ICC Finance Ltd*.[57] The facts of the case were as follows: In May 1992, the plaintiff, Mr Hanley, bought a car from Huet Motors Ltd. In August 1993, the car was repossessed by the defendants ICC Finance Ltd, who claimed to be the true owners of the car. It transpired that ICC Finance Ltd had bought the car from Huet Motors Ltd but that Huet Motors Ltd had retained possession of the car as a result of a lease agreement between ICC Finance and Fleetlink Ltd, a wholly owned subsidiary of Huet Motors Ltd.. The tax book had been given to a Mr McCarthy, who was director of both Huet and Fleetlink, for the purpose of taxing the car. ICC Finance was claiming the car back as Huet Ltd was in liquidation. The Circuit Court held that the plaintiff had obtained good title to the car and ordered its return, and this decision was upheld in the High Court. Huet Motors Ltd itself did not have a legal title to the car, but by virtue of s 25 of the Sale of Goods Act 1893 "it could and did give a good title" to the plaintiff.[58]

Kinlen J's judgment in this case is a relatively short one with little analysis of either the wording of s 25(1) or the policy behind it. It could easily be assumed, therefore, that the provision is relatively free of difficulty. In reality, however, s 25(1) of the 1893 Act has been the subject of much confusion in the courts.

For example, in *Staffordshire Motor Guarantee Ltd v British Wagon Co Ltd*[59] it was held that a second buyer claiming under this section must show that the seller was in possession as a seller, and not in any other capacity. Such an interpretation severely restricted the protection afforded to the third party: the legal title by which an individual is in possession, i.e. as owner, cannot continue once he has sold the goods. However, this narrow interpretation of the section was rejected by the Privy Council in *Pacific Motor Auctions v Motor Credits (Hire Finance) Ltd.*,[60] by the English Court of Appeal in *Worcester Works Finance Ltd v Cooden Engineering Co Ltd*[61] and by the Irish High Court in *Michael Hanley v. ICC Finance Ltd*.[62] Thus, if a seller continues

---

57 [1996] 1 ILRM 463.

58 [1996] 1 ILRM 463 at 468.

59 [1934] 2 KB 305. See also: *Eastern Distributors Ltd v Goldring* [1957] 1 QB 600.

60 [1965] AC 867. For commentary on this case see Thornely, "Sales by Sellers in Possession" [1965] 23 CLJ 181.

61 [1971] 3 All ER 708. See: Thornely, "Dispositions by Sellers in Possession" [1972] 30 CLJ 36; Goode, "The Dispositive Effect of a Seller's Repossession" (1972) 35 MLR 186.

62 [1996] 1 ILRM 463. Kinlen J states (at p 468) that he is "impressed" by the reasoning in *Worcester Works Finance* and prefers it to *Staffs Motor Guarantee Ltd.* Furthermore, the mere fact that the plaintiff succeeded in this case is an indication that the Irish High Court has rejected the interpretation of s 25(1) given in *Staffs Motor Guarantee Ltd.*

in possession the second buyer is covered by s 25(1), even though the seller has retained possession in a new capacity—either as bailee for the new owner or, in the case of wrongful possession, as a trespasser.[63]

However, in *Pacific Motor Auctions* the Privy Council limited the scope of the section by endorsing the position in *Mitchell v Jones*[64] that section 25(1) is inapplicable to cases where there has been a break in the continuity of physical possession. Thus, if S sells goods to B1, and B1 takes possession but later hands possession back to S—for example, by lending the goods to S, or giving them to S for safekeeping—and S sells the goods on to B2, then section 25(1) will be of no application. In this situation, the fact that S happened to sell the goods to B1 is irrelevant. The facts are simply those in which a bailee fraudulently misappropriates goods of the bailor.

This interpretation, however, arguably goes against the wording of the Act which provides for relief where the seller "continues *or* is in possession". Secondly, that such a decision was made after the Board declared that the object of the section is "to protect an innocent purchaser who was deceived by the vendor's physical possession of goods or documents"[65] is remarkable. A purchaser is equally deceived by a situation where there has been such a break in physical possession of the seller yet the court refused to protect him in such a case. This highlights the confusion as to what exactly is the policy of the legislature in this area.

A further difficulty concerns the requirement of "delivery or transfer . . . of the goods or documents of title". In *Nicholson v Harper*[66] it was held that no title would pass under s 25(1) where there was no physical delivery or transfer of possession. However this was rejected as bad law by the Australian High Court in *Gamer's Motor Centre v Natwest Wholesale Australia.*[67] Instead, there could be constructive or symbolic delivery not amounting to actual physical delivery. In the English case of *Gerson v Wilkinson*[68] it was accepted by both counsel and by the Court of Appeal that

63 The section applies even if the seller's retention of possession is unlawful. Section 25(1) does not state that the seller must possess the goods with the consent of the owner. See: *Worcester Works Finance Ltd v Cooden Engineering Co Ltd* [1971] 3 All ER 708 at 712–713.

64 (1905) 24 NZLR 932.

65 [1965] AC 867 at 886.

66 [1895] 2 Ch 415.

67 (1987) 163 CLR 236.

68 *MichaelGerson (Leasing) Ltd v Wilkinson and another* [2000] 3 WLR 1645. See also: *Forsythe International (UK) Ltd v Silver Shipping Co Ltd* [1994] 1 WLR 1334.

Gamer's Motor Centre was the applicable law and that delivery could be constructive for the purpose of s 25(1).[69] It was held that when the seller, who is in possession of goods after selling them to B1, sells them to a second buyer B2, but yet again retains possession, holding goods subject to a "sale and leaseback" agreement, then B2 has taken constructive delivery of the goods. Clarke LJ stated:

> "[I]t makes commercial sense to hold that such arrangements involve a transfer of constructive possession to the finance company who buys the goods and leases them back, such that the innocent finance company can take advantage of the provisions of section 24 of the Act of 1979."[70]

It has been argued that such an interpretation deprives the delivery requirement of any real meaning and furthermore that it disregards the policy of the statute.[71] However, in an area of law so full of anomalies and contradictions, such a decision for once in favour of the innocent purchaser should probably be welcomed.

Much of the academic debate surrounding s 25(1) has focused on technicalities, such as the examples above. However, most of these questions focus too much on the interpretation of the section and fail to ask if it should be there at all. Whilst it is good that the courts, in decisions such as *Pacific Motor Auctions,* have interpreted the section in a manner which renders it operable, it would be even better if Parliament redrafted the provisions to explain clearly what they mean. Does the section as it is now interpreted bear any resemblance to what it was originally intended to be? Is there any need for this section at all? What does it matter that the person who received possession from the owner was or was not in fact the same person who originally sold the goods to the owner? Is there really any difference between a situation where a seller retains possession and fraudulently resells the goods and one where a bailee takes possession and fraudulently resells them? In both situations the original owner has voluntarily parted with possession of the goods and entrusted them to a third party. If the policy of the statute is that in certain circumstances a purchaser should be allowed rely on possession, shouldn't it be clear why these circumstances are picked and not others? If the reasons behind the legislation are not clear to anybody it is inevitably going to result in the kind of mishmash of jurisprudence that has developed.

---

69 [2000] WLR 1645 at 1649. Sir Roy Goode QC represented the plaintiff.

70 [2000] 3 WLR 1645 at 1657.

71 Goode, *op. cit,* p 432.

Buyer in Possession

Section 25(2) of the 1893 Act deals with a situation where a buyer[72] who takes possession of goods resells the goods but doesn't pay for them:

> "Where a person having bought or agreed to buy goods obtains, with the consent of the seller, possession of the goods or the documents of title to the goods, the delivery or transfer by that person … of the goods or documents of title, under any sale, pledge, or other disposition thereof, to any person receiving the same in good faith and without notice of any lien or other right of the original seller in respect of the goods, shall have the same effect as if the person making the delivery or transfer were a mercantile agent in possession of the goods or documents of title with the consent of the owner."[73]

This section is generally meant to apply where the property in the goods remains with the seller, for example by the insertion of a retention of title clause into the contract,[74] and not where the property has in fact passed to the first buyer and that buyer has merely failed to pay the price. In this latter situation, the buyer will generally have a good title to pass on to the second buyer and the second buyer will not need to rely on s 25(2).

Section 25(2) may also apply where the seller lacked best title and thus did not pass the best title on to the first buyer or, consequently, on to the second buyer. This may occur where the seller's title is voidable and the seller resold after the title was avoided.[75] It may also occur where the goods are stolen from the original owner and passed on to the seller (and thus the first and second buyer) through a chain of sales. In this situation there is a difficulty with the wording of s 25(2) in that it provides that the effect of the transfer between the first and second buyer is as that it shall take

---

72 Section 25(2) only applies where there is a sale and not merely where there is a hire purchase agreement: see Bradgate, *op. cit,* p 429–430 and *Forthright Finance Ltd v Carlyle Finance Ltd* [1997] 4 All ER 90.

73 See also the similar exception in s 9 of the Factors Act 1889. In England, s 25(2) of the 1893 Act has been reproduced in s 25(1) of the 1979 Sale of Goods Act.

74 See for example: *Forsythe International (UK) v Silver Shipping Co and Petroglobe International (The Saetta)* [1993] 2 Lloyd's Rep 268. On retention of title clauses in general see : *Aluminium Industrie Vaasen BV v Romalpa Aluminium Ltd* [1976] 2 All ER 552.

75 In this situation, it would appear that the second buyer is protected by s 25(2) of the 1893 Act. Section 23 of the 1893 Act does not apply as it requires that the sale occurs *before* the first contract is avoided: see below.

place as though the "owner of the goods" expressly authorised the transaction. This seems to assume that the "seller" is the owner of the goods, and ignores the fact that the seller may not have had good title to pass on to the buyer. If s 25(2) were taken literally, the buyer would get title over and above the true owner of the goods, even if the goods were stolen from the owner in an outright theft. The ultimate purchaser of the goods would thus obtain good title through a thief. In *National Employers' Insurance Ltd. v Jones*[76] the House of Lords was constrained to interpret "owner" as in effect meaning "the seller." A similar conclusion had previously been reached in New Zealand[77] and Canada.[78] This means that if the goods were stolen from the original owner, the buyer will get the title of the seller, but not a better title than that of the original owner. This interpretation highlighted a lack of foresight on the part of those who drafted the section, resulting in the Court having to yet again interpret it against its natural and literal meaning in order to achieve a rational result. It has been commented that perhaps the real moral of this case is that a "thorough overhaul" of the Sale of Goods Act is necessary.[79]

A further difficulty with s 25(2) is that the second disposition has effect "as if the person making the delivery or transfer were a mercantile agent in possession of the goods or documents of title with the consent of the owner." This is in contrast with the s 25(1) relating to a seller in possession, which provides that the second disposition shall have effect as if it "were expressly authorised by the owner of the goods." In *Newtons of Wembly Ltd v Williams,*[80] it was held that the requirement in s 25(2) meant

---

[76] [1990] AC 24. For commentary on this case see, Gill, "Exceptions to the Nemo Dat Rule—A Problem Resolved" (1988) ILT 188; Battersby, (1991) 54 MLR 752; Thornely, "Thieves, Innocent Purchasers and Legislative History" [1988] 47 CLJ 358; Atiyah, Adams and MacQueen, *op. cit,* p 406–408; Bradgate, *op. cit,* p 431; The same problem exists with the wording of s 25(1) and it is now generally assumed that "owner" in the phrase "expressly authorised by the owner" must be taken to mean "the first buyer". This aspect of both ss 25(1) and 25(2) was the subject of much academic debate before this decision. See for example: Goode, *Commercial Law* (2nd eds, 1982), p 413–414; Atiyah, *The Sale of Goods* (3rd ed, 1966), p 163; Cornish, "Rescission without Notice" (1964) 27 MLR 472; Powles, "Stolen Goods and the Sale of Goods Act 1893 s 25(2)" (1974) 37 MLR 213; Battersby and Preston, "Stolen Goods and the Sale of Goods Act 1893 s 25(2)—A Rejoinder" (1975) 38 MLR 77; Powles, "Stolen Goods and the Sale of Goods Act, s 25(2)—A Surrejoinder" (1975) 38 MLR 83.

[77] *Elwin v O'Regan and Maxwell* [1971] N.Z.L.R. 1286.

[78] *Brandon v Leckie* (1972) 29 D.L.R. (3d) 633.

[79] Thornely, "Thieves, Rogues, Innocent Purchasers and Legislative Tangles" [1988] CLJ 15 at p 18.

[80] [1965] 1 QB 560. See however the earlier decision of *Lee v Butler* [1893] 2 QB 318. For commentary on *Newtons of Wembly Ltd v Williams* see: Thornely, "Sales by Persons with Voidable Titles and Buyers in Possession" [1965] CLJ 24.

that the second disposition would only take effect if the rogue buyer/seller were acting in the ordinary course of business—in other words the buyer "must somehow be treated as a notional mercantile agent".[81] This has been heavily criticised as it greatly reduces the scope of the section so as to deprive it of "any rational policy basis".[82] However, it is perhaps the wording of the Act itself that should be put under scrutiny and not the judges' conclusion. Whereas it may be true that it is "difficult to see how a person who is not a mercantile agent can act as if he were one",[83] it must be noted that the Act creates a distinction between the effect of the dispositions in s 25(1) and 25(2). Whereas the reasons for this distinction are not clear, the fact is that it remains and the courts have felt obliged to uphold the distinction. It was acknowledged that there are difficulties in deciding what constitutes an "ordinary course of business" when it is possible that the buyer has no business at all. The court seemed willing to be flexible in this regard, thus getting around the provision as best it could and holding the buyer was acting in the course of business, but the question as to the purpose of the distinction remains unanswered. The courts in Australia[84] and New Zealand,[85] however, have not felt as constrained as their English—and Northern Irish[86]—counterparts. In these jurisdictions the effect of a sale by a buyer in possession is the same as if the buyer were a mercantile agent and the sale was in the ordinary course of his business—as opposed to requiring him to actually be a mercantile agent. Yet again, therefore, the courts are faced with the dilemma of choosing between a literal but irrational interpretation of the provisions and a purposive interpretation that goes against its natural meaning. This dilemma could be avoided if provisions such as this were drafted clearly and sensibly by Parliament in the first place. In 1966, the English Law Reform Committee recommended reform of the provision but this has not yet been done.[87]

Sale Under a Voidable Title

Section 23 of the 1893 Act, which was applied by the Irish High Court in *Anderson v Ryan*,[88] enables a person with a voidable title to goods to transfer a good title to a

---

[81] Atiyah, Adams and MacQueen, *op. cit,* p 406.

[82] Goode, *op. cit,* p 437.

[83] Bradgate, *op. cit,* p 431.

[84] *Langmead v Thyer Rubber Co Ltd* (1947) SASR 29.

[85] *Jeffcott v Andrew Motors Ltd* [1960] NZLR 721.

[86] See: *Martin v Duffy* [1985] 11 NIJB 80.

[87] Twelfth Report, Cmnd. 2958, para 23 (1966).

[88] [1967] IR 34.

buyer in good faith and without notice of the seller's defect of title, provided he sells before his title is avoided. Goode has stated that this "is merely a specific application of the general rule of contract law that the right to rescind a contract is lost when an innocent third party has acquired an interest in the subject matter of the contract."[89]

In general, a party rescinds a contract by notifying the other party of the rescission. However, it is obviously going to be difficult to do this where the other party has disappeared, as will often be the case in this type of situation. Thus, in *Car & Universal Finance Co Ltd v Caldwell*[90] the Court of Appeal held that the owner can avoid the contract by doing all he can in the circumstances to communicate this to the other party, for example by asking the police to recover the goods. This decision greatly reduced the scope of this exception, as it meant that the contract is more likely to be avoided before the goods are sold on to the purchaser. However, an innocent buyer may still be able to get good title under s 25(2) of the Act.[91] The English Law Reform Committee[92] recommended reversal of the decision in *Caldwell* in 1966 but this has not been done either in England or here in Ireland. In Canada, in contrast, s 6.5(3) of the Canadian Uniform Sale of Goods Act would appear to go further than simply reversing the decision in *Caldwell*[93] by providing that the title passes to the purchaser even where the owner actually notifies the other party of the rescission and avoids the first contract.[94]

A further difficulty with s 23 is that it only applies where a title is voidable and not where the title is void. The distinction between these two situations can be hard to

---

89 Goode, *op. cit,* (3rd ed) p 425.

90 [1964] 2 WLR 600.

91 In *Newtons of Wembley Ltd v Williams* for example, s 23 was held not to apply as the first sellers had done all they could to avoid any title the first buyer had. The second buyer however was able to successfully rely on s 25(2). See Thornely, "Sales by Persons with Voidable Title and Buyers in Possession" [1965] CLJ 24.

92 Twelfth report, Cmnd 2958 (1966) para 16.

93 Indeed, the Ontario Law Reform Commission in its *Report on Sale of Goods* (1979), from which the Uniform Act developed, seems to give a limited approval to the *Caldwell* decision, commenting at p 287 that "it seems curious that the third party's position should depend on the accessibility of the rogue."

94 s 6.5(1) provides that a person with a voidable title has power to transfer a good title to a buyer who receives the goods in good faith, for value, and without notice of the defect in the title of the transferor. Section 6.5(3) provides that this rule applies "even though the owner has purported to avoid the sale to the transferor."

draw,[95] and it has been argued that the rights of the innocent purchaser should not depend on what is often merely a technicality.[96] Indeed, the English Law Reform Committee recommended that the distinction should be abolished in this context.[97] However, the Canadian Uniform Sale of Goods Act has resolved this problem, not by abolishing the distinction but by clarifying when a person is deemed to have a voidable title.[98]

Sale in Market Overt

A "market overt" is any market, established by grant, charter or statutory authority, which is held in a public place, with sales conducted openly and in public.[99] Section 22 of the Sale of Goods Act 1893 allows a *bona fide* purchaser to acquire good title when goods are bought in a market overt, even if the goods were originally stolen from their original owner. It states:

> "Where goods are sold in market overt, according to the usage of the market,[100] the buyer acquires a good title to the goods, provided he buys them in good faith and without notice of any defect or want of title on the part of the seller."

This rule originated in England in the Middle Ages,[101] as part of a policy designed to discourage private sales whilst encouraging trade in public: a purchaser who bought goods in a private or clandestine transaction would take the risk that the goods may be stolen, whereas a purchaser in open market would be assured of good

---

95 See for example the similar facts but different conclusions reached in *Ingram v Little* [1961] 1 QB 31 (contract void for mistake, section did not apply) and *Lewis v Avery* [1972] 1 QB 198 (contract voidable for misrepresentation, section applied.)

96 Bradgate, *op. cit,* p 428. See also the comments of Devlin LJ in *Ingram v Little* [1961] 1 QB 31 at 42.

97 Twelfth Report, Cmnd 2958 (1966) para 15.

98 s 6.5(2).

99 Every shop in the City of London is considered a market overt. See: Smith, "Valediction to Market Overt" (1997) *Am J Legal History* 225 at pp 242–245.

100 The requirement that the sale take place according to the usages of the market means, for example, that the purchaser only acquires good title as against the owner if the sale occurs in daylight hours: see *Reid v Commissioner of Police of the Metropolis* [1973] QB 551.

101 On the origins of the rule see: Smith, "Valediction to Market Overt" (1997) *Am J Legal History* 225; Davies, "Transferability and Sale of Goods" (1987) 7 *Legal Studies* 1 at pp 17–20; Hamilton "The Ancient Maxim *Caveat Emptor*" (1931) 40 *Yale LJ* 1133.

title.[102] If stolen goods were displayed for sale in an open market, the owner of the goods was expected to go to the market and reclaim the goods, preventing their purchase by a third party.[103] The mere fact that goods were on sale in open market was thus seen as evidence that the seller was the owner: the purchaser was entitled to suppose that "no person but the owner would dare to expose them for sale here, and, therefore, I have a right to assume that the shop-keeper has a right to sell them".[104] The market overt rule did not however apply where a thief was convicted: public policy here "seemed to favour the prosecution of thieves by giving the owner an incentive to recover the goods".[105]

It can easily be seen that the policy favouring the passing of good title in market overt is based on the presumption that a thief, lacking the means to transport stolen goods to the other end of the country, will be forced to sell goods at a local market which is easily accessible by the original owner of the goods.[106] However, the same difficulties of transport do not exist today, and "the goods may be at the opposite end

---

[102] Thus Coke stated: "The common law did hold it for a point of great policy, and behoveful for the Commonwealth, that fairs and market overts should be replenished and well furnished with all manner of commodities . . . And to that end the common law did ordain (to encourage men thereto) that all sales and contracts of anything vendible in fairs or market overt should not be good only between the parties but should bind that right had thereunto." From *Institutes* II 713, cited in Davies, "Transferability and Sale of Goods" (1987) 8 *Legal Studies* 1 at p 18.

[103] See, Hamilton, "The Ancient Maxim *Caveat Emptor*" (1931) 40 *Yale L J* 1133 at p 1147.

[104] per Blackburn J in *Crane v London Dock Co* (1864) 5 B & S 313; 33 LJQB 224.

[105] Davies, "Transferability and sale of goods" (1987) 7 *Legal Studies* 1 at p 19. This exception to the market overt rule can be found in s 24(1) of the Sale of Goods Act 1893: "Where goods have been stolen and the offender is prosecuted to conviction, the property in the goods so stolen revests in the person who was the owner of the goods, or his personal representative, notwithstanding any intermediate dealing with them, whether by sale in market overt or otherwise." This section was repealed in England by s 31(2) of the Theft Act 1968 which provides that title to property was not to be affected by reason only of the conviction of the offender. This repeal served to widen the scope of the market overt rule, giving the purchaser in a market overt "a virtually unimpeachable title." Smith, *loc. cit,* p 247.

[106] That this presumption was generally made can also be seen by the fact that the rule did not automatically apply to pass title in horses—which, of course, if stolen, can be easily transported and sold at a market far away from the locality of the original owner. Instead, certain statutory formalities had to be complied with in order to pass title: see for example, The Statute of 31 Elizabeth 12, concerning Sellers of Horses in Fairs and Markets, 1589. Furthermore, s 22(2) of the Sale of Goods Act 1893 explicitly states that "nothing in this section shall affect the law relating to the sale of horses." In England, these statutes (and s 22(2) of the 1893 Act) have since been repealed by s 10(2) of the Criminal Law Act 1967. See: Smith, *loc. cit,* p 242; Davies, *loc. cit,* p 19.

of the country, and sold, before [the owner] knows they are gone".[107] It is not realistic in modern conditions to expect an owner to scour all the markets in the country to reclaim his goods. Indeed, the owner may not even know where to look: it has been pointed out that it is virtually impossible to draw up a comprehensive list of all markets which would today be classified as "market overt".[108] Furthermore, the modern commercial world does not revolve around markets and fairs and many transactions occur in retail shops or at auction. It has been argued that the rule creates an unfair and unjustifiable distinction between public sales in markets, or shops in London, and other sale transactions which arguably are just as public and deserving of protection:

> "When originally introduced into the common law a rule which protected a purchaser of wool in the mediaeval fairs and markets was obviously a very reasonable one, but the justification for giving a purchaser of a car in Maidstone market (or any open shop in the City of London) a protection denied to a purchaser of a similar car in Portland Street is less obvious."[109]

The English Law Reform Committee in its 1966 Report said that the rule was capricious in its operation and recommended that the rule should either be abolished or extended to cover all retail sales at trade premises and sales by auction. The 1994 Department of Trade Consultation Paper similarly recommended that the rule should be abolished and replaced with a rule that would confer a good title on *bona fide* purchasers through retail outlets and auctions. However, the extension of the rule, whilst resolving some of the anomalies surrounding the rule, could not provide an answer to the strongest argument against the rule: namely that it appeared to condone theft and facilitate the sale of stolen goods:

> "In recent times . . . a rule designed to promote honesty among buyers and the integrity of the market came to be seen as providing a charter for thieves and fences, a perception highlighted by the theft of paintings by Gainsborough and Reynolds from Lincoln's Inn and their sale in Bermondsey market."[110]

107 Bradgate, *op. cit,* p 434.

108 Smith, *loc. cit,* p 248.

109 Gower, "Sale of Goods in Market Overt" (1949) 12 MLR 371.

110 Goode, *op. cit,* p 425.

The rule was thus abolished in its entirety in England in 1994,[111] as a result of lobbying by antiques dealers, auction houses, the police and politicians, wary of such a "national eccentricity" taken to an "unwelcome extreme".[112] This move was not without precedent, as other jurisdictions, which had originally based their Sale of Goods legislation on the English Act, had already repealed the equivalent of s 22 of the Act.[113] Other jurisdictions have simply never accepted the rule as part of their law.[114] More recently, the Law Reform Commission of Western Australia[115] and the Law Reform Commission of Hong Kong[116] have recommended the abolition of the rule, the latter commenting that the market overt rule is "in modern urban conditions, an anachronism which unreasonably penalises the innocent owner".[117]

However, it has been pointed out by a brave, lone few that "it makes nonsense of law reform to take aspects of chattels of a particular class and deal with it on its own".[118] Why insist on reforming one aspect of the law and then fail to deal with other situations equally open to challenge? Any reforms in this area should be wary of removing a degree of protection afforded a purchaser without first putting in place

---

111 Sale of Goods (Amendment) Act 1994.

112 Per Mr Richard Spring, Hansard Parliamentary Debates, 27 October 1993, Col 946.

113 For example, s 2 of the New Zealand Sale of Goods Amendment Act 1961 provides that "[t]he law relating to market overt shall not apply to New Zealand". In Victoria, the market overt rule was abolished in s 34 of the Second Hand Dealers and Pawnbrokers Act 1989.

114 The rule did not apply in Scotland (See s 22(3) of the Sale of Goods Act 1893) Wales (The Laws in Wales Act, 34 & 35 Hen. VIII, c.26, s 47, as amended by the Theft Act 1968, s 33(3)) or the United States after the colonial period. (See for example: *Towne v Collins* (1785) 14 Mass 500) See: Smith, "Valediction to Market Overt" (1997) *Am J Legal History* 225 at pp 225–226; Davies, "Transferability and the Sale of Goods" (1987) 7 *Legal Studies* 1 at pp 17–18. With the exception of British Columbia, none of the common law provinces in Canada has adopted the market overt rule, and even in British Columbia the doctrine has remained dormant: Ontario Law Reform Commission *Report on Sale of Goods 1979,* p 284. In Australia, the Sale of Goods Acts of Queensland, New South Wales, Northern Territory and Australian Capital Territory either do not include the rule or (for example, s 4(2) of the NSW Sale of Goods Act 1923) expressly exclude it. The market overt rule was abolished in Singapore by The Application of English Law Act 1993, although it is doubtful whether it applied before this: see Neo "Application of English Law Act 1993: Sale of Goods and *Nemo Dat*" [1994] *Singapore Journal of Legal Studies* 150 at pp 153–157.

115 Law Reform Commission of Western Australia, *Project No 89: Report on the Sale of Goods Act 1895* (1998), p 23.

116 Law Reform Commission of Hong Kong, *Contracts for the Supply of Goods* (2002), p 235.

117 *ibid*, p 234.

118 per Mr Roger Evans, Hansard Parliamentary Debates, Vol 246, Col 1341.

some form of substitute. They should take place, not in an isolated fashion as in England, but as part of an overall reform of the law in this area.

Possible Reforms

There is a general consensus that the *Nemo Dat* rule and the statutory exceptions thereto are in need of reform. It has been complained that "the statutory provisions, developed piecemeal and interpreted restrictively by the courts, do not in policy terms represent either a rational or a cohesive set of rules for balancing the conflicting interests"[119] and that their application depends "not on principles of equity or justice but on fine technicalities which have little rhyme and less reason".[120] It is clear that the problem with the current law does not lie solely with the amount of protection given to the purchaser—some would say this protection goes too far and the abolition of the market overt rule in many jurisdictions has served to reduce it further—but also with the basis of such protection. The policy of the 1893 Act is unclear and the circumstances in which it allows recovery tend to be arbitrary, technical and at times irrational.

Over the years, various different law reforms have been proposed by different institutions. Many of these involve the reduction of the current statutory provisions into a single basic principle, although there is a disagreement as to what exactly that principle should be! One recurring principle, which was suggested earlier in this article, is as follows: The purchaser should always have bought in good faith and without notice in order to have any claim to the goods. If, then, the owner of the goods is entirely blameless—for example in the case of theft—he should be entitled to the return of his goods. However, the purchaser should be protected where there is evidence that an owner was careless with his goods and gave possession to another who wrongfully sold them on, or where the normal rules of agency apply to pass on title. Such a principle can be found in s 6.4 (2) of the Canadian Uniform Sale of Goods Act. It states that an owner is precluded from denying the authority to sell of the person in possession of the goods where (a) he has failed to exercise reasonable care with respect to the entrustment of the goods and (b) the buyer has exercised reasonable care in buying the goods and has received the goods in good faith, for value and without notice of the defect in the title of the transferor or his lack of authority to sell the goods.

---

119 Goode, *op. cit,* p 424.

120 *Report of the Crowther Committee on Consumer Credit* (1974), Cmnd. 4596, para 4.2.8.

Reform proposals have not been limited to an "all or nothing" solution whereby one innocent party gets the goods and the other gets nothing. In *Ingram v Little* Devlin LJ suggested the possibility of apportioning the loss between the parties:

> "The relevant question in this sort of case . . . is . . . which of two innocent parties shall suffer for the fraud of a third. The plain answer is that the loss should be divided between them in such proportion as is just in all the circumstances. If it be pure misfortune, the loss should be borne equally; if the fault or imprudence of either party has caused or contributed to the loss, it should be borne by that party in the whole or in the greater part."[121]

This suggestion was rejected by the English Law Reform Committee as impractical[122]: how would the loss be apportioned and, in the case where there may be many parties and chains of transactions involved, between who? It is suggested, however, that these difficulties have been overcome in the area of contributory negligence in tort, and the principles involved there could be adaptable to this situation.[123] The wording of the formula given by Devlin LJ was perhaps unfortunate. He suggested that in a case of "pure" misfortune (i.e. simple larceny) the loss should be borne equally. The Law Reform Committee questioned why the owner should bear any part of the loss in this situation?[124] However this does not mean that apportionment should be rejected outright. Judicial discretion could have an important role here. The Committee though, feared the introduction of a wide judicial discretion in an area where it felt predictability is particularly important. It needs to be asked if such predictability comes at too high a price? It will not be much comfort to an innocent purchaser, such as that in *Newtons of Wembley v Williams,* when they lose on an irrational technicality, that at least the result is "predictable". Furthermore, it should be noted that the principle apportionment has been accepted in the Canada Uniform Sale of Goods Act, at least where both parties have failed to exercise reasonable care.[125]

There is another form of apportionment, based on unjust enrichment, which should not be ignored in this context. To give an example, where the owner of a

---

[121] *Ingram v Little* [1961] 1 QB 31 at 38.

[122] Twelfth Report, Cmnd. 2958.

[123] See for example: *Iarnrod Eireann v Ireland* (1996) 2 ILRM500; (1995) 2 ILRM 161.

[124] *op. cit,* para 10.

[125] s 6(3) of the Uniform Sale of Goods Act provides that in this situation "the court may allocate the loss between them and make such other order with respect to the goods as is fair in the circumstances."

Gainsborough painting worth £2 million voluntarily hands possession of it to a rogue in circumstances which should invoke an exception to the *Nemo Dat* rule, but the innocent purchaser of the painting pays only £100 for it, there is an argument that the law should prevent the unjust enrichment of the purchaser in this manner. It should be possible for the owner in these circumstances to pay the £100 to the purchaser and reclaim his painting. Authority for this idea can be found in the French Civil Code[126] and in texts as old as the Code of Hammurabi![127]

Before any reforms are implemented, however, it is important to compile empirical evidence as to the way in which the law operates. It has been commented that the continuing lack of such evidence "makes it difficult to justify positive proposals for change of a fundamental character".[128] Such evidence should include statistics as to the likelihood that either or both parties are covered by insurance,[129] although it seems more likely that the original owner would be insured against theft or fraud than the innocent purchaser would be insured against the risk that he might not have best possible title.[130] Where the owner is insured against theft or fraud, any reforms should bear in mind that any protection offered to the owner is more likely to constitute an advantage to insurance firms rather than the actual owners, particularly where the goods which have passed hands have a purely financial, as opposed to sentimental, value.[131] There would thus seem to be "good reason for giving greater

---

126 Article 2280 of the Civil Code provides that where a purchaser acquired goods in a fair or market or public auction or from a merchant who deals in those goods, the owner of the goods can recover the goods if he gives to the purchaser what the purchaser paid for it. See Nicholas, *French Law of Contract* (1982), p 78.

127 See s 287 of the Code of Hammurabi: "the purchaser shall take oath before god as to the silver he has paid: and the owner of the slave...shall give to the trader the silver he has paid; and shall recover his slave."

128 Atiyah, Adams and MacQueen, *op. cit*, p 413. Atiyah has strongly criticised the Law Reform Committee's 1966 Report for its lack of statistical evidence or factual basis: Atiyah, "Law Reform Committee: Twelfth Report" (1966) 29 MLR 541.

129 See: Atiyah, "Law Reform Committee: Twelfth Report" (1966) 29 MLR 541 at p 542.

130 It is arguable that even if the purchasers do regularly take out insurance on the risk of such a loss, that such insurance should not be necessary and merely increases costs. Once you have, in good faith, received and paid full value for goods you should not have to take account of the possibility that you may not have the best possible title.

131 The Law Reform Commission of Hong Kong has commented that it is important to remember that goods may have a sentimental value to their owner: Law Reform Commission of Hong Kong, *Contracts for the Supply of Goods* (2002), p 235.

protection under the law to [uninsured] *bona fide* purchasers than is done at present".[132]

There seems little point in reforming the legal position in Ireland without considering the viewpoints of other European states. Moves are currently afloat to harmonise European contract law,[133] and it may be that in a number of years reforms of the *Nemo Dat* will be instigated externally, from Brussels. Although the approach of the civil law has varied in the past,[134] in general the civil law protects the interests of the innocent purchaser over the interests of the original owner, such that the *Nemo dat* rule is the exception rather than the rule. This is reflected in Art 2279 of the French Civil Code which states that *"En fait de meubles, la possession vaut titre."*[135] Similarly, s 932 of the German Civil Code protects a purchaser who believes that a seller owns the goods and obtains possession of the goods and s 366 of the German Commercial Code protects a good faith purchaser of goods which he knew the vendor did not own, provided that the purchaser *bona fide* believed that the vendor was entitled to dispose of the goods on behalf of their owner.[136]

---

132 Atiyah, Adams and MacQueen, *op. cit,* p 413.

133 See: http://frontpage.cbs.dk/law/commission_on_european_contract_law/ (Accessed, 30 August 2005).

134 The *Nemo Dat* rule was an "established principle" of Roman law and was generally followed from the 13th century to the 18th century. See: Goode, *op. cit* (3rd ed) p 416.

135 This translates as "As far as movables are concerned, possession is equivalent to title." This provisions has the effect of enabling a bona fide possessor to obtain title immediately if he acquires the goods from a bailee and after three years if the owner has parted with the thing involuntarily. See Nicholas, *French Law of Contract* (1982), pp 78, 149.

136 See: Horn, Kotz and Leser (Translation by Weir), *German Private and Commercial Law: An Introduction* (1982), pp 176, 217. These provisions do not apply where the owner is the victim of theft.

Online Education and Copyright Law

by
Thomas Mohr*

> "At the moment when Charlemagne had begun to reign as sole king in the western regions of the world, two Irishmen happened to visit the coast of Gaul in the company of some British traders. These men were unrivalled in their knowledge of sacred and profane letters, at a time when the pursuit of learning was almost forgotten throughout the length and breadth of Charlemagne's kingdom and worship of the true God was at a very low ebb. They had nothing on display to sell, but every day they used to shout to the crowds who had collected to buy things: "If anyone wants some wisdom, let him come to us and receive it: for it is wisdom that we have for sale".[1]
>
> Notker the Stammerer, Monk of St Gall, 9th Century AD.

The above story is one of many that attest to the formidable reputation for learning enjoyed by the Irish in the early Middle Ages. The likes of Columbanus, Sedulius Scottus and Iohannes Eriugena were towering figures in the world of education in the period that is often given the unjust epithet the "Dark Ages". That such scholars had so completely mastered the learning of the classical world, despite coming from a distant island that had never been a part of the Roman Empire, was a constant source of amazement to continental Europeans. Anastasius, a papal librarian, remarked upon Iohannes Eriugena's extensive knowledge of Greek in a letter to Charles the Bald in 860. He concluded that "it is a wonderful thing how that barbarian, living at the ends of the earth, who might be supposed to be as far removed from the knowledge of this other language as he is from the familiar use of it, has been able to comprehend such ideas and translate them into another tongue".[2]

---

* This essay was awarded joint second place in the Law Society of Ireland, *Student Law Reform Essay Competition 2003.*

[1] Ó Cróinín, *Early Medieval Ireland 400–1200* (1st ed, Longman, London, 1995) p 220.

[2] *ibid,* p 228.

Modern technology has ensured that "living at the ends of the earth" is no longer the disadvantage it was in the distant past. The Internet has facilitated the proliferation of knowledge to such an extent that a person can now download, in a matter of minutes, more information than would have been contained in the libraries used by Iohannes Eriugena. There is little doubt that this new medium offers dazzling opportunities to contemporary Irish educators that their medieval counterparts could not have imagined in their wildest fantasies. Yet, many Irish educational institutions have hesitated to cross this bright new educational frontier as a result of another innovation that was unknown in medieval times, the law of copyright.[3]

Every person who has ever taught a class will be aware that it is often necessary to show students a photograph, illustration or diagram in order to illustrate a point, give an example or simply enliven the lesson. For the same reasons, it might be necessary to play a short clip from a film or a television programme to a class. Music teachers will not get far with their lessons and will rapidly lose their students' attention if they fail to play short musical excerpts as examples of what they are trying to explain. In the same way, a literature class may need to use works of poetry or extracts of prose, an engineering class may need technical diagrams and an information technology class may need portions of computer programs if they are to function properly. While educational institutions commonly make use of portions of such works in a physical classroom setting, they are apprehensive about doing so over the medium of the Internet as a result of fears of legal action being taken against them by a hostile copyright holder.

Every educational institution that plans to provide online courses will inevitably seek answers to the following questions:

(i) Can we incorporate a small portion of a copyright work into our online course, given that it is being used for an educational purpose, without risking legal action being taken for breach of copyright?

(ii) If the answer to the first question is "yes", how large can this portion be?

[3] This is unless one accepts the famous story of St Columba's illegal copying of a manuscript belonging to St Fintan. The resulting dispute was taken all the way to the High King who is supposed to have ruled "for every cow its calf, to every book its copy". It seems mandatory that every Irish law student must hear this charming story in their introductory lecture on copyright law. Nevertheless, even if the story is not apocryphal it should not be seen as having launched Irish copyright law.

An obvious way of overcoming these obstacles is to secure permission from the copyright holder to use the required portion of their work. However, while this might seem the obvious course of action, the reality is that it is often impractical. Anyone who has ever attempted to do this will be aware that even discovering the identity of the copyright holder can often be a labyrinthine process. When Pennsylvania State University attempted to secure permission to use a small portion of footage from the Bikini Atoll nuclear test for a physics lesson they rapidly became embroiled in the intricate maze of television and video copyright. They followed a trail of ownership from PBS to the American Federal Government to the camera operator who took the pictures in July 1946. Having done this, they had to ascertain whether or not the camera operator was in the employment of the Federal Government when he took the pictures or whether the filming was a "work for hire" done by a private company.[4] Such time-consuming and labour intensive research is clearly beyond the resources of most Irish educational institutions.

The Register of Copyright Licensing Bodies

The Irish Government has recently put in place a system that may ultimately provide educational institutions with some assistance in identifying an elusive copyright holder. In September 2002 a Register of Copyright Licensing Bodies was created and can now be accessed for a fee of €5 at the Office of the Controller of Patents, Designs and Trade Marks.[5] The Register is intended to provide an exhaustive list of all copyright licensing bodies operating in Ireland together with information relating to the copyright holders that they represent. Such licensing bodies may be able to assist educational institutions in identifying copyright holders and in negotiating permission to use copyright material. Obviously, such services would come at a price.

Notwithstanding the value of these innovations, it seems likely that much of the copyright material that Irish educational institutions would seek to use on their online courses would originate outside of the State. Foreign copyright holders may not be represented by a copyright licensing body operating in Ireland. Moreover,

---

[4] See Colyer, "Copyright Law, the Internet and Distance Education" (1997) 11(3) *The American Journal of Distance Education* 41 at p 54.
Also see <http://wbweb5.worldbank.org/disted/Policy/Institutional/copy-01.html> (accessed November 2002).

[5] The creation of the Register of Copyright Licensing Bodies was provided for by s 175 of the Copyright and Related Rights Act 2000 and was given effect by the Copyright and Related Rights (Register of Copyright Licensing Bodies) Regulations 2002 (SI No 463 of 2002).

there seem to be very few copyright licensing bodies, even outside of this jurisdiction, that deal with issues of copyright associated with films and television broadcasts. While the Register represents an important step in assisting with the identification of copyright holders, it does not represent a comprehensive solution to this problem. If online education is ever to achieve its enormous potential there is a real need for legal guidance as to what copyright material can be included in an online lesson and how much of it can be used if securing permission proves to be an impractical task.

The Current Status of Irish Law and Distance Education over the Internet

The most recent Irish statute dealing with copyright is the Copyright and Related Rights Act 2000. Regrettably, this statute does not deal with many of the issues that online educators are likely to encounter. Sections 53 to 58 provide for a number of limited exemptions with respect to the use of copyright material for educational purposes. These provisions allow literary, dramatic, musical and artistic works to be copied for educational use within very strict parameters. It should be emphasised that these provisions were not written specifically with the Internet in mind and their application to that medium is not always clear.

First, in order to benefit from the educational use exemption copying must be carried out in the course of instruction, in preparation for instruction,[6] or in the context of an examination.[7] Copyright in a work is not infringed by anything done for the purpose of an examination by way of setting questions, communicating questions to the candidates or answering questions.[8] It should be noted that copying need not be carried out by a teacher or a student to avail of the educational use exemption. It is enough that copying is being carried out "on behalf of a person giving or receiving instruction"[9] or "on behalf of an educational establishment for the educational purposes of that establishment".[10] This is important in the particular context of distance education as not all teachers are computer literate and may need the assistance of others to actually place the required information onto the Internet.

---

6 Copyright and Related Rights Act 2000, s 53(1).

7 *ibid* at s 53(5).

8 *ibid.*

9 *ibid* at ss 53(2)(a) and 53(4)(a).

10 *ibid* at ss 56(1) and 57(1).

The copyright in a literary, dramatic, musical or artistic work or the typographical arrangement of a published edition is not infringed by its being copied in the course of instruction or in preparation for instruction.[11] However, this does not apply to copying done by means of a reprographic process which includes photocopying and, more importantly in the context of online education, scanning.[12]

The copyright in a sound recording, film, broadcast or cable programme or an original database is not infringed by its being copied in the course of instruction or in preparation for instruction.[13] However, online educators should take note that this only applies when copying results in only a single copy being made.[14] In this context it should be noted that the Internet can be viewed at multiple locations all over the world. The question as to whether an item placed on the Internet would still constitute a single copy cannot be answered with complete certainty.

A fixation of a broadcast or cable programme, or a copy of such a fixation, may be made by or on behalf of an educational establishment for the educational purposes of that establishment without infringing copyright in the broadcast or cable programme, or in any work included in the broadcast or cable programme.[15] However, this will not apply where there is a licensing scheme and the person making the copy knew or ought to have been aware of the licensing scheme.[16]

In creating an anthology for educational use, the inclusion of a short passage from a literary, dramatic or musical work, original database or typographical arrangement of a published edition shall not infringe copyright in the work.[17] However, this is subject to the following conditions:

---

[11] *ibid* at s 53(1).

[12] *ibid* at s 53(2)(b). A special licensing scheme has recently been introduced in Ireland with respect to reprographic copying from books, journals and periodicals for educational purposes. This is operated by a non-profit making organisation called the Irish Copyright Licensing Agency. Under this scheme educational institutions can, in return for the payment of an annual tariff, obtain a licence to make reprographic copies within certain quantitative limits. See Copyright and Related Rights (Certification of Licensing Scheme for Reprographic Copying by Educational Establishments) (The Irish Copyright Licensing Agency Limited) Order 2002, SI No 514 of 2002 and <http://www.icla.ie>.

[13] *ibid* at s 53(3).

[14] *ibid* at s 53(4)(b).

[15] *ibid* at s 56(1).

[16] *ibid* at s 56(2). Such licensing schemes are dealt with by s 173 of the Act.

[17] *ibid* at s 54(1).

(i) The original work must have been lawfully made available to the public;[18]
(ii) The original work must not have been intended for use in educational establishments;[19]
(iii) The anthology must be intended for use in educational establishments and is so described in its title, or in any advertisements issued by or on behalf of the publisher;[20]
(iv) The anthology must consist mainly of material in which no copyright subsists;[21]
(v) No more than two excerpts from works by the same author which have been lawfully made available to the public by the same publisher may be included in an anthology within a period of 5 years.[22]

It cannot be overemphasised that a reproduction must always be accompanied by sufficient acknowledgement.[23] This stipulation also applies to inclusions in an anthology.[24] Persons dealing with materials in foreign languages should note that special care must be taken when translating a work. This is because an inept translation may be considered to constitute a breach of the author's moral rights.[25] Finally, a copy made for educational purposes that is subsequently sold, rented or lent, or offered or exposed for sale, rental or loan, or otherwise made available to the public may infringe copyright.[26] It is of particular importance that distance educators adhere to all the above requirements since they are working in a medium where the chances of an infringement being detected are much greater than any other.

The EU Information Society Directive

In addition to Irish domestic law it should be noted that the law of the European Union also provides exemptions, or rather "exceptions", as EU drafters prefer to call

---

18 *ibid.*

19 *ibid.*

20 *ibid* at s 54(1)(a).

21 *ibid* at s 54(1)(b).

22 *ibid* at s 54(2).

23 *ibid* at ss 53(2)(c), 53(4)(c) and 54(1)(b) (relating to anthologies) and 57(1) (relating to reprographic copying).

24 *ibid* at s 54(1)(b).

25 This is contrast to the UK, where the integrity right expressly excludes translations. See Clark, *Irish Copyright and Design Law* (1st ed, Butterworths, Dublin, 2001).

26 Copyright and Related Rights Act 2000, ss 53(7), 56(3) and 57(5).

them, with respect to uses in an educational context. The Information Society Directive[27] allows Member States to provide for exceptions to reproduction rights and rights of communication to the public of works when the use is for the sole purpose of illustration for teaching or scientific research.[28] It should, however, be noted that the educational exceptions given in the Directive are contingent on the activity in question being of a non-commercial nature. However, the Directive clarifies that the non-commercial nature of the activity in question will be determined by that activity as such. The organisational structure and the means of funding of the establishment concerned are not decisive factors in this respect.[29] The Directive also emphasises the obligation to identify the source of the material used, including the author's name, unless this proves to be impossible.[30]

While it is important that distance educators be aware of such provisions it should be noted that EU Directives, in common with Irish statutes, do not specifically answer the question distance educators are most interested in having answered. How much of a copyright work can be used without the need to pay royalties to the copyright holder? In this context, the area of existing law of most interest to distance educators can be found in a legal concept known as "fair dealing".

Fair Dealing

The law takes into account the need to achieve a balance between the copyright holder's intellectual property rights over a work and the public's right to use the ideas contained within the work for a number of limited purposes. To achieve this balance, Irish law has recognised "fair dealing"[31] as a defence against infringement of copyright. In determining whether the use of certain materials constitutes "fair dealing" the following factors are weighed and balanced:

- (i) The purpose of the use. (Is it commercial or educational non-profit?);
- (ii) The nature of the copyright work itself;
- (iii) The quantity or substantiality of the segment of the work being used in relation to the whole;

[27] Directive 2001/29/EC of the European Parliament and of the Council of 22 May 2001 on the harmonisation of certain aspects of copyright and related rights in the information society, OJ L 167.

[28] *ibid* at Art 5(3)(a).

[29] *ibid* at Art (42).

[30] *ibid* at Art 5(3)(a).

[31] Copyright and Related Rights Act 2000, ss 50 and 51.

(iv) The effect of the use on the potential market for the original work. (Will it compete with or in some way damage the market for the original work?).

In order to constitute "fair dealing" the copyright material must be used in the context of one of the permitted uses. These permitted uses are:

(i) Research or private study[32];
(ii) Criticism or review[33];
(iii) Reporting current events.[34]

There is an enduring and commonly held legal myth that "fair dealing" always permits the use of 10 per cent of a piece of copyright material without fear of infringement. The truth is that there is no reference to such a 10 per cent permissible limit in the Copyright and Related Rights Act, 2000 or in any other legislation. "Fair dealing" is determined on the basis of the four criteria given above. For example, the use of a number of film clips that constitute less than 10 per cent of a film will not be seen as "fair dealing" if those clips give away vital plot twists and thus damage the film's potential market. Likewise, taking just a few seconds of footage from a copyright recording of a football match would be unlikely to constitute "fair dealing" if those few seconds included all the goals scored. In short, the "fair dealing" analysis is qualitative as well as quantitative in nature. Lord Reid, in *Ladbroke (Football) Ltd. v William Hill (Football) Ltd.,* went as far as saying: "If he does copy, the question whether he has copied a substantial part depends much more on the quality than on the quantity of what he has taken".[35] While there have been few Irish cases in this area, there are a number of cases emanating from other common law jurisdictions that illustrate this principle.

Sillitoe and Others v McGraw-Hill Book Company (UK) Ltd.[36] involved an action for infringement of copyright in a series of study notes for "O" Level students. The plaintiffs alleged that the study notes had reproduced substantial parts of Alan Sillitoe's short story the "Loneliness of the Long Distance Runner", of Laurie Lee's

---

32 *ibid* at s 50(1).

33 *ibid* at s 51(1).

34 *ibid* at s 51(2).

35 [1964] 1 All ER 465 at 469.

36 [1983] FSR 545.

book "Cider with Rosie" and of George Bernard Shaw's play "Saint Joan" without the permission of the copyright holders. According to the plaintiffs, the defendants had reproduced 10 per cent of the short story in question and five per cent of the book and play. The defendants disputed these figures and gave their own quantitative analysis of how much of the contents of each work had been reproduced. Nevertheless, the decision of Judge Mervyn Davies emphasised that the quality of the material reproduced was also a factor to be considered. "It is plain that substantiality is a question of fact and degree determined by reference not only to the amount of the work reproduced but also to the importance of the parts reproduced. Judged by that test, after reading the quoted extracts in the context of the original work, there is no doubt in my mind that The Runner Notes do reproduce substantial parts of the original work."[37] He made similar findings with respect to the remaining two works.

In the New Zealand case of *Longman v Carrington*[38] the authors and publishers of a number of books on technical drawing alleged infringement of copyright by an educational institution. A tutor had photocopied extracts of drawings and texts from copyright works and published them as a soft-cover book for the use of his students. The court made a number of quantitative analyses in deciding whether or not substantial reproduction had taken place. It examined how many individual drawings had been taken from every book and from particular chapters within those books. It also estimated how many pages of drawings and text had been taken from each book. Finally, it attempted to calculate the percentage that the copyright material constituted in relation to the total contents of the original works. In spite of this, the court's decision that substantial reproduction had taken place was largely based on a qualitative analysis. The court inferred that the tutor had chosen the best available drawings from the copyright works in creating his guide for his students. Doogue J noted that an expert witness had stated that the drawings taken were "fundamental and basic to that part or that aspect of engineering drawing under consideration".[39] The tutor himself admitted that he only copied "useful and significant portions of the books" which were fundamental to his course.[40]

While these cases might be interesting from an academic perspective it should be noted that they only serve to add to the difficulties faced by the distance educator.

37 *ibid* at 549.

38 [1991] 2 NZLR 574.

39 *ibid* at 580.

40 *ibid.*

Establishing the principle that "fair dealing" involves a qualitative, in addition to a quantitative, analysis only serves to add to the complexity of the concept of "fair dealing". It means that its scope becomes less, rather than more, certain. In any case, while the educational use exemptions contained in the Copyright and Related Rights Act 2000, in the EU Information Society Directive and the concept of "fair dealing" provide some guidance to educational institutions they do not address many of the most serious questions that are of particular relevance to distance education over the Internet.

Some Copyright Problems that are Relevant to Distance Education Over the Internet

The greatest difficulty faced by distance educators is that the Copyright and Related Rights Act 2000 makes no specific reference to education over the Internet and gives little guidance with respect to the problems that face this new form of education. In spite of the fact that the 2000 Act is a relatively new piece of legislation, it barely mentions the word "Internet" in any of its 376 sections.[41] The main problems encountered by educational institutions that wish to initiate online courses are as follows:

(i) When the Copyright and Related Rights Act 2000 refers to the use of a work in or at an "educational establishment" is the legal meaning of this term confined to a physical space or can an "educational establishment" exist in cyberspace?

(ii) How much of a piece of text, music or audiovisual recording can be placed on an educational web site without risking a breach of the copyright holder's intellectual property rights? Can a photograph or an illustration be displayed in their entirety? It is all very well to refer educational institutions to "fair dealing" but this is a vague concept and there are few guidelines and very little case law as to its application with respect to the Internet. This question is likely to be of interest to all institutions offering multimedia educational courses whether these are provided over the medium of the Internet or by other technological means.

[41] I am only aware of three instances in which the term is used. Sections 40 and 205 stipulate that copyright holders and performers respectively are entitled a making available right which expressly applies to the Internet. The third reference is contained in s 38, which stipulates that provisions for licences of right in respect of sound recordings do not apply to the Internet.

(iii) What safeguards must the educational institution put in place in order to prevent persons who are not registered students from accessing the online classes that incorporate portions of copyright works? Do educational institutions have a duty to adopt a copyright policy and make it known to their staff and students?

(iv) There is no legislative guidance as to how long an online lecture or tutorial that incorporates a portion of copyright material can be displayed on the web. Can it remain on the Internet indefinitely or must it be removed after a certain period of time has elapsed? Obviously, the longer it remains on the Internet the more likely it is to be accessed by an unauthorised person.

In the absence of any clear legislative guidance in this area, a number of what can only be termed "legal myths" have arisen to fill the void. The commonly held legal myth that "fair dealing" always permits the use of 10 per cent of a piece of copyright material has already been examined. There is also an erroneous assumption that copyright law only applies to big multi-national corporations and not to individuals. Another myth is the extremely dangerous belief that copyright law does not apply to the Internet in any capacity. According to this view "the Internet is the modern-day version of the wild frontier or the Old West—no laws apply and it's every man for himself".[42] In addition, many people believe that material that is placed on the Internet is *ipso facto* in the public domain and, therefore, can be freely used by other web users without breaching copyright law. The truth is that while the Internet might be a relatively recent invention which has created significant challenges for copyright law to cope with, there is no doubt that it applies to the Internet just as it applies to materials in print and to television broadcasts. A number of organisations publish exclusively on the Internet and have a strong interest in protecting the commercial viability of their web publications. As far as the law is concerned, these organisations are as entitled to protect their intellectual property rights as those who use more established means of relaying information. It is also no longer safe to assume that copyright law does not protect a work that does not carry a copyright notice.

Giving full credit to the author of the original work, while at least precluding any accusations of plagiarism, does not grant any form of immunity with respect to

---

[42] "Internet Top Myths" <http://www.law.duke.edu/copyright/face/softint/myths.htm> (Accessed November 2002).

breaches of copyright. The fact that the use of a portion of a work might constitute "free advertising" is also no defence in relation to a breach of copyright.

The Need for Reform

There is little doubt that the current state of the law provides insufficient guidance for educational institutions interested in offering courses over the medium of the Internet. The uncertainty that results from this lack of guidance inhibits educational institutions from taking full advantage of modern technology to expand their activities into an area with such revolutionary potential. Many institutions may refrain entirely from stepping onto such uncertain ground as a result of a dread of deep legal pitfalls. Those who do take the step may take an excessively conservative path as a result of such fears. This may lead them to omit material that would both enliven and clarify what they are attempting to teach, thus damaging the quality of their courses.

Some Preliminary Steps

There are a number of preliminary steps that educational institutions can immediately take to minimise the risk of legal action being taken against them as a result of incorporating small portions of copyright material into their online classes. First, all material posted onto the Internet should be proofread beforehand to ensure that it is free of plagiarised material and to ensure that all copyright works are identified. If copyright items are discovered, their owners should be identified if this is reasonably possible and an effort made to secure permission. If copyright material is to be used in an online lecture or tutorial it is imperative that it be directly related to the relevant subject matter and be of real assistance to the teaching content of the lecture or tutorial in question. Although it may seem an obvious point, educational institutions should ensure that the portions of copyright materials used do not come from copies that they know or have reason to believe were not lawfully made or acquired.

It is important that the distance education web site be secure with a password or pin number for registered students. If any legal exemptions with respect to educational purposes are to be maintained it is imperative that only registered students can access the site. If possible, technological measures should be put in place to prevent students from sharing the online material with unauthorised persons. The first page of any distance education transmission should include a notice informing students that materials used in connection with the course may be subject to copyright protection. Students should also be informed that they might be liable for any use of the materials outside the sphere of their own studies that infringe the rights of the copyright holder. Finally, the material on the distance education web site should only be accessible to students for a limited period of time. In other words, online lectures or tutorials containing copyright material should be removed from the web site at regular intervals.

A Legislative Solution

While such basic guidelines may provide a useful start for educational institutions seeking to create online courses, they are clearly insufficient to completely allay all their fears of breaching copyright law. In order to remove this constraint from a form of education with such enormous potential it is necessary to initiate a process of consultation with interested parties on what can be done to ensure that copyright issues do not stifle it in its cradle. The participants in this process should include educational institutions, libraries, publishers, filmmakers, recording companies, television production companies, media associations, software publishers, photographers' associations, artists' associations, authors' associations, copyright licensing bodies, representatives from the relevant Government Departments and, of course, copyright lawyers. The large number of participants together with the complexity of the issues involved mean that this is likely to be an extremely time-consuming process. The length of time required to draft the legislation that may eventually result from the final report of this consultation process would cause further delay. Bearing all this in mind, it is essential that this process begin in the very near future to ensure that Irish educational institutions are not left behind in entering the new arena of online education.

In spite of all these difficulties, some comfort can be taken from the fact that legislation in this area has already been produced in the jurisdiction whose software, media and entertainment industries dominate the globe. The Technology, Education and Copyright Harmonization Act 2002 (also known as the TEACH Act) was signed into law by President George W Bush on 2 November 2002.[43] The TEACH Act attempts to clarify the terms and conditions under which non-profit educational institutions may use copyright materials in distance education, which includes distance education over the Internet, without permission from the

[43] The long title of this Act is "An Act to amend chapter 1 of title 17, United States Code, relating to the exemption of certain performances or displays for educational uses from copyright infringement provisions, to provide that the making of copies or phonorecords of such performances or displays is not an infringement under certain circumstances, and for other purposes".

copyright holders and without the payment of royalties. The value of this American statute, from an Irish perspective, is that it not only provides a measure of guidance as to the direction that future Irish legislation should take but is also definite proof that consensus can be reached in this complex area.

The central theme of the TEACH Act is that it envisages a system of distance education that derives its basic format from traditional classroom teaching. The Act specifies that the portions of copyright material used must be "an integral part of the class experience, controlled by or under the actual supervision of the instructor and analogous to the type of performance or display that would take place in a live classroom setting".[44] It assumes that lessons will occur in separate instalments and that the copyright portions that are used will be incorporated into the online lecture in much the same way that such materials would be used in face-to-face classes, i.e. real-time use. This means that instructors can only use such portions of a copyright work as could be utilised in the limited time allowed by a lecture or tutorial. They would not be permitted to place entire works for students to access for their own private study or include chapters from textbooks or other materials "which are typically purchased or acquired by the students".[45]

The TEACH Act assumes that structures will be put in place to limit the instructional programme to students enrolled in the course "to the extent that is technologically feasible".[46] They are also obliged to implement technological systems that seek to prevent unauthorised dissemination of the copyright material incorporated into the instructional programme. To further minimise this risk, the TEACH Act envisages a system whereby the online lectures or tutorial would be removed and placed into storage after a certain period of time has elapsed. According to the Act, material should not be available on a network "for a longer period than is reasonably necessary to facilitate the transmissions for which it was made".[47] Once the material is placed in storage it may continue to be accessed by registered students for a limited period of time, presumably in a library or some other on-site facility.[48] It should also be noted that the Act's stipulation that online classes using portions of copyright material must be used "solely for... students officially

---

[44] TEACH Act, s 1(b)(2).

[45] *ibid.*

[46] TEACH Act, s 1(b)(1).

[47] TEACH Act, s 1(b)(2).

[48] *ibid.*

enrolled in the course for which the transmission is made"[49] means that the classes cannot be made available to the general public for promotional purposes:

The TEACH Act expressly permits the use of:

(i) Performances of non-dramatic literary works;
(ii) Performances of non-dramatic musical works;
(iii) "Reasonable and limited portions" of performances of any other work including dramatic works and audiovisual works;
(iv) Displays of any work "in an amount comparable to that which is typically displayed in the course of a live classroom session".[50]

The Act also specifies that the following materials may not be used in creating an online course.

(i) Works that are marketed "primarily for performance or display as part of mediated instructional activities transmitted via digital networks", i.e. somebody else's online course;
(ii) Performances or displays which were accessed through copies "not lawfully made or acquired" under American Copyright Law if the educational institution either knew or had reason to believe that these copies were not lawfully made or acquired.[51]

There are also restrictions on converting analog materials into a digital format.[52]

The American Act imposes a number of duties on educational institutions and their component parts. The educational institution must "initiate policies regarding copyright".[53] Although it does not specify what these policies should be, it is clear that they must be in accord with the demands of the TEACH Act and other pieces of US copyright legislation. The institution must also provide informational material regarding copyright which should be distributed to "faculty, students and all relevant staff members".[54] In addition, students must be provided with a notice

49 TEACH Act, s 1(b)(1).

50 *ibid.*

51 *ibid.*

52 TEACH Act, s 1(c)(1).

53 TEACH Act, s 1(b)(1).

54 *ibid.*

informing them that materials used in connection with the course may be subject to copyright protection.[55] It seems to be enough here to give a brief statement outlining basic copyright information to students. This notice could appear in the opening frame of an online course or could be attached to the instructional material in some other way that ensures that every student sees it. Finally, it should be noted that the Act imposes a duty on instructors to oversee the preparation of materials for their classes.[56] The portions of copyright material that they incorporate into their online classes should be "directly related and of material assistance to the teaching content of the transmission".[57]

Difficulties with Following the American TEACH Act

While the TEACH Act will undoubtedly prove an important guide to other legislatures in dealing with the copyright problems that accompany online education, it is not without its flaws, which Irish legislation should seek to avoid. First, the TEACH Act allows educational institutions to keep a limited number of copies of an instructional programme that contains copyright material. These copies may be stored and retrieved for future use. It also protects educational institutions from any liability that might result from "transient or temporary storage of material".[58] However, the Act says nothing about any entitlements on the part of the person who created the instructional material to keep a copy for their own personal use. This might include presenting the material at conferences or at job interviews. Irish legislation should provide for such personal copies which would allow educators to receive the credit they deserve for their work. Secondly, the TEACH Act provides no guidance as to how much of a given copyright work can be legitimately used under "fair dealing". As mentioned earlier, this is not an easy question to answer since "fair dealing" involves a qualitative as well as a quantitative analysis. Nevertheless, this is the question that educational institutions are most interested in having answered and the TEACH Act is of little assistance here.

An Interim Solution while awaiting an Irish TEACH Act

As mentioned earlier, the greatest problems in creating legislation to clarify the demands of copyright law in relation to online education are the length of time

---

55 *ibid.*

56 *ibid.*

57 *ibid.*

58 TEACH Act, s 1(b)(2).

required to achieve consensus among all interested parties and the delay caused by the drafting of the legislation itself. The American TEACH Act was only drafted after years of campaigning by American educational institutions and libraries. Even after Congress finally began to pay attention many years were to elapse before the TEACH Act was finally signed into law. In the interim, Irish educational institutions can make use of the exemptions provided by the "fair dealing" provisions of the Copyright and Related Rights Act 2000. However, as mentioned earlier, "fair dealing" is an extremely vague concept which does not provide much specific guidance to educators. Is it possible to provide some guidance to Irish educational institutions while awaiting the arrival of legislation? One possible solution would be to immediately begin the consultative process among the interested parties mentioned above in order to draft a set of "fair dealing" guidelines that could be used by educational institutions as an informal guide and could form the bones of an eventual Act of the Oireachtas. Once again Ireland has an American precedent to follow in this respect.

In recognition of the difficulties faced by educational institutions with respect to making use of the American concept of "fair use", a similar though not identical equivalent of Irish "fair dealing", a group of American publishers, authors and educators came together to agree on an interpretation of "fair use" that would provide specific guidelines for educators to follow and be reasonably sure that they were not violating copyright law. In 1996 these guidelines were finalised as the "Fair Use Guidelines for Educational Multimedia Established by Congress of the United States" and were adopted as part of a non-legislative report by a Subcommittee of the American House of Representatives.[59] In addition, these guidelines were also endorsed by a number of organisations representing copyright holders in the educational, artistic, industrial and entertainment spheres.

As their name suggests, these guidelines are aimed at educators who are involved in the development of multimedia projects. The guidelines expressly provide that they apply to distance education over an educational institution's secure electronic network, whether the lessons are given in real-time, for after class review or for self-directed study, provided that:

[59] Adopted on 27 September 1996 by the Subcommittee on Courts and Intellectual Property, Committee on the Judiciary, US House of Representatives. A copy of these guidelines is available on Pennsylvania State University's web site at <http://www.libraries.psu.edu/mtss/fairuse/guidelines.html> (Accessed 21 January 2004)

> "there are technological limitations on access to the network and educational multimedia project (such as password or PIN) and provided further that the technology prevents the making of copies of copyrighted material".[60]

The guidelines further provide that if the educational institution's network or the technology used to access the educational multimedia project cannot prevent the duplication of the portions of copyright material used, the project may be used over an otherwise secure network for a limited period of 15 days.

The American concept of "fair use", in common with the Irish concept of "fair dealing", is complicated by the fact that it requires a qualitative as well as a quantitative analysis. In spite of this, the American Fair Use Guidelines do provide a number of quantitative limits which they consider to constitute "fair use". It should be emphasised that these guidelines are not legally binding, even in the USA. However, it is likely that the American courts and their Irish counterparts would take them into account as evidence of persuasive effect in view of the fact that these guidelines represent an interpretation of "fair use" endorsed by such a large number of organisations concerned with copyright protection. It should, however, be noted that the guidelines state that "fair use and these guidelines shall not supersede licenses and contractual obligations".

The American guidelines set out the following "fair use" limits:

Motion Media

Up to 10 per cent or three minutes, whichever is less, in the aggregate of a copyright motion media work may be reproduced or otherwise incorporated in a multimedia project.[61]

Text Material

Up to 10 per cent or 1000 words, whichever is less, in the aggregate of a copyright piece of text material may be reproduced or otherwise incorporated in a multimedia project. An entire poem of less than 250 words may be used, but no more than three

---

60 s 3.2.3 of the "Fair Use Guidelines for Educational Multimedia Established by Congress of the United States".

61 *ibid* at s 4.2.1.

poems by one poet, or five poems by different poets from any anthology may be used. In respect of poems of greater length, 250 words may be used but no more than three excerpts by a poet, or five excerpts from different poets from a single anthology may be used.[62]

Music, Lyrics and Music Video

Up to 10 per cent, but in no event more than 30 seconds, of the music and lyrics from an individual musical work (or in the aggregate of extracts from an individual work), whether the musical work is embodied in copies, or audio or audiovisual works, may be reproduced or otherwise incorporated as part of a multimedia project.

The guidelines also specify that any alterations to a musical work shall not change the basic melody or fundamental character of the work. This stipulation was probably inserted to avoid any breach of the author's moral rights.[63]

Illustrations and Photographs

The guidelines emphasise the difficulty in defining when the reproduction or incorporation of photographs or illustrations constitutes "fair use" because, as noted above, "fair use" usually precludes the use of a work in its entirety. However, the guidelines provide that a photograph or an illustration may be used in its entirety but no more than five images by a photographer or an artist may be reproduced or otherwise incorporated as part of an educational multimedia project. They further provide that where photographs and illustrations from a published collective work are being used, no more than 10 per cent or 15 images, whichever is less, may be reproduced or otherwise incorporated as part of an educational multimedia project.[64]

Numerical Data Sets

Up to 10 per cent or 2500 fields or cell entries, whichever is less, from a copyright database or date table may be reproduced or otherwise incorporated as part of an educational multimedia project. The guidelines define a "field entry" as a "specific item of information, such as a name or Social Security number, in a record of a

---

62 *ibid* at s 4.2.2.

63 *ibid* at s 4.2.3.

64 *ibid* at s 4.2.4.

database file". A "cell entry" is defined as "the intersection where a row or column meet on a spreadsheet".[65]

Computer Programs

The guidelines note that "the reproduction or decompilation of copyright computer programs and portions thereof, for example the transfer of underlying code or control mechanisms, even for educational uses, are outside the scope of these guidelines.[66]

The quantitative limits given above apply to each educator or student's multimedia projects for the same academic semester, cycle or term. The term "in the aggregate" used above is said to mean "the total amount of copyrighted material from a single copyrighted work that is permitted to be used in an educational multimedia project without permission under these guidelines".[67] The guidelines demand that students be instructed to keep to these limits and have the reasons why they should do so explained to them.[68]

Conclusion

To conclude, I would like return to the story of the two Irishmen offering their wisdom to the crowds of a Carolingian market town that was mentioned at the beginning of this paper. Their activities eventually reached the ears of a curious Emperor Charlemagne who summoned them to his presence. Greatly impressed with their learning, he immediately employed them as educators at his court and later sent them to continue this work in key parts of his extensive dominions.[69] Their success is but one of many examples of the high esteem in which Irish education and learning was held throughout the Western world in the Early Middle Ages. If their example is to be emulated in the 21st century the Irish legislature must ensure that concerns over issues of copyright do not stop Irish educational institutions from entering a new educational arena that is not confined by land frontiers or by stretches of sea. As things stand, American educational institutions

[65] *ibid* at s 4.2.5.

[66] *ibid* at s 6.6.

[67] *ibid* at s 4.2.

[68] *ibid.*

[69] Ó Cróinín, *Early Medieval Ireland 400–1200* (1st ed, Longman, London, 1995), p 220.

can now stride into this arena with the guidance of groundbreaking legislation to light their path while their Irish counterparts must continue to grope through the shadows. Until this situation is remedied any aspirations of introducing the online world to modern Irish education and learning will be left to stumble their way along unknown and uncertain paths.

The Road Not Taken

by

Ray Ryan and Des Ryan*

In April 1978, Irish criminal law underwent a significant change. The Court of Criminal Appeal ("the CCA") expressly adopted a subjective test for the defence of provocation on a charge of murder. It is indeed surprising that, in all the years prior to and following that decision, the Supreme Court has never once yet had to consider the ambit of the defence of provocation. Despite the absence of a guiding statement from the Supreme Court, the Oireachtas has yet to enact legislation specifically addressing the nature of the defence of provocation in Irish law. Rather, we have had to content ourselves in this jurisdiction with comments made *obiter* by the CCA more than 25 years ago in the case of *People (DPP) v Sean MacEoin.*[1]

That the House of Lords has ruled on this issue on several occasions in the last decade is indicative of the level of confusion which the defence causes for English judges and juries alike. Regrettably, all the evidence points to a similar state of confusion when the defence is pleaded in our Central Criminal Court. As the comprehensive analysis provided in Chapter 4 of the Law Reform Commission's recent Consultation Paper on Homicide: *The Plea of Provocation*[2] demonstrates, the law of provocation is in need of urgent reform. Indeed, the inherent difficulties in the statement of law provided by Kenny J in *MacEoin* have become all too apparent in recent cases. In the case of *People (DPP) v Stephen Davis,*[3] Hardiman J, speaking for the CCA, went as far as to reveal that it was "with some trepidation that the court

* This essay was awarded a prize by the Law Society of Ireland, for the *Student Law Reform Essay Competition 2003.*

1 [1978] IR 27.

2 LRC CP 27–2003 (hereafter "LRC Consultation Paper").

3 [2001] 1 IR 146.

ventures into [the] territory of provocation".[4] Hardiman J went on to remark that *MacEoin* had created "a good deal of difficulty in practice in dealing with cases where provocation is, or is claimed to be, an issue".

The fundamental problem with the "subjective" approach espoused by Kenny J in *MacEoin* is the proportionality stage in the test enunciated. This requirement effectively renders defunct the very subjectivity which the Court in *MacEoin* sought to embrace. Little wonder, then, that subsequent decisions demonstrate the formidable difficulties of applying *MacEoin.* These difficulties might be resolved either via legislation or by judicial intervention. If the latter, the CCA could, at the next available opportunity, certify a point of law of exceptional public importance to be considered by the Supreme Court. This certified question would invite the Supreme Court to grapple with what Stannard has termed the "insuperable difficulties"[5] that stem from *MacEoin.* Alternatively, legislation could be enacted to circumvent the current law. In this vein, the Bill introduced in recent months to reform our archaic insanity laws is of potential significance when considering how best to reform the law of provocation. In considering the precise ambit of the revised subjective test, we note the significance of the recent *volte face* in England, with a majority of the Appellate Committee, delivering the advice of the Privy Council on appeal from Jersey, having recently rejected the approach in *DPP v Smith.*[6]

Provocation and *MacEoin*

In *MacEoin,* the accused had killed Patrick Hyland with a hammer, both men having consumed large quantities of alcohol. MacEoin asserted that there had been a hostile verbal exchange between the two, and that Hyland then attacked MacEoin with the hammer. At trial in the Central Criminal Court, Butler J directed the jury that the accused could not avail of the defence if he had intended to kill the deceased or to cause really serious bodily injury. This direction being manifestly erroneous, the appeal would have to have been allowed solely on this ground. However, the CCA took the opportunity to consider the nature of the provocation defence in Irish law. Dispensing with any objective requirement on the grounds that such an approach was "profoundly illogical", Kenny J set out the following model direction to be given to juries when provocation was an issue:

---

4 At 154.

5 Stannard, "Making Sense of *MacEoin*" (1998) ICLJ 26.

6 [2001] 1 AC 146.

> "The prosecution must establish beyond reasonable doubt that the accused was not provoked to such an extent that, having regard to his temperament, character and circumstances, he lost control of himself at the time of the wrongful act."

However, Kenny J proceeded to attach the significant proviso of "proportionality" to the "purely subjective" test. The added requirement was that there be a "reasonable relation" between the provocation and the force employed by the accused: "If the prosecution prove beyond reasonable doubt that the force used was unreasonable and excessive having regard to the provocation, the defence fails".

We will argue that these two strands of this test are inconsistent and impossible to reconcile. This dichotomy is responsible for the ensuing confusion that has prevailed in this area. This argument is further explored below. First, however, it is necessary to revisit two seminal cases from England decided prior to *MacEoin.* We believe that these cases are most instructive if we are to understand that the CCA was well-intentioned, but ultimately misguided, in *MacEoin.*

A Legacy of Confusion

The CCA delivered judgment in *MacEoin* on 17 April 1978. Just 11 days earlier, on the 6 April, the House of Lords had decided the seminal case of *Reg v Camplin,*[7] where a significant gloss was placed on the objective test for provocation as it had existed in English law up to that date. The unfortunate clash in the timing of these two decisions can only be lamented: it is clear from a reading of *MacEoin* that the decision in *Camplin* had not yet come to the attention of counsel. Had there been a longer interval between the two decisions—or had technological research resources been as refined as they are today—it seems certain that the very parameters of the analysis in *MacEoin* would have been significantly altered. For, in *Camplin,* their Lordships ruminated at length upon the nature of the defence, with particular emphasis on the merits of retaining the objective standard, with certain special modifications. Thus it was that *Camplin,* arguably the most important decision on the law of provocation ever to be handed down by the House of Lords, was to receive no analysis by the CCA in *MacEoin.* The "insuperable difficulties for Irish judges"[8] to which *MacEoin* gives rise, will be explored below. First, however, it is necessary to analyse the decision of House of Lords in *Camplin* in order to appreciate the backdrop against which the present confused state of Irish provocation law was to originate.

---

[7] [1978] AC 705.

[8] Stannard, above, n 5.

From *Bedder* to *Camplin*

Prior to the passing of the 1957 Homicide Act in England, the test for the defence of provocation was purely objective. No account could be taken of the personal characteristics of the accused; rather, the benchmark by which a defendant was judged was that of the reasonable man. The test was whether the accused was provoked, and, if so, whether or not a reasonable man would have acted similarly. Needless to say, such a stringent objective test was apt to lead to instances of peculiar unfairness. Nowhere was such hardship better exemplified than in the 1954 case of *Bedder*,[9] a case which can be viewed as the high-water mark of the objective test. There, the accused, who was sexually impotent, had killed a prostitute who had taunted him about his impotence and who had kicked him in the groin area. The House of Lords held that in such a case, the jury could have no regard for the accused's peculiar sexual problem. In assessing the reasonableness of his conduct, the jury must consider what the reasonable man would have done in the circumstances. Since a man of ordinary virility would not have been provoked to kill another due to taunts about sexual impotence, the defence of provocation could not succeed. Accordingly, the accused's conviction for murder was upheld.

Understandably, the decision in *Bedder* prompted considerable criticism and led to the passing in England of the 1957 Act. This restated the law on provocation and permitted the jury to have cognizance of the circumstances of the accused when considering whether the reasonable man would have acted as the accused did. However, the extent to which the Act imported a subjective element into the English law of provocation remained unclear. In the seminal case of *Camplin*, a unanimous House of Lords expressly confirmed that the 1957 Act did introduce certain subjective elements into the test for provocation. In *Camplin*, the respondent, a boy of 15, killed the deceased by hitting him over the head with a chapatti pan. He pleaded provocation on the grounds that he had been buggered by the deceased, who had then taunted him. The trial judge directed the jury that they must consider whether the provocation had been sufficient to make a reasonable man, and not a reasonable youth of 15, in the circumstances act as the respondent had done. The jury convicted the respondent of murder. The Court of Appeal allowed the appeal and substituted a conviction of manslaughter. An appeal to the House of Lords was dismissed, their Lordships holding that the jury were entitled to consider those factors, including the age and physical characteristics of the accused, which in their opinion would affect the gravity of

[9] [1954] 2 All ER 801.

the taunts and insults and the degree of self-control to be expected of him as a reasonable person.

For our purposes, the important point to be gleaned from the above overview is this: by the time the CCA gave judgment in *MacEoin* the precedent of *Bedder* was no longer considered to be good law. The CCA, as we have explained, was patently unaware of this ground-breaking development. Charleton has said of the decision in *MacEoin* that some of the relevant authorities were not cited to the Court, that the Court took it upon itself to introduce a test for provocation without precedent in the common law world and that it made use of an out-of-date textbook.[10] We can be fairly certain that the CCA would have preferred the modified objective test set out in *Camplin* to the unjust orthodoxy of *Bedder*. The reason the Court charted a new course of pure subjectivity lies, it is suggested, in its determination to "rout" the bitter harshness of *Bedder*. There is good reason for concluding that *MacEoin*, so far from representing an informed and authoritative innovation in Irish law, is fatally undermined by its unfortunate timing which precluded the Court from noting the landmark shift effected in English law just days previously.

The Inadequacy of the *MacEoin* Formulation

The difficulty with the Court's judgment in *MacEoin* is the blatant incongruity between the adoption of a "subjective" test and this simultaneous requirement of proportionality. To muster support for his rejection of an objective test, Kenny J points to several policy arguments which expose the dangers of objectivity. Ironically, such arguments are equally applicable to the proportionality requirement, which Kenny J regards as constituting a core aspect of the defence.

A string of recent cases supports this contention. The first of these is *People (DPP) v Mullane*.[11] At issue at trial was whether the accused had lost self-control. Counsel for the defence inquired how the issue of proportionality could be connected to a loss of self-control, a state which seemed to fly in the very face of proportionality. The trial judge described this as "an interesting question" but stressed to the jury that *MacEoin* was the law in Ireland, and reiterated the very wording of the *MacEoin* judgment in his direction to the jury. The accused was convicted and appealed to the CCA. Quashing the conviction and ordering a

[10] Charleton, *Criminal Law: Cases and Materials* (1992), at para 4.156.

[11] Unreported, Court of Criminal Appeal, 11 March 1997.

retrial, the Court held that while the passage in Kenny J's judgment dealing with proportionality might on its own suggest the application of an objective standard, it must be read in the context of the whole judgment, in the course of which Kenny J expressly rejects an objective standard. The Court further expressed its disapproval of the fact that the trial judge had quoted verbatim from *MacEoin*, which judgment, it said, was only intended as a guide and which should not be treated as though it were contained in a statute.

Stannard says of the CCA in *Mullane* that it "refused to allow the proportionality requirement introduced in *MacEoin* to introduce through the back door what had been so firmly expelled through the front".[12] That is, the court refused to interpret one isolated passage from the judgment in such a way that would fly in the face of everything that preceded and succeeded this passage. However, we would argue that this approach to *MacEoin* is open to criticism. The decision of the CCA in *Mullane* to simply disregard Kenny J's comments on proportionality in *MacEoin* is less than helpful since it provides no guidance on how to reconcile Kenny J's enunciation of the subjective test, on the one hand, with this requirement of proportionality, on the other.

This confusion has continued to characterise the case law. In the case of *DPP v Keith Kelly*,[13] Barrington J, speaking for the CCA, provided a telling indication of the problems caused by *MacEoin.* Having conceded that Kenny J's words in that case had caused great difficulties for trial judges, Barrington J concluded that judges in the Central Criminal Court should direct juries to the effect that *MacEoin* is the law, but that they should refrain from quoting from the speech of Kenny J!

The apparent opposition of Hardiman J in *Davis* to allowing the defence of provocation to succeed where it would offend public policy to do so adds a further problematic dimension to the Irish position. Whilst it may well be contrary to public policy to allow a "concession to human frailty" in road rage cases or cases where racist supremacists lose control (to take the two examples cited by Hardiman J in *Davis*) developing a list of exceptions to the defence does not sit easily with the "purely subjective test" that is apparently at the core of the defence in Irish law. In this regard, it is instructive to consider recent developments in the jurisprudence of the English courts *vis-à-vis* the subjective requirement.

---

12 Stannard, above, n 5.

13 [2000] 2 IR 1.

The Rise and Fall of *DPP v Smith*: Does *Holley* Represent a Possible Compromise?

With the decision of a majority of the Appellate Committee in *DPP v Smith*,[14] it appeared that English law was moving towards a far greater degree of subjectivity than had been espoused by the House in *Camplin*. The key question for resolution by the House of Lords in *Smith* was whether, in the English law of provocation, consideration could be given to the accused's particular characteristics not only in assessing the gravity of the provocation but also in considering the accused's ability to retain self-control. A similar question had divided the Judicial Committee of the Privy Council some four years earlier in *Luc Thiet Than*.[15] In *Luc*, the majority, led by Lord Goff, held that, construing *Camplin*, the only characteristics which could be considered when assessing the ability of the accused to retain self-control were age and sex. These were the only two characteristics which had been expressly mentioned in *Camplin*. A powerful dissenting voice in *Luc* had been that of Lord Steyn, who took the opposite view in order "to accord with justice and with common sense". Lord Steyn held that any peculiar characteristics of the accused were relevant in considering the effect of the accused's personal characteristics upon his ability to retain self-control.

This approach of Lord Steyn in *Luc* found favour with the majority of the Appellate Committee in *Smith*. Lord Hoffmann drew attention to the following important passage from the speech of Lord Diplock in *Camplin*, who had delivered the leading judgment in the *Camplin* case:

> "In strict logic there is a transition between treating age as a characteristic that may be taken into account in assessing the gravity of the provocation addressed to the accused and treating it as a characteristic to be taken into account in determining what is the degree of self-control to be expected of the ordinary person with whom the accused's conduct is to be compared. But to require old heads upon young shoulders is inconsistent with the law's compassion to human infirmity to which Sir Michael Foster ascribed the doctrine of provocation more than two centuries ago."

Lord Hoffmann deemed this "a most important passage" and drew attention to several points. First, he noted that Lord Diplock had said that youth may be taken

---

14 [2001] 1 AC 146.

15 [1997] AC 131. See Virgo, "Provocation: Muddying the Waters" [2001] CLJ 23.

into account because the principle of compassion to human infirmity, as the jury drawing on their experience may apply it, requires one to do so. Tellingly, Lord Diplock did not state that this same principle of compassion to human frailty—upon which the law of provocation has been traditionally based—could not (and did not) apply to other characteristics. As Lord Hoffmann observed, had Lord Diplock wished to say this in *Camplin*, nothing could have been easier. In a similar manner, Lord Diplock had expressly rejected in *Camplin* the distinction between the effect of age on the *gravity of the provocation* and on the *power of self-control* on the grounds that it was "of too great nicety" for application by a jury. At no stage did Lord Diplock say that this was not equally true of other characteristics. As such, Lord Hoffmann was confident that the correct interpretation of *Camplin* was that regard can be had to individual characteristics of the accused in assessing not only the gravity of the provocation but also in considering the accused's ability to retain self-control.

The *Smith* decision apparently represented a milestone in English provocation law. However, it was subjected to heavy criticism. Strong dissenting judgments in the case were delivered by Lords Millett and Browne-Wilkinson, and the position of the majority came in for considerable academic criticism by commentators.[16] In its Consultation Paper on the *Defence of Provocation* issued in October 2003, the Law Reform Commission considered the approach it adopted in the *Smith* case and concluded that the decision should not be incorporated into Irish law, on the grounds that the defence of provocation is not best suited to cases involving mentally ill defendants. With respect, this concern of the LRC has been entirely vindicated by the recent *volte face* in England from the approach of the majority in Smith. In the recent decision of the Privy Council in *Attorney General for Jersey v Holley*,[17] a majority of the Board rejected the *Smith* approach and reverted to that adopted by the majority in *Luc*. Though discussion of *Holley* is outside the scope of the present piece, the authors suggest that the approach of the majority is preferable to the (admittedly powerful) dissenting positions adopted by Lords Bingham, Hoffmann and Steyn in *Holley*. Significantly, it is the majority approach in *Holley* which echoes the reform proposed by the LRC.[18] The LRC proposes that the jury, having first

---

[16] See for example Smith [2000] *Crim LR* 1005; Gardner and Macklem, "Compassion without Respect: Nine Fallacies in *R v Smith*" [2001] *Crim LR* 623; Gardner and Macklem, "Provocation and Pluralism" (2001) 64 MLR 815; Stannard, "Towards a Normative Defence of Provocation in England and Ireland" (2002) 66 JCL 528.

[17] [2005] UKPC 23.

[18] At para 7.32 of the Consultation Paper.

assessed the gravity of the provocation on the accused taking into account his or her individual characteristics, would then be required to consider whether the accused ought to have responded as he or she did, as judged by ordinary community standards of self control and proportionality, "rather than by a vague, individualized criterion derived from his or her personal characteristics".[19]

Conclusion

It is submitted that such proposals, if adopted, would do much to add clarity and cogency to Irish law. A consideration of the sustained criticism to which *MacEoin* has been subjected reveals the weaknesses of the decision and the so-called "purely subjective" test it seemed to espouse. As noted above, this pure subjectivity is both an unattainable and an artificial objective that has served only to obscure Irish law. Its rejection will both simplify and ameliorate the criminal law.

It is of course possible to identify other features of the criminal law system which, if themselves subject to reform, could only serve to effect improvements in the area of provocation. Perhaps the most obvious of these is the current mandatory life sentence imposed for murder. Undoubtedly, this has a significant impact on a defendant's choice to have recourse to the defence of provocation. As such, it is arguable that the mandatory sentence has essentially resulted in the over-use of what was originally a defence of extraordinarily narrow and confined parameters. Interestingly, the former Chief Justice, writing extra-judicially, was a strong advocate of the abolition of the mandatory life sentence.[20]

The recent rejection of *Smith* by a majority of the Privy Council in *Holley* is a stark reminder that judicial attempts to clarify the law of provocation are often doomed to further complicate the existing confusion. Ideally, reform in this jurisdiction should be achieved through the intervention of the Oireachtas. Some years ago, Mr Paddy MacEntee SC, QC,—in his then capacity as Chairman of the Bar Council—remarked that "the legislature has been disposed to vacate certain areas of their legislative functions where unpopular decisions were for one reason or another unavoidable".[21] It is to be hoped that the LRC Consultation Paper will provide a much-needed impetus for legislative reform in this sphere. Until such reform is effected, the troubling legacy of *MacEoin* will cast a long shadow over the defence of provocation in Irish law.

---

19 *ibid.*

20 Keane, "The Mental Element in Murder" (2002) 52(1) NILQ 1.

21 See Boland, (1996) 47(3) NILQ 260.

Constitutional Right or Chimera? Reforming the Right of Access to a Lawyer

by
Elizabeth Campbell*

Recent years have seen a marked expansion in the capacities of the Irish State at the pre-trial stage of the criminal process. Notwithstanding the inherent imbalance of power that exists in the relationship between the accused and the State, various measures have been introduced which purport to facilitate the expeditious investigation of crime, arguably to the detriment of the rights of the accused. On first glance, the constitutional right of access to a lawyer, which accrues to a suspect when detained for questioning, has the potential to compensate, to some extent, for this disparity in power. Nevertheless, when examined in more detail, it becomes apparent that, although this right purports to equalise the relationship between the two parties, in fact, it is so circumscribed as to render it of little effect. Reform of the law is urgently required, so as to preclude further attrition of the rights of the accused.

The rights of the suspect in Garda custody have been compromised by a number of legislative provisions, which substantially extend detention periods and erode the right to silence. While a suspect may be detained for up to 12 hours under s 4 of the Criminal Justice Act 1984, s 9 of the Criminal Justice Act 2006 permits a Garda, not below the rank of chief superintendent, to authorise detention for a further 12 hours.[1] Moreover, s 2 of the Criminal Justice (Drug Trafficking) Act 1996 sanctions

* This essay was awarded joint second by the Law Society of Ireland, *Student Law Reform Essay Competition 2006*. Elizabeth Campbell is a PhD candidate at University College Cork.

[1] This amendment mirrors the recommendations of the *Report of the Expert Group Appointed to Consider Changes in the Criminal Law which were Recommended in the Garda SMI Report* (The Leahy Report) (Dublin: Stationery Office, 1998). Nevertheless, the Human Rights Commission has stated that "the case for an increase of a further 12 hours without judicial supervision in the case of *all* arrestable offences has not been made and that it is not strictly necessary." Human Rights Commission, *Observations on the Scheme of the Criminal Justice Bill 2003*, 14 January 2004, p 18.

a repressive and lengthy period of detention of up to 168 hours, as does s 50 of the Criminal Justice Act 2007, which applies to certain firearm offences, murder involving the use of a firearm or an explosive, and murder of a Garda, prison officer or head of state. The introduction of these powers was marked by a paucity of empirical evidence to substantiate the claim that lengthy detention furthers the successful investigation and resolution of crime.[2] In addition, the right to silence of the accused in the course of police interrogation has been eroded in a considerable sense. While the traditional motivation behind the right to silence was "to avoid the risk of untrue confessions being obtained from a person while in police custody",[3] more recently, the imperatives of crime control have outweighed notions of due process in the context of this right.[4] The right to silence is perceived as assisting the guilty to evade the full rigours of the law,[5] and so there are a number of statutory provisions which penalise the accused for remaining silent. For example, s 52(1) of the Offences against the State Act 1939[6] permits a Garda to demand a full account of the movements and actions of a detained suspect during a specified period of time.[7] In addition, inferences may be drawn from the failure of the accused to account for marks or substances on his person, or for his presence at a particular place, when asked to do so by a garda who reasonably believes that this may be attributable to his participation in the commission of the offence.[8]

---

[2] See Dáil Debates, 2 July 1996, Vol 467, Col. 2330. *Criminal Justice (Drug Trafficking) Bill, 1996: Report and Final Stages per* Mr O'Donoghue.

[3] *Heaney v Ireland* [1994] 3 IR 593, *per* Costello J.

[4] The crime control/due process dichotomy in the justice system was developed by Herbert Packer in *The Limits of the Criminal Sanction* (Stanford: Stanford University Press, 1968), where he presented and analysed these two oppositional normative models of the criminal process.

[5] A submission by the Gardaí to the Joint Committee on Justice, Equality, Defence and Women's Rights stated that "The present status of the right to silence is an historical relic and harks back to a previous age when suspects were deemed to be of limited intelligence. It is untenable that in serious crimes such as murder and rape, theft or fraud, suspects can refuse to disclose their whereabouts when questioned and courts cannot draw inferences from this. It is not a question of compelling anyone to speak but rather informing the court of a refusal and empowering it to draw inferences and take appropriate note." Submission by the Association of Garda Sergeants and Inspectors to the Joint Committee on Justice, Equality, Defence and Women's Rights, 8 December 2003.

[6] The constitutionality of s 52 was upheld in *Heaney v Ireland* [1994] 3 IR 593 (HC); *Heaney v Ireland* [1996] 1 IR 580 (SC).

[7] This power pertains to any offence under the Offences against the State Acts and any scheduled offences. Failing to give such information, or giving false information, is an offence for which a person may be imprisoned for no longer than six months.

[8] Sections 18 and 19, Criminal Justice Act 1984. The constitutionality of these provisions was upheld in *Rock v Ireland and the Attorney General* [1997] 3 IR 384.

Inferences may also be drawn under s 30 of the Criminal Justice Act 2007 (inserting a new s 19A into the 1984 Act) from the failure of the accused to mention any fact on which he later relies in his defence, if that fact was one which he could reasonably have been expected to mention when questioned.[9]

The lengthening of detention periods and the attenuation of the right to silence of the accused has shifted the balance in the State/accused relationship further in favour of the State. Thus, the right of access to a lawyer in custody gains more significance, given its capacity to remedy this inequity. The presence of a lawyer during interrogation acts as a protective device which guarantees that statements are not made as a result of compulsion or coercion, and ensures that the accused receives sufficient legal advice.

The right of a detainee to access a lawyer was recognised in a number of cases in the 1970s and 80s.[10] Moreover, s 5(1) of the Criminal Justice 1984 Act provides that any person detained under s 4 of the Act shall be informed by the member in charge of the Station in which he is held that he is entitled to consult a solicitor.[11] Nevertheless, the right of access to a lawyer was not recognised as constitutional in nature by the Irish courts until 1990, in *DPP v Healy*.[12] Finlay CJ noted that the logic behind this right is to ensure that the suspect has sufficient independent advice so as to allow him to make a free decision regarding his attitude to interrogation or to the making of any statement.[13] In addition, the availability of advice from a lawyer was

---

[9] This section repeals s 7 of the Criminal Justice (Drug Trafficking) Act 1996 and s 5 of the Offences against the State (Amendment) Act 1998. While the original inference-drawing provisions in the 1984 Act pertain to the accused's response to the questions of the Gardaí, s 19A impose an especially onerous task on the suspect, who must envisage what particular facts are likely to be used by him in his defence. It is arguable that this may result in injustice, due to the fact that the accused may forget to mention certain facts or details on which he seeks to rely in his defence.

[10] See *In Re Emergency Powers Bill, 1976* [1977] IR 159; *People v Shaw* [1982] IR 1; and *People (D.P.P.) v Conroy* [1986] IR 460.

[11] Section 9 (as amended) provides that this provision applies to the Offences against the State Act 1939 and to detention under s 19A of the 2007 Act. In addition, article 8 of the Criminal Justice Act, 1984 (Treatment of Persons in Custody in Garda Síochána Stations) Regulations 1987 provides that an arrested person shall without delay be informed in ordinary language of his entitlement to consult with a solicitor. In *DPP v Spratt* [1995] 1 IR 585, the High Court concluded that the right to be informed of the right of access to a solicitor for an accused person in Garda custody was not a Constitutional right.

[12] *DPP v Healy* [1990] 2 IR 73.

[13] *ibid*, p81.

characterised by the Court as contributing towards some measure of equality in the position of the detained person and his interrogators.[14] The Court stressed that this right was such an important and fundamental standard of fairness in the administration of justice that it must be deemed to be constitutional, and that to regard it as merely legal would undermine its significance and the completeness of its protection.[15]

Nevertheless, despite these persuasive arguments in favour of the right of access to a lawyer during interrogation, this right was classified only as one of reasonable access. A right of reasonable access means that once the solicitor arrives at the Garda station in which the suspect is detained, that individual has an immediate right to be told of the arrival and, if he so requests, immediate access.[16] Finlay J noted that postponement or delay in this regard could only be justified for reasons, which when objectively viewed from the perspective of the interest or welfare of the detained person, would be seen as valid by a court.[17]

Although the Court of Criminal Appeal in *People (DPP) v Connell* stressed that the Gardaí are prevented from obstructing the right of the suspect to a lawyer,[18] thereby strengthening the protection accorded to the right, the "reasonable" caveat has provided fertile ground for the delimitation of the scope of the right by the Irish courts. While it has been contended that the constitutional status accorded to this right implies that the scope for denial is strictly limited,[19] it is evident from the case-law that the courts have interpreted the right of access to a solicitor in a restrictive manner. For example, Gardaí are permitted to interrogate the suspect before the solicitor has arrived, provided that they are making *bona fide* attempts to provide the individual concerned with a lawyer, and they are not obliged to defer the arrest of a suspect until such time as the solicitor is likely to be available.[20] Furthermore, denial of access to a solicitor to the notes of the interrogation of his client does not render

---

14 *ibid.*

15 *ibid.*

16 *ibid.*

17 *ibid.*

18 *People (DPP) v Connell* [1995] 1 IR 244.

19 Walsh, D. *Criminal Procedure* (Thomson Round Hall, Dublin, 2002) p 272.

20 *People (DPP) v Buck* [2002] 2 IR 268.

detention unlawful.[21] These examples of the circumscription of the right of access to a lawyer add credence to the blunt suggestion that the right is, in effect, "generally worthless".[22]

However, the recent case of *O'Brien v DPP* may give ground for hope in this regard.[23] When the defendant in *O'Brien* requested access to a solicitor after his arrest, the Gardaí recommended a busy sole practitioner, who could not attend the Garda station until more than seven hours after the time of arrest. The Court held that the detention of the defendant had been rendered unlawful by the choice of a solicitor in circumstances where the Gardaí knew, or ought to have known, that there would be a substantial delay in his arrival. The defendant's constitutional rights had been breached by the failure to provide him with a solicitor within a reasonable time. Nevertheless, the Court determined that once the defendant's constitutional rights had been restored by the receipt of advice from a solicitor, his continued arrest and detention were proper and valid, and so statements made after the arrival of the solicitor were admissible as evidence.

While *O'Brien* may indicate the burgeoning of a more expansive interpretation of the right of access to a lawyer, the right is still categorised by the Irish courts as a right of reasonable access. Reform of the law in this area, to provide for an unqualified right of access to a lawyer when in Garda custody, would provide the most concrete and efficacious means of ensuring that the rights of the accused are safeguarded, and that the balance in the State/accused relationship does not swing too far in favour of the State. The grounds expounded by the Supreme Court in *Healy*, justifying the recognition of a right of reasonable access to a lawyer, in fact mandate a comprehensive constitutional right to have one's solicitor present during the whole of the interrogation.[24] Indeed, the European Committee for the Prevention of

---

21 *Lavery v The Member in Charge, Carrickmacross Garda Station* [1999] 2 IR 390. Breen and MacEntee contend that "[t]he overall effect…of the Lavery case, is that while the 1998 Act encroaches seriously upon the right to silence of a person in custody, there is to be no adequate safeguards to protect the person in custody from an abuse of the system." Breen, F. and MacEntee, P. "The Right to Silence in Light of *Deaglan Lavery v the Member-in-Charge, Carrickmacross Garda Station* 1999 (5) 1 *Bar Review* 6, 8.

22 White, J. "The Confessional State – Police Interrogation in the Irish Republic" Part 1 (2000) 10(1) *Irish Criminal Law Journal* 17, 18.

23 *O'Brien v Director of Public Prosecutions*, unreported Supreme Court, 5 May 2005.

24 White, J. "The Confessional State – Police Interrogation in the Irish Republic" Part II (2000) 10(2) *Irish Criminal Law Journal* 2, 3.

Torture has recommended in its past three reports to Ireland that the right of access to a lawyer should include the right to have the lawyer present during police interrogations.[25] Acknowledging such a right would ensure that the suspect has adequate legal advice so as to facilitate a free decision concerning the making of any statement, and would create a degree of equality between him and his interrogators.

In the US, as a result of the seminal case of *Miranda v Arizona*, a detainee has a constitutional right to be questioned in the presence of his lawyer if he so wishes.[26] The rationale behind this judgment proves elucidatory in assessing the need to expand the interpretation of the right of access to a lawyer in Ireland. In *Miranda*, Warren CJ stressed that for statements obtained from a suspect who is being interrogated in custody by the police to be admissible and constitutionally valid, the suspect must be informed that he has a right to the presence of an attorney throughout questioning.[27] Unless sufficient protective devices, such as the presence and advice of a lawyer, are employed to dispel the compulsion inherent in custodial surroundings, no statement obtained from the defendant can truly be the product of his free choice.[28] Moreover, the Court recognised that the presence of counsel during interrogation may reduce the dangers of untrustworthiness if the accused divulges information to the police, and may reduce the likelihood of coercion.[29] Significantly, the US Supreme Court concluded that as preliminary advice given to the accused by his lawyer can be overcome by the secret interrogation process, the right to legal advice involves not only a right to consult with the lawyer before questioning, but also to have counsel present during any questioning if the defendant so desires.[30]

---

25 Report to the Government of Ireland on the visit to Ireland carried out by the European Committee for the Prevention of Torture and Inhuman or Degrading Treatment or Punishment (CPT) from 20 to 28 May 2002 CPT/Inf (2003) 36, para 22; Report to the Irish Government on the visit to Ireland carried out by the European Committee for the Prevention of Torture and Inhuman or Degrading Treatment or Punishment (CPT) from 31 August to 9 September 1998 CPT/Inf (99) 15, para 22; Report to the Irish Government on the visit to Ireland carried out by the European Committee for the Prevention of Torture and Inhuman or Degrading Treatment or Punishment (CPT) from 26 to 5 October 1993 CPT/Inf (95) 14 para 43.

26 *Miranda v Arizona* (1966) 384 US 436.

27 *ibid*, p 466.

28 *ibid*, pp 457–8.

29 *Miranda*, p 470.

30 *ibid.*

Thus, it may be seen that the Court in *Miranda* grounded its decision on three significant effects of the constitutional right of access to a lawyer; namely the right's ability to prevent the accused from being compelled or coerced to confess, its ability to preclude the mistreatment of the accused by the interrogators, and its ability to ensure that the accused is furnished with adequate legal advice. The first facet of the right, concerning the prevention of false confessions, has particular pertinence in the Irish context, given that the current limited interpretation of the right of access, coupled with the inherent pressures of interrogation, the extensive powers of detention and the limitations on the right to silence, may lead to a suspect confessing to an offence for which he was not responsible. Indeed, the notorious Kerry Babies case[31] and the confession of Dean Lyons to the brutal Grangegorman murders[32] provide stark examples of the danger of false confessions in this jurisdiction.

The second element of the right of access to a lawyer focuses on its ability to prevent the mistreatment of the accused by the interrogators. Although cases of physical harm are not commonplace in Ireland, they are not unheard of,[33] and furthermore, the potential for unreasonable psychological pressure to be exerted is ever-present in the interrogation process. Whilst it may be argued that the audio-visual recording of police interrogations, as provided for by the Criminal Justice Act 1984 (Electronic Recording of Interviews) Regulations 1997, provides an adequate safeguard against the possibility of ill-treatment of suspects in custody, a number of caveats attach to these regulations. For example, only Garda stations which have electronic recording equipment installed are affected by these regulations.[34] Furthermore, the interview does not have to be recorded if the recording equipment is broken or in use at the

31 For an interesting examination of the relevant psychological techniques that were evident in the interrogation in the notorious Kerry Babies case, see O'Mahony, P. "The Psychology of Police Interrogation" in O'Mahony, P. (ed.) *Criminal Justice in Ireland* (Dublin: Institute of Public Administration, 2002) pp534–6.

32 Dean Lyons was a homeless young heroin addict with a history of psychiatric problems, who falsely admitted, under the pressure of police interrogation, to the murder of two women in Dublin in 1997. Charges against him were dropped when another man confessed to those and other murders, providing accurate and specific details of the manner in which the women were killed, and of the house in which the murders took place. A Commission of Investigation has recently been established to examine the circumstances arising from the making of his confession and the adequacy of the Garda assessment of the reliability of his confession.

33 It has been reported that €6 million was paid out, mainly in out-of-court settlements, to 70 victims of Garda assault and wrongful arrest between 1999 and 2003. See "Time to hold garda to account", *Irish Times,* 19 July 2003.

34 Reg 3(1).

time of the interview,[35] or if recording it is "not practicable". Although the Third Report of the Steering Committee on Audio and Audio/Video Recording of Garda Questioning of Detained Persons, which analysed interviews which took place from January to November 2003, reported that 96 per cent of interviews which fall within the remit of the Regulations were recorded,[37] the Courts have been less positive in their appraisal of the scheme. In *Director of Public Prosecutions v Diver*, Hardiman J, giving the judgment of the Supreme Court, contended that the claim that such recording now takes place in 96 per cent of garda interviews is not evident in the appellate courts.[38] Moreover, as O'Mahony notes, the taping of interviews, although necessary, is not sufficient to guard against "the machinations of corrupt or over-zealous and under-critical police interrogators."[39] However, regardless of the efficacy of the scheme of interview-recording in Ireland, the fundamental nature of the rights involved necessitates the presence of a lawyer throughout the course of the interview so as to protect suspects from being mistreated in custody.

The final element of the right of access to a lawyer which was emphasised by the court in *Miranda* was its capacity to ensure that the accused is given adequate legal advice to make informed decisions as to his response to questioning. This is particularly important, given the various provisions in this jurisdiction which restrict the right to silence and permit the drawing of inferences. Moreover, when these restrictions on the rights of the accused are considered in conjunction with the claim that police practice is to define reasonable access as amounting to one hour in every six in detention,[40] the significance of a more expansive interpretation of the constitutional right of access to a lawyer in Ireland is thrown sharply into focus. Recognition of this right would guarantee that the legal advice delivered is thorough and not limited by time constraints.

Reforming the law in this area, so as to provide for a constitutional right of access to a lawyer without qualification, is fundamental in order to defend and preserve the

---

[35] Reg 4(3)(a)(i) and (ii).

[36] Reg 4(3)(b).

[37] Third Report of the Steering Committee on Audio and Audio/Video Recording of Garda Questioning of Detained Persons, (Department of Justice: September 2004) p 9, para 2.5.2.

[38] *Director of Public Prosecutions v Diver*, unreported, Supreme Court, 29 July 2005.

[39] O'Mahony, P. "The Psychology of Police Interrogation", above, n 31, p 525. Indeed, in the case of Dean Lyons, part of his interrogation was video-taped, in which he seems incoherent and ready to confess to every charge put to him. However, the incriminating statements were not video-recorded.

[40] White, above, n22, p 18.

rights of the accused individual. However, such reform would necessitate the concomitant creation of a panel of duty solicitors, in accordance with the suggestion of the Incorporated Law Society of Ireland, referred to in the 1998 Report of the European Committee for the Prevention of Torture,[41] to ensure that each suspect is accorded the legal advice that is his right. Indeed, as long ago as 1978, the O'Briain Report recommended the establishment of a duty solicitor scheme.[42] The Report noted that the exercise by arrested persons of the right of access to a solicitor seems to have received "less than the whole-hearted co-operation of the Gardaí" and suggested that this stemmed from the feeling among investigating officers that the inevitable consequence will be a direction to say nothing in reply to Garda questioning.[43] Although the Criminal Legal Aid Review Committee recommended against the introduction of a duty solicitor scheme in Ireland,[44] the non-statutory Garda Station Legal Advice Scheme was commenced in February 2001. Under this scheme, where a person is detained in a Garda station for the purpose of the investigation of an offence, without sufficient means to pay for a consultation with a solicitor, the consultation will be paid for by the State.[45] Entrenching the duty

[41] Report to the Irish Government on the visit to Ireland carried out by the European Committee for the Prevention of Torture and Inhuman or Degrading Treatment or Punishment (CPT) from 31 August to 9 September 1998 CPT/Inf (99) 15, para 23. In addition, the CPT noted in its most recent report that formal arrangements are not yet in place for the appointment of solicitors for detained persons who do not have their own lawyer, and that some persons waived their right to legal assistance as they felt that the proposed solicitors were not independent from the police. Report to the Government of Ireland on the visit to Ireland carried out by the European Committee for the Prevention of Torture and Inhuman or Degrading Treatment or Punishment (CPT) from 20 to 28 May 2002 CPT/Inf (2003) 36 para 21.

[42] *Report by the Committee Appointed by The Government to Recommend Certain Safeguards for Persons in Custody* (Stationery Office, Dublin, 1978) para 40, p 14.

[43] Para 32, p 12.

[44] *Final Report of the Criminal Legal Aid Review Committee* (Stationery Office, Dublin, 2002) p 27, para 3.8. This reluctance was also evident in the *Report of Committee to Enquire into Certain Aspects of Criminal Procedure* (the Martin Committee Report) (Stationery Office, Dublin, 1990) p 44 which was "less than sanguine regarding the operation of a duty solicitor scheme in practice", due to the failure of solicitors to attend the police station and also due to the poor quality of professional advice. It is of interest to note that a 24 Hour Duty Solicitor Scheme was introduced in England and Wales by means of the Police and Criminal Evidence Act, 1984 (PACE), to ensure that suspects being questioned by the police have access to free legal advice at all times.

[45] The scheme, which applies to detention under the provisions of the Offences against the State Acts 1939–1998, the Criminal Justice Act 1984 and the Criminal Justice (Drug Trafficking) Act 1996, has a strict means test for qualification.

solicitor scheme in legalisation would further the rights of the accused, and would represent a fundamental element of the reformed constitutional right of access to a lawyer.

The inherent inequities in the relationship between the State and the accused, which are extant in the context of arrest, detention and interrogation, are aggravated by the protracted periods for which individuals are detained, and by the encroachments on the right to silence. The limited interpretation of the constitutional right of access to a lawyer in custody serves to further compound the imbalance in this relationship and compromises the rights of the individual. Reforming this entitlement, so as to render it more comprehensive and useful, in contrast to its present emasculated form, would mitigate, to a considerable extent, other restrictions on the rights of the accused. As Ashworth noted, the State should take no more power over a person at this stage than is absolutely necessary for the carrying out of the proper functions of law enforcement.[46] Expanding this fundamental right of the individual would not preclude the investigation of crime, but would serve to enhance and protect the rights of the individual, during the course of police interrogation.

[46] Ashworth, A. *The Criminal Process: An Evaluative Study* (Clarendon Press, Oxford 1994), p 26.

Saying Nothing at All—Sales by Description in Consumer Transactions

by

Brian Foley*

Introduction

Section 13 of the Sale of Goods and Supply of Services Act 1893[1] implies a condition into every contract for sale of goods by description that the goods sold shall correspond with the description offered of those goods. Without dwelling on many of the substantive elements of this provision, this essay argues that the law relating to sale of goods by description has become self-defeating to the point of utter redundancy and is in urgent need of reform. Indeed, the need for reform is an extremely compelling one. It seems reasonably obvious that in response to widespread consumer dissatisfaction, government policy in relation to consumer protection is more visible then ever.[2] In a society fuelled by increased wealth and marked by consequent increased consumer spending, the law of consumer protection is coming under increased pressure and scrutiny. One response to the problems in consumer law can be seen in the Attorney Generals approval of the restatement of the Sale of Goods legislation—a commendable effort to bring increased clarity to this increasingly important body of law.[3] In perhaps a bolder move, the Department of

* LL.B. (Trinity), Barrister-at-Law, Postgraduate Student, Trinity College. This article was revised while in receipt of a grant from the Irish Research Council for the Humanities and Social Sciences and is a revised version of the essay that won first place in the Law Society of Ireland *Law Reform Essay Competition* in 2004. Many thanks are owned to Eoin O'Dell of the law school in Trinity, who helped me sort out some of the murkier issues of contract relevant to sales by description.

[1] As substituted by s 10 of the Sale of Goods and Supply of Services Act 1980.

[2] The Office of the Director of Consumer Affairs *Price Awareness Campaign* is an example of this. See "Sustaining Progress: Price Awareness Campaign", Press Release, 2 November 2003, (ODCA).

[3] The Sale of Goods Restatement was certified by the Attorney General on 27 February 2003 under s 2(1) of the Statute Law (Restatement) Act 2002. It restates the 1893 Act and Pt II of the 1980 Act.

Enterprise, Trade and Employment has created a Consumer Strategy Group charged with development of a National Consumer Policy which has recently made its first report. In short, consumer law reform is on the agenda.

If, however, we are placing so much emphasis on the consumer area and if we are providing what is in essence a partial code of consumer protection—shouldn't we be getting it right? This essay argues that unless specific attention is drawn to the flaws of widely used interpretations of s 13 then consumer law will remain tainted by a degree of uncertainty intolerable in the present climate and unsuitable to restatement.

Some Terminology in Contract

Essential to contract law is the distinction between the terms of a contract and pre-contractual statements intended to be of no contractual effect.[4] The latter are usually referred to as mere representations. These are the kind of statements that are normally associated with the zealous, but not ill-minded salesperson—"mere puffs". Suffice it to say for present purposes that whereas breach of a term can be loosely said to be a breach of contract and attract the remedies associated with such,[5] a breach of a mere representation is a different beast altogether, generally said not be actionable outside of extra elements such as fraud or negligence. For example, in *T & J Harrison v Knowles & Foster*[6] a description of ships as being of 460 tonne deadweight had been made in pre-contract discussions. This did not get included in any memorandum of sale, and therefore under the strict dichotomy of term/representation, the Court of Appeal held that the description was not a "term of the contract". Thus, the fact that the ships were really 360 tonnes was not actionable as a breach of contract.

However, it is not always easy to draw the line between a pre-contractual and a contractual statement. In many cases the pre-contractual statement or representation will transcend its non-contractual status and become (depending on your preference) a warranty, collateral warranty or collateral contract. The practical consequence is that those representations then become contractual promises of themselves.[7]

---

4 See generally the discussion in *Carey v Independent Newspapers (Ireland) Ltd.*, Unreported, High Court, 7 August, 2003 (Gilligan J), at 10–12.

5 Leaving aside a remedy based on negligence on the basis of *Hedley Byrne & Co Ltd v Heller & Partners Ltd* [1964] AC 465; [1963] 2 All ER 575.

6 [1918] 1 KB 608.

7 For a recent example see *Hagen & others v ICI Chemicals and Polymers Ltd and others* [2002] IRLR 31.

The Problem

One conservative approach to s 13 is to argue that it only applies where the description of the goods offered is itself part of the contract. To put it another way: a description, such as "strong and sturdy", must transcend the potential label of mere representation and become contractual terms for s 13 to operate. On this view s 13 is given an utterly implausible construction. It merely provides that the seller has to comply with his contract, whatever that was. Therefore, if a court insists that the description be a term of the contract, and not some kind of pre-contractual statement, then the section is an extended nullity. But could a court seriously argue that legislation specifically designed to improve consumer protection actually does nothing?

In *Harlingdon & Leinster Enterprises v Christopher Hull Fine Art*[8] it was argued that a sufficient basis for the operation of s 13 was that a description of a painting as being by a certain artist was such as to induce the bargain. The Court of Appeal rejected this argument, holding that this inducement was not enough to make the transaction a sale by description. Rather, the Court of Appeal held that the description had to be influential so as to become an essential term of the contract. Now, sometimes one sees proposals for an alternative reading of *Harlingdon*—that the real requisite of s 13 is not a contractual description, but rather reliance on whatever description is offered.[9] This cannot be supported. Nourse LJ was quite clear in this respect: "the description must have a sufficient influence in the sale to become an essential term of the contract and the correlevative of influence is reliance."[10]

Therefore, (at least on the strength of *Harlingdon*) it is simply not sufficient to argue that s 13 becomes effective when reliance on the description has been proven. Whereas one must rely on the description, this is because *Harlingdon* understands reliance not in some factual sense but because it is only such reliance that proves that the description is itself a term of the contract.[11] Thus, Harlingdon advances the utterly implausible construction of s 13: unless the description is contractual then

---

[8] [1990] 1 All ER 737. There were somewhat similar facts in *Leaf v International Galleries* [1950] 2 KB 86, where Denning LJ seemed to be of the opinion that a representation had to be a term of the contract in order to found misrepresentation. But he did note it was a rescission claim and specifically not one in warranty nor on the Sale of Goods Acts.

[9] This is just what White seems to do in her *Commercial Law* (Thomson Round Hall, Dublin, 2002), at p 251.

[10] [1990] 1 All ER 737 at 744.

[11] *Cf* White, *op. cit*, at 251.

there is no remedy based on s 13. If the description was contractual, there would be a remedy. But that of course means that s 13 means nothing except that "breach of contract is actionable" and therefore offers none of the consumer protection that it can reasonably be supposed to.

The Traditional Solution

The *Heilbut*[12] decision has traditionally been understood to mean that pre-contract statements should generally not be allowed to be classed as terms of the contract themselves. However, the modern cases (particularly those decided by Lord Denning[13]), notably *Oscar Chess v Williams*[14] and *Dick Bentley Productions Ltd v Harold Smith (Motor) Ltd*,[15] are less restrictive. They show a tendency to accept a representation made in connection with a sale of goods as in fact a warranty.[16] In *Oscar Chess*, for example, Denning LJ (as he then was) said that if an innocent bystander would reasonably infer a warranty, then the courts would. Similarly, in *Dick Bentley*, when the Master of the Rolls, Lord Denning, said that where a representation is made in the course of dealings for the very purpose of inducing the buyer to contract, it is a *prima facie* ground for inferring that it was a warranty and therefore contractual. Generally speaking, it does seem that "... an affirmation at the time of the sale is a warranty, provided it appears as evidence to be so intended."[17] This modern tendency is often offered as the counter-balance to interpretations of s 13 such as that offered in *Harlingdon.*[18] That is to say, it is argued by some that the requirement for the description to be part of the contract is offset by the courts general willingness to view representations, and thus descriptions, as terms of the contract.

It is submitted that this is an insufficient solution. As opposed to answering the problem of s 13, these cases in fact fuel it. When applied to s 13, the modern

[12] [1913] AC at 37.

[13] In addition the case discussed below, see also *J Evans & Son (Portsmouth) Ltd v Merzario* [1976] 2 All ER 930 at 933; [1976] 1 WLR 1078 at 1081 and *Esso Petroleum Co Ltd v Mardon* [1976] 2 All ER 5 at 13; [1976] QB 801 at 817.

[14] [1957] 1 All ER 325; [1957] 1 WLR 370.

[15] [1965] 2 All ER 65; [1965] 1 WLR 623.

[16] A tendency noted with apparent approval by Gilligan J in *Carey*, cited above at n 4, at 11.

[17] Per Holt CJ in *Cross v Gardner* (1689) 1 Show. 68, 89 ER 453 cited in *Pasley v Freeman* (1789) 3 Term. Rep, 51 100 ER 450.

[18] See for example Goode, *Commercial Law* (2nd ed, Penguin, 1995), at p 303.

tendency to view pre-contractual statements in consumer transactions as warranties merely submits to the manifest illogic of the *Harlingdon* approach. Consider the following dictum of Lord Haldane in *Heilbut*—"It is contrary to the general policy of the law of England to presume the making of such a collateral contract in the absence of language expressing or implying it."[19] The opponents of this point then cite the modern authority and argue that descriptive language can in fact amount to a collateral contract. But this cannot remove the problem—it only escapes it. There is simply nothing in the terms of s 13 that requires a description to be a contractual term. The mere fact that related doctrines in contract may be twisted with a sympathetic hand just adds to the absurdity of the *Harlingdon* approach. Indeed, by relying on these cases as the cure to the problem of s 13, one is implicitly admitting that the *Harlingdon* interpretation is, in fact, correct. There should be no need to argue, however easy the argument, that a description in a consumer transaction should be contractual. Merely by making that argument the clear purpose and logic of s 13 is submitted to an undesirable conceptual tautology.

Further, the argument that the "Denning" representation cases can surmount the *Harlingdon* problem cannot avoid the possibility that in some cases it will be held not to apply. As a somewhat *ad hoc* concession to the rigours of the term/representation distinction, it therefore suffers from its own inherent nature and cannot offer the certainty and clarity that consumer protection law so desperately needs.

Potential Explanation of the Problem

Why has this happened? How can such an implausible construction be put on such a plain provision? One explanation is that the description provision, when it is actually applied, is more rigorous than the terms as to fitness for purpose and merchantable quality.[20] Generally speaking, any discrepancy with description is

[19] [1913] AC 30 at 37; [1911–13] All ER 83 at 85. See also per Lord Moulton [1913] AC 30 at 47; [1911–13] All ER 83 at 90–91: "It is evident, both on principle and on authority, that there may be a contract the consideration for which is the making of some other contract. 'If you will make such and such a contract I will give you one hundred pounds', is in every sense of the word a complete legal contract. It is collateral to the main contract, but each has an independent existence, and they do not differ in respect of their possessing to the full the character and status of a contract. But such collateral contracts must from their very nature be rare."

[20] s 14 of the Sale of Goods Act 1893 (as substituted by s 10 of the Sale of Goods and Supply of Services Act 1980) implies undertakings as to the merchantable quality and fitness for purpose of goods.

actionable.[21] This rigour in application was perhaps felt to somewhat offset the other shortcomings of the provision. However, far more likely is that by duplicating the *Heilbut* philosophy, the Court of Appeal in *Harlingdon* suffers from a marked confusion between the concept of reliance in contract law generally and the very specific protectionist provisions in the Sale of Goods Act. If we take the *Harlingdon* case in its best possible light it is somewhat plausible to argue that descriptions under s 13 "look and feel like" the kind of statements that would historically be classed as representations. Of course, they are not—but it is easy to see just how the mistake is made. If one thinks that a description is essentially a representation, then the natural response would seem to be to try and figure out the extent to which it can be said that that statement forms part of the contract. The problem can be illustrated by reference to *Howard Marine & Dredging Co Ltd v A Ogden & Sons (Excavations) Ltd*.[22] Here in relation to a dredging contract, the capacity of the barges to be used had been exaggerated in pre-contract discussions. Bearing in mind that this was a case about misrepresentation *per se*, consider the following dictum from Shaw LJ:

> "I must confess that I was at one time inclined to the view that, as Mr O'Loughlin's answer could be regarded as part of the description of the subject-matter of the charter, there was a sufficient basis for regarding it also as giving rise to a warranty as to the carrying capacity of the barges".

In other words, in non-consumer or "regular" contract law, the live issue in *Howard Marine* was whether a factual description could found a warranty, or more specifically, a collateral warranty. Leaving aside any substantive criticism of the collateral warranty doctrine, one should be able to see how similar it appears to the s 13 problem. It seems arguable that the courts are merely reacting to a "description" in the way that normal contract law is accustomed to and failing to recognise the very special nature of s 13.

A Different Approach

We can now revisit the plain terms of s 13 to put the problem in its starkest form. The section implies a condition that where goods are sold by description, there is an implied condition that those goods meet that description. We have seen that it is conceptually incoherent to require that the description be an express term of the

[21] See Goode, *Commercial Law, op. cit*, p 303. See also, *Arcos Ltd v E. A. Ronaasen & Sons* [1933] AC 470.

[22] [1978] 2 All ER 1134; [1978] QB 574.

contract for that renders the section useless. We cannot take this approach seriously. It is submitted that the following approach is preferable. The question of whether a sale is by description or not is a matter of fact. One simply asks the question of whether the sale was one by description. Of course, there can be legal wranglings over just what a description is, but that's the stuff of law and nothing to be afraid of.[23] If there has been, in fact, a sale by description, then there is simply implied into the contract for sale, a term that the goods sold, meet that description. In other words, whether it is an express term or a mere representation does affect whether the sale is by description or not. This simple factual approach has the relatively modest merit of giving s 13 practical effect.

Has This Been Done Already?

In *Beale v Taylor*[24] a car was advertised by the description "Herald convertible, white, 1961, twin carbs", which disguised the fact that it was actually two halves of different Herald models welded together. Sellars LJ recognised that no warranties were made with this description, but nevertheless held it a sale by description. Whereas this recognises the merit of the factual approach outlined above, the problem is of course that *Harlingdon* came over 20 years later, indicating that the law is far from settled. Indeed, that *Beale* has not been treated as settling the issue is clear from the more recent case of *Pritchard v Cook*,[25] where Evans LJ held:

> "The authority of *Beale v Taylor* shows that there is scope for the implication of such a term when there is a sale of specific goods, combined with a description of those goods or part of them. However, it is unnecessary to go into that in the present case because, [the] primary case is that the contents of the specification were given contractual effect in the present case. If they were and there was an express term by incorporation, then he succeeds on the ground that there is a breach of that term. If he fails on the basis that there was no such term, then he does not suggest that he could succeed by the alternative route of s 13. I therefore shall say nothing more about it".

The latter portion of the dicta clearly indicates that the plaintiff would have succeeded had he shown that the descriptions were contractual. If he did that, s 13

[23] See for example *Reardon Smith Line Ltd v Yngvar Hansen-Tangen* [1976] 3 All ER 570.

[24] [1967] 3 All ER 253; [1967] 1 WLR 1193.

[25] Unreported, 4 June 1998, Court of Appeal, Evans LJ with Hale J (as she then was) agreeing.

was superfluous. However, if he could not establish that the descriptions were contractual "then he does not suggest that he could succeed by the alternative route of s 13". Although the point was not argued, it would seem, therefore, that there is some lingering doubt over whether *Beale* or *Harlingdon* is the law.

Of course, without precedent on the matter, the Irish jurisdiction has the luxury of deciding which approach to follow on the merits. To my knowledge no Irish case has decided on the proper construction of s 13.[26] It is submitted that if consumer protection is to have a healthy future these kinds of conceptual incoherencies need to be ironed out and the factual approach outlined above, and seemingly followed in *Beale* should be adopted. One may retort that the modern judicial practice has been to "bypass"[27] this problem by treating descriptions as contractual, but it is no solution to the compelling need for conceptual clarity and guaranteed certainty to rely on an essentially escapist judicial practice. Pending concrete decision on the matter, a provision that potentially offers protection to a great number of consumer transactions is tainted with a degree of uncertainty unsuitable to any legislation. Indeed, given the courts, lack of opportunity for comment on s 13, and on the Sale of Goods Acts as a whole, legislative intervention in the aftermath of the Restatement is entirely appropriate.[28] If modern consumer law is to move forward, and if the Restatement is to signal a progressive and democratising development strengthening the laws new and commendable commitment to increased accessibility,[29] then this uncertainty needs to be removed to make the law certain, intelligible and sensible.

---

[26] It has been considered in one reported case: *Duffy v Sutton (Trading as Sutton Tel-el-Kebir Dairy)* [1955] IR 248, where the point under discussion here was not raised. In the Circuit Court decision of *O'Connor v Donnelly* [1944] *Ir. Jur. Rep.* 1 at 6, Davitt J held that the buyer had to "really and ultimately [rely] upon the description". It is far from clear, however, whether he meant merely that one had to rely on the description or whether the description had to form part of the contract itself. It is reasonably arguable that a "sale by description" should include some degree of reliance for the sale to be really "by" description. Whether that description needs to be a part of the contract however, is another matter altogether.

[27] Goode, *op. cit*, p 304.

[28] Indeed, it is perhaps unfortunate that the Restatement programme did not also include a modicum of reform. It is of course worthwhile to get the Sale of Goods Acts all into a convenient place, but one may query the point of restating some points of law that are of dubious worth.

[29] See the Law Reform Commission, *Report on Statutory Drafting and Interpretation: Plain Language and the Law* (LRC 61–2000).

The potential for the highly artificial construction of s 13 put forward in *Harlingdon* should be deliberately and clearly remedied by a simple legislative *caveat*, that nothing in s 13 is to be taken to require a description to be a term of the contract. An amendment to that simple and modest effect would remove the problem and be a strong and positive statement of this Government's admirable commitment to consumer protection.

The Role of the Attorney General as Guardian of the Public Interest

by
Darren Lehane*

The office of Attorney General is one of the great constitutional offices of State. Described as a meeting place of diverse legal, political and constitutional functions,[1] the Attorney General is both legal adviser to the Government and guardian of the public interest. Yet despite the importance of the office, the appointment of a new Attorney General, according to one commentator, usually generates as much excitement as the "arrival of a new assistant principal officer in the Labour Market Vital Statistics Division of the Central Statistics Office".[2]

On those rare occasions when the full glare of public attention is focused on the office, concern often arises. The question is asked how one official, a political appointee, can successfully juggle the two different and often conflicting roles of both legal adviser to the Government and guardian of the public interest. The solution proffered by the courts is that the Attorney General is completely independent of the executive in the exercise of his quasi-judicial functions as guardian of the public interest.[3]

This paper examines the role of the Attorney General as "guardian of the public interest". It outlines its scope and traces its development from its origins as an element of the sovereign's prerogative through to the present day. In particular, it considers whether this prerogative power survived the creation of the State and concludes that it did not.

---

* BCL, LLM (NUI), Barrister-at-Law. This essay was awarded a prize by the Law Society of Ireland for the *Student Law Reform Essay Competition 2004.*

[1] Bradley, Book Reviews (1965) *Cambridge Law Journal,* 296.

[2] O'Toole, "McDowell's arrival as AG a most significant assignment", *Irish Times,* July 9 1999.

[3] See Lehane, "*A Legal Janus: Resolving the Conflict between the Attorney General's Functions as Guardian of the Public Interest and Legal Advisor to the Government*" (2004) ISLR 48.

Guardian of the Public Interest

Article 30 of the Constitution gives constitutional status to the office of Attorney General. However, it does not deal with the Attorney General's role as guardian of the public interest. Section 6 of the Ministers and Secretaries Act 1924 provides the statutory basis for the Attorney General's role as guardian of the public interest. Section 6(1) vests in the Attorney General the powers, duties and functions formerly vested in or exercised by the Irish Law Officers of the Crown prior to the establishment of Saorstát Éireann. This includes the assertion or protection of public rights and all powers, duties and functions connected with the same. It is in this capacity, as an officer of the public, rather than as legal advisor to the Executive, that the Attorney General is raised to the level of an organ of State under Art 6 of the Constitution.[4]

There exists no comprehensive list of all of the functions which the Attorney General carries out as "guardian of the public interest".[5] However, it may be said to include all those functions, which the Attorney General carries out on behalf of the public independently of the Executive. Using this test, there may be said to be two categories of function. The first category consists of those functions which have led to the creation of his position as guardian of the public interest. Into this category falls the Attorney General's role as public prosecutor, his role in the assertion and protection of public rights, his role in relation to charities and his functions in relation to the administration of the estates of deceased persons born in extra-marital relationships. The second category consists of those functions which have been assigned to the Attorney General because of his role as guardian of the public

---

[4] See *McLoughlin v Minister for Social Welfare* [1958] IR 1 at 16 per Kingsmill Moore J Norton-Keyshe makes a similar point in his comprehensive study of the English Law Officers, *The Law and Privileges relating to the Attorney General and Solicitor General of England* (London, 1898). At p 76 he states: "The Attorney General has historically been the officer of the King and represented his interests; at the same time, under the guise of representing the nation, he has usurped for the benefit of the Crown many privileges, which he would not, as representing the Crown alone have obtained.

[5] The Office of the Attorney General provides no guidance, the *Statement of Strategy 1999–2002* (Dublin, 1999), the *Guide to the Functions and Records of the Office of Attorney General* (Dublin, 2001) and the Attorney General's website (www.gov.ie/ag) provide no list of the functions carried out by the Attorney General as "guardian of the public interest". Similarly, although the Constitution Review Group devotes a section to the guardian of the public interest function, it provides no guidance to what duties are contained within that rubric. This may be contrasted with the detailed guidance given to prosecutors on when it will be in the public interest to prosecute and when it will be not. See DPP, *Statement of the General Guidelines for Prosecutors* (Dublin, 2001), pp 9–16.

interest. Into this category falls his role under the Extradition Acts 1965–1994, the Coroners Act 1962 and the Courts and Courts Officers Acts 1995.[6]

Development of the Attorney General's Role as Guardian of the Public Interest

Although the term "guardian of the public interest" is of relatively recent vintage, first being coined by Professor Edwards in 1964, the role of the Attorney General in the assertion and protection of public rights is of great antiquity.[7]

Its origins are to be found in the character of the King who as *parens patriae*, or father of the country, was charged with a duty to ensure that justice was done to each of his subjects.[8] This was accomplished through the establishment of courts of justice where an individual subject could go to enforce his rights. However, certain classes of person, such as minors and those with mental disabilities, were unable to do this for themselves, so the Crown as *parens patriae* took responsibility for ensuring that their rights were enforced. In addition, the Crown as *parens patriae* was responsible for upholding the law for the general public benefit.

---

[6] Casey, *The Irish Law Officers* (Dublin, 1996), pp 145–148, suggests that where the Attorney General appears in constitutional litigation pursuant to Ord 60 of the Rules of the Superior Courts, he does so as guardian of the public interest. However, it could also be argued that Ord 60 exists merely to ensure that the Government through its legal advisor is made aware of constitutional challenges to legislation so that it is given the opportunity to defend them. Support for this conclusion may be discerned from President Roosevelt's attempts to insert a similar provision into US federal law. As Cope & Kinsky, *Franklin D. Roosevelt and the Supreme Court* (Boston, 1965) note, Roosevelt argued that this was necessary as under the existing practice the federal courts could rule on the validity of federal statutes without the executive being afforded any opportunity to defend their measures. This conclusion is supported by the fact that the Attorney General invariably argues for the constitutionality of the impugned legislation.

[7] Edwards, *The Law Officers of the Crown* (London, 1964), p 286.

[8] See Halsbury's *Laws of England, Vol. 8(2) Constitutional law and Human Rights Law*, p 226 for a definition of *parens patriae*: "As Liege Lord and Protector of his subjects, the Monarch enjoys the prerogative right of taking Care of the persons and estates of minors and, mentally disordered persons and of supervising charities, although the exercise of those powers has been delegated by the Monarch or assigned by Statute to various authorities." The earliest recorded use of the term *parens patriae* is that of Lord Nottingham in *Attorney General v Peacock* 1674/5, Reports of the Cases of Lord Nottingham, (Seldon Society, Vol. 73, ed. D. Yale) p 209. See also De Smith, *Judicial Review of Administrative Action* (London, 1959), p 386–388.

This power was eventually delegated to the Lord Chancellor who, as the keeper of the King's conscience, was seen as the appropriate officer to dispense this prerogative jurisdiction on behalf of the King.[9] Similarly, the power to assert this prerogative jurisdiction in the Lord Chancellor's court was vested in the King's Law Officer, the Attorney General, who exercised it on behalf of the King.[10]

The pre-independence Irish courts repeatedly stressed that the Attorney General had no inherent *parens patriae* powers. It was merely as the forensic representative of the Crown that the Attorney General was charged with upholding the public interest.[11]

In *Attorney General v Mayo County Council*,[12] the plaintiff sued the defendants because they had obstructed a public road. The Irish Court of Appeal held that the Attorney General, as the Law Officer of the Crown, was entitled to bring the action because that office was charged with the protection and assertion of public rights.[13] A similar conclusion was reached in *Attorney General (Duffy) v Appleton*.[14] In this case, the Attorney General, at the suit of the Irish Branch of the Dental Association, alleged that a company had been formed for fraudulent purposes contrary to the Dentists Act 1878. The Irish Court of Appeal found for the plaintiff. Porter MR summed up the position of the Attorney General in such cases as follows: "the public interests are committed to the care of the Attorney General, as representing the Crown, and in that way he represents the public".[15] In *Weir v Fermanagh County*

---

[9] Historically, the Lord Chancellor was a clergyman who, in addition to conducting the King's business, served as his confessor.

[10] In *Ludlow Corporation v Greenhove* (1827) 1 Bli. NS 17 at 48, the House of Lords stated that: "The King is to be considered as the *parens patriae*; that he is the protector of every part of his subjects, and that therefore, it is the duty of his officer, the Attorney General, to see that justice is done to every part of those subjects."

[11] This is also the modern position in the United Kingdom. Wade & Forsyth, *Administrative Law* (8th ed, Oxford, 2000), p 570, describe the position as follows: "The foundation of this procedure is in the interest of the Crown as *parens patriae*, in upholding the law for the general public benefit. The Crown is concerned to see that public bodies, public trusts and charities should not exceed or abuse their powers or their funds; to abate public nuisances; and to prevent the law being flouted. The court may always restrain such abuses at the Attorney General's instance."

[12] [1902] 1 IR 13.

[13] [1902] 1 IR 13 at 20 *per* Porter MR.

[14] [1907] 1 IR 252.

[15] [1907] 1 IR 252 at 257 *per* Porter MR.

Council,[16] the plaintiff, a farmer, sought an injunction to restrain the defendants from building a road. The Irish Court of Appeal held that the action failed as the plaintiff had no *locus standi* and therefore was not legally competent to sustain the action without the joinder of the Attorney General. Palles CB stated that: "the rule in relation to such a suit is unquestioned: the Plaintiff, or at least one of the plaintiffs, must be represented by the Crown, who sues by his officer, the Attorney General."[17]

Following independence, the powers, duties and functions of the old Law Officers of the Crown were vested first in the Law Advisor to the Provisional Government and then in the Attorney General of Saorstát Éireann. This situation was regularised following the enactment of the Ministers and Secretaries Act 1924, s 6(1) of which set out the powers, duties and functions of the office. This provides:

> "There shall be vested in the Attorney General of Saorstát Éireann the business, powers, authorities, duties and functions formerly vested in or exercised by the Attorney General for Ireland, the Solicitor General for Ireland, the Attorney General for Southern Ireland, the Solicitor General for Southern Ireland, the Law Advisor to the Lord Lieutenant of Ireland and any or all of them respectively, and the administration and control of the business, powers, authorities, duties and functions of the branches and officers of the public services in connection with the representation of the Government of Saorstát Éireann and of the public in all legal proceedings for the enforcement of law, the punishment of offenders and the assertion or protection of public rights and all powers duties and functions connected with the same respectively, together with the duty of advising the Executive Council and the Several Ministers in matters of law and legal opinion."

The Supreme Court considered s 6(1) in *Moore v Attorney General*.[18] The Court divided the subsection into two parts. The first part endows the Attorney General with the necessary powers, authorities, duties and functions by reference to the old Law Officers of the Crown. The second part assigns to the Attorney General the administration of the public business, and the offices and officers connected with the office, especially the representation of the Government and of the public in the legal proceedings mentioned therein.

---

16 [1913] 1 IR 193.

17 [1913] 1 IR 193 at 198.

18 [1930] IR 471.

The Court held that the authority of the Attorney General to assert and protect public rights flowed from the first part of the subsection. The Court then proceeded to examine the position of the former Law Officers in relation to the assertion and protection of public rights from the time of the personal kingship to the time of the impersonal Crown, when the Court was synonymous with the community.[19] The Court was of the view that the Attorney General developed from his early position of King's Attorney to his ultimate position of Attorney General to the public under the "guise" of the Crown.

The 1937 Constitution does not refer to the Attorney General's role as "guardian of the public interest".[20] However, in *Attorney General v Dublin Tramways*, the High Court held that the role of the Attorney General in the assertion and protection of public rights had survived the enactment of the Constitution.[21]

Parens Patriae and the Expulsion of the Prerogative from Irish Law

Although the Attorney General's *parens patriae* powers were held to have survived both the creation of the State and the 1937 Constitution, in *Moore v Attorney General* and *Attorney General v Dublin Tramways*, it is submitted that there is a problem here which, while it would not have been apparent to the Court in those cases, clearly undermines their decisions. This problem is caused by later decisions in which the courts have held that none of the royal prerogatives survived the enactment of the 1937 Constitution.

---

19 [1930] IR 471 at 495 *per* Kennedy CJ.

20 This may be said to be curious given that Hamilton CJ speaking extra-judicially said that the responsibilities of the Attorney General as legal advisor to the Government "'paled into insignificance' when compared to his role as guardian of the public interest". See McGarry, "Mr. Justice Whelehan sworn in as new President of the High Court", *Irish Times* (16 November 1994). It could be argued that this omission is not due to any deliberate oversight but to the fact that in 1937 the main way in which the Attorney General acted as "guardian of the public interest" was as public prosecutor. The Constitution expressly refers to this in Article 30.3. As the wider implications of the Attorney General's role in the assertion and protection of public rights have only become apparent in the last decade or so, it is therefore not surprising that the drafters of the Constitution omitted to include any reference to them. Support for this conclusion may be found from a perusal of the Dáil debates on the draft Constitution, which shows that there was a clear awareness of the Attorney General's role as "guardian of the public interest". For example, Mr John A Costello TD referred to the Attorney General as "the person who looks after the rights of the people". 67 Dáil Debates col 17 (12 May 1937).

21 [1939] IR 590 at 597 *per* Maguire P.

In *Byrne v Ireland*,[22] the Supreme Court ruled that the royal prerogative of immunity from suit did not survive the enactment of the Constitution of 1922. In *Webb v Ireland*,[23] which dealt with the issue of whether the State inherited the Crown's prerogative right of treasure trove, the Supreme Court ruled that no royal prerogative had survived the enactment of the Constitution of 1922.

It has already been shown that the Attorney General's, in relation to the assertion and protection of public rights, jurisdiction flowed from his position as forensic representative of the King. In such cases, the Attorney General exercised a prerogative power on behalf of the King. However, if we apply *Byrne* and *Webb* it would appear that this prerogative power, along with the rest of the royal prerogative, ceased to exist in 1922. Therefore, it could not have been transferred from the Law Officers of the Crown to the Attorney General of the Saorstát in 1924.

In addition, even if it had existed in 1924 it would still be vulnerable to challenge because s 6(1) did not vest the Crown's *parens patriae* in the newly established Saorstát. It simply changed the official responsible for its exercise. In *Moore v Attorney General*,[24] the Supreme Court was quite clear on this point. It expressly rejected the argument that the source of the *parens patriae* power derived from the second half of s 6(1), holding that it flowed from the first half of the subsection, from the old Law Officers of the Crown.[25]

The Supreme Court accepted that this *parens patriae* power was vested in the Crown but suggested that this was a mere fiction, the impersonal Crown being merely a way of describing the people whose powers were now vested in the Saorstát. However attractive this argument might seem, the Supreme Court rejected it in *Byrne* and *Webb* by holding that none of the prerogative powers had been transferred from the Crown to the people in the manner suggested by Kennedy CJ in Moore.[26]

The logic in this argument would appear to be unassailable, but it was rejected by the High Court in *Campus Oil Ltd. v Minister for Industry and Commerce (No. 2)*.[27]

---

22 [1970] IR 241.

23 [1988] IR 353.

24 [1930] IR 471.

25 [1930] IR 471 at 495 *per* Kennedy CJ.

26 [1930] IR 471.

27 [1983] IR 88.

Here it was argued that the traditional role of the Attorney General in the assertion and protection of public rights as outlined in s 6(1) of the Ministers and Secretaries Act 1924, did not survive the enactment of the Constitution. The High Court rejected this. It held that the Attorney General was the appropriate person to assert and defend the public interest stating that "This is clear from a number of decisions both prior and subsequent to the present Constitution."[28] Curiously, the Court did not refer to *Byrne v Ireland*.[29] As a result, it would appear its precedential value is lessened particularly in light of the Supreme Court's affirmation of *Byrne* in *Webb v Ireland*.[30]

However, later courts have not addressed the prerogative issue at all and opted instead to follow *Campus Oil*.[31] The most recent case in this area is the decision of the Supreme Court in *Attorney General v Lee*.[32] In this case, the defendant refused to attend a coroner's inquest. The Attorney General, as guardian of the public interest sought an order compelling the defendant's attendance at the inquest. In the course of his judgment for the Court, Keane CJ gave the following explanation of the role of the Attorney General in such circumstances.

> "There is no doubt that such a jurisdiction exists. It has for long been recognised that… the Attorney General is also the guardian of the rights of the public, and the courts will enable him to perform that role by the granting of injunctions or other appropriate relief where the other remedies available for ensuring that the law is complied with are plainly inadequate. This had been recognised in the case of the Attorney General in Ireland prior to 1921 and the same considerations applied to the Attorney General of the Irish Free State [and] the office of Attorney General created by the Constitution."

It is submitted that the Irish Courts have consistently misinterpreted s 6(1) of the 1924 Act. They have consistently drawn the authority of the Attorney General in the assertion and protection of public rights from the second part of the subsection. This

---

28 [1983] IR 88 at 101 *per* Keane J (as he then was).

29 [1970] IR 241.

30 [1988] IR 353.

31 See *Attorney General and the Minister for Posts and Telegraphs v Paperlink* [1984] ILRM 373; *Attorney General (Society for the Protection of Unborn Children) v Open Door Counselling Ltd* [1988] IR 593; *Attorney General v X* [1992] 1 IR 1; *Attorney General v Hamilton* [1993] ILRM 81.

32 [2000] 4 IR 298.

is despite the fact that Kennedy CJ expressly rejected this argument in *Moore* and held that the power of the Attorney General here flowed from the first part of the subsection, which vested in the Attorney General the powers of the Irish Law Officers of the Crown. As such, it is submitted that the legal basis for the role of the Attorney General in the assertion and protection of public rights and as protector of charities is inherently suspect.[33]

Salvaging the Attorney General's Role as "Guardian of the Public Interest"

The role of the Attorney General in the assertion and protection of public rights could be retrieved in a number of ways. The most obvious is to ground the Attorney's authority in the field of public rights in the Constitution. Another route would be by statute. The Oireachtas could replace s 6(1) of the 1924 Act with a new section, which outlines the role of the Attorney General in this area without reference to the powers, duties and functions of the old law officers of the Crown, the Attorney General of Saorstát Éireann or the present Attorney General, tainted as they are with unconstitutionality. Alternatively, the Attorney General could be taken out of the equation altogether and confined to his primary task of advising the Government, and a new office, specifically charged with the protection and the assertion of public rights along the lines of a director of public proceedings could be set up.[34] One method of achieving this would be to vest the "guardian of the public interest" function in constitutional matters in the newly established Human Rights Commission (HRC),[35] which because of the definition of human rights in its

33 Implicit support for this conclusion may be drawn from Art 30. Although it was generally accepted in 1937 that the prerogative powers of the King were vested in the State. It could be argued that the reason the drafters of the Constitution included such a detailed provision on the Attorney General, who had received no mention in the 1922 Constitution, was to ground his authority as public prosecutor in the people and not the Crown. As already noted, it was in this capacity that the Attorney General was generally understood to act as guardian of the public interest in 1937.

34 This is advocated by Professor David Gwynn Morgan of University College Cork. See Morgan, "Attorney General's juggling act must be ended" *Irish Times*, 15 March 1993, 'No major problem in separating AG's roles' *Irish Times*, 16 March 1993. However, the Constitution Review Group and the All-Party Oireachtas Committee on the Constitution did not think this was necessary by virtue of the small amount of time, five per cent, taken up by Attorney General in the discharge of this role. See All-Party Oireachtas Committee on the Constitution, Eighth Progress Report (2003) at 38–39.

35 This was advocated by the first President of the Commission, Mr Justice Donal Barrington, in a paper entitled "The Development and Work of the Human Rights Commission" delivered at a *Law and Policy Seminar* in UCC on 15 November 2001.

governing statute has nearly the same roving jurisdiction in the field of public rights as the Attorney General.[36]

However, it is clear that whatever solution is used, some action has to be taken in order to ensure that the Attorney General's role as guardian of the public interest continues to be exercised.

[36] s 2 of the Human Rights Commission Act 2000 defines human rights as: "Rights liberties and freedoms conferred on, or guaranteed to, persons by the Constitution and as the rights liberties and freedoms conferred on, or guaranteed to, persons by any agreement, treaty or convention to which the State is a party and which has been given the force of law in the State or by a provision of any such agreement, treaty or convention."

The Urgency for Legal Regulation of the Practices of Cloning and Stem Cell Research

by
Geraldine Cleere*

"The ability to turn blood into liver would be the envy of the alchemists of former times. Turning stem cells into 'therapeutic gold' will probably rest on our ability to identify the mechanisms by which tissue-derived stem cells respond to environmental cues and execute new developmental decisions."[1] To develop legislation for such an area as cloning and stem cell research is a governmental nightmare. An ethical minefield coupled with the rapid advances in the area ensures most governments place the issue on the long finger until it can be ignored no longer. The Irish Government has indeed fallen foul of this rule. The issue has come before it in a European context recently, and this alone caused a major storm. With no, domestic legislation in the area and an increasing bio-pharmaceutical presence in this country it is an area which must be legislated for, and soon. After all, "controls, regulations and safeguards are far better than a free-for-all".[2]

On 23 February 1997, Dolly the sheep was cloned by Scottish scientists. It was from that point that genuine ethical concerns were raised about the possibility of cloning humans. With so much publicity surrounding the field of genetics and its related areas it is little wonder that much of the terminology inherent with the area is confused, and it is difficult for the lay person to determine one practice from another. It is true that cloning and stem cell research are very much related, but from a procedural and an ethical point of view the differences between the two are quite significant.

---

* BA, LL. B, LL.M Candidate, University College Cork. This essay was awarded joint second place in the Law Society of Ireland, *Student Law Reform Essay Competition 2004.*

[1] Orkin, *Nature Medicine,* November 2000, Vol 6, Number 11, p 1212 at 1213.

[2] Former An Táiniste, Mary Harney, quoted in Fionán Sheehan, "Fianna Fáil Split deepens over stem cell research", *Irish Examiner*, 26 November 2003.

Cloning

There are two main categories of cloning, reproductive cloning and therapeutic cloning.

"Reproductive cloning" is the technology used to generate a specimen that has the same nuclear DNA as another currently or previously existing specimen, be it animal or human, and may simply be defined as a way of producing a genetic twin of an organism without the need for sexual reproduction. Dolly the sheep was created by reproductive cloning technology. The process involves the transfer of a cell nucleus to an unfertilized egg, the nucleus of which has been removed and its development stimulated by a small electrical current. Once the cloned embryo reaches a suitable stage it is transferred to the uterus of a female host, where it continues to develop until birth. This process does not create an identical twin of the creature that supplied the nucleus, only a genetic twin. There are many inherent risks with this type of cloning with scientists believing that errors or incompleteness in the process cause the high rates of death, deformity, and disability observed among creatures cloned.

"Therapeutic cloning" or embryo cloning is the creation of human embryos for use in research. The goal of this process is not to create cloned human beings but, rather, to harvest stem cells that can be used to study human development and to treat disease. The creation procedure is the same as for reproductive cloning, the transfer of a nucleus of one cell to the unfertilized egg, the nucleus of which has been removed. The difference is in the procedure after this. While the intention in reproductive cloning is that the embryo be implanted and develop into a human baby, in therapeutic cloning the embryo is allowed to develop for about five days, until the "blastocyst"[3] stage is reached, at which point the stem cells are harvested for research.

Stem Cell Harvesting and Research

Stem cells are of reported importance to medical researchers as they can be used to generate virtually any type of specialised cell in the human body. The fertilized egg is allowed to divide for five days, at which point the stem cells are extracted from the egg. It must be noted that the extraction process destroys the embryo, which raises a variety of ethical concerns. Many researchers hope that one day stem cells can be used to serve as replacement cells to treat heart disease, Alzheimer's, cancer and other diseases.

---

[3] The "blastocyst" is a hollow, fluid-filled ball of cells.

For the most part embryonic stem cells for research are obtained from embryos donated by persons with an excess following a course of IVF treatment and so these embryos are destined to be destroyed anyway. However, where the numbers of IVF surplus embryos being donated are insufficient there are instances where embryos have been cloned for the purpose of harvesting stem cells for use in research.

As the embryo develops it goes through several stages. Following fertilization, the embryo is a single cell. This is comprised of half male genetic material and half female genetic material. This zygote undergoes a series of cell divisions. When the developing embryo has divided to about 100 cells it is known as a blastocyst. Of these cells in the blastocyst, some go on to form both embryonic cells, which may develop into a human baby under the right circumstances, and non-embryonic cells, which go on to form such things as the placenta and the umbilical cord. It is impossible to say what percentages of these blastocyst cells form which tissue. Within the blastocyst is a population of cells from which embryonic stem cells can be harvested. At this stage the cells are still relatively undifferentiated.[4] There is no trace of human structure such as a nervous system. At about 14 days after fertilisation, and only following implantation, the cells begin to become differentiated into more specialised cell types, and the "primitive streak", from which the central nervous system eventually develops, begins to appear.[5]

The Current Law

Ireland currently has no legislation which bans or regulates the practices of cloning and stem cell research. In Ireland, should an organisation be found engaging in such activities, the matter would be dealt with as being contrary to the Constitution and indeed natural law. The Constitution guarantees a right to life[6] and a right to bodily integrity. It would need to be proved that the practices being undertaken are contrary to these rights in order for an injunction, restraining the organization, to be obtained. But this might be too late. Such proceedings take time, certainly longer than it takes to implant a cloned embryo. What would be the remedy to such a

---

[4] "Undifferentiated" means the cells have not become specialised and can develop into any type of human tissue.

[5] Scientists in general believe this is the first stage at which the cells are recognisable as any form of person.

[6] Article 40.3 of Bunreacht na hÉireann 1937.

situation?[7] With no legislation to determine the boundaries and sanctions, the legal conundrum would begin.

The sole guidelines in relation to this area exist in the governance of the medical professions. The Medical Council of Ireland published its sixth edition of its guidelines on ethics in 2004,[8] which stated that:

> "The creation of new forms of life for experimental purposes or the deliberate and intentional destruction of in-vitro human life already formed is professional misconduct."[9]

This has the effect of banning medical professionals from participating in any process relating to the destruction of an embryo for the purposes of stem cell research, or indeed for any reason.

Those embryos which are created must only be used for the purposes of implantation in IVF treatment.[10]

However, these guidelines apply solely to the medical profession acting in such capacity and are in no way binding on any member of the scientific community.

There is no evidence at this point to suggest that either cloning or stem cell research is being carried out in this jurisdiction but the biotechnology market in this country is currently booming. In such a fast-paced research area there is little point in trying to play catch-up. The stakes are too high.

The EU

This issue is ongoing at European level but it must be stressed that any decisions taken by the EU in relation to the funding of such research will not be imposed on any of the Member States. The issue before the EU is whether or not to allow funds under the 6th Framework Programme to be applied to cloning or stem cell research.

---

7 Because there is judicial recognition that the constitutional right to life encompasses the unborn child, abortion is not a valid remedy.

8 Medical Council of Ireland, *A Guide to Ethical Conduct and Behaviour*, 6th edition, 2004.

9 *ibid* at p 35.

10 *ibid.*

It has decided that funding may be given to stem cell research projects, but only where the embryos used are those which are left over from IVF treatment and would otherwise be destroyed. Other stringent prerequisites will all need to be satisfied before an ethics review group and before any funding for a particular research project will be approved. Embryonic stem cells can only be derived from embryos that are donated for research by parents who gave their fully informed consent. The parents donating these embryos shall be forbidden from making any financial gain. Research will be funded only when it is demonstrated that it meets important research objectives. There must be no adequate alternative available to researchers. Traceability of stem cells and anonymity of donors must be guaranteed. Finally, the EU will not fund human embryonic stem cell research in a particular country where such practice is forbidden by that Member State.

Other Jurisdictions

Other jurisdictions have recently put legislation in place to regulate the practices in their own country. There are striking differences between the positions taken by different countries in their regulation of the area. These differences largely reflect contrasting cultural and religious traditions. Reproductive cloning is either illegal or prohibited in all countries which have relevant legislation.

In Britain, the use of embryos and creation of embryos for use in stem cell research and other areas of genetic research are permitted under the Human Fertilisation and Embryology Act 1990. This legislation was enacted primarily to regulate the practice of *in vitro* fertilisation, but the regulatory authority[11] set up by the Act is also empowered to license research on human embryos. Under the Act research on embryos older than 14 days is prohibited. All research must be undertaken under license from the HFEA. A license may not be granted unless two tests have been satisfied: first that the use of embryos is necessary and they cannot be obtained by other means, and second, the research must be necessary or desirable for one of the specified purposes.

In the US, President Bush has authorised federal funding for research on human embryonic stem cells, but only if they were derived from stem cell lines established before 9 August 2001.[12] It is generally up to individual States to put in place their

[11] The Human Fertilisation and Embryology Authority (HFEA).

[12] This is the date of the Act and so the creation of further embryos past this date will not qualify for funding. The research is not expressly banned in the USA.

own regulations in relation to research on embryos, and therefore funding is the sole method of regulation of such practices from a federal point of view. Some states have no regulations in place and therefore little control over what takes place in private research facilities.

In Australia, the House of Representatives Standing Committee on Legal and Constitutional Affairs, following a two-year enquiry, published a report recommending a ban on the creation of embryos solely for research purposes, allowing the extraction of stem cells from spare IVF embryos and banning reproductive cloning.

Recommendations

It is a slight anomaly, but even though stem cell research and cloning are inextricably linked, the two are very much separate and distinct, and each stands alone without the other. The decision to regulate these practices is difficult as the area is fraught with many scientific, religious, ethical and legal matters.

Reproductive Cloning

Bunreacht na hÉireann 1937 guarantees the right to life of all citizens[13] and upholds the family as the primary institution of society.[14] The constitutional and social implications of permitting such a practice are endless.

Dolly the sheep was hailed a scientific success story, but she was sheep number 277. The previous 276 perished from abnormalities at different stages of development or were simply discarded. Putting this on a human scale, the implications are terrifying. We are human beings, not scientific guinea pigs.

In this jurisdiction, the Constitution describes the family as the primary social group in society.[15] Cloning does not subscribe to a mother or father in the conventional sense. The closest the clone would conceivably come to a family would be a series of ambiguous relationships. These concerns are merely the tip of the iceberg, an iceberg submerged in very murky waters. What rights would the clone have? Would it have

---

[13] Article 40.3.2 of Bunreacht na hÉireann 1937.

[14] Article 41.1 of Bunreacht na hÉireann 1937.

[15] *ibid.*

any of the rights of a normal person? Would it merely be treated as the results of an experiment, to be discarded or destroyed once it has yielded all of the useful scientific evidence it can?

Reproductive cloning is a dangerous game. It is no longer an issue of animal testing or lab rats; it is a matter of human life. To endorse such a practice or not make it a grave crime would be making a mockery of the sanctity of human life,[16] the right to bodily integrity[17] and the concept of the family,[18] all guaranteed by the Constitution. It would be a failure of the State to uphold the fundamental rights guaranteed to all by the Constitution. Reproductive cloning is wrong, full stop! It has been banned or criminalised in all other jurisdictions, and this ought to be the position here. It is recommended that any efforts to carry out such a procedure within this jurisdiction be punishable as a criminal offence with a severe sentence attached.

Stem Cell Research using Surplus IVF Embryos

The decision as to whether or not this type of research ought to be permitted is more difficult. As already pointed out, stem cell research involves the harvesting of embryonic stem cells from an early embryo in order for research as to their efficacy to be carried out. Scientists believe these stem cells may hold the key to providing cures to degenerative diseases such as Parkinson's disease, Alzheimer's disease and cancer. The moral and legal issues in this area derive from the fact that the harvesting of the stem cells destroys the embryo. Therefore the question which must be asked in respect of this type of research is: are these early embryos afforded the right to life?

The Roman Catholic Church claims that all life is sacred and must be protected from the time of conception.[19] The reasoning behind this view is that from the point of conception the embryo, in whatever form, is a person and so its right to life should be guarded as with all other persons. This is a somewhat romantic view and one which society cannot reasonably claim to subscribe to. It is a fact that a very high percentage of conceived embryos perish in the body prior to implantation and indeed even in more advanced pregnancies where a woman miscarries or the pregnancy fails through complications, and there is no public mourning of the loss of these embryos or babies. Of course this is not to suggest that such a loss is not

[16] Article 40.3 of Bunreacht na hÉireann 1937.

[17] *ibid.*

[18] Article 41.1 of Bunreacht na hÉireann.

[19] *An Opportunity Not To Be Lost*, Catholic Communications Office (Dublin, 2002).

traumatic for the family, it is a time of great grief. Nonetheless, society does not hold the death of an embryo in early development in near the same regard as a baby in the late stages of pregnancy or post birth.

It is also worth noting that the "morning after pill" is permitted in this jurisdiction. This pill effectively destroys the embryo.[20] In permitting the use of the morning after pill, the Government and society are suggesting the right to life is not absolutely given to the very early embryo.

The embryos used are destined for destruction, not because they are an experiment but because they are left over from IVF treatment, a legal procedure. At the point of their creation they were intended for life, but this life is contingent on being selected for implantation. Since they are never going to become implanted and develop into a living person, they are merely to be destroyed. Should their creation not be allowed to serve some purpose?

It is not denied that the IVF embryo is a potential person, but should this in itself mean it has a right to life? A person below the age of 18 is a potential voter, but this does not extend to them a right to vote. A law student is a potential lawyer, but this does not give he or she a right to practice law. These rights are contingent, respectively, upon reaching 18 or becoming qualified as a barrister or a solicitor. The right to life of an embryo ought to be contingent upon it becoming implanted in the womb of its mother. Furthermore, it is widely accepted in the scientific world that the embryo only begins to develop a primitive streak at around 14 days. If the scientific view was to be followed, as it seems to be in many jurisdictions, the harvesting of stem cells would only be permitted on embryos below 14 days old.

It is recommended that the scientific view be taken in respect of surplus IVF embryos being made available for research.

Of course the strict line laid down by the EU should be taken, with strict laws governing the area. Among other things, the donor parents must give their fully informed consent, they must not receive any monetary reward, they must remain anonymous and the organizations conducting the research must undergo strict checks and testing by a board of ethics to ensure that only genuine research projects

---

[20] The "morning after pill" works in two ways. First, it aims to prevent ovulation and thus fertilisation and, secondly, should the egg become fertilized the embryo is prevented from implanting in the uterus and therefore the embryo dies in the body.

receive licensing and the activities of these organisations must be constantly monitored by this board to ensure that no rogue activities are undertaken.

Therapeutic Cloning

This area is very much the middle ground between the issue of reproductive cloning and stem cell research using surplus IVF embryos. The public policy considerations in relation to therapeutic cloning are not quite as compelling as with reproductive cloning. Here the cloning process would begin as for reproductive cloning but the development of the cloned embryo would end at the blastocyst stage.[21] The embryo would be created only to harvest stem cells. Generally this type of cloning is only used where there is a shortfall in the amount of surplus IVF embryos being donated, but it is sometimes used to research the development of early embryo and genetic research.

Many people subscribe to the view that this type of cloning is acceptable. The embryo is treated the same way as a surplus IVF embryo in that the stem cells are removed at an early stage, which ends development of the embryo. The stem cells are used for valuable research, and this is no different than using the embryos left over from IVF. This is not so.

The creation of an embryo for the express purpose of destroying it is contrary to all the laws of nature. It is believed that this type of cloning may be putting the country on a slippery slope. If the cloning of embryos is allowed, what then if one "accidentally" becomes implanted? Criminal sanctions or not, the damage has been done.

It is not that there is no alternative. Surplus IVF embryos are a viable option, and they are created originally for human reproductive purposes. There are those who argue that the cloned embryos would only be used where there is a shortfall in the number of IVF embryos donated, but this can hardly be a reason for justifying such a procedure. Indeed it ensures more value is attached to those IVF embryos which are donated, and emphasis will need to be placed on refining techniques in order to ensure there is no wasting of donated embryos. For this reason it is recommended that the cloning of embryos for use in research be banned and a criminal sanction

[21] The "blastocyst stage" is reached between the five and fourteen day mark, when the embryo is a small, hollow ball of cells.

attached to it, albeit not so severe as the punishment for attempts at reproductive cloning. However, this view might be reviewed in the future should the position regarding availability of embryos change.

Conclusion

> "...Rights given by the Constitution must be considered in accordance with concepts of prudence, justice and charity, which may gradually change and develop as society changes and develops and which fall to be interpreted from time to time in accordance with prevailing ideas...The Constitution did not seek to impose for all time, the ideas prevalent or accepted with regard to these virtues at the time of its enactment."[22]

Thus, the law must move with the times. This may be a controversial area, but regardless of the feelings of the public and the Government, it must be legislated for in one way or another in the very near future.

The Constitution of Ireland upholds the sanctity of life, and a failure to expressly ban the cloning of human embryos for any purpose would be a failure to uphold these rights. There are no reasons to clone humans. After millions of years it is safe to say the human race has accepted the ritual of conventional reproduction. To interfere with the most natural of processes can only result in bad things. But in recognising the dangers of modern science, the Oireachtas must also acknowledge its rewards. The right to life as guaranteed by the Constitution is a prominent consideration, but another consideration must be the benefits of stem cell research. No entity shall be denied the right to life, save for the common good.

The human race has been handed a gift in the discovery of the medical potential of stem cells, but in order to explore the full potential of this therapeutic gold the proper legislation must be put in place. The potential for abuse of all these areas is far too great. Without legislation, and with a growing biopharmaceutical presence, this jurisdiction could become a cloning playground. Legislation must be forthcoming.

After all, there is little point in closing the stable door after the horse has bolted.

---

[22] *per* O'Higgins CJ *The State (Healy) v Donoghue* [1976] IR 325 at 347.

The Exception (Im)proves the Rule: Reforming the Irish Law of Hearsay

by

Ray Ryan and Des Ryan*

Prior Inconsistent Statements: The Case for Reform

It has been said that the rules relating to the admissibility of hearsay evidence in a criminal trial "resemble an old-fashioned crazy quilt made from patches cut from a group of paintings by cubists, futurists and surrealists".[1] The hearsay rule has been described by Professor Wigmore as "that most characteristic rule of the Anglo-American law of evidence — a rule which may be esteemed, next to jury trial, the greatest contribution of that eminently practical legal system to the world's methods of procedure".[2] Leaving aside considerations of doctrinal certainty, this branch of the law has been characterised by the restrictive, molecular nature of its development, with judges generally being unwilling to amidst evidence not embraced by the limited exceptions previously recognised by the common law. We submit, however, that the law of evidence can be reformed for the better if the Irish courts are prepared to place principle above precedent. We submit that the rules in this area of law may desirably be reformed by judicial as opposed to legislative action: not least because it is the courts that have been exclusively responsible for the development of the criminal hearsay rules in this jurisdiction to date. Our concern is that an overly restrictive attitude to the admissibility of hearsay evidence can serve, on occasion, to frustrate the effective operation of our criminal justice system. For present purposes, we confine our analysis to the prior inconsistent statement exception to the hearsay rule. We suggest that a recent controversy has served to highlight that this exception

* This essay was awarded joint second place in the Law Society of Ireland, *Student Law Reform Essay Competition 2004.*

[1] Moran and Maguire, "Looking Backwards and Forwards at Evidence" (1937) 50 *Harv L Rev* 909 at 921.

[2] *Wigmore on Evidence* (Boston, Little Brown and Co, 1940), Vol V, p 28.

could, with profit, be introduced into Irish law. The dramatic collapse of a murder trial at the Central Criminal Court some months ago has sharply focused attention on the effectiveness of our criminal justice system.[3] The collective amnesia allegedly experienced by several key prosecution witnesses in that particular case, after what Mr Justice Paul Carney was to describe as "suspicious goings-on" in his court, can only be regarded as most disturbing. These events, which the vastly experienced presiding trial judge considered unprecedented, understandably focused attention on the effectiveness of the administration of justice. There were calls in some quarters for increasing recourse to be had to the Special Criminal Court. It is unquestionably true that the non-jury court — where security is at a premium — constitutes an important alternative court in which to try certain individuals in respect of whom the standard administration of justice is deemed insufficient to conduct an effective prosecution. But as commentators search for an effective bulwark against the recurrence of the events of a few months ago, there is an entirely different legal response that is hugely more attractive and likely to be more effective. The Irish law of evidence should be reformed so as to permit the introduction into evidence, in the presence of specified safeguards, of statements made by a witness, notwithstanding that the witness has recanted his statement at trial. This rule, which pertains in other common law systems, is known as the prior inconsistent statement exception to the hearsay rule. It is the purpose of the present article to explore the manner in which courts in other jurisdictions — particularly Canada — have developed the prior inconsistent statement exception so as to address the very problems encountered in the recent controversy at the Central Criminal Court. We seek to analyse the legitimacy of the reasoning behind this extension of the hearsay rule in evidence and to consider its potential application in the law of evidence in this jurisdiction.

The Hearsay Dangers

Hearsay evidence is evidence of out of court statements sought to be admitted to prove the truth of their contents. This species of evidence is presumptively inadmissible because of the dangers that accompany it. Foremost among such dangers are the absence of an oath when the statement is made, the inability of the trier of fact to assess the demeanour and therefore the credibility of the maker of the statement and the inability to cross-examine the maker. In the course of a well-

[3] See, *inter alia*, "A Case of Collective Amnesia", *Irish Times*, 8 November 2003; "A Challenge for Criminal Justice", *Irish Times*, 4 November 2003; "Limerick man walks free after murder trial collapses", *Irish Times*, 3 November 2003.

known judgment of the Supreme Court over 40 years ago, Kingsmill Moore J stressed that:

> "There is no general rule of evidence to the effect that the witness may not testify as to the words spoken by a person who is not produced as a witness. There is a general rule, subject to many exceptions, that evidence of the speaking of such words is inadmissible to prove the truth of the facts which they assert...This is the rule known as the rule against hearsay."[4]

The Exception (Im)Proves the Rule

Although accompanied by dangers, hearsay evidence may be the best or the only available evidence going to some critical fact in issue. The out-of-court statements made by the witnesses in the controversial trial at the root of the present public debate provide a classic example of such a case. The courts in all common law jurisdictions, including Ireland, have etched out a number of important exceptions to the hearsay rule in recognition of the fact that in certain cases the interests of justice demand the introduction of hearsay evidence. The crucial test underpinning the acceptance of all such exceptions is that the dangers inherent in admitting the evidence must be outweighed by the unfairness which would be engendered to the integrity of the trial process by its exclusion. It is this very tension which has led other common law jurisdictions to expand the scope of the rule to allow for the admission of prior inconsistent statements where such statements would previously have been excluded on the grounds of incompatibility with the hearsay rule. The more relaxed approach allows the admission of prior statements not just for the issue of credibility, but also for the truth of their contents. It was exactly for this latter purpose that the High Court of Australia admitted such evidence in the leading decision in that jurisdiction, *Driscoll v The Queen.*[5] A similarly liberal approach had been taken much earlier by Judge Learned Hand in *Di Carlo v United States,* [6] where Judge Learned Hand expressed the expansive flexibility of the prior statement exception in the following terms:

> "The latitude to be allowed in the examination of a witness, who has been called and proved recalcitrant, is wholly within the discretion of the trial

---

[4] *Cullen v Clarke* [1963] IR 368, at 378.

[5] (1977) 137 CLR 517.

[6] (1925) 6F.2d 364.

> judge. Nothing is more unfair than to confine a party under such circumstances to neutral questions. Not only may the questions extend to cross-examination, but, if necessary to bring out the truth, it is entirely proper to inquire of such a witness whether he has not made contradictory statements at other times. He is present before the jury and the [jury] may gather the truth from his whole conduct of contradictory answers he may have made at other times...The possibility that the jury may accept as truth the earlier statements in preference to those made upon the stand is indeed real, but we find no difficulty in it. If from all that the jury see of the witness, they conclude that what he says now is not the truth but what he said before, they are nonetheless deciding from what they see and hear of that person and in court. There is no mythical necessity that the case must be decided only in accordance with the truth of words uttered under oath in court."[7]

The principles espoused in the above passage, though remarkable for their liberality, should be interpreted with caution. It is submitted that, in shaping a reformed approach to prior inconsistent statements, the Irish courts must tread delicately along the precarious fault-line between embracing flexibility, on the one hand, and giving rise to the classic hearsay dangers described above, on the other. In striving to achieve this goal of balance, it is submitted that the Irish courts could most profitably learn from developments to the rule in Canada. It is to that jurisdiction that we now shift focus.

Prior Inconsistent Statements and the Supreme Court of Canada

The Supreme Court of Canada dramatically reformed its approach to prior inconsistent statements some 12 years ago in the celebrated case of *The Queen v KGB.*[8] The facts may be briefly stated. The accused and three of his friends were involved in a fight with two men. In the course of the fracas, one of the young men produced a knife with which he stabbed another man in the chest, killing him. The four youths fled the scene. Three of them were subsequently interviewed separately by the police and, with their consent, the interviews were video-recorded. In the course of their statements, the men told the police that the accused had made

---

[7] *ibid* (emphasis added).

[8] [1993] 1 SCR 740.

statements to them in which he acknowledged that he thought he had caused the death of the victim by the use of a knife. At the trial, the three youths withdrew their earlier statements and said that they had lied to the police to exculpate themselves from possible involvement. The trial judge had no doubt that the recantations were false, but withdrew the case from the jury on the ground that their earlier statements could only be used to impeach the witnesses' credibility and that, in the absence of any other evidence, the accused must be acquitted. This was upheld by the Court of Appeal. Prior to the hearing in the Supreme Court of Canada, the three witnesses pleaded guilty to perjury as a result of their testimony at trial.[9] The question which faced the Supreme Court was whether the law of evidence should be changed so as to allow the introduction into evidence of these statements to prove their truth, where certain criteria were met. A unanimous Supreme Court emphatically answered this question in the affirmative. The Court held that the old common law rule ("the orthodox rule"), limiting the use of prior inconsistent statements to impeaching the credibility of the witness, should be replaced by a new rule recognising the changed means and method of proof in a modern society. But the court also laid down safeguards designed to protect accused persons in their enjoyment of a constitutional presumption of innocence, stressing that a reformed rule must "carefully balance the accused's interests in a criminal trial with the interests of a society in seeing justice done".[10] In particular, the Court was careful to point out that a reformed rule must address the typical hearsay dangers of admitting prior inconsistent statements for the truth of their contents *viz* the absence of an oath or solemn affirmation when the statement was made, the inability of the trier of fact to assess the demeanour, and therefore the credibility, of the declarant when the statement was made, and the lack of contemporaneous cross-examination by the opposing party. Following its earlier landmark decisions in the cases of *Khan*[11] and *Smith*,[12] the Court emphasised that statements, in order to be admissible, must have a substantial probative value, must come within a circumstantial guarantee of trustworthiness, and there must be a necessity for the evidence.[13] Lamer CJC stated that there would be a sufficient

[9] It is worth noting at this point that perjury proceedings have been instituted in the Limerick case referred to above: see "Three to face court over trial collapse in Limerick", *Irish Times*, 28 July 2005.

[10] [1993] 1 SCR 740 at 762.

[11] *R. v Khan* [1990] 2 SCR 531.

[12] *R. v Smith* [1992] SCR 915.

[13] Further, the Court took the view that these core criteria need to be adapted to suit the context of the case under consideration, holding that, as a threshold matter, the prior inconsistent statements would only be admissible if they would have been admissible as the witness's sole testimony, lest what would be excluded as the witness's primary evidence be admitted under the reformed rule simply because the witness had recanted.

circumstantial guarantee of trustworthiness to allow the jury to make substantive use of the statement where: (1) the statement is made under oath, solemn affirmation of solemn declaration following an explicit warning to the witness as to the existence of severe criminal sanctions for the making of false statements; (2) the statement is videotaped in its entirety; and (3) the opposing party, whether the Crown or the defence, has a full opportunity to cross-examine the witness at trial in respect of the statement. Alternatively, Lamer CJC opined, "other circumstantial guarantees of trustworthiness may suffice to render such statements substantively admissible, provided that the judge is satisfied that the circumstances provide adequate assurances of reliability in place of those which the hearsay rule traditionally requires".[14]

Canadian "Principled" Approach Finds Welcome in Ireland

Significantly, the Irish Supreme Court addressed the principled approach to the law of evidence adopted in Canada in the 1999 case of *Re MK, SK and WK*.[15] The Court seemed, through obiter comments, to be impressed with the reasoning in the seminal Canadian Supreme Court decision in *Khan*. *Khan*, which concerned an alleged sexual assault by a doctor upon a three-year-old child, is identified as the starting point of the principled approach to the hearsay rule in Canada. McLachlin J (as she then was) stressed the need for increased flexibility in the interpretation of the hearsay rule to permit the admission into evidence of statements made by children to others about sexual abuse and framed the admissibility test into two core criteria. McLachlin J explained that necessity for these purposes "might be interpreted as 'reasonably necessary'".[16] As to reliability, this criterion was capable of taking into consideration a range of factors in the particular case, such as, *inter alia*, timing, demeanour, and the personality, intelligence or understanding of the child. Significantly, McLachlin J declined to draw up "a strict list of considerations for reliability or to suggest that certain categories of evidence (for example the evidence of young children on sexual encounters) should always be regarded as reliable".[17]

Examining this approach of McLachlin J in *Khan*, the Irish Supreme Court in *Re MK, SK and WK* seemed convinced by the decision to admit the evidence of the

---

[14] [1993] 1 SCR 740 at 792.

[15] [1999] 2 IR 99; [1999] 2 ILRM 321.

[16] [1990] 2 SCR 531 at 593.

[17] *ibid.*

child. Keane J (as he then was) said that "there is undoubtedly much to be said for adopting this approach to the admissibility of such evidence".[18] Notably, Keane J. also addressed the issue of whether such important reform of the law of evidence is properly within the remit of the judiciary. Although Keane J reached no definite conclusion on the desirability of judicial creation of a new exception to the hearsay rule, Keane J stated that "if the law in *R v Khan* were to be adopted in this jurisdiction, it would represent an important additional exception to the rule against hearsay".[19] Further hope that the principled approach enunciated in *Khan* might be followed in this jurisdiction is to be gleaned from the opinion of Denham J in the same case. Denham J stated that the hearsay rule was adopted to protect the trial process, but that new exceptions to the rule were capable of being recognised.[20] She felt that the unique nature of wardship proceedings necessitated such an exception, although the reliability threshold had not been satisfied in the instant case. This approach is encouraging. Denham J's express recognition that certain cases can—because of the peculiar evidential difficulties which they throw up—"necessitate" recourse to a more flexible approach to the hearsay rule, provides a most promising mechanism for resolving the type of difficulties encountered by the Special Criminal Court in recent months. While it is true that *MK* was restricted to the issue of wardship proceedings, we would submit that the flexible approach of the Supreme Court evinced in that case is sufficiently broad to encapsulate other species of case. It is instructive to bear in mind in this context that *Khan* itself appeared at first to apply only in cases of child sexual abuse, only to be extended by the Supreme Court of Canada very shortly thereafter, not only in *KGB* itself but also in the landmark *Smith*[21] and *Starr*[22] decisions.

Recent Developments: *KGB* Considered in the Court of Criminal Appeal

It is therefore of great interest, then, that the Court of Criminal Appeal in a recent case has arguably indicated its willingness to adopt this very approach. In *DPP v McArdle*,[23] Keane CJ appeared receptive to a consideration of how *KGB* might

---

[18] [1999] 2 IR 99 at 135; [1999] 2 ILRM 321 at 355.

[19] *ibid.*

[20] [1999] 2 IR 99 at 108; [1999] 2 ILRM 321 at 331.

[21] [1992] SCR 915.

[22] [2002] 2 SCR 144.

[23] Unreported, Court of Criminal Appeal, 13 October 2003 (Keane CJ, O'Sullivan and O'Higgins JJ).

potentially apply in an Irish setting and demonstrated his respect for the intellectual rigour of the Supreme Court of Canada's analysis in that case, referring to the judgment of Lamer CJC as "exhaustive". Although the factual context of *McArdle* ruled out the possibility of applying *KGB*, it is submitted that the treatment accorded to the judgment of Lamer CJC in that case is a cause for optimism and that, should an appropriate case present itself, it will be viewed as embracing the inclusion of the *KGB* approach into the Irish law of evidence. Moreover, it may be of significance that Keane CJ did not indicate any concern that such a reform would more properly be a matter for the legislative branch of the government; *a fortiori* since the same judge, in the *Re MK* case discussed above, had aired doubts about whether such law reform was a matter for the courts. In addition, although the Court of Criminal Appeal held that the *KGB* rule could not be applied on the facts of *McArdle*,[24] the strong impression from the judgment of the court is that *KGB* might well be followed in this jurisdiction when the appropriate case presents itself.

Conclusion

The traditional rigidity with which the hearsay rule has been applied has "frequently proved unduly inflexible in dealing with new situations and new needs in the law".[25] The recent events in the Central Criminal Court relating to recantation by witnesses bear out the truth of this proposition with devastating clarity. In response to these events, the coalition government has vowed in recent months to provide all resources necessary for the effective prosecution of crime. Indeed, it is conceded that the recent publication of the Criminal Justice Bill 2004, proposing the very reform being canvassed for here, may, if enacted into law, render somewhat moot the preceding case law analysis of potential for reform.[26] Nonetheless, we submit that this reform would be better left to the judicial branch of government. The old hearsay rules are, after all, judge-made laws, thereby lending themselves to judicial reform,[27] and were the appropriate case to present itself, the Supreme Court would have the opportunity to rule in a manner similar to its Canadian counterpart that such evidence is

24 Keane CJ noted that no *voir dire* had been conducted at trial in this case and that the prosecution had not sought to have the prior statements admitted.

25 *R. v Khan*, *op. cit.*, *per* McLachlin J at 570.

26 The same reform has been effected in English law via s 119 of the Criminal Justice Act 2003, which entered into force in 2005.

27 As Lamer CJC stated in *KGB*: "The guidelines which direct this Court's exercise of its jurisdiction to overrule its previous decisions adopting the orthodox rule do not suggest that it should do anything other than what it thinks best in reconsidering the orthodox rule": [1993] 1 SCR 740, 781.

admissible once certain key safeguards are satisfied. The objective of these safeguards is to ensure that a balance be struck between the accused's interests in a criminal trial and the interests of society in seeing that justice be done. The rights enjoyed by accused persons need to be zealously guarded, and we are indeed fortunate that they are accorded such scrupulous protection by the courts in this jurisdiction. But this commentary has sought to argue that the current rules of evidence have tilted the scales too heavily in favour of the accused, at the expense of the people's right to have crime prosecuted effectively. What is needed is judicial intervention; and it is to the Canadian lead in *KGB* that our judges should turn. In his recent judgment in *McArdle*, examined above, Keane CJ has arguably left the door open for just such a reform. The prior inconsistent statement exception to the hearsay rule thus awaits a (not-too-distant?) future restatement.

Lording It: Reforming the Mode of Address Used Before the Superior Courts

by
Brian Conroy*

One aspect of Irish court procedure that non-lawyers find surprising, if not downright bizarre, is the mode of address used towards judges in the Superior Courts. The man on the Cabra omnibus, weaned on *Matlock* and *The Practice*, tends to assume that judges should be addressed as "Your Honour". Failing this, laymen at least expect lawyers to use a term that is not evocative of the British aristocracy. Yet it remains the case that, in the infant years of the 21st century, a visitor to court will hear counsel peppering their addresses with references to "My Lord" and "Your Lordship". It would appear that this area of court procedure is over-ripe for reform.

In the first section of this piece I will explore the historical origins of this mode of address in order to assess whether there is any legitimate reason for its continued use. The second section describes the political and other pressures that have frustrated attempts to abolish the traditional mode of address since the coming into force of the Irish Free State Constitution. The argument of the third and final section is that, in the light of the demonstrated ineffectiveness of reform brought about in any other manner, the only feasible means of changing the mode of address is via a mandatory and unambiguous legislative provision.

Historical Origins

The obvious assumption would be that the mode of address, "My Lord", was brought here by the British in the wake of their colonisation of Ireland and was supposed to indicate the aristocratic standing of the judiciary. On this basis it is easy to dismiss the use of the phrase as completely inconsistent with the manner in which

* This essay was awarded first place in the Law Society of Ireland, *Student Law Reform Essay Competition 2005.*

justice should be administered in a modern republic. Academics and practitioners seem to have avoided setting their thoughts on this matter in writing, but several politicians have made it clear that the above is their understanding of the antecedents of this mode of address. In a 1995 Dáil debate, Mr John O'Donoghue TD, later to become Minister for Justice Equality and Law Reform, dismissed the traditional mode of address as a colonial hangover:

> "Symbolic vestiges of what one might describe as old Victorian decency have no place in post-colonial Ireland. The time has come to express the view that this is a young Republic in a new Europe and that the addressing of a judge as "my Lord" is now arcane, belongs to a different age. We do not have nobility or lords, in so far as there are lords my understanding is that they are attached to the British House of Lords."[1]

Probably unbeknownst to himself, Mr O'Donoghue was echoing the following (somewhat more strident) comments made by a Mr Sherwin TD in a parliamentary debate of more than thirty years before:

> "I deplore hearing people falling over themselves, worshipping judges and justices. It all reminds me of the past. I am very fond of reading history and I have just finished Serjeant Sullivan's book on the courts in Ireland. Apart from the fact that we are now a Republic I do not think that we should persist in this servile form of address. If they addressed people by titles like that in France during the Revolution they would be sent to the guillotine immediately."[2]

However, reacting to Mr Sherwin's comments in the course of the same debate, Mr Thomas F. O'Higgins TD drew a very different picture of the history of these modes of address, finding their origin in the ecclesiastical law of this country:

> "It was suggested here on the Second Reading that to address a judge as "my Lord" or to refer to him in the third person as "Your Lordship" was in some way a remnant of some alien view and in some way servile and servient. Of

---

1 459 Dáil Debates Col 1219, of 12 December 1995, on the Report Stage of the Courts and Courts Officers Act 1995.

2 191 Dáil Debates Col 2155, of 27 July 1961, on the Committee Stage of the Courts (Supplemental Provisions) Bill, 1959. It may be suggested that Mr O'Higgins's fierce defence of the traditional practice derived at least in part from his long and distinguished association with the barrister's profession.

course, it has nothing to do whatever with the practice in the British courts and it is well that that should be said.

It is part of the tradition which arises from the fact that the forms in our courts are associated exclusively with Canon Law and with the Ecclesiastical Courts and the title "my Lord" has come to us from the fact that in the years gone by it was the practice in the Ecclesiastical Courts that applied. As frequently the presiding person in the old Ecclesiastical Court was a bishop, the title and style of address—"my Lord"—was associated with these courts. Although our conventions and relations between citizens are no longer based on the Canon Law, it has survived into the ordinary law of the land. That is history and those who have taken part in the Second Reading, thinking that they were having a tilt at something British, should re-examine the way they are aiming their lances because they are not tilting at anything British; they are tilting at something which is part of our Christian heritage in this country. I do not think that any Christian in this country of any denomination who recognises bishops in his religion would regard it as being in any way wrong or servile or in any way improper to address a bishop as "my Lord". That is the recognised mode of address."[3]

Quite apart from the fact that in modern Ireland there would be almost as many objections to drawing a mode of address from a religious as from a colonial context, it is not clear that Mr O'Higgins's analysis of the phrase's historical origins is entirely persuasive. The terms "lord" and "lordship" were unknown in the Brehon courts, and only began to be used here in courts that constituted a part of the administration of British justice. Hence, although the use of this mode of address probably *was* inspired by the practice of canon law, it seems to have been drawn from the ecclesiastical courts of Britain.[4] Therefore it would appear that the historical origins of this mode of address were *both* religious and colonial.

Regardless of arguments as to its historical derivation, it is clear that the phrase, "My Lord", is now generally perceived as having connotations of servility and colonialism. Thus, the less stigmatised phrase, "Your Honour", was adopted in the courts of

[3] *ibid*, at para 2153.

[4] See Chap 8 of Kelly, *A Guide to Early Irish Law* (Dublin, 1988); also Hogan and Osborough ed., Brehons, *Serjeants and Attorneys: Studies in the History of the Irish Legal Profession* (Dublin, 1990).

Australia, New Zealand and the United States following independence.[5] It has been observed that the procedure before the Dáil Courts that existed in Ireland between 1920 and 1924 was distinguished by an "absence of sonorous titles", so presumably the phrase was not used in those courts.[6] Furthermore, it appears that bishops in the Roman Catholic and Anglican Churches should now be addressed either as "The Most Reverend" or "The Right Reverend". The only religious figures who may still occasionally be addressed as "My Lord" are those Church of England bishops who are members of the House of Lords.[7] Hence any religious significance which the phrase once possessed has now disappeared, leaving it to be associated almost exclusively with a servile attitude towards the British nobility.

The above seems enough to demonstrate that the modes of address currently used have a very strong association with the British aristocracy that makes their use inappropriate in a modern republic. If any more imperatives for reform be needed, at least two exist. First, it may be suggested that the expressions "lord" or "lordship" are unsuitable when a female judge is presiding. It has been reported that Ms Justice Mella Carroll refuses to use the title and insists on being addressed as "Judge".[8] The option of calling female judges "My Lady", which has been adopted in England,[9] is not reasonably available here because this would move us even further towards a situation where Irish judges appear to claim aristocratic standing. Second, there is the small matter of Article 40.2.2 of the Constitution, which provides that "[N]o title of nobility or of honour may be accepted by any citizen except with the prior approval of the Government." It may be argued that the use of the current modes of address conflicts with the spirit if not the letter of this provision.[10] This is not to claim that a constitutional challenge to the modes of address would have any chance of succeeding, but merely to emphasise how inconsistent with the ethos of our Constitution the current practice is.

---

[5] It may also be relevant to note that the prescribed mode of address before the Supreme Court of Canada was changed from "My Lord/Lady" to "Justice", in 2001. See Law Society of British Columbia, *Benchers' Bulletin*, September/October 2001.

[6] Kotsonouris, *Retreat from Revolution: The Dáil Courts, 1920–1924* (Dublin, 1994), at p 133.

[7] Montague-Smith, *Debrett's Correct Form* (revised edition, London, 2002).

[8] *Irish Times*, 9 April 1991.

[9] See, for example, the 2002 *Consolidated Criminal Practice Direction of the English High Court and Court of Appeal*, at Chapter II.13

[10] This second point was in fact made by the current Minister for Justice Equality and Law Reform, Mr Michael McDowell TD, at para 1220 of the parliamentary debate of 12 December 1995, cited above.

Attempts at Reform Since 1922

Since the demise of British rule here, elements in the legislature, recognising the inappropriate nature of the traditional modes of address, have tried repeatedly to reform them. At the time of the Dáil Debates on the Bill which was eventually to become the Courts of Justice Act 1924, there was fierce opposition from those deputies who had links with the Bar of Ireland, as well as from Labour deputies and from several independents, to what were perceived as attempts by the Government to harness the independence of the judiciary. As regards the Superior Courts, this resistance centred around the issue of mode of dress and of address: it was felt that the Bar and the Bench should be free to decide on the robes to be worn and, more pertinently for our purposes, the judicial titles used, "without even the *nihil obstat* of the Minister".[11]

When the Bill reached the Seanad, Lord Glenavy, who was then chairman of the Judiciary Committee (having previously been both Lord Chief Justice and Lord Chancellor of Ireland), was invited to vacate the chair so that he could give his fellow Senators his views. He proceeded to launch a withering attack on s 35(6) of the Bill, which purported to give the Minister for Home Affairs power to make orders in respect of, *inter alia*, the mode of address to be used towards judges:

> "I think the real purpose and object will be found in paragraph 6 of Clause 35, because the Minister for Home Affairs is to provide for the mode of address to be adopted to the judges and the robes and official dress to be worn by the Bench and Bar. There is the whole part of Hamlet, in my opinion, and the only specific object or purpose for which this thing could be inserted. The sooner that clause is out of the Bill, and a corresponding clause dealing with other Courts, the better, in my opinion, for the credit of the Government. It will make for the removal of any possibility of their coming in conflict, in fact the certainty of their coming at a very early stage in conflict, with the Bar and the Bench, and, above all, for preserving, in this respect, the sanctity of our Constitution, which has given us, as I have said, a prize and privilege invaluable beyond conception if preserved in its integrity, but one that can be very easily weakened and dissipated by constant encroachment. I am very proud and very jealous of the traditions and honour of the Irish Bench and Bar."[12]

The opposition to the provision must have fallen on deaf ears at the time because s 35(6) of the Bill duly became law. However, probably fearing that further outcries

[11] Kotsonouris, *op. cit,* at p 115.

[12] See *Seanad Debates,* Vol 2, at para 417, of 16 January 1924.

were certain to follow such action, the Government deemed it impolitic to interfere with the traditional modes of address for the time being. The Minister did go on in due course to make provision for the modes of address before the Superior Courts in the guise of Ord XXX, r 1 of the Rules of the High Court and Supreme Court, 1926, which provided as follows:

> "1. Every Judge of the Supreme Court and the High Court may be addressed therein in the manner at present in use, or by the Irish equivalent thereto."

Thus the *status quo ante* was preserved, and judges continued to be addressed as "My Lord".[13] Of course, the rules did give counsel the option of addressing a judge as "A Thiarna Breithimh". However, beginning a pattern that has been repeated up to the present day, in practice the overwhelming majority of barristers refused to replace the traditional mode of address with its less stigmatised Irish equivalent.

The above situation continued undisturbed until the initiation of the Courts (Miscellaneous) Provisions Bill 1959. The Fianna Fáil Government of the time had expressed its fervent desire to see the use of the expressions "lord" and "lordship" discontinued, primarily because of the concerns voiced above in relation to their colonial and servile overtones. Section 45 of the 1959 Bill aimed to force the Bench and Bar to substitute less deferential and more "Gaelic" modes of address for these expressions. The proposed s 45 was phrased as follows:

> "45–(1) The Chief Justice shall be addressed in court as "A Phríomh-Bhreithimh".
>
> (2) Each other judge and justice of the District Court shall be addressed as "A Bhreithimh".
>
> (3) Where a court consists of more than one judge, they shall be addressed as "A Bhreithiúna"."

Predictably, the proposed provision was vehemently opposed both by opposition politicians and by the legal profession. Whilst an interesting aspect of the Dáil debates on the measure was that many of its opponents seemed more exercised about the

13 It should be noted that the Minister's power to make orders relating to the mode of dress and address before the Superior Courts was transferred to the Superior Courts Rules Committee by s 68 of the Courts of Justice Act 1936. In addition, according to later parliamentary debates, Hugh Kennedy, then Chief Justice, did express his wish to have the traditional modes of address reformed in the mid-1930s but nothing was done.

inelegant Irish in which it was phrased than by its substance, the primary focus of the outcry was again the claimed interference with the independence of Bench and Bar.

The proposed s 45 was eventually deleted from the Bill at the Report Stage, ostensibly because the Superior Court Rules Committee had undertaken in any event to substitute new modes of address for the old expressions. The new prescribed modes of address were contained in the High Court and Supreme Court Mode of Address Rules, 1961, which provided as follows:

> "The Judges of the Supreme Court, the High Court (including the Central Criminal Court), and the Court of Criminal Appeal respectively shall be addressed, in Irish or English, by their respective titles and names, and may be referred to, in Irish, as "an Chúirt", or, in English, as "the Court"."

The Government of the time clearly believed that the result of the new rules would be that the old colonial mode of address would be discontinued. In the words of Mr Charles Haughey TD,[14] the new rules were "acceptable to the Government which was anxious to see the expressions 'lord' and 'lordship' discontinued."[15]

Had the professed goal of the changes made to the court rules in 1961 been achieved, only the most gnarled of practitioners would now even recall a time when judges were addressed as lords and lordships. However, as we shall see in the last section, the provisions of the court rules as to mode of address have essentially been ignored in practice for well over 40 years.

The Reform Needed

The provisions of the Mode of Address Rules, 1961, were replicated in the body of the Rules of the Superior Courts, 1962. These provisions then became Ord 119, r 1 of the Rules of the Superior Courts, 1986, the text of which is almost identical to the text of the Mode of Address Rules, 1961, reading as follows:

> "The Judges of the Superior Courts shall be addressed in Irish or English by their respective titles and names, and may be referred to, in Irish as "An Chúirt" or, in English, as "The Court"."

---

14 Mr Haughey was one of the chief movers behind the proposed reforms.

15 191 Dáil Debates Col 1892, of 26 July 1961, on the Committee Stage of the Courts (Supplemental Provisions) Bill 1959.

It appears that the first clause of the above provision has had almost no effect in practice. Barristers in the High and Supreme Courts almost invariably address judges either as "My Lord" or, less frequently, as "The Court". Anecdotal evidence suggests that only a tiny minority of barristers ever use the mode of address, "Judge...", when appearing before the Superior Courts. Thus, amending the court rules has had little if any impact on the modes of address actually used in the courts, meaning that the result anticipated and desired by those who proposed these reforms has not come about.

There has been one recent initiative aimed at rectifying this situation. When the Courts and Courts Officers Bill 1995 was being debated in the Dáil, Mr John O'Donoghue TD proposed an amendment to that Bill, to be phrased as follows:

> "7.—From the date of operation of this Act, a judge sitting in any Court shall be addressed as 'Bhreitheamh' or 'Judge'."[16]

Ms Nora Owen TD, the Minister for Justice at the time, opposed the proposed amendment, relying on the traditional argument that undertaking such reform via legislation would interfere with the independence of the Bench and Bar. However, she was willing to concede that the aim of the proposed amendment was a laudable one, stating as follows:

> "I accept the principle behind the amendment, to ensure that with the passage of time the procedures of the court are modernised...[but it] is a matter of procedure that comes within the responsibility of the rules committee, which is made up of judges and others."[17]

It is worth recording that the current Minister for Justice, Mr Michael McDowell, also professed to support the aim of the amendment, but again argued that the Superior Court Rules Committee was the appropriate organ to deal with such reform, stating as follows:

> "I support the spirit of the amendment... The time has come for this matter to be regularised, but I suggest that the proper place to do so is in the rules of the courts... I strongly endorse the spirit of Deputy O'Donoghue's

16 459 Dáil Debates Col 1219, of 12 December 1995, on the Report Stage of the Courts and Court Officers Act, 1995, *op. cit.*

17 *ibid*, at Col 1221.

> proposal that the titles used are effectively Anglo-Norman titles which are not appropriate any more."[18]

The suggested amendment was eventually withdrawn. However, at least from the text of the debate, the whole discussion on the point seemed to be predicated on the mistaken view that the Rules of the Superior Courts then in force, provided that practitioners must address judges as "lord" or "lordship" and that these Rules could be amended so as to change the practice. The parties involved were either unaware or had forgotten that the Rules had in fact been changed more than 30 years before and the practice of calling judges "My Lord" survived merely as a matter of convention. Hence the point that the Rules Committee could do nothing more to reform court practice in this area was never raised. This writer would venture that, had the true situation with regard to the Rules been brought to the attention of the parties involved in the debate, a less deferential attitude to Bench and Bar might have been adopted.

It is abundantly clear on the basis of the above that those responsible for regulating the modes of address, i.e. the legislature and the Superior Courts Rules Committee, have indicated their preference for reform. The stumbling block has been the difficulty in forcing the Bar to change its practice. In keeping with the King's Inns motto of *nolumus mutari*,[19] counsel appearing before the courts have clung to the traditional mode of address, many of them perhaps unaware that this approach to addressing the judge has long since been devoid of a textual foundation.

It is submitted that the only realistic means of changing the mode of address used in practice is through a statutory provision that makes it mandatory for counsel to address the court using the simpler and less stigmatised phrase, "Judge", or, in the Irish language, "A Bhreitheamh". Whilst objections to such an interference with the independence of the profession could again be raised, this possibility should not be of decisive importance, given the demonstrated readiness of the legislature to intervene in other areas of court practice.[20] Opponents of reform could legitimately argue that, if changing the court rules has not changed the practice, there is no reason why a statutory amendment should do so. But this ignores the fact that a legal

---

18 *ibid*, at Col 1220.

19 "Never shall we change".

20 See s 49 of the Courts and Court Officers Act 1995, which provides that "A barrister or solicitor when appearing in any court shall not be required to wear a wig of the kind heretofore worn or any other wig of a ceremonial type".

practitioner is more likely to pay heed to a legislative provision than to a mere rule, being aware more than anybody of the risks involved in law-breaking. It would be a brave and foolhardy barrister who would continue to address a judge as "My Lord" in the face of a legislative provision that could be used by the Court or by opposing counsel to take the wind out of his sails at any time.

Conclusion

One final objection to legislative intervention in this sphere might echo Juliet: "What's in a name?" She desperately wanted names not to matter. A cynic might argue that the manner in which we address the judiciary is of no importance because what matters is the substance of the decision handed down.[21] But as Juliet discovered to her cost, names do matter, and it is important that Irish court practice does not continue to be blighted by the use of a nomenclature that is objectionable both because of its colonial connotations and its unsuitability in a modern context where men and women of all backgrounds may sit on the bench. Therefore, a legislative amendment abolishing and replacing the old modes of address once and for all would be a welcome and necessary reform.

[21] In the parliamentary debates of 27 July 1961, relating to the Courts (Supplemental Provisions) Bill, 1959, *op. cit*, at Col 1867, Senator Michael Hayes, a professor of Modern Irish language and literature in UCD, appeared to adopt the attitude referred to here, arguing that there was no necessity to tamper with tradition and that the Government should leave well alone: "[The modes of address] could have been left alone. It is evidence of the slave mind to get rid of them. They are all part of our history. The fact that we have judges as a result of Acts passed by the Irish Parliament and appointed by an Irish Government is sufficient."

The Guys from Out of Town: Expert Witnesses—A Law Reform Proposal

by
Níamh Howlin*

> As science advances and it is increasingly possible to establish the truth or otherwise of certain difficulties by technical process, so the courts have more need of experts to explain to them what they have done, why, and what conclusions they draw from the results of their inquiries.[1]

The realm of the expert witness is ever expanding, and includes such provinces as scientific and technical matters, mental conditions, banking, finance, medicine, genealogy, engineering, handwriting, music, art, literature, professional and trade practices and standards, and foreign law. The list is virtually endless.[2] In Ireland, the expert witness represents a growing industry — there are "professional" expert witnesses, directories of expert witnesses, and companies specialising in the training of expert witnesses.[3] All of this in spite of Lord Woolf's 1996 recommendation that

---

* B.C.L. (NUI), Ph.D. Candidate, University College Dublin. The author acknowledges the support of the Irish Research Council for the Humanities and Social Sciences. This essay was awarded a prize by the Law Society of Ireland for the *Student Law Reform Essay Competition 2005.*

[1] Field, in *The Law of Evidence in Scotland* (1998), at p 335.

[2] For a more detailed discussion of the instances where expert testimony may be given, see McGrath, *Evidence* (Thomson Round Hall, 2005) at pp 313–318. See also *Murphy on Evidence* (8th ed, 2003), at pp 384–388.

[3] For example, La Touche Bond Solon Training Ltd., based in Dublin. The question of whether a witness qualifies as an expert is one for the trial judge. Traditionally, experts were not required to have formal qualifications, but an increase in specialisation over the past 50 years has resulted in experts having "a particular expertise or experience in the particular area, which is based on a special study or his day-to-day experience". Expert witnesses generally boast impressive credentials, either in the form of a number of years' experience or a lengthy list of recognised qualifications, and the level of qualification will be material in any given case.

the appointment of "well-seasoned" experts ought to be discouraged. It has been noted that "if the litigation stakes are high enough there never seems to be a shortage of impressively credentialed experts arrayed on opposing sides".[4]

This article outlines some of the problems associated with expert witnesses and their testimony, and tenders some possible solutions thereto. It should be noted that, whilst in this jurisdiction the expert witness features largely in civil litigation, for comparative and historical purposes our attention will not be limited to the civil sphere.

Origins and Raison D'etre

The *raison d'être* of expert evidence is to furnish the finders of fact[5] with specialised or scientific information likely to be outside their knowledge and experience. The duty of the expert witness was described in *Davie v Edinburgh Magistrates*[6] as being the duty:

> "to furnish the judge or jury with the necessary scientific criteria for testing the accuracy of their conclusions, so as to enable the judge or jury to form their own independent judgment by the application of these criteria to the facts proved in evidence".[7]

Popular belief would have us suppose the expert witness to be a relatively modern creature.[8] However, accounts of expert witnesses date back as far as 1345.[9] By the end of the 17th century, judges were beginning to recognise the need for expert

4 Heerey, "Expert Evidence and the Australian Experience" (2002) *Bar Review* 7 (3) at p 166.

5 Before the passing of the Courts Act 1988, all civil actions in the High Court entailed the right to a jury. Section 1 of that statute, however, now limits this to cases of defamation, and the less common actions such as assault, false imprisonment and civil prosecution. Article 38 of *Bunreacht na hÉireann* entitles any person charged with a "non-minor" criminal offence to be tried by a jury. In all other cases, the judge will make findings both on matters of law and on issues of fact.

6 (1953) Sess. Cas. 34.

7 *ibid., per* Cooper LJ.

8 See Basten, "The Court Expert in Civil Trials" (1977) 40 MLR 174.

9 (1353) *Anon.* Lib. Ass. 28, pl 5, cited in Holdsworth, *A History of English Law* Vol 10 (Methuen & Co., 1938), at p 212, n 4. For further discussion of the origins of the expert witness, see generally, Howlin, "The Special Jury: A Solution to the Expert Witness Problem?" (2004) 12 ISLR 19.

testimony on some points.[10] This is illustrated in the growing reliance on expert testimony from about 1650 onwards, particularly the opinions of physicians in criminal cases.[11] Many of the cases in which witnesses' opinions were admissible became the centres of bodies of law.[12] By the late 18th century, the expert witness had begun to assume its modern guise, and operated alongside emerging rules of evidence familiar to the modern lawyer.[13] By the early years of the 19th century, it was beyond doubt that the expert witness represented an exception to the general exclusion of opinion evidence and had become a permanent facet of the law of evidence.[14]

Flaws in the System

Partiality

Lack of objectivity is a problem inherent in the expert witness system. In a situation where the expert is called upon to testify for one side or the other, bias is sometimes inevitable. There is also the issue of divided loyalties. As Blom-Cooper notes:

> "Inevitably, the expert owes a duty to the party which is hiring him or her and paying for the opinion given to the court. It is likewise true that the expert is assisting the process of justice and as such owes a duty to the court."[15]

Knowingly or unknowingly, the expert colours his or her testimony, and becomes a "hired champion"[16] for one side or the other. A party may further influence expert

---

10 Holdsworth, *A History of English Law* Vol 5, *op. cit,* at p 419.

11 For example, see the cases of *Alsop . Bowtrell* (1620) Cro. Jac. 541, 542; 79 ER 464; *R v Pembroke* (1678) 6 Howell's State Trials 1309 at 1337–1341; *R v Green* (1679) 7 Howell's State Trials 185 at 186; *R v Coningsmark* (1682) 9 Howell's State Trials 21; and *R v Cowper* (1699) 13 Howell's State Trials 1126–1135.

12 One such area was opinion as to handwriting. See Wigmore, *Evidence in Trials at Common Law* (Vol 3 Little, Brown and Co, 1940), at §1991; and Holdsworth, *A History of English Law* Vol 9, *op. cit,* at p 212.

13 See *R v Heath* (1744) 18 Howell's State Trials at 68–84; and *R v Ferrers* (1760) 19 Howell's State Trials at 942–944.

14 See *Beckwith v Sydebotham* (1807) 1 Camp. 116; 170 ER 897 *per* Lord Ellenborough.

15 Louis Blom-Cooper, "Experts and Assessors: Past, Present And Future" (2002) 21 CJQ 341.

16 Learned Hand, "Historical and Practical Considerations Regarding Expert Testimony," in (1901) 15 *Harv. Law Rev.* 40 at p 53.

evidence by requiring his expert to revise his opinions so that the final report would be more to the party's liking.[17] Commentators have been quick to point out that expert witnesses do not wilfully misrepresent their position, but that;

> "their judgements become so warped by their regarding the subject in one point of view, that even when conscientiously disposed they are incapable of forming independent opinion."[18]

During the mid-1990s,[19] Lord Woolf expressed concern that "experts sometimes take on the role of partisan advocates instead of neutral fact-finders or opinion-givers."[20] Zimmerman is concerned that expert evidence "may also be influenced by what has become known as 'expert shopping'".[21] This entails the consultation of successive experts until the party in question receives the desired opinion.

Aside from the financial benefits, the expert may also be induced by such compelling considerations as his or her professional reputation and, in some cases, a strong attachment to some stereotypical professional attitude. McGrath considers it unsurprising that in a number of recent decisions, the courts have found it necessary to "emphasise the requirement of objectivity on the part of experts and to lay down some guidelines with regard to their evidence".[22]

Usurpation of the Role of the Fact Finder

Experts give evidence, and do not decide the issue; that is the role of the jury[23] or the judicial fact finder. With regard to cases where there is no jury, Blom-Cooper

---

[17] See the recent English decision of *Jackson v Marley Davenport Ltd* [2004] EWCA Civ 1225; [2005] C.P.Rep. See also *Beck v Ministry of Defence* [2003] EWCA 1043.

[18] Taylor, *Treatise on the Law of Evidence* (12th ed, 1931), at p 59.

[19] In his 1995 interim report, Access to Justice: Interim Report to the Lord Chancellor on the Civil Justice system in England and Wales. London: HMSO1995: 192, 183, and again in his final report in 1996, Access to Justice: Final Report to the Lord Chancellor on the Civil Justice system in England and Wales. London: HMSO, 1996: 139.

[20] Although Lord Woolf was discussing the traditional English system, it is, for this purpose, identical to our own.

[21] Zimmerman, *op. cit,* at p 295.

[22] Mc Grath, *op. cit,* at p 324. See the English decision, *National Justice Compania Naviera S.A. v Prudential Assurance Co. Ltd.* [1993] 2 Lloyd's Rep. 68 (The "*Ikerian Reefer*" case), where Cresswell J, at 81-82, outlined some of the duties and responsibilities of expert witnesses.

[23] See *Phipson on Evidence* (12th ed, 1976), at p 486. See also Keane, *The Modern Law of Evidence,* (4th ed, 1996), at p 464.

observes that "[e]ven nowadays there is more than a hint from the judiciary that experts must not trespass on the court's lawn".[24]

Expert testimony as to the ultimate issue in a case is problematic.[25] Traditionally, witnesses were prohibited from giving opinion evidence as to the ultimate issue.[26] The risk that the expert witness might encroach upon the jury's territory, and "contribute the major premise",[27] has resulted in a general exclusionary rule.[28] Unfortunately, the ultimate issue rule tends to be applied in an inconsistent and *ad hoc* manner.[29]

In the 1960s, the English case of *DPP v AB & C Chewing Gum*[30] marked an encroachment on the common law rule that an expert witness may not be asked questions which are for the court to decide. Attempts have since been made by the judiciary to delineate the respective territory of the expert witnesses and the jury.[31]

---

24 Blom-Cooper, *op. cit,* at p 346.

25 In the US, for some time the Federal Rules of Evidence permitted experts to testify on ultimate issues, both in criminal and civil cases. FRE (702) permitted expert evidence if "scientific, technical or other specialised knowledge" will assist the trier of fact. But because it appeared that such testimony was being accorded too much weight by the jury, FRE (704) now states that "ultimate issues are matters for the triers of fact alone."

26 See *R v Wright, op. cit.*

27 Learned Hand, *op. cit,* at p 51.

28 See *Hayes v Doman* [1899] 2 Ch. 13 *per* Lindley MR p 24.

29 See McGrath, *op. cit,* at pp 316-317.

30 (1967) 131 JP 373; [1968] 1 QB 159. In a prosecution under the Obscene Publications Act 1959, the net issue was whether "battle cards" sold with packets of chewing gum were likely to deprave and corrupt children. The court admitted the evidence of a child psychiatrist as to the likely impact of the material on children. The fact that the publication in question involved children was cited as a vital factor in coming to this decision—it was acknowledged that in an ordinary case, the jurors would be capable of judging the likely effect of a publication. Cannon and Neligan, *Evidence* (Thomson Round Hall, Dublin, 2002) describe this case as unique, whilst Keane, in *The Modern Law of Evidence* (4th ed, 1996), at p 164-165 is of the opinion that it is "highly exceptional and confined to its own circumstances".

31 For example, in *R v Anderson & Neville* [1971] 3 All ER 1152, Widgery J excluded the evidence of a defence witness to the effect that a written article was not obscene as it did not have a tendency to deprave and corrupt. The evidence was excluded on the ground that whether or not the article was obscene was a question for the jury. In another English case, *R v Turner* [1975] QB 834, the court specified that matters that could be considered to fall within the ambit of ordinary human experience were for the jury to determine. In that case, the matter in question was the accused's reaction to the news of his partner's alleged affairs with other men. An Irish authority in this area is *DPP v Paul Kehoe,* unreported, Court of Criminal Appeal, O'Flaherty J, 6 November 1991. Kehoe, accused of

Despite what McGrath dubs "the eclipse of the ultimate issue rule", it ought to be emphasised that the courts remain "quite conscious of the dangers of uncritical acceptance of the evidence of experts going to the issues in the case".[32]

Undue Weight

Following from the above is the problem of juries attaching undue weight to expert evidence in certain cases. The credibility of expert testimony will vary, depending on the expert's qualifications, expertise, their investigations and methodology, and the extent to which the facts on which their opinion is based are grounded in evidence.

For example, the Court of Criminal Appeal[33] has relatively recently indicated that the problem of undue weight goes hand in hand with DNA evidence.[34] Also illustrative of the problem of over-reliance on expert testimony is the recent controversy surrounding Professor Sir Roy Meadow. Once considered one of Britain's most eminent paediatricians, Meadow was recently stuck off by the General Medical Council having been found guilty of serious professional misconduct over his "seriously misleading"[35] testimony in a case which resulted in the life imprisonment of a mother wrongly convicted of murdering her two baby sons.[36] Her conviction

---

murder, invoked the defence of provocation. A psychiatrist was called upon as an expert witness. O'Flaherty J was of the opinion that the expert served only to regurgitate "in a fuller way" what the accused had already stated—that is, that he had been annoyed and upset at the time. O'Flaherty J went on to say that the psychiatrist had "overstepped the mark" by stating that the accused had not intended to kill the victim and that he believed he was telling the truth. Such matters were, in O'Flaherty J's opinion, "four-square within the jury's function". See also *R v Jennion* [1962] 1 WLR 317. See also the Australian case of *Murphy v the Queen* (1988-89) 167 CLR 94 at 110. In non-jury cases, the problem of the expert eclipsing the trial judge is equally as grave. A series of cases from the early 1990s demonstrates the courts' increasing awareness of this problem: *F (Orse C) v C* [1991] 2 IR 330, *per* Keane J at 344; *KWT v DAT*, *per* Murphy J at 21-22; and *Murnaghan Bros. v O'Maoldomhnaigh* [1991] 1 IR 455, *per* Murphy J.

32 *ibid.*

33 *People (DPP) v Allen* [2003] 4 IR 295 at 299.

34 When DNA evidence is introduced in court, it is always explained by an expert witness.

35 *The Guardian,* 23 June 2005, available online at <http://society.guardian.co.uk/nhsperformance/story/0,8150,1512227,00.html>

36 See *R v Clark*, Chester Crown Court, Harrison J, 9 November 1999. An initial appeal against this conviction was dismissed by the Court of Appeal (Criminal Division) comprised of Henry LJ, Bracewell & Richards JJ on 2 October 2000.

was overturned on appeal in 2003.[37] Perhaps more worryingly, this does not appear to be an isolated case.[38]

In an area of such scientific esotericism, a jury could jump to the conclusion that the evidence is flawless, which, of course, it is not. The obligation rests on the trial judge to warn the jury against relying too heavily on such testimony.

The Battle of the Experts

Another problem inherent in the expert witness system is the fact that a situation often arises whereby the experts for each side are of entirely contradicting opinions.[39] Opinions are by definition subjective, and scientific facts are themselves the product of social construction. In a jury trial, the jurors are faced with the difficulty of choosing one expert testimony over another, and are not necessarily equipped to make such an evaluation.[40] As one commentator[41] put it:

> "how can the jury judge between two statements each founded upon an experience confessedly foreign in kind to their own? It is just because they are incompetent for such a task that the expert is necessary at all."[42]

Similarly, McGrath notes that:

> "[w]here there is a conflict of evidence between experts who put forward conflicting theories of how particular events may have occurred, it is not the role of the tribunal of fact to resolve that controversy".[43]

---

37 *R v. Clark* [2003] EWCA Crim 1020; [2003] 2 FCR 447.

38 What have been termed the "Meadow cases" consist of Sally Clark (served three years after being wrongly convicted of killing her two sons), Angela Cannings (served 18 months after being wrongly convicted of killing her two sons), Donna Anthony (served six years after being wrongly convicted of killing her son and daughter) and Trupti Patel (cleared of killing three of her children). See BBC, 25 July 2005, available online at <http://news.bbc.co.uk/2/hi/health/4685511.stm>.

39 See Fennel, *The Law of Evidence in Ireland* 2nd Ed (LexisNexis, Dublin, 2003) p 170.

40 For a discussion of this, see Sven Timmerbeil, "The Role of the Expert Witness in German and US Civil Litigation," in 9 Ann. Surv. Int'l. & Comp. L. 163; Caroline Fennel, *The Law of Evidence in Ireland* (2nd ed), p 169, and Learned Hand, *op. cit.* This problem was recently discussed by the High Court of Australia in *Velveski v The Queen* [2002] 76 ALJR 402.

41 Learned Hand, *op. cit,* at p 54.

42 *ibid.*

43 McGrath, *op. cit,* at p 323.

Rather, the court, and accordingly, the finder of fact must "apply common sense and a careful understanding of the logic and likelihood of events to conflicting opinions and conflicting opinions".[44] However, this might not always be possible in jury cases.[45]

Mark Twain described the expert as being "some guy from out of town". The expert holds a certain power over the jury—their very label commands attention and respect.[46] Jurors faced with opposing expert testimony resort, at times, to favouring the expert with the most impressive credentials.[47] Fennel[48] also suggests that the personality and presentation of expert witness may also be a factor in the jury's decision. This highlights the need for experienced expert witnesses who can simplify their science and convey their opinion to a jury in a straightforward and clear-cut manner. This, however, has given rise to a breed of "expert expert witnesses," whose considerable courtroom experience and, in some cases, formal training, has exacerbated the problem of exorbitant fees and costs.

Expense

That the expert witness is an expensive luxury is a fact well known to practitioners. Zuckerman notes "the high and uncontrollable cost of expert evidence,"[49] while Jackson similarly describes the expert witness system as "a huge area of delay and expense."[50] Criticism of the high cost of the expert witness was evident in the 1995 English case *Liddell v Middleton,*[51] where Stuart-Smith LJ averred, "[i]n my judgment the expert witnesses have contributed nothing to the trial in this case

44 *Best v Wellcome Ltd.* [1993] IR 421.

45 Another problem, related to this, is the issue of poor-quality expert evidence. Miles J Vigilante, "Screening Expert Testimony After *Kumho Tire Co. v Carmichael*" (2000) 8 JLPOLY 543, discusses some standards to be in applied by judges in deciding whether or not to allow the presentation of expert testimony to the jury.

46 Champagne, in "Expert Witnesses in the Courts: An Empirical Examination", 76 Judicature 5, 8 (1992), revealed that in the US, 65 per cent of jurors surveyed stated that testimony of expert witnesses influenced the outcome of litigation.

47 See Heerey, "Expert Evidence and the Australian Experience," in (2002) *Bar Review* 7(3), p 166.

48 *The Law of Evidence in Ireland* (2nd ed), p 171.

49 AAS Zuckerman, "Disclosure of Expert Reports" 24 (2005) CJQ 293 at p 293.

50 Carol Jackson, "The Uses and Abuses of Experts and Their Evidence" 2000 JPIL 19.

51 TLR 17 July 1995.

except expense." More recently, Lord Woolf, MR commented that "[t]he cross-examination of expert witnesses at the hearing, even in a substantial case, can be very expensive."[52]

Expert witnesses are remunerated for their time and expertise, and the price duly reflects their level of proficiency. In cases where several expert witnesses are called, the costs can be crippling for the losing side.[53] The cost to the parties in civil actions and the State in criminal cases can be spectacular.

Alternatives to the Current System

Trial by Judge

Some Solutions

Judges recognise that they may require assistance and training in order to master the issues in cases involving complex technical evidence. In cases where the judge makes the finding of fact, the education of the judiciary seems to be an obvious solution. It is rare for a judge to have specialised training in areas other than the law. There are, however, indications of change, with members of the judiciary seeking to increase their own knowledge in certain fields, and thus diminish the need to rely heavily on experts.[54] In addition to this, Struve claims that "[b]etter training in scientific principles will assist judges in assessing whether to admit the testimony of party-retained experts".[55] In the US, the Federal Judicial Centre has published a Reference Manual on Scientific Evidence designed to educate judges.[56] The advantages of providing the judiciary with a basic understanding of economics, financial transactions, medical issues, and so on, are obvious, but such a proposition clearly has its limitations.

---

52 *Daniels v Walker* [2000] 1 WLR 1382 at 1388.

53 In 1999, one could, for example, expect to pay in the region of €508 (£400) per day plus expenses, in addition to an hourly rate of about €127 (£100) for researching and preparing reports, for a recruitment consultant or an occupational physician to testify in court. These figures are taken from *The Role of the Expert Witness,* (Daly ed, Dublin 1999), pp 87–145.

54 For example, in 2001 the Law Council of Australia held a one-day seminar on economic issues for judges and practitioners. See also Basten, "The Court Expert in Criminal Trials – A Comparative Appraisal" (1977) 40 *Mod L Rev* 174 at p 190.

55 Struve 'Doctors, The Adversary System, And Procedural Reform In Medical Liability Litigation" 2004 72 FDMLR 943, at p 1006.

56 See Struve, *op. cit,* at p 1006.

Heerey[57] recommends the appointment of assessors to act as advisors to the judge, helping him or her to understand complicated evidence. This would be of considerable use in cases necessitating an understanding of complex machinery or highly technical equipment and processes. However, it would be imperative to ensure such assessors or advisors were of the utmost independence as they would be a part of the decision-making process. There is also the problem of securing a suitable advisor for each case. It would be costly and impractical to source advisors with expertise in a large number of areas. It is suggested that were such a proposal to be adopted, the persons in question could be placed on some sort of a rotating register.[58] Even aside from these drawbacks, consideration must be given to the constitutional difficulty which might be presented by Art 34.1, which provides that "[j]ustice shall be administered in courts established by law by judges appointed in the manner provided by this Constitution".

In a similar vein, Basten[59] advocates the appointment of "expert judges"—that is, the appointment of an expert in a specialised scientific field to act as a judge in the resolution of a particular dispute.[60] However, the desirability of taking the decision-making power out of the hands of the judiciary is questionable, and such a move would most likely be met with hostility from several quarters. Furthermore, the inevitably inordinate costs involved in such an undertaking would be difficult to justify.

A Proposed Alternative

In 1977, it was suggested by Martin[61] and Kantrowitz[62] that a "science court" be established, consisting of a group of experts qualified and equipped to deal with

---

57 *Expert Evidence and the Australian Experience* (2002) *Bar Review* 7(3), at p 166.

58 Previously, assessors like this were restricted to Admiralty cases, but in England, s 71 of the Supreme Court Act 1981 and s 63 of the County Court Act 1984 provide for the appointment of persons who, by virtue of some special skill, knowledge or experience, sit with a judge during court proceedings to answer any questions that may be posed by the judge during court proceedings on the area in which they are expert.

59 Basten, "The Court Expert in Criminal Trials – A Comparative Appraisal" (1977) 40 *Mod L Rev* 174 at p 190.

60 For example, a tax consultant could decide upon issues of revenue fraud.

61 Martin, "The Proposed Science Court," (1977) 75 *Mich. L. Rev* 1058 at pp 1064–1069.

62 Kantrowitz, "The Science Court Experiment: Criticism and Responses" (1977) 33 *The Bulletin of the Atomic Sciences* 44.

technical or scientific evidence and to evaluate the various arguments. The problem with this proposal, however, is that if a science court were to exist in conjunction with and in addition to the existing courts system, the cost of trying cases involving technical evidence would be greatly increased. Furthermore, since 1977, the prevalence of this type of case has increased in proportion with technical and scientific advances. More recently, Lang[63] argued in favour of the establishment of medical courts. She contends that "certain matters are more efficiently handled by specialists…because nonspecialized courts generally operate slowly and have long dockets".

If the science court model were to be adopted, it would need to operate as a division of the existing courts. An example of a specialised court in this jurisdiction is the Commercial Court. Established in 2004 as a division of the High Court,[64] it deals exclusively with cases concerning such issues as patents and trademarks, construction, insurance, contractual disputes and appropriate judicial review.[65] There are currently three judges[66] who sit in the Commercial Court, each of whom has considerable experience in dealing with such issues. The court itself is equipped with specialised electronic equipment, and cases are more stringently managed and quickly processed.

The advantages of such specialisation are manifold. Lang[67] claims that "specialization allows for reliance on judicial expertise, which can expedite the decision making process and thereby increase efficiency." This reduces the need for expert witnesses to explain the issues involved.[68] Specialised judges can become experts in a specific area of law, which may result in more accurate findings.

---

63 Lang, "A New Approach to Tort Reform: An Argument For The Establishment of Specialised Medical Courts" (2004) 39 GALR 293 at p 310.

64 SI No 2 of 2004, now contained in Ord 63 (a) of the Rules of the Superior Courts 1986, as amended.

65 A requirement for having one's case transferred to the Commercial Court is that the value of the claim exceeds €1 million. This requirement does not apply in respect of judicial review and cases concerning trademarks and patents and may be waived in respect of the other categories (under Ord 64A, r 1(b)).

66 Kelly, Finlay-Geoghegan and Clarke JJ.

67 *op. cit.*

68 Lang also argues that specialised courts would be a cheaper alternative to the current system.

Trial by Jury

Previous Proposals

In this jurisdiction, the expert witness features mainly, albeit not exclusively, in civil litigation. In such cases, juries are relatively rare.[69] As such, the difficulties traditionally associated with reconciling experts and jurors arise relatively infrequently, compared with the problems arising between experts and judges. Nevertheless, it is submitted that this is still a problem worth addressing, especially given the fact that expert evidence in criminal prosecutions appears to be on the increase.

In the United States, the jury is still a feature of the civil trial, and the expert witness is heavily relied upon in US civil litigation. Accordingly, the problems with the expert witness in the jury trial have received considerably more attention in the US than in this jurisdiction. For example, attempts have been made to remedy the problem of bias in the expert witness by providing for their appointment by the court.[70] The court may appoint an expert when factual issues arise that would be better solved with the support of scientific knowledge, and the parties have no influence over the court's choice of expert. In theory, this sounds like an ideal solution, as the expert is rendered independent of the parties. The reality is, however, that court-appointed expert witnesses are rarely used in US civil litigation. In addition, it is doubtful whether such a system would be desirable in criminal prosecutions as the expert would effectively be employed by the State, putting his or her independence in jeopardy.

Casey[71] notes that in England, the Woolf reforms have to a certain degree eliminated the need for expert witnesses, have codified the role of the expert witness and have extended the adversarial nature of expert testimony. These reforms are now contained in the Civil Procedure Rules 1999, which allow the court itself to decide whether expert evidence is needed. The parties have no right to rely on expert evidence

---

[69] s 1 of the Courts Act 1988 provides that trial by jury is limited to cases of defamation and the less common actions such as assault, false imprisonment and civil prosecution.

[70] A similar suggestion had already been made over a century ago by Learned Hand, *op. cit.* He recommended the appointment only of official experts as witness, similar to the civil law system, or the appointment of an expert by the judge in addition to the parties' experts. The latter suggestion he lauded as the most viable.

[71] Patricia Casey, "Expert testimony in court". Available online at <http://apt.rcpsych.org/cgi/content/full/9/3/177>.

without the court's permission, and all expert witnesses, regardless of who calls them, have an overriding duty to the court. In appropriate cases, the court may order the parties to appoint a single joint expert, thus avoiding a conflict of expertise. If the parties are unable to agree on a single expert, then the court may make the appointment.[72]

Blom-Cooper notes that the court-appointed expert has tended not to be utilised in major litigation.[73] The appointment of a single joint expert (or the court-appointed expert, including the assessor) avoids the potential of bias or even perceived bias. However, as he points out, "the single joint expert, freed from the shackles of partisanship must nevertheless perform his task of thoroughness. Who … will ensure that that duty is properly performed?"[74]

Whilst reviewing the English civil justice system, Lord Woolf had cause to consider at length the French concept of the *expert judiciaire.* Although he did not advocate the adoption of the civil system wholesale into English law, the 1999 Civil Procedure Rules were, to a certain extent, influenced by the French system. In France, whenever the court considers that a report by experts is necessary, it is ordered by a judgment clearly setting forth the objects of the expertise.[75] Three experts are then appointed, unless the parties can agree upon a single one.[76] The experts may be challenged on the same grounds as any other witness.[77] The necessary documentation is laid before them[78] and they make a single report to the court, even if they express different opinions. The court is not bound to adopt the opinion of the experts,[79] and if not satisfied with the report, new experts may be appointed.[80]

The German Civil Procedure Code (ZPO) distinguishes between lay witnesses and court experts. In German civil litigation, an expert is not a witness; rather, he or she

---

72 *Cosgrove v Pattison* [2001] CP Rep 68 examined the principles to be applied when a party seeks to call further expert evidence after the appointment of a joint expert.

73 *op. cit* at 349.

74 Blom-Cooper, *op. cit,* at p 345.

75 Code Proc. Civ. Art. 302.

76 *ibid,* Art 303.

77 *ibid,* Art 310.

78 *ibid,* Art 317.

79 *ibid,* Art 323.

80 *ibid,* Art 322. For a further discussion of the French expert system, see Bodington, *French Law of Evidence* (London, 1904), at p 102.

provides a separate form of evidence. The expert is selected by the court[81] from a list. The judge retains the discretion whether or not to follow the views of the court-appointed expert.[82] There is also scope for the parties to hire their own experts, but the courts are generally sceptical about the testimony of such experts. Their opinion tends to be valued at considerably less than that of the court expert, and this is reflected in the fact that party-appointed witnesses cannot testify at all. A disadvantage of this system is the close relationship between the court and the court expert, who seems to be the *de facto* decision maker.[83]

Over the past 100 years, several proposals have been proffered by US academics and institutions for the improvement of the expert witness system. For example, early in the twentieth century, Judge Learned Hand proposed the establishment of special juries of experts.[84] He suggested that such bodies would evaluate the evidence and recommend decisions on scientific issues. It was his opinion, however, that these bodies should co-exist with normal jury trials. Again, a problem with this was the additional costs involved in setting up and maintaining a permanent panel of experts. Wigmore[85] has also suggested the substitution of "an official jury of experts" in appropriate cases but acknowledged the impracticability of such a proposal in the US.

The American Academy for the Advancement of Science (AAAS) proposes the introduction of Court Appointed Scientific Experts (CASE).[86] Under this scheme, a committee would be established to assist court experts on a case-by-case basis.[87] It seems that the CASE is intended to operate in conjunction with the expert witness, which, it is submitted, would serve merely to exacerbate the existing difficulties.

The Proposed Alternative

Until early in the 20th century, cases concerning matters of technical or specific expertise were tried by special juries.[88] The special jury was, in effect, a jury of

---

81 ZPO §404.

82 ZPO §286.

83 For further discussion of the German system, see Sven Timmerbeil, "The Role of Expert Witnesses in German and US Civil Litigation" in Ann. Surv. Int. & Comp L, Spring 2003.

84 Learned Hand, *op. cit,* at p 56.

85 Wigmore, *Evidence in Trials at Common Law* Vol 2, (1979), p 762.

86 See < http://www.aaas.org/spp/case/case.htm>.

87 Harris, "Testimony for Sale – The Law and Ethics of Snitches and Experts" (2002) 22 *Pepp L Rev* 1 at pp 2-3. This project is currently being evaluated by the Federal Judicial Centre.

88 Other cases were tried by common juries.

experts, similar to those later proposed by Hand,[89] Martin[90] and Kantrowitz.[91] The major distinction, however, was that the special jury operated *alone*—it was the only trier of fact in the case. The special jury did not operate in conjunction with a trial jury; it was the trial jury.[92]

Other types of specialised jury in the 19th century included the market jury,[93] which dealt with cases concerning weights and measures, and trade-related disputes, the jury of matrons,[94] which determined pregnancy, and the jury *de medietate linguae,*[95] which decided cases concerning non-nationals.

It is submitted that the special jury may be a pragmatic solution to many of the problems inherent in the present system. A major advantage of re-introducing the special jury system would be the fact that the jury would no longer be wholly

---

89 *op. cit.*

90 *op. cit.*

91 *op. cit.*

92 Although the precise origins of the special jury are unknown, it enjoyed considerable popularity in the 19th century, until its abolition in 1927 (in this jurisdiction, s 66 of the Juries Act 1927 abolished both special and common juries). For further detail on the special jury, see Howlin, "The Special Jury – A solution to the Expert Witness Problem?" (2004) 12 ISLR 19; Oldham, "The Origins of the Special Jury," (1983) 50 U *Chicago LR* 137; and Oldham, "Special Juries in England: Nineteenth Century Usage and Reform" (1987) 8 *J Legal Hist.* 148 at p 149.

93 This was a group responsible for ensuring that market regulations and trade by-laws were observed. They ensured all weights and measures complied with the law. Examples of breaches of regulation are the sale of underweight bread, and meat-blowing (literally, pumping air into a joint of meat with a bellows to give the appearance of a larger joint). See for example the cases of *Wallis v Keogh* and *Walls v Loudon,* reported in *The Anglo Celt,* 1 December 1853. These were prosecutions for selling meat that was unfit for consumption. The market jurors in these cases were called upon to testify as to the sate of the meat and the general practices of meat vendors.

94 Until the mid-19th century, if it were shown that a convicted female in a criminal case was pregnant, the death sentence would be postponed until after the birth of her child. A jury of 12 matrons, or married women, were appointed, under the writ *de ventre inspiciendo,* literally to "inspect the belly" of the prisoner and make a finding as to whether or not she was "quick with child". See Oldham, "The Origins of the Special Jury" (1983) 50 *U Chicago LR* 137 at pp 171–172, and Forbes, "A Jury of Matrons" (1988) 32 *Med Hist* 23.

95 Literally, the jury "of the half-tongue". Until 1870, a non-national, or alien defendant, was entitled to a jury *de medietate linguae,* meaning that half of the jurors were also aliens. For a more detailed discussion, see Oldham, *op. cit,* at pp 167–171. This evolved as a consequence of prejudice against Jews, and was introduced as a means of improving relations, particularly in matters of trade, with the Jewish community.

ignorant of the increasingly specialised evidence produced in both civil and criminal cases. It is acknowledged, however, that because of the major social changes since the 19th century, the special jury model would have to be modified somewhat. In the past, the criteria for special jurors revolved mainly around property qualifications, as the Victorians equated wealth with intelligence.

The 19th century special jury was comprised of persons who qualified *generally* as special jurors. Whether it would be better to have a jury consisting wholly of persons from a particular job or profession, or simply a jury composed of experts generally,[96] is open for debate. Whilst the former would most probably have less difficulty in reaching a decision, there is the disadvantage that such a jury would not be representative of society at large. Yet, under the present system, the jury does not represent a social cross section, thus such an argument loses some credibility: s 9 of the Juries Act 1976 excludes and excuses numerous broad categories of persons from jury duty.[97] After the various categories are excluded, along with anyone else who presents a "good reason", one is left with a group mainly consisting of semi-skilled and unskilled workers and non-professional employees; the people, it would appear, whose jobs can be done by somebody else. This undoubtedly creates a non-representative jury. If jury members were to represent a more balanced cross-section of society, there would be less need for expert witnesses.

Other modifications to the special jury system would also be imperative. How such juries would operate within the current legal system poses some interesting theoretical and logistical questions. For example, in the 19th century, there were separate jurors' lists for special and common jurors, and the inconvenience entailed was one of the very reasons cited for the abolition of the system.[98] It is submitted that

---

96 For example, a jury composed of persons who have attained either a third-level education or some formal specialised training or apprenticeship.

97 The County Registrar can exclude members of the Oireachtas, members of the Council of State, the Comptroller and Auditor General, the Clerks of Dáil Éireann and Seanad Éireann, persons in Holy Orders, ministers, vowed members of religious orders living in religious communities, full-time sheriffs, ships' masters, aircraft pilots, persons aged between 65 and 70, doctors, dentists, nurses, midwives, vets and pharmacists who are actually practicing. Other persons may be entitled to be excluded if they can show that their actions cannot reasonably be filled by anybody else, for example, the staff of the Houses of the Oireachtas, civil servants, chief executive officers, employees of local authorities, heath boards and harbour authorities, school-teachers and university lecturers. The Registrar can also exclude other persons if he or she is satisfied that there are "good reasons" for doing so.

98 See Dáil Éireann, vol. 18, 15 February 1927, Orders of the Day. Juries Bill 1927 – Second Stage, *per* Mr O'Higgins.

a mere amendment of the existing jury lists would be a more appropriate and cost-effective means of determining and identifying those persons duly qualified.

Another suggested deviation from the old system would be to have juries consisting of a mix of expert and non-expert jurors, rather than a complete divide. Such was the practice in Scotland in the 19th century; one third of the jurors were "special", whilst the rest were "common". This would result in a more representative jury than one consisting, for example, entirely of doctors. On a more practical level, the idea of removing 12 qualified doctors, for example, from their surgeries for a period of days is absurd. It is submitted that having four or perhaps six expert jurors on a given jury would have the desired effect; they would understand the evidence, and could simplify it and relay it to their fellow jurors at some stage during the trial.

At present, there is no state remuneration for those called upon for jury service, but s 29 of the 1976 Act provides that employees and apprentices will receive their usual wages or salary for such days as they are absent as a result of a jury summons. There is no provision for the remuneration of employers or the self-employed. It is submitted that if provision were made for the payment of, say, the minimum wage, or the cost of remunerating a replacement or a locum, such persons would be better able to partake in jury service. It would undoubtedly be cheaper to pay a day's average wages to such persons than continuing to pay exorbitant fees charged by similar persons acting in an expert witness capacity.

It has been suggested that permanent panels of experts be established for the resolution of technical cases.[99] It is submitted that a better solution would be to continue with the present rotation system of jury summonses so that cases continue to be decided by what one hopes are independent and disinterested citizens rather than by individuals who are essentially making a living out of it.

Conclusion

The future is indeed bleak for expert witnesses. Their weaknesses are manifold; they are costly, time-consuming, and potentially biased. They often encroach upon the jury's territory, and they regularly conflict with one another. Their *raison d'être* is to explain complicated and specialised evidence to jurors or judges who are inexperienced in such matters. If the standards of expertise of both the jury and the

[99] See Martin, *op. cit.* at pp 1064–1069, Kantrowitz, *op. cit,* and Learned Hand, *op. cit.*

judiciary were raised, the role of such experts would be rendered nigh on redundant. In the context of the jury trial, this end may best be achieved by a resurrection of the special jury. In cases tried by the judge alone, increased specialisation and education of judges appears to be the ideal solution.

No Talismanic Incantation: "Subject to Contract" in Irish Law

by
Neil Maddox*
Martin Canny**

This article proposes to analyse the current state of the law in Ireland on the status of agreements made "subject to contract", and in particular the difficulties that arise when a note or memorandum containing this phrase is proffered for the purpose of satisfying the requirements of the Statute of Frauds. In addition, the question is asked as to whether the Irish courts have rowed back from the decision of the Supreme Court in the seminal case of *Boyle v Lee*[1] since it was handed down over a decade ago.

In the last thirty years, actions for specific performance brought on foot of alleged contracts for the sale of land, have been of perpetual headache to judges, academics and conveyancers alike. This is due in no small part to the confused and often conflicting precedents in this and the neighbouring jurisdiction regarding the interpretation to be given to the phrase "subject to contract".[2] It is an area of law that has been of major concern to solicitors since it was, for many years, a belief of practitioners that the insertion of the phrase in their letters would always be sufficient to protect their client from being bound by an open contract. This view was shattered by the decision of the English Court of Appeal in *Law v Jones*,[3] which held that the insertion of the rubric "subject to contract" in a document was not

---

* B.C.L. Ph.D. (N.U.I.), Barrister at Law. This essay was awarded joint second place in the Law Society of Ireland, *Student Law Reform Essay Competition 2005*.

** B.C.L., LL.M. (N.U.I.), Barrister at Law.

1 [1992] ILRM 65; [1992] IR 555.

2 Generally see Farrell, *Irish Law of Specific Performance* (Dublin, 1994), pp 91–107; Clark, *Contract Law in Ireland* (4th ed, Dublin, 1998), pp 33–36, 95–96.

3 [1974] Ch 112.

necessarily fatal to that document being used to satisfy s 2 of the Statute of Frauds. The reasoning employed in that case was categorically rejected by the Irish Supreme Court in *Boyle v Lee.* However, the strict approach laid down in *Boyle* has not been applied enthusiastically in subsequent decisions and a degree of uncertainty still exists as to the precise legal effect the phrase has when contained in correspondence.

The Alarm Bells Ring: The Influence of *Law v Jones*

The modern source of these difficulties date from the early 1970s, when the English Court of Appeal decided *Griffiths v Young*[4] and *Law v Jones,* which appeared to reject the long established notion that the presence of the "subject to contract" rubric in a document prevented it from being used as evidence of an agreement. Instead, oral evidence could be adduced to prove that the phrase had been waived or was not fatal to the finding of a concluded contract. Such a document could then be proffered as the note or memorandum of the agreement necessary under the Statute. The case earned the plaudit of sounding "an alarm bell in the offices of every solicitor in the land".[5] Buckley LJ (Scrutton LJ concurring)[6] felt that the memorandum of agreement need not acknowledge the existence of a contract, as this could be established by extraneous evidence.[7] It was held that a letter written by the defendant to confirm an increase in the price agreed could be read together with earlier correspondence marked "subject to contract" to form a memorandum of the second agreement. Although the meaning of the dicta in *Law v Jones* are far from clear, they do create a precedent for disregarding the strict rule that the appearance of the "subject to contract" rubric anywhere in a chain of correspondence is sufficient to prevent the parties being bound. Instead, the approach taken is to look at the context in which the phrase appears and construe it accordingly. In many cases, this would necessarily lead to a finding that the parties contemplated the execution of a formal agreement as a condition of their already concluded contract. In such an instance, the phrase would not amount to a denial of the contract existing.

Of more pique to conveyancers, however, was the idea that parol evidence could be introduced to remove the phrase from a memorandum where there was a subsequent oral waiver, thus allowing the evil which the Statute of Frauds was intended to prevent. The danger of such a precedent lies in the uncertainty it creates around

---

4 [1970] Ch 675.

5 *Tiverton Estates v Wearwell* [1975] Ch 146 at 159.

6 Russell LJ gave a dissenting judgment whose reasoning would later be approved in *Tiverton.*

7 *Law v Jones* at 124–125.

contracts for the sale of land. Whereas prior to 1973, the widely held view was that the presence of the rubric was sufficient to immunise one's client from an action for specific performance, it was now far from clear. Each individual transaction would have to be examined in detail to determine if a sufficient memorandum of agreement existed. Uncertainty created litigation and this would be disastrous for conveyancers and their clients. While a different Court of Appeal effectively overruled the decision at the first available opportunity,[8] such an approach can still be attractive to a judge who wishes to hold a gazumper to his word. In the years that followed, the Irish Supreme Court seemingly adopted the reasoning of *Law v Jones*. In *Casey v Irish Continental Bank*,[9] the court found that the oral agreement had not been concluded "subject to contract" and that this phrase was unilaterally inserted subsequent to the bargain being made. Kenny J held that this was an unauthorised variation of the concluded agreement.[10] This reasoning is identical to that in *Law v Jones* where Buckley LJ noted that 'where a principle has entered into a binding contract, neither he nor his solicitor can thereafter deprive it of its binding effect by treating it as "subject to contract"'.[11] The court went further in *Kelly v Park Hall Schools*,[12] where a memorandum of agreement written "subject to contract" was used to evidence a concluded oral contract and as a note of that contract sufficient to satisfy s 2 of the Statute. The relevant clause stated that "...we have agreed terms, subject to contract..." Hamilton J (as he was then) in the High Court[13] said the problem was dealt with in a long line of authority which established that the mere fact that the parties to a bargain stipulate that it shall be subsequently set down in a formal written document does not, necessarily, lead to the conclusion that no final oral agreement has been reached.[14] While the insertion of the "subject to contract" rubric may sometimes deny such an oral agreement, it may also, in the court's view, merely state the intention that the terms of the oral contract be set down in writing.

---

[8] Lord Denning MR could not convince his colleagues that they would not be bound by a previous decision of the court which was erroneous. However, the three judges accepted the principle that, as between two conflicting decisions, they may decide which to follow and *Law v Jones* was regarded as conflicting with prior authority which required the memorandum of agreement to recognise the contract, *Tiverton v Wearwell*, at 160–161; Stamp LJ at 171; Scarman LJ at 172–173.

[9] [1979] IR 364.

[10] This passage in *Casey* is problematic as Kenny J refers to his judgment in *Law v. Roberts* [1964] IR 364 as lending support for this view. On reading the case, however, there is no reference at all to the phrase "subject to contract". See also Keane J's observations in *Mulhall v Haren* [1981] IR 364 at 372.

[11] At 124.

[12] [1979] IR 340.

[13] His decision was subsequently affirmed by the Supreme Court.

[14] At 348.

From *Tiverton* to *Boyle v Lee*

In *Tiverton v Wearwell*, Lord Denning MR stated his view that *Law v Jones* had been incorrectly decided.[15] Of critical importance to his thinking was the fact that the case set a dangerous precedent whereby oral testimony could be introduced to contradict the written record. He wrote of the dishonest plaintiff who:

> "...can now assert an oral contract in conversation with the defendant before the solicitor wrote the letter and then rely on the letter as a writing to satisfy the statute, even though it was expressly "subject to contract" or, alternatively, the plaintiff can assert that after the solicitor wrote the letter he met the defendant and in conversation orally agreed to waive the words "subject to contract"."[16]

This really is the crux of the issue. To admit a document, or a series of connected documents, which in no way acknowledge the existence of an agreement, as evidence of an oral contract proved by oral testimony is to expose the prospective vendor to tremendous danger of being bound unfairly and is to ride roughshod over the principles the Statute of Frauds seeks to uphold. Furthermore, Lord Denning did not believe that a phrase such as "we have agreed, subject to contract", as a matter of construction, could ever reveal a different intention than a phrase which explicitly denied the existence of an agreement. It could not, therefore, in any case, be interpreted as meaning the parties had concluded an oral contract.[17]

In the Irish High Court case of *Mulhall v Haren*,[18] Keane J (as he was then) was presented with the two conflicting English Court of Appeal decisions. He opted to follow *Tiverton*, in spite of the fact that the Irish Supreme Court, in both *Casey* and *Kelly*, had appeared to favour Buckley LJ's approach in *Law v Jones*. In an exhaustive

---

[15] He felt that the "offer cases", which required only the terms to be set down in writing and no acknowledgment, either express or implied, of the conclusion of a bargain, as stretching the literal construction of the Statute of Frauds and as of little application as these cases were decided to provide a just result in law at a time when equity could not have assisted the purchaser, *Tiverton*, at 158–159.

[16] at 160. Stamp LJ similarly observed that "the statute would not afford a shield against perjured testimony if it did not require the note or memorandum upon which it insists to recognise the existence of the alleged agreement, while as a matter of construction what is required is a memorandum 'of the' agreement upon which the party is charged", at 171.

[17] *ibid.*

[18] [1981] IR 364.

examination of the authorities, Keane J drew a distinction between cases where the "subject to contract" rubric was used and cases where the parties use alternative language which contemplates the execution of a formal agreement.[19]

He noted that where a solicitor used a phrase such as "please let us have draft contract for approval", then the court could undertake an examination of the intentions of the parties when inserting this stipulation. It could, if the evidence allowed, treat the request for a written contract as being no more than a condition of an already concluded oral bargain.[20] However, where the sale was stated to be "subject to contract", a long line of precedent, beginning with *Winn v Bull*,[21] seemed to dictate that such an examination could never take place and the presence of the phrase in a document is always inconsistent with the existence of a binding agreement.

Thus, where "subject to contract" appears in a document, it would be inappropriate to construct its meaning. Rather, from this line of authority, the presence of the phrase is always inconsistent with a binding agreement. Keane J distinguished the two seemingly conflicting Supreme Court decisions by observing that neither *Kelly* or *Casey* expressly overruled *Tiverton* or, indeed, any of the cases forming the *Winn v Bull* line of authority. He concluded that if the Court had intended to overrule such an important body of law, it would have said so.[22] His only concession to the weight of these two binding precedents was to note that the existence of the "subject to contract" phrase in a written document was inconsistent with a binding contract, save in the most exceptional cases.[23]

This precedential conflict was finally addressed directly by the Supreme Court in the seminal decision in *Boyle v Lee*, which sought to restore some certainty to the law concerning contracts for the sale of land. While the case was decided on the ground that there was no concluded agreement, as no deposit had been agreed, the court offered valuable *obiter dictum* on the effect of the "subject to contract" rubric in a written memorandum containing all the essential terms. Four of the five judges

[19] See Kenny J in *Law v Roberts*.

[20] Keane J at 375.

[21] (1887) 7 Ch. D. 29.

[22] He regarded *Kelly* as a special case decided on its own particular facts. He stated further that *Casey* did not lay down any principle which was generally applicable.

[23] At 386.

unequivocally rejected the idea that a document, or series of connected documents, containing the phrase could ever satisfy the statute. Finlay CJ,[24] in a lucid exposition of the law stated that, even where oral evidence could establish a concluded agreement, the presence of the phrase "subject to contract" in correspondence renders that documentation unable to comply with the Statute. He accepted that this would allow a vendor, in certain cases, to avoid the terms of a bargain but felt this was a far more a preferable position than the alternative approach which would allow amendment or deletion of the only written record by oral evidence.[25] Nor did he think that the exceptional circumstances" envisaged by Keane J in *Mulhall* could ever allow the phrase "subject to contract" be given anything other than a literal construction.[26]

The Alarm Bells Silenced? Decisions of the Superior Courts after *Boyle v Lee*

The intention of the Supreme Court in *Boyle v Lee* was to clearly resolve the uncertainty that had developed in relation to the legal effect of a document containing the phrase "subject to contract". However, the courts have seemed reluctant to apply the full rigours of the decision, not least because of the harshness which its strict application would present to a frustrated purchaser of land who had been gazumped. The case clearly set down two points; first, the presence of the phrase in the memorandum of agreement is always inconsistent with the existence of a binding contract and secondly, the meaning of the phrase must always be interpreted literally to deny such an agreement—its meaning should never be discovered by its context, as had occurred in *Law v Jones*, *Casey* and *Kelly*. Both rules have been undermined by recent pronouncements of the High Court and Supreme Court.

---

24 Hederman J concurring; McCarthy J approved of *Tiverton v Wearwell* and agreed with the chief-justice's observations on the "subject to contract" issue in broadly similar terms, at 79–80.

25 at 76–77.

26 Hederman and McCarthy JJ agreed with the chief-justice's analyses; O'Flaherty and Egan JJ differed slightly with the former accepting that, in certain limited circumstances, the phrase may not deny the existence of a contract but "there must be cogent evidence of a contrary intention before such a phrase is put to one side". He still described both *Kelly* and *Casey* as exceptional and confined to their own facts and stated that he did not believe that the incantation "subject to contract" possessed any "talismanic" properties, at 88–89; Similarly, McCarthy J does not agree with Keane J's allowing for exceptional circumstances, at 80; Egan J is the sole judge who explicitly approves of Keane J's view of the two cases as exceptional circumstances, at 95.

In *Embourg v Tyler Group Ltd*[27] Blayney J said that "whenever there is a sale, 'subject to contract', no binding contract comes into existence until contracts have been exchanged. Each case must be decided on its own facts". This appeared to be a return to a context based attitude to interpreting the rubric and this break from *Boyle v Lee* has found favour in subsequent cases. In *Supermacs (Ireland) Ltd v Katesan (Naas) Ltd*,[28] a motion was brought by the plaintiffs to strike out the proceedings for specific performance on foot of an alleged contract for the sale of land as having no chance of success. Evidence was produced that the solicitors had marked their earlier correspondence "subject to contract", but the Supreme Court did not believe that this was necessarily fatal to the existence of a binding contract and struck out the motion. Hardiman J observed:

> "In my view it is plainly arguable that the use of this rubric by the solicitors does not preclude the existence of a 'done deal' between the parties themselves...In so far as it is contended that the plaintiffs are estopped by the use of the rubric form from asserting a completed and enforceable agreement this seems to me to be plainly a matter for evidence at the trial."[29]

Similarly, Geoghegan J, while accepting that the use of the phrase may be helpful to the defendants at the ultimate hearing, stated that it did not lead to a definite conclusion that the parties intended there to be no concluded agreement. Both judgments appear to leave the possibility open for the finding of a binding oral contract where the written record, on a literal construction at least, denies its existence. The same approach was taken in the High Court by O'Donovan J, in the almost identical case of *Moran v Oakley Park Developments*,[30] where he too refused to strike out an action for specific performance where the solicitors correspondence was marked "subject to contract".[31] However, it should be noted that in *Shirley*

[27] [1996] 3 IR 480.

[28] [2001] 1 ILRM 401.

[29] At 409.

[30] Unreported, High Court, 31 March 2000.

[31] Similar language was used in *Dekra Erin Teo v Minister for the Environment* [2002] 2 ILRM 30, where O'Neill J held that the acceptance of a tender, both verbally and in writing, could in no way lead to the conclusion that a final decision to award the contract had not been made as "the most obvious meaning of the phrase in the context it was used was that the decision to award was subject only to the formal execution of the contract itself" at 53. See also O'Dell, "Contract Law" *Annual Review of Irish Law 2001* (Dublin, 2002), p 147.

Engineering v Irish Telecommunications Investment,[32] Geoghegan J, in the High Court, stated that the inclusion of the phrase in a document meant that in "virtually all circumstances" no binding agreement existed, but this would still appear to allow for "exceptional circumstances" which the majority disapproved of in *Boyle v Lee.*

In all of these cases, the court may have been concerned that to apply *Boyle*, would deny the plaintiffs any chance of establishing an act of part performance at the trial as there could be no concluded contract. Perhaps, as Judge Buckley suggests, the application of the case is restricted to disputes involving the Statute of Frauds and not to cases where an act of part performance is in issue.[33]

In *Jodifern v Fitzgerald*,[34] Barron J also appeared to depart from a strict application of the case by stating that the meaning of the phrase depends on whether it is found at the head of the document or in its body. If it is the former, it governs the entire document and will prevent it from being capable of satisfying the requirements of the Statute of Frauds, whereas if it is the latter, then its effect will be a matter of construction.[35] This seems to be clearly at odds with the line of authority which commenced with *Winn v Bull* and was approved of in *Boyle* and dictates that the court may not engage in such an inquiry.

Conclusion

Recent pronouncements of the Superior Courts make it clear that the insertion of the phrase "subject to contract" in correspondence does not prevent those documents from being used to satisfy s 2 of the Statute. In that sense, the decisions of the majority of the Supreme Court in *Boyle v Lee* have not been followed. However, this does not mean that the Irish courts have whole heartily embraced the approach of *Law v Jones.* While judges have used language reminiscent of that authority in recent cases, it would seem unlikely that any document containing the words "subject to contract" could satisfy s 2 of the Statute in all but the most exceptional cases. As long

---

[32] Unreported, High Court, 2 December 1999. This case is also authority for the proposition that the use of the phrase in verbal communications does not attract the same strict rules as when it is used in written correspondence and the court may discover its meaning in the context it was used, at 3–4.

[33] Buckley, *"Part Performance Lives" in Liber Memorialis: Professor James C Brady Breen*, Casey and Kerr (eds), (Dublin, 2001), p 117.

[34] [2000] 3 IR 321.

[35] [2000] 3 IR 321 at 331.

as the phrase relates to the agreement in issue, it would seem to be inadmissible as a note or memorandum of the agreement for the purposes of the Statute. However, uncertainty still exists and it would be advisable to take certain precautions when entering into correspondence. The phrase should always be inserted at the head of the document. It should clearly refer to the agreement in question and not to any prior or subsequent agreement. It should also refer to the whole of the contract and not simply to a part of it. While failure to follow any of these guidelines would not necessarily lead to the document being used as evidence of an agreement, it would seem wise to be careful in light of the reluctance of the judiciary to exercise the inherent jurisdiction of the courts to strike out claims for specific performance which have no chance of success in all but the clearest cases.

Reforming the Law on Double Jeopardy

by
Gerard Coffey*

The common law principle against retrials[1] expressed by the pleas in bar, *autrefois acquit* and *autrefois convict*, proscribes the retrial of an accused person for the same criminal offence subsequent to a lawful acquittal or conviction following a trial by a court of competent criminal jurisdiction.[2] This principle evolved throughout the development of the common law in response to the inherent deficiencies in criminal procedure and the draconian punishments imposed by Anglo-Saxon law[3] and subsequently by the common law[4] for the commission of most criminal offences.

---

* B.A. (U.L.), LL.B. (N.U.I.), Ph.D. (N.U.I.), Research Officer in Criminal Justice, Centre for Criminal Justice, School of Law, University of Limerick. The views expressed in this essay are those of the author and not necessarily those of the Centre for Criminal Justice. This is an updated version of an essay awarded second place in the Law Society of Ireland, *Student Law Reform Essay Competition 2005*, while the author was reading for a Ph.D in Law at NUI Galway.

1 Commonly referred to as the "rule against double jeopardy".

2 At common law, the principle against double jeopardy was expressed by the four pleas in bar, *autrefois acquit, autrefois convict, autrefois attaint* and former pardon. This essay will focus on the pleas in bar, *autrefois acquit*, and *autrefois convict*, these being the most relevant to contemporary criminal procedure.

3 Pollock and Maitland, *The History of English Law: Before the Time of Edward I* (vol 1, 2nd ed, Cambridge University Press, Cambridge, 1968), p 452, provide the following description of the punishments imposed during the reign of the Anglo-Saxon kings: "When punishment came it was severe. We read of death inflicted by hanging, beheading, burning, drowning, stoning, precipitation from rocks; we read of loss of ears, nose, upper lips, hands and feet; we read of castrations and flogging and sale into slavery; but the most gruesome and disgraceful of these torments were reserved for slaves."

4 See Plucknett, *A Concise History of the Common Law* (5th ed, Butterworth, London, 1956), p 15 stating: "...the period of Anglo-Saxon law extended later than the Norman Conquest, and at least as the year 1100 or thereabouts. We therefore see that in the reign of Henry I the law was substantially Anglo-Saxon and administered by the sheriffs locally according to ancient custom (which was certainly not the same all over the country). As yet there was very little that could be called 'common law'."

Indeed, the death penalty was frequently imposed for the commission of most criminal offences throughout the development of the common law.[5] Fundamental aspects of the criminal trial process, such as representation and calling witnesses, were solely to be utilised by the prosecution thus placing the accused at a certain disadvantage in the criminal justice process during the medieval period.[6] It was not uncommon for the trial court and the prosecution to collude, dismiss the case and re-indict the accused for the same criminal offence so as to enhance the possibility of securing a conviction.

However, in consideration of contemporary criminal procedure and the development of criminal justice systems in liberal democracies, the continued unconditional application of the common law principle against retrials for the same criminal offence following an acquittal has arguably been negated in circumstances where fresh and viable evidence of the accused's guilt is subsequently discovered. The preservation of the principle without exception may result in some individuals being "acquitted" of offences for which they are in all probability, guilty.[7]

Rationale of Double Jeopardy

The justification for the development of the common law principle against retrials was succinctly described in *Green v United States*,[8] *per* Black J in the following terms:

> "The underlying idea, one that is deeply ingrained in at least the Anglo-American systems of jurisprudence, is that the State with all its resources and power should not be allowed to make repeated attempts to convict an individual for an alleged offence, thereby subjecting him to embarrassment, expense and ordeal and compelling him to live in a continuing state of anxiety and insecurity, as well as enhancing the possibility that even though innocent he may be found guilty."[9]

Enhancing the possibility that an innocent person may be found guilty, through the multiplicity of trials for the same offence, is fundamental to what double jeopardy

---

[5] See Radzinowicz, *A History of English Criminal Law and its Administration from 1750* (Vol I – The Movement for Reform) (London, Stevens, 1948), pp 3–8.

[6] See Plucknett, *A Concise History of the Common Law* (5th ed, Butterworth, London, 1956), pp 434–437, and generally pp 424–441.

[7] See further Goodhart, "Acquitting the Guilty" (1954) 70 *Law Quarterly Review* 514.

[8] (1957) 355 US 184 (SC).

[9] (1957) 355 US 184 at 187–188 (SC).

jurisprudence was designed to prevent. Friedland,[10] one of the classical writers on double jeopardy jurisprudence,[11] explains that:

> "In many cases an innocent person will not have the stamina or resources effectively to fight a second charge. And, knowing that a second proceeding is possible an innocent person may plead guilty at the first trial. But even if the accused vigorously fights the second charge he may be at a greater disadvantage than he was at the first trial because he will normally have disclosed his complete defence at the former trial. Moreover, he may have entered the witness-box himself. The prosecutor can study the transcript and may thereby find apparent defects and inconsistencies in the defence evidence to use at the second trial."[12]

Accordingly, it is essential that the State, with its greater capacity and resources in comparison to those available to the accused, should not be afforded repeated attempts to convict an accused for the alleged commission of the same criminal offence subsequent to an acquittal or conviction following a trial on the merits by a court of competent criminal jurisdiction.

The application of the principle against double jeopardy not only prevents the retrial of accused persons for the same criminal offence following a trial on the merits, but also serves to enhance public confidence in the effective administration of the criminal justice system. Retrials for the same criminal offence subsequent to an unsuccessful prosecution where the State had failed to establish the guilt of the accused, despite the availability of sufficient evidence of guilt, may result in public confidence in the competence of the police and the prosecution authorities in the investigation and prosecution of crime being eroded. In *Connelly v DPP*,[13] Lord Devlin having outlined the injustices associated with multiple trials for the alleged commission of the same criminal offence, explained that:

> "There is another factor to be considered, and that is the courts' duty to conduct their proceedings so as to command the respect and confidence of the public."[14]

---

[10] Friedland, *Double Jeopardy* (Clarendon Press, Oxford, 1969).

[11] See also: Sigler, *Double Jeopardy: The Development of a Legal and Social Policy* (Cornell University Press, Ithaca, New York, 1969); Thomas, *Double Jeopardy: The History, the Law* (New York University Press, New York, 1998).

[12] Friedland, *Double Jeopardy* (Clarendon Press, Oxford, 1969), p 4.

[13] [1964] AC 1254 (HL & PC).

[14] [1964] AC 1254 at 1353 (HL & PC).

Likewise, Friedland[15] explains that:

> "It is not just the accused that is protected by the rule, but the legal system itself. By preventing harassment and inconsistent results, the rule assists in ensuring that court proceedings, to use Lord Devlin's phrase, 'command the respect and confident of the public.' Moreover, the rule conserves judicial resources and court facilities."

Thus, a fair and just balance must be achieved between the common law[16] right of the accused not to be placed twice in jeopardy for the same offence and the collective interests of society in the detection, prosecution and punishment of offenders.[17]

Retaining the *Status Quo*

Double jeopardy jurisprudence, as developed by the common law, operates to restrict the authority of the State against multiple prosecutions for the same offence of individuals who have previously been tried and acquitted or convicted by a court of competent criminal jurisdiction following a trial on the merits. The injustice in the case of a retrial in these circumstances is the risk that the prosecution with its superior resources would enervate the resilience of an accused into pleading guilty or securing a conviction solely through persistence rather than on the merits of the particular case.[18]

Retrying individuals who have been formerly acquitted increases the likelihood of convicting the innocent particularly due to adverse pre-trial publicity in view of the subsequent emergence of "new and compelling evidence" of the accused's guilt. The issue of adverse pre-trial publicity arose for consideration in *DPP v His Honour Judge Kevin Haugh and Charles J. Haughey (No 2)*,[19] where Carroll J held that while the Central Criminal Court had the authority to grant an order for adjournment in criminal trials, this was not necessarily final in the nature of an order of prohibition

---

15 Friedland, *Double Jeopardy* (Clarendon Press, Oxford, 1969), p 4.

16 The common law principle against double jeopardy may also enjoy constitutional status under the provisions of Art 38.1 of the Constitution.

17 In *Deaton v Attorney General* [1963] IR 170, a crime was described in terms a public offence or an offence against the State.

18 See further Note, "Trial by Persistence" (1952) 4 *Stanford Law Review* 537.

19 [2001] 1 IR 162 (HC).

or indeed a permanent stay on the criminal proceedings against the accused and furthermore that it was for the trial judge to decide the issue as to whether there was an unavoidable injustice of trial against the accused.[20]

It is the function of the trial judge to determine the issue of adverse pre-trial publicity and, accordingly, whether or not a criminal trial should proceed at that point in time or, alternatively, whether the trial should be stayed until such time as the adverse effects of pre-trial publicity is deemed to have faded from the memories of prospective jurors. The significance of this is that a conviction following a retrial in circumstances where the jury were biased by the presence of adverse pre-trial publicity (effectively prejudging the case) would be open to challenge on appeal as the accused would be deemed not to have had a fair "retrial". However, this scenario may be averted by the imposition of reporting restrictions[21] or the application of the *sub judice* rule.[22]

If the State is afforded the opportunity to retry an accused for the same criminal offence *ad infinitum*, the prosecution may perhaps have recourse to "jury-shopping"[23] until a "conviction" is finally obtained, a procedure that may infringe the constitutional right to natural justice, particularly if a second jury is aware that

---

[20] [2001] 1 IR 162 at 168-169, Carroll J explained that: "The possibility of asking prospective jurors at the time of empanelling a jury to say whether in view of adverse publicity they would not be able to bring an open mind to the trial and if so to inform the trial judge if chosen, was never canvassed before the respondent. It may be that there would not be an unavoidable unfairness of trial unless the procedure of allowing jurors to disqualify themselves because of the effect of adverse publicity, was followed. However … it is the trial judge who must decide the question of whether there is an unavoidable unfairness of trial and there is no requirement of law that an attempt to empanel an unbiased jury must first be made." See further O'Donnell, "The Jury on Trial: Reflections on *DPP v Haugh*" (2000, July) 5(9) *Bar Review* 470.

[21] s 82 of the Criminal Justice Act 2003 (UK) provides for reporting restrictions in the interests of justice where an application is made by the prosecution to quash an acquittal, where new and compelling evidence of the accused's guilt discovered, in order that a retrial may proceed. Section 83 of the 2003 Act provides that it is an offence to breach a restriction on publication order, punishable by fine "not exceeding level 5 on the standard scale".

[22] See Law Reform Commission of Ireland, *Report on Contempt of Court* (LRC 46–1994), chap 6 "The *Sub Judice* Rule", pp 33–46.

[23] In *Swisher v Brady* (1978) 438 US 204 at 216 (S.C.), Burger J delivering the opinion of the US Supreme Court referring to the Fifth Amendment guarantee against double jeopardy, explained that: "The Double Jeopardy Clause also precludes the prosecutor from enhancing the risk that an innocent defendant may be convicted by taking the question of guilt to a series of persons or groups empowered to make binding determinations."

the accused has previously been tried and acquitted for this same criminal offence. Indeed, a strong argument against permitting retrials for the same offence is that the first trial may be considered by the prosecution to be a "dry run" or "dress rehearsal" in preparation for a subsequent opportunity to secure a conviction.[24] Moreover, by affording the DPP the opportunity to prosecute the accused on more than one occasion for the same criminal offence may also permit the inference that this will strengthen their case by coaching witnesses to alter their testimony so as to enhance the prosecutions' assertion of the accused's guilt during the course of the retrial.[25]

An obvious adverse consequence of permitting retrials for the same criminal offence following an acquittal is the elongation of criminal trial process to the detriment of the accused, a process that may violate the accused's constitutional right to a speedy trial.[26] The English Law Commission recommended that a retrial should proceed "on grounds of new evidence" in the interests of justice so long as the prosecution acts "with reasonable dispatch" from the time the new evidence was discovered.[27] Section 84(2) of the Criminal Justice Act 2003 (UK) provides

---

[24] See Roberts, "Double Jeopardy Law Reform: A Criminal Justice Commentary" (2002) 65 *Modern Law Review* 393 at p 398 stating: "Increased risk of wrongful conviction is compounded...by the prospect of the prosecution enjoying an unfair tactical advantage at a second or subsequent trial. Having become privy to the defendant's arguments and strategy in the first proceedings, the prosecutor would be forewarned and forearmed at the second attempt. Merely presentational improvements in the prosecution's case, though irrelevant to the underlying merits, might nonetheless increase the likelihood of conviction, simply because the prosecutor's arguments have had the benefit of a previous 'dress rehearsal'".

[25] This issue was addressed in *United States v Scott* (1978) 437 US 82 at 105, n 4 (SC) where the United States Supreme Court *per* Brennan J delivering the opinion of the Court explained that: "There are a number of reasons a retrial enhances the risk that 'even though innocent, [the criminal defendant] may be found guilty....A retrial affords the Government the opportunity to re-examine the weaknesses of its first prosecution in order to strengthen the second. And, as would any litigant, the Government has been known to take advantage of this opportunity. It is not uncommon to find that prosecution witnesses change their testimony, not always subtly, at second trials."

[26] The right to a trial within a reasonable time of arrest and detention has been recognised as an unspecified constitutional right under Art 38.1 of the Constitution; see *In Re Singer* (1963) 97 ILTR 130; *State (O'Connell) v Fawsitt* [1986] IR 363; "a fair and public hearing within a reasonable time" is also provided for by Art 6(1) of the European Convention on Human Rights.

[27] Law Commission for England and Wales, Report No 267, *Double Jeopardy and Prosecution Appeals* (Cm. 5048, 2001), para 4.90(3).

that an accused shall be indicted within two months after an order for retrial, unless the Court of Appeal (Criminal Division) gives leave for an indictment beyond this period.

The requirement of a speedy trial may be satisfied once the accused is put on trial within a reasonable period of time following his indictment for the criminal offence charged. However, the requirement that a criminal trial proceeds with reasonable period of time should not prevent the prosecution from presenting fresh and compelling evidence of the accused's guilt, even if a significant period of time has elapsed[28] since the accused's acquittal, provided that once this new evidence has been discovered the accused is charged and tried expeditiously. In other words, the accused must be tried within a reasonable period of time from the date he is arrested and charged with the alleged commission of a criminal offence, otherwise the prosecution may be estopped from proceeding with the criminal trial by an order of prohibition.

An important issue to be considered against any proposed reforms of the principle against double jeopardy is that if a truly innocent individual has been charged, prosecuted and acquitted, he is compelled "to live in a continuing state of anxiety and insecurity"[29] due to the possibility of a retrial for the same criminal offence. An accused in these circumstances may be compelled to live in a continued state of anxiety and distress with the prospect having to undergo a retrial for the same offence at some future unspecified point in time.

Throughout the course of a criminal trial, an accused is afforded many substantive and procedural rights, whether statutory, constitutional or common law rules, to ensure a fair determination of the charges against the accused following a trial on the merits.[30] However, these substantive and procedural rights essential to a fair and impartial trial of an accused, and the contemporary modes of sentencing,[31] should

---

[28] There are currently a number of war crimes tribunals investigating atrocities which occurred decades previously such as the ICTY (The Hague, The Netherlands) and the ICTR (Arusha, Tanzania).

[29] *Green v United States* (1957) 355 US 184 at 187-188 (S.C.) *per* Black J.

[30] See *Report of the Constitution Review Group* (Stationery Office, Dublin, 1996), pp 191–193.

[31] See O'Malley, *Sentencing Law and Practice* (2nd ed, Thomson Round Hall, Dublin, 2006), chaps 20–27.

not *per se* justify the absolute abolition or indeed a relaxation of the common law principle against retrials for the same criminal offence.[32]

The justifications against reform of double jeopardy jurisprudence may be summarised by stating that the retention of the *status quo* demands greater efficiency and effectiveness from both the police and the prosecution authorities in the investigation and prosecution of offenders. If the police are mindful that a subsequent criminal trial against the accused may proceed in the event that the first trial does not result in a conviction then further (complete) investigations, such as to consider other suspects, prior to the initial criminal trial may not be deemed necessary. Likewise, the prosecution may perhaps be inclined to proceed with an indictment against the accused at an earlier stage of the investigative process rather than wait for a complete investigation by the police. Thus, the quality of police investigations and the effectiveness of prosecutions by the State may perhaps deteriorate over time and there is a real possibility that innocent defendants would be convicted.[33] Moreover, the disparity of capacity and resources between the prosecution and the accused in a criminal trial necessitates the application of *res judicata* following a trial on the merits in the interests of justice so as to prevent the unwarranted harassment of an accused through repeated attempts by the State to convict.

Proposals for Reform

Double jeopardy jurisprudence imposes a legal restraint on the State against retrials for the same criminal offence following an acquittal in circumstances where fresh and compelling evidence of the accused's guilt subsequently emerges. Consequently, some individuals who in all likelihood are guilty of committing serious criminal offences cannot be re-indicted, tried and punished for their criminal transgressions.

---

32 See Hall, "Objectives of Federal Criminal Procedural Revision" (1942) 51 *Yale Law Journal* 723 at p 729 stating: "...there is the fallacy of arguing that because the accused had so few rights in the 16th and 17th centuries, therefore he has too many rights now."

33 Fisher, "Double Jeopardy, Two Sovereignties and the Intruding Constitution" (1961) 28 *University of Chicago Law Review* 591 at p 593-594 writes: "If the prosecutor can, at his election, render a previous trial meaningless, serious consequences would follow. In the first place the prosecutor might be tempted to proceed with an inefficiently or incompletely prepared case when he knows that he will have a chance to do better or to present additional evidence in the second prosecution."

While an "acquittee" may well boast[34] of his guilt subsequent to an "acquittal" or may perhaps confess[35] to his crimes, he cannot be retried for the same criminal offence owing to the common law principle against double jeopardy. If, however, the accused had given evidence on oath during the course of the former criminal trial and now confesses to the crimes previously charged in the indictment for which he has been formerly acquitted, he may of course be charged with perjury,[36] unless of course he had exercised his right to silence,[37] but this is of little consequence to the victim or indeed the victim's family in the case of homicide.

The United Kingdom has been to the forefront[38] with proposals for reforming the common law principle against retrials for the same criminal offence following an acquittal,[39] and these reforms have recently been effected by the relevant provisions

[34] Friedland, *Double Jeopardy* (Clarendon Press, Oxford, 1969), p 5, n 1 cites the following examples: the British Columbia case of *Heathman*, Toronto *Globe and Mail*, 28 and 29 January 1964; *Leffer* (1936) 67 CCC 330 (Ont SC).

[35] Consider Ronnie Knight, who confessed that he had got away with murder when he and the Krays were acquitted of the gangland murder of Alfredo Zomparelli; see Knight, *Memoirs and Confessions* (Blake Publishing, 1998).

[36] Interestingly, in a recent high-profile Australian case, *The Queen v Carroll* [2002] HCA 55, the accused was charged and convicted of murder in 1985, this conviction being overturned on appeal. Further evidence of his guilt was subsequently discovered however the accused could not be charged with the same criminal offence (murder) but instead was charged with perjury on the basis that he had lied under oath at the former criminal trial. His conviction for perjury was quashed on appeal as it was deemed by the High Court of Australia to have infringed the accused's right against double jeopardy.

[37] The accused is entitled to exercise the unspecified constitutional right to silence, this being a corollary of the specified constitutional right of freedom of expression as provided for by Art 40.6.1°i. of the Constitution of Ireland 1937; see *Rock v Ireland* [1997] 3 IR 484; *Heaney v Ireland* [1996] 1 IR 580; Hogan, "Constitutional Law: The Right to Silence after *National Banks* and *Finnerty*" (1999) 21 *Dublin University Law Journal* 176; Langbein, "The Historical Origins of the Privilege Against Self-Incrimination at Common Law" (1994) 92 *Michigan Law Review* 1047.

[38] Proposals for a relaxation of the common law principle against retrials are also underway in Australia, *Discussion Paper on Issue Estoppel, Double Jeopardy and Prosecution Appeals Against Acquittals* (March 2004), and New Zealand, *Acquittal Following Perversion of the Course of Justice* (Report 70, 2001). However, it is unlikely that the law on double jeopardy will be reformed in the United States in view of the fact that this common law principle enjoys constitutional status by virtue of the Fifth Amendment to the United States Federal Constitution which, *inter alia*, provides "nor shall any person be subject for the same offence to be twice put in jeopardy of life or limb".

[39] See: Law Commission for England and Wales, Report No 267, *Double Jeopardy and Prosecution Appeals* (Cm. 5048, 2001); Law Commission for England and Wales, Consultation Paper No 156, *Double Jeopardy* (1999).

of the Criminal Justice Act 2003 (UK).[40] The provisions of the 2003 Act dealing with reform of double jeopardy are best described as a comprehensive eradication of this archaic principle of criminal procedure and provide for a retrial of approximately 30 "qualifying" serious criminal offences,[41] carrying a sentence of life imprisonment. The Act gives the prosecution the right of appeal against an acquittal with the objective of seeking a retrial where "new and compelling evidence" of the accused's guilt subsequently emerges. Furthermore, while the European Convention on Human Rights makes provision for the prohibition against retrials for the same offence in the same state,[42] provision is also made for a retrial for the same criminal offence "if there is new or newly discovered facts, or there has been a fundamental defect in the proceedings, which could affect the outcome of the case".[43]

The spur to reform in the United Kingdom was directly associated with the bungled attempt to prosecute the five white youths who in all likelihood are guilty of the murder of black teenager Stephen Lawrence in 1993.[44] The five accused in this case were "acquitted" as a consequence of police incompetence in the investigation of the murder in addition to the ineffective prosecution of the case by the DPP.[45] The

---

40 Part 10, ss 75–97 of the 2003 Act; see Ward and Davies, *The Criminal Justice Act 2003: A Practitioner's Guide* (Jordans, Bristol, 2004), chap 11. The provisions of the 2003 Act effectively modifies the operation of the common law principle against double jeopardy in the United Kingdom. The 2003 Act has been used as the model for the proposed reform of double jeopardy jurisprudence in Australia.

41 These "qualifying offences" are provided for in Sched 5 to the Criminal Justice Act 2003 (UK). These include: offences against the person; sexual offences; drugs offences; criminal damage offences; war crimes and terrorism; and conspiracy. The procedure for making an application for a retrial for a "qualifying offence" is comprehensively set out in Pt 10 of the Criminal Justice Act 2003 (UK).

42 European Convention on Human Rights, Protocol 7, Art 4(1).

43 European Convention on Human Rights, Protocol 7, Art 4(2).

44 See: Bridges, "The Lawrence Inquiry – Incompetence, Corruption, and Institutional Racism" (1999) 26(3) *Journal of Law and Society* 298; Docking and Tuffin, "Racists Incidents: Progress Since the Lawrence Inquiry" *Home Office Online Report* (42/05), available at:
http://www.semperscotland.org.uk/reports/RacistIncidentsProgressSinceLawrenceHoReport4205.pdf.

45 Three of the five youths were prosecuted in 1996 by private prosecution which resulted in an "acquittal" due to the absence of conclusive evidence—this was a directed acquittal by the trial judge. The remaining two youths were discharged at the committal stage of the prosecution. The Stephen Lawrence case was the seminal case for reforming double jeopardy jurisprudence in the past decade in the United Kingdom.

public disquiet that followed the "acquittal" of the five youths resulted in the Home Secretary, Mr Jack Straw MP, instigating an official inquiry in 1997. The MacPherson Inquiry,[46] which investigated the death of Stephen Lawrence, made a number of recommendations, the most significant of which was that the common law principle against double jeopardy should be abandoned where fresh evidence of the accused's guilt subsequently emerges which makes the prosecution's case substantially stronger, in conjunction with the evidence adduced during the course of the former trial.[47]

The first "acquittal" under the relevant provisions of the Criminal Justice Act 2003 (UK) has been successfully challenged. The Director of Public Prosecutions, Ken McDonald QC, gave his consent to the Crown Prosecution Service on 10 November 2005 to refer the case of William "Billy" Dunlop, formerly acquitted of murder, to the Court of Appeal (Criminal Division), which now has the power to quash an "acquittal" and order a retrial where there is fresh and compelling evidence of guilt. Mr Dunlop was twice tried in 1991 for the murder of Julie Hogg, the first trial resulting in a "hung jury", and he was acquitted following the retrial. However, Mr Dunlop was convicted in 2000 on a charge of perjury and sentenced to six years imprisonment having confessed in prison that he had murdered the victim.[48] On 11 September 2006 Dunlop pleaded guilty, and on 6 October 2006 he was sentenced to life imprisonment with a minimum tariff of 17 years. The outcome of this seminal double jeopardy reform case may determine whether "acquittees" of murder and other serious criminal offences may also be retried, particularly in consideration of the fact that the National Crime Faculty (UK) has estimated that there are

---

[46] MacPherson Inquiry, *The Stephen Lawrence Inquiry – Report of an Inquiry by Sir William MacPherson of Cluny* (Cm. 4262, 1999). The MacPherson Inquiry concluded that the police investigation failed to examine eyewitness accounts of the murder for several days, and had failed to secure forensic evidence—moreover, the police investigation failed to take action into lines of inquiry that were clearly available following the murder. It is widely believed that there was institutionalised racism among the investigating members of the police force.

[47] MacPherson Inquiry, *The Stephen Lawrence Inquiry – Report of an Inquiry by Sir William MacPherson of Cluny* (Cm. 4262, 1999), recommendation 38 reads: "That consideration should be given to the Court of Appeal being given power to permit prosecution after acquittal where fresh and viable evidence is presented."

[48] Dunlop confessed to the murder and mutilation of Julie Hogg to a prison officer in a taped conversation, while serving a seven-year term of imprisonment in Moreland Prison for a serious assault on another victim.

approximately 35 individuals formerly acquitted of murder in the UK who may eventually be retried for the same offence if fresh and compelling evidence of their guilt is discovered.[49]

The presumption of innocence is an integral part of a fair trial and has been accepted as an unspecified constitutional right under the Constitution[50] in addition to being a specified right under Art 6(2) of the European Convention on Human Rights.[51] The significance of the presumption of innocence for the purposes of reforming double jeopardy jurisprudence is that in order to quash an acquittal the reviewing court would have to be satisfied that there is a *prima facie* case that the accused would be convicted following a retrial for the same criminal offence. What is significant in this respect is that the term used by proponents for reform is "new and compelling" evidence of the accused's guilt necessitating a retrial, not "conclusive" evidence of the accused's guilt, which could prejudge the outcome of a retrial and accordingly the accused's constitutional right to natural justice. Indeed, flowing from this is the issue of adverse pre-trial publicity,[52] which may suggest that the accused is being retried in consideration of new evidence which is conclusive of his guilt, thereby pre-empting the jury verdict following a retrial.[53] The significance of this is that the trial court must be impartial in the adjudication process and apply the principles of natural

49 *The Guardian,* 11 November 2005, Rosie Cowan, crime correspondent (online version available at: http://www.guardian.co.uk/print/0,3858,5330933-104770,00.html). Fresh and compelling evidence of guilt may be discovered using contemporary forensic techniques such as DNA, facial mapping technology and voice recognition technology.

50 Article 38.1 of the Constitution of Ireland 1937.

51 Article 6(2) provides that: "Everyone charged with a criminal offence shall be presumed innocent until proved guilty according to law."

52 See further Duffy, "Pre-trial Publicity, Prejudice, and the Right to a Fair Trial" (1994) 4 *Irish Criminal Law Journal* 113. Sections 82 and 83 of the Criminal Justice Act 2003 (UK) provide for reporting restrictions and the imposition of criminal sanctions where the media is deemed to have published adverse pre-trial publicity which could render a second trial unfair and subject to challenge on appeal (if the accused was convicted). Alternatively, the *sub judice* rule could be applied.

53 Consider the potential for adverse pre-trial publicity if the five youths accused of the murder of Stephen Lawrence were to be retried for the same criminal offence. Would it be possible to empanel an impartial jury who were unaware of the media coverage prior to the first criminal trial, not to mention the media coverage, which would undoubtedly be associated with a retrial? Indeed there is a real possibility that the retrial of such a high-profile case would become *cause célébre* with the associated political and public pressure for a "conviction".

justice so as to ensure that proper procedures are followed.[54] It is imperative that the terminology used by the reviewing court pertaining to the subsequent emergence of fresh evidence of the accused's guilt does not rebut the presumption of innocence. Would a relaxation of the common law principle against retrials for the same offence constitute substantial inroads into the presumption of innocence which is essential to a fair trial? Can it be said that the jury when determining the guilt or innocence of an accused on a retrial would be impartial if they have knowledge of the fact the reviewing court had concluded that there was "conclusive" fresh evidence of the accused's guilt? Once the reviewing court has decided that the accused should be retried on the basis of new and compelling evidence of his guilt, a certain consequence is that the accused would be unable to avoid the suspicion of guilt. This undoubtedly produces an inherent imbalance during the course of the retrial between the prosecution and the defence. Therefore, it is important for the reviewing court to use the correct terminology when quashing an acquittal and ordering a retrial, i.e. that there is "new and compelling evidence" (not conclusive) of the accused's guilt, which when taken in conjunction with the evidence adduced during the course of the former criminal trial, makes the prosecution's case against the accused substantially stronger.

Assuming the Law Reform Commission of Ireland ultimately reviews the law on double jeopardy with a view to relaxing the principle against retrials, reference could be made to the Supreme Court of Nigeria decision in *Okoduwa v The State*,[55] where the Court indicated that the following guidelines should be satisfied before a retrial would be ordered:

- That there has been such an error in law or an irregularity in procedure that neither renders the trial a nullity nor makes it possible for the appeal court to say that there has been no miscarriage of justice;
- That apart from the error of law or irregularity in procedure the evidence before the court discloses a substantial case against the accused;

---

[54] The principles of natural (constitutional) justice stipulate that the tribunal or court which is adjudicating the case must be impartial (*nemo iudex in causa sua*) and give each litigant a fair opportunity to present their version of the case (*audi alteram partem*); see Hogan and Morgan, *Administrative Law in Ireland* (3rd ed, Round Hall Sweet & Maxwell, 1998), chaps 10 and 11.

[55] [1990] LRC (Const.) 337 at 346 (SC) *per* Nnanami JSC.

- That there are no special circumstances which would make it unjust to put the accused on trial a second time;
- That the offence for which the accused is charged and their consequences are serious in nature; and
- That to refuse an order of retrial would occasion a greater injustice than to grant it.

These guidelines are not necessarily comprehensive and may be modified accordingly. Thus, when considering an application on behalf of the prosecution for a retrial, the following issues should be considered:

- The seriousness and prevalence of the offence;
- The probable duration and expense of a new trial;
- The ordeal to be undergone for a second time by the accused;
- The lapse of time since the alleged commission of the offence and its effect on the quality of the evidence; and
- The nature of the case of the prosecution against the accused as disclosed in the evidence at the first trial, whether substantial or not.[56]

Therefore, proposed reforms of double jeopardy jurisprudence should take into consideration that the interests of society should not simply be to convict the guilty but also to ensure that criminal trials are conducted in a fair and just manner. This is fundamental to produce fair and equitable judgments and to enhance public confidence in the effective administration of the criminal justice system by prosecuting and convicting those individuals who in all probability are guilty of the commission of serious criminal offences.

In order to ensure that applications to retry an accused for the same criminal offence are not made without any real prospect of securing a conviction, the English Law Commission[57] recommended that a "consent requirement" should be an integral part of this process. This procedure is necessary to eliminate impulsive applications

---

[56] [1990] LRC (Const.) 337 at 346 (SC).

[57] The Law Commission for England and Wales, Report No 267, *Double Jeopardy and Prosecution Appeals* (Cm. 5048, 2001), para 4.99 recommended: "...that it should be necessary to obtain the consent of the Director of Public Prosecutions, in person, before making an application for an acquittal to be quashed on grounds of new evidence."

by the prosecution for a retrial based on new evidence.[58] Indeed by filtering out these unmeritorious claims, this procedure would serve to prevent the congestion of the criminal courts in addition to the avoidance of the unwarranted harassment of the accused through repeated attempts to convict him of the alleged commission of the same criminal offence.[59]

Once the DPP has consented to an application[60] for the quashing of an erroneous acquittal, the next stage in the process of seeking a retrial is a hearing by the reviewing court whose function would be to establish whether new and compelling evidence of the accused's guilt warrants a retrial; in other words, in conjunction with the evidence adduced during the course of the former criminal trial is it highly probable that a conviction would be secured against the accused.[61] Assuming that the Irish Supreme Court[62] is ultimately vested with the responsibility of reviewing new evidence of the accused's guilt, the accused should be put on notice and, accordingly, will have the opportunity to challenge this before the reviewing court. However, the negative aspect of this procedure is that the reviewing court or other established body whose function will be decide if the "new and compelling" evidence warrants a retrial

---

58 See Fisher, "Double Jeopardy, Two Sovereignties and the Intruding Constitution" (1961) 28 *University of Chicago Law Review* 591 at 593–594 stating: "If the prosecutor can, at his election, render a previous trial meaningless, serious consequences would follow. In the first place the prosecutor might be tempted to proceed with an inefficiently or incompletely prepared case when he knows that he will have a chance to do better or to present additional evidence in the second prosecution."

59 s 76(3) of the Criminal Justice Act 2003 (UK) requires the prosecutor to first obtain the consent of the DPP before an application may be made to the Court of Appeal (Criminal Division) to quash an acquittal, which would clear the way for a retrial. Under the provisions of s 79(4) of the 2003 Act the DPP may also reopen an acquittal following a private prosecution; this provision may result in the retrial of the individuals acquitted following a private prosecution for the murder of Stephen Lawrence.

60 s 76(5) the Criminal Justice Act 2003 (UK) permits only one application to review an acquittal with the objective of seeking a retrial for the same offence.

61 s 77(1) of the Criminal Justice Act 2003 (UK) provides that the Court of Appeal (Criminal Division) may quash an acquittal on the application of the prosecution, with a right of appeal to the House of Lords available to both the acquitted person and the prosecutor under s 81 of the 2003 Act (amending s 33 of the Court of Appeal Act 1968 (UK)).

62 The most likely option for a reviewing court would be the Court of Criminal Appeal, however, s 4 of the Court and Court Officers Act 1995 apparently provides for the eventual abolition of this Court with "powers" jurisdiction and function being transferred to the Supreme Court.

for the same criminal offence may not have the opportunity to hear direct evidence and observe the demeanour of witnesses so as to determine the veracity of their evidence. During the course of a criminal trial, witnesses giving oral testimony are subjected to cross-examination in order to test the veracity of their testimony. However, the reviewing court may only examine the transcript of the former criminal trial in conjunction with the fresh evidence of the accused's guilt. Likewise, an expert witness, such as a DNA analyst, may not be as convincing under cross-examination as opposed to an unchallenged presentation of evidence against the accused to the reviewing court. Nevertheless, the essential point of reviewing new evidence of the accused's guilt is to determine whether an exception should be made to the common law proscription against retrials. Once the reviewing court has determined that the new evidence of the accused's guilt in conjunction with the original evidence adduced during the course of the initial criminal trial warrants a retrial, it is then for the defence during the course of the retrial to undermine the cogency of the prosecution entire case against the accused. This may be achieved by providing a rational explanation of this "new and compelling evidence", thereby negating the prosecution's contention that the accused is in fact guilty of the criminal offences for which he had been formerly acquitted.

If fresh and viable evidence of a defendant's innocence is discovered subsequent to a conviction, this will be admitted in the interests of justice on application to the appellate court for an order to quash the conviction on the basis that it cannot be sustained in the light of fresh and viable evidence of the accused's innocence.[63] Is it in the interests of the preservation of a just and ordered society that individuals should continue to be at liberty where new and compelling evidence of their guilt is discovered, albeit following a trial on the merits resulting in an "acquittal"? Does the subsequent emergence of fresh evidence of the accused's guilt following an "acquittal" undermine the legitimacy of such an acquittal with the result that an exception to the common law principle against retrials should be made?[64] Of course

[63] In the United Kingdom, retrials were introduced by s 1 of the Criminal Appeal Act 1964 where a conviction had been quashed on the basis of fresh evidence. Also, the Criminal Cases Review Commission, which investigates possible miscarriages of justice (England, Wales and Northern Ireland) assesses whether convictions or sentences should be referred to an appellate court.

[64] Dennis, "Rethinking Double Jeopardy" [2000] *Criminal Law Review* 933 at p 945 writes: "We are however used to the idea that new evidence of innocence, a previously unknown alibi witness for example, calls into question the legitimacy of a conviction. It suggests that a mistake has been made that calls for investigation and possible rectification. Similarly the emergence of significant new evidence of guilt calls into question the legitimacy of an acquittal. It suggests likewise that a mistake

what must also be considered is that the subsequent discovery of new evidence such as DNA, voice identification technology, facial mapping recognition technology, fingerprints, blood samples, reliable witnesses, etc, establishing that the accused was at the crime scene is not, however, conclusive evidence of guilt.

Proposed reforms of double jeopardy jurisprudence in Ireland[65] should not only consider the interest and rights of the accused but also those of society in convicting and punishing those who are undoubtedly guilty of the commission of serious criminal offences.[66] Any meaningful debate on the reform of double jeopardy law must be composed with the interests of both the prosecution and the accused being equally considered. However, high-profile cases[67] that may call for swift changes in the law,[68] should not dictate an injudicious response by the legislature in favour of a

has been made. Why should we not investigate and if necessary rectify the mistake, so as to lead to a retrial? It is not apparent now that a different verdict on a second trial would be inconsistent, given significant new evidence. The criminal justice system exists to enforce the criminal law, and the correct enforcement of the criminal law against those whom we have reason to believe may be guilty is a matter of state policy. The interests of justice seem therefore to call for a retrial in these circumstances. A retrial will resolve the legitimacy problem of the first acquittal and forward the aims of criminal justice if the defendant is in fact guilty."

65 See the remarks by the Minister for Justice, Equality and Law Reform pertaining to reforming the common law principle against double jeopardy (Rebalancing Criminal Justice - Remarks by Tánaiste in Limerick, 20 October 2006 available at: http://www.justice.ie/80256E01003A02CF/vWeb/pcJUSQ6UTMDB-en).

66 Devlin, *The Enforcement of Morals* (Oxford University Press, Oxford, 1965) p. 22 explains that: "… the criminal law exists for the protection of individuals….But the true principle is that the law exists for the protection of society. It does not discharge its function by protecting the individual from injury, annoyance, corruption, and exploitation; the law must protect also the institutions and the community of ideas, political and moral, without which people cannot live together."

67 A most notable example being the Australian High Court case, *The Queen v Carroll* [2002] HCA 55. This involved the conviction of the defendant in 1985 for murder, which was later overturned on appeal. New and compelling evidence of the accused's guilt was subsequently discovered by the police, however, in compliance with the common law principle against retrials, the accused could not be retried with the same criminal offence but was alternatively charged and convicted for perjury on the basis that he had lied about his involvement in the murder while giving testimony during the former criminal trial. However, the perjury conviction was quashed on appeal as it was deemed by the High Court of Australia to have infringed the principle against double jeopardy.

68 Dworkin, "Hard Cases" (1975) 88 *Harvard Law Review* 1057.

coherent detailed examination if the core issues involved in double jeopardy law reform.[69]

It is essential for the criminal justice system to keep pace with the advancements made in forensic science. Moreover, as fresh and viable DNA and other scientific evidence can expose wrongful convictions, this evidence could also form the basis of an application for a retrial of the accused formerly acquitted for the same criminal offence.[70]

Retrospective Effect

The principle of non-retroactivity provides that parliament shall not declare acts (or omissions) to be criminal offences which were not criminal offences at the time of their commission (or omission).[71] Provision is made for the principle of non-retroactivity in the Constitution of Ireland[72] and also the European Convention on Human Rights.[73] Neither of these provisions places any legal impediment against retroactive criminal procedure. Accordingly, if the common law principle against retrials is ultimately reformed in Ireland permitting retrials for the same criminal offence following an acquittal, this will not *per se* infringe the principle against non-retroactivity.

The English Law Commission has recommended that the proposed exception to the common law principle against double jeopardy have retrospective effect,[74] and this

---

69 Roberts, "Double Jeopardy Law Reform: A Criminal Justice Commentary" (2002) 65 *Modern Law Review* 393 at p 396 explains that: "As the debate is taken forward into the policy arena, clear thinking and principled argument will be at a premium, the more so because double jeopardy reform has become entangled in the public mind with highly-charged issues of racist violence and police effectiveness in the aftermath of Macpherson. Every lawyer knows that hard cases make bad law."

70 Albeit in strictly limited circumstances.

71 See further Beddard, "Retrospective Crime" (1995, May) *New Law Journal* 663.

72 Article 15.5.1° of the Constitution provides: "The Oireachtas shall not declare acts to be infringements of the law which were not so at the date of their commission."

73 Article 7.1 of the European Convention on Human Rights *inter alia* provides: "No one shall be held guilty of any criminal offence on account of an act or omission which did not constitute a criminal offence under national or international law at the time it was committed."

74 Law Commission for England and Wales, Report No 267, *Double Jeopardy and Prosecution Appeals* (Cm. 5048, 2001), para 4.56.

has been adopted by the 2003 Act.[75] Whether or not retrospective effect would violate the common law principle of legality[76] and the Constitution of Ireland is a matter of debate. Allowing an exception to the double jeopardy prohibition does not create any new substantive criminal offence but merely makes an alteration to an aspect of criminal procedure which is permissible without offending the principle of legality. The significance of retrospective effect of the proposed relaxation of the common law principle against double jeopardy is that procedures for harvesting forensic evidence may not have been available at the time of the alleged commission of the criminal offence.

Retrospective effect of the proposed reforms of the law on double jeopardy is essential because in many cases the criminal offences may have been committed decades previously, bearing in mind that contemporary techniques for gathering forensic evidence may not have been available at the time of the commission of the offence.[77]

Tentative Conclusions

The rationale for the development of the principle against retrials at common law no longer exists. Consequently, the proscription against retrials for the alleged commission for the same criminal offence could be relaxed where the interests of justice require that the accused undergoes a second trial, albeit in strictly limited circumstances, where new and compelling evidence of his guilt subsequently emerges.

Double jeopardy jurisprudence is as much rooted in the need for finality in litigation as it is with the concern for justice. However, although it may be said that public interest requires finality in the criminal justice process, this cannot override the

75 Section 75(6) of the Criminal Justice Act 2003 (UK) provides that the double jeopardy reform provisions "applies whether the acquittal was before or after the passing" of the 2003 Act.

76 The principle of legality prevents the creation of criminal offences applicable retrospectively. It is encapsulated in the maxims *nullum crimen sine lege* and *nulla poena sine lege*; see further O'Malley, "Common Law Crimes and the Principle of Legality" (1989) 7 *Irish Law Times* 243.

77 See Third Report of the Home Affairs Select Committee (1999-2000) HC 190, "The Double Jeopardy Rule" at para 54, stating: "Retrospection will be a controversial area if legislation is brought forward to amend the double jeopardy law. Without retrospection, the change would take years to have any impact and would leave a sense of frustration about past cases. Time limits would further restrict the benefits of such a change and there is a risk that the strongest cases for a retrial would happen to fall just outside the limits chosen."

greater public interest of convicting those who have committed serious criminal offences.

If the law on double jeopardy is ultimately reformed, thereby permitting retrials following an "acquittal", would this be the norm in every case with the result that public confidence in the administration of criminal justice would be eroded? The prosecution should be afforded one further opportunity to retry the accused for the same criminal offence, but only in circumstances where new and compelling evidence of the accused's guilt has emerged subsequent to an acquittal. If double jeopardy jurisprudence is completely abolished then an accused could potentially be retried for the same criminal offence *ad infinitum.* Proposed reforms of double jeopardy jurisprudence are not advocating a complete abolition but rather a relaxation of the principle against retrials, albeit in strictly limited circumstances, where new and compelling evidence of the accused's guilt is discovered subsequent to an acquittal.

Although criminal justice systems in liberal democracies generally operate efficiently resulting in just and equitable verdicts of acquittal or conviction, there is nevertheless a *lacuna* in the law whereby an acquittee cannot be retried for the same criminal offence where new and compelling evidence of his guilt subsequently emerges, such as DNA scientific evidence, fingerprints, evidence from voice recognition or facial mapping technology or witnesses. Is it in the interests of a just and ordered society that individuals who are most likely guilty of heinous criminal offences should be immune from further prosecution because of the continued unconditional application of this principle of the common law?

The proper implementation of the policies underlying double jeopardy jurisprudence necessitates simultaneous solutions of several interdependent problematic issues pertaining to substantive and procedural law. These are not likely to be addressed in any single superior court decision, with the result that a resolution of the prevalent inadequacies of double jeopardy jurisprudence by judicial determination is undoubtedly burdensome and improbable. Therefore, a legislative response to reforming the law on double jeopardy is desirable whereby the common law proscription against retrials for the alleged commission of the same criminal offence would be relaxed albeit in strictly limited circumstances where fresh and compelling evidence of the accused's guilt subsequently emerges.

Conclusion

In the final analysis, since the rationale for the development of double jeopardy jurisprudence no longer exists, the unconditional adherence to the common law principle against retrials for the same criminal offence should be relaxed where, in the interests of justice, the accused is required to undergo a second trial for the same criminal offence in consideration of the discovery of new and compelling evidence of his guilt. However, it is essential to provide a *caveat*, that only one retrial should be permitted for the same criminal offence. Indeed, if the principle against double jeopardy was entirely abolished, as opposed to a relaxed in strictly limited circumstances, then an accused could potentially be retried for the same criminal offence *ad infinitum*, something which may be expected in totalitarian states, not in liberal democracies. Thus, what is proposed is a relaxation of double jeopardy jurisprudence where new and compelling evidence of the accused's guilt subsequently emerges which in conjunction with the evidence adduced during the former criminal trial substantiates the prosecution's assertions of the accused's guilt.[78] The proposed relaxation of the proscription against retrials would also serve to enhance public confidence in the criminal justice system where individuals who are most likely guilty of the commission of serious criminal offences are tried and punished accordingly, thereby obviating the necessity for "private vengeance" where an accused has been "acquitted" notwithstanding compelling evidence of his guilt.[79] Reforming the law so as to permit retrials for the same criminal offence does not involve the creation new substantive criminal offences but merely amends a principle of criminal procedure. Consequently, there is no legal impediment against the retrospective effect of double jeopardy law reform. In the absence of legislative intervention, the *status quo* remains.

---

78 Permitting only one retrial (for the same criminal offence) would also serve to ensure efficiency by the police in the investigation of crime prior to the initial criminal trial and the effective prosecution of the evidence against the accused during the course of the criminal trial.

79 See Holmes, *The Common Law* (Dover Publications, New York, 1991), Lecture I, "Early Forms of Liability", pp 2-3 stating: "It is commonly known that the early forms of legal procedure were grounded in vengeance. Modern writers have thought that Roman law started from the blood feud, and all the authorities agree that German law begun in that way."

Reforming the Leave Procedure on Appeal to the Court of Criminal Appeal

by
Genevieve Coonan*

Introduction

If a person wishes to appeal his conviction to the Court of Criminal Appeal ("hereafter CCA"), s/he must first seek leave from the trial judge to do so. This involves applying to the trial judge for a certificate stating that his case is "fit for appeal".[1] Where this is refused, then the convicted person, if still desirous of bringing an appeal, must appeal that refusal to the CCA.[2] The CCA will then, in theory, decide whether leave should be granted, and if it should be, the court will at some later point decide the appeal. The fundamental point to note is that the law, as it stands, provides for a leave stage. There is no automatic right of appeal to the CCA.

There are, however, several pressing problems with the leave stage in criminal appeals. Primarily, it has become arbitrary and meaningless and fails to serve any real or apparent purpose.[3] It does not seem to act as any real filter, as one may believe a leave stage is supposed to. Nor do trial judges seem to give any real consideration as to whether a case is or is not fit for appeal. Refusals of leave are the norm. The consequence of this is that the criminal process takes on an air of unreality. One gets convicted, and one then goes to the CCA which then in turn treats the leave stage as

* This essay was awarded a prize by the Law Society of Ireland for the *Law Reform Essay Competition 2005*.

[1] Section 31(i) of the Courts of Justice Act, 1924.

[2] Section 31(ii) of the Courts of Justice Act, 1924.

[3] It has been noted that, "it does not conform to the reality of the conduct of cases in the Court of Criminal Appeal and performs no meaningful purpose" – see The Working Group on the Jurisdiction of the Courts, *The Criminal Jurisdiction of the Courts* (May, 2003), at p 163, para 645.

the actual hearing of the case. Indeed, it has been somewhat wryly noted that "a non-legal reader of the press is likely to believe that this refusal has some actual effect."[4]

So, it should be clear that some reform is necessary. Indeed, such an objective is even more compelling when considered in the light of recent governmental policy to improve the "comprehensibility" and "accessibility" of criminal legislation.[5] In response to this, the Working Group on the Jurisdiction of the Courts recommended the abolition of the leave stage. In this essay it will be submitted that this is a "step to far" and is motivated by a largely unsubstantiated reading of the European Convention on Human Rights. It is submitted that retention of the leave stage, coupled with a reform of its function and role, can serve a very necessary purpose in alleviating some of the workload of the CCA. The prospect of relieving even a small part of the enormous burden the exponential growth in the criminal law has placed on the judiciary must surely rank as an important reason for reform in its own right.

Problems with the Leave Stage

It was remarked above that the primary difficulty with the leave procedure is that in reality it serves no real purpose. In most cases, the trial judge refuses the certificate granting leave without any real examination of the grounds of appeal or elaboration on the reasons for refusal.[6] Further, if an application for leave reaches the CCA, it is, for all intents and purposes, treated as the appeal itself. Indeed, this practice tends to obscure the fact that leave to appeal should only be granted if the test in s 32 of the Courts of Justice Act 1924 is met.[7] That is to say that the trial judge must apply the terms of s 32 (which we will discuss in more detail in a moment) in order to decide if leave should be granted. The CCA, however, rarely makes any reference to the actual legislation which provides the test as to whether a case is, or is not, a suitable case for appeal. In short it seems that the CCA simply hears appeals from the lower courts without a leave stage at all.

---

[4] The Working Group on the Jurisdiction of the Courts, *The Criminal Jurisdiction of the Courts*, (May, 2003), at p 162, para 642.

[5] *See* below at p 4. Also see the Law Reform Commission, *Consultation Paper on Statutory Drafting and Interpretation: Plain Language and the Law*, LRC-CP14-1999 (Dublin, 1999), at p viii.

[6] As the Working Group has noted, "in almost all cases, the trial judge simply refuses the application". Although, it must be noted that it also conceded that it is not unknown for a trial judge to grant a certificate – "it is merely infrequent" – *see* The Working Group on the Jurisdiction of the Courts, *The Criminal Jurisdiction of the Courts* (May, 2003), at p 162, para 642.

[7] The Working Group on the Jurisdiction of the Courts, *The Criminal Jurisdiction of the Courts* (May, 2003), at p 162, para 643.

So why is this? It is submitted that the first explanation for this situation is that the actual test applicable in s 31 is wholly indeterminate. It is incredibly difficult to discern what it actually requires. Section 31(i) requires a trial judge to be satisfied that a case is "fit for appeal" in order for leave to be granted. If this certificate is refused, the applicant must apply to the CCA who, pursuant to s 32, must be satisfied that either:

> a question of law is involved, or where the trial appears to the court to have been unsatisfactory, or there appears to the court to be any other *sufficient ground* of appeal.[8]

Therefore, a trial judge must be able to recognise those cases that are "fit for appeal" without any guide as to applicable criteria of "fitness" and the CCA must then be satisfied that a "sufficient ground of appeal" exists.[9] The fact that differing language is used in both provisions is already a cause for some concern. These concerns are further aggravated if one considers the power of the CCA to order summary dismissal of an appeal under s 5 of the Criminal Procedure Act, 1993. In order to avoid summary dismissal under s 5, the appellant must satisfy a standard which is higher than that required for the granting of leave pursuant to s 31. As has been noted, leave may only be granted where a question of law is involved, where the trial appears to the court to have been unsatisfactory, or there appears to the court to be any other *sufficient ground* of appeal.[10] Under s 5 on the other hand, the Registrar of the Court may refer an application for summary determination where it "does not

[8] Section 32 of the Courts of Justice Act 1924. Despite the fact that, as will be discussed later, it is unclear whether the standards to be applied under s 31(i) and s 32 are the same, for the purposes of this argument, the author proposes to set aside that discussion and use the wording of the latter here as it provides a greater elucidation of the purpose of the leave stage.

[9] In addition to these problems, differences between the wording of s 31(i) and s 32 may also create difficulties. Although it is arguable that both require the same standard to be applied by the trial judge and CCA, it is also arguable they do not. Although, on one interpretation it could be argued that the "fitness" requirement encompasses all those requirements set out under s 32, one must nevertheless ask the question — if that was the case, why was no explicit reference made of such? Why were the criteria set down in s 32 made in relation to both provisions?

[10] Section 32 of the Courts of Justice Act 1924. Despite the fact that, as will be discussed later, it is unclear whether the standards to be applied under ss 31(i) and 32 are the same, for the purposes of this argument, the author proposes to set aside that discussion and use the wording of the latter here as it provides a greater elucidation of the purpose of the leave stage.

show *any substantial ground* of appeal".[11] Clearly, there is a difference between "substantial" grounds and "sufficient" ones.[12] Indeed, it seems anomalous to allow an appeal to be dismissed summarily for failure to satisfy a standard which is higher than that required for its dismissal during ordinary leave stage.

Indeed, the apparent difference in standards tends to remind one of similar differences in judicial review. For instance, whereas "ordinary" Order 84 judicial review requires a "sufficient interest", judicial review of planning decisions requires a "substantial interest". Simons has remarked that these different standards have had some probably unforeseen effects:

> It would appear that there has been a considerable narrowing of the gap between the leave stage and the substantive hearing, with the application for leave to apply for judicial review in respect of the planning legislation approximating more closely to that of the substantive hearing in conventional judicial review than to a leave application...In order to maintain the façade of some qualitative distinction between the two hearings, the High Court has had to resort to ingenuity.[13]

The relatively simple conclusion one can draw from this is that if the s 5 test, in fact, represents a higher standard than that required to get leave in the first place, then does that not go some way towards narrowing the gap between the leave stage and the hearing of the appeal itself? Indeed, if this is the case, how long will it be before the CCA becomes the object of criticism for "resorting to ingenuity" in order to "maintain the façade" of a tiered leave stage?[14]

There is one quite reasonable response to all this. If, for the moment, we focus on the "sufficient ground" test, the objection may run that in judicial review under

---

[11] Section 5(1) of the Criminal Procedure Act 1993.

[12] For example, the new standard to be satisfied at the leave stage for judicial review of planning matters pursuant to s 50 of the Planning and Development Act, 2001, is that of a "substantial interest". Compare that to the standard set for conventional judicial review proceedings, which is that of a "sufficient interest" – see Supreme Court's decision in *G v DPP* [1994] 1 IR 374, at pp 377–378. The difference between the two standards has been discussed in the Law Reform Commission's *Consultation Paper on the Judicial Review procedure* (LRC CP 20-2003).

[13] Simons, G, *Planning and Development Law*, at 378.

[14] This is assuming of course that s 5 is applied alongside ss 31(i) and 32. However, just like those provisions, it seems that s 5 too has yet to be applied.

Order 84, the applicant must show an "arguable case" and "sufficient interest".[15] These requirements can hardly be said to be precise, and yet the courts have applied them in a more or less consistent manner. So, what basis could on have for criticising the language of ss 31 and 32? If the relatively imprecise tests in judicial review can be applied in a more or less comprehensible manner, then why cannot the same be said about the tests at the leave stage in criminal appeals? The answer is that in judicial review, the courts have the relative luxury of applying the requirements of "arguable case" and "sufficient interest" in light of the fact that the purpose of the leave stage in such proceedings is to afford a "screening process of litigation against public authorities and officers".[16] The point is simply that judicial review has the benefit of *G v DPP* and other authorities which clearly spell out the rationale of the leave stage. Therefore, relatively indeterminate phrases such as "arguable case" and "sufficient interest" can be rendered relatively determinate because one knows what purpose they are meant to serve.

However, in the context of the criminal appeal process there is no such stated rationale. Why is there a leave stage? Is it there to weed out frivolous and vexatious cases? Or is the requirement to seek leave from the trial judge (with three days, it may be added) designed for administrative reasons—perhaps with a view to speeding up the appeals process? Indeed, the difficulty in understanding the rationale for the criminal leave stage is exacerbated by the presence of s 5 of the Criminal Procedure Act, 1993 which was discussed in brief above. The Working Group has argued that the purpose of s 5 is to "enable a certain number of utterly frivolous or unmeritorious appeals to be disposed of at an early stage by a single judge".[17] Whatever one may think about this, it creates the relatively disconcerting notion that a case which is "fit for appeal" is actually not a case with a "substantial ground of appeal". Further, if the purpose of the s 5 requirement (which it must be remembered is an *addition* to the ss 31 and 32 requirements) is to weed out utterly frivolous claims, then does this mean then that the function of the leave stage itself is *not* to weed out such claims? If this is the task of the CCA, then what is the function of the trial judge? If s 5 weeds out unmeritorious claims, then the leave stage seems to have no function.

---

15 *See* Order 84, rule 20(1) of the Rules of the Superior Courts 1986. Also see the dicta of Denham J in *G v DPP* [1994] 1 IR 374, at pp 377–378.

16 Per Denham J in *G v DPP* [1994] 1 IR 374, at p 382.

17 The Working Group on the Jurisdiction of the Courts, *The Criminal Jurisdiction of the Courts*, (May, 2003), at p 163, para 646.

To draw the strings together, the provisions governing the leave procedure are badly drafted. They do not offer any guide as to just what precise standard to be applied nor do they cast any light on the rationale or function behind the leave stage. They make it difficult to apply the requirements of leave and this is supported by the failure of the courts to apply them.[18] So, reform is clearly necessary—but what kind of reform?

If It Ain't Broke—Don't Fix It

It has to be conceded that compliance with the requirement of leave is a mere formality with no meaningful purpose.[19] If the trial judge rejects (which he or she invariably does) the application for leave, then if the ground of appeal is well founded, the CCA will treat the application for leave as the hearing of the appeal itself. Therefore, one may retort that "if it ain't broke, don't fix it". In other words, the system, practically speaking, does not block cases that are fit for appeal. However, this pragmatic approach to law reform is at odds with prevailing legislative policy. The legislative impetus is clearly behind rendering legislation more "comprehensive" and "accessible" to the non-lawyer. A statute fails to achieve these objectives where its operation is arbitrary, without meaning and confusing to the general public. The government's zeal for this kind of "democratising" reform can be seen in a number of areas. For example, the Statute Law Revision Bill, due to be enacted later this year, seeks to repeal a number of obsolete antique laws, which have long fallen into disuse.[20] Indeed, it has been remarked of the leave stage that "a non-legal reader of the press is likely to believe that this refusal has some actual effect."[21] The "if it ain't broke" mentality is simply incompatible with the function of regulation and

[18] Indeed, this argument is supported by the fact that the leave requirement is a mere formality with no concrete connection to the provisions governing leave. The Working Group has also noted that s 5 of the 1993 Act has never been used—see The Working Group on the Jurisdiction of the Courts, *The Criminal Jurisdiction of the Courts* (May, 2003), at p 163, para 646.

[19] The Working Group on the Jurisdiction of the Courts, *The Criminal Jurisdiction of the Courts*, (May, 2003), at 162, paras 642–643.

[20] Including the Statute of Winchester, 1285, the Pillory Abolition Act, 1816 (allowed offenders to pay fines rather than spend time in the stocks), the Adulteration of Coffee Act, 1718 (sought to prevent the addition of water, grease or butter to roasted coffee to increase its weight), the Chimney Sweepers and Chimneys Regulation Act, 1840 (prohibited persons under age of 21 from engaging in such work) and the Children's Dangerous Performances Act, 1879—see Hennessey, M, *The Irish Times*, 26 November, 2004.

[21] The Working Group on the Jurisdiction of the Courts, *The Criminal Jurisdiction of the Courts*, (May, 2003), at p 162, para 642.

legislation in a modern democratic society. Simply because the appeals procedure seems to "work" on a day-to-day basis cannot, and should not, cast a sheet of ignorance over the flaws of the system.

Proposals for Reform

In its report on *The Criminal Jurisdiction of the Courts*, the Working Group on the Jurisdiction of the Courts[22] has recommended the outright abolition of the leave stage. In the remainder of this essay, it is argued that this is a step too far, and an alternative proposal is put forward. First, of course, some analysis of the Working Group's reasoning is necessary.

It is clear that the Working Group was influenced by the fact that the leave stage is an "entire fiction". However, in the end it seemed swayed by the fact that, even if substance was given to the leave procedure, it was unsure whether its retention would have any "practical" value. That is to say, the Working Group felt that the retention of any tiered-aspect to criminal appeals would not serve any purpose. The first critique one may make of this conclusion is that the Group failed to consider any evidence of whether a leave stage can save Court time. Although it did note that the British equivalent of the CCA grants leave in only about a quarter of all cases,[23] it had no regard to the recent *Review of the Crown Office List*,[24] which revealed that the leave procedure in judicial review applications in England had led to a significant saving in court time, which would otherwise have been taken up hearing unmeritorious claims.[25] It also failed to note the Law Reform Commission's suggestion that the leave stage provided a useful mechanism for achieving case management.[26] Maybe one should not be too hard on the Working Group in this respect. After all, this evidence was in the area of public law judicial review. However, it does emphasise one point. The Working Group clearly wanted to "get rid" of the leave stage. It did not consider whether its retention could serve any practical

---

[22] As set out in The Working Group on the Jurisdiction of the Courts, *The Criminal Jurisdiction of the Courts*, (May, 2003).

[23] The Working Group on the Jurisdiction of the Courts, *The Criminal Jurisdiction of the Courts*, (May, 2003), at p 162, para 643.

[24] Lord Chancellors Department (London, 2000).

[25] *ibid.*

[26] Law Reform Commission, *Consultation Paper on the Judicial Review Procedure* (LRC CP 20-2003), at p 12.

purpose. This, it is submitted, was a mistake. The Working Group failed to see the potential the leave stage could have in providing a solution to a different problem the CCA is experiencing at present.

An endemic problem in the criminal appeals process relates to the drafting of notices of appeal. Each appeal to the CCA must contain a reasonably detailed (although not as detailed as an affidavit may be) outline of the grounds of appeal. The CCA itself has issued a stern practice direction scorning counsel for sloppiness in the timely submission of the notice of appeal.[27] Indeed, the Working Group has noted that many notices of applications for leave to appeal against conviction do not, in practice, include properly formulated grounds of appeal. This is usually because convicted persons often want to change legal representation after the trial and as a result, submit their own applications from prison. As, at present, the CCA hearing of the leave stage is effectively treated as the appeal itself, there is no difference between the time it takes to hear an appeal and an application for leave to appeal. Thus, it is likely that notices of appeal will also oftentimes be badly drafted. In fact, the Working Group has noted that,

> In practice, the appellants or applicants send almost all notices of appeal or applications from prison. They use the printed forms but they rarely formulate any recognisable, legally relevant grounds of appeal.[28]

It went on to note that:

> A possible and practical approach would be to introduce a rule to the effect that, where the notice of appeal does not contain the grounds, the appeal will not be treated as effective and that no further steps shall be taken to process it until properly stated grounds are lodged.[29]

In light of these remarks, it is clear that a procedure to ensure that notices are well drafted would be a welcome one.

A reformed leave procedure could carry out this function. In short, it is submitted that it would be workable and sensible for the trial judge to fulfil a screening function

---

[27] *Practice Direction on Written Submissions on Legal Issues*, 11 December, 2000.

[28] The Working Group on the Jurisdiction of the Courts, *The Criminal Jurisdiction of the Courts*, (May, 2003), at p 152, para 603.

[29] At p 154, para 610.

in evaluating the extent to which notices of appeal are properly drafted. The trial judge would have no function in respect of the merits of the grounds stated therein, but would restricted to deciding whether the grounds were sufficiently stated in order to allow the CCA to fulfil its appellate function. This proposal has several worthwhile consequences. In the first place, it would go some way towards meeting the concerns of the CCA in respect of badly drafted notices of appeal. As it stands, the CCA has no ability to "send back" notices of appeal for re-drafting and this has caused great problems once the matter comes to trial. The sole fact that the CCA had to warn counsel against introducing grounds of appeal on the day of trial tends to prove this. It is submitted that it is just and sensible that the CCA should be able to assume that the document submitted to it constitutes the appellants proper grounds of appeal, and that the document is, to put it bluntly, "good to go".

Second, it would remove the trial judge from having any role in considering the merits of an appeal. As it stands, it is arguably approaching objective bias that the trial judge should have any role in deciding whether the trial he has just conducted was faulty or not.

Third, the problem of "prisoners" notice of appeal will be removed. As the Working Group noted, the desire to change counsel pursuant to a conviction sometimes leads prisoners to draft their own notices. However, there is no intermediary body to check these notices. The CCA must simply take them as they get them. That is surely unsatisfactory and time consuming for one of the busiest courts in the land.

Fourth, as he is familiar with the facts of the case, the trial judge will be able to determine whether the grounds disclose enough information about the case to enable the CCA to discharge its function. Thus, it is submitted that if a convicted person wishes to appeal his conviction he must first submit his notice of appeal to the trial judge for evaluation. If the notice of appeal meets the appropriate standards of clarity and expression then this appeal must be automatically forwarded to the CCA. Under this procedure, there is no role for the trial judge to refuse an appeal "on the merits".

To achieve this worthwhile reform of the leave stage, several matters must be addressed. In the first instance, it will be clearly necessary to abolish the requirement that an appellant obtain leave to appeal from the CCA in the event that the trial judge refuses it. Under the proposed system, the trial judge will have no such function. The requirement of obtaining a certificate that the case is "fit" for appeal from the trial judge should be retained. However, a case that is "fit" for appeal should be understood as one that is accompanied by a properly drafted and completed notice of appeal. So, the definition of "fitness" should require adherence to a particular format, as well as the inclusion of relevant legal grounds and terminology. Although a judge may have regard to a model notice of appeal (perhaps to be set out in a Schedule attached to s 31), failure to strictly follow that model should not prevent an appeal from progressing. In summary, the definition should be general enough to leave the question of satisfaction of this requirement largely at the judge's discretion,[30] while also leaving him in no doubt about the intention behind this requirement.

As the law stands, an application for leave to appeal must be made to the trial judge within three days of the conviction. It is submitted that if the trial judge's function is to be reformed as suggested, this time period is too short. However, if the above proposals for reform were implemented, the task of submitting one's notice of appeal within three days to the trial judge would be hard to carry out. Instead, a more realistic time frame should be implemented. Indeed, the advantages of this may be seen elsewhere—as the Working Group has noted, a failure to submit properly formulated grounds can result in an appeal becoming side-tracked. It may be listed to explain delay or adjourned generally with liberty to re-enter.

ECHR Compatibility

The Working Group argued that any restrictions on the right of appeal may be incompatible with the European Convention on Human Rights. Whilst it is true that Article 2 of Protocol 7 states that such a right exists, it continues to state that this right can be subject to domestic regulation. Indeed, as Jacob and White point out, the travaux preparatories of Protocol 7 indicates that the regulatory power reserved to the State was designed to allow the English leave procedure to remain consonant with Convention obligations. Further, the proposals for reform advanced here to do not strike at the "core" of the right to appeal but merely regulate it in the manner which Protocol 7 allows. There is no denial of the right to appeal by requiring compliance with a set of procedures which make the very right itself workable.

Conclusion

The Minister for Justice recently introduced proposals for the creation of a Criminal Law Codification Advisory Committee. The establishment of this body was the main

[30] After all, with their legal expertise, it is likely that judges would be in the best position to ascertain whether a notice of appeal is badly drafted or not.

recommendation in a report of an expert group on the codification of the criminal law, received by the Minister in December, 2004. Welcoming its publication, the Minister has said:

> The publication of th[is] report paves the way for the transformation of our criminal law into a comprehensive body of knowledge that meets the often-cited codification objectives of making the law more accessible, comprehensible, consistent and certain.[31]

It is submitted that the Criminal Law Codification Advisory Committee should pay particular attention to reforming the leave procedure. Codification is a sensible endeavour, but it makes little sense to waste time and resources codifying a useless law. It is submitted that proposals for reforming the leave stage to ensure proper procedural compliance serves very worthwhile goals. It answers the concerns of the CCA in respect of poorly drafted notices of appeal and will alleviate part of the CCA's ever increasing work-load, whilst at the same time remaining true to Ireland's obligations under the ECHR.

[31] Coulter, C, *The Irish Times*, 29 December, 2004.

Gender and the Formation of a Marriage: Tying the Knot, or Tied up in Knots?

by
Paul Hutchinson*

"*Tempora mutantur, et nos mutamurin illis*"[1]

Marriage was defined[2] by Lord Penzance in *Hyde v Hyde and Woodmansee*[3] as "the voluntary union for life of one man and one woman to the exclusion of all others".[4] This was cited with approval by Costello J in the High Court case of *B v R*,[5] and by the Supreme Court in *Murray v Ireland*.[6] However, it is a troublesome formula. It provides little assistance in light of the difficult questions posed since the mid 20th century about the gender make-up of marriage — namely the issues of same-sex unions, and the position of transsexuals in the marital unit.

---

* LL.B. (Dub.), Final Year Degree student at the King's Inns. My thanks are due to Dr Fergus Ryan, Trinity College Dublin Law School, for whom this paper was originally written as part of his course on Family Law. Any errors that appear are the responsibility of the author alone. This essay was awarded a prize by the Law Society of Ireland for the *Student Law Reform Essay Competition 2005*.

[1] "Times are changing, and we are changing with them" (Ovid).

[2] See Cretney and Masson, *Principles of Family Law* (6th ed, Sweet and Maxwell, 1997), at p 51–54.

[3] [1861–1873] All ER 176.

[4] The case concerned the refusal by the English Matrimonial Court to recognise as valid a polygamous marriage contracted in Salt Lake City, Utah by a Mormon as it did not amount to a marriage "as understood in Christendom" (despite being valid under the *lex loci*) and hence the suit seeking enforcement of matrimonial duties and relief for a breach of matrimonial obligations was ill-conceived. See also, *Morrison v Sadler* 821 NE 2d 15 (Indiana Court of Appeal, 2003).

[5] [1995] 1 ILRM 491.

[6] [1985] IR 532. See generally, Shatter's *Family Law* (Butterworths, 1997), at p 151.

Dissent at the perceived lack of willingness by the courts in the United Kingdom and America to embrace change has been persistently vocal[7] in media and academic discourse. For example, Veitch notes that "the existing law continues to mirror [those] outdated and questionable assumptions."[8] However, these remain dissenting voices only, and a widespread change in public opinion seems, as yet, elusive.

The issue of gender in the formation of a marriage has two distinct limbs:

(i) Whether transsexuals are considered members of their original or assumed sex for the purposes of marriage.
(ii) Whether same-sex marriages should be recognised in law?
(iii) Wider issues about the impact of transsexuality on a person's legal status remain similarly unresolved,[9] but are distinct from the scope of this essay.

The Position in the United Kingdom and Ireland

The leading common law judgment is that of *Corbett v Corbett (Otherwise Ashley)*.[10] The fact that the leading case is a 30-year-old decision is itself an ominous sign in any analysis of the law in this area. The case concerned the validity of a marriage between a Scottish aristocrat and the 1960s model April Ashley, a male to female transsexual who had undergone gender reassignment surgery prior to the marriage. The marriage ultimately failed and the petitioner sought a decree of nullity partly on the ground that the parties were both male and therefore lacked capacity to marry. In the course of the trial, medical experts gave evidence that there were a number of competing tests as regards a person's gender encompassing both the physical and the psychological.[11] Ormrod LJ delivered the judgment of the Court, which held that as regards one's "legal" gender, the relevant test was a purely biological one determined at birth by reference to three factors: the chromosomal, anatomical and gonadal features of the subject. The Court further reasoned as follows:[12]

---

[7] See Moloney, "Give Gay Couples 'Marriage' Rights, Ministers are Urged", *Irish Independent*, 4 June 2003; Kinsley, "Marriage is the next Thing on the Agenda as Homosexuals seek Equality", *Irish Times*, 7 July 2003; Ashley and Wilson, "Gay Rights: Legal Boost for Same-Sex Partners Heralds Social Revolution", *Guardian*, 30 June 2003; and "The War over Gay Marriage", *Newsweek*, 7 July 2003.

[8] Veitch, "The Essence of Marriage – A Comment on the Homosexual Challenge" (1976) 5 *Anglo-American Law Review* 41.

[9] For example, the status of such individuals' birth certificates and other official documentation.

[10] [1971] P 83 (PDA); [1970] 2 All ER 33.

[11] See Diduck and Kaganas, *Family Law, Gender and the State* (Hart Publishing, 1999), at p 49.

[12] [1970] 2 All ER at 48.

> "Sex is clearly an essential determinant of the relationship called marriage, because it is and always has been recognised as the union of one man and one woman. It is the institution on which the family is built, and in which the capacity for natural heterosexual intercourse is an essential element."

The decision has been heavily criticised and indeed it this is understandable. As Diduck and Kaganas point out:[13]

> "This positivistic form of legal reasoning demonstrates a conservative approach to the judicial role and the power of judicial rhetoric to accept a contention as axiomatic and thus dismiss any need for evidence to prove it or legal authority to validate it."

This approach became the standard for determining legal gender in the wake of the *Corbett* decision. In *R. v Tan,*[14] the defendant attempted an imaginative defence to a charge of being a man living of the earning of prostitution on the basis he had undergone a sex-change operation and was now a woman. In the Court of Appeal, Parker J followed precedent and gave the argument little weight, rejecting the "submission without hesitation" despite the contention that the defendant was "philosophically or psychologically or socially female".[15]

In *Bellinger v Bellinger,*[16] Johnson J in the English High Court[17] declined the opportunity to depart from *Corbett* in refusing a declaration that a man and his transsexual wife were validly married. The Court refused to be persuaded that advances in medical science made the existing test redundant. The Court accepted the Attorney General's submission that parliamentary intervention was required for a change in the law to come about.[18]

The leading modern Irish decision is that of McKechnie J in the High Court case of *Foy v An t-Ard Chlaraitheoir & others.*[19] The Applicant here was a dentist, Dr Lydia

---

[13] Diduck and Kaganas, *op. cit,* at, 50.

[14] [1983] 2 All ER 12

[15] *ibid* at 19.

[16] *The Times,* 22 November 2000.

[17] Family Division.

[18] See also *R v Registrar General for Births, Deaths and Marriages for England and Wales, ex parte P and G* (*Independent,* 22 February 1996) where the Queen's Bench Division once again upheld the *Corbett* test.

[19] Unreported, High Court (McKechnie J), 9 July 2002.

Foy, who was registered at birth as being of the male sex with the chosen Christian name of Donal Mark. The Applicant married, and fathered two children, but contended that from a young age he suffered from a gender identity crisis, and underwent gender-reassignment surgery in 1992. The Applicant sought a High Court declaration to the effect that that Applicant was born female, but with a congenital disability which was both unidentified and undiscovered, and an order rectifying what was alleged to be a fundamental error in the record of the applicant's birth. McKechnie J refused to accept the argument that brain differentiation is a scientifically proven indicator of gender and instead followed the English authorities, which favour purely biological indicators.[20] On the issue of preserving the integrity of public records, McKechnie J held that[21]:

> "Every modern society must be entitled to have a means of obtaining and thereafter recording vital particulars which surround the birth of its citizens and all others born in its country. The resulting register is a document of historical value, being current only at the date of birth and not beyond. It is no more than that. It is not a continuum record of one's travels through life or even of the most important and most significant events of that journey. It is, it has been said 'a snap shot' of matters on a particular day and does not purport to be otherwise".

The decision in *Foy* was subject to some unfortunate timing[22] as the *prima facie* conflicting European Court of Human Rights decision in the *Goodwin* case[23] was delivered a mere two days later. However, perhaps *Foy* can be distinguished on its facts in that it concerned amendments to personal official documents charting historical events in an individual's life. The impact of *Goodwin* is assessed below, but perhaps reconciliation can be found in limiting State interference in a person's rights by registering their assumed gender on future official documents while reserving the right the leave documents created prior to gender-reassignment surgery in their unaltered state. Under this analysis, a post-operative transsexual would have no grounds for insisting upon amendment of official documents before any surgery, and it would therefore follow that the State would be vested with the right to record an individual's gender as it was at a given point in time. To do otherwise is to endorse a fiction.

---

20 *ibid* at para 121.

21 *ibid* at para 170.

22 See Ryan's editorial [2002] 4 IJFL 1.

23 Unreported, ECHR 7th July 2002—discussed below.

Judicial statements on the legal prohibition of homosexual, or "same-sex", marriages are scarce. However, the illegality of such marriages is undoubtedly implicit from the cases which focus on gender-reassignment—one need only think back to the unequivocal terms of Lord Penzance's definition of "marriage" in *Hyde v Hyde*. However, on 9 November 2004, McKechnie J in the High Court granted a lesbian couple leave to judicially review a decision by the Revenue Commissioners to treat them as unmarried for taxation purposes.[24] The result of the substantive hearing is awaited with anticipation.

The Position in the United States

It is instructive to examine the transatlantic experience on the issue, as the focus of the legal analysis has been same-sex marriage, as opposed to the treatment of post-operative transsexuals. The traditional common law starting point can be seen from the decisions of *Anoymous v Anonymous*[25] and, more importantly, in "the precedent-setting"[26] *Baker v Nelson*,[27] which concerned the rights of transsexual persons and same-sex couples to marry respectively. In *Baker*, the constitutionality of the Minnesota licensing statute was upheld and a prohibition on same-sex marriages implied via statutory reference to "words of heterosexual import." The Court found that there had been no violation of the 14th Amendment.[28] The Minnesota Supreme Court noted that marriage had always been considered "a heterosexual union" and pointed to procreation as the purpose behind the institution. Justice Peterson was adamant that the Petitioners' argument that the right to marry without regard to the sex of the parties is a fundamental right of all persons and that

---

24 Zappone & Gilligan v Revenue Commissioners; see Carolan, "Lesbian Couple Can Challenge Status", *The Irish Times*, 10 November 2004.

25 325 NYS 2d 499 (New York Supreme Court, 1971).

26 Green and Long, *Marriage and Family Law Agreements* (Shepard's and McGraw-Hill, 1984), at p 33.

27 191 NW 2d 185 (Minnesota Supreme Court, 1971).

28 The Fourteenth Amendment to the US Constitution was ratified on 9 July 1868 and designed to give full legal effect to the Emancipation Proclamation. The first clause reads as follows: "All persons born or naturalized in the United States, and subject to the jurisdiction thereof, are citizens of the United States and of the State wherein they reside. No State shall make or enforce any law which shall abridge the privileges or immunities of citizens of the United States; nor shall any State deprive any person of life, liberty, or property, without due process of law; nor deny to any person within its jurisdiction the equal protection of the laws." See *Dean v District of Columbia* 653 A.2d 307 (DC, 1995).

restricting marriage to only couples of the opposite sex is irrational and invidiously discriminatory was unpersuasive, and not supported by United States Supreme Court authority.[29]

> "The institution of marriage as a union man and woman, uniquely involving the procreation and rearing of children within a family, is as old as the book of Genesis. [The case of] *Skinner v. Oklahoma ex rel. Williamson*... stated in part: 'Marriage and procreation are fundamental to the very existence and survival of the race.' This historic institution manifestly is more deeply founded than the asserted contemporary concept of marriage and societal interests for which petitioners contend. The due process clause of the Fourteenth Amendment is not a charter for restructuring it by judicial legislation."

This analysis remains the prevalent one, as evidenced by the decision of the New York Appellate Division in *Storrs v Holcomb*,[30] which cited a "political, cultural, religious and legal consensus" opposed to the recognition of same-sex marriages as demonstrated by the long tradition of marriage as traditionally understood (i.e. between a man and a woman) amongst the states of the Union.

In *Jones v Hallahan*,[31] the Kentucky Court of Appeal affirmed the decision of a lower court in refusing a marriage licence to two lesbians on the basis that the ceremony proposed "is not marriage." Similarly, in *Adams v Howerton*,[32] "immediate relative" immigration status was refused to an Australian man who claimed to be the spouse of an American man on foot of having participated in a ceremonial "marriage" conducted by a clergyman in Colorado.

However, the decision in *Adams* must be read in light of the decision in *Braschi v Stahl Associates*,[33] which allowed the surviving partner of a gay man to inherit his rent-controlled property as a "close family member". However, this was limited by *Gajovski v Gajovski*,[34] where the Ohio Court of Appeal refused to terminate a

[29] 191 NW2d 185 (Minnesota Supreme Court, 1971) at para 2 (edited by author).

[30] 645 NYS2d 286 (New York Appellate Division, 1996).

[31] 501 SW2d 588 (Kentucky Court of Appeal, 1973).

[32] 486 F Supp 1119 (Central District California 1980).

[33] 74 NY2d 201 (New York Court of Appeals, 1989).

[34] 610 NE2d 431 (Ohio Court of Appeals, 1991).

maintenance order in favour of the petitioner's ex-wife on the basis that she was in "concubinage" with a third party. The Court found that this was impossible for the same reasons that she could not marry another woman.[35] While these cases are interesting barometers of judicial attitude, they largely concern questions of statutory interpretation and therefore tend to avoid the central issue of the gender competent of the marital unity.

As regards the rights of transsexual persons to marry, there is some competing authority at play. The New Jersey Superior Court held in *MT v JT*[36] that a transsexual could marry as the transition from female to male that she had undergone preserved the status of marriage as a union between one man and one woman. The Court in the course of its judgment stated:[37]

> "[W]e must disagree with the conclusion reached in *Corbett* that for the purposes of marriage sex is somehow irrevocably cast at the moment of birth, and that for adjudging the capacity to enter marriage, sex in its biological sense should be the exclusive standard…[A] person's sex or sexuality embraces an individual's gender, that is, one's self-image, the deep psychological or emotional sense of sexual identity and character. Indeed, it has been observed that the "psychological sex of an individual", while not serviceable for all purposes, is "practical, realistic and humane".

However, in *Landrach, Re,*[38] the Ohio Probate Court came to the opposite conclusion, denying a man who had undergone gender re-assignment surgery the right to marry another man as it would in effect amount to an illegal same-sex marriage.[39]

An interesting modern analysis of the issue of gender and the formation of a marriage is evident from the Hawaiian Supreme Court case of *Baehr v Lewin.*[40] The Court was frank about the judicial task facing it, Judge Levison noting that[41]:

---

35 See also the decision in *FitzPatrick v Sterling Housing Association* [1999] 3 WLR 1113.

36 355 A.2d 204 (New Jersey Superior Court, Appellate Division, 1976).

37 *ibid* at 209.

38 573 NE2d 828 (Ohio Probate Court, 1987).

39 A similar conclusion was reached in *Estate of Gardiner, In Re,* 42 P3d 120 (Kansas Court of Appeals, 2002).

40 852 P.2d 44 (Hawaii Supreme Court, 1993).

41 *ibid.*

> "[T]he precise question facing this court is whether we will extend the *present* boundaries of the fundamental right of marriage to include same-sex couples, or, put another way, whether we will hold that same-sex couples possess a fundamental right to marry."

The Court held that the applicant couples did not enjoy "a fundamental constitutional right to same-sex marriage arising out of the right to privacy or otherwise",[42] but rather that the State laws prohibiting same-sex marriages were unconstitutional in light of the equal protection clause of the Hawaiian Constitution, unless the State could demonstrate "compelling" public interest in the law's continuance. The case was sent back to be retired the Hawaiian State Court[43] found the relevant statute unconstitutional and without justification.[44] The decision had potentially radical consequences in the United States as the US Constitution provides for "full faith and credit" to be given to the internal administrative and judicial decisions of the individual States. However, this was prevented by an amendment to the Hawaiian Constitution, which restricted the right to marry to heterosexual couples and provided for diluted recognition of Hawaiian civil partnerships by way of compromise.[45]

However, in February 2004, the Massachusetts Supreme Court found in the case of *Goodridge v Massachusetts Department of Public Health*[46] that the State "failed to identify any constitutionally adequate reason" for denying homosexual couples the right to marry. The Massachusetts state legislature was given six months to amend local marriage laws to accommodate this change. However, even as the first marriage licences are issued[47], campaigning has begun for a referendum set for 2006 to amend the Massachusetts Constitution and formally outlaw same-sex unions.[48]

---

[42] A similar conclusion was reached in the Arizona decision of *Standhardt v Superior Court ex. rel. County of Maricopa* 77 P 3d 451 (Ariz. App. 2003).

[43] Judge Kevin Chang in December 1996.

[44] http://www.lgirtf.org/newsletters/Winter97/W3.html (visited 1 February 2003). The decision was subsequently upheld on appeal.

[45] See the Defense of Marriage Act 1996. An almost identical decision was reached in the Alaskan case of *Brause v Bureau of Vital Statistics*, 1998 WL 88743 (Alaska Supreme Court, 1998), but this too was superseded by a swift amendment to the Alaskan State Constitution.

[46] 440 Mass. 309; 798 NE2d 941 (2003).

[47] Kilroy, "First US Gay Marriages Take Place", *Irish Times*, 17 May 2004.

[48] http://www.cnn.com/2003/LAW/11/18/samesex.marriage.ruling (visited 29 January 2004).

In 2004, a Federal Marriage Amendment, which would constitutionally define marriage as consisting "only of the union of a man and a woman" and prohibiting state legislatures from making their own determinations on marriage for same-sex couples, was voted down by both the House and Senate, however this constitutional amendment was reintroduced in the Senate on the 24 January 2005 and is pending at the time of writing.[49]

The European Court of Human Rights—The Impetus for Change?

The European Court of Human Rights[50] has taken an initially cautious approach when dealing with the issue of transsexuality and marriage. However, recent developments, in line with advances in medical understanding, have "marked the reversal of previous caselaw".[51]

In *Rees v United Kingdom,*[52] the applicant was born a female but from an early age started to develop male characteristics. She began hormone treatment and changed name. Thereafter, the applicant lived, for all intents and purposes, as a man. In 1974, the applicant underwent gender re-assignment surgery and in 1980, tried to have his personal identity documents altered to reflect his assumed gender, however the Registrar General refused to alter his birth certificate as no clerical error had occurred at its creation. The applicant claimed that there had been a breach of Art 8[53] and Art 12[54] of the Convention. In applying a margin of appreciation to the issue, the ECHR held that no violation of either article had occurred:[55]

49 See http://www.hrc.org/Template.cfm?Section=Federal_Constitutional_Marriage_Amendment&Template=/TaggedPage/TaggedPageDisplay.cfm&TPLID=23&ContentID=17018 and http://en.wikipedia.org/wiki/Federal_Marriage_Amendment (both viewed 20 August 2005).

50 Hereafter the ECHR.

51 Ryan, *loc. cit,* at 1.

52 (1987) 9 EHRR 56.

53 Art 8 of the European Convention on Human Rights reads: "Everyone has a right to respect for his private and family life, his home and his correspondence."

54 Art 12 of the European Convention on Human Rights reads: "Men and women of marriageable age have a right to marry and to found a family, according to the national laws governing the exercise of this right."

55 (1987) 9 EHRR 56.

> "[I]t must for the time being be left to the respondent State to determine to what extent it can meet the remaining demands of transsexuals. However, the Court is conscious of the seriousness of the problems affecting these persons and the distress they suffer...The need for appropriate legal measures should therefore be kept under review having regard particularly to scientific and societal developments."

In *Cossey v United Kingdom,*[56] the applicant was born a male but later underwent the necessary hormonal treatment and operation, and subsequently went on to become a successful model.[57] She wished to marry her Italian fiancé but was informed by the Registrar General that she would be considered male for these purposes. In a subsequent relationship, she purported to marry another man in a London synagogue. The relationship broke down, and the applicant sought a decree *nisi* from the High Court. The Court found the marriage to be void on the ground that it was conducted between two male persons, and the applicant contended that a violation of human rights. However, the Court felt it was unable to distinguish the *Rees* case:[58]

> "The Court has been informed of no significant scientific developments that have occurred in the meantime; in particular, it remains the case – as was not contested by the applicant – that gender reassignment surgery does not result in the acquisition of all the biological characteristics of the other sex."

Furthermore, as regards the alleged violation of Art 12, the Court held: "[a]s to the applicant's inability to marry a woman, this does not stem from any legal impediment and...it cannot be said that the right to marry has been impaired as a consequence of the provisions of domestic law".[59]

A number of subsequent decisions point to a change in direction for the ECHR. Firstly, the decision of *B v France*[60] held that although the substance of the case was indistinguishable from *Rees* and *Cossey,* the French authorities had breached their

56 (1991) 13 EHRR 622.

57 Interestingly, her career peaked with a role as a "Bond girl" in the film "For Your Eyes Only".

58 *ibid* at 503.

59 *ibid* at 504.

60 (1992) 16 EHRR 1.

margin of appreciation in delimiting the applicant's rights to privacy and awarded her damages. In *Sheffield and Horsham v United Kingdom,*[61] the ECHR held that the UK authorities had failed in their duty to set up "appropriate legal measures…to keep the area under review".[62]

However, it was only in the case of *Goodwin & I v United Kingdom*[63] that a major shift in the law occurred. The case concerned a complaint by a male to female post-operative transsexual who alleged that the failure of the British authorities to allow the birth certificates of transsexuals to be amended to reflect their assumed identity infringed her rights under Art 8 insofar as the embarrassment of her unaltered birth certificate effectively precluded her from obtaining certain benefits (for example, life insurance). She furthermore contended that her right to marry (as protected by Art 12) had been infringed by the same failure.

The ECHR indicated a move away from the reliance on congruent biological factors in determining an individual's gender, and held that such factors could no longer be decisive in denying legal recognition to the change of gender of a post-operative transsexual [64]:

> "The medical and surgical acts…were indeed carried out under the supervision of the national health authorities. Nor, given the numerous and painful interventions involved in such surgery and the level of commitment and conviction required to achieve a change in social gender role, can it be suggested that there is anything arbitrary or capricious in the decision taken by a person to undergo gender re-assignment. In those circumstances, the ongoing scientific and medical debate as to the exact causes of the condition is of diminished relevance."

The ECHR was of the opinion that it followed that a State has a duty to reflect this change in gender on the personal documents of the individual.[65]

---

61 [1998] ECHR 69 (30 July 1998).

62 *ibid* at para 60.

63 [2002] ECHR 583 (7 July 2002).

64 *ibid* at para 81.

65 *ibid* at paras 86–88. The personal records would appear to include: driving licences; medical records; student records, revenue and insurance records, and (crucially in light of the *Foy* decision) birth certificates.

The ECHR furthermore accepted that the terms of Art 12 of the Convention refer "in express terms to the right of a man and woman to marry", but assessed the impact of the "congruent biological features" gender-identity test as follows:[66]

> "The Court has therefore considered whether the allocation of sex in national law to that registered at birth is a limitation impairing the very essence of the right to marry in this case. In that regard, it finds that it is artificial to assert that post-operative transsexuals have not been deprived of the right to marry as, according to law, they remain able to marry a person of their former opposite sex."

While finding no objective justification for barring the transsexual from enjoying the right to marry under any circumstances, the ECHR nevertheless held that it is for the contracting State to determine the conditions under which a person claiming legal recognition as a transsexual establishes that gender reassignment has been properly effected.[67]

It is worth noting that, as a result of this decision, the legal impediments to transsexuals seeking to wed and homosexual couples hoping to do likewise diverge. The *Goodwin* decision clearly removes the conceptual barrier to transsexual persons as regards the formation of a valid marriage, but the tenor of the judgment is to accept advances in medicine and understanding of the psychology of sexual identity to bring these persons within the existing definition of marriage. The decision does not elasticise the definition of marriage to include a wider combination of genders *per se*. It merely obliges the State to consider persons who undergo the full rigors of gender reassignment as full members of their assumed gender.[68] A shift in legal attitude appears to have taken place for transsexual persons,[69] rescuing them from "legal and social *no-man's land*".[70]

As regards homosexual couples, it seems that the definition of marriage itself is the obstacle and potential change raises a number of different arguments and concerns from both sociological and legal perspectives.

---

66 *ibid* at para 101.

67 *ibid* at para 103.

68 Presumably including the right to marry that membership of that gender entails.

69 Although, as the decisions of the ECHR are not directly binding, it remains to be seen how it will be received in domestic law.

70 Ryan, "Marriage at the Boundaries of Gender: The 'Transsexual Dilemma' Resolved?" [2004] 1 IJFL 15 at 16.

Sociology and Same-Sex Marriages

Whether or not recognition of homosexual marriages is sociologically desirable is subject to fierce academic debate.[71] Wilson dismisses the idea that a parallel can be drawn between this issue and racial integration[72] as "popular attitudes toward sexuality are [anyway] quite different from those about race".[73] The essence of his argument is that one of fertility—not that capacity for child-rearing, or desire to have children is a pre-condition for a valid heterosexual marriage, but rather an acknowledgment of the heterosexual marital unit as (in his opinion) the best environment for this purpose:[74]

> "The role of raising children is entrusted in principle to married heterosexual couples because after much experimentation – several thousand years, more or less – we have found nothing that works as well. Neither a gay nor a lesbian couple can of its own resources produce a child; another party must be involved"

Mohr argues the contrary[75] and concentrates instead on an analysis of the essence of marriage to prove that each of the constituent elements he identified can be fulfilled by gay or lesbian couples.[76] On the child-rearing issue, he points out that there is no prohibition on heterosexuals who are incapable of having children marrying, nor is there any particular endorsement of polygamous marriages which can be very efficient child-rearing units.[77]

---

71 As indeed does the issue have moral and religious implications, for example see: Lichfield, "Pope Calls for Battle against Gay Marriages", *Irish Independent*, 1 August 2003, and "Bush Condemns Push for Same Sex Weddings", *ibid.* The author has endeavoured to avoid such argument, save where it has a legal philosophical bearing (see below).

72 See Wilson, "Against Homosexual Marriage" in *Morals, Marriage and Parenthood* (Houlgate ed, Wadsworth Publishing Company, 1999), at pp 78–81.

73 Wilson, *loc. cit*, at 79.

74 Wilson, *loc. cit*, at 80. As against this, the fact that an inability to procreate is not a bar to a valid heterosexual marriage must be borne in mind.

75 Mohr, "The Case for Gay Marriage" in Houlgate (ed.), *op. cit*, at pp 81–87.

76 Mohr states that gender-equality is, by definition, fulfilled by same-sex couples and that the legal recognition of relationship "based on the presence and blending of necessity and intimacy" can similarly be attained.

77 Mohr, *loc. cit*, at 83.

Coltrane makes a different, but nevertheless interesting, point.[78] He notes that none of the competing theories linking State, family and gender[79] offer a full description of family policy in modern, Western nations and that there is an evolutionary link between change in social custom and change in the law; "it is also true that when taken-for-granted practices associated with marriage begin to change, pressure mounts to change marriage laws".[80]

Legal Philosophy and Same-Sex Marriages

The question must also be viewed from a jurisprudential perspective. In a fully functioning democracy, the laws of the land are meant to reflect the moral norms of its people. As Abrahams dryly puts it; "the man on the Clapham omnibus…is a fairly sophisticated fellow these days".[81] As such, if a fundamental shift in public attitude to a social issue such as the gender-makeup of the marital unit occurs, this should resonate in the government elected by those people and duly the change in the law should come to pass. In a very real sense, popular silence on a supposedly burning area of reform is indicative of acquiescence of the *status quo*. This issue was alluded to quite properly by Lord Hope in the Scottish Court of Sessions case of *T, Petitioner, Re*[82] where he stated that:

> "Where public policy stands on homosexuality is a matter for the court to determine from the material placed before it and then to apply, so far as relevant, to the facts of the case. So the judge may examine such material as the intendment of the Act and decisions and dicta in other cases in order to discover objectively what, if anything, public policy has to say on the issue. In that exercise he is performing a judicial function on behalf of the court. What he must not do is permit his own personal views, or his own private beliefs, to affect his judgment"

Would it then be an undemocratic leap for the judiciary to pre-empt a definite shift in the public appreciation of the marital norm? Surely if reform of the law in this

78 Coltrane, *Gender and Families* (Pine Forge Press, 1998), at pp 134–159.

79 Namely the pluralist, conflict and patriarchy theories.

80 Coltrane, *op. cit*, at 150.

81 Abrahams, *Morality and the Law* (Calder and Boyars, 1971), at p 15.

82 (1997) SLT 724 at 736. This passage was quoted with approval by Waite LJ in the English Court of Appeal decision of *Fitzpatrick v Sterling Housing Association* [1998] FLR 6 at 18.

area weighed heavily on the majority of Irish persons' minds it would be a pressing election issue. The link between societal morality (such that it exists) and the law is an interesting but complex one. Fuller points to the "view of man implicit in the internal morality of law"[83] in his analysis of the substantive aims of law, while Foot concludes pithily that:[84]

> "[*m*]*oral judgment* is for the most part a term of art. What is clear is that the expression of approval and disapproval is part of the complex phenomenon we call *morality*, and that if approval and disapproval are essentially social…then the morality we are trying to analysis is so too."

It is not the purpose of this essay to resolve the question of the precise nature of the relationship between law and collective morality. Suffice to note the theoretical tension between advocating radical social change on one hand, and the risk of undemocratic usurpation of what could be viewed as a statement of public morality —or perhaps more accurately public approval.

Conclusion

In 2002, the British Lord Chancellor[85] announced proposals to accommodate transsexual people who can show they have taken "decisive steps towards living fully and permanently in their acquired gender".[86] There is much speculation in Britain as to whether the recognition of same-sex unions may be imminent[87] and, indeed, a consultation process began in the summer of 2003 to discuss whether a full civil partnership system would be appropriate in that jurisdiction.[88] This approach enjoys a major advantage over the current all-party Oireachtas Committee on the Constitution's current consultation process on what constitutes the "family" under

---

83 Fuller, *The Morality of Law* (Revised Edition, Yale University Press, 1969), at pp 162–167 generally; quote at p 162.

84 See Foot, *Approval and Disapproval* in *Law, Morality and Society: Essays in Honour of HLA. Hart* (Hacker and Raz eds, Clarendon Press, 1977), at p 229; quote at p 246 (emphasis in original).

85 Lord Irvine of Laird.

86 These changes will make it possible for such persons to marry in their assumed gender, claim state pensions at the appropriate age and request "updated" birth certificates: See http://www.lawtutorsonline.co.uk/news.htm.

87 The City of London Mayor, Ken Livingstone, for example, introduced a civic blessing scheme during his first term as a symbolic statement of his political beliefs on the subject.

88 "Gay Marriages: What Could Change?" http://www.bbc.co.uk/2/hi/uk_news/2549845.stm (visited on 1 February 2003).

Article 41 insofar as the equivalent British process is significantly more targeted than the Irish counterpart. The gender component in the marital unit is related to changing attitudes to the traditional family unit,[89] but the issue is characterised by conceptual complexities which are unique and demand distinct public attention.[90]

This confusing issue has troubled jurisdictions beyond those discussed hitherto. Australia,[91] New Zealand[92] and Scotland[93] have similarly disjointed jurisprudence, whilst the Netherlands[94] Belgium,[95] Canada,[96] Spain[97] and most recently, South Africa[98] are the only jurisdictions to formally recognise same-sex civil unions. There has been recent pressure from European Parliament when, on 8 June 2005, the Parliament voted to adopt a report on the protection of minorities and anti-discrimination policies in the EU, which urges that same-sex "marriages" which are legal in some member states receive recognition in all EU countries.[99] This adds an

---

89 Bacik, "Time to Re-Evaluate what Constitutes the Irish Family", *Irish Independent*, 28 May 2003.

90 See Sheridan, "A Modest Proposal", *Irish Times*, 7 June 2003.

91 The Australian Marriage Act 1961 and the Family Law Act 1975 are largely silent on the point because the male/female requirement is regarded as "axiomatic". The question involves an interpretation of s 51(xxi) of the Australian Constitution, and given that a similar result was reached in *Secretary DSS v SRA* (1993) 118 ALR 467 as was by the ECHR in *Goodwin* perhaps a trend is in the offing. See Finlay, Bailey-Harris and Otlowski *Family Law in Australia* (5th ed, Butterworths, 1997), at p 102–103.

92 In New Zealand a liberal attitude was taken in the question of the legal status of transsexuals in *Attorney General v Othuhu Family Court* [1995] 1 NZLR 603, where the view was taken that there was "no social advantage" in refusing to recognise marriages involving transsexuals and that it merely "confirms the factual reality" (See Diduck and Kaganas, *op. cit*, at p 53).

93 In Scotland, Clive considers that "there can be no doubt" that a marriage would be void if the parties were not respectively man and woman (Clive, *The Law of Husband and Wife in Scotland* (4th ed., W. Green, 1997), at p 76).

94 Article 30(1) of the Dutch Civil Code permits marriage between "persons of different sex or the same sex".

95 "Same-Sex Marriages: Belgium says *We Do*" See http://www.smhcom.au/articles/200/01/31/1043804509778.html (visited on the 1 February 2003).

96 Reuters, "Six of Canada's Ten Provinces Permit Gay Marriages", *Irish Times*, 6 November 2004.

97 "Spanish MP's Approve Gay Marriages", see http://news.bbc.co.uk/2/hi/europe/4636133.stm (visited on the 20 August 2005).

98 *Minister of Home Affairs and Another v Marie Adriaana Fourie and Another*, Unreported, (Constitutional Court) Case no. 232/2003.

99 See http://www2.europarl.eu.int/omk/sipade2?SAME_LEVEL=1&LEVEL=4&NAV=X&DETAIL=&PUBREF=-//EP//TEXT+TA+P6-TA-2005-0228+0+DOC+XML+V0//EN (visited on the 20 August 2005).

element of immediacy to the debate and fuels speculation that our membership of the European Union may ultimately result in the domestic recognition of same-sex unions contracted elsewhere in the EU, a highly controversial, if remote, prospect.[100]

Regardless of the socio-moral position, it is clear that the current legal position suffers from a distinct lack of clarity and an internal inconsistency of rationale. This, in and of itself, is unsatisfactory. It is paradoxical that an institution so central and familiar to us defies ready definition. This is not to necessarily say that wholesale change to the nature of marriage[101] is itself desirable or mandated. However, there must be a realisation that the time has come to subject old assumptions about the nature of marriage to public scrutiny.

I respectfully submit the following proposals for reform:

(i) A statutory re-evaluation of the decision in *Foy v An t-Ard Chlaraitheoir* in light of the *Goodwin* case.
(ii) The amendment of official documents of post-operative transsexuals prospectively.
(iii) A statutory definition of "marriage", determined by as inclusive a process of public consultation as possible, and by referendum if necessary.

Fundamental change in the nature of the marital unit is a profound societal change, and not one to be embarked upon lightly. For change to realistically and democratically occur, the advocates for change will have to stop being the vocal minority and become the voice of the majority, otherwise, as it was succinctly put by Ward LJ in the Court of Appeal decision of *Fitzpatrick v Sterling Housing Association*[102]:

> "[i]nteresting though these developments may be, they are no more than straws in the wind."

[100] Currently, the decision of the Barron J in the High Court decision of *Conlon v Mohamed,* Unreported, High Court, 25 July 1986 is authority for the refusal to recognise a foreign union contracted under the *lex loci celebrationis* where such union would not constitute a valid common law marriage.

[101] For example, the full recognition of same-sex unions.

[102] [1998] 1 FLR 6 at 36.

Garda Diversion of Young Offenders: An Unreasonable Threat to Due Process Rights?

by

Liz Campbell*

Diversion programmes play a significant role in the field of youth justice as an alternative to the conventional court process, and aim to prevent the entry of the child into the formal justice system. The long-established practice of diverting certain young offenders from prosecution ensures that children are not drawn into the criminal justice system and are not given a criminal record.[1] A non-statutory diversion programme entitled the Garda Liaison Scheme was established in Ireland in 1963, which diverted less serious young offenders from prosecution.[2] This scheme was placed on a statutory footing by Part 4 of the Children Act 2001, an Act which represents a major reform of the law pertaining to youth justice. Whilst a diversion programme has been established under Part 8 of the Act which concerns children who are being prosecuted for a crime, this article will concentrate solely on the pre-trial diversion programme, given the particular issues of due process which arise in this regard.

Whether the purported benefits of the Garda diversion programme outweigh any infringements on the rights of the child will be considered. Firstly, a brief elucidation of the salient provisions of Part 4 will be given. Then the application of the programme to date will be examined, to establish the measure of success of the scheme. Next, the issue of whether traditional due process rights are relevant or necessary in the context of the Garda diversion programme will be explored. Whether the factors differentiating the diversion programme from court proceedings

---

* This essay was awarded a prize by the Law Society of Ireland for the *Student Law Reform Essay Competition 2004*.

[1] Goldson, "Wither Diversion? Interventionism and The New Youth Justice" in *The New Youth Justice* (Goldson ed, Russell House, 2000, Dorset, UK), p 35.

[2] *Annual Report of the Committee Appointed to Monitor the Effectiveness of the Diversion Programme, 2004*, p 8.

are so significant as to warrant the application of a modified rights framework which departs from the conventional due process model will be assessed. Finally, a proposed legislative amendment which would permit the fact of participation in the diversion programme to be cited in court and which has the capacity to alter the tenor of the debate in a fundamental sense will be considered.

The Diversion Programme

While there is no absolute right to be admitted to the diversion programme, s 18 of the Act states that any child (that is, any individual less than 18 years of age) who has committed an offence and accepts responsibility for his criminal behaviour shall be considered for admission unless the interests of society otherwise require. Section 23 stresses that for a child to be admitted, he must accept responsibility, consent to the process and have attained the age of criminal responsibility.[3] The participation of the child in the programme must be in his best interests and not inconsistent with the interests of society and any victim.

Section 25 of the Act provides for the issuance of an informal or formal caution to every child admitted to the programme. An informal caution is administered by a juvenile liaison officer (JLO) in a Garda Síochána station or in the child's home.[4] A formal caution is usually administered in the Station by a member of the Garda Síochána not below the rank of inspector or by a JLO. Both an informal and formal caution must occur in the presence of the child's parents or guardian. A formal caution generally entails supervision of the child for 12 months. Furthermore, under s 26, the victim may be invited to attend the administration of a formal caution, at which the child may be invited to apologise and make reparation.

Section 29 facilitates the convening of a family group conference (FGC), a method of dealing with youth crime first propounded in New Zealand with the enactment of the Children, Young Persons and their Families Act 1989.[5] Section 32 states that

---

[3] s 52 of the Act raised the age of criminal responsibility to 12 years and imposed a rebuttable presumption that a child who is not less than 12 but under 14 years of age is incapable of committing an offence.

[4] A JLO is a Garda who receives special training in the area of youth justice, and works mainly in plain clothes. O'Dwyer, "Juvenile Crime and Justice in Ireland" in *Juvenile Justice Systems: An International Comparison of Problems and Solutions* (Bala, Hornick, Snyder, and Paetsch, Toronto: Thompson Educational Publishing Inc, 2002), p 159.

[5] See Hassall, "Origin and Development of Family Group Conferences" in *Family Group Conferences – Perspectives on Policy and Practice (*Hudson, Morris, Maxwell, & Galaway, eds New South Wales: Federation Press, 1996), pp 17–36.

the conference is to be attended by the child and his parents, while the victim and other individuals may also be invited. The conference seeks to mediate between the victim and the offender, and thus incorporates a restorative justice element. The restorative model proposes that crime should be treated holistically, as a conflict between members of a community, where the locus of justice is not a courtroom but rather the community of the transgressor.[6] The presence of the victim is not vital but is seen as significant in making the child recognise his offence and in influencing the future behaviour of the child. The conference seeks to establish why the child became involved in criminal behaviour that gave rise to his or her admission to the programme and discusses how the child may be prevented from becoming involved in such behaviour in the future. The FGC considers whether the period or level of supervision of the child should be varied taking into account the educational or employment circumstances of the child, his leisure activities, his family relationship and his attitude to the programme, the offence and the victim.[7] Furthermore, an action plan, including provision for an apology or reparation to the victim, or participation by the child in a particular activity or training course, is formulated at the conference.[8] The conference may reconvene to consider compliance with the terms of the action plan.

An incentive to participate in the Garda diversion programme is provided by s 48, which renders inadmissible in subsequent court proceedings an admission of responsibility, or evidence of participation in the programme. Nevertheless, as will be detailed, a proposed amendment to this provision would remove this impetus to participate, and would alter the concept of diversion on which the programme purports to be predicated.

The Success of the Programme

Prior to the commencement of Part 4 of the Children Act in May 2002, an evaluation of the pilot programme of cautions and conference for young offenders was carried out by the Garda Research Unit.[9] This research, which examined 68 cases in the pilot programme, suggests that the initiative should be expanded. Various

[6] Johnstone, *Restorative Justice – Ideas, Values, Debates* (Willan Publishing, 2002, Devon, UK), p 11.

[7] s 38.

[8] s 39.

[9] O'Dwyer, *Restorative Justice Initiatives in the Garda Síochána – Evaluation of the Pilot Programme* (Garda Research Unit, Research Report No. 4/01, 2001).

elements of the pilot programme were assessed and the general conclusions reached were positive. The involvement of the offenders in the process was deemed to be at a good level, while the participation of the offender's family and the victim was even higher.[10] The involvement in decision-making was also higher for the other participants than for offenders.[11] However, positive average changes were reported in the demeanour of the offenders, although some negative changes in behaviour were also recorded. The greatest average changes were recorded in respect of feeling remorse, accepting responsibility and being apologetic, and feeling self-conscious.[12] The offender was able to make up for what he did in the majority of cases, and also accepted responsibility for his behaviour. Moreover, most offenders demonstrated that they understood how the victim felt and indicated that they were sorry. Furthermore, the vast majority admitted that their behaviour was wrong and undertook to stay out of trouble in the future.[13] In addition to the positive feedback recorded as regards the offenders, victim satisfaction was also high, with 95 per cent of victims indicating their satisfaction with the programme.[14]

A committee to monitor the effectiveness of the programme and review all aspects of its operation was established in accordance with s 44 of the Act. The 2004 Report of the Committee indicates that a total 20,607 cases were referred to the diversion programme in that year.[15] However, only 177 restorative cautions and conferences took place from May 2002 to the end of 2003, although this represents an increase of 59 from the 2003 total of 118.[16] As a total of 3,385 formal cautions were administered in 2004 alone, along with 10,511 informal cautions, it is evident that restorative cautions and conferences represent a tiny proportion of the cases dealt with by the police in the context of youth crime.[17] This fact may be explained by the additional time required to hold such cautions and conferences, given the need to engage with the participants and the preparation required.[18] As noted in the report,

---

10 *ibid*, pp 19–20.

11 *ibid*, p 20.

12 *ibid*, pp 23–4.

13 *ibid*, pp 26–7.

14 *ibid*, p 29.

15 *Annual Report of the Committee Appointed to Monitor the Effectiveness of the Diversion Programme*, 2004, p 9.

16 *ibid*, p 11 and Appendix C, p 21. See *Annual Report of the Committee Appointed to Monitor the Effectiveness of the Diversion Programme*, 2003, p 17.

17 *2004 Annual Report*, p 13.

18 *ibid*, p 9.

research is required to examine the level of recidivism among children who participate in the diversion programme.

The paucity of statistical analysis concerning the diversion programme means that the effectiveness of the approach is uncertain. However, the review of the pilot programme indicates a degree of success in terms of participation and involvement in the programme. Nevertheless, it is questionable whether the potential benefits of the scheme justify any possible infringements on the due process rights of the child.

The Due Process Rights of the Child

In the context of court proceedings involving children, certain due process rights and basic procedural safeguards must be respected, as outlined in Art 40 of the UN Convention on the Rights of the Child (CRC)[19] and Art 7 of the UN Standard Minimum Rules for the Administration of Juvenile Justice.[20] The preservation of such rights is necessitated by the need to safeguard the dignity and the human rights of the child in the face of inherently punitive and coercive judicial proceedings. The possibility of a custodial sanction being imposed after the judicial process and the serious curtailment of rights associated with a penal sentence indicate that the upholding of due process rights is imperative. Article 40(3)(b) of the CRC provides that the child's human rights and legal safeguards must be fully respected during non-judicial measures for dealing with children who are accused of having committed a crime or who have done so. Nevertheless, it is questionable whether the same due process rights apply in the context of the diversion programme as do in judicial proceedings, given that the outcome of the programme does not have the capacity to restrict so acutely the rights of the child. Furthermore, the benefits associated with the diversion programme, including its informal nature and the capacity for frank and direct conversation between the offender and the victim, may warrant the application of altered standards. By examining three specific rights, namely the right to the presumption of innocence, the right to legal representation, and the right to an independent and impartial hearing, this article determines the extent to which the Garda diversion programme erodes the rights of the accused child, and seeks to establish whether this can be justified given the considerable benefits which accrue from the application of such an approach.

---

19 United Nations Convention on the Rights of the Child, A/RES/44/25.

20 United Nations Standard Minimum Rules for the Administration of Juvenile Justice (Beijing Rules), G.A. Res. 40/33 (1985).

Presumption of Innocence

The first due process right of the child to be considered which may be compromised by the Garda diversion programme is the presumption of innocence. While the importance of this right in court proceedings is apparent, given the possibility of a custodial sentence being imposed, its significance is less clear in the context of the diversion programme. Section 18 of the 2001 Act provides that consideration for admission to the programme is dependent on the child accepting responsibility for his criminal behaviour. In addition, under s 30(2), the consent of the child is required before a caution is administered, while the consent of his parent or guardian is required for the convening of a conference with the child's views being ascertained in this regard. These requirements indicate that the child waives his right to the presumption of innocence by declaring his guilt before entering the programme, a confession which rarely occurs in the presence of a lawyer. In addition, this disclosure may not be sufficient to convict the child of the offence in court as it may not indicate the intention of the child at the time of the offence and so avoids the legal requirement of *mens rea.*[21]

It may be argued that the presumption of innocence is an indispensable right which ensures that a vulnerable child is not coerced into making a false statement, either by a desire to protect a friend or to end the interview with the police. As it is conceivable that a child may refuse to cooperate with the gardaí in the stressful and oppressive surroundings of the station, the presumption of innocence ensures that this reticence is not interpreted as an expression of guilt. Furthermore, the reality of the child's consent to participate is also problematic, given that significant pressure may be exerted on him to partake in the programme by his parents or by the police.[22] The application of the right to the presumption of innocence in the context of the programme protects the child from such coercion.

Conversely, it may be claimed that applying the presumption of innocence in the context of diversion does not protect the child, but rather stymies the aim of the

---

21 Cunneen, "Thinking Critically about Restorative Justice" in *Restorative Justice – Critical Issues* (McLaughlin, Fergusson, Hughes, & Westmarland (eds), London: Sage Publications, 2003), p 189; Johnstone, above, n 6, pp 30, 34.

22 Ashworth, "Responsibilities, Rights and Restorative Justice" (2002) 42 *British Journal of Criminology* 578 at 587; Dumortier, "Neglecting Due Process for Minors: A Possible Dark Side of the Restorative Justice Implementation", paper presented at the Ancillary Meetings of the 10th United Nations Congress on the Prevention of Crime and Treatment of Offenders, Vienna, Austria (10–17 April 2000), p 6.

programme. In the traditional adversarial system, the defendant, even if responsible for the offence of which he is accused, may be advised to plead not guilty so as to exploit a legal lacuna or technicality. Such a strategy may prevent the offender, if in fact guilty, from accepting moral responsibility for the crime. The acknowledgement of responsibility for an offence and the resultant dialogue between the offender and the victim lies at the core of restorative justice which underpins the diversion programme. The aim of the programme is to divert the child from future offending, and this is only possible if the child takes responsibility for and acknowledges the consequences of his actions. In addition, the argument that the child's admission may not be adequate to secure a conviction in the courts fails to consider that the diversion programme differs from a judicial process both in its aims and its outcome, and therefore that the application of modified standards is acceptable in this regard.

Any reservations about the pressure brought to bear on a child to admit guilt or to consent to participation may be assuaged by s 23 of the 2001 Act, which permits the child to avail of legal advice before being admitted to the diversion programme, as provided for in the UN Basic Principles on the Use of Restorative Justice Programmes.[23] The meeting with the lawyer serves as an appropriate forum at which the guilt of the child can be discussed and any issues in this regard aired. At this juncture, if the child has falsely confessed, he may retract his statement and explain his reasons for not telling the truth. Permitting the child to talk to a lawyer at this stage of the process mitigates any harshness associated with the attrition of the presumption of innocence.

Legal Representation

While the child is entitled to consult a lawyer before the initiation of the diversion programme, there is no right to be represented by a lawyer during the course of an FGC. While the basis for the former entitlement is understandable, given the restriction on the right to the presumption of innocence, it is questionable whether legal representation throughout the course of a conference is necessary to protect the rights of the child. In favour of such an approach, it may be argued that the police, the victim, and the family of the accused may represent a formidable and potentially punitive group, against whom the child needs support. The pressure exerted on the child may be excessive, and a lawyer, acting on behalf of the child, would ensure that the child is not subjected to an overly stressful confrontation. In addition, the

23 UN Preliminary Draft Elements of a Declaration of Basic Principles on the Use of Restorative Justice Programmes in Criminal Matters, ECOSOC Res 2000/14, Issue No 12.

issue of proportionality is pertinent in this regard, as the participants to the conference, including the victim and the police, determine the length or level of supervision of the child under s 38 and formulate an action plan according to s 39(1). A disproportionately onerous action plan could be devised in the FGC due to the input of a retaliatory victim or police officer.[24] The presence of a lawyer arguably acts as a bulwark against the imposition of an excessively burdensome action plan and guards against the development of an oppressive atmosphere in the conference.

However, as Hudson *et al* note, a system of formal legal representation impedes the ability of victims and offenders to talk directly to each other.[25] The success of the diversion programme is predicated on the notion of frank and direct communication; therefore, the programme should strive for face-to-face discussion so as to aid the healing process for the victim and to discourage reoffending by the child by personalising the effects of his actions. FGCs seek to fully involve all the parties to a crime, in contrast to the formal justice system in which the offender and victim can become peripheral due to the dominant role played by legal professionals.[26] Therefore, permitting a lawyer to represent the child during an FGC would have a detrimental effect on the dynamic of the conference and would negate the conference's beneficial elements. The child would be likely to avoid true participation in the conference and would not contribute in a meaningful way. Furthermore, the presence of a lawyer would be likely to import a degree of formality to the proceedings due to the manner in which she may instruct her client and also due to the use of legal terminology.

Although it is feasible that the proportionality and fairness of the final action plan may be compromised by the input of the police and the victim, the attendance of a lawyer at an FGC is not the most efficacious means of guarding against this possibility. A reasonable and effective way to ensure that the rights of the child are safeguarded throughout the conference and that the outcome is proportionate, without jeopardising the core aims of the programme, would be to facilitate the attendance of an independent advocate at the FGC. This advocate would not adopt the adversarial role of a lawyer but would, rather, assist and guide the child in a non-

24 Dignan, "The Crime and Disorder Act and the Prospects for Restorative Justice" (1999) *Criminal Law Review* 48 at p 56.

25 Hudson *et al.*, above, n 5, p 230.

26 Jackson, "Family Group Conferences in Youth Justice: The Issues for Implementation in England and Wales" (1998) 37 *Howard Journal of Criminal Justice* 34 at p 38.

confrontational manner so as not to imperil the fundamental objectives of the diversion programme. This compromise ensures the adequate protection of the child's rights but does not threaten the informality of the conference and its concomitant benefits.

Independent and Impartial Hearing

The right of the child to an independent and impartial hearing is the final right to be considered. It is arguable that this fundamental principle, which is provided for in the context of judicial hearings in Art 40(2)(b)(iii) of the CRC, is threatened by the active role played by the Garda Síochána in the diversion process. The facilitator of the FGC, who convenes the conference, decides where it is to be held and determines who attends, is either a JLO or another member of the Gardaí.[27] Considerable benefits accrue from specifically using trained JLOs, due to their knowledge of the law and their credibility with young people.[28] Moreover, s 46(1) provides that each facilitator shall receive adequate and appropriate training to ensure the proper and efficient discharge of his duties. This provision may prove sufficient in ensuring that the facilitators act appropriately and in an unpartisan manner. Furthermore, as McCold highlights, a police-based model is regarded as more serious by the participants when compared with a process facilitated by a volunteer mediator, and the police are more likely to be successful in securing compliance with the action plan.[29]

Despite these advantages of the police-led model of diversion, it is questionable whether a police officer can satisfy the terms of the UN Basic Principles on Restorative Justice which stress that "facilitator" means a fair and impartial third party.[30] The central role played by the police in both the investigation and the quasi-adjudication of the offence represents a basic conflict of interest and compromises the right of the child to a fair and neutral hearing. A similar worry has been expressed by Goldson in the context of the diversion scheme in place in England and Wales,

---

[27] ss 31–33.

[28] O'Dwyer, above, n 9, p 43.

[29] McCold, "Police-Facilitated Restorative Conferencing – What the Data Show", paper presented to the Second Annual International Conference on Restorative Justice for Juveniles, Florida Atlantic University, and the International Network for Research on Restorative Justice for Juveniles, Fort Lauderdale, Florida (7-9 November, 1998), p 11.

[30] above, n 23.

where the decision whether to issue a reprimand, a final warning or to prosecute under the Crime and Disorder Act 1998 is vested solely in the police.[31] Although the training given to each facilitator may improve the likelihood of his remaining impartial, the police may adopt authoritarian tactics in dealing with the young offender. Indeed, there is significant potential for the facilitator to become the leader of the conference and renounce his disinterested role, as indicated by the research conducted by O'Mahony and Doak.[32] In contrast, empirical evidence collated by McCold refutes the claim that police may be incapable of being neutral facilitators and may fall into controlling behaviour patterns.[33]

To ensure that the right of the child to an independent and impartial hearing is not threatened, it is imperative that the role of the police is strictly circumscribed. Whilst it is evident that many members of the Gardaí have a wealth of experience in the area of diversion and youth justice, the danger posed to the rights of the child is sufficiently strong to necessitate the participation of an external facilitator, perhaps a community representative, trained in mediation. Although it is conceded that this would also pose difficulties, as picking individuals who are properly representative of the community is itself a challenging task,[34] the importance of preserving the independence of the facilitator and of the conference cannot be understated. Permitting the JLO to attend the FGC and to play an active role in the formulation of the action plan would be an acceptable compromise, as the presence of a police officer would emphasis the gravity of the process, while the pivotal role of facilitator would remain impartial.

It has been argued that the restriction on the presumption of innocence is not so serious as to warrant the alteration of the diversion programme. Moreover, the limitation on the right to legal representation may be mitigated by the attendance of an independent advocate at the FGC. Finally, it has been suggested that to ensure the protection of the right of the child to an independent and impartial hearing, the role of facilitator should be adopted by a specially trained individual from outside the ranks of the Gardaí. However, the possible rescission of the important safeguard in

---

31 Goldson, above, n 1, pp 37–38.

32 O'Mahony and Doak, "Restorative Justice – Is More Better? The Experience of Police-Led Restorative Cautioning Pilots in Northern Ireland" (2004) 43 *Howard Journal of Criminal Justice* 484 at 490.

33 McCold, above, n 29, p 8.

34 Crawford and Newburn, "Recent Developments in Restorative Justice for Young People in England and Wales" (2002) 42 *British Journal of Criminology* 476 at 482 *et seq.*

the Children Act 2001 concerning the admissibility of evidence relating to the diversion programme may necessitate the revision of the preceding arguments on the importance of traditional due process rights in the context of the Garda diversion programme.

Admissibility of Evidence Concerning the Diversion Programme

As previously noted, s 48 of the 2001 Act precludes the admissibility in criminal proceedings of evidence concerning the acceptance of responsibility for an offence or the participation of a child in the diversion programme. However, s 31 of the Criminal Justice Bill 2004 seeks to amend this protection by providing that where a court is considering a sentence to be imposed in respect of an offence committed by a child after participating in the diversion programme, the prosecution may inform it of the child's acceptance of responsibility, the offending behaviour or the child's involvement in the programme. The adoption of this proposed amendment would, in essence, alter the core precept of the programme, *viz* to divert the child from the formal criminal justice process.

Permitting evidence which pertains to diversion to be mentioned in court compromises the aims of the programme, as it would result in the programme becoming the first stage in, rather than an alternative to, the formal justice process. If the scheme becomes, to all intents and purposes, an element of the formal system, then it is arguable that no compromise can be reached *vis-à-vis* due process rights. If participation in the programme may be cited in court at a later stage, this may have serious repercussions for the child, in that involvement in the programme may result in a more serious sentence being passed. Therefore, if this fundamental alteration to the programme is enacted, the child must accrue identical due process rights to those applicable in the courtroom.

Conclusion

This article, by focusing on three specific rights, examined whether the Garda diversion programme unduly threatens the due process rights of the young offender. The aim of a diversion programme based on the precepts of restorative justice is to move away from the formalised courtroom environment and to replace it with an alternative method of dealing with youth crime. The insistence on and imposition of traditional legal rights locates the process in the adversarial model, and thwarts true restorative and constructive dialogue by concern for formalistic legal entitlements. Furthermore, not all conventional due process rights are necessary to guarantee the protection of the child's dignity and rights in the programme. Nevertheless, it is imperative to ensure that the benefits associated with the diversion programme are not negated by the possibility that participation in the programme may be cited in court. The adoption of the proposed amendment would alter the programme in an essential way, and so would necessitate the imposition of traditional due process rights.

Recording and Representation: The Interrogation of Suspects in the Irish Pre-Trial Process

by
Yvonne Marie Daly*

Introduction

The right to pre-trial legal advice in Ireland was first recognised as being of constitutional origin by the Supreme Court in *People (DPP) v Healy.*[1] However, the members of the Court expressly reserved opinion as to whether or not it encompassed a right to have one's solicitor present throughout Garda interrogation. The right as articulated in *Healy* was one of "reasonable access" to legal advice only, and later courts have held, often with rather blunt exploration of the issues, that it does not in fact include a right to the presence of one's legal adviser during garda interview.[2]

In March 1990, the Martin Committee, reporting on certain aspects of criminal procedure, concluded that there was no need for a suspect to be entitled to have his legal representative present if garda interrogations of suspects were to be the subject of audio-visual recording.[3] Provision for such recording was made under s 27 (1) of the Criminal Justice Act 1984. However, it took until 1997, almost 13 years later, for the necessary regulations, the Criminal Justice Act 1984 (Electronic Recording of Interviews) Regulations 1997,[4] to be brought into force.

---

* B.C.L., Doctoral Candidate, Trinity College Dublin. This essay was awarded joint second place for the Law Society of Ireland, *Student Law Reform Essay Competition 2006.*

1 [1990] 2 IR 73.

2 e.g, *Lavery v Member-in-Charge, Carrickmacross Garda Station* [1999] 2 IR 390, wherein it was further declared (at 396) that an accused's solicitor is not entitled to be given updates or running accounts of the progress of garda investigations.

3 *Report of the Committee to enquire into Certain Aspects of Criminal Procedure* (Dublin: Stationery Office) March 1990.

4 hereinafter referred to as "the 1997 Regulations" or "the Regulations".

This essay revisits to some extent the conclusion of the Martin Committee and examines whether, in fact, the introduction of such recording does negate the need to recognise a right to have one's solicitor present during garda interrogation. Certain suggestions for reform of the law in this area are proffered accordingly.

The 1997 Regulations

The 1997 Regulations relate to the questioning of persons arrested and detained pursuant to s 30 of the Offences against the State Act 1939; s 4 of the Criminal Justice Act 1984; and s 2 of the Criminal Justice(Drug Trafficking) Act 1996.[5] Section 27 of the 1984 Act provides that a failure to comply with any provision of the Regulations shall not of itself render a person (presumably a garda) liable to civil or criminal proceedings or render inadmissible in evidence anything said during questioning, "without prejudice to the power of the court to exclude evidence at its discretion". This proviso automatically undermines the effectiveness of the Regulations in the protection which they claim to offer to a suspect detained in Garda custody.[6] Furthermore, the regulations themselves are weak in their protection of suspects' rights and provide for quite a number of exceptions from the general rule that interviews ought to be recorded.

Regulation 4 provides that interviews with persons arrested and detained under the relevant provisions shall be electronically recorded, except where:

> "(i) the equipment is unavailable due to a functional fault, or
> (ii) the equipment is already in use at the time the interview is to commence, and the member in charge considers on reasonable grounds that the interview should not be delayed until the fault is rectified or the equipment becomes available; or
> (iii) where otherwise the electronic recording of the interview is not practicable."[7]

---

[5] Reg 3.

[6] It is notable that the 1984 Act offers moderately stronger support to the 1997 Regulations than it does to the Criminal Justice Act 1984 (Treatment of Persons in Custody in Garda Sìochána Stations) Regulations 1987, but it is nonetheless submitted that the support of the 1997 Regulations in the parent statute is poor.

[7] Reg 4(3).

In some cases the courts appear to have been quite lenient in accepting the reasoning of gardaí for an absence of audiovisual recording of interviews. One of the earliest cases which dealt specifically with the 1997 Regulations and the effect of their breach was *People (DPP) v Holland*.[8] The appellant in this case was convicted of having £100,000 worth of cannabis in his possession for sale or supply and was sentenced to 20 years imprisonment. On the same date as the accused's arrest, his solicitor had also been arrested. Furthermore, the accused was brought to, detained and questioned in Lucan Garda station, which did not have electronic recording equipment. It was argued on his behalf that the gardaí had brought him there on purpose in order to deprive him of the possibility of having his interview audio-visually recorded. The gardaí contended that the offence under investigation was one in a series of other offences which were being investigated at that time and that the centre of these investigations was Lucan Garda station.

The Special Criminal Court held that the reasons advanced by the gardaí for the decision to detain the appellant at that particular Garda station were reasonable and that, as there is no statutory obligation to record an interview in a station which is not equipped with the relevant audiovisual facilities, there was no breach of the 1997 Regulations in this case. The Court of Criminal Appeal upheld these findings but noted that if it had been established in the trial court, which it had not in this case, that there was a deliberate attempt by the gardaí to deprive the suspect of the benefit of having an electronic recording made of his interview, then that would indeed be a "serious matter". McGrath has suggested that "Although the Court [in Holland] did not explicitly indicate that a deliberate attempt to circumvent the Regulations would result in the exclusion of any inculpatory statements…such statements should be excluded as being taken in breach of fundamental fairness by reason of the deprivation of a procedural protection to which the accused would otherwise have been entitled".[9]

In the later case of *People (DPP) v Connolly*,[10] the question of audiovisual recording of Garda interviews did not arise directly on the facts. However, Hardiman J made some interesting comments on that matter. He stated, for example, that the audiovisual recording of interviews is routine in most first world common law countries and that "its failure to become routine, or even remotely to approach that

[8] Unreported, Court of Criminal Appeal, 15 June 1998.

[9] McGrath, *Evidence* (Thomson Round Hall, Dublin, 2005), paras 8–149.

[10] [2003] 2 IR 1.

status in this country, nearly 20 years after statutory provision for it was first made has ceased to be a mere oddity and is closely approaching the status of an anomaly".[11] The learned judge also noted that a very high percentage of criminal trials centre around a hard fought issue—a "trial within a trial"—in regard to the admissibility of statements which are often the main focus of the prosecution case. He pointed to the findings in Ontario, Canada (which were first quoted in the Martin Committee report in 1990) that the introduction of audio-visual recording of police interrogations had almost ended the need for such admissibility battles as a routine part of criminal cases.[12]

Perhaps most interestingly, Hardiman J went on to state that "[t]he courts have been very patient, perhaps excessively patient, with delays in this regard. The time cannot be remote when we will hear a submission that, absent extraordinary circumstances (by which we do not mean that a particular garda station has no audio-visual machinery or that the audio-visual room was being painted), it is unacceptable to tender in evidence a statement which has not been so recorded".[13]

In the recent case of *DPP v Diver*,[14] Hardiman J referred back to his judgment in *Connolly*, reiterating the "central importance" of audiovisual recording of Garda interviews to ensure fairness to the accused. He supported his call for a greater emphasis on such recording with the criticism that "gardaí have regularly avoided audio visual recording, made selective notes, and breached the clear and simple regulations for the treatment of persons in custody…"

It is submitted, however, that the need for audiovisual recording in order to ensure fundamental fairness to the accused is best illustrated by the case of *People (DPP) v Paul Kelly*,[15] which came before the Special Criminal Court in January 2005. Part of the defence argument on behalf of the accused, who had been arrested and detained under the Offences against the State Act 1939, was that two interviews with him

[11] [2003] 2 IR 1 at 17–18.

[12] Grant, "The Audio-Visual Taping of Police Interviews with Suspects and Accused by Halton Regional Police Force, Ontario, Canada" – quoted in the *Report of the Committee to Enquire into Certain Aspects of Criminal Procedure* (the Martin Committee) March, 1990.

[13] [2003] 2 IR 1 at 18.

[14] Unreported, Supreme Court, 29 July 2005.

[15] Unreported, Special Criminal Court, 26 November 2004—see *Irish Times*, Monday 17 January 2005.

which took place on the 2 July 2003 were tainted with unfairness to such an extent that their content was inadmissible in evidence. There were several grounds on which the fairness of the interviews was challenged including the fact that they took place in a Garda station in which audio-visual recording facilities were not available.

The Special Criminal Court held that the interviews, overall, were tainted with unfairness and the products thereof were accordingly inadmissible. In regard to the fact that the accused was not brought to a Garda station equipped with audio-visual recording facilities, the Court held that as gardaí were aware that during his detention the accused would be interviewed about allegations that he was a member of the IRA and that s 2 of the Offences against the State (Amendment) Act 1998 which allows for inferences to be drawn from silence in the pre-trial period, would be invoked, it would have been preferable for the interview to have been video-taped. The Court felt that the two relevant gardaí ought to have recognised that fact and brought the suspect to an appropriate Garda station.

The evidence of the gardaí was to the effect that they had brought the accused to Dundalk Garda station so that he would be near his family and legal advisers, and while the Court accepted that this was reasonable, it nonetheless had grave reservations about the failure to bring the accused to a station which had audio-visual recording equipment. The members of the Court noted that there is no legal obligation to do so and therefore the accused's detention was at all times lawful; however, it doubted whether it was fair. It believed that, while there was no statutory obligation to do so, where it was possible to bring a suspect to a Garda station with audiovisual facilities, basic fairness required that that be done with a prisoner whom it is intended to interview invoking s 2 of the 1998 Act.

Section 2 of the 1998 Act is only one of several statutory provisions in operation in Ireland which significantly curtail the accused's right to silence in the pre-trial period. Sections 18 and 19 of the Criminal Justice Act 1984 and s 7 of the Criminal Justice (Drug Trafficking) Act 1996 also allow for inferences to be drawn at later trial from the failure of the accused to answer certain questions or provide certain information at garda interview. While these provisions have been accepted by the courts both domestically[16] and on a European level,[17] it is submitted that their operation needs to be both fair and transparent. It is therefore submitted that interviews which

[16] *Rock v Ireland* [1998] 2 ILRM 35.

[17] *Murray v United Kingdom* (1996) 22 EHRR 29.

involve the employment of such provisions must be properly recorded. To this end, it is suggested that the 1997 Regulations ought to be amended so as to include a compulsory duty on gardaí to ensure that if a suspect is to be interviewed, and ss 18 and 19 of the Criminal Justice Act 1984, s 2 of the Offences against the State (Amendment) Act 1998 or s 7 of the Criminal Justice (Drug Trafficking) Act 1996 are to be employed, such interview must be audio-visually recorded. Failure to record such interview should result in the exclusion of any statements made therein or evidence of the accused's silence. This would considerably strengthen the current weak protection of the accused rights and would ensure that proper procedures were at all times adhered to by the gardaí. It would be preferable that such a provision be applied to all interviews, but perhaps the first step towards this is to apply the provision to potential inference-drawing interviews. Surely it is time to insist on audiovisual recording in such cases.

Even if this important reform is accepted, the question still remains as to whether recording of Garda interrogations provides sufficient protection for the rights of the accused. Does the audio-visual recording of Garda interviews truly negate the need to recognise a right to the presence of one's legal adviser throughout?

Recording versus Representation

In the Irish Government's response to the 2002 Report of the European Committee for the Prevention of Torture and Inhuman or Degrading Treatment or Punishment (the CPT), it stated that "...the electronic recording of interviews is now well established" and "...over 220 interview rooms have been ...equipped in up to 130 Garda stations and these are fully operational".[18] While there are a total of 702 Garda stations in this jurisdiction at present, it appears that only 167 stations have detention facilities and are actually used to detain and interview suspects.[19] Recording facilities have been installed and are operational in 79 per cent of these detention stations (132 stations). While this is not perfect, the Steering Committee on Audio and Audio/Video Recording of Garda Questioning of Detained Persons has declared that it "...is assured that, with the putting in place of additional units

---

18 Response of the Government of Ireland to the report of the European Committee for the Prevention of Torture and Inhuman or Degrading Treatment or Punishment (CPT) on its visit to Ireland from 20 to 28 May 2002 (available at http://www.cpt.coe.int/documents/irl/2003-37-inf-eng.htm).

19 Report of the Steering Committee on Audio and Audio/Video Recording of Garda Questioning of Detained Persons (Dublin, Stationery Office, September 2004), para 2.2.1.

in a very small number of stations which already have facilities, there are a sufficient number of Garda stations, in all Garda Divisions, to ensure that all interviews as specified in the Regulations are recorded".[20] As discussed above, this has not always been the case given the exceptions allowable under the current Regulations.

The government also stated in its response to the CPT's 2002 Report that the Electronic Recording Regulations were under review and that new regulations "...are likely to be made this year [2003]." In the Steering Committee's 2004 Report it made a number of recommendations to the Government for inclusion in any new regulations. One recommendation was that the recording of an interview could be interrupted or discontinued by order of a chief superintendent, or more senior officer, where he believes on reasonable grounds that there is a real and substantial risk to the life of any person and that insistence upon the electronic recording of the interview gives rise to this risk.[21] Beyond this, few major changes to the Regulations were put forward by the Committee and no changes have been made by the Government to date.

In any case, the CPT has generally expressed the view that while it considers that "the introduction of audio-visual recording of interviews as an additional safeguard is a most welcome development; ...it remains persuaded of the importance, in the interests of the prevention of ill-treatment, of the possibility for lawyers to be present during interviews...".[22] This view has been reiterated to the Irish Government on a number of occasions, despite the Government's submission that the introduction of audio-visual recording is a preferable alternative to the recognition of a right to have one's legal representative present throughout interview.

Interestingly, while there has been no similar study done in this jurisdiction, evidence exists in Scotland to suggest that the introduction of electronic recording of police interviews there led to an increase in the number of suspects making statements outside of the police station. In the 1982 report of the Scottish Home and Health Department on a two year pilot scheme of audio-taping police interviews in Dundee and Falkirk[23] (the SHHD Report), evidence showed that the percentage of suspects

---

[20] *ibid,* at para 2.2.3.

[21] *ibid,* at para 1.7.2.

[22] Report to the Government of Ireland on the visit to Ireland carried out by the European Committee for the Prevention of Torture and Inhuman or Degrading Treatment or Punishment (CPT) from 20 to 28 May 2002 (available at http://www.cpt.coe.int/documents/irl/2003-36-inf-eng.htm), para 22.

[23] "Tape-Recording of Police Interviews: Interim Report – the first 24 months" (Scotland, 1982).

making relevant statements prior to arrival at the police station rose from 14 per cent before the introduction of recording to 44 per cent after its introduction.

In their analysis of that report, McConville and Morrell[24] looked at the effect of the case of *H.M. Advocate v McFadden*,[25] wherein statements made during a taped interview with the accused were deemed inadmissible in evidence as the court ruled that parts of the interview had been improperly conducted. The authors suggest that this judgment was taken by the police as a rejection of their interrogation methods and that instead of rectifying those problems in the interview room the result was, rather, an increase in the questioning of suspects off-tape with a more formal approach subsequently adopted in the interview room on-tape. McConville and Morrell further observe that while it had generally been assumed that "once taping was introduced, beneficial consequences, including desirable changes in police behaviour, would necessarily result. Few...appreciated how the actual changes in police behaviour might in fact succeed in neutralising the reform".[26] They suggest that, rather than improving police interrogation methods, police are likely to continue with their former methods of interrogation off-tape while adopting a formal approach on-tape which would be more acceptable to both public and judicial scrutiny.[27]

Another issue which must be alluded to is the fact that the taping of an interview provides only a retrospective record of what transpired in the interview room. While this may well enhance the ability of the court to assess the evidence and may be hoped to encourage better police standards of behaviour and interview technique, as well as decreasing the need for a trial-within-a-trial in regard to the admissibility of statements made, it ought to be remembered that the presence of audio-visual recording equipment does nothing to redress the imbalance of power between the suspect and his interrogators. Furthermore, a video camera cannot explain certain complicated legal concepts to a suspect as they arise in the course of an interview.

The need for the accused to be at all times aware of his rights, and the need to redress the imbalance of the interrogation room were both noted by Finlay CJ in the seminal

---

24 McConville and Morrell, "Recording the Interrogation: Have the Police Got it Taped?" [1983] *Crim LR* 125.

25 Unreported, 1980.

26 McConville and Morrell, "Recording the Interrogation: Have the Police Got it Taped?" [1983] *Crim LR* 125 at 158.

27 See also McConville, "Videotaping Interrogations: Police Behaviour on and off Camera" [1992] *Crim LR* 532.

case of *People (DPP) v Healy* and indeed appear to have been the main rationale on which the Supreme Court in that case recognised a constitutional origin for the right to legal advice in the pre-trial period.[28] While these issues were employed in *Healy* to support the recognition of the basic right to consult with a solicitor, White argues that they equally support a prohibition on "*incommunicado interrogation*"[29] and in fact mandate a broader acceptance of the right which would allow for the presence of solicitors during interrogation.

It is submitted then that even an improved system of audio-visual recording of Garda interviews would not be enough to redress the imbalance of the interrogation room or strengthen the rights of the accused in the pre-trial period, which are so essential to the overall fairness of the accused's trial. In order to ensure such fairness, it is submitted that the right to have one's legal representative present throughout Garda interrogation ought to be recognised. For clarity, this could and should be declared by statutory enactment.[30]

Reform

The accused in this jurisdiction currently stands in a precarious position in the pre-trial period, particularly if he is to be questioned under certain inference-drawing provisions which exist within current Irish legislation. He is not entitled to have his legal adviser with him throughout the duration of his questioning by members of the Garda Síochána, and while provision exists for the audio-visual recording of such questioning, the Regulations governing same are malleable and weak in application.

It is high time for reform of this area, not only to ensure fairness to the individual accused at each trial, but also to uphold the integrity of the criminal justice system

---

28 per Finlay CJ in *Healy:* "The availability of advice from a lawyer must…be seen as a contribution, at least, towards some measure of equality in the position of the detained person and his interrogators." He also spoke of the need to ensure that a suspect is informed of his rights so as to reach a "truly free decision as to his attitude to interrogation or the making of any statement" [1990] 2 IR 73 at 81.

29 See White, "*The Confessional State – Police Interrogation in the Irish Republic*" Part I [2000] 10 (1) ICLJ 17 and Part II [2000] 10 (2) ICLJ 2.

30 Note: In England and Wales, a solicitor is entitled to remain with the suspect throughout the interview period. He may only be required to leave the interview if his conduct is such that the interviewer is unable to properly to put questions to the suspect: see the Police and Criminal Evidence Act, 1984 Code of Practice C Arts 6.8–6.11.

as a whole. It is submitted that the 1997 Regulations should be amended to at least make it compulsory to audio-visually record Garda interviews with suspects where inferences may be drawn at later trial from their silence in the pre-trial period.

However, even if this were to occur, or even if all Garda interviews with suspects were to be compulsorily audio-visually recorded, the scales would still be tipped against the accused. Unlike the conclusions of the Martin Committee, it is submitted that the audio-visual recording of Garda interrogations does not negate the need to recognise the right to have one's legal adviser present throughout.

It is notable that the members of that Committee in 1990 linked the right to legal advice with the right to silence stating that "the right to remain silent depends, insofar as its implementation in practice is concerned, in large measure on the unfettered exercise of the right of access to legal advice".[31] Perhaps if the members of that Committee had foreseen the increasing incursions on the right to silence which have become a part of the Irish legal landscape they would have been of a different opinion in regard to the need to recognise the right to have one's solicitor present throughout interrogation. The suggestion of the O'Briain Committee ought perhaps to be considered instead. In its 1978 Report, that Committee recommended that once a detained person had consulted with his solicitor such solicitor "should be entitled, as of right, to attend any subsequent interrogation as an observer".[32]

It is submitted that such a right ought to be recognised, by way of statutory enactment, in regard to all suspects. However, if this does not occur, the least that ought to be accepted is that those who may have their silence later used against them under one of the inference-drawing provisions of the Criminal Justice act 1984, the Criminal Justice (Drug Trafficking) Act 1996 or the Offences Against the State (Amendment) Act 1998 ought to be entitled to have their solicitor present throughout the duration of their interrogation.

Only in this way can we truly ensure, as the Supreme Court originally sought to do in *Healy*, that the accused is at all times aware of his legal rights, thereby ensuring the

---

[31] Report of the Committee to enquire into Certain Aspects of Criminal Procedure (March 1990), p 31.

[32] Report of the Committee to Recommend Certain Safeguards for Persons in Custody and for Members of an Garda Síochána (Dublin: Stationery Office, 13 April 1978) para 55 Further to this, the chairman of the Committee, Mr Justice Barra O'Briain, in an addendum to the Report, stated that he could think of no way of guaranteeing that ill-treatment of persons in Garda custody would not take place "except by providing, as far as practicable, the surveillance of an independent eye-witness throughout that custody" (Chairman's Addendum).

voluntariness of any statements made by him, and that there is a fair balance in the interrogation room between the interrogators and the arrested suspect. Once more, the dictates of fairness to the individual accused and the need to uphold the integrity of the criminal justice system as a whole, surely necessitate such reform.

The Law of Infanticide in Ireland: A Cry for Reform

by

Darina Flynn*

Introduction: The Tragedy of Infanticide

"The murder of infants is among the most disquieting of crimes, at least to the sensibilities of the modern world in which standards of civilization are generally associated with the protection of the defenceless and innocent."[1] The Infanticide Act 1949 defines infanticide as the killing of a child under the age of twelve months by its biological mother. Infanticide is a distinctly tragic form of child killing in which the law must often strive for compassionate justice rather than uncompromising retribution. Nonetheless, the State is constitutionally obliged to protect and vindicate the right to life of every citizen, including the infant child.[2] Even more shocking than the tragic details of infanticide cases is the apparent ambivalence of society towards the loss of infant life—an attitude that is reflected in our legal system's treatment of mothers who kill.

* This essay was awarded a prize by the Law Society of Ireland for the *Student Law Reform Essay Competition 2006.*

[1] Ogle and Maier-Katkin, "A Rationale for Infanticide Laws" (1993) *Crim. L.R.* 903 at p 903.

[2] Article 40.3.2 Bunreacht na hÉireann: "The State shall, in particular, by its law protect as best it may from unjust attack and, in the case of injustice done, vindicate the life, person, good name, and property rights of every citizen." Article 40.1 Bunreacht na hÉireann: "All citizens shall, as human persons, be held equal before the law. This shall no be held to mean that the State shall not in its enactments have due regard to differences of capacity, physical and moral, and of social function." The application of these constitutional Articles with respect to minors was upheld in the following cases: *North Western Health Board v H.W. and C.W.*; unreported, Supreme Court, Hardiman J, 8 November 2001; O' Donoghue (a Minor) suing by his mother and next friend *O'Donoghue v The Minister for Health, Minister for Education, Ireland and the Attorney General*, unreported, High Court, 27 May 1993; *G v An Bord Uchtala* [1980] IR 32 at 52.

The 1949 Act provides that women who commit infanticide, in circumstances that would otherwise amount to murder, may be tried and punished for the lesser offence of manslaughter. By distinguishing the crime of infanticide as less culpable than all other killings, the law devalues the lives of society's most dependant and vulnerable members. This issue has received inadequate attention and should be a priority item on any legal reform agenda. Furthermore, this controversial law is founded on unsound and outmoded notions of mental disturbance, is arbitrarily restrictive and does not have any significant procedural advantages for the accused.[3] The infrequent use of the current infanticide law in Ireland,[4] in addition to more fundamental criticisms of its underlying ideological and medical rationales, has led many to question its validity.[5] The Irish legislature is in the process of introducing the defence of diminished responsibility into law, which will be available as a partial defence to reduce murder to manslaughter where an offender kills in a state of significant mental impairment.[6] This defence would treat infanticidal mothers with the compassion they deserve without allowing the loss of an infant's life go unrecognised by the law. Now is an ideal time to abolish the 1949 Infanticide Act as the diminished responsibility defence could then be formulated to specifically ensure infanticide cases could be accommodated within its remit. Thus, it is proposed here

---

[3] The New South Wales Law Reform Commission, Report 83: *Partial Defence to Murder: Provocation and Infanticide* (1997), notes that the social, medical and legal bases on which the infanticide provisions are based have all been called into question in recent times.

[4] "The crime [of infanticide]...according to statistics, is least common in Ireland": http://www.newadvent.org/cathen/08001b.htm (last visited 22 February 2006)*;* see also O'Donnell, "Lethal Violence in Ireland, 1841 to 2003: Famine, Celibacy and Parental Pacification" (2005) *45 Brit. J. Criminology* 671: "baby killing [in Ireland] dropped rapidly in the decade after the Famine. There was then a long period of slow decline and, by the mid-twentieth century, this category of violent death had virtually disappeared from the official records." O'Donnell notes that infant mortality rate in Ireland fell from 99 to 6 per 1000 live births between 1900 and 1995. He attributes this decline in baby killing to changing social factors in Ireland and a marked increase in celibacy after the Famine of 1854–1850.; The New South Wales Law Reform Commission, Report 83: *Partial Defence to Murder: Provocation and Infanticide* (1997) reported that the infanticide law is very rarely used in New South Wales; In the UK, the Law Commission, Consultation Paper No 177: *A New Homicide Act for England and Wales?*(28 November 2005) reported that use of the law on infanticide is infrequent in England and Wales.

[5] Including: Clarkson, *Understanding Criminal Law* (3rd ed, Sweet & Maxwell, London, 2001); Ashworth, *Principles of Criminal Law* (3rd ed, Oxford University Press, Oxford, 1999); New South Wales Law Reform Commission, Report 83: *Partial Defence to Murder: Provocation and Infanticide* (1997).

[6] The Criminal Law (Insanity) Bill 2002, currently at second stage in Dáil Éireann.

that the law on infanticide should be abolished, conditional on the more general defence of diminished responsibility being available for women whose responsibility for killing their children is reduced by reason of mental impairment.

A Historical Perspective on Ireland's Infanticide Law: The Need for Compassionate Justice

The Irish law on infanticide is contained in the Infanticide Act 1949, which provides that any woman who wilfully causes the death of her child, being a child under the age of twelve months, in circumstances that would otherwise amount to murder, may for that offence be tried and punished for manslaughter providing at the time of the act or omission the balance of her mind was disturbed by reason of her not having fully recovered from the effect of giving birth to the child or by reason of the effect of lactation consequent upon the birth of the child.[7]

Traditionally, legal retribution for mothers who killed their children was extremely harsh. The Bastardy Act 1624 allowed for the presumption that the death of any illegitimate child was caused by its mother, who would be executed without any requirement of proof that she had killed the child. This draconian measure remained the law for almost 200 years, but after its repeal in 1803, mothers who killed their children were still found guilty of capital murder and thus sentenced to death. Infanticide was reasonable frequent at that time due in part to the stigma of illegitimacy, poverty, loss of employment and desertion unmarried mothers commonly faced.[8]

---

[7] Ireland's 1949 Act is modelled on the Infanticide Act 1938 in the United Kingdom, which has been followed in many other Commonwealth countries. For example, similar provisions exist in the Australian states of Victoria (Crimes Act 1958, s 6), New South Wales (Crimes Act 1900, s 22A), Western Australia (Criminal Code s 281A) and Tasmania (Criminal Code Act 1924, s 165A), as well as various other common law countries such as Canada (Criminal Code ss 233, 237, 663) and New Zealand (Crimes Act 1961, s 178).

[8] New South Wales Law Reform Commission, Report 83: *Partial Defence to Murder: Provocation and Infanticide* (1997); UK Law Commission, Consultation Paper No 177: *A New Homicide Act for England and Wales?* (28 November 2005). Mary Raftery refers to the "Taliban-like moral climate" of mid-20th century Ireland, where "those [single mothers] without money ended up in mother and baby homes, where the regime was often punitive and the moral condemnation absolute.": Raftery, "Babies born in shame", Irish Times, 12 January 2006; see also Goulding, *The Light in the Window* (revised edition, Poolbeg, 2004). Goulding worked as a nurse for nine months in the Bessboro mother and baby home in Cork, run by Sacred Heart nuns. In this book she recounts how women could leave within weeks of giving birth if they paid one hundred pounds to the nuns, a substantial sum at the time. Otherwise, they had to spend two years in the institution, working to pay off their keep.

Public unease with the harshness of punishment in such cases mounted throughout the mid to late 19th century as society became increasingly aware of the social stigma and poverty experienced by mothers of illegitimate children. Sympathetic juries became increasingly unwilling to convict these mothers and most death sentences passed on such women were commuted to life imprisonment.[9] Judges and juries were continuously circumventing the law in order to exercise mercy. Widespread concern that this was making a "solemn mockery"[10] of the judicial process motivated the introduction of the Infanticide Act in 1949. The Irish legislature, in passing the 1949 Infanticide Bill into law, repeatedly emphasised the unnecessary cruelty of making infanticidal mothers endure the trauma of a murder trial and the pronouncement of a death sentence where it is clear to the Court, but not perhaps to the accused, that

---

Elsewhere, their "sentence" could be up to three years. The most distressing cases of single mothers were those who became caught within Magdalen laundries, in some cases for most of their lives—a fate set aside for the poorer classes. Times, however, have changed. A recent decline in the Church's influence on Irish society has coincided with the emergence of more cosmopolitan values and uninhibited lifestyles. Premarital sex is no longer taboo and single motherhood is now an accepted reality. In a review of the One-Parent Family Payment (OPFP) introduced in 1997, the Department of Social, Community and Family Affairs providing statistical insight into the growing trend of single motherhood in Ireland. Some of its findings are as follows: There has been a dramatic rise in Ireland and in other countries in the number of births outside of marriage. The EU rate in 1960 was 5.1 per cent of all births, rising to 23.4 per cent in 1995. In Ireland, births outside marriage rose from 1.6 per cent in 1960 to 8.5 per cent in 1985 and 24.8 per cent in 1996 (Drew, 1999). In 1999, 30.9 per cent of births were to single mothers (16,461 out of a total of 53,354. For women who did not marry, the other alternative was adoption. During the 1960s there was an increase in the number of non-marital births, and the proportion adopted rose steadily (McCashin, 1996). However, the number of adoptions has declined, possibly due to the changes which have taken place in societal attitudes towards lone parents and the availability of social welfare supports. In 1986, non-marital births accounted for almost one out every ten births in Ireland. By 1994, the incidence had increased to one in five. In 1999, the incidence had increased further to one non-marital birth out of every 3.2 births in the country: http://www.welfare.ie/publications/opfpreview.pdf Department of Social, Community and Family Affairs, *Review of OPFP,* 3 November 2003 (last visited 22 February 2006. The persistent application of an infanticide law that fails to reflect social reality is thus biased against other members of society and clearly undermines the sanctity of infant life.

9 UK Law Commission, Consultation Paper No177: *A New Homicide Act for England and Wales?* (28 November 2005); The New South Wales Law Reform Commission, Report 83: *Partial Defence to Murder: Provocation and Infanticide* (1997).

10 Walker, *Crime and Insanity in England: Volume One, The Historical Perspective* (1965), at p 130.

such sentence will most likely be commuted.[11] An infanticide conviction enables judges to sentence as though for manslaughter rather than murder, which carries with it a discretionary sentence and thus offers a more compassionate method of dealing with women temporarily disturbed by the impact of childbirth.

The Forgotten Victim's Perspective

In its quest to ensure the compassionate treatment of mothers who kill, the current law on infanticide has forsaken equality and failed to meet the constitutional imperative to protect and vindicate the right to life of every citizen. Article 40 of Bunreacht na hÉireann declares that "all citizens shall, as human persons, be held equal before the law" and furthermore that "the State shall...by its laws protect as best it may from unjust attack and, in the case of injustice done, vindicate the life...of every citizen."[12] The Infanticide Act 1949 is inconsistent with these constitutional principles. Regarding the equality provision, any act that singles out infanticidal mothers as less culpable than other killers implies that a baby's life is more expendable and their killing less serious than that of persons over 12 months. Moreover, the current law on infanticide cannot be said to demonstrate the State protecting or vindicating the lives of babies "as best it may." It is the role of the law to defend the defenceless and protect the weak from exploitation by the strong. An infant child has no voice of its own and relies on the care and good will of others for survival.[13] Through prioritising the rights of mothers who kill, over the lives of their babies, the State is failing in its role to protect the most vulnerable in society.[14]

[11] *Dáil Debates* Cols 265–283; *Seanad Debates* Cols 1471–1477. The reasons for introducing the 1949 Infanticide Act were very similar to those given for introducing the law on infanticide into British law. Major DeValera, one of the few voices of dissent regarding the ratification of the Infanticide Act in Ireland, remarked he "would not be too happy blindly to subscribe to anything resulting from the traditions of English liberal thought on this matter.": *Dáil Debates* Col 276.

[12] See above, n 2.

[13] "[according to the Home Office, Criminal Statistics England and Wales 1989] the age group most at risk of death by homicide are those aged under one year...The rate for this age group in 1989 was 29 per million population aged under one year; conversely, the age group least at risk was those aged five and over but under 16.": Morris and Wilczynski, "Parents Who Kill their Children" (1993) *Crim. L.R.* 31.

[14] In the 1949 Dáil Debates regarding ratification of the Infanticide Bill, only one speaker vociferously objected to the Bill on the grounds it devalued infant life. Major de Valera argued, "I do not see why there should be any objection to the full formalities of the trial. I do not see why such a terrible thing as the killing of a child should not be dealt with as a solemn and extremely serious procedure...I would urge that we should recognise that murder is murder.": *Dáil Debates* Cols 277–278.

The Flawed Medical Basis of Infanticide Law

The Infanticide Act 1949 requires that in order to be convicted of infanticide, the balance of the mother's mind must be disturbed by reason of her not having fully recovered from the effect of giving birth to the child or by reason of the effect of lactation consequent upon the birth of the child. This medical basis of infanticide is the subject of ongoing controversy amongst legal and psychological experts.[15]

It is now widely agreed that lactational insanity is a fiction whose inclusion in infanticide legislation was motivated by a desire to medically justify extending infanticide beyond the first few weeks of birth.[16] In 2004, the Victoria Law Reform

---

[15] Abolitionists argue that the law on infanticide medicalises a condition in order to absolve the accused from moral blame. Professor Walker has characterised the Act as a process of "myth-making by legislation": Walker, *Crime and Insanity in England: Volume One, The Historical Perspective* (1965), at p 136; Some critics have claimed that the law on infanticide exemplifies a wider pattern of neutralising female guilt, responsibility and dangerousness, to obviate the need for punitive or custodial sanctions: Allen, "Rendering Them Harmless" in *Gender, Crime and Justice* (Carlen and Worrall eds, 1987); In the UK, the Law Commission, Consultation Paper No177: *A New Homicide Act for England and Wales?* (28 November 2005), notes however that postpartum depression has been the subject of a great deal of psychiatric research and there is a close relationship between postpartum psychosis and major affective disorder. Thus, notwithstanding criticism of the psychiatric basis of the law on infanticide, many have argued that the policy of mitigation for mothers who kill their infants can be justified in psychiatric terms. See for instance, Ogle and Maier-Katkin, "A Rationale for Infanticide Laws" (1993) *Crim. LR* 903 at pp 905–909; and Wheelwright, "Nothing in Between: modern cases of infanticide" in *Infanticide: Historical Essays on Child Murder and Concealment, 1550–2000* (Jackson ed.) Ashgate, Aldershot, UK, 2002); There is at present, however, no official diagnosis of postpartum illness. The term was taken out of the Diagnostic and Statistical Manual of Mental Disorders published by American Psychiatric Association in the early 20th century, and in 1972 the World Health Organization also took it out of its International Classification of Diseases. Ogle and Katkin claim that psychiatrists are unable to agree on the nature and aetiology of these psychoses and that is why they were removed from World Health Organisation's International Classification of Diseases and the Diagnostic and Statistical Manual of Mental Disorders published by American Psychiatric Association: Ogle and Maier-Katkin, "A Rationale for Infanticide Laws" (1993) *Crim. LR* 903. Whatever the reason, there is at present no official diagnosis of postpartum psychosis anywhere in the world, and as the UK Law Commission, Consultation Paper No177: *A New Homicide Act for England and Wales?* (28 November 2005) notes, "legal theory as to whether there is a valid psychiatric basis for the defence continues to be polarised accordingly."

[16] Walker, *Crimes and Insanity in England* (University Press, Edinburgh, 1968), at p 132; Ward notes that "lactational insanity" was typically a condition of "overworked and poorly fed women" often suffering from anaemia. Overwork, malnutrition and anaemia were all common conditions among working class mothers of the 1930s. Indirectly, thus, the 1938 Infanticide Act [UK] took account of the social conditions which probably lay behind the violent acts of some depressed mothers, but by

Commission recommended the removal of the reference to lactation from the current legislative definition of infanticide and in 2005 the UK Law Commission made the same recommendation.[17]

The excuse that the balance of the mother's mind is disturbed by the after-effects of childbirth is the subject of more lively debate. Ogle and Katkin note that although the incidence of depression during the post-partum period can be regarded as fact, this does not justify a unique law on infanticide as most people experience transient depression, the occurrence of which is no more frequent or intense in new mothers.[18] More serious post-partum psychiatric illnesses exist in one or two per one thousand post-partum women.[19] However, Morris and Wilczynski note that such a serious post-partum psychiatric illness is very rarely the cause of a woman killing her child.[20] In reality, infanticide is more regularly applied to women suffering from the psychological and social stresses of child birth and child rearing or from pre-existing mental conditions.[21] Indeed, the legislative definition of infanticide does not explicitly require a psychosis or severe mental illness be proven, but rather a disturbance of the balance of the mind.[22] Thus, many non-psychotic mothers who kill their children may be dealt with under the current infanticide law.

---

putting the defence on a medical footing the Act reassured those who were concerned lest "it should be thought that taking the life of an infant child is not as serious a form of murder as taking the life of anybody else.": Ward, "Legislating for Human Nature: Legal Responses to Infanticide, 1860–1938" in *Infanticide: Historical Essays on Child Murder and Concealment, 1550–2000* (Jackson ed, Ashgate, Aldershot, UK, 2002), at p 249.

[17] The Victorian Law Reform Commission, *Defences to Homicide: Final Report* (2004); UK Law Commission, Consultation Paper No177: *A New Homicide Act for England and Wales?* (28 November 2005).

[18] Ogle and Maier-Katkin, "A Rationale for Infanticide Laws" (1993) *Crim. L.R.* 903.

[19] *ibid.*

[20] Morris and Wilczynski note that estimates are that this occurs in about 5 cases per year. Research shows about half the women who plead guilty or are convicted of infanticide aren't suffering any identifiable form of mental illness: Morris and Wilczynski, "Parents Who Kill their Children" *Crim. L.R.* (1993); Ogle and Katkin note that whilst it's inappropriate to dismiss the link between childbirth and mental illness as a myth created by the authors of the Infanticide Act, this doesn't mean that every person, or even woman, who kills a child is actually suffering from a disturbance of the balance of the mind. Indeed, a study by psychologist P.T. d'Orban of 89 women charged with murder or attempted murder of their kids, found that only 24 suffered from psychotic illness: Ogle and Maier-Katkin, *ibid.*

[21] New South Wales Law Reform Commission, Report 83: *Partial Defence to Murder: Provocation and Infanticide* (1997).

[22] Infanticide Act 1949.

The Arbitrarily Restrictive Provisions of Infanticide Law

The Infanticide Act 1949 limits the application of infanticide to natural mothers of an infant victim less than 12 months of age. However, as noted above, research shows that mental disturbance following child birth is more often due to a pre-existing mental illness or the social and psychological disturbances of child care rather than a specific post-partum mental illness.[23] This being the case, other groups of offenders are arguably just as vulnerable and deserve to be treated with the same compassion as the biological mother. These include killers of children over twelve months, adoptive parents or other primary carers, and male offenders.[24]

Moreover, the above-mentioned stresses of pre-existing mental illness or the social and psychological disturbances of child care are not restricted to a year after the birth. The 12-month age limit is considered by the UK Law Commission to be "necessarily arbitrary."[25] However, there is little agreement amongst different countries' legal systems as to what the appropriate cut off age should be.[26]

---

23 See above, nn 20 and 21.

24 *Doughty* (1986) 83 Cr App R 319 provides an example of a case in which a father killed an infant. In that case, the British Court of Appeal held that the persistent crying of a 17-day-old baby could in theory amount to provocation (although they fully expected a jury to reject this on the merits). This case provides an interesting contrast to infanticide cases. The father, who was said to be "caring and affectionate", had attempted to silence the child by covering his head with cushions and kneeling on them, thus killing him. He had his conviction for murder quashed and one of manslaughter substituted. He received a sentence of five years' imprisonment. The UK Law Commission, Consultation Paper No 177: *A New Homicide Act for England and Wales?* (28 November 2005), at p 227, questions why the defendant father in *Doughty* didn't receive a much lower sentence, as would a mother convicted of infanticide in similar circumstances. One possible reason given by the Commission is that the circumstances in which mothers kill their infants differs from that of men (and possibly other carers) who kill infants and this difference may justify a disparity in treatment. However, this is not a strong enough justification. Morris and Wilczynski note that whilst there is a common perception that women and men commit filicide for very different reasons and in very different circumstances (the very existence of the offence of infanticide is an example of this) we do not know this. Nonetheless, "men are perceived as "wicked" and in need of punishment rather than as victims in need of sympathy, support and psychiatric treatment...[In contrast] women are assumed to be inherently passive, gentle and tolerant; and mothers are assumed to be nurturing, caring and altruistic. It's and easy step therefore to assume that a 'normal' woman ... must have been 'mad' to kill her own child.": Morris and Wilczynski, "Parents Who Kill their Children" (1993) *Crim. L.R.* 31.

25 UK Law Commission, Consultation Paper No177: *A New Homicide Act for England and Wales?* (28 November 2005).

26 For example, the Malaysian age limit is less than 12 months (Penal Code (Malaysia), s 309A). In New Zealand, the offence of infanticide applies where the mother kills any of her children under the

The result of these restrictions on age and relationship is often unjust and illogical and some commentators have proposed their removal from the Infanticide Act.[27] For instance, in 2004, the Victorian Law Reform Commission recommended retention of the infanticide law, but recommended a modification of the definition to include 'disturbance of the mind as result of either not having recovered from effect of giving birth or any disorder consequent on child birth,' increasing the age limit of the victim to two years, and application of the law to a woman who kills her older child due to mental disturbance caused by the birth of her younger child.[28] Similarly, in 2005 the UK Law Commission supported the retention of the infanticide law but argued that the age limit of the child should be raised to two years.[29] These proposals address some of the current anomalies of the infanticide law caused by the arbitrarily restrictive definition. However, the extension of the age limit amidst wide international divergence on the issue should be regarded with caution.[30] Furthermore, whilst the Victorian Law Reform Commission's expanded definition of infanticide acknowledges motivating factors other than severe post partum depression, by removing infanticide from its biological base it raises the problematic issue of whether infanticide can justifiably be limited to biological mothers. Thus, neither of these proposals would eliminate the complexities of this controversial law,

age of ten (Crimes Act 1961 (NZ), s 178). Victoria, Australia is considering extending the age limit to two years (Crimes (Homicide) Act 2005, s 5); However, the law of both New Zealand and Victoria contains no defence of diminished responsibility. The 1938 Infanticide Act (UK) created the 12-month limit to counteract the unjust arbitrariness that resulted from the 1922 Infanticide Act's restriction to "newborns." However, as the UK Law Commission in its Consultation Paper No 177: *A New Homicide Act for England and Wales?* (28 November 2005) noted, there may be deserving cases above the 12-month limit and thus such injustices may still exist.

[27] Some illogical results include, for instance, where a new mother whose mind is disturbed by the effects of giving birth in killing her own infant simultaneously kills someone else's infant for whom she is caring at the time. In such circumstances, there would be a presumption that her disturbed balance of mind had caused her to kill her own infant, and she could plead or be charged with infanticide. In relation to the other infant, however, she would be forced to rely on the defence of diminished responsibility; a similar situation arises where there are two children—one of whom is under twelve months and the other whom is over twelve months. The law on infanticide also doesn't extend to the woman who does not succeed in killing her child but merely injures it. Such a mother would be charged with attempted murder: New South Wales Law Reform Commission, Report 83: *Partial Defence to Murder: Provocation and Infanticide* (1997).

[28] The Victorian Law Reform Commission, *Defences to Homicide: Final Report* (2004)

[29] See above, n 25.

[30] See above, n 26.

but would further diminish an already fragile legal recognition of the sanctity of infant life.

Perceived Procedural Advantages of Infanticide Law

A common argument in favour of the infanticide law is the theoretically significant procedural advantages it affords the accused.[31] The woman on trial avoids the distress of both a murder charge and the prospect of being tried for murder, and furthermore the burden of proving infanticide rests with the prosecution.

The trauma a murder trial imposed on female offenders was a primary motivation for passing the 1949 Infanticide Act.[32] At that time, there was a mandatory sentence of death for murder. However, this has since been changed to life imprisonment[33] and thus the defendant must no longer endure the distress of the judge donning his black cap to proclaim a sentence of death. In addition, the prosecution may accept a plea of guilty to manslaughter where a woman is charged with murder and there is clear evidence of mental disturbance. The prosecution may also choose to exercise its discretion by laying an indictment for manslaughter, instead of murder, where the accused clearly suffered from an impaired mental capacity. Thus, the abolition of the current law on infanticide would not create any significant procedural disadvantages for female defendants.

Undoubtedly any trial, whether it is for manslaughter or murder, will be a traumatic experience for the defendant. However, this is insignificant in comparison to the tragic loss of innocent life and may be a necessary price to pay in order to ensure that that life is vindicated. "We are dealing with a fundamental question of right and wrong. In dealing with such a subject one has to approach it fundamentally in a different way from what I might call merely procedural matters."[34]

---

[31] The Victorian Law Reform Commission, *Defences to Homicide: Final Report* (2004); UK Law Commission, Consultation Paper No 177: *A New Homicide Act for England and Wales?* (28 November 2005); New South Wales Law Reform Commission, Report 83: *Partial Defence to Murder: Provocation and Infanticide* (1997).

[32] *Dáil Debates* Cols 265–283; *Seanad Debates* Cols 1471–1477.

[33] However, the Irish Law Reform Commission, in its *Report on Sentencing* (August 1996), recommended that mandatory and minimum sentences of imprisonment for indictable offences be abolished.

[34] Major de Valera, *Dáil Debates* Col 276.

The Solution: Diminished Responsibility

"The availability of diminished responsibility will allow juries treat cases in a more sympathetic and humane way."[35] Diminished responsibility, due to be enacted into Irish law as part of the Criminal Law Insanity Bill 2002, will be available as a partial defence to reduce murder to manslaughter where an offender kills in a state of significant mental impairment.[36]

Section 5(1)) of the Criminal Law Insanity Bill 2002 provides that "where a person is tried for murder and the jury or, as the case may be, the Special Criminal Court finds that the person – (a) did the act alleged, (b) was at the time suffering from a mental disorder, and (c) the mental disorder was not such as to justify finding him or her not guilty by reason of insanity, but was such as to diminish substantially his or her responsibility for the act, the jury or court, as the case may be, shall find the person not guilty of that offence but guilty of manslaughter on the ground of diminished responsibility."

The use of this defence in infanticide cases would ensure that the law continues to treat infanticidal mothers with compassion, through the application of uniform standards which would simultaneously give appropriate recognition to the tragic loss of infant life.

Nonetheless, the possibility of merging diminished responsibility and infanticide is a source of some controversy. The UK Law Commission has objected that diminished responsibility would not be wide enough to cover all infanticide cases as it requires a mental disturbance of greater severity than that currently required under infanticide.[37] It has been argued that some women convicted of infanticide would not be able to meet the definition of "mental disorder" in the Mental Health Act 1983 (UK), s 1, and thus would not be able to rely on the defence of diminished responsibility.[38] However, the New South Wales Law Reform Commission has countered that the defence of diminished responsibility as provided for in s 2 of the Homicide Act 1957 (UK) does not require the accused to prove a mental disorder as defined in the Mental Health Act 1983 (UK).[39] Moreover, the Irish defence could be

---

[35] Mr Kett, 171 *Seanad Debates* Cols 776–778.

[36] Criminal Law (Insanity) Bill 2002, s 5.

[37] See above, n 25.

[38] Wilczynski, *Child Homicide* (Greenwich Medical Media Ltd, London, 1997), at p 157.

[39] New South Wales Law Reform Commission, Report 83: *Partial Defence to Murder: Provocation and Infanticide* (1997), above, n 22.

modelled on a broader version than the UK law to ensure it has the scope to accommodate all infanticide cases. One example of a broader version of diminished responsibility is that proposed by the New South Wales Law Reform Commission, whose amended definition of the defence of diminished responsibility was drafted with the specific intent of accommodating all cases justifiably falling within existing infanticide provisions.[40]

The New South Wales Law Reform Commission's proposed reformulation is as follows: "A person, who would otherwise be guilty of murder, is not guilty of murder if, at the time of the act or omission causing death, that person's capacity to: (a) understand events; or (b) judge whether that person's actions were right or wrong; or (c) control himself or herself, was so substantially impaired by an abnormality of mental functioning arising from an underlying condition as to warrant reducing murder to manslaughter. 'Underlying condition' in this subsection means a pre-existing mental or physiological condition other than of a transitory kind."'[41]

Disorders such as depression or post partum paranoid psychosis, which might constitute the basis of an infanticide plea, would be characterised under the Commission's recommended reformulation of diminished responsibility as an "abnormality of mental functioning" affecting the accused's capacity to understand events, to judge right from wrong, or to control herself. This statutory definition of diminished responsibility is much more detailed than that which is proposed in the Irish Criminal Law Insanity Bill (2002) and provides an ideal model for the Irish legislature to follow in ensuring the Irish defence has the scope to accommodate all infanticide cases.

One of the principle difficulties with the current law of infanticide is the flawed medical principles on which it is based.[42] Diminished responsibility would have the advantage of not limiting the type of mental disturbance which might give rise to the crime of infanticide to conditions that resulted directly from the effects of giving birth and thus would be widely available to mothers who kill in a state of

---

[40] New South Wales Law Reform Commission in Recommendation 4, Report 82: *Partial Defences to Murder: Diminished Responsibility* (May 1997).

[41] *ibid*, s 3.43.

[42] Refer to s 4 in the text, above.

genuine mental distress.[43] However, by requiring that the offender be suffering from a significant mental impairment, this law would ensure justice is served through sufficient retribution on mothers whose baby suffers death by their rational hand.

In contrast to the arbitrarily restrictiveness of the current infanticide law,[44] the defence of diminished responsibility imposes no restrictions on eligible offenders or victims but instead allow appropriate consideration of the effect of mental impairment on each individual offender's culpability. Reliance on diminished responsibility would also increase uniformity of the law as the defence is a current fall-back for those who do not fall within the restrictive provisions of the Infanticide Act.[45]

Regarding the perceived procedural advantages of an infanticide law,[46] the UK Law Commission noted that postnatal depression is frequently undetected and thus untreated in clinical practice because women do not report their symptoms to health professionals.[47] This would make it difficult for an infanticide defendant to discharge the burden of proof of diminished responsibility. Debate regarding the reverse onus in insanity cases and the general rule that the prosecution must prove its case is a significant source of current legal controversy and it has been argued that the current situation is difficult to justify.[48] The Irish legislature could thus have the burden of proof rest on the prosecution in the defence of diminished responsibility.[49]

---

[43] It has been suggested that as a result of the restriction on the types of mental disturbance giving rise to the crime of infanticide to those that result directly from the effects of giving birth, medical experts frequently feel compelled to alter their diagnoses to ensure conformity with the legislative requirements: Lansdowne, "Infanticide: Psychiatrists in the Plea Bargaining Process" (1990) 16 *Monash University Law Review* 41 at p 54; New South Wales Law Reform Commission, Report 83: *Partial Defence to Murder: Provocation and Infanticide* (1997), notes that the defence of diminished responsibility would not require medical experts to distort their diagnoses in order to reflect what are essentially outmoded notions of mental illnesses in childbirth.

[44] Refer to s 5 in the text, above.

[45] See above, n 25.

[46] Refer to s 6 in the text, above.

[47] See above, n 25.

[48] McAuley, *Insanity, Psychiatry, and Criminal Responsibility* (Round Hall Press, Dublin, 1993), at pp 95–96.

[49] This would be in accordance with one of the recommendations made by the UK Butler Committee in its *Report on Mentally Abnormal Offenders* (1975).

The law on diminished responsibility is narrower than the law on infanticide in one respect in that it requires a causal connection between the accused's mental impairment and the killing of the victim, whereas infanticide does not express such a requirement. However, proof of causation is central to the notion of criminal responsibility and thus while diminished responsibility may be more restrictive in this regard, it is submitted that this does not place too heavy a burden on the accused.

In 1997, the New South Wales Law Reform Commission proposed the abolition of the infanticide law conditional on there being a defence of diminished responsibility in some form in New South Wales.[50] This is in accordance with the position advocated throughout this essay and is the most appropriate form of legal action. The use of this defence in infanticide cases would not only vindicate the baby's life by treating the infanticidal mother the same as all other killers with diminished responsibility but also—aside from any moral implications—would render the Infanticide Act wholly redundant.

Conclusion: A Time to Answer the Silent Victims' Cries

Controversy regarding both medical and moral aspects of the infanticide law has fuelled academic debate, and several Commonwealth jurisdictions have recognised the need for legal reform.[51] However, there is a persistent failure by commentators to consider the issue of infanticide from the victims' perspective. Supporters of the current infanticide law speak of a desire to spare the mother any undue trauma, which they regard as more important than respect for the right to life of those mothers' infant children. Even abolitionists' scathing criticisms of the Infanticide Act focus on medical and ideological arguments, largely ignoring the fundamental issue of the tragic loss of infant life. The very concept of a law on infanticide undermines the sanctity of infants' life and their right to equal treatment before the law. Such a law cannot be allowed to exist in Ireland, and its enduring statutory presence reveals a condemning flaw in the Irish legal system. It is too easy to ignore the silent victims of these crimes, and it requires a brave legislature to challenge the status quo and advocate for those babies that otherwise have no voice. However, the time to address this issue is now. By removing the Infanticide Act 1949 from Irish law, incoming

[50] New South Wales Law Reform Commission, Report 83: *Partial Defence to Murder: Provocation and Infanticide* (1997).

[51] See above, n 31.

legislation on diminished responsibility can be formulated specifically to ensure the accommodation of all potential infanticide cases within its remit. Until the Infanticide Act is abolished the threat of future injustices shall continue to be upheld in Irish statute books, whilst the unheard cries of innocent infant victims remain silenced forever.[52]

[52] Note from the author: Since this essay was submitted, there have been some important developments in the law relating to infanticide in Ireland. On the 12th of April 2006, the Criminal Law (Insanity) Act 2006 came into force. Two final-stage amendments are worth nothing. Firstly, the defence of diminished responsibility is provided for in s 6 of the 2006 Act, which now contains an additional subsection regarding women found guilty of infanticide (see s 6 (3)):

> **6.**—(1) Where a person is tried for murder and the jury or, as the case may be, the Special Criminal Court finds that the person—
> (a) did the act alleged,
> (b) was at the time suffering from a mental disorder, and
> (c) the mental disorder was not such as to justify finding him or her not guilty by reason of insanity, but was such as to diminish substantially his or her responsibility for the act, the jury or court, as the case may be, shall find the person not guilty of that offence but guilty of manslaughter on the ground of diminished responsibility.
> (2) Subject to section 5(4), where a person is tried for the offence specified in subsection (1), it shall be for the defence to establish that the person is, by virtue of this section, not liable to be convicted of that offence.
> (3) A woman found guilty of infanticide may be dealt with in accordance with subsection (1).

Secondly, section 22 of the 2006 Act now amends the Infanticide Act 1949 as follows:

> **22.**—Section 1(3) of the Infanticide Act 1949 is hereby amended—
> (a) in subsection (3)(c), by the substitution of "by reason of a mental disorder (within the meaning of the Criminal Law (Insanity) Act 2006)" for "by reason of the effect of lactation", and
> (b) by the substitution of "as for manslaughter and, on conviction may be dealt with under section 6(3) of the Criminal Law (Insanity) Act 2006 as if she had been found guilty of manslaughter on the grounds of diminished responsibility" for "and punished as for manslaughter".

"Man, I Feel Like a Woman!" A Proposal for the Legal Recognition of Transsexualism in Ireland

by

Maebh Harding and Mark Murphy*

On 9 July 2002, the High Court missed an opportunity to bring Irish jurisprudence on marriage law and human rights in line with other common law jurisdictions and the European Convention on Human Rights. In *Foy v An tArd Chláiritheoir*,[1] McKechnie J ruled that people living with transsexualism were not entitled to rectify their birth certificates to acknowledge their new gender, and, as a result, not entitled to remarry in their new identity.

This paper examines the stark divergence of Irish law from other Western jurisdictions in light of the *Foy* case. The authors contend that Irish law in this area is in serious need of legislative reform in order to accord proper human rights to people suffering from transsexualism.

What is transsexualism?

Transsexualism has been reported since antiquity. It occurs when an individual finds her or himself to be of the opposite sex to that indicated by their own body. People living with transsexualism undergo irreversible sex affirmation treatment on their own initiative because of their compelling need to experience sexual harmony between body and their innate sexual identity (otherwise called neurological, psychological or brain sex).[2]

---

* This essay was awarded first place in the Law Society of Ireland, *Student Law Reform Essay Competition 2006.*

1 *Foy v An tArd Chláiritheoir & Ors* [2002] IEHC 116.

2 Wallbank, "*Re Kevin* in Perspective" (2004) 9 *Deakin Law Review* 461.

Transsexualism occurs in up to 2.5 per cent of the population.[3] Many people with transsexualism only affirm their innate sex later in life and may have married and borne children in their first naturally assigned sex. This creates complicated legal issues as regards marriage rights and the status of children.

Terminology

The language surrounding transsexualism has been influenced by cultural prejudice, ignorance and mystification. Indeed, one of the major criticisms of the English Gender Recognition Act 2004 has been its use of pejorative terms to describe people suffering with transsexualism. In Australia, the recent public trial of *Re Kevin*[4] required the experience of transsexualism to be explained in an affirmative and intelligible way.[5] Following suit, this essay proposes the use of affirmative language in the drafting of statutes.

The noun "transsexual" should not be used but, rather, a person living with transsexualism.

The "legal sex" of a person refers to the sex first assigned to the person at birth by a medical practitioner following casual inspection of the person's external genitalia. It is recorded amongst the particulars of the legal identity of that person in the birth register of the state.

The sex a person living with transsexualism identifies with is known as the "innate sex" or "brain sex" of the individual.

When a person with transsexualism lives a public life consistent with their innate sex they are said to have affirmed their sex (i.e. an affirmed female is an individual who was born male but lives as a woman).

All medical treatment is referred to as "sex affirmation treatment". Once a person has undergone irreversible sex-affirmation treatment, such a person is said to be "a person of transsexual background".

---

[3] Conway, "How often does transsexualism occur?" www.lynnconway.com.

[4] [2001] *Fam CA* 1074.

[5] Wallbank, "Difference on Trial—Transsexualism in Family Law and De Facto Relationships Litigation" Law Council of Australia for Family Law, www.familylawsection.og.au.

Why does Transsexualism Occur?

A distinction must be made between transsexualism and other phenomena such as transgender expression, transvestism, homosexuality and mental disorders described as "gender dysphoria".[6]

People who do not identify with their legal sex but do not seek to live as the opposite sex are known as *trans* (e.g. transvestites). People who live a large part of their lives as the opposite sex to their legal sex but do not desire complete and irreversible sex affirmation treatment are known as *transgender*. Sexuality is a totally different issue to transsexualism; the sexuality of people suffering from transsexualism varies with the individual.

Transsexualism itself is a form of an intersexual condition.[7] The physiology of the human brain is sexually differentiated at birth just like genitalia and is fixed and unalterable by the completion of infancy.[8] The biological explanation for the condition distinguishes it from psychological disorders such as "gender dysphoria" and gender identity disorder. Medical science traditionally pathologised transsexualism and treated it as a psychological disorder. This outdated view has dominated the law in respect of transsexualism and is epitomised by the English decision of *Corbett v Corbett*,[9] examined below.[10] Many transsexual people are not mentally ill and have no sense of unease with their gender.

---

[6] The categorisation used in this essay is that of the "trans" rights campaigner Stephen Whittle,[7] Vice-President of the British Press-for-Change campaign. See www.pfc.org.uk

[7] "Intersex" occurs where a physical examination on birth concludes that the child is of indeterminate sex.

[8] Michel, "A Psycho-Endocrinological Overview of Transsexualism" (2001) 145 *European Journal of Endocrinology* 365.

[9] [1971] P 83.

[10] Transsexualism was not recognised as a distinct medical category until 1968, when it appeared as a separate heading in the *Index Medicus* (Amercian Medical Association, 1968). Sectioning into mental hospitals, aversion therapy and ECT were used in its treatment. In 1980, transsexualism was entered in the American Psychiatric Association's revised edition of the Diagnostic and Statistical Manual of Registered Mental Illness as *Gender Identity Disorder*, which was defined as psychological problems stemming from a sense of unease with one's gender. In the UK, Harry Benjamin introduced guidelines on treating transsexualism to the general medical community in 1954. Throughout the 1950s and 1960s trans-people in the UK were understood to have a congenitally-based condition and were entitled if appropriate to have their birth certificates corrected and marry. The pathologisation of transsexualism and the disenfranchisement of trans-people in the UK occurred in the 1970 case of *Corbett v Corbett*, in which medical evidence of congenital disposition, which had formerly been accepted in courts of law, was now ignored. See further Playdon, *Intersection Oppressions: Ending Discrimination against Lesbians, Gay Men and Trans People in the UK* (Oxford, Portland, Oregon 2004).

The disorder model of transsexualism is gradually being overtaken, as many commentators, judges and medical professionals come to the conclusion that the condition of transsexualism is not mere delusion. In *Re Alex,*[11] Nicholson CJ declared himself to be uncomfortable with such diagnosis, and in *Re Kevin,*[12] the medical evidence accepted by the court expressly declared that Kevin's identification with the opposite sex was not as a result of mental ill health or delusion.

This is not to say that disorders such as *gender dysphoria* and *gender identity disorder* do not exist, but rather that they are different to transsexualism, which is an intersexual condition. One of the flaws of the British Gender Recognition Act of 2004 was expressing transsexualism solely in these terms.

We should allow transsexualism to be perceived as a natural aspect of human diversity rather than a disorder. The truly important role of psychiatrists and psychology in the diagnostic process is to rule out disorders or illness. Any legislation should steer away from branding all individuals with transsexualism as suffering from mental disorders.

Treatment by the Courts

The courts have approached the issue of transsexualism in three ways:

(i) "Exclusive" judgments such as *Foy, Bellinger v Bellinger*[13] and *Corbett* focus on biological sex at birth in accordance with the *Corbett* criteria.[14] These judgments focus on the causes of transsexualism rather than the effects. They also assume that an affirmed male would never be able to fulfil stereotypical sexual roles within a marriage[15] and are thus very genitocentric. They are uncritical of the proposition that transsexualism is a form of mental ill-health and do not allow recognition of the new sex.

---

11 [2004] *Fam CA* 297, [2].

12 [2001] *Fam CA* 1074 at [46].

13 *Bellinger v Bellinger* [2003] UKHL 21.

14 Examined below.

15 *Corbett* [1971] at 83.

(ii) "Social Justice" decisions such as *Attorney-General v Otahuhu Family Court,*[16] *Goodwin*[17] and *I*[18] do not attempt to address the causes of transsexualism. They reject the *Corbett* approach and determine that surgically affirmed people with transsexualism should be able to marry in their affirmed sex. They are based on a pragmatic acceptance of the existence of people with transsexualism but do not provide any legitimacy for people with transsexualism to be allowed change gender.

(iii) "Inclusive" cases such as *Re Kevin, Estate of Gardiner*[19] and *Re Anonymous*[20] place the individual in the sex he/she most resembles and identifies with. They ground the decision in contemporary medical science and connect transsexualism with other inter-sexual conditions. Any legislative effort should follow this approach.

Legal Problems

There are relatively few situations in which it is necessary for a court to determine someone's sex. In most areas of law gender is irrelevant. However, employment law, marriage law and certain criminal offences are dependent on gender and most legal systems use gender as a means of categorisation.

The Legal Definition of Sex

The only Irish case to address this issue fully was the recent decision of *Foy v An tArd Chláraitheoir,* which is currently awaiting a second High Court review in light of the *Goodwin* decision. The applicant, although living as a woman for ten years by the time her action came to court, had lived as a man for around 45 years, married, and had children with his wife before undergoing sex affirmation surgery in 1992. Dr Foy sought an order of *certiorari* quashing the refusal of the Registrar of Births, Deaths & Marriages to amend her birth certificate to display her new female gender and name. The Registrar had indicated that such could only be granted where an administrative mistake on a birth certificate was required to be rectified, according

---

16 [1995] 1 NZLR 603.

17 *Goodwin v UK* [2002] 2 FCR 577.

18 *I v UK* [2002] 2 FCR 613.

19 No 85,030, 11 May 2001, Court of Appeals, Kansas.

20 293 NYS 2d 834 (1968).

to the Registration of Births and Deaths (Ireland) Act 1863 as amended, and the 1880 Regulations made there-under. Alternatively, Dr Foy sought a declaration that this legislative framework was unconstitutional, in that it breached her rights to dignity, privacy, equality and her right to marry.

Interestingly, the 1880 Regulations did not dictate any specific guidelines as regards determining sex at birth. To fill the void, the Registrar had adopted the policy laid down in *Corbett,*[21] which was based on the four established medical indicia of gender:

(i) chromosomal factors;
(ii) genital factors[22];
(iii) gonadal factors[23];
(iv) psychological factors.

Ormrod J's reasoning in *Corbett* was based on four points[24]:

(i) Sex is fixed at birth and cannot be changed by natural development or surgical intervention.
(ii) Gonadal, chromosomal and genital tests at birth determine the sex. Psychological sex is irrelevant.
(iii) In determining a person's sex for the purpose of marriage, the capacity for heterosexual intercourse with their partner is crucial.
(iv) Certainty as to sex is crucial for the law.

Corbett became the leading case on the legal definition of sex in England and Wales and many other countries.[25] Ormrod J acknowledged that his test would not provide an assignation of sex for some intersex people and left such cases to another day.

---

[21] *Corbett v Corbett* [1970] 2 WLR 1306.

[22] i.e. the presence or absence of testes or ovaries.

[23] Including internal sex organs.

[24] The learned judge said in summary: "the law should adopt in the first place, the first three of the doctors' criteria, i.e. the chromosomal, gonadal and genital tests, and if all three are congruent, determine the sex for the purpose of marriage accordingly, and ignore any operative intervention.", *Corbett v Corbett* [1970] 2 WLR 1306 at 1325.

[25] e.g. *B v B* 355 NYS 2d 712 in USA and *W v W* [1976] 2 SALR 308 in South Africa.

In *W v W (Nullity: Gender)*,[26] Charles J reconsidered the legal position of intersex people. Charles J proposed that in cases where the *Corbett* factors did not all point in one direction, other factors such as secondary sexual characteristics should be considered. By permitting secondary sexual characteristics and psychological factors into account Charles J appears to reject the assertion in *Corbett* that sex is fixed at birth and cannot be changed. It has been suggested that the *W v W* test is inconsistent with the *Corbett* approach.[27]

This list was approved in *Bellinger*,[28] but no indication was given of how to weigh the six factors when they point in different directions. It is a matter for the judge's discretion. Some commentators indicate that in conflicting situations the individual's psychological attachment to one sex or the other is likely to be regarded as crucial.[29]

In the 30 years following Ormrod J's decision, its exclusive focus on the three "corporal" indicia for determining gender came in for extensive criticism by the medical community, in light of advances made in scientific understanding, which advances were acknowledged by McKechnie J in *Foy*. In particular, a new criterion for gender assessment known as "brain differentiation" had gained widespread support.[30]

---

26 [2001] Fam 111.

27 Chau and Herring, "Men, Women, People: The Definition of Sex" (Oxford, Portland, Oregan 2004).

28 *Bellinger v Bellinger* [2003] UKHL 21.

29 Chau and Herring, "Men, Women, People: The Definition of Sex" (Oxford, Portland, Oregan 2004).

30 Brain differentiation as a theory centres around a particular part of the hypothalamus, the central subdivision of the bed nucleus of the stria terminalis (BSTc), which is responsible for biological functions such as hunger, appetite, respiration, cardiac system, sexual activity and sexual behaviour. It has been shown that the (BSTc) was larger in "normal men" than in "normal women", and also shown that in the six male to female transsexuals looked at in one particular study, the size of their (BSTc) was found to be within the female range, not within the male range. Studies on laboratory rats, testified to by experts at trial and discussed in the judgment of McKechnie J at p 80 *et seq*, have shown that the BSTc plays an essential role in masculine sexual behaviour and in the regulation of gonadotrophin release, which is related to gender formation in the foetus. However this finding was heavily qualified by the study itself which conceded that "there has been no direct evidence that the BST has such a role in human sexual behaviour but our demonstration of a sexually dimorphic pattern in the size of the human BSTc, ... indicates that this nucleus may also be involved in human sexual or reproductive functions." Professor Gooren, a specialist in endocrinology, gave evidence before McKechnie J that the word *"may "*, is too loose and should be replaced by the word *"likely"*. The court held nevertheless that the qualifications deprived the study of any conclusive weight, and that the traditional view of gender should remain unimpeached.

McKechnie J, after an extensive and considered review of the expert scientific evidence before the court, decided that brain differentiation was not yet sufficiently proven to be elevated to the status of the other "sex indicators". As a result, the "traditional" view of gender—as a matter decided irrevocably at birth—would remain.[31]

The authors contend that the traditional method of determining sex at birth should remain but flexibility in regards to inter-sex individuals should be ensured. Children born of indeterminate sex should be allowed a number of years to decide their gender in line with current medical practice.

Right to Change One's Birth Certificate

In *Foy*, McKechnie J held that one's birth certificate is a historical, not a transient, document.[32] Its value to society, the court held, is crucial to marriage rights and rights of succession and motherhood, amongst others. The court therefore found it reasonable for the domestic law of this State to have in place a system of registration upon birth including an entry as to sex, unassailable by the coming to light of a subsequent transsexual condition.

However, the birth register is assailable as it stands. Adoptees are furnished with a new birth cert at the time of their adoption. Such a system could work for people suffering from transsexualism and is in fact the system recently introduced in the UK by the Gender Recognition Act 2004.

The European Court of Human Rights, in *Goodwin v UK* and *I v UK*,[33] held that post-operative trans-people have the right under Art 8 and 12 of the Convention to be recognised by the law as being of the sex they claim to be and that sex is not necessarily defined at birth.[34] By not allowing people with a transsexual

[31] *Foy v An tArd Chláiritheoir & Ors* [2002] IEHC 116; 83-97.

[32] A birth certificate, the Court said, is "...not a continuum record of one's travels through life or even of the most important and most significant events of that journey..." *ibid* at 125.

[33] [2002] 2 FCR 577; [2002] 2 FCR 613.

[34] Article 8 of the ECHR says: "(1) Everyone has the right to respect for his private and family life, his home and his correspondence. (2) There shall be no interference by a public authority with the exercise of this right except such as is in accordance with the law and is necessary in a democratic society in the interests of national security, public safety or the economic well-being of the country, for the prevention of disorder or crime, for the protection of health or morals, or for the protection

background to register their affirmed sex Ireland is out of line with the rulings of the ECHR.

The authors contend that people with a transsexual history should be furnished with a certificate confirming their new gender from the date of compete sex affirmation surgery. The surgery would be confirmed by a medical practitioner practising in the state. The new certificate would be linked to the original birth record by a confidential system similar to the current adoptive Index.

Right to Marry

In Irish marriage law, gender remains a crucial determinant of status and capacity.[35] McKechnie J reaffirmed in *Foy* that "marriage as understood by the Constitution, by statute and by case law refers to the union of a biological man with a biological woman".[36] The extension of this rule has been the denial of the right to marry to people with a transsexual background.

In *Foy*, the court found no breach of the constitutional right to equality. As no transsexuals could marry, they were all treated the same by the State. As regards the obvious inequality between, say an affirmed female and a biological female, McKechnie J simply concluded that a difference "unquestionably exists".[37]

However, *W v W* rejected the view that sexual intercourse was a key element in defining sex for the purposes of marriage by pointing out that there is much more to marriage and to individual identity than sexual intercourse. This approach appears to be correct. Sexual intercourse is not key to marriage. Non-consummation or impotence renders a marriage voidable rather than void. Without the necessity for "normal" sexual intercourse in marriage the genito-centric approach of *Corbett* does not seem to be justified.

---

of the rights and freedoms of others." Article 12 of the ECHR says: "Men and women of marriageable age have the right to marry and to found a family, according to the national laws governing the exercise of this right."

35 Ryan, "Marriage at the Boundaries of Gender: The 'Transsexual Dilemma' Resolved?" [2004] IJFL.

36 *Foy v An tArd Chláraitheoir* [2002] IEHC 116 at 130.

37 The learned judge said that: "A person with a transsexual background could never entirely shed his/her biologically ordained characteristics, nor fully acquire those of their new gender."

Foy also rejects the claim based on the right to marry as people with a transsexual background could still marry people of their original opposite gender. In *Goodwin* the ECtHR pointed out that this was a disingenuous argument as the applicant in that case would never wish to marry such a person. The court expressly noted that neither biological nor psychological criteria on their own suffice but that the court must look at the totality of facts and condition of the individual as of the date of marriage.

In *Re Kevin,*[38] Chisholm J held that *all* relevant matters needed to be considered when assessing an individual's sex, not just the person's biological and physical characteristics at birth, as in *Corbett,* but also: the person's life experiences, including the sex in which he or she is brought up and the person's attitude to it; the person's self-perception as a man or woman; the extent to which the person has functioned in society as a man or a woman; any hormonal, surgical or other medical sex reassignment treatments the person has undergone, and the consequences of such treatment; and the person's biological, psychological and physical characteristics at the time of the marriage, including (if they can be identified) any biological features of the person's brain that are associated with a particular sex.[39]

As a result of *Re Kevin,* transgender persons' assigned sex is now recognised for the purposes of validating their marriages in Australia.

In the case of *Attorney-General v Family Court of Otahuhu,*[40] New Zealand family law took a giant leap forward as regards transsexual rights. Ellis J simply held that post-operative transgender persons were entitled to marry in their new gender.

By refusing to accept the effect of gender reassignment on marriage Ireland remains out of step with international developments and finds itself in breach of the European Convention on Human Rights.

The authors submit that Irish legislation should allow people to marry based on their sex at the time of marriage. This would not require any change to marital law but would be the logical progression of the introduction of new gender certificates. If the new spouse is not aware or is deceived as to the individual's transsexual history, that should make the marriage voidable.

---

38 *Re Kevin* [2001] *Fam CA* 1074.

39 *ibid* at para 330.

40 [1995] 1 NZLR 603.

Validity of a Previous Marriage

In some jurisdictions, people with transsexualism have only been permitted to correct their legal identity if they agree to divorce their spouse or have not been married.[41] Thus married people with transsexualism fall victim to a misplaced homophobia. The withholding of the right to an accurate legal identity from a person of transsexual background because that person desires to continue to honour a marriage has nothing to say about the sexuality of that couple at the time of marriage and is inhumane and against public policy that seeks to ensure the stability of the family.

In New Zealand in *Otahuhu,*[42] Ellis J held that the validity of a marriage should be determined by reference to the situation at the date of that marriage, not at the dates of birth of the parties to the marriage.[43] As a result, the validity of a prior marriage of a transsexual would not be affected by gender reassignment surgery.

Since criticism by the ECtHR of French law in this area by the ECHR in *B v France,*[44] France has allowed people to register their affirmed sex. While the Cour de Cassation has yet to decide on the right to marry in the new affirmed sex, it has decided on what should happen to an existing marriage: nullity or divorce is open to a spouse if transsexualism has been concealed.

The authors contend that the validity of an existing marriage simply makes sense if at the time of the marriage both parties were of opposite sexes. The concealment of a transsexual condition by one of the parties would make the marriage voidable.

Guardianship and Children

In *Foy,* McKechnie J argued that changing the applicant's birth certificate might render Dr Foy's marriage with Mrs Foy a nullity, and render his two daughters legally fatherless as well as non-marital, a proposition the judge considered "...

41 e.g. Germany: *Gesetz über die Änderung der Vornamen und die Feststellung der. Geschlechtszugehörigkeit in besonderen Fällen (Transsexuellengesetz oder „TSG")* 10 September 1980 (BGBl I S. 1654).

42 *AG v Otahuhu Family Court* [1995] 1 NZLR 603.

43 *ibid* at 607.

44 CEDH 25 mars 1992 aff Botella/France JCP 1992; (1992) 16 EHRR 1.

demonstrably impossible and therefore false".[45] Walsh J's fear, expressed while sitting as a judge of the ECtHR in *B v France,*[46] that it would be "the height of absurdity" to change a father into a mother, is understandable. The constitutional rights of the family under Art 41 and 42 thus militated against Dr Foy's claim.

A provision of the German *Transsexuellengesetz*[47] which is particularly instructive from an Irish perspective is SS 11 which states that parent-child relationships formed before the gender change will not be affected. The successful transsexual will remain as the father or mother of any children born or adopted before the decision is made final, and lines of inheritance due to sex are not affected. SS 12 ensures that existing pension rights and other benefits will be untouched and this includes the rights of a former spouse to pension benefits. It really can be that simple: it is possible to circumnavigate the concerns voiced by McKechnie J in *Foy* and Walsh J in *B v France*, if the legislative will is present. In any event, if Irish law adheres to the principle of spousal equality in parenting,[48] then perhaps parental gender is less relevant than one might think.

If the suggestions of this article were followed, children of the marriage would still be constitutionally protected as the marriage would still be valid. If the marriage was declared null because of the concealment of the transsexual condition the constitutional status of the children would be protected by the Status of Children Act 1987 s 46(i) and s 46(iv) in relation to voidable marriages. The parent with a transsexual history would still be the legal guardian of the children.

Pre-operative Claim to Gender Recognition

People living with transsexualism who are unable to undergo irreversible surgery due to age or ill-health are generally precluded from the right to have their legal sex reassigned.[49]

---

45 *Foy v An tArd Chláiritheoir* [2002] IEHC 116 at 127. Indeed Dr Foy's two daughters were notice parties to the application.

46 (1992) 16 EHRR 1 at 51.

47 *Transsexuellengesetz (TSG)*, above.

48 *Tilson v AG* [1951] IR 1.

49 Female-to-male reassignment surgery in particular can give rise to complications and, in some cases, can be life-threatening.

In Germany, until a very recent judgment of the Federal Constitutional Court,[50] pre-operative transgender persons could not register their partnerships with partners who were of the same legal gender. Such was considered "same-sex marriage". The applicant in that case was pre-operative female, living with a female partner.[51] When they married, the applicant discovered that her acquired female identity had reverted upon marriage to her original male identity in accordance with the 1981 law. As a result, she applied for a registered partnership, but this was refused as registered partnerships were only available to same-sex couples. All possible avenues were closed.

The Constitutional Court found that this refusal violated the right to one's first name and intruded upon the intimate sphere of the person. Interestingly, the Court recognised that many pre-operative transsexuals in Germany do not desire to undergo full surgery and held that their gender identity nonetheless has to be respected by the law. The Court also noted that the 1981 TSG is outdated in its expectation that all transsexuals will be heterosexual, noting that there are many transsexuals who are in fact homosexual in their acquired gender identity.

The authors suggest a dual regime whereby those people who have undergone irreversible sex affirmation treatment need only evidence that treatment to the state registrar in order to be reassigned. Those unable to do so because of health risks could make an exceptional application to an expert panel in order to have their legal sex reassigned on either a permanent or provisional basis on the ground of hardship.

Children are the best example of pre-operative transsexuals whose new gender should be recognised without surgery. In Australia, as a result of the recent decision of *Re Alex*,[52] young people with transsexualism and their parents/guardians are required to obtain the approval of the Family Court of Australia before such children can receive medically approved, non-surgical, hormonal treatment for their condition (even if such treatment has been approved by the child's parents).[53]

---

[50] Bundesverfassungsgericht 1 BVL 3/03 (available at http://www.bundesverfassungsgericht.de/entscheidungen/ls20051206_1bvl000303).

[51] In other words, the applicant had been born a "man" but lived as a female and had availed of the opportunity to change his legal name and create a female legal identity without undergoing surgery. In Germany this is called the "small solution", with full surgery being the "big solution".

[52] *Re Alex (Hormonal Treatment for Gender Identity Dysphoria)* [2004] *Fam CA* 297.

[53] Before *Re Alex* such treatment was available with parental consent after proper diagnosis by medical practitioners.

The court compared treatment of adolescent transsexualism to sterilisation for mentally ill young persons and other procedures which have no therapeutic benefit for the young person concerned, or present a parent/child conflict of interest.

The authors contend that judicial approval for non-surgical treatment is unnecessary as diagnosis and treatment of transsexualism is in the child's best interests. Requiring a court order makes the process expensive and arduous for the family. Children should be provisionally recognised in their affirmed sex before surgery upon application to the expert panel, just as pre-operative adults are.

Why the Law Needs to be Changed

As we have seen from our extensive comparative analysis, Ireland finds itself in an increasingly isolated position regarding transsexual marriage rights and in breach of the ECHR. But the simple fact that so many other jurisdictions have modernised their law is not conclusive of the matter. We propose to look finally at the normative arguments for law reform in this area: why should people with a transsexual history be allowed a birth certificate registering their new gender? Why should they be allowed to marry?

The reality is that gender remains, even today, a significant determinant of social status. As one's gender is required in applying for many of the benefits of living in the Irish State,[54] an Irish citizen with a history of transsexualism is forced either to admit that they are "not who they say they are" or face criminal sanction.[55] McKechnie J suggested that administrative bodies should cease to require copies of birth certificates, but it is submitted that this is no solution and avoids the bigger issue. Those with a transsexual history should not be subjected to such intrusions on their privacy by the State, semi-State bodies or private enterprises, especially when there is little corresponding benefit to wider society. Allowing them a second birth certificate recognising their new gender would relieve them of having to face such enduring embarrassment.

The right to marry is one of the most sacred in the constitutional canon. It is the strongest legal bond two private individuals can create, making their loving

---

[54] *Viz,* pensions benefits, etc, and, of course, marriage.

[55] McKechnie J in *Foy* noted that the applicant had had to produce her birth certificate for a conferral by St Patrick's College, Maynooth, and even to register for a FÁS course.

relationship public. Marriage, furthermore, has always been a social relationship. If procreation is not a necessary feature of that relationship,[56] then the fact that a marriage involving a person with a history of transsexualism would be childless is surely irrelevant. That said, the rights of spouses obviously require adequate legal protection. As outlined in our legislative proposal, marriages failure to reveal one's transgender status before marriage would render that marriage voidable at the instance of the other spouse.

Two loving individuals are currently prohibited under Irish law from entering into marriage if the sex of one is the result of a surgical operation designed to correct what is medically recognised as an accident of birth. Similar in all other respects to any heterosexual couple, the "transsexual couple" are excluded from the joys of marriage afforded to those lucky enough not to have had to face the trials of transsexualism. Simple legislation giving legal identity to affirmed gender, as outlined above, can represent a recognition on the part of the State that transsexualism is another dimension of human sexual identity, and welcome into the community a minority that has been marginalised for far too long.

Summary of Proposals

(i) People suffering from transsexualism should not be automatically considered to be suffering from mental disorders.

(ii) Any legislation relating to transsexualism should use affirmative and intelligible language.

(iii) Gender should be recorded on the birth register in the normal way, but with flexibility as regards intersex children who would be allowed to delay registration.

(iv) Gender should be reassigned upon presentation of certificate of full gender affirmation surgery.

(v) Where gender affirmation surgery is not possible, an expert panel will review the case and see if permanent or provisional reassignment is desirable.

(vi) A new "gender recognition certificate" will be issued, identical in appearance to an ordinary birth certificate. There will be an indicator placed on the original birth register entry, showing that the legal sex has been superseded, but invisible under data protection law.

---

56 Neither sterility nor infertility (nor indeed an absence of desire for progeny) are grounds under Irish law for a marriage being void.

(vii) Upon receipt of a new gender recognition certificate, the person with a transsexual background will be able to marry in their new sex.

(viii) A marriage dating from before the affirmation treatment will remain valid but voidable at the instance of the other spouse.

(ix) Any children of such a marriage will retain their constitutional status as children of that marriage.

(x) The person with a transsexual history will remain the legal guardian of their children.

Public Participation and the Regulation of Forestry Development in Ireland—A Call for Reform

by

Michael JS Moran*

Introduction

Although once completely covered by forests, exploitation and climate change down through the ages left Ireland with just 1 per cent of its surface area covered by forestry in 1900. In 1903, State forestry development commenced, and until the mid 1980s, almost all plantations in Ireland were established by the State. The methods of increasing the national forest cover then changed, however, and in the last two decades, instead of purchasing and planting land, the State has provided grant aid for private landowners to plant their own lands or to acquire new lands for planting.

Since the early 1990s, generous European Union funding programmes have meant that private afforestation[1] has increased dramatically, making forestry a major industry in Ireland. Today, the Government's strategic plan for forestry, entitled, *Growing for the Future,*[2] provides for a national afforestation target of 20,000 hectares per annum which, if met, will mean that by 2030, 17 per cent of Ireland will be under forest. Such a rate of land use change is unparalleled in recent Irish history

* Michael JS Moran, Sophister, LL.B Candidate, Trinity College Dublin. This essay was awarded a prize by the Law Society of Ireland for the *Essays on Reform Competition* 2006.

[1] Afforestation is defined as the direct human-induced conversion of land that has not been forested for a period of time (the definition in the Kyoto Protocol is 50 years) to forested land.

[2] (Government Publications Stationery Office, Dublin, 1996). According to the Forest Service, overall forest cover is now in the region of 10 per cent. Public funding of over €888 million has been spent supporting this strategic plan since 1996. See Department of Agriculture, *Annual Review and Outlook 2005/2006* (Government Publications Stationery Office, Dublin, 2006), p 74.

and, if realised, will undoubtedly result in the most significant alteration of the character of the Irish landscape for many centuries.[3]

In light of this high scale of environmental metamorphosis, the need for adequate regulatory legislation and public participation in environmental decision making is greatly increased. In the course of the present essay, it is proposed to analyse current inadequacies in Irish forestry law, to outline why reform is necessary and to suggest the nature of reform required, especially in the area of public participation.

Irish Forestry Regulation at Present

The treaties of the European Union do not provide for a common forestry policy in the Community; consequently, forestry remains an area of competency for Member States. Local Authority planning permission is not required in respect of initial afforestation.[4] Instead, the legal situation regarding forestry development in Ireland has been traditionally regulated by the Forestry Acts 1946–1988. In 2001, however, to facilitate compliance with the European Court of Justice ruling in *Commission v Ireland*,[5] the Environmental Impact Assessment Regulations (SI No 538 of 2001)[6] were signed into force. These regulations introduced a new statutory consent system for forestry development and provided for consultation with prescribed bodies and

---

[3] The period 1996–2003, saw an average annual afforestation rate of just over 14,000 hectares per annum, rather than 20,000 which had been planned. Bacon points out, however, that reform of the Common Agricultural Policy and the introduction of the single payment will see targets being met and have a "significant positive impact on the attractiveness of forestry compared to agriculture sufficient to provide adequate land for an afforestation programme of 20,000 hectares per annum as planned." Bacon, *A Review and Appraisal of Ireland's Forestry Development Strategy* (Peter Bacon & Associates, Economic Consultants, September 2004).

[4] The Local Government (Planning & Development) (Amendment) Regulations (SI No 539 of 2001) removed initial afforestation from the planning control system under the Planning Acts.

[5] *Commission v Ireland* [1999] ECR I-5901. In this decision (which arose from afforestation on the Pettigo plateau in County Donegal), the ECJ held that the EIA thresholds adopted by Ireland in relation to initial afforestation exceeded the discretion available to Ireland under Directive 85/37/EEC, in that they did not take into account "the nature, location or cumulative effect of projects below these thresholds". See Mc Hugh & Gallagher, *Trees Forests and the Law in Ireland* (Coford, 2004), p 89.

[6] European Communities (Environmental Impact Assessment) (Amendment) Regulations (hereinafter SI No 538 of 2001).

members of the public prior to granting approval for afforestation in environmentally sensitive areas.[7]

When questioned on the inadequacies of Government policy in this area of law, members of the Government are now quick to point to this new system as providing the necessary protection for environmental concerns and as sufficiently safeguarding public involvement in forestry development.[8] In reality, however, the new system is far from sufficient and, as we shall now see, many inadequacies remain in Irish forestry law.

Present Inadequacies in Irish Forestry Development Regulation

There is currently no mechanism in Ireland for the public or for stakeholders with environmental responsibilities to object to forestry development. The only mechanism available at present is to object to the grant support for afforestation, which an individual landowner may be eligible to apply for through the Department of Agriculture; and this mechanism itself is only available in limited circumstances.

Although SI No 538 of 2001 provides for a public consent system, the type of cases processed under the SI are only those where the site is within a proposed NHA, SAC, SPA or national park, contains an archaeological site or feature with intensive public

---

[7] Pt 5 of SI No 538 of 2001 sets out the details of the new afforestation consent system. Article 8 of the Regulations specifies that the system requires the approval of the Minister for initial afforestation (excluding planting within the curtilage of a house). Article 10(1) provides for consultation with prescribed bodies including the Environmental Protection Agency, Dúchas, An Taisce and Bord Fáilte Article 11 provides for public consultation and requires the Minister to publish notice of all applications which have been referred to one or more statutory consultees in at least one newspaper circulating in the district in which the land is situated, and to which the proposed afforestation relates. Article 11(2) specifies the information to be contained in such notice. This information includes the reference number, the nature and extent of the proposed afforestation, that the application and a map of the site may be inspected and that submissions or observations may be made in writing to the Minister within three weeks of the publication of the notice. The Forestry (Transfer of Departmental Administration and Ministerial Functions) Order 2003 (SI No 691 of 2003) has now transferred all responsibility in this regard from the Minister for Communications, Marine and Natural Resources to the Minister for Agriculture, Food and Forestry.

[8] See Comments of Minister for Agriculture and Food (Mary Coughlan) Dáil Debates Thursday 23 June 2005: "All forestry operations in Ireland must be carried out in full compliance with the code of best forest practice … In addition, further regulation is provided through SI No 538 of 2001, which introduced a statutory consent system with regard to initial afforestation."

usage or is within a prime scenic area in the county development plan, or is within an area listed in the inventory of outstanding landscapes.[9] In reality, only approximately 8 per cent of applications fall within this category.

While the Forest Service[10] has a policy of public notification for all afforestation applications exceeding 2.5 hectares, regardless of whether they fall under the provisions of SI No 538 of 2001 or not, this seems futile as the notification given is deficient in information and does not specify that submissions or observations may be made to the Forest Service by members of the public or other bodies.[11] In fact, the Forest Service has refused to accept objections not falling within the 8 per cent referred to above.[12] Consequently, in 92 per cent of Irish forestry development applications, the law does not provide for public consultation and there is no way for anyone to object.

Given that initial afforestation is exempt from the planning control system set out in the Planning Acts, the fact that adequate public participation is not provided for in such a huge proportion of forestry development is most alarming. In addition, there is evidence that the provisions of SI No 538 of 2001 are not being strictly complied with in relation to the small number of applications which do fall within these provisions.[13]

---

[9] Minister for Agriculture (Mary Coughlan) Dáil Debates Tuesday 21 June 2005.

[10] The Forest Service is responsible for ensuring the development of forestry within Ireland in a manner and to a scale that maximises its contribution to national socioeconomic well-being on a sustainable basis that is also compatible with the protection of the environment.

[11] This is a specified requirement under Pt 5, Art 11(2) of SI No 538 of 2001 and would appear to be one of the main reasons behind the public notification requirements in the first place.

[12] See Forestry Network News <www.friendsoftheirishenvironment.net/main/index.php> (last visited January 2006).

[13] Art 12 of the Regulations provides that the Minister is to consider submissions received from the general public and other organisations in coming to his decision on the application. Once the decision has been reached, the legislation requires that notification of the decision shall be given to the applicant and to any other person or body who made a submission or observation, in accordance with Arts 10 or 11, and shall specify, *inter alia*, the main reasons and considerations on which the decision is based. However, it has been stated that adequate notification of decisions is not being made to individuals and bodies, such as An Taisce and Local Authorities, who forward submissions on applications. This is in direct contravention of the legislation and prevents anyone, aside from the applicant, from appealing the decision. In addition, it calls into question the legality of afforestation approvals already granted where such approvals may have been made in breach of legislation. See Clerkin, *Participation by Local Authorities in the Afforestation Consent System* (An Taisce, November 2003).

While appeals are accepted following a decision with regard to sites which come under the provisions of SI No 538 of 2001, the appeals procedure in place has no statutory basis and is handled instead by an administrative unit of the Forest Service. This means that there is no legislation to govern how appeals should be processed or who should adjudicate on them. In contrast, statutory appeals procedures are provided for in planning regulations, aquaculture licences, waste licences and other land development regulations. This lack of a statutory appeal procedure could amount to a breach of Art 6 of the European Convention of Human Rights, given the precedent set down in *Zander v Sweden.*[14]

Aside from the lack of provision for public involvement, there is no requirement in Irish forestry law for road signs to be erected at the site of a proposed forestry development specifying details of the application submitted with regard to the site. In addition, although SI No 538 of 2001 reduced the threshold for Environmental Impact Assessment ("EIA") from 70 hectares to 50 hectares, in practice it appears that no EIAs are undertaken. If a landowner plants adjacent blocks that come over the threshold, he may not have to undertake an EIA provided a 500-metre gap exists between the blocks. Similarly, cumulative planting is not considered; thus, if adjacent blocks are planted by different landowners which exceed the threshold, an EIA is not required—each plantation is treated as a single unit, with no relationship to other, existing plantations.[15]

A further inadequacy in Irish forestry law is the requirement that, without exception, afforested land must be 100 pre cent reforested following clearfell.[16] In such circumstances, there is no provision for public consultation; consequently, the environmental damage caused by inappropriate forestry in the past is being reinforced and perpetrated.

---

[14] *Zander v Sweden* [1993] IIHRL 103. Although the existence of judicial review could be sufficient to remedy this failure, *Alconbury Developments Ltd v Secretary of State for the Environment, Transport and the Regions* [2003] 2 AC 295 considered.

[15] In 2005, the European Commission notified a Reasoned Opinion because of Ireland's practice in this area. See generally, Hickie, *Site Audit of Private Afforestation Applications* (An Taisce, November 2004).

[16] s 41, Forestry Act 1946. The European Commission is currently addressing concerns to Ireland in relation to this replanting requirement. Perhaps the main concern of the Commission is that, formally, actions under the Forestry Act 1946 are not subject to the requirements of the Habitats Directive (92/43/EEC), due mainly to the issue of conformity of national legislation.

Finally, Irish forestry law at present fails to provide for sufficient planting of broadleaf trees and of native Irish woodland.[17] The plantation species of preference has been the Sitka spruce, and planting policy has focused almost exclusively on non-native conifers to the near exclusion of native Irish trees. One of the main reasons for this is, perhaps, that the Forest Service has a dual purpose of promoting the achievement of "critical mass" in the timber processing sector and of regulating sustainable forestry development.[18] It would seem that such a dual purpose involves a clear conflict of interests.

Why Should Forestry Law Provide for Public Participation and Regional Differences in Attitude in the Matter of Private Afforestation?

On a small island nation, land is an especially limited resource. Public involvement in how we develop that land is an essential feature of a democratic State. The noble concepts of generating increased social capital, of expanding participatory democracy and of upholding the environmental rights of the public are now key issues in the development of a more fair and just society. Without allowing members of the public access to justice in environmental matters such as forestry development, we are merely paying lip service to these worthy concepts. Indeed, more notably, we are contravening the Aarhus Convention,[19] an international agreement which lays down a set of basic rules to promote citizens' involvement in environmental matters.

While it is acknowledged that allowing for public participation usually involves increased time and costs and sometimes creates a platform for the crank in society

---

17 The State Forestry Board, Coillte, was established under The Forestry Act 1988. While initial afforestation plays an increasingly small part of the Coillte's activities, it is replanting more than 11,000 hectares of clear-felled plantations every year, with less than 8 per cent broadleaves. See Lewis, "*Broadleaves? Not in our Lifetimes!*" in An Taisce Magazine, Summer 2006, p 16. The planting of exotic conifers often has negative impacts on the environment including the creation of a higher risk of insect infestation and disease, a greater need for pesticide usage and a greater likelihood of forest fires due to the resin content of such non-native species.

18 Critical mass relates specifically to a scale of timber production large enough to make true competition and the operation of market forces possible, and to support a range of processing industries.

19 The European Aarhus Convention, adopted in Aarhus, Denmark in 1998, which establishes that sustainable development can be achieved only through the involvement of all stakeholders and requires that each party guarantees the rights of access to information, public participation in decision-making and access to justice in environmental matters.

who tries to prevent all development often for frivolous reasons, these problems are greatly outweighed by the need to cater for the common good of society and the best interests of the environment. Indeed, such problems are also reduced by employing a clear statutory framework setting down time limits and procedures for the regulation of public participation.

Not all proposed land development, be it residential, industrial, commercial or agricultural enjoys the full support of all environmental stakeholders. Statutory-based public participation is a vehicle for creating pro-active debate between Government, developer, environmental organisations and the public. Such debate eventually provides for better decision making and more appropriate land use in the long term.

In Ireland at present, it would appear that decision making in regard to forestry landscape and planning design is ultimately made by professionals, including foresters, landscape experts, ecologists and planners. There is an immense need, however, that such decision making should, to a greater extent, reflect the needs, expectations, perceptions, attitudes and preferences of the public. In particular, regional differences should be taken into account and provided for.

In their regional study, entitled *Afforestation in Ireland: Regional Differences in Attitude,*[20] O'Leary *et al* point out that there are strongly contrasting preferences and attitudes towards afforestation in different regions of Ireland, with some regions positively disposed towards forestry and other regions highly critical of it. O'Leary *et al* go on to state that such diverging relationships highlight the need to develop regionally applicable forestry strategies and policies rather than attempting to use a universal solution crudely applied at a national level.

In his report on non-agricultural use of the countryside, Coeterier stresses that:

> "the development of a satisfactory planning strategy for the countryside cannot only be determined top-down by the national or even provincial government, because the allocation of new activities has to be fine-tuned to local conditions."[21]

---

20 O'Leary, McCormack and Clinch, *Afforestation in Ireland: Regional Differences in Attitude* (Department of Environmental Studies, University College Dublin, December 1999).

21 Coeterier, *Non agricultural use of the countryside in the Netherlands: What is local opinion?* (Landscape and Urban Planning, 1994) 29, pp 55–256.

Consequently, increasing the national forest cover should be governed by bottom up planning—an objective which can only be achieved by providing for public involvement in environmental decision making.

Disadvantages of Forestry When Developed Without Adequate Legislation and Public Involvement

Before proposing the various reforms needed in Irish forestry law, it is necessary to first set out the adverse effects of forestry development where adequate land use regulations are not in place and where consultation with those whose environment is to be affected is not provided for.

Improper forestry development can have significant negative and often irreversible effects on the landscape. Forestry can be visually intrusive if not developed in suitable locations. The planting of non-native conifers often results in a uniform dark appearance on the landscape which can discourage tourism—the lifeblood of many rural communities. The impact of afforestation on the Irish countryside is especially noticeable due to the small scale of the landscape.

Forestry development can also be hugely damaging to the environment, especially if it takes in acid sensitive locations. Fertilising plantations established on soil with poor capacity to hold phosphorus may lead to the nutrient enrichment of run off waters. In June 2005, Ireland was condemned by the European Court of Justice for not having an authorisation system in place for aerial spraying of phosphorus in connection with forestry.

Forestry development, unlike most other forms of development, is heavily grant aided. Previous grant systems have caused long-term problems such as overgrazing and soil erosion. Expensive measures have had to be introduced in an attempt to solve these intractable problems. A balance must be achieved between economic returns and conservation of the environment.

With our high afforestation rate, archaeological sites have come under increasing threat from forestry. Where traditional landscapes are being transformed, there must be additional protection for their inherent features. Forestry development must take place with due regard to archaeology and heritage, and not just that which is already recorded.

A further feature of inappropriate forestry, constructed without public involvement, is the isolation of rural dwellings. The lack of community-based participation in the past has meant that many small communities have been "planted in", increasing the abandonment of rural farms, contributing to the depopulation of the villages and causing a reduction in the quality of life for those who remain. It should also be noted that forestry can cause extensive damage to roads during planting and harvesting.

Proposals for Reform of Irish Forestry Law

In order to develop a regulatory framework for the orderly development of forestry in Ireland, encompassing sufficient public participation and recognizing the need to protect the environment, the following proposals for reform are put forward:

The Forestry Acts need to be amended to provide a modern workable legislative framework to safeguard the expansion of forestry in Ireland. While it is understood that a review of the Forestry Acts has been under way for some time, this review appears to be taking a disproportionate amount of time to complete and a new Forestry Bill has not yet been finalised. Reform of our forestry laws is a matter of utmost urgency given the present rate of forestry development in Ireland under existing inadequate legislation.

The new Forestry Act must provide for a broader and more effective public consent system than is presently in place and must also provide for a statutory appeals procedure. The broadening of the consent system must allow for the receipt of submissions and observations on all forestry applications, not just those deemed by the Minister to be environmentally sensitive, as is the position at present. This system must allow for public objection to all forestry development itself and not just objection to grant aid for afforestation. In addition, the new Act must take into account the cumulative effects of private plantations on the landscape and thereby herald a change in the present situation where each plantation is treated as a single unit with no relationship to other existing plantations. The new Forestry Act should require the erection of a notice at the site of a proposed plantation similar to that presently required for planning applications under the Planning Acts.

The Act should also seek to create links between afforestation and the Rural Environment Protection Scheme (REPS).[22] In addition, given the apparent lack of

---

22 REPS is a scheme designed to reward farmers for carrying out their farming activities in an environmentally friendly manner and to bring about environmental improvement on existing farms. The objectives of the scheme are to establish farming practices and production methods which reflect the increasing concern for conservation, landscape protection and wider environmental problems; protect wildlife habitats and endangered species of flora and fauna; and produce quality food in an extensive and environmentally friendly manner.

Forest Service control over non-grant aided afforestation, the new Act must provide for the establishment of a system which will also ensure this form of forestry development is also regulated.[23]

The provisions of the new European Commission Regulation 1698/2005 on support for rural development should be considered in drafting the new Act as this regulation may entail a specific planning process for grant aided forestry.[24] In addition, the widening of the consultation process must reflect the principles set out in the Aarhus Convention.

Irish forestry policy must be updated to reflect modern scientific advances. The focus on critical mass should be reduced to balance competing economic and environmental objectives. Legislation should provide that each county develops a forestry strategy tailored to local conditions. A national land use policy should be developed which the aim of improving integration between all those engaged in land use, including those involved in forestry development. Such an all-embracing land use policy is preferable to allowing economically-driven farming practices dictate the use to which land is put.

The functions of the Forest Service, which presently involve both regulating forestry development and promoting it, must be separated. As Bacon has suggested, the role of the Forest Service should be limited by statute to regulatory and supervisory functions.[25]

Statutory consultees and environmental organisations should be involved in the afforestation consent system in a more efficient manner than at present. The working relationship between the Forest Service and these organisations should be improved in light of a common aim to develop forestry in a sustainable and environmentally friendly manner.

---

23 When viewed relative to granted aided forestry, non-grant aided forestry seems somewhat insignificant. Christmas tree plantations, however, may constitute one example of non-grant aided planting.

24 Art 50 of Regulation 1698/2005 contains certain dispositions regarding the designation of areas eligible for support as an element of the Rural Development Programmes to be proposed by Member States for Community support between 2007 and 2013. This may well entail a specific planning process for grant aid to forestry.

25 Bacon., *op. cit.*

While it is acknowledged that there may be good reasons for 100 per cent replanting of clear-felled forestry, this strict statutory requirement, under the Forestry Act 1946, must be removed from Irish law in order to prevent the replication of initial damage caused by inappropriate development in the past. Greater attention must also be placed on achieving a 30 per cent broadleaf target for Irish forestry. More native woodland must be created and the planting of exotic species should gradually be reduced. The increased planting of broadleaf and native species must be an aim provided for in any reform of Irish forestry law.

Advantages of Forestry When Developed With Adequate Legislation and Public Involvement

In spite of a most favourable climate for growing trees, Ireland remains one of the least forested countries in the European Union.[26] Creating, maintaining and replacing forestry in accordance with a suitable legislative framework and an adequate consultation process is vital. Once the reforms set out above have been put in place, continued forestry development is both necessary and beneficial for Ireland.

Annual turnover in the forestry sector is in the order of €800 million; therefore, forestry plays an important role in the Irish economy. Approximately 16,000 landowners are now engaged in forestry. In addition, 3,780 people are employed in forest crop establishment and harvesting, and in excess of 6,000 are employed in timber processing in Ireland.[27] Much of this employment is based in rural communities throughout the country.

Forestry provides a number of environmental benefits. It plays an important role in the carbon cycle as forestry plantations sequester carbon and act as carbon sinks to reduce global warming. Under Kyoto,[28] Ireland is committed to limiting the growth

---

26 The average tree cover in the European Union is in the region of 35 per cent. It is interesting to note that six thousand years ago, native forests of oak, ash, elm, birch, rowan, scots pine, alder and hazel flourished across Ireland. Therefore, the most authentic Irish landscape is diverse native woodland. Indeed, the economy of Ireland under the Gaelic order was largely based on the forests. This great resource was the provider of raw materials, medicine, weapons, tools, charcoal, food, spirituality and wisdom. It is true that as many as 40,000 Irish place names still exist which are connected to the forest, although today they are often drastically out of context with either deforestation or exotic plantations nearby.

27 Bacon., *op. cit.*

28 The Kyoto agreement sets out legally binding targets agreed by governments in 1997 to reduce emissions of green house gases under the United Nations Framework Convention on Climate Change.

in emissions of greenhouse gases to 13 per cent above its 1990 output. Increased forest coverage can help reduce our net emission of greenhouse gases and contribute towards achieving compliance with our Kyoto commitments. Forests also act as atmospheric filters removing pollutants from the atmosphere. In addition, developed forestry reduces soil erosion by wind and water and controls land slips. All in all, forestry is essential for our environmental wellbeing.

In addition, forests may be developed as recreational and leisure facilities. They can become interesting visitor attractions offering peaceful walks and exercise opportunities. Such benefits are often referred to as the "non-timber" benefits of forestry.[29] The aesthetic value of forestry can enhance the landscape and make a region more attractive as a place in which to live and work.

Finally, forests play an important role in the conservation and development of biodiversity in the countryside. They also provide habitats for diverse species of birds and wildlife and are fertile sanctuaries for flora.

Conclusion

It is clear from the issues addressed in this essay that urgent reform is needed in Irish forestry law. While Ireland has a long history of public participation in relation to planning decisions, dating back to the introduction of the Planning and Development Act 1963 and strengthened by the Planning and Development Act 2000, this is not the case in the area of forestry regulation.

At present, the legislation in place is inadequate and does not provide for public participation or objection for approximately 92 per cent of forestry development applications. Procedural justice and the environmental rights of the public are being sidelined, with increased timber production being placed as a priority. The Forest Service's role in achieving critical mass contradicts its role as an impartial regulator, with the result that the views of environmental organisations on sustainable forestry are not being heard. Given the high rate of afforestation and its position as the central agent in Irish land use change, these problems have serious consequences for our environment.

---

29 The total economic value of forest recreation in Ireland is approximately €503 million. This is divided between domestic forest visitors (€268 million) and overseas walking and cycling tourists at €138 million, with the non-market value of forest recreation valued at €97 million. See Department of Agriculture, *Annual Review and Outlook 2005/2006* (Government Publications Stationery Office, Dublin, 2006).

Forestry is very necessary for Ireland, and we should be grateful that the European Union continues to play a very significant role in Irish forestry development. However, without addressing existing problems and implementing necessary reform, we risk undermining future negotiations with the EU on funding for forestry programmes. Indeed, we may find ourselves facing infringement proceedings because of our continuing sub-standard practices in terms of forestry development regulation and public involvement in the afforestation consent system.

Trees are a natural part of the landscape and so should have an important place in land use development. Since forestry decisions made today, however, have environmental, ecological and social impacts for over five to six decades and longer, we must be always mindful of the adverse consequences of inappropriate tree planting. Embracing wholeheartedly the notion of public participation and providing adequate land development regulation is the key to achieving sustainable forestry into the future.

"The best friend on earth of man is the tree: when we use the tree respectfully and economically we have one of the greatest resources of the earth."[30]

30 Frank Lloyd Wright, American architect 1867–1959. See <www.fbbcustom.com/smart.html> (last visited January 2006).

Pre-emptive Costs Orders and the Public Interest—A Law Reform Proposal

by
James Mulcahy*

Introduction

The system of costs allocation in Ireland follows the so-called English rule, i.e. the losing party pays the costs of both sides.[1] Our civil law system has its roots in the conventional model of litigation, the "bilateral private dispute model",[2] and the procedural law has been shaped to a large extent by this model. The old assumptions regarding economic incentives to litigate do not apply[3] in public interest litigation and, therefore, the procedures are not suitable.[4] If public interest litigation is to develop in this jurisdiction, the costs rules must be examined, debated and ultimately reformed. The following quote, although uttered in the Australian context, has a particular resonance in Ireland:

> "Relaxing the traditional requirements for standing may be of little significance unless other procedural reforms are made ... There is little point in opening the doors to the courts if litigants cannot afford to come in. The general rule in litigation that 'costs follow the event' is in point. The fear, if unsuccessful, of having to pay the costs of the other side (often a government

---

* BCL (NUI), LL.M. This essay was awarded a prize by the Law Society of Ireland for the *Student Law Reform Essay Competition* 2006.

1 This is in contrast with the "American rule" under which parties pay their own costs regardless of the outcome of the case.

2 Chakrabarti, Stephens and Gallagher, "Whose Cost the Public Interest" (2003) *Public Law* 697.

3 Friedlander, "Costs and Public Interest Litigation" (1995) 40 *McGill Law Journal* 56 at p 103.

4 For a detailed discussion on the differences between conventional litigation and public interest litigation see, Whyte, *Social Inclusion and the Legal System — Public Interest Law in Ireland* (Dublin, IPA, 2002), p 58.

instrumentality or wealthy private corporation), with devastating consequences to the individual or environmental group bringing the action, must inhibit the taking of cases to court. In any event, it will be a factor that looms large in any consideration to initiate litigation."[5]

Public Interest Litigation

Any person seeking to promote litigation taken to vindicate the public interest will necessarily have to address questions about the scope of public interest law — what is the public interest it seeks to vindicate? The term "public interest law" originally related to attempts to use the law on behalf of disadvantaged and marginalised groups[6], and this remit is discernible in recent Irish literature.[7] It may also refer to cases taken by, for example, environmental groups and it is in this area that some reform of the costs rules has taken place in Ireland.[8] For the purposes of this discussion, a wider definition will be used to embrace challenges to legislation, practice or policy of public authorities which is of wide, or potentially wide, application or consequence.[9] As is readily appreciable, a large number of cases taken will involve cases concerning the fair and efficient administration of justice or those taken by or on behalf of groups whose interests are not adequately addressed by the "democratic" process.[10] The benefit of public interest litigation is that it provides the court with an opportunity to judicially review legislation, governmental policy and decisions of other public bodies to ensure compliance with the Constitution. The purpose of judicial review is, according to Monahan, "to ensure that the political process is open to those of all viewpoints on something approaching an equal basis."[11]

Pre-Emptive Costs Orders: Current Law

Until recently, the Irish courts have been reluctant to grant *locus standi* to non-governmental organisations, but in the recent judgment of Gilligan J of the High

---

[5] Justice Toohey, formerly of the High Court of Australia, at an address to a NELA conference on environmental law in 1989.

[6] Whyte, *ibid*, at p 1.

[7] Litigation on behalf of the disadvantaged is the subject of Whyte, *ibid*; Cousins, *A Report on Public Interest Law and Litigation in Ireland* (2005).

[8] Australian Law Reform Commission, *Costs Shifting – Who Pays for Litigation*, (1995) ALRC 75.

[9] This accords with the definition used in Chakrabarti, Stephens and Gallagher, above, n 2, at p 712.

[10] "Democratic" is used here to refer to the majoritarian organs of State, i.e. the Oireachtas and the Executive.

[11] Monahan, "Judicial Review and Democracy: A Theory of Judicial Review" (1987) 21 *University of British Columbia Law Review* 87 at p 89.

Court,[12] the Irish Penal Reform Trust were held to have *locus standi* to represent mentally ill prisoners in legal proceedings against the State. However, while the rules relating to standing may be relaxed, the costs barrier will stand firm.[13] The cost of taking a legal action was cited as the primary and most significant barrier to public interest litigation in the Cousins report.[14] This barrier is multi-faceted, but primarily consists of the inability to pay lawyers' fees and also the fear that one may have to pay the costs of the other side if unsuccessful. Indeed, the prohibitive nature of costs may help explain the extremely small number of public interest cases brought before the Irish courts. In 2003 and 2004, 3.5 per cent of all cases brought in the High and Supreme Courts were public interest cases.[15]

It is important at this juncture to set out the rules that govern the making of costs orders. The Irish courts have a general discretion in costs matters, granted to them by Ord 99, r 1(1) of the Rules of the Superior Courts, 1986. The general rule stated in subsections (3) and (4) of r 1 is that unless otherwise ordered, costs follow the event. Rule 5 provides that costs may be dealt with at any stage of the proceedings and an order for the payment of costs may require the costs to be paid notwithstanding that fact that the proceedings may have not been concluded.

The judiciary affirmed their jurisdiction to make "pre-emptive costs orders" (PCOs) in the High Court decision of *Village Residents v An Bord Pleanala,*[16] which is an order granted in advance of litigation that protects the applicant from having to pay costs, regardless of the outcome of the litigation. Despite this recognition, the High Court held that such orders should only be granted in the most exceptional of circumstances. Laffoy J laid down the criteria for obtaining a PCO and relied heavily on those enunciated by Dyson J in the English case of *R v Lord Chancellor, exp. Child Poverty Action Group*[17] (*CPAG*). In *Village Residents* the applicant sought, *inter alia,* a pre-emptive costs order. This order was not granted because the challenge was not a "public law challenge in the sense that that concept was explained by Dyson J [in

[12] *Irish Times,* 3 September 2005.

[13] Costs is mentioned as being one of a series of barriers to public interest litigation in the Cousins' Report, above, n 6, pp 21–25.

[14] *ibid* at p 21.

[15] *ibid* at p 43. The definition used in the Cousins report, which relates solely to the interests of vulnerable and disadvantaged groups, is narrower than the definition used in this discussion. However, as the report notes, a slightly broader definition would not significantly increase this level.

[16] [2000] 2 ILRM 59.

[17] *R v Lord Chancellor ex p Child Poverty Action Group* and *R v DPP exp. Bull* [1999] 1 WLR 347.

CPAG]"[18] as the members of the company bringing the challenge were held to have a private interest in the outcome of the application. Laffoy J approved of the Dyson's conception of a public law challenge:

> "The essential characteristics of a public law challenge are that it raises public law issues which are of general importance, where the applicant has *no private interest* in the outcome of the case. It is obvious that many, indeed most, judicial review challenges do not fall into this category ... because, even if they do raise issues of general importance, they are cases in which the applicant is seeking to protect some private interest of his or her own."[19] [emphasis added]

In addition, Laffoy J said that as she did not have a sufficient appreciation of the merits of the application, she could not conclude that it would be in the public interest to make a PCO. This argument (the pre-maturity argument), coupled with the prohibition on private interests, makes it extremely difficult for public interest litigants to obtain a costs order that will effectively enable their challenge. The private interests prohibition was recently reaffirmed by the High Court in *Dunne v Minister for the Environment and Local Government,*[20] although the plaintiff did receive a favourable costs order in this case as the litigation raised a question of general importance and the plaintiff did not have a private/personal in the outcome.[21] However, this case did not involve an application for a pre-emptive costs order.

It is submitted that prohibition on private interests and the pre-maturity argument are irrational and unsound. The courts, of course, have legitimate concerns about the opening of the floodgates. However, these barriers must be proportionate and legitimate.

Inadequacies in the Current Law

The Prohibition on Private Interests

The prohibition on private interests is a wholly disproportionate response to the threat of a "litigation explosion"[22]. While *Village Residents* did accept that the

---

[18] *Per* Laffoy J, above, n 15.

[19] Above, n 16, at p 762.

[20] [2005] IEHC 79.

[21] The litigation concerned the impact of the construction of the south eastern route motorway on the archaeological site at Carrickmines Castle.

[22] Friedlander, above, n 3, at p 92.

litigation need not involve issues as grandiose as a "heritage protection issue or an environmental issue" to be worthy of protection, the court did hold that their jurisdiction would only be exercised in favour of litigants acting in a "selfless, disinterested spirit."[23] This prohibition supposes that the public interest character is wholly tarnished by the presence of a private interest on the part of the person bringing the case. That the scope or consequence of the litigation has remained unchanged is irrelevant. The problem with this approach is that it buys into the false dichotomy which accepts that public and private interests operate distinctly and to the exclusion of the other.[24] This is tantamount to saying that the presence of a private or personal interest is necessarily improper, and the exercise by the courts of its jurisdiction to grant PCOs will only be possible when some "altruistic stranger"[25] decides to bring a case. Chakrabarti *et al.* suggest this prohibition is "nonsensical" and "deeply flawed" and call for its abandonment.[26] There is a considerable lack of clarity in the present arrangement: does a company incorporated to initiate litigation on behalf of some cause necessarily have a private interest in the litigation and must, therefore, be refused an order? Whyte concludes that pre-emptive costs orders will "probably be restricted to *Crotty*-type litigants raising issues that effect all citizens equally."[27] While the rules relating to standing are increasingly being liberalised,[28] one may recognise the inconsistency between the prohibition and the traditional approach of the court concerning standing, which requires a litigant to have a private interest in the action.

The Pre-Maturity Argument

The pre-maturity argument is apparently more difficult to dispute as one can appreciate the difficulty a judge may have in determining whether litigation is actually in the public interest before the trial. This is a result of the alleged inability of judges in cases to separate the assessment of the public interest status of a case from the determination of the merits of the challenge and this has been described at the most unfortunate aspect of the *CPAG* decision.[29] The merits of bringing a claim

23 Costello, "Costs Principles and Environmental Judicial Review" (2000) 35 *Irish Jurist* 121 at p 135.

24 Thomas, "Costs in Public Interest Cases" (2001) October *Legal Action* 21.

25 Above, n 2, at p 712.

26 *ibid.*

27 Above, n 4, at p 92.

28 See above, n 11 and Whyte, *ibid*, at pp 62–86.

29 Above, n 2, at p 704.

can be assessed at the interlocutory stage and the courts regularly make the distinction in relation to interlocutory injunctions. To grant an interlocutory injunction, the courts do not have to satisfy themselves that the claimant has a *prima facie* case or is likely to succeed at a full trial of the action.[30] The court must only be satisfied that the plaintiff's case is not frivolous or vexatious and that there is a serious question to be tried. It may be contended that the nature of an interlocutory injunction is distinct from that of a PCO because the latter involves a judgment that carries financial implications for the other side. The judicial hesitation regarding PCOs is to a large degree related to the fear that such an order may be revealed to have been inappropriate in light of the facts of the case. According to Costello, "only in exceptional cases will the courts be able to make the decision the legal issue is one of such importance that no order in costs would be made against the applicant."[31] However, interlocutory injunctions can carry financial implications for the other side, for example, where the injuncted party must cease trading until the conclusion of the trial. Furthermore, the courts, through the employment of the *Mareva* injunction,[32] have been willing to freeze the assets of a defendant in order to prevent them from dissipating or removing assets prior to trial. The standard of proof required for a *Mareva* injunction is the same as that for an interlocutory injunction, i.e. a substantial question to be tried rather than the requirement to show a *prima facie* case.[33] Add to this the fact that *Mareva* injunctions are generally granted *ex parte,* and one begins to realise that the judiciary can and does differentiate between the merits of bringing a case and the actual merits of that case.

Reform

Why Reform is Necessary

Many factors contribute to the current underdeveloped state of Irish public interest law, for example, legal education, unfavourable standing rules, etc. Despite this, costs remain the primary barrier to the development of public interest law and litigation.

---

30 The "*prima facie*" standard was rejected by the House of Lords in *American Cyanamid Co. v Ethicon Ltd.*[1975] AC 396 and by the Irish Supreme Court in *Campus Oil v Minister for Industry and Commerce* [1983] IR 88. See, Delany, *Equity and the Law of Trusts in Ireland* (3rd Edition, Dublin, 2003), Ch 13.

31 Above, n 22, at p 136.

32 Taking its name from *Mareva Campania Naveria v International Bulkcarriers* [1975] 2 Lloyds Rep 509.

33 *Countyglen v Carway* [1995] 1 IR 481; *O'Mahony v Horgan* [1995] 2 IR 411.

One may question the desirability of legislation and policy being challenged by community groups, interest groups and lobbyists in the courts. The argument may be forwarded from many quarters that the use of the courts by such groups to vindicate the public interest is a misuse of the courts system as the political sphere is the appropriate forum. The judiciary may feel uncomfortable with their courtrooms being used to fight political battles and that the promotion of public interest litigation, in a sense, validates the licence of interest groups to clog up the courts system with test cases. Nevertheless, it is submitted that the use of the courts to challenge policy and acts of public authorities is an essential element in our democratic system. The separation of powers inherent in our Constitutional order necessarily mandates a system of checks and balances between the organs of State[34] and judicial review is the exercise of, *inter alia*, control by the courts over public power.[35] The contention that use of the courts to vindicate the public interest is illegitimate is an extension of the argument that judicial review, generally, is anti-democratic. This argument is, however, based upon the misconception that crude majoritarianism and democracy are synonymous. In a liberal democracy, such as Ireland, the will of the majority, represented in the legislature and the executive, is subject to the rule of law and moderated by a Constitution which emphasises the protection of the rights and freedoms of individuals and minorities. Thus, recourse to the courts for review of legislation, policies and practices is valid and does not constitute a usurpation of the democratic process.

Once it is understood that public interest litigation is desirable as well as being legitimate, one may ask whether pre-emptive costs orders are an effective method of enabling this form of litigation. While the creation of a public interest legal culture will require much more than PCOs,[36] they do break down the very immediate and often insurmountable costs barrier. Judicial leadership is needed on this issue as well as a willingness to confront its challenges and explore its possibilities.[37]

Possible Reforms

Chakrabarti *et al* submit that the granting of PCOs should be governed by a two-fold test, with the two requirements being cumulative: "(i) is this a public interest

[34] Cousins, *above* n 6 at p 9.

[35] De Blacam, M, *Judicial Review* (Butterworths, Dublin, 2001).

[36] See generally, Cousins, *above* n 6.

[37] Chakrabarti *et al*, *above* n 2 at p 703.

case[38] ... and (ii) does the defendant's superiority in terms of its financial capacity to bear the costs of the litigation create an inequality of arms?" This approach not only avoids the private interest prohibition and the pre-maturity argument but also focuses on the nature of the case taken rather the characteristics of the litigant. This is the appropriate level at which to screen cases, and the above proposal ensures that marginal or frivolous challenges will not receive an order.

The Irish Law Reform Commission dealt briefly with the issue of pre-emptive costs orders[39] and recommended that the courts continue to exercise their jurisdiction to make them only in exceptional circumstances. The Commission's cautiousness mirrors that of certain commentators[40]: however, it recommends that courts should, in certain circumstances, "indicate at an initial stage of proceedings the likely outcome in relation to costs while not committing itself absolutely on the issue."[41] Costello says of this approach:

> "while the applicant will have a legitimate expectation which, although reversible, must be afforded sufficient weight when the court exercises its ultimate costs jurisdiction.[42]"

This approach is desirable in circumstances where the determination of the public interest status of a challenge can only be made in light of some evidence to be presented in the trial. However, in most cases the public interest status of a challenge will be obvious. The Australian Law Reform Commission has been more progressive in relation to costs orders and has proposed the introduction of public interest costs orders, which could be granted by any court or tribunal provided it is satisfied that:

- "the proceedings will determine, enforce or clarify an important right or obligation affecting the community or a significant sector of the community
- the proceedings will affect the development of the law generally and may reduce the need for further litigation

---

38 A dual working definition of a public interest case is used, each being sufficient independently: "(a) it involves a real (as opposed to manufactured or academic) human rights complaint; (b) it involves a real (as opposed to manufactured or academic) challenge to legislation, policy or practice of wide or potentially wide application or consequence, or exciting wide controversy."

39 Law Reform Commission, "Report on Judicial Review Procedure", LRC71–2004 at p 64.

40 Costello, above, n 22, at p 136.

41 Above, n 38, at p 67.

42 Above, n 22, at p 136.

- the proceedings otherwise have the character of public interest or test case proceedings

> A court or tribunal may make a public interest costs order *notwithstanding that one or more of the parties to the proceedings has a personal interest in the matter.*" [emphasis added][43]

The appeal of such orders is that they can be awarded pre-emptively and do not prevent relief where a litigant has a private interest. The Commission also recognised the potential benefit of indicative costs orders where the court could not determine the status of a challenge at the interlocutory stage.[44] The recommendations of the Australian Law Reform Commission have not yet been implemented. The Australian judiciary have been reluctant to liberalise the rule regarding the availability of PCOs despite the decision in *Oshlack v Richmond River Council*,[45] which had been characterised by commentators as authority for allowing the court to advert to a concept of public interest litigation in making a determination as to costs. Kirby J in the High Court of Australia rejected the Council's contention that the floodgates would be opened if litigants could bring cases without a costs penalty where such litigation proved unsuccessful. He agreed with the trial judge, Stein J, who believed that experience showed that what could reasonably be expected was "little more than a modest flow barely wetting the wellies."[46] While the *Oshlack* principles were intended to enjoy a broad application, subsequent decisions have rejected the public interest litigation consideration.[47]

In South Africa, the basic principles of costs allocation are similar to Ireland; however, the exceptions to the general rule that costs follow the event are quite different. The courts in numerous cases have not awarded costs against an unsuccessful litigant who raises questions of constitutional law in cases against the State. To do otherwise would have a "chilling effect"[48] on other potential litigants. In the case of *Die Oranje Vrystaate vir Staatsondersteinde Skole v Premier van die Provinsie Vrystaate*[49] the court

---

[43] Australian Law Reform Commission, above, n 7, Ch 13.

[44] *ibid* at 2.34.

[45] [1998] HCA 11, HC (Aus).

[46] (1994) 82 LGERA 236 at 245.

[47] See Edwards, "Costs and Public Interest Litigation after *Oshlack v Richmond River Council*" [1999] *Sydney Law Review* 27.

[48] *Motsepe v CIR*, CCT 35/96, Constitutional Court (1997) at p 30.

[49] (1998) 3 SA 692.

employed a two-part test; first, whether the complaint was frivolous or vexatious and, secondly, whether the applicants had any improper motives in bringing the proceedings. The definition of "frivolous and vexatious" is narrowly interpreted, which has resulted in no costs orders being made against unsuccessful applicants even when they were unlikely to succeed.[50] Despite this, the courts have warned against the bringing of spurious challenges. Whether the litigant has a private/personal interest is not an issue. Chakrabarti *et al* have praised the South African model. However, they do recognise a problem that relates to the difficulty of making a distinction between a spurious challenge and a "worthy failed human rights" argument after the trial.[51] They suggest that this determination should be made at the permission stage and pre-emptive costs orders would provide an opportunity to make the distinction.[52] Clearly, if certainty of risk is to be promoted in order to prevent a "chilling effect" the litigant should be aware of the status of his case before the trial.

Concluding Remarks & Reform Proposal

The High Court in *Village Residents* recognised that certain challenges taken in the public interest warrant special protection by the courts from costs orders. Though the Court was not philosophical about this development, one may assume that it realises that, in certain cases, public interest litigation is desirable and should benefit from a pre-emptive costs order. It may be argued that the Court was merely stating this jurisdiction as a corollary of their discretion in costs matters. However, the conditions placed on the granting of this order demonstrate that it was intended to be used by public interest litigants, but in what was, perhaps, a moment of judicial nervousness, almost impenetrable barriers were positioned to defend against the presumed inevitable flood of claims. As explained above, the arguments used to justify this approach are irrational, disproportionate and militate against the spirit of the pre-emptive costs order. It should be noted that law reform regarding costs and public interest litigation is not solely the concern of the judiciary. The civil legal aid system in Ireland[53] should be expanded to cover cases taken in the public interest as, has been done in the United Kingdom.[54]

---

50 Above, n 2, at p 709.

51 *ibid.*

52 *ibid.*

53 See generally on the problems with the civil legal aid scheme, Free Legal Advice Centres, *Access to Justice: A Right or a Privilege?* (Dublin, 2005).

54 See Smith "The UK experience of test cases and the Human Rights Act 1998", a speech given at "Public Interest Law in Ireland" Conference; Dublin, 6 October 2005.

The potential of pre-emptive costs orders must be realised and the following proposal allows the court to exercise control over the granting of pre-emptive costs orders so only the deserving challenges benefit. The courts, when exercising their discretion, should continue to follow the general rule that costs follow the event. They should depart from this general rule when the case is taken in the public interest, i.e. where it involves a genuine challenge to legislation, policy or practice of a public authority which is of wide or potentially wide application or consequence. This definition necessarily excludes redundant and frivolous challenges. Although a favourable costs order to an unsuccessful public interest litigant granted after the trial is welcomed, pre-emptive costs orders are more effective in enabling public interest litigation. The presence of a private/personal interest should not impact upon the public interest character of a challenge. When making a pre-emptive costs order, the courts should not have regard to the substantive merits of the claim or whether the litigant is likely to succeed. They should base their decision on the merits of bringing the claim, i.e. whether it falls to be classified as a public interest challenge so defined. Where the determination of the status of a challenge is dependent upon some evidence to be produced at trial, the court should indicate that a favourable costs order will be granted to the litigant, unless the evidence does not confirm its public interest status. The failure of a litigant to receive a PCO should not prejudice their application for a favourable costs order after the trial. The granting of pre-emptive costs orders should be contingent on the ability of the defendant to pay the costs bill and the courts should have regard to the effect the payment of costs would have on the plaintiff if unsuccessful.

Index

B

C

D

E

F

H

J

O

P

T